Perth •

St Andr

Dunfermline •
Abercorn • Dalmeny •
Edinburgh • Inver

• Glasgow

Clyde

Tweed

E

N

Annan

• Ballantrae

La

Kirkcudbright •
• Dundrennan
Holm Cultr
• Torpen
• Whithorn

• St Bees
• Calder Br.

Cartmel •
Furness Abbey •

Chester •

0   50   100 km

THE ANGLO-NORMAN NORTH

yninghame
Dunbar
gton
dingham
Edrom
Fishwick
Berwick
Norham
Lindisfarne (Holy Island)
Farne Is.
es
Ednam
Kelso
Roxburgh Bamburgh Ellingham
Wooler
Alnwick
Whittingham
Holystone
Brinkburn
Tyne
Morpeth
Wark
Ponteland
Ovingham Tynemouth
Hexham
Bywell Newcastle
l
n
Wear Durham
Tees
Guisborough
Whitby
Richmond
Ure
Northallerton
Hackness
Lastingham
Rievaux Helmsley
Scarborough
irkby Lonsdale
Byland
Newburgh
Malton
Fountains
Kirkham
Wharram-le-Street
Kirkhammerton
York
Bridlington
vley
Pocklington
Kirkstall
Beverley
Selby
North Ferriby
Howden
Pontefract
Nostell
Trent
Roche
Laughton en
le Morthern
Louth Park
Worksop
Stow
Southwell

ANGLO-NORMAN DURHAM

DURHAM

1093–1193

Aerial view of the peninsula of Durham
Photo © University of Newcastle-upon-Tyne

ANGLO-NORMAN DURHAM

DURHAM

1093–1193

EDITED BY

David Rollason
Margaret Harvey
Michael Prestwich

THE BOYDELL PRESS

First published 1994
The Boydell Press, Woodbridge
Reprinted in paperback 1998

ISBN 0 85115 390 9 (hardback)
ISBN 0 85115 654 1 (paperback)

The Boydell Press is an imprint of Boydell & Brewer Ltd
PO Box 9, Woodbridge, Suffolk IP12 3DF, UK
and of Boydell & Brewer Inc.
PO Box 41026, Rochester, NY 14604–4126, USA

British Library Cataloguing-in-Publication Data
Anglo-Norman Durham, 1093–1193
I. Rollason, D.W.
942.8602
ISBN 0–85115–390–9

Library of Congress Catalog Card Number: 94–18926

Printed in Great Britain by
St Edmundsbury Press Ltd, Bury St Edmunds, Suffolk

Contents

PART ONE: THE MONKS AND THE PRIORY

PART TWO: CHURCH ARCHITECTURE IN ANGLO-NORMAN DURHAM

PART THREE: THE PRINCE BISHOPS

PART FOUR: SCHOLARSHIP AND MANUSCRIPTS

TO THE MEMORY OF
H. S. OFFLER
(1913–1991)
Professor of Medieval History in
the University of Durham

Acknowledgments

We are grateful to the following for permission to reproduce illustrations in this volume:

Society of Antiquaries of London (cover illustration), the Bodleian Library, Oxford (pls. 2a–b, 3a), the Dean and Chapter of Durham (pls. 2c, 3b–d, 4a–c, 5b, 6–10, 52, 64–5, 79, 86, 88, 91–4), the Master and Fellows of University College, Durham (pl. 15); Durham University Library (pl. 5a), the British Library (pls. 67, 87, 89–90), the Conway Library of the Courtauld Institute of Art (pls. 31, 66), Canon M.H. Ridgway (pl. 31), the National Monuments Record (pl. 83); Cambridge University Air Photographic Collection (pls. 84–5); Professor N. McCord and the University of Newcastle upon Tyne (pl. 80), Mr Tom Middlemass (pls. 11–12); Dr David Rollason (pls. 53–8, 68), Professor Malcolm Thurlby (pls. 72–4, 77). All other plates are by the authors of the papers.

We are particularly grateful to Professor Norman McCord for allowing us to use his aerial photograph for the frontispiece to this paperback edition.

The publication of this book has been assisted by a grant from The Scouloudi Foundation in association with the Institute of Historical Research.

Preface

This book is based on papers read to a conference held in Durham on 13–18 September 1993 to mark the nine hundredth anniversary of the foundation of Durham Cathedral. The conference, which was one of a series of celebratory events taking place throughout 1993, was attended by well over two hundred people, and even more came in very inclement weather to hear the series of public lectures associated with the conference. The result was a striking demonstration of the interest and excitement aroused by Durham and its cathedral. The conference attracted specialists in a range of disciplines as well as non-specialists with a more general interest in the subject. The papers, lectures, and discussions of the very full four-day programme were absorbing; and all the insights gained into the manifold interests and fascination of the conference's subject were riveting.

One great scholar was constantly in mind, and the seminal character of his work was underlined by the continual references to it made in papers on very different aspects Durham's history. Professor H.S. Offler, who died in 1991, has been sorely missed in Durham and elsewhere, but never more so than at this conference devoted to a subject so close to his interests and dear to his heart. To him this volume is dedicated in respectful and affectionate memory.

The editors wish to take this opportunity to express their thanks to the individuals and institutions who have made the conference and this publication possible. These include: the contributors themselves for the time and effort involved in preparing and delivering papers, and for their patience with the editors; Dr Anne Orde, who has checked through and polished the entire text, correcting many errors and inconsistencies; Mrs Maggie Prestwich and Mrs Lynda Rollason for all their work in the preparations for publication; St John's College and especially Mr Martin Clemmett for making the running of the conference so smooth; Mrs Gillian Ivy, Mr Trevor Woods, and Mrs Yvonne Beadnell for help with the illustrations (the last of these drew the maps in the endpapers); colleagues in the University and in the History Department and especially Mrs Joan Pearce, Ms Janet Forster, Mrs Susan Duncan, and Ms Helene Rusby for their forebearance and for their very considerable assistance; and to Messrs Boydell and Brewer, and especially to Dr Richard Barber, for their work on the publication, and above all for their support and their willingness to undertake publication at an early stage.

We have attempted to standardize spellings and the system of references, but we should like to emphasize that no attempt has been made to reconcile the views expressed here. Readers will find different opinions and approaches, and this is entirely right and proper, given the importance of the subject matter and the vigour of the research devoted to it. The index has been designed with a view to facilitating cross-references between papers and we hope that it will materially assist readers.

David Rollason
Margaret Harvey
Michael Prestwich
Durham, March 1994

List of Plates

List of Figures

Abbreviations

AN	*Anglo-Norman Studies: Proceedings of the Battle Conference of Anglo-Norman Studies*, 1–11, ed. R. Allen Brown (1979–89), 12, ed. Marjorie Chibnall (1990); continued from 1983 as *Anglo-Norman Studies*
Ant. J.	*Antiquaries Journal*
Arch.	*Archaeologia*
Arch. Ael.	*Archaeologia Aeliana*
Arch. J.	*Archaeological Journal*
ASA	H.M. and Joan Taylor, *Anglo-Saxon Architecture* (3 vols., Cambridge, 1965–78)
ASC	*Anglo-Saxon Chronicle*, cited *sub anno* (*s.a.*) and, where necessary, by the conventional manuscript sigla, A–G; ed. J. Earle and C. Plummer, *Two of the Saxon Chronicles Parallel* (2 vols.; Oxford, 1892–9); trans. D. Whitelock *et al.*, *The Anglo-Saxon Chronicle* (London, 1961), and in *EHD*, I, pp. 145–61
ASE	*Anglo-Saxon England*
BAACT	British Archaeological Association Conference Transactions
BIHR	*Bulletin of the Institute of Historical Research*
BL	London, British Library
BM	London, British Museum
BNJ	*British Numismatic Journal*
Bodl.L	Oxford, Bodleian Library
CCCC	Cambridge, Corpus Christi College
CCSL	Corpus christianorum, series latina (Turnhout, 1953–)
CHE	*The Church Historians of England*, III, part ii, *containing the Historical Works of Symeon of Durham*, trans. J. Stevenson (London, 1855)
CR	*Chronicles of the Reigns of Stephen, Henry II and Richard I*, ed. R.J. Howlett (4 vols., RS 82; 1884–90)
CTC	Cambridge, Trinity College
CUL	Cambridge University Library
Cuthbert	*St Cuthbert, his Cult and his Community to AD 1200*, ed. Gerald Bonner, David Rollason and Clare Stancliffe (Woodbridge, 1989)
Cuth. virt.	Reginald of Durham's *'Little Book' about the Wonderful Miracles of the Blessed Cuthbert which were Performed in Recent Times*, cited by chapter; ed. James Raine, *Reginaldi monachi Dunelmensis libellus de admirandis beati Cuthberti virtutibus quae novellis patratae sunt temporibus* (SS 1; 1835). Page references where given are to this edition

DAJ	*Durham Archaeological Journal* (formerly *TAASDN*)
DB	*Domesday Book* (2 vols., Record Commission; 1783)
DCDCM	Durham Cathedral, Dean and Chapter Muniments (now housed in the Archives and Special Collections, Durham University Library)
DCL	Durham, Dean and Chapter Library
DCM	R.A.B. Mynors, *Durham Cathedral Manuscripts to the End of the Twelfth Century* (Oxford, 1939)
DEC	*Durham Episcopal Charters, 1071–1152*, ed. H.S. Offler (SS 179; 1968)
De miraculis	*Capitula (liber) de miraculis et translationibus sancti Cuthberti*, Concerning the Miracles and Translations of St Cuthbert. This is a collection of twenty-one miracle stories relating to St Cuthbert and composed in the late eleventh and twelfth centuries. They are cited here from the edition by Thomas Arnold in *Sym. Op.* I, 229–61, and II, 333–62. Arnold assigned to each miracle a chapter number and this is used in references in the present volume with in brackets a page reference to his edition; for example, *De miraculis*, ch. 4 (*Sym. Op.* I, 241). The *De miraculis* were also edited (under the title *Historia translationum sancti Cuthberti* in *Symeonis Dunelmensis Opera et Collectanea*, ed. J. Hodgson Hinde (SS 51; 1868), pp. 158–201. There, however, Arnold's ch. 7 was printed as ch. 18 with consequential effects on the numbering of the miracles. Although Arnold's edition is cited in this volume as the most often consulted, Hinde's numbering is followed in Bertram Colgrave's discussion of the *De miraculis* in his 'The Post-Bedan Miracles and Translations of St Cuthbert', in *The Early Cultures of North-West Europe*, ed. Cyril Fox and Bruce Dickins (Cambridge, 1950), pp. 307–32.
DIV	*De iniusta uexacione Willelmi episcopi primi per Willelmum regem fil<l>ium Willelmi magni regis.* The definitive edition of this text is likely to be the one prepared by Professor H.S. Offler, which at the time of publication of this volume is forthcoming in the Camden Series. Thanks to the kindness of Mrs E. Offler, Dr Philpott has in his contribution been able to quote from Professor Offler's typescript; since that edition is not yet published, however, page references throughout the volume are given to the edition and translation in *English Lawsuits from William I to Richard I*, ed. R.C. van Caenegem (Selden Society, 106; London, 1990), no. 134 (pp. 90–106); for example, *DIV*, p. 101. Another edition is in *Sym. Op.* I, 170–95.
DUL	Durham University Library
EEMF	Early English Manuscripts in Facsimile
EHD, I	*English Historical Documents, c.500–1042,* I, ed. D. Whitelock (2nd edn; London, 1979)
EHD, II	*English Historical Documents 1042–1189*, II, ed. D.C. Douglas and G.W. Greenaway (London, 1953)
EHR	*English Historical Review*

ESC	*Early Scottish Charters prior to A.D. 1153*, ed. A.C. Lawrie (Glasgow, 1905)
Fl. Wig.	*Florentii Wigorniensis monachi Chronicon ex chronicis*, ed. Benjamin Thorpe (English Historical Society, 2 vols.; 1879–80)
FPD	*Feodarium Prioratus Dunelmensis*, ed. W. Greenwell (SS 58; 1871)
HE	*Baedae Historia ecclesiastica gentis Anglorum*, Bede's *Ecclesiastical History of the English People*, cited by bk. and ch.; see *Bede's Ecclesiastical History of the English People*, ed. and trans. B. Colgrave and R.A.B. Mynors (Oxford, 1969); and *Venerabilis Baedae Opera historica*, ed. C. Plummer (2 vols.; Oxford, 1896).
Hinschius	*Decretales pseudo-Isidorianae et Capitula Angilramni*, ed. P. Hinschius (Leipzig, 1863)
HR	*Historical Research* (formerly *BIHR*)
HReg	*Historia regum*, the History of the Kings, ed. *Sym. Op.* II, 3–283; trans. *CHE*, pp. 425–617. Since *HReg* is mainly arranged as a series of annals under years, the principal form of reference is *sub anno* (*s.a.*). For the years 849–947, however, the text offers two parallel series of annals one after the other, so that *s.a.* references alone are not sufficient. Nor are they adequate in the case of very long annals. The normal of form of reference in this volume is therefore to the year of the annal followed where necessary by page numbers in brackets referring to *Sym. Op.* II; e.g. *HReg, s.a.* 950 (p. 94).
HSC	*Historia de sancto Cuthberto*, the History of St Cuthbert. This is cited in the edition by Thomas Arnold in *Sym. Op.* I, 196–214. References are normally to the section numbers assigned to it by Arnold with page numbers referring to his edition in brackets where these are necessary; e.g. *HSC*, § 16 (p. 205).
JBAA	*Journal of the British Archaeological Association*
JEH	*Journal of Ecclesiastical History*
JTS	*Journal of Theological Studies*
LDE	*Libellus de exordio atque procursu istius hoc est Dunelmensis ecclesie*, On the Origin and Progress of this Church of Durham, attributed to Symeon of Durham. The most widely consulted edition at the time of publication of this volume is that by Thomas Arnold in *Sym. Op.* I, 3–169; there is a translation in *CHE*, pp. 621–711. The text is also known as *Historia Dunelmensis ecclesie*, the History of the Church of Durham, although this has no manuscript authority. It is referred to in this volume under its authentic title, shortened as necessary to *Libellus de exordio* (abbreviated *LDE*). The text is divided into books and chapters in its third earliest manuscript, CUL, MS Ff.1.27, and this division, although unique to that manuscript, was adopted by Arnold and has wide currency. It is therefore used here, coupled where necessary with page numbers in brackets which relate to *Sym. Op.* I. A new edition and translation is to be published shortly as Symeon of Durham, *Libellus de exordio atque procursu istius, hoc est Dunelmensis ecclesie* (On the Origin and Progress of this Church of

Durham), ed. and trans. David Rollason (Oxford, forthcoming). This will mark the book and chapter breaks in Arnold's edition so that easy reference can be made to it from the present volume.

Liber Vitae   BL, Cotton MS Domitian VII. This abbreviation refers to the facsimile published as *Liber Vitae Ecclesiae Dunelmensis: A Collotype Facsimile of the Original Manuscript*, ed. A. Hamilton Thompson (SS 136; 1923), which is cited by folio number (pencil folio number is specified in those parts of the manuscript where there is a pencil and an ink foliation). A printed text is to be found in *Liber Vitae Ecclesie Dunelmensis nec non Obituaria duo ejusdem ecclesie*, ed. J. Stevenson (SS 13; 1841), which also prints material from DCL, MS B.IV.24 and BL, MS Harley 1804.

MAADC   *Medieval Art and Architecture at Durham Cathedral*, ed. Nicola Coldstream and Peter Draper (BAACT for 1977; London, 1980)

MGH   *Monumenta Germaniae Historica*

NC   *Numismatic Chronicle*

Offler,   Preface and introduction to H.S. Offler's edition of *DIV* (Camden
'Introduction'   Series, forthcoming)

Offler,   H.S. Offler, 'The Tractate *De iniusta vexacione Willelmi epsicopi
'Tractate'   primi*', *EHR* 66 (1951), pp. 321–41

Orderic   *The Ecclesiastical History of Orderic Vitalis*, ed. Marjorie Chibnall (6 vols.; Oxford, 1969–80)

PL   *Patrologiae cursus completus, series latina*, ed. J.P. Migne (221 vols.; Paris, 1844–64)

Regesta   *Regesta Regum Anglo Normannorum*, I, ed. H.W.C. Davis; II, ed. C. Johnson and H.A. Cronne; III and IV, ed. H.A. Cronne and R.H.C. Davis (Oxford, 1913–70)

Rites   *Rites of Durham*, ed. J.T. Fowler (SS 107; 1902)

RRS   *Regesta Regum Scottorum 1153–1424*, I, ed. G.W.S. Barrow; II, ed. G.W.S. Barrow and W.W. Scott (Edinburgh, 1960–71)

RS   Rolls Series (Rerum Britannicarum medii Aevi Scriptores or Chronicles and Memorials of Great Britain and Ireland during the Middle Ages)

Script. Tres   *Historiae Dunelmensis scriptores tres: Gaufridus de Coldingham, Robertus de Graystanes, et Willielmus de Chambre*, ed. James Raine (SS 9; 1839). This also contains an appendix of 355 documents relating to the history of Durham cathedral and priory.

Sym. Op.   *Symeonis monachi Opera omnia*, ed. T. Arnold (2 vols., RS 75; 1882–5)

SS   Surtees Society

TAASDN   *Transactions of the Architectural and Archaeological Society of Durham and Northumberland*

TRHS   *Transactions of the Royal Historical Society*

V. Barth.   Geoffrey of Durham, *Vita Bartholomaei Farnensis*, ed. *Sym. Op.* I, 295–325.

VCH	Victoria History of the Counties of England
V. Godr.	*Libellus de vita et miraculis S. Godrici, heremitae de Finchale, auctore Reginaldo monacho Dunelmensi*, ed. Joseph Stevenson (SS 20; 1847)
V. Godr. Gal.	Geoffrey of Durham, *Vita Sancti Godrici auctore Galfrido*, ed. *Acta Sanctorum Bollandiana*, ed. Socii Bollandiani (3rd edn.; in progress, Paris and elsewhere, 1863–), May V, pp. 70–85.
YAJ	*Yorkshire Archaeological Journal*

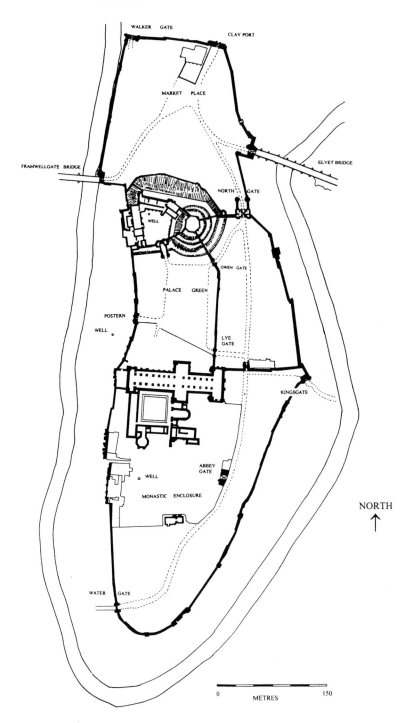

Fig. 1. Durham, plan of the peninsula, showing the site of the Cathedral, Castle and defences.

INTRODUCTION

The cathedral of Durham has long been recognized as one of the greatest Anglo-Norman achievements, but it is only one of Durham's many claims to a central and enduring place in the study of the Anglo-Norman period. These include: the long and well-documented history of the religious community there and of its principal saint, the hermit of the Farne Island and the bishop of Lindisfarne, Cuthbert (d.687); the role of Durham in the political and religious history of northern England; the well-preserved episcopal fortress-residence which faces the cathedral across Palace Green; the richness of Durham Cathedral Priory's library, many of the manuscripts of which survive, a considerable number in Durham itself; and the diversity and depth of its scholarship and literary culture. Yet despite all this no book had ever been devoted to Anglo-Norman Durham before 1993, when the nine hundredth anniversary of the laying of the foundation stones of Durham Cathedral prompted the preparation of the papers which were read to a conference in that year and now form the substance of this book. The key-note of it is its interdisciplinary approach: specialists in a range of disciplines here present their observations, insights, and conclusions which are often arrestingly complementary.[1]

Our knowledge of the early history of Anglo-Norman Durham is largely based on the work known as 'The Origin and Progress of this Church of Durham' (*Libellus de exordio et procursu istius, hoc est Dunelmensis ecclesie*), a work which was written between 1104 and 1109, almost certainly by the Durham monk Symeon.[2] This work is the first to describe how the religious community of St Cuthbert, having fled from its original home on the Holy Island of Lindisfarne in 875 and having been settled for more than a century at Chester-le-Street to the north of Durham, finally moved in 995 to Durham, where the episcopal see was established where it still is. Lindisfarne had of course been founded as a community of monks, but by the time of its move to Durham it was a community of secular, married clerks. These clerks, although they had been reformed by the first post-Conquest bishop of Durham, Walcher (1071–80), were expelled from Durham in 1083 by his successor Bishop William of St Calais (1080–96), and replaced by a Benedictine community which had established itself in 1073–4 under the leadership of

---

[1] Two papers relating to this period were published in this volume's predecessor, *St Cuthbert, his Cult, and his Community to AD 1200*, ed. Gerald Bonner, David Rollason, and Clare Stancliffe (Woodbridge, 1989). They are: Alan Piper, 'The First Generations of Durham Monks and the Cult of St Cuthbert', pp. 437–46, and Victoria Tudor, 'The Cult of St Cuthbert in the Twelfth Century: The Evidence of Reginald of Durham', pp. 447–67.
[2] Guidance notes on the editions of various Durham texts which are liable to cause confusion can be found in the list of abbreviations.

three monks from Evesham and Winchcombe at the ruined monasteries of Jarrow and Monkwearmouth. It was this new Benedictine community of Durham, Durham Cathedral Priory, which was to serve the cathedral until the Dissolution of the Monasteries.

After an introductory essay on the place of Durham in the cultural development of the Anglo-Norman world, the first part of this book is devoted to this new monastic community. Contributors address: the background to its establishment, first with regard to the place of Durham in the general context of eleventh-century church reform and then in relation to the refounding of ancient abbeys in Yorkshire, which was an offshoot of the refoundation of Jarrow and Monkwearmouth – and of Durham Cathedral Priory itself; the attitudes of the Durham monks to the clerks who were expelled to make way for them in 1083; the debt which the monks owed to eremitical traditions and the role of hermits vis-à-vis the priory; the texts and manuscripts they possessed, above all in relation to the Durham Martyrology and the work of a scribe who is here identified for the first time with the historian Symeon of Durham; and the production of forgeries at Durham. Under this last heading, new light is cast not only on the forged charters of the late eleventh century, but also on the account of Bishop William of St Calais's trial, the claim of which to be contemporary with the event is here defended with new evidence.

The second part of the book is concerned with Durham Cathedral as a building. Contributors consider: the general development of early Romanesque architecture in the North-East (with radically new interpretations of a number of buildings previously considered pre-Conquest); the relative contributions of Bishop St Calais as patron of the cathedral and of the anonymous master mason; the place of Durham in the development of Gothic west facades; the design and function of Durham's remarkable Galilee Chapel; the architectural provision for the cult of St Cuthbert, based on a petrological study of the floor of the feretory; the form of Durham's twelfth-century rood screen, here reconstructed for the first time; and the wide influence of the cathedral's architecture in the churches of England and Scotland. The wide influence of Durham is a theme which emerges in other parts of the book also.

The third part of the book concerns the bishops of Durham in the eleventh and twelfth centuries, opening with reinterpretations the careers of two of the most important, William of St Calais and Ranulf Flambard. The latter's role in government, which is evaluated here, inevitably made him an important figure in English history. Three papers are then concerned with one of the most important themes of Durham's history – and of nothern England in general – in this period: relations with the Scots, considered here in terms of connections with the Scottish kings, the place in particular of King Malcolm III, who is said in one source to have been present at the dedication of Durham Cathedral, and Scottish influence on Durham. Other papers then consider: the position of Durham during Stephen's reign, not least with regard to the usurpation of the bishopric by King David I's chancellor; the case of the bishopric of Carlisle, which was of great interest to Durham and whose history forms an interesting parallel to that of the see of

Durham; the episcopal mint at Durham, which has never been previously studied in detail; the survey of the bishopric's lands known as Boldon Book, the evidence of which for the organisation of those lands is here re-interpreted; and the remarkable fortress-residence of the bishops at Durham, studied here both in detail with phased drawings offering a new interpretation of its development, and in general terms in relation to contemporary episcopal palaces and castles.

The final section turns to the scholarship and manuscripts of Anglo-Norman Durham. The first two papers emphasize how influential Durham was, particularly amongst the Cistercian monasteries of Yorkshire, but also among other northern religious houses. The significance of particular Durham styles of ornamentation is evaluated, and challenging discussions are devoted to the question of which scholarly manuscripts, particularly manuscripts of historical texts, were produced at Durham. In this connection, exciting conclusions are offered regarding one of the earliest manuscripts of Symeon of Durham's *Libellus de exordio*, as well as about one of the most important of all English medieval manuscripts of historical texts, Cambridge, Corpus Christi College, MS 139. Two final papers deal first with the great illuminated Bible of Bishop Hugh of le Puiset, and secondly with the neglected Old English poem on Durham itself, which is here shown to be of a quite unexpected level of sophistication.

The richness and diversity of these papers bears witness not only to the vigour of research in the various disciplines represented, but also to the richness, fascination, and inspiration of its subject. The papers also bear witness to the enduring scholarship of the dedicatee of this volume, the late Professor of Medieval History in the University of Durham, H.S. Offler, to whose wide-ranging contributions to scholarship, repeatedly acknowledged in these papers, it is a memorial.

Durham and the Anglo-Norman World

DONALD MATTHEW

T HE FIRST STONE of Durham cathedral was laid on 11 August 1093. Until this year, no centenary of the event has been an occasion of celebration. Admittedly a hundred years ago, Archdeacon Hamilton asked the Dean and Chapter to do something to mark the event, but an unenthusiastic proposal to hold a religious service was quickly abandoned. The chapter agreed instead that it would be more appropriate to honour the consecration of the church (whenever that might have been).[1] A hundred years before that, the Dean and Chapter were so little mindful of the foundation as to be engaged in ruthless renovations to the building, which involved demolishing the chapter house and planning to remove Bishop Puiset's Galilee chapel. Much to their surprise they found themselves at the centre of bitter public criticism from a group of outraged London antiquaries.[2] These men were pioneers of a quite new movement for the appreciation of medieval buildings. Until then, at Durham, as elsewhere, the care of such buildings had been a purely local responsibility. Those in charge naturally thought first of their own comfort and convenience, and were not aware of any need to take aesthetics into account. It has therefore taken 900 years to celebrate the foundation of the new Durham cathedral as a national monument. The wish to do so tells us in the first instance something important about our own age. Before turning to twelfth-century Durham in particular, it may be helpful to try to outline these modern attitudes towards the twelfth century in general.

1 DCDCM, Chapter Minute Book 1890–98, pp. 124–5, 3 December 1892; p. 148, 3 June 1893. I owe these references to the kindness of Mr Pat Mussett and Mr Alan Piper. Bishop Foss Westcott was sufficiently interested in the cathedral building to make a sketch of the sanctuary knocker when he went to Durham; see Arthur Westcott, *Life and Letters of B.F. Westcott* (2 vols., London, 1903).
2 T.H. Cocke, 'Pre-Nineteenth Century Attitudes in England to Romanesque Architecture', *JBAA*, 3rd ser. 36 (1973), pp. 72–97, especially pp. 90–2. On Wyatt, see R.A. Cordingley, 'Cathedral Innovations: James Wyatt Architect at Durham Cathedral 1795–97', *Transactions of Ancient Monuments Society* 3 (1955), pp. 31–55.

I

In the past generation or so, historians right across Europe have developed a special affection for the twelfth century and its renaissance. This is mainly because it is now thought of as being the time when a distinctively European culture first began to take shape. Surfacing first in a great new effort for church reform, this itself developed a programme for a new kind of education in schools, and eventually universities. This new learning in turn had a marked impact on the emergence of a new vernacular literary culture, first of all in French and mainly for the upper classes. Courtly manners and the cult of chivalry duly encouraged a new style of social behaviour, with important consequences, particularly for relations between the sexes. In England, historians have also discerned the creation, after the Norman Conquest, of a new kind of political organization, which established for the first time some institutions still familiar: the royal exchequer, the common law and the notion of privilege, confirmed by royal authority, best known from Magna Carta. To us, therefore, the twelfth century naturally seems an age of innovation, creativity, full of promise, but not yet so systematized or refined as to have lost the earthy vitality of the barbarian period. One of the finest expressions of this twelfth-century spirit is exemplified for us by Romanesque architecture, with its magnificent, ample forms and firm control of exciting sculptural decoration. In England there is no better example of this than Durham, and Durham holds its own in any competition for ranking the finest churches in Romanesque Europe. No wonder that in 1993, to celebrate the foundation of Durham cathedral seems entirely justified.

There are, however, various ways of marking satisfaction with the past. It would be possible to concentrate on praise and thanksgiving for an age that provided so generously for our present aesthetic satisfactions, and we might be inclined to view the twelfth century accordingly as a kind of golden age reflected in its art forms. A historical conference about twelfth-century Durham invites us to go deeper than this. We are expected to set its achievements in context and see them not necessarily as reflections of a particularly favoured era, and more like affirmations often realised in spite of adverse circumstances. To reconsider how contemporaries had to live with their own times is to rediscover the complexity of their experience, their vicissitudes, even decade by decade, and their perennial anxieties about the future. They obviously could draw no comfort for their present worries from the idea that later generations would admire their works of art.

If modern experience is anything to go by, it is probable that there were some people in twelfth-century Durham who did not approve or admire the new cathedral and could have remembered with nostalgia the fine church built by Bishop Aldhun which Bishop St Calais had destroyed in 1092. Reginald of Durham in the mid-twelfth century went out of his way to allude to the former White Church with two towers, claiming that it was already so admirable that it pointed forward to the finer one to come, which is however praised only as appropriate to the great merits of the saint within.[3] Prior Laurence, who described the site of Durham and the castle at great length, mentions our cathedral only in connection with the Scottish occupation, when the soldiers used the church as a kitchen and a refectory.[4] The merits of Durham cathedral in the twelfth century could in no way depend upon respect for its venerable age, since it was starkly new. Bishop Flambard, who cleared the buildings and residents from Palace Green,[5] certainly thereby made it possible to admire the north flank of the great building, but this was obviously not for aesthetic reasons. Anyway, the cathedral in the twelfth century must have most often looked more like a building site. Almost as soon as it appeared to be finished, Bishop Puiset determined to leave his mark on its austere beauties by adding an annexe in the style of his own age, if not at the east end, then in the west.[6] Since there were confident critics of grandiose buildings in the twelfth century and some who thought modest churches or the venerable buildings associated with the great saints of the past were preferable to such novelties,[7] it is not entirely fanciful to believe that even in those days Durham had some tetchy old codgers who deplored the present and idealised the past. Where there is innovation on the scale we find in the twelfth century, there is also bound to have been resistance to change, defence of what was attacked and nostalgia for the good old ways. As in our own day, men disagreed about the times they lived in, what needed to be changed and what was worth striving for.

Durham cathedral can so easily come to epitomise Norman England for us that it is useful to remember how unlike the rest of England Durham really was. The bold geometrical patterns of the nave columns themselves make Durham quite unlike 'typical' English Norman churches.[8] William the Conqueror, who could stretch the administrative resources of his kingdom as far as the Tees for the compilation of Domesday Book, left Durham out of his account. Whatever the reasons,[9] this alone put Durham in a different position from any other part of the kingdom not only in the twelfth century, but also for historical purposes. The Conqueror was admittedly strong enough to make appointments to the see of

3 *Cuth. virt.*, ch. 16 (p. 19).
4 *Dialogi Laurentii Dunelmensis monachi ac prioris*, ed. James Raine (SS 70; 1880) bk. I, lines 271–454. *Script. Tres*, Appendix no. xxxvi, p. lii.
5 *Sym. Op.* I, 140.
6 *Script. Tres*, p. 11; Geoffrey of Coldingham, ch. vii. Pope Alexander III confirmed Durham's right to collect one *denarius* a year from every *domus* of the people of the Haliwerfolc for building expenses, 8 August 1164.
7 *Corpus Iuris Canonici*, ed. Ae. Friedberg, Pars 1: *Decreta Magistri Gratiani* (Leipzig, 1879), col. 710–11 causa 12: 2, 71: 'Multi aedificant parietes et columnae ecclesiae subtrahunt marmora nitent auro splendent laquearia gemmis altare distinguitur et ministrorum Christi nullo electio est.' See also *Gothic Art 1140–c.1450 Sources and Documents*, ed. T.G. Frisch (2nd edn; Toronto, 1987), 'Twelfth Century Critics of the New Architecture', pp. 30–3. I owe this reference to the kindness of Miss Anne Lawrence.
8 E. Fernie, 'The Spiral Piers of Durham Cathedral', *MAADC*, pp. 49–58.
9 Although there are various explanations possible for the omission of the lands of St Cuthbert from Domesday Book, the most persuasive is the fact that there was no county organization in 'county Durham' in 1086.

Durham, but bishops had to be capable of coping there without the expectation of invoking regular royal help. Bishop Walcher, who himself became earl of Northumberland in 1075, did not even have a local military commander to help him.[10] When later the military responsibilities of the earldom were assumed by others, the bishop was not relieved of the duty to defend his own possessions in the region.[11] His spiritual authority still nominally extended over an immense district stretching between Tees and Forth and from sea to sea.[12] Though the size of his fortune cannot be measured in Domesday terms, no one doubts that the bishopric was one of the wealthiest in England. The exercise of 'regalian' rights made the bishop effectively 'king' in what were in fact the lands of the old Bernician kingdom.[13] By the time of the Norman Conquest the bishopric, which then straddled northern England and southern Scotland, had to acknowledge two kings. It was therefore the greatest marcher lordship in the British Isles. Bishops of Durham not surprisingly saw more of the kings of Scotland than of the kings of England but were duly mindful of the need to treat both diplomatically. Since King David of Scotland was eventually frustrated in the one Scots attempt to appoint a bishop to the see, Durham cannot be considered generally vulnerable to Scottish encroachment, but bishops appointed in such an exposed position had to be both strong men and yet loyal if the king of England was to leave them so much freedom. Durham's bishops in this period, St Calais, Flambard, Puiset, were by any measure remarkable men. Their exploits and characters were described by contemporary chroniclers at some length.

At the core of the diocese lay the shrine of St Cuthbert, former bishop of Lindisfarne, whose body had been disinterred twelve years after his death and found to have been miraculously preserved from decay. Treasured at Lindisfarne

[10] *LDE*, bk. 3, ch. 23 (p. 114), and *HReg, s.a.* 1075 (pp. 207–8).

[11] Between 1080 and 1189, no bishop of Durham was also earl of Northumberland. For Puiset's acquisition of the office of earl, see G.V. Scammell, *Hugh du Puiset, Bishop of Durham* (Cambridge, 1956), pp. 49–50.

[12] When Lothian was ceded by the kings of England to the Scots, it is not clear that the bishop of Chester le Street/Durham immediately lost his episcopal jurisdiction between the Tweed and the Forth. Eventually, the bishop of St Andrews assumed responsibility in Lothian, but there is no evidence of this until 1150, when Bishop Robert confirmed for Durham grants of churches at Swinton and Fishwick made by King Edgar (1097–1107) without any reference to episcopal authority. Likewise, in 1094 King Duncan II gave Durham Tynninghame and Broxmouth north of the Tweed. The kings' grants indeed make more sense at that time, if they still took Durham's rights at least in some parts of the territory across the Tweed for granted. For a general view of this question, see M. Morgan, 'The Organization of the Scottish Church in the Twelfth Century', *TRHS*, 4th ser. 29 (1947), pp. 135–49. G.W.S. Barrow, 'The Anglo-Scottish Border', *Northern History* 1 (1966), pp. 21–42, suggested that the Scots had *de facto* occupied Lothian in the 940s but did not discuss the implications of this for episcopal jurisdiction.

[13] *Cuth. virt.*, ch. 95 (p. 210). The wealth of the diocese is discussed by Scammell, *Puiset*, pp. 194–219, who estimates the bishop's annual revenue at the end of the twelfth century as £3,000. Laurence refers to the wealth of the district, instancing the resources of the mines, the forests, the corn and honey, and especially its wonderful supplies of horses; see also *Dialogi Laurentii*, bk. 2, lines 167–230.

until the Vikings made life intolerable for the monks there, it had been carried away for safety in 875 by a group of monks and clergy called the congregation of St Cuthbert. For more than two hundred years in various places and at Durham after 995, this congregation had not only looked after the body of Cuthbert and other relics and books, but also provided for the continuity of the diocese and the institutional life of the bishopric. It was still keeping records of the see's property and of the miracles performed by St Cuthbert after the Norman Conquest.[14] The congregation was abruptly dissolved when Bishop St Calais installed a community of Benedictine monks in his cathedral in 1083 because he considered them more appropriate custodians of Cuthbert's shrine. This certainly provoked both distress and indignation, but in the long run the old congregation's reputation was effectively besmirched and its achievements did not receive adequate recognition. The monks who took their place disapproved of them for not living according to formal Benedictine rules and for allowing the clergy to be married. Thanks to the congregation's efforts, however, Cuthbert's reputation had been kept alive through a very troubled period. Though his cult was strongest in the north, it had in this period also penetrated into southern England. The spiritual radiance of Cuthbert in northern England counted for at least as much as the physical resources of the bishopric in making Durham the heart of the region. Cuthbert's miraculous powers provided for the security of his lands and the health of his people, kept enemies at bay and punished violators of his rights; respect for the saint had inspired further gifts. When Durham monks thought about Cuthbert's position in the Norman kingdom, they believed him capable of inspiring fear and trembling even in the Conqueror.[15] The only other old English saints they thought of comparable significance were Etheldreda, royal foundress of Ely, and Edmund, the martyred king of East Anglia.[16] In the north Cuthbert had no rival.

After the Conquest, the new Norman bishop, Walcher, had received a group of monks from Evesham who asked permission to resettle the old monasteries of Jarrow and Wearmouth, centres of the great Northumbrian church, associated with Bede and old English learning. Walcher was later credited with the intention to transfer these southern monks to Durham but had not done so when he was brutally murdered at Gateshead in a local insurrection in 1080.[17]

---

[14] B. Colgrave, 'The Post-Bedan Miracles and Translations of St Cuthbert', *The Early Culture of North-West Europe: H.M. Chadwick Memorial Studies*, ed. C. Fox and B. Dickins (Cambridge, 1950), pp. 307–32 (miracles 5,6,7 of between 1065 and 1083). H.H.E. Craster 'The Patrimony of St Cuthbert', *EHR* 69 (1954), pp. 196–8, discusses the property belonging to the congregation of St Cuthbert, but not the limits of the bishop's authority. Given that the Durham diocese derived from Lindisfarne it may have been still more 'Irish' in style than 'Roman' in the eleventh century, so vague boundaries would be expected. See also D. Bethell, 'English Monks and Irish Reform in the Eleventh and Twelfth Centuries', *Historical Studies* 8 (Dublin, 1971), pp. 111–35.

[15] *LDE*, bk. 3, ch. 19.

[16] *Cuth. virt.*, chs. 19, 112, and 115 (pp. 38, 251, 260).

[17] For Aldwin of Winchcombe and two monks from Evesham, see *LDE*, bk. 3, chs. 21–2. Aldwin may have had Irish connections: see Bethell, 'English monks', especially p. 127.

The Conqueror's decision to replace the murdered Walcher with a monk was decisive for the future of Durham. It is not easy to explain why he did so, because although St Calais was by origin a Norman he had gone to Maine to enter the monastery of St Calais there, hence the name by which he is known. He had only recently been elected abbot of St Vincent in Le Mans when the Conqueror offered him Durham at the other end of the Norman dominion nearly five hundred miles away. William of St Calais must somehow have impressed the king as being vigorous, independent and a great organiser; capable therefore of coping on his own in border lands.[18] Although the posting to Durham was dangerous and cannot have been much coveted by any conventionally ambitious clergyman, by 1080 the king could not actually afford to lose another prelate in the north. The new bishop would need great qualities. What St Calais had done to impress the king remains a mystery, but he was certainly tough. After his part in the succession dispute in 1088, he proved capable of standing up to both William Rufus and Archbishop Lanfranc.[19] If it seems surprising that such a prelate should have been found in the Norman border lands, his monastic profession should not be considered incidental. A community of committed monks under a powerful head which could establish itself in alien lands, would take deep institutional root. St Calais obviously believed that what Durham needed was just such a monastic community. Unlike the southern English monks whom he took from Jarrow and Wearmouth for the new cathedral priory, St Calais had not come north with moist eyes at the thought of Cuthbert, Bede or the Northumbrian golden age. He did not however straightway begin a new church for his monastic community, and when after only five years their bishop was driven into exile for his political intransigence, his community must have felt rather uneasy. But when he returned determined to rebuild and refurbish his cathedral in 1091, the process of promoting the cult of Cuthbert on the grand scale was launched in magnificent style. By 1104, the new church was ready for the ceremony of translating the body of the saint to its new shrine and a spate of new miracles confirmed the saint's blessing on his new custodians.[20] Although the new bishop, Flambard, was suspected of being less than enthusiastic,[21] the new monastic community had vindicated St Calais's vision and the early uncertainties were over. The monks were no doubt very optimistic about their future.

---

[18] For William of St Calais, there is an extended essay by L. Guilloreau, 'Guillaume de Saint Calais', *Revue historique et archéologique du Maine* 74 (1913), pp. 209–32, and 75 (1914), pp. 64–79.

[19] 'De iniusta vexatione', in *Sym. Op.* I, 170–95.

[20] The translation of 1104 was very widely reported at the time. The fullest account is *De miraculis*, ch. 7. See B. Colgrave, 'The Post-Bedan Miracles', p. 317 (miracle 18), for texts and manuscripts.

[21] *De miraculis*, ch. 7 (p. 254) from BL, MS Harley 1924: 'At episcopus non facile his accommodans fidem, omnino judicabat incredibile corpus quamlibet sanctum tamen humanum per tantum temporis, id est per quadringento decem et octo annos ab omni corruptionis labe intactum perdurare.' Laurence of Durham nevertheless left a flowing tribute to Flambard as bishop (*Dialogi Laurentii*, ed. Raine, bk. 2, lines 231–42).

II

Thanks to its monastic status, the cathedral became part of a great religious network stretching across England and the continent, to Rome and beyond, which radically broke with the long period of Northumbrian isolation. Thanks to the monks who wrote the histories, collected the books, treasured the archives, erected the buildings and consolidated their hold on the north for over four hundred years, more has been preserved of the medieval past here than elsewhere in Britain. This has provided historians with as impressive and comprehensive a collection of historical evidence as could ever be hoped for.[22] The monastic character of the cathedral was not unique, but most English cathedrals with monks after the Conquest had only reverted to the practices of the tenth-century English church reform, which had not affected northern England at all. At Durham, the idea that Benedictine monks from southern England knew better than the local clergy how to do Cuthbert honour will initially have seemed quite offensive. The fellowship the monks established with other monasteries and great men in church and state was important for proving their credentials. To put up a new building may itself be considered a symbol of the new order.

Amongst the books and records of this period must be counted the *Liber Vitae*, an altar book originally recording the names of the persons who had wished to be remembered in the prayers of the Lindisfarne community in the ninth century.[23] Bishop St Calais revived the practice of enrolling the names of the monks and of others who valued the monks' prayers. From this record and other documents of the period,[24] a list of Durham 'friends', as we should say today, can be drawn up. It includes the names of all the Norman kings of England and of the kings of Scotland. New names were added regularly for most of the twelfth century. Great nobles, like Robert, count of Meulan, his wife, and son, Robert, earl of Leicester, and his wife occur alongside Scottish nobles, Henry, earl of Northumberland, his wife and sons, Earl Duncan of Fife and the Scots king's seneschal. Later in the century, famous individuals like the justiciar, Ranulf Glanville, the author, Walter Map, and Herbert of Bosham were enrolled. Foreign prelates, Bishop Henry of Troia in south Italy or Cardinal Odalrinus, envoy of Pope Paschal II, appear alongside William the Moneyer of Newcastle, possibly the community's banker, and Aefwold, the London bell-founder. Little can be made of the names on their own, even of those of the famous. One interesting point to emerge is the number of women, queens and countesses or just wives named in it. Although stories of Cuthbert insisted that the saint could not bear the presence of women in his

---

[22] For the cathedral manuscripts see *DCM*. For the archives of the Dean and Chapter, see *The Muniments of the Dean and Chapter of Durham, a Report to the Pilgrim Trustees* (1939).
[23] *Liber Vitae*.
[24] For other manuscripts, see *Liber Vitae Ecclesiae Dunelmensis*, ed. J. Stevenson (SS 13; 1841): ('Liber Vitae' BL, Cotton MS Domitian VII.2 and obituaries from DCL, MS B.IV.24 and BL, MS Harley 1804).

church,[25] his misogyny did not discourage female devotion or bar their acceptance into the fraternity. Bishop St Calais himself saw to it that the anniversaries of both his mother's and father's deaths were remembered at Durham. The community of St Cuthbert was built up like an ever-growing family.

If we can only go so far in explaining how these individuals came to be connected with Durham, more can be said of other religious institutions which became part of the fraternity. Many of the great English Benedictine houses and some French ones, Fécamp, Caen, St Taurin of Évreux, St Calais itself and St Nicholas of Angers exchanged promises with Durham to pray for the souls of one another's monks. Surviving calendars from some of the English monasteries, like Chertsey, Thorney, Croyland, and St Augustine's Canterbury, show also that feasts of prominent Durham saints, Cuthbert, Oswald, and Bede, were duly celebrated there.[26] As far away as Monte Cassino itself, the Durham feast of St Oswald was observed in the calendar, though not that of Cuthbert, probably because his feast on 20 March was also the vigil of the feast of St Benedict.[27] This coincidence may have been inimical to the celebration of the cult, except in such places as had special reasons to cultivate Cuthbert's memory.

Durham's surviving calendars show that this kind of spiritual association helped to introduce Durham itself to cults of saints from other places.[28] Before the Conquest Durham had obviously honoured such saints as Cuthbert, Oswald, Aidan and Wilfrid. But the commemorations of Bede and of Boisil, Cuthbert's teacher, were probably added when Alfred brought their relics to Durham from Jarrow and Melrose.[29] Some feast days in the old Durham calendar were probably taken from the Old English martyrology, even before the see was moved from Chester le Street. This source would easily account for the great number of Roman saints in it, like Fabian, Sebastian, Pancras and Petronilla, as well as some from northern France: Germanus of Auxerre or Quentin from Picardy. But Durham may have owed to the influence of Walcher its first foreign bishop, who came from Liège, its respect for such saints as Amand, the apostle of the Belgians, or Vedast from Flemish Arras, even the twin saints Medard and Godard, held in great honour at Soissons. Similarly, Bishop St Calais must surely have been responsible for the names of St Calais, who had founded his original monastery in Maine, as well as St Julian, bishop of Le Mans. The feast of the translation of St Nicholas of Myra to Bari, an event which occurred only in 1087, may not have taken long to arrive in Durham, for the town church had already been dedicated to him.

---

[25] For Cuthbert's misogyny according to the monks of Durham, see *LDE*, bk. 2, chs. 7–9; and *Cuth. virt.*, chs. 62, 74, 100, and 119 (pp. 122, 151–4, 223, 265).

[26] F. Wormald, *English Kalendars before AD 1100* (Henry Bradshaw Society 72; 1934), pp. 2–13 for the printed text of Bodl.L, MS Digby 63, and *English Benedictine Kalendars after AD 1100* (Henry Bradshaw Society 77; 1939), pp. 161–79.

[27] A. Muratori, *Rerum Italicarum Scriptores*, VII (Milan, 1725), col. 936 (excerpta ex antiquo martyrologio Casinensis ecclesiae): 'Non. Aug. in Brit. S. Owaldi regis Anglorum'.

[28] Wormald, *English Benedictine Kalendars*, pp. 161–79.

[29] For Alfred the Priest, son of Westou, grandfather of Ailred of Rievaulx, see *LDE*, bk. 3, ch. 7. Compare Hexham's view of Alfred's enterprises, in *HReg, s.a.* 781 (pp. 47–50).

Nicholas had become very popular in mid-eleventh-century England, perhaps again under influences from the Low Countries.[30]

There was a close association between the celebration of the saints' feast days and the possession of relics associated with the saints. Which came first, acquisition of the relics or veneration of the feast cannot be shown: only some connection between the two. In spite of its possession of such a great relic as Cuthbert's incorruptible body, Durham did not hesitate to go on adding to its relic collection throughout the twelfth century as a regular part of keeping up its contacts across the Catholic world.[31] Queen Margaret of Scotland had been a great benefactress. Not content with the Gospel book and cross she had herself given them, the monks also obtained some hair and one of her teeth after her death in 1093. St Malachy, bishop of Armagh, who died in 1148, is represented in the Durham relic lists by some hair, a comb (*pecten*) and some finger nails (*unguibus*); his friend, St Bernard of Clairvaux, by some hair and a rib-bone; St Godric of Finchale, the local hermit, by his coat of mail, girdle and beard; Bartholomew, hermit of Farne, who died in 1193, by some hair; St Amphibalus, a martyr companion of St Alban, whose relics were discovered in 1185,[32] by some dust (or ashes, *pulvus*). There were also various relics of St Nicholas of Bari, some bones of St Exuperius, bishop of Bayeux, a tooth of St William of York, who visited Durham shortly before his death in 1154, and some relics of Becket, perhaps obtained through the influence of the Durham 'friend', Herbert of Bosham. Some oil from the miraculous icon of St Mary of Sarcinay in Syria, a cult of the crusading period, could have also been acquired in the twelfth century.[33] Anyway, the community's stock of venerabilia was notably increased in this period and some of these relics came from great distances. Reginald of Durham has a story that when Prior Roger urged pious pilgrims to bring back marble slabs from their travels so that Durham could be paved in Roman style, one burly knight, Harpin of Thornley, duly obliged;[34] by comparison, it would be no hard task for other pilgrims to collect samples of hair or teeth belonging to the holy men of the age.

Reginald's story of the marble pavement is told in the context of a miracle performed at sea by Cuthbert. It is worth noting in connection with Durham's contacts abroad that communication with the continent was not necessarily

---

[30] For the cult of St Nicholas see C.W. Jones, *Saint Nicholas of Myra, Bari and Manhattan* (Chicago, 1978). Durham had, exceptionally early, an illustrated life of St Nicholas; see V. Ortenberg, *The English Church and the Continent in the Tenth and Eleventh Centuries* (Oxford, 1992), p. 73. Some idea of the changes at Durham may be derived by comparing the kalendars printed in Wormald, *English Kalendars*, pp. 2–13 from Bodl.L, MS Digby 63 and *English Benedictine Kalendars*, pp. 161–79 from DCL, MS Hunter 100.

[31] J. Raine, *Saint Cuthbert* (Durham, 1828), pp. 120–30. C.F. Battiscombe, *The Relics of Saint Cuthbert* (Oxford, 1956), pp. 112–14, for the printed text of the twelfth-century relic list with references to the later lists.

[32] For Amphibalus, see Matthew Paris, *Chronica Majora*, ed. H.R. Luard (6 vols., RS 57; 1866–82), II, 301–8 (*s.a.* 1178).

[33] P. Devos, 'Les premières versions occidentales de la légende de Saidnaia', *Analecta Bollandiana* 65 (1947), pp. 245–78.

[34] *Cuth. virt.*, ch. 75 (pp. 154–7).

dependent, as we might at first think, on traversing the rest of England en route. If Durham itself seems distant from the coast, Jarrow, Wearmouth and the Farne islands are not and Hartlepool was the principal port of the diocese. The cult of Nicholas is closely linked to the sea and sailors who invoked his help in storms. Godric, himself a great traveller in his earlier days, composed a lyric prayer in English to Nicholas.[35] Many of Cuthbert's own twelfth-century miracles were done for those in distress at sea. Ailred of Rievaulx, on return from a regular visit to Cîteaux, commended Cuthbert in a great storm at sea to Cistercian abbots travelling back with him.[36] The cult of Cuthbert in Norway had crossed the North Sea and prayers for the liturgical celebration of the feast of his translation were used by the cathedral in Trondheim.[37] Bishop Walcher had come from the Low Countries; Bishop Puiset in 1173 secured a force of Flemish mercenaries directly across the sea during the war between his kings.[38] The monks had close relations with the sailors of Farne and of Berwick. They had ships of their own.[39] It would be unwise to discount the ease of Durham's maritime communications as a factor in opening up the community to outside influences. The miracle stories which focus on the hazards of maritime transport demonstrate how familiar an experience it was and by implication encourage its use, at least by those faithful enough to have confidence in divine power to protect them.

Durham's part in the religious community of early twelfth-century Europe inevitably brought its affairs to more general knowledge. St Bernard of Clairvaux, for example, took an interest in the monks' attempts to claim the right to elect their new bishop in 1140, used his good offices at the Roman curia on their behalf and then characteristically urged the monks to elect the candidate he favoured, Master Laurence, the chief negotiator at Rome.[40] In practice, the affair at Durham was settled by purely local interests, but Bernard's interventions are a reminder that in the twelfth century election disputes could acquire international importance. The

[35] *V. Godr.*, Godric's poem to St Nicholas is the earliest known lyric in English to have been written after 1066. It was copied in BL, MS Royal 5.F.VII, fol. 85r, Geoffrey's Latin Life of Godric, and printed by Joseph Hall, *Selections from Early Middle English 1130–1250* (Oxford, 1920), part I, p. 5; part II, pp. 241–5.
[36] *Cuth. virt.*, chs. 1, 16, 26, 83, 88 (pp. 1–3, 32, 60, 175–7, 188).
[37] C. Hohler, 'The Durham Services in Honour of St Cuthbert', in Battiscombe, *The Relics of Saint Cuthbert*, pp. 155–91. For Nidaros (Trondheim) see pp. 161–2 and E. Eggen, *The Sequences of the Archbishopric of Nidaros* (Copenhagen, 1968). For Norway and St Cuthbert see also *Cuth. virt.*, chs. 32, 52, and 112, and BL, MS Harley 1924, fol. 70v. As a young man Prior Turgot went into exile in Norway; see *HReg, s.a.* 1074 (pp. 202–4).
[38] Roger of Howden, *Chronica Magistri Rogeri de Houedene* (4 vols., RS 51; 1868–71), II, 63.
[39] *Cuth. virt.*: for Berwick, chs. 30, 68; for Farne miracles, chs. 23, 27, 29–34, 58, 62, 78, 101–2, 111, 117–20 (pp. 67–77, 116–17, 162–3, 226–9, 247–8, 262–6). For Durham's own ships see B. Colgrave, 'The Post-Bedan Miracles', pp. 316–17 (miracle 17), and for exemptions from tolls in ports, *Script. Tres*, Appendix no. xxx, p. xlix. Bishop Puiset had had a *magna navis*; see *The Chancellor's Roll, 8 Richard I*, Pipe Roll Society 42, ed. D.M. Stenton (1930), p. 253.
[40] T. Rud, *Codicum manuscriptorum ecclesiae cathedralis Dunelmensis catalogus classicus* (Durham, 1825), pp. 208–9, from DCL, MS B.IV.24.

1140s were unhappy years for Durham because King David of Scotland attempted to consolidate his position in northern England and violated the sanctuary of St Cuthbert. Laurence in his Latin poetry gave expression at some length to the misfortunes of the city and the exile forced upon him personally,[41] but the rest of England may not have been much interested. David's incursions into England had begun after the death of King Henry I at the end of 1135, and his depredations were described at length by northern historians.[42] Yet William of Malmesbury, the greatest English historian of the time, curiously paid them no attention, although in the 1120s he had naturally included a section on Durham in his history of English bishoprics. He had then described the site of the city and the river Wear and given a history of the see which emphasised the role of Cuthbert, and more recently of St Calais, in establishing monks there. His account ends, however, with the great translation ceremony of 1104 and his own prayer to Cuthbert.[43] Although Malmesbury travelled extensively for his studies, there is actually nothing in his work to substantiate the belief that he had visited Durham himself.[44] What he wrote could have all been taken from written sources such as Symeon's history. Whereas, therefore, we must allow for the exchange of information and books between Durham and other monasteries about matters of ecclesiastical interest, it did not follow that Durham's problems were understood or its vicissitudes followed with close attention outside the region. It had been drawn into the wider world but was still left to cope as it could. Hence, no doubt, the sense of helpless bewilderment that descended on Durham when William Cumin and the Scots occupied the city between 1141 and 1144.

III

The political rupture between the kings of England and Scotland in the twelfth century which threatened the security of the Durham diocese was only the most obvious of the ways in which the older pattern of life in the north was disintegrating. English royal interventions in Scotland to strengthen the authority of Queen Margaret's sons to the succession brought a new stability to the borders, followed by infiltration of Anglo-Norman families and customs into the Scottish kingdom. This in turn gave King David confidence that Cumbria and Northumberland at

---

[41] *Dialogi Laurentii*, ed. Raine, bk. 1, lines 428–30.

[42] G.W.S. Barrow, *David of Scotland (1124–1153): The Balance of Old and New* (Stenton Lecture, Reading, 1985), provided a very different view of David, and set contemporary records in a proper context. For Cumin, see also A. Young, *William Cumin: Border Politics and the Bishopric of Durham* (Borthwick Papers 54; York, 1978).

[43] William of Malmesbury, *De Gestis Pontificum Anglorum*, ed. N.E.S.A. Hamilton (RS 52; 1870), 'Lib. III De episcopis Dunelmi', pp. 266–76. There are signs of west country influence on Malmesbury's view of Durham. It is inexplicable why he should state that Bishop St Calais died at Gloucester, rather than Windsor. The most likely source of most of his information about the bishop is the *LDE* which he gutted for his own purposes and amended as he saw fit.

[44] R.M. Thomson, *William of Malmesbury* (Woodbridge, 1987), p. 74.

least, if not more of northern England, could be absorbed into the new style Scottish kingdom. This was resisted, the bishop of Durham himself contributing the construction of Durham and Norham castles to the defence of the region; King William II began the castle on the Tyne at Newcastle.[45] These military activities were not at all in the tradition of the Cuthbertine church. The monks of Durham began to think of themselves as a weak community exposed to Scottish violence and this reinforced their sense of being Englishmen living at the extremity of the kingdom. In this connection it is interesting to note how Reginald of Durham writes about King Stephen.[46] Surprisingly he is not blamed for the misfortunes his reign brought to Durham itself. The monks insisted on believing that their future lay with England and that the king would have surely delivered them had he not been prevented from doing so. There was no question whatever of accepting Scottish dominion, though in some ways this might have made more sense in local terms.

One of the consequences of Scottish reorganization in the borders was that Lothian became subject to the ecclesiastical authority of the bishop of St Andrews instead of that of Durham.[47] This was not, however, the only intrusion into its spiritual monopoly that Durham had to endure. The brief period of Robert Mowbray's earldom of Northumberland was sufficient for him to introduce some monks of St Albans into a priory-church at Tynemouth, to the great indignation of Durham monks who considered it their property. They claimed that Cuthbert punished not only the earl for his temerity with forfeiture and imprisonment, but also Abbot Paul of St Albans with an early, miserable death.[48] But Tynemouth Priory was never recovered by the Durham monks. Then there were the encroachments of the archbishop of York to deplore. The church of Hexham was revived as a religious community of Austin canons by Archbishop Thomas II and, though Hexham did not escape altogether from the cultural influence of Durham, it did not hesitate to resuscitate its own historical traditions.[49] Thus at Hexham the defeat of Malcolm Canmore in 1079 was attributed to the power of Hexham saints, Bishop Acca and others, whereas at Durham, Cuthbert was held responsible for this.[50] Then there was the creation of a new see at Carlisle in 1133, which threatened to cut Durham off from the west coast, formerly part of Cuthbert's Patrimony.[51] Though the new see had only a precarious life in the twelfth century,

---

[45] *HReg, s.a.* 1072 (p. 199, Durham castle built by William I); *HReg, s.a.* 1080 (p. 211, Newcastle founded by Robert Courthose); and *HReg, s.a.* 1121 (p. 260, Norham castle built by Bishop Flambard).

[46] *Cuth. virt.*, chs. 29, 64, 67, and 90 (pp. 65–6, 127, 134–5, and 193–4).

[47] For this see notes 12 and 39 above.

[48] *LDE*, bk. 4, ch. 4, and *De miraculis*, ch. 13 (*Sym. Op.* II, 345–7).

[49] *HReg, s.a.* 740 (p. 340), and *s.a.* 1112 (p. 247).

[50] *HReg, s.a.* 740 (pp. 36–8) for Acca, and *De miraculis*, ch. 10 (*Sym. Op.* II, 338–41) for Cuthbert. The *Vita sancti Eatae Haugustaldensis episcopi*, ed. J. Raine (SS 8; 1838), pp. 121–5, shows that Archbishop Thomas II was frustrated when he tried to translate Eata's bones from Hexham to York in 1113.

[51] For Cuthbert and Carlisle, see *Two Lives of Saint Cuthbert*, ed. and trans. B. Colgrave

its shadowy existence was an irksome indication of new boundaries being drawn through Durham's old northern empire.

Uneasiness about Durham's position went even deeper. The cathedral priory had come into being during the comparatively short period after the Conquest when Benedictine monasticism had reached its highest point in public esteem. From the early twelfth century, monasticism began to suffer from criticisms within the monastic order itself that the rule of St Benedict had been overlaid by improper accretions and was not being observed as was originally intended. In England the bishops, once they began to exercise their episcopal duties in the Norman kingdom with some confidence, discovered that they needed archdeacons and other administrative staff to help them, rather than the support of monastic chapters. The monks tended to have very tiresome ideas about the respect due to them and a preference for choosing more monks as bishops. Increasingly, new cathedral schools were appearing in twelfth-century England and France which offered better training for future bishops and episcopal servants than the monasteries could do. In England, the difficulty of the relationship between bishops and monks was made worse precisely because so many English cathedral chapters, including Durham, were composed of monks. Since it proved impossible in practice to dislodge these monastic chapters from the cathedrals until the English Reformation, the bishops began to build up a body of assistants alongside the chapters and tensions between these different interests in the church make up a large part of its domestic history in this period.[52]

The new learning of the schools also began to have an effect on the intellectual, moral and religious outlook for all men, monks included. The religious certainties of the Cuthbertan age so willingly embraced by Bishop St Calais began to shift uneasily under his successors. Durham never again saw a monk made bishop there. Rufus's minister, Flambard, was already suspected of being lukewarm in his appreciation of Cuthbert's miraculous powers and the meticulous account given of the translation ceremony in 1104 is clearly intended to dispel any possible doubt that the body of Cuthbert could have been miraculously preserved in his coffin for over four hundred years. The impact of these different experiences at Durham in the twelfth century meant that the community, despite all its famous achievements, was far more anxious, disturbed and unhappy than we are at first inclined to assume. The promise of the St Calais era was not, to their way of thinking, fulfilled.

The most eloquent and disturbing expression of how the 1140s had upset the community can be found in the Latin poetry of Laurence, a native of Waltham in Essex who had come north to be professed as a monk.[53] His verse, modelled on the

(Cambridge, 1940), pp. 116, 122, and 124 (anonymous life), and p. 242 (Bede's life). The loss of Durham's rights in Carlisle (and Teviotdale) was attributed in the first continuation of *LDE* to the period of Flambard's exile in 1100 (*Sym. Op.* I, 139).

52 Scammell, *Puiset*, p. 132.

53 *Dialogi Laurentii*, ed. Raine: on Waltham bk. 3, lines 329–440. For Laurence see also A. Hoste, 'A Survey of the Unedited Work of Laurence of Durham with an Edition of his Letter to Aelred of Rievaulx', *Sacris Erudiri* 11 (1960), pp. 249–65.

Latin classics, itself demonstrates the high level of accomplishment possible at Durham by his time and proves that the impressive collection of Latin literature kept in the monastic library[54] had real impact on the community. Laurence's dialogues in verse also prove the influence on him of the new scholastic style of study. The abstract character of his religious meditations and his professed obsession with his own death belong to a quite different tradition from that of the old Northumbrian church. His verses on St Cuthbert are respectful,[55] but there is not that expectation in them of any miraculous interventions of the kind found in the many Durham miracle stories. Since Laurence's dialogues present him in conversation with his friends, he did not think of himself as an entirely isolated figure in his community, though it does seem very likely that few monks shared his intellectual outlook. Yet taken alongside the evidence of library lists and books surviving from Durham, his works are proof of the great intellectual activity in the cathedral at this time. Apart from classical literature, its possession of works of law, theology, and medicine all make it impossible to ignore the great transformation of the scholastic interests of the monks, and their contacts with the schools of France and Italy. This put them in the forefront of the new learning, if not as pioneers, at least as willing pupils.[56]

The most independent of Durham's own intellectual activities was the writing of history, an interest that was widely cultivated all over post-Conquest England. Yet this interest seems to have been much more sustained at Durham than anywhere else in England.[57] At Malmesbury, William had no successors. But at Durham, beginning even before the Conquest, through Symeon and his continuators, the author of the *De iniusta uexacione*, to Reginald, and into the thirteenth century with Geoffrey of Coldingham, the writing of history was assiduously carried on across the generations as nowhere else. It was certainly an example to other churches, like the new community established at Hexham, and it must have been an inspiration to other well-known northern historians, Ailred of Rievaulx, William of Newburgh, and Roger of Howden. Though no one Durham writer can be claimed to have equalled the achievements of William of Malmesbury in restoring the Bedan historical tradition, no one could pretend that Durham ever needed to be prompted as to the importance of Bede. Before the Conquest his bones had been brought from Jarrow and deposited in the same coffin as St Cuthbert. They were honourably uncovered in 1104 and Bishop Hugh built for them in his new Galilee chapel a marvellously ornamented shrine.[58] The works of Bede and other

---

[54] 'Vetus Catalogus librorum qui in armariolo ecclesiae Cathedralis Dunelmenis olim habebantur', in DCL, MS B.IV.24 printed in *Catalogi ueteres librorum ecclesie cathedralis Dunelm*, ed. B. Botfield (SS 7; 1838), pp. 1–10.

[55] *Dialogi Laurentii*, ed. Raine, pp. 69–71: poem and prayer.

[56] *Catalogi*, ed. Botfield, for medicine, p. 6; for Gratian law books, p. 7; for English books, p. 5. Reginald's work on Cuthbert shows the effects of his medical learning and of his familiarity with classical mythology, presumably from his reading of the Latin classics.

[57] H.S. Offler, *Medieval Historians of Durham* (Inaugural Lecture; Durham, 1958), p. 6, was less impressed by the Durham historical tradition.

[58] *Script. Tres*, pp. 11–12. For the copying of Bede's *Vita S. Cuthberti* in the twelfth century,

Durham writers past and present were copied and preserved in the community and it is legitimate to suppose that they were also read and appreciated. The importance of intellectual activity at Durham was such that in the thirteenth century it was alone amongst the Benedictines in founding a college in Oxford for the benefit of its own monks.[59] We are surely justified in thinking that medieval Durham was a monastery where individual talents and learning were valued and promoted.

The English historical outlook in the twelfth century has been linked with a national desire to rescue the English traditions and past from French disrespect or indifference. The Durham monks were probably more often speakers of English than of French. A French-speaking clerk was picked out in one of Reginald's stories, presumably as unusual, and significantly was involved in an act of disrespect to a relic of St Cuthbert.[60] There are several pieces of Old English writing in twelfth-century Durham manuscripts, including a poem on the site of the city and the distinguished saints and kings honoured there, and a translation of the Benedictine rule.[61] In the twelfth-century library list, the books in English have a section to themselves.

Yet French must also have been familiar in the community. There were Frenchmen named in the Boldon Book as settled in the district.[62] A Durham calendar in the Bodleian Library has annotations of an astronomical character in French and a memorandum in French on the amount of money left at Cuthbert's shrine at Epiphany 1198.[63] There is an early copy of Wace's verse life of St Nicholas and an even more recent work: the vernacular sermons of Maurice de Sully, bishop of Paris, who must have been known personally to Bishop Puiset. How the two languages lived side by side at Durham we do not know, but monks who moved at all outside the region are bound to have spoken French on occasion. It is only

see M. Baker, 'Medieval Illustrations of Bede's Life of St Cuthbert', *Journal of Warburg and Courtauld Institutes* 41 (1978), pp. 16–49, especially p. 17.

[59] M.W. Sheehan, 'The Religious Orders 1220–1370', in *The History of the University of Oxford*, Vol. I, *The Early Oxford Schools*, ed. J. Catto (Oxford, 1984), p. 216 for foundation of Durham College in 1286.

[60] *Cuth. virt.*, ch. 47 (pp. 96–7).

[61] E. van Kirk Dobbie, *The Anglo-Saxon Minor Poems* (New York, 1942), p. 27, and notes 151–3. The sole surviving manuscript of the text is CUL, MS Ff.1.27. H.S. Offler, 'The Date of "Durham" ', *Journal of English and Germanic Philology* 61 (1962), pp. 591–4, argued that there were no good historical reasons why the poem must have been written after the translation of 1104 and thought it could well have been written in the late eleventh century before the monks were introduced at Durham in 1083. See also C.B. Kendall, 'Let Us Now Praise a Famous City', *Journal of English and Germanic Philology* 87 (1988), pp. 507–21.

[62] *Boldon Buke*, ed. W. Greenwell (SS 25; 1852), pp. 28, 31–2, 34, 36.

[63] C.A. Robson, *Maurice de Sully and the Medieval Vernacular Homily* (Oxford, 1952). Bodl.L, MS Douce 270 contains a calendar as printed in F. Wormald, *English Benedictine Kalendars*, pp. 161–79 from Cambridge, Jesus College, MS Q.B.6., the Sully sermons, a French translation of the Elucidarium attributed to Anselm, and Wace's metrical life of St Nicholas. On fol. ii v there is a note showing that the book was at Durham in 1197: 'lan del Encarnacion nostre Seigneur m c xcvij le ior de la Tephanie furent sor le fiertre saint Cuthbert c et vij besanz et xlv aneals'.

nationalistic prejudice to suppose that contemporaries would have regarded relations between their languages as antagonistic rather than as complementary. Both, like Latin itself, had their appropriate place. There was then no assumption that one language could fulfil all requirements.

For the most part, our view of late twelfth-century Durham depends on Durham records themselves, but there are a few clues as to the nature of Durham's reputation in those days found in other writers. In the history written by William, canon of Newburgh near Ampleforth, for example, as in Malmesbury more than half a century earlier, Durham is noticed mainly because of the activities of the bishops (a habit still with us), but Newburgh was not interested in Cuthbert as Malmesbury had been.[64] One of the events treated at most length in his chronicle is the death of Bishop Hugh of le Puiset who is openly criticised for his worldly life. Newburgh was very unfavourably impressed by the bishop's political ambitions and his castle-building. Of his works of piety he mentions only the leper hospital founded near Durham not, however, in mitigation, but because he alleged the bishop had built it by misappropriating funds. Puiset's personal eminence and qualities over forty years may be considered sufficient explanation for the attention he received.[65] By the end of the twelfth century, it was very commonly the case that the worldly lord had become the personification of his fee, even to the eclipse of its spiritual patron. In Rome itself, the pope had become of more consequence than St Peter. Bishop Hugh, who was a regular visitor in Normandy and at Rome, must have made the name of Durham known and surely secured respect for it as a see of great consequence. He himself had had his promotion to the bishopric confirmed by Pope Anastasius IV in 1154 when it was widely criticised in Cistercian circles.[66] Some thirty papal bulls were issued for Durham in Bishop Puiset's time.[67] He even received from Alexander III a detailed account of the famous Venice peace-talks in 1177, as one whom it was fitting to keep informed.[68] When he died, his death was entered for regular commemoration at Rouen cathedral.[69] At Durham, if not at Newburgh, such a magnificent bishop as Hugh would have been admired for enhancing its reputation.

Even Newburgh's own religious ideals were not totally outraged by what Durham had become under Bishop Hugh. He records his own visit to the aged hermit, Godric, in his last years at Finchale and acknowledged that Godric's saintly

---

[64] William of Newburgh, *Historia Rerum Anglicarum*, ed. R. Howlett (RS 82; 1884).

[65] Ibid., bk. 4, chs. 4–5 (pp. 303–5) and ch. 27 (pp. 371–2); bk. 5, chs. 10–11 (pp. 436–42).

[66] Scammell, *Puiset*, p. 16.

[67] *Papsturkunden in England*, ed. W. Holtzmann (Abhandlungen der Gesellschaft der Wissenschaften zu Göttingen, dritte Folge n. 14; 3 vols., Berlin, 1930–52), II, 111–26.

[68] Alexander III's letter 'Exigunt gratissimae' addressed to Roger, archbishop of York, and Bishop Hugh, 26 July 1177, from *Gesta Regis Henrici Secundi Benedicti Abbatis*, ed. W. Stubbs (2 vols., RS 49; 1867), I, 188–90; P. Jaffé, *Regesta Pontificum Romanorum* II (Leipzig, 1886), n. 12891.

[69] M. Bouquet, *Recueil des Historiens des Gaules et de la France*, XXIII, ed. MM de Wailly, Delisle and Jourdain (Paris, 1894), 'e Rotomagensis Ecclesiae Necrologio', p. 358.

reputation was properly appreciated at Durham itself since a senior monk was sent regularly to instruct Godric and offer him the holy sacrament.[70] Godric had become a very important figure at Durham itself. His great age and simplicity of life won him devotion and prompted concern at Durham to be of help to him. Prior Thomas encouraged Reginald of Durham to keep notes about the holy hermit; Thomas's successor, Germanus, himself wrote a life of the hermit which was later used by another monk, Geoffrey, in his biography. Reginald's own very long work on Godric was completed after Godric's death in 1170, probably after Reginald had abandoned, unfinished, a collection of stories about Cuthbert. Godric did not, of course, have anything like Cuthbert's reputation, but for many years he was a living example of the holy hermit Cuthbert himself had been.[71] He was a contemporary, impressive in his independence and obviously with many incredibly interesting stories to tell. It is not surprising that Durham monks allowed themselves to be fascinated. There may also be another important aspect. Perhaps the eremitical tradition of the older monasticism continued to be important at Durham. A priory was established at Lindisfarne. More significant still monks from Durham and others regularly sought solitude in the Farne islands where they felt Cuthbert's presence was very close. Durham's greatest historian, Symeon, appears to have taken in religion the name of one of the most famous of all recluses. Moreover, this strongly ascetic streak in monasticism held great attractions for monks of the Cistercian order like Ailred of Rievaulx or Bernard of Clairvaux; it also informed William of Newburgh's religious views. Did the monks of Durham show favour to hermits as much to impress the austere communities of monks and canons springing up in the new Northumbria north and south of the border as to maintain a strand of their own inheritance?

However significant in its own terms and for marking the end of an earlier era, the interest in contemporary hermits could not nourish the Durham community spiritually as the Cuthbert stories had done. More than any other one source the miracles wrought by their saint, as recorded at Durham, bring to life the hopes and fears of the age. All over the north there appear to have been men and women devoted to his cult, particularly, it seems, in those churches dedicated to him.[72] The list of these compiled by Prior Wessington in the fifteenth century[73] would, in fact, have been the same if made in the twelfth century. Most of the eighty-three churches concerned are in the north of England or southern Scotland. The incumbents of these churches may have considered it a point of honour to visit Durham, eager to tell extraordinary stories about what Cuthbert's powers had effected in their own parishes. The monks of Durham gratefully made use of such stories as

[70] Newburgh, *Historia Rerum Anglicarum*, pp. 149–50.

[71] See note 35. *Cuth. virt.* shows that Cuthbert was a more powerful intercessor, chs. 113, 124, and 126 (pp. 255, 270, and 272).

[72] *Cuth. virt.*, chs. 20, 57, 64–5, 68–73, 84–8, 129, and 132–40 (pp. 41–4, 115, 126–34, 138–51, 177–82, 275–8, and 280–90).

[73] A. Hamilton Thompson, 'The Manuscript List of Churches Dedicated to Saint Cuthbert Attributed to Prior Wessyngton', *TAASDN* 7, part 2, (1936), pp. 151–77.

additional proof of Cuthbert's continuing interventions. Outside these favoured parishes Cuthbert does not seem to have been more widely known. One knight in Leicestershire had learned to honour Cuthbert while in the service of Bishop Geoffrey Rufus, forty years earlier.[74] Ailred of Rievaulx, who had learned to venerate Cuthbert from his own father, encouraged Reginald's project of collecting the miracle stories, himself composed a work in praise of Cuthbert and, on his return from the annual chapter at Cîteaux, commended the powers of Cuthbert as an intercessor at sea.[75] Cuthbert's reputation as a miracle-worker in storms was, however, unlike Nicholas's, localised in the North Sea, and most of the storm stories were gathered in the Farne Islands. Cuthbert's dominion was essentially confined geographically to the old Northumbria.

Bede was naturally the most important authority for the life and miracles of St Cuthbert.[76] But the community which looked after Cuthbert's body had kept records in the tenth and eleventh centuries of the saint's continuing intercessions on their behalf.[77] After the foundation of the monastic priory in the cathedral, a much more deliberate effort was made to write up the wonderful events by which Cuthbert had continued to assure the monks of his protection. The monks' new foreign connections had some influence here for a collection of these stories was made for a French house and the monks seem to have borrowed from some French centre like Le Mans the idea of illustrating manuscripts of their local saint's life.[78] An elaboration of seven Cuthbert miracles earlier than 1072 was written up after 1083, and another collection of miracles belonging to Rufus's reign was put together shortly after 1104.[79] Later a Durham writer compiled a short account of Cuthbert from all these materials,[80] and from the mid-twelfth century Reginald began to collect yet another set of wonder-stories.[81] Before he finished, this amounted to another 141 stories, far exceeding that of any of his predecessors. Each of Reginald's stories were for the most part small works of art in their own

[74] *Cuth. virt.*, ch. 128 (p. 274).

[75] *Cuth. virt.*, as note 36.

[76] *Two Lives of Cuthbert*, ed. Colgrave. The anonymous life is only known from continental manuscripts.

[77] B. Colgrave, 'The Post-Bedan Miracles' showed that the *Historia de S. Cuthberto* provided miracles attributed to the ninth century and H.H.E. Craster, 'The Red Book of Durham', *EHR* 40 (1925), pp. 504–32 argued that the chronicle contained in the lost Book of the High Altar was written 1072–83 (p. 531). *Cuth. virt.*, ch. 19 (p. 41), is a record of a miracle recorded by the *veterani canonici* from before 1083.

[78] M. Baker, 'Medieval Illustrations', and F. Wormald, 'Some illustrated manuscripts of the Lives of Saints', *Bulletin of the John Rylands Library* 35 (1952–53), pp. 248–66.

[79] B. Colgrave, 'The Post-Bedan Miracles' identified a first group of miracles (his chs. 1–4) and others (chs. 5–7) relating to the period before 1072 but written up after 1083, and a second group (chs. 8–17) relating to events under William Rufus which was probably written up with the encouragement of Prior Turgot. The wonders of the translation ceremony of 1104 provided three more (chs. 18–20).

[80] 'Brevis relatio de sancto Cuthberto' in BL, Cotton MS Nero A.II and Bodl.L, MS Laud 491, printed in *Symeon of Durham*, ed. H. Hinde (SS 51; 1867), pp. 223–30.

[81] *Cuth. virt.*

terms, with long introductions of a moralistic or theological character indicating what kind of point each particular miracle would illustrate. The main part of the story usually concluded by referring specifically to the original witnesses of the miracle and sometimes compared it with a similar miracle told in scripture or of another saint. In the many stories relating to cures Reginald, perhaps illustrating here the impact of recent medical studies, gave the most minute descriptions of the physical condition of the sick or injured person. In the several cases he gives of wrongful imprisonment, he similarly enlarged on the harrowing details of the victim's sufferings. Although the work has a very long and learned preface, it lacks a formal conclusion and since its last few miracles were short and unelaborated it looks as though Reginald did not actually complete the task he had originally set himself. By the time he gave up, he was clearly uneasy about the powerful new cult of Becket at Canterbury.[82] This in fact put paid to any earlier hope at Durham of promoting Cuthbert as England's greatest saint.

The very number of miracles Reginald collected hints at some anxiety to silence any doubt. Cuthbert was a saint of a bygone era and at Durham it had become important to insist on his effective miraculous powers in a new age. Reginald's many examples, his reference to parallel miracles worked by better known saints, Nicholas of Bari, Martin of Tours, even Leonard of Limoges,[83] and the learned elaboration of his introductions introduces us to the heart of the problem as it seemed at Durham; Cuthbert was coming to look like a very regional figure from a remote Northumbrian age quite alien to the new kind of world the monks of Durham had to live with, indeed wished to live with. Was it for this reason that Reginald stressed so often that when he appeared in visions to impress his devotees, Cuthbert wore pontifical vestments of contemporary impressiveness, almost never the garb of the hermit he had in fact been most of his real life?[84] And when the monks heard about the Irish legend of Cuthbert's birth into a royal line of Irish kings, why did they so quickly adopt this spurious material into their own long hallowed traditions, adding the element of noble birth to a saint who so obviously had appealed in the past to a different kind of sensibility?[85]

Reginald's own compatriots could show themselves singularly indifferent to

---

[82] *Cuth. virt.*, chs. 112, 114–16, and 125–6 (pp. 251–2, 236, 260, 261–2, 271).

[83] For comparisons with Nicholas, see chs. 27, 29–31, and 71; with Martin, chs. 104 and 88; with Benedict, ch. 103; Leonard, ch. 79; Peter, ch. 70; Lawrence, ch. 108; Christ, chs. 14, 23; various figures from the Old Testament, chs. 12, 21, 28, 64, 73.

[84] *Cuth. virt.*, chs. 23, 38, 68–9 (pp. 52, 82, 140, 141).

[85] 'Libellus de nativitate sancti Cuthberti de historiis Hybernensium excerptus et translatus', printed in *Miscellanea Biographica*, ed. James Raine (SS 8; 1838), pp. 61–87. M.H. Dodds, 'The Little Book of the Birth of St Cuthbert', *Arch. Ael*, 4th ser., 6 (1929), pp. 52–94 provides a commentary and translation. D. Bethell, 'English Monks and Irish Reform', gave no reasons for ascribing this curious work to Prior Laurence (p. 123, n. 79). H.H.E. Craster, 'The Red Book of Durham', p. 507, shows that London, Lincoln's Inn, MS 114, item 7, is superior to that used by Raine in his edition. See also P. Grosjean, 'The Alleged Irish Origin of Saint Cuthbert', in Battiscombe, *The Relics of Saint Cuthbert*, pp. 144–54.

Cuthbert's merits unless monks of Durham enlightened them. The bishop's architect, a man of Durham called Richard the Engineer, put great faith in an amulet he carried bearing the name of Saviour until, confiding this faith to one of the monks, he was persuaded that a relic of St Cuthbert was a more reliable source of strength.[86] As close to Durham as Brancepeth, a poor man falsely accused, imprisoned and loaded with chains, called on his local saint, St Brendan, for help. According to the story told by Reginald, St Brendan duly led him out of his dungeon, but left him at the gate of the prison itself where St Cuthbert took over his release, because Cuthbert, as Brendan himself admitted, was more famous, more powerful and much more outstanding and effective as a miracle-worker.[87] The Durham stories contain many indications of how widely contemporaries cast around for effective miracle-workers and how hard the Durham community itself worked to promote the superior merits of Cuthbert. These tales themselves show that they could not take general respect and faith for granted.

From Reginald's work on Cuthbert we do, however, receive the most vivid impressions of contemporary life in the city, cathedral and places associated with the saint, particularly the country churches in outlying regions where the old faith in the saints' powers may have resisted scepticism elsewhere. From other sources we may learn about the striking individuals who were bishops, even about priors at Durham. But only in Reginald can we read about individual monks, the sacrists, Bernard and Benedict, with their pride in the interior decorations of the church for which they were responsible;[88] the cellarer, Uhtred, anxious about his declining stock of provisions, who had to be reassured by the sub-prior;[89] poor Brother John who could not resist the temptation to take a closer peek at Cuthbert's Gospel book, though he had not reverently abstained from food or made due liturgical ablutions;[90] Brother Robert of St Martin, a former knight, who simply could not learn to read, eventually threw his psalter at Cuthbert's tomb in disgust;[91] the equally impassioned steward, Brother John, who was thrown from his mount when it was frightened because John's youthful attendants raced their horses on the way back from Newcastle. John was so seriously injured in the groin that he was advised to submit to surgery, but he refused because he could not endure the ignominy of being mocked as a eunuch.[92] Reginald's monks had their own duties and their own worries. They must have often repeated the stories of the wonders they knew about, and Reginald perhaps encouraged them to do this round the fire in winter as a way of paying their personal tribute to their holy patron and advancing his collection. Other stories of Cuthbert's wonders were more occasionally narrated to the monks sitting in chapter when they received visitors, like those from Norway or

---

[86] *Cuth. virt.*, chs. 54, 47 (pp. 94–8, 111–12).
[87] *Cuth. virt.*, ch. 46 (pp. 92–4).
[88] *Cuth. virt.*, chs. 27, 36–7, 51, 80, 91 (pp. 61, 79–81, 107, 165–8, 197–201).
[89] *Cuth. virt.* ch. 106 (pp. 236–9).
[90] *Cuth. virt.*, ch. 91 (pp. 197–201).
[91] *Cuth. virt.*, ch. 76 (pp. 158–60).
[92] *Cuth. virt.*, ch. 103 (pp. 229–31).

the Low Countries, who reported the cures or deliverance attributed to the intervention of their saint.[93] There were naturally stories featuring Durham itself, particularly from those who had suffered in the local gaol, but escaped because of Cuthbert's miraculous powers to lead them out of prison or cause their fetters to rust away.[94] Cuthbert had cured a blind old lady,[95] a fantasising youth who jumped around the banks of the Wear[96] and another who was struck seriously on the head when the clapper of one of the cathedral bells crashed from the tower.[97] (On feast days, Reginald tells us, the local lads were very enthusiastic bell-ringers.)[98] Without Reginald's enthusiasm for Cuthbert, we would be much less well informed about twelfth-century Durham.

Yet all Reginald's efforts could not disguise the fact that the world was changing in so many ways that the monks could do nothing about. Durham had been relegated to the periphery of the powerful new kingdom shaped by the Angevins. Henry II had insisted on extending his royal enquiry into crime to the bishop's immunity.[99] Becket, Henry II's greatest opponent became, in death, the most famous of all English saints. He would thereafter overshadow Cuthbert, except perhaps residually in the farthest north. Cuthbert had been the venerable saint of the old Northumbrians. When Northumbria was partitioned between England and Scotland, Cuthbert's natural constituency fell apart. The monks of Durham did what they could to infuse new life into that old order, but the times were against them. Their brave and baffled efforts to deal with the problems of their times made the twelfth century a challenging period for Durham. Their ultimate failure should not be attributed to their lack of will. Nor indeed did they fail to sense the challenge of the age. For historians looking back after nine hundred years, there is the fascination of seeing how men in those days did strive to make something positive of the difficult situation facing them.

Twelfth-century Durham must not be thought of as an impossibly ideal time. It was as worrying as any period has ever been. The monks who cultivated a simple faith in their patron saint discovered that this was hardly sufficient to give them the pre-eminence and security for their church that they hoped for. But even if they did not ultimately succeed, they gave every sign of fighting on to the end for the values they believed in. Though they became provincial to the main lines of English development, they knew how to create the cathedral as a magnificent testimonial to the great Northumbrian tradition. It was admittedly only the outer

[93] *Cuth. virt.* There are many references to the narration of miracles to the monks: chs. 17, 19, 63, 76–7, 94, 106–7, 113–14, 128, 134–5.
[94] *Cuth. virt.*, chs. 20, 46, 49, 50, 90, 93, 95.
[95] *Cuth. virt.*, chs. 121, 123.
[96] *Cuth. virt.*, ch. 122.
[97] *Cuth. virt.*, ch. 92 (pp. 201–4).
[98] *Cuth. virt.*, ch. 92 (p. 202): 'Illi tamen, qui de Dunelmo nati fuerant, campanariorum pulsandorum periciae noticiam et artis scientiam plus habebant. Nempe usus exercitati operis dabat noticiae scientiam et artem cognitionis.'
[99] *Script. Tres*, Appendix no. xxxi, p. l.

shell of which the core was Cuthbert's shrine, and that shrine was broken up centuries ago at the Reformation. But the twelfth-century building, which is still visible, can lead us on in our historical imaginations to glimpse Durham as it was in the Anglo-Norman world.

PART ONE

The Monks and the Priory

English Cathedral Communities and Reform in the Late Tenth and the Eleventh Centuries

JULIA BARROW

I N THE TENTH and eleventh centuries English cathedral communities underwent fundamental changes. These would provide enough material for a monograph (so far only Canterbury has received attention on this scale).[1] But before this
can be attempted it is necessary to go behind the existing interpretations and
reassess what the sources tell us, and the area where such a re-evaluation is most
needed is the question of reform, since the views of the reformers, where they were
successful, have too often been adopted uncritically by historians.

Durham cathedral offers an excellent point of entry into the subject, because it
underwent three distinct phases of development which encapsulate the changes in
English cathedrals over the period *c.*960–*c.*1100. These phases are mapped out for
us in the early twelfth-century *History of the Church of Durham* attributed to
Symeon (the *Libellus de exordio*), a text which needs to be interpreted carefully to
allow for the author's ideological standpoint, one of staunch Benedictine partisan-
ship:[2]

(a) from the departure of the community of St Cuthbert from Lindisfarne up to the
time of Bishop Walcher (1071–80) we see a group of clerics, mostly hereditary,
with bishops who had in some cases taken monastic vows (according to the *Libellus
de exordio* all but two had done so, but we know from another source that Aldhun,
one of the 'monastic' bishops, had a daughter).[3]

(b) under Bishop Walcher, and at his instigation, we see the adoption of a more
strictly ordered canonical life, with the main change being in liturgical practices:
'When (Walcher) found clerks in that place he taught them to observe the custom
of clerks in the day and night offices.'[4]

[1] N.P. Brooks, *The Early History of the Church of Canterbury* (Leicester, 1984).
[2] *LDE*; on the community of St Cuthbert, see W. Aird, 'The Origins and Development of
the Church of St Cuthbert, 635–1153, with Special Reference to Durham in the Period
*c.*1071–1153' (unpublished Ph.D. thesis, Edinburgh University, 1991); E. Craster, 'The Patrimony of St Cuthbert', *EHR* 69 (1954), pp. 177–99; *The Relics of St Cuthbert*, ed. C.F.
Battiscombe (Oxford, 1956), and *Cuthbert*.
[3] *LDE*, bk. 2, ch. 6 (p. 58), ch. 20 (p. 78), bk. 3, ch. 6 (p. 86), ch. 9 (p. 91), and ch. 18 (p.
106); *De obsessione Dunelmi* (*Sym. Op.* I, 217).
[4] *LDE*, bk. 3, ch. 18 (p. 106).

(c) under Bishop William of St Calais (1081–96) in 1083, we see the expulsion of the secular clerics and their replacement with Benedictine monks.[5] The author of the *Libellus de exordio*, taking a similar line to earlier Benedictine writers, presented this final change as justified both by the 'unclean living' (i.e. marriage) of the clergy and by the fact that the Lindisfarne community had originally been monastic, as stated by Bede and other early sources. This had indeed been so, but the author of the *Libellus de exordio* failed to realise that the term 'monastic' before the tenth century was so elastic that it could refer to any sort of ecclesiastical community.[6] Instead, he assumed that it meant 'Benedictine'.

In what follows I want to concentrate on the two trends which at Durham were exemplified by the reforms of Bishop Walcher and Bishop William: organised *uita communis* for secular canons, and the introduction of Benedictine monks into cathedrals. The two phenomena were linked: both show a desire on the part of the Anglo-Saxon higher clergy to catch up with continental developments, and both were meant to make the running of cathedrals, in particular from a liturgical viewpoint, more efficient and disciplined. Firstly, however, the political background must be sketched, since English episcopal churches in the tenth century had suffered profound upheavals.

Very few dioceses were unaffected by political events in this period. The south-eastern sees and those in western Mercia were least affected. Everywhere else there was change. The two Wessex dioceses were subdivided in 909–10 to mirror the shire system more exactly. Wiltshire and Berkshire were removed from the see of Winchester to form the new see of Ramsbury, while Sherborne lost the south-western peninsula, which became the see of Crediton, and also Somerset, which became the see of Wells, to retain only Dorset. This scheme must have been instigated by Edward the Elder, though with assistance from Archbishop Plegmund, who apparently had the task of obtaining papal permission for the change.[7]

Meanwhile the two East Anglian sees had disappeared in or after the 870s, with the area coming under the supervision of the bishop of London in the first half of the tenth century.[8] The diocese of Leicester was moved to Dorchester between 869 and 888.[9] Episcopal succession in the see of Lindsey is impossible to trace between the 870s and the 950s and was re-established only briefly in the mid-tenth century:

---

[5]   *LDE*, bk. 4, chs. 2–3 (pp. 120–3).
[6]   *Pastoral Care before the Parish*, ed. J. Blair and R. Sharpe (Leicester, 1992), esp. J. Blair and R. Sharpe, 'Introduction', pp. 1–10, at pp. 3–4, and S. Foot, 'Anglo-Saxon Minsters: a Review of Terminology', pp. 212–25.
[7]   N.P. Brooks, *Early History*, pp. 210–13.
[8]   D. Whitelock, *Some Anglo-Saxon Bishops of London* (Chambers Memorial Lecture, 1974; London, 1975), pp. 18, 20; reprinted in her *History, Law and Literature in 10th–11th Century England* (London, 1981).
[9]   R.A. Hall, 'The Five Boroughs of the Danelaw: a Review of Present Knowledge', *ASE* 18 (1989), pp. 149–206, at p. 167; F.M. Stenton, *Anglo-Saxon England* (3rd edn, Oxford, 1971), pp. 437–8.

the see was merged with that of Dorchester after 1011.[10] Out of the whole area of Danish settlement York alone preserved its line of archbishops, and, after the permanent conquest of the Scandinavian kingdom of York by Eadred in 954, the archbishopric was, up to 1016, held in tandem with a Southumbrian see – Dorchester until 971 and then Worcester.[11] The northernmost diocese of the Anglo-Saxons, Lindisfarne, underwent the most dramatic upheaval of all, as the bishop and clergy moved across northern England in the late ninth century. Here, continuity was preserved through the devotion of the clerical community to their patron saint, and through the assistance of one of the Scandinavian York kings.[12]

It has until very recently been customary to blame the Danes for the ills (often hypothetical rather than actual) afflicting the English church in the ninth and tenth centuries. In particular the disruptions in the diocesan map have been laid at their door: 'There can be no question that the Danish invasions of the ninth century shattered the organisation of the English church' (Stenton); 'The reasons most commonly alleged for Oswald's pluralism are the poverty of the see of York and its inhabitants. The Viking invasions had made large areas of eastern and northern England pagan at worst, missionary country at best' (Rosalind Hill and C.N.L. Brooke).[13] A more critical approach to the sources has been urged by Pauline Stafford, but no one has yet provided the much-needed analysis of the Danish impact on the English church.[14]

In fact, many Danes seem to have been intensely pious, often from quite early in the settlement period. The significant number of new parish foundations in the Danelaw in the tenth century, and the wealth of Anglo-Scandinavian funerary carvings found at church sites all over northern England,[15] show us how the richer Danes adopted the beliefs and social observances of their neighbours. Earlier still,

[10] S.R. Bassett, 'Lincoln and the Anglo-Saxon See of Lindsey', *ASE* 18 (1989), pp. 1–32, at pp. 22–5.
[11] D. Whitelock, 'The Dealings of the Kings of England with Northumbria in the Tenth and Eleventh Centuries', in *The Anglo-Saxons: Studies in Some Aspects of their History and Culture Presented to Bruce Dickins*, ed. P.A.M. Clemoes (London, 1959), pp. 70–88, at pp. 73–6; eadem, 'Wulfstan at York', in *Franciplegius*, ed. J.B. Bessinger and R.P. Creed (New York, 1965), pp. 214–31, at pp. 214–15; both articles reprinted in Whitelock, *History, Law*; Janet Cooper, *The Last Four Anglo-Saxon Archbishops of York* (Borthwick Papers 38; York, 1970), pp. 1–2.
[12] See works cited in n. 2 above, and, in addition, D.W. Rollason, *Saints and Relics in Anglo-Saxon England* (Oxford, 1989), pp. 144–52, 197–202.
[13] Stenton, *Anglo-Saxon England*, p. 433; R.M.T. Hill and C.N.L. Brooke, 'From 627 until the Early Fourteenth Century', in *A History of York Minster*, ed. G.E. Aylmer and R. Cant (Oxford, 1977), p. 16.
[14] P. Stafford, *Unification and Conquest* (London, 1989), p. 181; R. Fleming, 'Monastic Lands and England's Defence in the Viking Age', *EHR* 100 (1985), pp. 247–65, is challenged by D. Dumville, 'Ecclesiastical Lands and the Defence of Wessex in the First Viking Age', in idem, *Wessex and England from Alfred to Edgar* (Woodbridge, 1992), pp. 29–54.
[15] P. Stafford, *The East Midlands in the Early Middle Ages* (Leicester, 1985), pp. 184–6; J.T. Lang, 'Anglo-Scandinavian Sculpture in Yorkshire', in *Viking Age York and the North*, ed. R.A. Hall (Council for British Archaeology, Research Report no. 27; London, 1978), pp. 11–20; idem, *Corpus of Anglo-Saxon Stone Sculpture, III, York and Eastern Yorkshire* (London, 1991).

there is evidence for high-ranking Danes taking an interest in, or at least showing tolerance to, churches and saints' cults in the late ninth and the early tenth centuries. From the mid-890s coins bearing the name of St Edmund (killed by the Danes in 869) were circulating widely in areas under Scandinavian control;[16] in the early tenth century pennies were minted at York and Lincoln bearing respectively the names of St Peter and St Martin.[17] This coinage was probably controlled by local Scandinavian rulers, and this suggests that at the least they were tolerant of Christian ideology. The strongest Scandinavian support for a saint's cult came from Guthfrith, king of York, who gave the community of St Cuthbert a site for a new episcopal church at Chester-le-Street.[18] Finally, clerics of partly Danish descent were obtaining the highest offices in the English church in the first half of the tenth century.[19]

In these circumstances, the fates of the East Anglian and the East Midlands sees seem especially surprising. Surely the Danes would have been happy to see them filled – obviously by bishops of their choice? But the Danes lacked control of the Southumbrian metropolitan see. New bishops for Dunwich, Elmham, Leicester and Lindsey would have to be consecrated by the archbishop of Canterbury, which in political terms meant that they would have to meet the approval of the kings of Wessex. More probably, Alfred and his successors determined to bring the lines of episcopal succession under their own control, not only to prevent the Danes from further consolidating their political power, but also to extinguish any possibility of a revival of the kingdom of Mercia. Dorothy Whitelock and Janet Cooper have argued convincingly that the reason for the see of York being held in plurality was because the English kings wanted to ensure the loyalty of the archbishops of York.[20] As Stenton, Whitelock and Stafford have all remarked, the unification of England was not a foregone conclusion, and no-one was more aware of this than Eadred and his successors.[21]

It seems likely, therefore, that giving the bishop of London temporary charge of East Anglia, moving the see of Leicester to Dorchester (within the orbit of Wessex by the late ninth century), and allowing the see of Lindsey to disappear for half a century were acts of political opportunism by the Wessex kings. If there is a genuine basis to the letter of Pope Formosus addressed to the bishops of England between 892 and 896, urging them not to allow sees to remain unfilled, it might perhaps have been inspired by a complaint from clerics in eastern England that

---

[16] *Medieval European Coinage, I, The Early Middle Ages, 5th–10th Centuries*, ed. P. Grierson and M. Blackburn (Cambridge, 1986), pp. 319–20.

[17] Ibid., pp. 322–3; Rollason, *Saints and Relics*, p. 157.

[18] *Historia de sancto Cuthberto*, § 13 (*Sym. Op.* I, 203); E. Cambridge, 'Why did the Community of St Cuthbert settle at Chester-le-Street?', in *Cuthbert*, pp. 370–2, 385–6.

[19] Oda, archbishop of Canterbury from 942 to 958 (*Historians of the Church of York and its Archbishops*, ed. J. Raine (3 vols., RS 71; London, 1879–94), I, 404; Oskytel (archbishop of York, 956–71) has a partly Danish name.

[20] See works by D. Whitelock and J. Cooper cited in n. 11.

[21] Ibid., and F.M. Stenton, 'The Founding of Southwell Minster', in *Preparatory to Anglo-Saxon England*, ed. D.M. Stenton (Oxford, 1970), p. 365.

they were being starved of bishops.[22] After 954 it was possible for the southern kings to control the church as far north as the Tees. Chester-le-Street was too far north to come under their direct control, but it had built up good relations with them in the first half of the tenth century, when it wanted to fend off domination from Scandinavian York on the one hand and from the Scottish kingdom on the other.[23]

The events we have observed affected the cathedral communities of the tenth and eleventh centuries much more seriously than their bishops. All the sees which had been moved, or newly founded, faced the problems of acquiring land and building up networks of friendship with thegns and nobles. They were often placed in grossly unsuitable sites, far away from burgeoning urban centres.[24] The Wessex kings carefully avoided planting new sees in burhs.[25] As a result, cathedral communities were often economically marginalised. Worst of all, they often had no saints' cults, which made it much harder for them to build up clientages among the local landowning classes. Ramsbury and Dorchester, for example, were quite unable to emulate the community of St Cuthbert, which used its saint's cult to establish a huge network of friendship, recorded in the Durham *Liber Vitae*, across northern England and southern Scotland.[26] Not surprisingly, only a few English cathedral communities established cultural reputations in the last century before the Norman Conquest.

Having sketched the impact of political events on cathedrals we may now turn to the question of reforming trends: which ones were available in the tenth and eleventh centuries and how effective were they? There were two alternative types of reform to hand, Benedictine monasticism and an ordered life for secular canons, as developed by Carolingian legislation. The former had a great impact on England. Cathedrals which became Benedictine remained monastic until the Reformation. They were also extremely influential, forming the careers of many late-Saxon bishops and providing a model for the conversion of further cathedrals (Durham and Rochester) in the late eleventh century.[27] The latter trend (an ordered life for secular canons) had almost no impact during the period *c*.900–1050.[28] I shall here

---

[22] *Cartularium Saxonicum*, ed. W. de G. Birch (4 vols., London, 1885–9), no. 573, discussed by Brooks, *Early History*, pp. 212–13.
[23] D.W. Rollason, 'St Cuthbert and Wessex: the Evidence of Cambridge, Corpus Christi College MS 183', in *Cuthbert*, pp. 413–24; idem, *Saints and Relics*, pp. 146–51.
[24] Cf. the famous criticisms expressed by William of Malmesbury in his *De Gestis Pontificum Anglorum*, ed. N.E.S.A. Hamilton (RS 52; 1870), pp. 133, 148, 175, 182, 200, 307, 311, discussed by F. Barlow, *The English Church 1000–1066* (2nd edn, London, 1979), pp. 164–5.
[25] *An Atlas of Anglo-Saxon England*, ed. D. Hill (Oxford, 1981), pp. 85–6. Note that the only tenth-century episcopal sees which coincide with burhs listed in the Burghal Hidage are Worcester (a later addition to the text), and Winchester, both early episcopal foundations in Roman walled sites.
[26] *Liber Vitae*; J. Gerchow, *Die Gedenküberlieferung der Angelsachsen* (Berlin and New York, 1988), pp. 109–54, comments only on the entries up to the ninth century.
[27] Durham (1083) and Rochester (1080): D. Knowles, *The Monastic Order in England* (2nd edn., Cambridge, 1963), pp. 169, 177.
[28] M.McC. Gatch, 'The Office in Late Anglo-Saxon Monasticism', in *Learning and Literature*

look at the rules for secular canons and their diffusion in England before comparing their success with that of the Benedictine Rule.

In the tenth and eleventh centuries there was no indigenous English attempt to devise a pattern of life for the clergy. Possible models for cathedral communities were, however, provided by a range of continental texts. The legislation of Louis the Pious at Aachen between 816 and 819 had established separate rules for secular canons (the *Institutio canonicorum* or Rule of Aachen), nuns (*Institutio sanctimonialium*), and monks (the Benedictine Rule with additional customs drawn up by Benedict of Aniane).[29] Soon afterwards, a hybrid rule for canons was compiled out of the Rule of Aachen and its parent text, the mid-eighth century Rule of Chrodegang (bishop of Metz). This hybrid text is known as the Enlarged Rule of Chrodegang.[30] There is evidence for some circulation in England of the Rule of Aachen and more particularly of the Enlarged Rule of Chrodegang: we may look at each in turn.

Rule of Aachen

No entire text of this Rule can be shown to have existed in pre-Conquest England. This is in strong contrast to its distribution on the continent, where roughly fifty manuscripts of the text survive from the period before *c.*1100.[31] Only eight chapters of the Rule of Aachen are known, or can be surmised, to have been transmitted in England before 1066, and these are incorporated into other texts. Chapter 145, the final chapter of the rule, which is intended to summarize the whole work, occurs in Latin in two pre-Conquest English manuscripts, and was translated into English by Archbishop Wulfstan II of York to form part of the final recension of his Institutes of Polity.[32] Secondly, seven chapters of the Rule of Aachen, in whole or in part, are to be found in the thirteenth-century Rule of St Paul's, drawn up by Dean

in *Anglo-Saxon England: Studies Presented to Peter Clemoes*, ed. H. Gneuss and M. Lapidge (Cambridge, 1985), pp. 341–62, at p. 343; cf. also J. Semmler, 'Le monachisme occidental du VIIIe au Xe siècle: formation et réformation', *Revue bénédictine* 103 (1993), pp. 68–89, at pp. 86–9, and R. Schieffer, *Die Entstehung von Domkapiteln in Deutschland* (Bonn, 1976), pp. 242–60.

[29] *Institutio Canonicorum Aquisgranensis* and *Institutio Sanctimonialium Aquisgranensis*, in *Concilia Aevi Karolini*, ed. A. Werminghoff (MGH Concilia II/1; Hanover, 1904), pp. 308–421, 422–56; *Corpus Consuetudinum Monasticarum*, I, ed. K. Hallinger (Siegburg, 1963), pp. 501–36. Frankish legislation on common life for clerks found an echo in the cathedral communities of Canterbury and Winchester in the ninth century: Brooks, *Early History*, pp. 155–9 and *Cartularium Saxonicum*, ed. Birch, no. 544.

[30] B. Langefeld, 'Die lateinische Vorlage der altenglischen Chrodegang-Regel', *Anglia* 98 (1980), pp. 403–16, updates some of the findings of A. Werminghoff, 'Die Beschlüsse des Aachener Concils im Jahre 816', *Neues Archiv* 27 (1902), pp. 605–75, at pp. 646–51.

[31] Catalogued by A. Werminghoff, MGH Concilia II/1, pp. 310–11, with supplement by R. Schieffer, *Die Entstehung von Domkapiteln*, pp. 249–50, n. 105.

[32] Cf. D. Whitelock, 'Archbishop Wulfstan, Homilist and Statesman', *TRHS*, 4th ser. 24 (1942), pp. 42–60, at pp. 47–8, reprinted in Whitelock, *History, Law, Die "Institutes of Polity, Civil and Ecclesiastical"*, ed. K. Jost (Bern, 1959), pp. 248–55 and also pp. 12–13.

Ralph Baldock.[33] Both Dorothy Whitelock and C.N.L. Brooke have argued that the likeliest time for this material to have come to London was in the tenth century, under Bishop Theodred (926–951/3), Bishop Dunstan (959), or Wulfstan (bishop of London 996–1002 before becoming archbishop of York).[34]

It is worth looking closely at the content of the chapters of the Rule of Aachen chosen for incorporation into the Rule of St Paul's and the Institutes. Dorothy Whitelock, C.N.L. Brooke and Frank Barlow have stated that they were self-contained rules, but I would argue that this is not so. The seven chapters selected for the Rule of St Paul's are essentially moralizing and hortatory, not prescriptive. Chapters 94, 99 and 100 consist of excerpts from Jerome's letter to Nepotianus concerning the life of the cleric, and from Isidore's *De Ecclesiasticis Officiis*. These texts say that clerics ought to be men of moderation, chastity, and discretion. Chapter 124, which quotes Jerome and Gregory the Great, urges canons to dress simply and respectably, but makes no specifications. Chapter 131 gives guidelines for the behaviour of canons in choir, but chapter 132 moves far away from the prescriptive, warning singers in choir to be mindful of the presence of angels around them. These excerpts do not form a Rule governing daily life: they appear to have been selected to encourage the canons of St Paul's to set themselves apart from laymen. It is significant that there is no *horarium*, although this could have been obtained from the Rule of Aachen.

Similarly, Wulfstan's quotation of chapter 145 in the Institutes cannot be interpreted as a rule for the canons of York Minster.[35] Firstly, it has to be placed in the context of Wulfstan's treatise. The Institutes propose ideals of behaviour for different social groups. Chapter 145 suited Wulfstan's purposes fairly well, since it summarizes ideal behaviour for clerks living in communities. Secondly, although it is prescriptive, it is so only in a very general way. It recapitulates the two great commandments and some of the ten commandments; it orders canons to share one dormitory and one refectory, to be prompt at prayers, to be silent during meals or else listen to reading, to practise crafts by which they can earn their living, and to live according to a Rule. But these prescriptions do not add up to a structured daily timetable, nor are there guidelines about the enforcement of discipline, or the appointment of officials. Wulfstan made similar general prescriptions in Aethelred's 1008 law code. Here too the canons are told to live regularly, sleep in one

---

[33] *Registrum Statutorum et Consuetudinum Ecclesiae Cathedralis Sancti Pauli Londinensis*, ed. W. Sparrow Simpson (London, 1873), pp. 38–43. See also C.N.L. Brooke, 'The Earliest Times to 1485', in *A History of St Paul's Cathedral*, ed. W.R. Matthews and W.M. Atkins (London, 1957), pp. 12–15 and 363, who points out that these chapters are from the Rule of Aachen, not the Enlarged Rule of Chrodegang.

[34] Brooke, 'Earliest Times', p. 13; Whitelock, *Some Anglo-Saxon Bishops of London*, pp. 28–9. Brooke thinks Theodred brought the Rule of Aachen to St Paul's, Whitelock is uncertain.

[35] Against Barlow, *English Church*, pp. 71, 73, 228, and Whitelock, *Some Anglo-Saxon Bishops of London*, pp. 27–8.

dormitory and eat in one refectory,[36] but there is no sign of the production and distribution of copies of rules for canons which would have made this possible.

Enlarged Rule of Chrodegang

The other canonical rule available in Anglo-Saxon England was the enlarged Rule of Chrodegang in eighty-four chapters. Brigitte Langefeld has traced the origins of this text: the original compilation was made in the Carolingian Empire not long after 816. The earliest surviving manuscript (Paris, Bibliothèque Nationale, MS lat. 1535, fols. 113v–149v) is West Frankish, and datable to the second quarter of the ninth century. Before the middle of the tenth century the text, slightly altered, had reached England, where a copy was made (Brussels, Bibliothèque Royale, MS 8556–63, fols. 1–38v) at an unidentifiable centre in the South East.[37] In the second half of the tenth century Winchester cathedral, newly turned into a Benedictine community by Aethelwold in 964, took an interest in the text. Aethelwold undertook the task of collecting the texts connected with the reforms of the Frankish church by Louis the Pious. Monastic texts were of primary importance, to assist with the drafting of *Regularis concordia*, but the Enlarged Rule of Chrodegang would have helped to provide ideas both about the organization of the liturgy and about the disciplinary role of the bishop within his cathedral community, a topic not touched on in monastic literature hitherto.[38]

Winchester acted as a centre for distributing this text to a wider audience. Helmut Gneuss and Walter Hofstetter have shown from textual and linguistic evidence that the Enlarged Rule of Chrodegang was translated into Old English at Winchester, and from here copies went to Christ Church, Canterbury, and, in the mid-eleventh century, to Exeter.[39] Here the text and translation were copied under the direction of Bishop Leofric, an Anglo-Saxon who had been educated in Lotharingia. This is our first and only firm evidence for this rule being applied in a community of secular canons in England.[40]

We can summarize our knowledge of the use of the Rule of Aachen and the Enlarged Rule of Chrodegang in England as follows: interest in the former was restricted to short, moralizing extracts, while interest in the latter was strongest in Benedictine centres until the mid-eleventh century. Wulfstan's legislation shows that he wanted to impose a common way of life on groups of clergy, but this

---

[36] *Councils and Synods with Other Documents Relating to the English Church, I,* ed. D. Whitelock, M. Brett and C.N.L. Brooke (2 vols., Oxford, 1981), I, 348.

[37] Langefeld, 'Die lateinische Vorlage der altenglischen Chrodegang-Regel', p. 407; eadem, 'A Third Old English Translation of Part of Gregory's Dialogues, This Time Embedded in the Rule of Chrodegang', *ASE* 15 (1986), pp. 197–204.

[38] Wulfstan of Winchester, *The Life of Saint Aethelwold,* ed. M. Lapidge and M. Winterbottom (Oxford, 1991), pp. lii–lx, xciii–xciv.

[39] H. Gneuss, 'The Origin of Standard Old English and Aethelwold's School at Winchester', *ASE* 1 (1972), pp. 63–83; W. Hofstetter, *Winchester und das spätaltenglische Sprachgebrauch* (Munich, 1987), pp. 94–100.

[40] Barlow, *English Church*, p. 214.

required a major programme of building, education, and dissemination of texts to be put into effect.

Evidence for such practical measures can be seen a little later in the eleventh century, when Wulfstan's successor at York, Aelfric Puttoc (1023–51), started to build a refectory and dormitory at the minster church of Beverley.[41] However, these were not completed until the pontificate of his successor but one, Ealdred (1061–9), who tried to introduce *uita communis* into York Minster, Southwell and Beverley.[42]

With Ealdred of York and Leofric of Exeter we move into the era of Lotharingian influence on the English church, which began under Edward the Confessor. Ealdred was inspired by a visit he had made to the Empire in 1054, when he had spent some time as a guest of Archbishop Hermann of Cologne. What chiefly impressed him were the liturgical practices in the Cologne churches, and his reforms in the archdiocese of York were chiefly intended to raise liturgical standards: 'He heard, saw, and committed to memory many things which belong to the dignity of ecclesiastical observance, many things which belong to the rigour of the Church's teaching, which he afterwards caused to be observed in the churches of the English.'[43] Ealdred's reforms were part of a wider trend visible in the English church in the middle decades of the eleventh century: the importation of manpower and ideas from the Empire, and more specifically from Lotharingia.[44] Several (though not all) of the bishops of Lotharingian origin or education instituted *uita communis* for their cathedral clergy. Leofric did so when he moved his see from Crediton to Exeter in 1050, Giso at Wells between 1061 and 1088.[45] Bishop Walcher of Durham, a Lotharingian, started to build what are described in the *Libellus de exordio* as *monachorum habitacula*,[46] but which were probably intended to be communal living-quarters for clerks. Walcher, like Ealdred, placed liturgical reforms at the top of his agenda. According to the *Libellus de exordio*, he ordered the Durham clerks to adopt 'the clerical manner' of performing the day and night offices. 'For beforehand they had rather imitated the custom of monks at these, as they had always learnt from their ancestors, as has been said above, who had been reared and brought up among monks.'[47] Obviously, these archaic 'monastic' customs would not have had anything in common with the practices of reformed Benedictine houses in the tenth and eleventh centuries, but equally they could not have been close to Walcher's own expectations of clerical liturgical

---

[41] *Historians of the Church of York*, ed. Raine, II, 353–4.

[42] Ibid., II, 345, 353–4, and 107–8; Stenton, *Preparatory to Anglo-Saxon England*, p. 369.

[43] *Historians of the Church of York*, ed. Raine, II, 345. Cf. also M. Lapidge, 'Ealdred of York and MS Cotton Vitellius E xii', in his *Anglo-Latin Literature 900–1066* (London and Rio Grande, 1993), pp. 453–67.

[44] Barlow, *English Church*, pp. 156–7.

[45] On Leofric, see ibid., p. 214. On Giso, see *Historiola de Primordiis Episcopatus Somersetensis*, in *Ecclesiastical Documents*, ed. J. Hunter (Camden Society 8; London, 1840), p. 19.

[46] *LDE*, bk. 3, ch. 22 (p. 113).

[47] *LDE*, bk. 3, ch. 18 (p. 106): the author was trying to emphasize the 'monastic' origins of the community as much as possible.

practices, shaped by his experiences in Lotharingia. The Durham clergy did in fact possess a collectar designed for secular clergy in northern France, but according to its most recent editor, Alicia Correa, they used it as a quarry of materials, rather than as a text to be followed to the letter.[48]

Walcher had another community of secular clergy to preside over, at the collegiate church of Waltham in Essex, which was granted to him by William I.[49] Waltham already had strong Lotharingian connections, since Earl Harold Godwineson had appointed to the community the schoolmaster Adelard, a Liégeois who had been trained at either Utrecht or Maastricht (*Traiectum*). Adelard is said by the author of the twelfth-century history of Waltham, the tract *De inuentione Sanctae Crucis*, to have established in the church 'the laws, institutes, and customs, both in ecclesiastical and secular matters, of the churches in which he had been brought up'.[50] The *De inuentione* also shows that the Rule of Aachen had had a strong influence on the organisation of the church's estates, though this had been adapted to make room for the idea, already to be found in some English secular communities, that lands should be divided between canons. However, *uita communis* cannot have been observed very strictly at Waltham, since Adelard himself was married with a son who succeeded him.[51]

Lotharingian influence on the eleventh-century English church was extensive, but is only just beginning to receive attention in modern analyses.[52] There are several reasons why it has been undervalued. It was short-lived, and was overwhelmed by the work of Norman and other French ecclesiastics.[53] Moreover, acceptance of Lotharingian ideas was half-hearted. By contrast, Benedictine reformers were more effective. Furthermore, although Benedictine cathedral chapters accounted for only a small minority of English cathedral communities as late as the 1070s, they dominated through their wealth and their cultural influence.

We can now turn to the question of Benedictine reform ideals in cathedral communities. Since over the last twenty years there has been a significant re-evaluation of the process of the tenth-century monastic reform in England, it is necessary to summarize very briefly the process by which Winchester, Worcester, Sherborne and Canterbury became Benedictine, and then I should like to outline

---

[48] *The Durham Collectar*, ed. Alicia Correa, Henry Bradshaw Society 107 (1992), p. 77.

[49] *LDE*, bk. 3, ch. 23 (p. 113); *The Early Charters of Waltham Abbey 1062–1230*, ed. R. Ransford (Woodbridge, 1989), p. xxiv and also nos. 5, 10.

[50] *The Foundation of Waltham Abbey*, ed. W. Stubbs (Oxford and London, 1861), ch. 15, p. 15.

[51] Ibid., ch. 15, p. 16 and ch. 25, p. 35.

[52] Barlow, *English Church*, esp. pp. 45–6, 82–3, 156–7; V. Ortenberg, *The English Church and the Continent in the Tenth and Eleventh Centuries* (Oxford, 1992), pp. 41–94; J. Barrow, 'A Lotharingian in Hereford: Bishop Robert and the Reorganisation of the Church of Hereford' in BAACT for 1989, ed. D. Whitehead (forthcoming).

[53] T. Webber, *Scribes and Scholars at Salisbury Cathedral, c.1075–c.1125* (Oxford, 1992), esp. pp. 114–29, and John Le Neve, *Fasti Ecclesiae Anglicanae 1066–1300*, IV, *Salisbury*, ed. D.E. Greenway (London, 1991), pp. xxi–xxvi (though the statement on p. xxiv that Amalarius's *Liber Officialis* was used as a Rule is mistaken, since the work is simply a commentary on the liturgy).

the main areas in which the Benedictines made a distinctive contribution to the English church.

Benedictine monasticism was not an obvious choice for cathedral chapters, which were supposed to be served by clerks. The starting point of the conversion process was the appointment of Aethelwold, a committed Benedictine, as bishop of Winchester in 963. Patrick Wormald has shown how Aethelwold interpreted Bede's *Historia ecclesiastica* to make it appear that monastic bishops and communities of monks in episcopal churches were normal features of the Anglo-Saxon church in the seventh and eighth centuries.[54] More generally, the word *monasterium*, widely used in early Anglo-Saxon England to mean any kind of religious community,[55] was helpful to Aethelwold, who naturally assumed that all these communities had degenerated from the Benedictine ideal, and that they all ought to be brought back to a state of ascetic purity. In particular he was opposed to clerical marriage, widespread in late Anglo-Saxon England (and later), which he saw as pollution of holy places. Indeed, the words 'clerk' and 'canon' are associated in his writings with the words 'lascivious' and 'filth'.[56] In his eyes, the only form of disciplined, celibate manpower available to conduct services consisted of Benedictine monks.

Aethelwold expounded his views systematically in his writings, especially the proem to *Regularis concordia*, the charter issued by Edgar for New Minster in 966, and the account of Edgar's establishment of monasteries.[57] In addition to Aethelwold's hostility to clerks, other frequent themes are the insistence that bishops should be elected from within monastic communities, and that kings should be the final arbiters in disputes.

At Winchester Old Minster the clerks were expelled in 964 and replaced by monks.[58] In the three other cathedrals which became Benedictine before the Conquest the conversion was slower and less dramatic. At Worcester, Oswald (961–92) created a double community by building a second church, St Mary's, next to the existing cathedral, St Peter's. Monks start to occur in the witness lists to genuine leases of Oswald from 977, which suggests that St Mary's probably came into use in the 970s. It is likely that the whole community was only completely Benedictinized in the middle of the eleventh century.[59] For Sherborne we have less information,

---

[54] P. Wormald, 'Aethelwold and his Continental Counterparts: Contact, Comparison, Contrast', in *Bishop Aethelwold: his Career and Influence*, ed. B. Yorke (Woodbridge, 1988), pp. 13–42, esp. pp. 40–1.

[55] On the meaning of the term *monasterium*, see the articles cited in n. 6 above; cf. also P. Sims-Williams, *Religion and Literature in Western England, 600–800* (Cambridge, 1990), esp. chs. 5 and 12.

[56] *Councils and Synods I*, ed. Whitelock, I, 121, 125, 126, 136, 150.

[57] For some of Aethelwold's texts, see ibid., I, 119–54; for editions of Regularis Concordia, see *Regularis Concordia*, ed. T. Symons (Edinburgh and London, 1953), and *Corpus Consuetudinum Monasticarum* VII/3, ed. K. Hallinger (Siegburg, 1984), pp. 61–147.

[58] Cf. Wulfstan, *Life of Saint Aethelwold*, pp. xlv–xlvii, 30–3.

[59] For the events at Worcester see J. Barrow, 'How the Twelfth-Century Monks of Worcester Perceived their Past', in *The Perception of the Past in Twelfth-Century Europe*, ed. Paul Magdalino (London and Rio Grande, 1992), pp. 53–74, and eadem, 'The Community of

but the process of monasticization seems to have been carried out by Wulfsige, a
protégé of Dunstan, after he became bishop in 993.[60] At Canterbury the process
was clearly hesitant. Already under Dunstan (archbishop 959–88), Benedictine-
inspired liturgical materials were being copied there,[61] but there is no specific
reference to monks at Christ Church until the 1020s, as Nicholas Brooks has
shown.[62] Likewise, Alan Thacker has pointed out how slow the community of
Christ Church was to build up the cult of Dunstan: he attributes this to conserva-
tive attitudes among the cathedral clergy who 'lacked the stimulus provided by
reform'. This initial lack of interest in a saint's cult is significant, for Benedictine
houses were keen to promote saints' cults, especially where the saints were monks
or nuns.[63]

The process of conversion to Benedictine monasticism was the subject of a
wealth of documentation, often tendentious and some of it, even as early as the
early eleventh century, involving forgery.[64] This phenomenon has greatly complicated the process of disentangling the events of the tenth-century reform, but is
worth studying in itself because it shows us an important aspect of the process: the
self-justification of the reformers demanded, but in turn also nourished, a much
higher degree of literacy and learning than had been found in English churches for
some time.[65]

The main aim of the Benedictine reformers appears to have been to improve
liturgical standards. The liturgy was overhauled to bring it into line with continental practice: Helmut Gneuss has shown how in this period continental calendars,
the Gallican Psalter, the New Hymnal, computistic manuals, and Amalarius's *De
officiis ecclesiasticis* (a commentary on aspects of the liturgy) were introduced into
England, and that this was almost exclusively a monastic phenomenon.[66] Secular
communities showed little interest in liturgical developments until the

Worcester Cathedral, 961–c.1100', in Proceedings of the Oswald of Worcester Millenary
Conference, ed. N.P. Brooks (forthcoming), and literature cited in both articles.
[60] *Charters of Sherborne*, ed. M.A. O'Donovan (London, 1988), no. 11, pp. 39–40; this
charter, issued by Aethelred, has some curious features: see notes ibid., pp. 41–4.
[61] Brooks, *Early History*, pp. 252–3; Jane Rosenthal, 'The Pontifical of St Dunstan', in *St
Dunstan: his Life, Times and Cult*, ed. N. Ramsay, M. Sparks, and T. Tatton-Brown (Woodbridge, 1992), pp. 143–63.
[62] Brooks, *Early History*, pp. 255–6; cf. also the reference in Anglo-Saxon Chronicle, *s.a.*
1011, to the members of the communities of Christ Church and St Augustine's Canterbury, as
'ealle tha gehadodan men' rather than specifically as monks: *The C Text of the Old English
Chronicle*, ed. H.A. Rositzke (Bochum-Langendreer, 1940), p. 61.
[63] A.T. Thacker, 'Cults at Canterbury: Relics and Reform under Dunstan and his Successors',
in *St Dunstan: his Life*, ed. Ramsay, pp. 221–45, at p. 239; cf. also Rollason, *Saints and Relics*,
pp. 177–83.
[64] Brooks, *Early History*, p. 257; J. Barrow, 'How the Twelfth-Century Monks of Worcester',
pp. 56, 72.
[65] Brooks, *Early History*, pp. 266–78, esp. pp. 275–6; F.A. Rella, 'Continental Manuscripts
Acquired for English Centres in the Tenth and Early Eleventh Centuries: a Preliminary
Checklist', *Anglia* 8 (1980), pp. 107–16; H. Gneuss, 'A Preliminary List of Manuscripts
Written or Owned in England up to 1100', *ASE* 9 (1981), pp. 1–60.
[66] H. Gneuss, 'Liturgical Books in Anglo-Saxon England and their Old English Terminology',

mid-eleventh century; the Durham Collectar did not inspire the community of St Cuthbert to make great changes to their services.[67]

An important part of monastic life was devotion to saints, especially monastic saints. Hence the particular stress in the late tenth and the eleventh centuries on the leading figures of the tenth century monastic reform – Aethelwold at Winchester, Oswald at Worcester and Wulfsige at Sherborne.[68] Communities of secular clergy were not uninterested in saints, but they tended not to have the educational or liturgical resources to develop cults fully. Only north of the Tees could the community of St Cuthbert, well out of reach of marauding Benedictine relic-hunters in the south, preserve the cult of Cuthbert and also raid other churches in the vicinity for further supplies of relics.[69]

Finally, we should consider the impact of the Gregorian papacy on English cathedrals in the second half of the eleventh century. If we look at papal correspondence with England over the period from the tenth to the early twelfth century, we can see that there are very few genuine papal confirmations of ecclesiastical possessions and rights until the time of Calixtus II (1119–24).[70] Here we need to consider the undated privilege, supposedly issued by either Pope John XII or John XIII, giving Aethelwold licence to reform Winchester.[71] None of Aethelwold's works proposes a role for the pope in monastic reform. We can contrast this with the behaviour of Abbo of Fleury, who forged a papal privilege in the 990s and then obtained a genuine one from Gregory V to confirm it.[72] The reason for the difference in attitudes between Abbo and Aethelwold is that the former felt that the best way to deal with bishops was to obtain exemptions limiting their involvement with monastic houses, while the latter felt that the best method was to turn the bishops into monks.

The dating of the Winchester privilege has long been recognised as

in *Learning and Literature in Anglo-Saxon England*, ed. M. Lapidge and H. Gneuss (Cambridge, 1985), pp. 91–141, esp. p. 94.

[67] *The Durham Collectar*, ed. Correa, pp. 77–9, 91–2, 107–11.

[68] C. Talbot, 'The Life of St Wulfsin of Sherborne by Goscelin', *Revue bénédictine* 69 (1959), pp. 68–85, and Rollason, *Saints and Relics*, p. 229; A.T. Thacker, article in Proceedings of the Oswald of Worcester Millenary Conference, ed. N.P. Brooks, forthcoming; Wulfstan, *Life of Saint Aethelwold*, pp. xcix–cxliii.

[69] Rollason, *Saints and Relics*, pp. 144–52, 211–12; *LDE*, bk. 3, ch. 7, on the activities of Alfred Westou; *The Relics of St Cuthbert*, pp. 40ff; M.K. Lawson, *Cnut: the Danes in England in the Early Eleventh Century* (London, 1993), pp. 140–1.

[70] See *Regesta Pontificum Romanorum*, ed. P. Jaffé, 2nd edn by S. Loewenfeld et al. (2 vols., Leipzig, 1885–8), I, 464–701, and *Papsturkunden in England*, ed. W. Holtzmann (3 vols., Abhandlungen der Gesellschaft der Wissenschaften zu Göttingen, Phil.-hist. Klasse; Berlin, 1930–52), passim.

[71] *Papsturkunden 896–1046*, ed. H. Zimmermann (2 vols., Veröffentlichungen der Österreichischen Akademie der Wissenschaften 174, 177; Vienna, 1984–5), I, 416–18, no. 212, with a proposed date of 971, and *Councils and Synods I*, ed. Whitelock, I, 109–13 (not cited by Zimmermann), with a proposed date of 963. In both editions the document is assumed to be genuine.

[72] On Abbo's forgery, see M. Mostert, 'Die Urkundenfälschungen Abbos von Fleury', in *Fälschungen im Mittelalter* (6 vols., MGH Schriften 33; Hanover, 1988–90), IV, 287–318.

problematical.[73] The document refers to Aethelwold as a 'brother bishop'. Aethelwold was consecrated 29 November 963; John XII was deposed and replaced by Leo VIII 4 December 963; John briefly returned to Rome in February 964 at about the time that Aethelwold expelled the clerks (19 February). There would not have been time for Aethelwold to make such a request. John XIII only became pope in the autumn of 965. The dating is not the only suspicious aspect of the document. Felix Liebermann noted that it makes use of *Regularis concordia*, written no earlier than 965.[74] The most serious difficulty, however, is that though the drafter knew some of the phrases laid down by the *Liber Diurnus*, he was not aware that this text prescribes different honorific vocabulary for kings and emperors.[75] The ascription of *imperii dignitas* to Edgar only twenty months after the imperial coronation of Otto I proves that the document is bogus. Finally, the privilege bears a close resemblance to three of the Canterbury forgeries (St Augustine's 5 and 9 and Christ Church 1).[76] This suggests that it was forged in collaboration with Canterbury scribes, probably between the 1070s and the 1120s.

With the Winchester privilege out of the running, we can see that from c.900 to 1050 papal correspondence with England was limited to a few letters disciplining bishops, bestowing *pallia*, or ordaining penance in manslaughter cases.[77] English churches did not seek papal confirmations of their possessions, perhaps because in Anglo-Saxon law-courts the documents which were required to protect property rights were ones notifying transactions as they were made, rather than confirmations of gifts from assorted donors. However, just before the Conquest, two bishops with Lotharingian connections, Leofric of Exeter and Giso of Wells, sought papal privileges. Leofric wanted permission to move his see from Crediton to Wells in 1050, and Giso wanted a general confirmation of the possessions of the

---

[73] For the two most recent editions of the privilege see n. 71 above. The privilege has been accepted as genuine by W. Levison, *England and the Continent in the Eighth Century* (Oxford, 1946), pp. 196–8; C.N.L. Brooke, 'The Canterbury Forgeries and their Author', *Downside Review* 68 (1950), pp. 462–76, at pp. 467–8; P. Wormald, 'Aethelwold', p. 34.

[74] F. Liebermann, 'Aethelwolds Anhang zur Benediktinerregel', *Archiv für das Studium der neueren Sprachen und Literaturen* 108 (1902), pp. 375–7; cf. also Hanna Vollrath, *Die Synoden Englands bis 1066* (Paderborn, 1985), pp. 449–53, accepting Liebermann's case but arguing that the document might yet be genuine, and issued in 967.

[75] On the Winchester privilege's use of some of the phrases in *Liber Diurnus*, see Levison, *England and the Continent*, pp. 196–8; see also *Liber Diurnus Romanorum Pontificum*, ed. H. Foerster (Bern, 1958), p. 181; for papal documents addressed to or mentioning kings in this period see *Papsturkunden*, ed. Zimmermann, nos. 10–11, 21, 49, 55, 58, 73, 132, 438. All lack references to *imperium*, in contrast to no. 154, ibid., dated 12 February 962, for the emperor Otto I.

[76] Brooke, 'The Canterbury Forgeries', 467–8; S.E. Kelly, 'Some Forgeries in the Archive of St Augustine's Abbey, Canterbury', in *Fälschungen im Mittelalter*, IV, 347–69, esp. 366. Kelly, like Brooke, is of the opinion that the Canterbury forgeries are modelled on the Winchester privilege and that the latter is genuine.

[77] *Cartularium Saxonicum*, ed. Birch, nos. 573, 1069; *Councils and Synods, I*, ed. Whitelock, I, 231–7; R.A. Aronstam, 'Pope Leo IX and England: an Unknown Letter', *Speculum* 49 (1974), pp. 535–41; eadem, 'Penitential Pilgrimages to Rome in the Early Middle Ages', *Archivium Historiae Pontificiae* 13 (1975), pp. 65–83.

church of Wells in 1061.[78] The Wells privilege stands at the beginning of a great series of papal confirmations for English churches, but until the early twelfth century it seems to have had few, if any, genuine followers. Papal privileges for English Benedictine houses in the eleventh century are either forgeries,[79] or at least highly suspicious.[80] The Benedictine houses awoke rather late to the idea of obtaining papal privileges, but when they realised how useful these could be, they put their developing historiographical skills to use in making their numerous forgeries believable.[81]

By examining the distribution of rules for secular canons and comparing their influence with that of the Benedictine Rule, we can reassess the impact of reforming trends in the tenth and the early eleventh centuries and work out a chronology for them. Until the mid-eleventh century, interest in rules for monks and canons was shown (if we look only at cathedral churches) principally by Winchester. Winchester was the earliest cathedral to become Benedictine and it possessed the most influential school and scriptorium. The Benedictine reform was conducted without any recourse to the papacy, an institution which only started to play a prominent part in the lives of English monastic houses in the early twelfth century. Non-Benedictine cathedrals, which had weak institutional structures, were much less affected by reform, and even when *uita communis* was imposed on some of them in the middle of the eleventh century it was (Exeter cathedral apart) short-lived.

---

[78] Barlow, *English Church*, pp. 82–3. For the bull obtained by Leofric, see *Councils and Synods, I*, ed. Whitelock, I, 524–5, no. 70; for the bull obtained by Giso, see *Papsturkunden in England*, ed. Holtzmann, II, no. 1, dated 1061.

[79] E.g. *Regesta Pontificum Romanorum*, ed. Jaffé, nos. 4257 and 4462, discussed briefly *Papsturkunden in England*, ed. Holtzmann, I, 229; ibid., I, no. 2; *Regesta Pontificum Romanorum*, ed. Jaffé, no. 4543, discussed briefly by R.H.C. Davis, 'An Unknown Coventry Charter', *EHR* 86 (1971), pp. 533–97; *Papsturkunden in England*, ed. Holtzmann, II, no. 2, discussed by G. Scammell, *Hugh du Puiset, Bishop of Durham* (Cambridge, 1956), pp. 300–7.

[80] E.g. the letters of Alexander II for Canterbury and Winchester cathedrals: Helen Clover, 'Alexander II's Letter *Accepimus a quibusdam* and its Relationship to the Canterbury Forgeries', in *La Normandie bénédictine au temps de Guillaume le Conquérant*, ed. G.-U. Langé (Lille, 1967), pp. 417–42.

[81] Most recently on Eadmer and Canterbury, see R.W. Southern, *St Anselm: a Portrait in a Landscape* (Cambridge, 1990), pp. 352–64, esp. p. 360, and also idem, 'The Canterbury Forgeries', *EHR* 73 (1958), pp. 193–226; cf. use of *LDE* in *Papsturkunden in England*, ed. Holtzmann, II, no. 2.

The Monastic Revival in Yorkshire: Whitby and St Mary's, York

JANET BURTON

AFTER THE FOUNDATION of Durham Cathedral Priory in 1083 its monks continued to keep the *Liber Vitae* in which the community of St Cuthbert had, since the ninth century, recorded the names of those whom they commemorated especially in their prayers. Among the entries made in the years shortly after 1083 were the names of two monastic communities in Yorkshire: Lastingham and Hackness.[1] Although these two were not destined to become permanent monastic sites, they played a significant, if short-lived, role in the re-establishment of regular life in the North in the wake of the Norman Conquest and settlement. By 1093, when the foundation stone was laid for the cathedral at Durham, Lastingham had ceased to be monastic; Hackness probably functioned as a cell; and regular life in Yorkshire was concentrated at Selby, at York, and possibly – though as we shall see not certainly – at Whitby.[2] My concern in this paper is with two of the Yorkshire houses, not the first after the Conquest – for priority of foundation must go to the hermit settlement of the monk Benedict of Auxerre which under royal patronage grew to be the abbey of Selby – but rather with Whitby and St Mary's, York, which were both products of that same northern revival which resulted in the monastic recolonization of Northumbria and the foundation of a Benedictine priory in Durham. I would like to look at three themes which the Yorkshire experience shares with Durham: first, the part played in the revival by devotion to the Anglo-Saxon heritage, a sense of the integrity of the past; second, the importance of the eremitical tradition, that is, the notion of withdrawal, as hermits, from the secular world, and a stress on simplicity and poverty; and third, the part played by politics in the formation of northern monastic life, how Whitby and York fit into the power structure of northern England. Whitby and York in a sense form counterpoints to Durham; but we shall see how and why the development of monasticism, the outcome of the northern revival, was somewhat different between the Humber and the Tees and farther north. What will emerge from this examination is that the conflict which surfaced from time to time throughout the history

---

[1] *Liber Vitae*, fol. 48r/v; noted in D. Bethell, 'The Foundation of Fountains Abbey and the State of St Mary's, York in 1132', *JEH* 17 (1966), pp. 1–27, at p. 18.
[2] There may also by this date have been a Cluniac priory in the south of the county at Pontefract; however, a more precise date of foundation than *c.*1090 cannot be assigned.

of monasticism between cenobitism, the communal religious life, and eremiticism, where the emphasis is on the individual striving for spiritual perfection in retreat from the world, was fully apparent in the Yorkshire part of the revival; and that the tension between the aspirations of the monk-founders and those whose support turned their primitive settlements into fully-fledged Benedictine communities, was not easily resolved.

The sources for the foundation of Whitby do not admit easy interpretation or reconciliation. The briefest, and probably the earliest statement comes in the *Libellus de exordio et procursu Dunelmensis ecclesie*, otherwise known as the *Historia Dunelmensis Ecclesie*, attributed to Symeon of Durham. Symeon's history, which covers the years up to 1096, was completed by 1107.[3] In this account, Whitby and York receive mention as part of the northern pilgrimage of three men: Aldwin, prior of the Benedictine abbey of Winchcombe (Gloucestershire), and two monks of another Midland house, Evesham, named Aelfwig and Reinfrid. Symeon places the refoundation of Whitby firmly in the context of the revival of monastic life in the North which resulted from their journey, and which led to the restoration of the ancient monasteries of Monkwearmouth and Jarrow and to the creation of a monastic cathedral at Durham. Durham is Symeon's main concern, and the mention of Reinfrid's foundation at Whitby and the establishment of an abbey in York is almost incidental.

There are three other narrative accounts which deal with the early history, or elements of the early history, of Whitby and the York abbey. Two derive from Whitby itself, and the third from St Mary's. The first of these is a Memorial of the foundation and benefactions of Whitby, a brief narrative covering the years up to 1176, which was copied into one of the two abbey cartularies.[4] The manuscript is a composite one, but the section containing the Memorial appears to be of a twelfth-century date and may therefore be roughly contemporary with the original composition. A second Whitby source, a more problematic one of uncertain date, survives only in seventeenth-century transcripts in two Dodsworth manuscripts.[5] Clearly the late date of this witness to the text makes difficult an assessment of its reliability and it can be used only with caution.

The final narrative introduces a key figure in the story, Abbot Stephen of St Mary's, York. Indeed it is a narrative ascribed in the text to the abbot himself. Some historians, notably J.C. Atkinson, editor of the Whitby cartulary, and David Knowles, rejected Stephen's narrative as spurious. This was partly because of its

---

[3] *LDE*, chs. 56–7 (pp. 108–13); translated in *CHE*, pp. 692–6. See also *HReg, s.a.* 1074 (pp. 201–2).
[4] The Memorial is contained in the Whitby cartulary among the Whitby Literary and Philosophical Society, Strickland MSS, on deposit at Whitby Museum; printed in *Cartularium Abbathiae de Whiteby*, ed. J.C. Atkinson (SS 69, 72; 1879 for 1878, 1881 for 1879), I, 1–10. On the surviving cartularies of Whitby see G.R.C. Davis, *Medieval Cartularies of Great Britain* (London, 1958), pp. 118–19.
[5] MS now lost, formerly in the possession of the Cholmley family; printed in *Cart. Whit.*, I, xxxviii–xxxix from Bodl.L, MS Dodsworth 159, fol. 115v; another copy survives in Bodl.L, MS Dodsworth 9 (*Monasticon Boreale*), fols. 127–9.

manuscript – the text printed by Dugdale in the *Monasticon Anglicanum* derived from a thirteenth-century manuscript where there was confusion between Stephen and a later abbot, Simon de Warwick;[6] but they were also suspicious of certain details in Stephen's account which seemed inconsistent with the Whitby narrative, that is the Memorial of the foundation and benefactions. Other historians, however, notably Alexander Hamilton Thompson and William Farrer, editor of the first three volumes of *Early Yorkshire Charters*, were inclined to accept Stephen's account as reliable.[7] Moreover, the manuscript tradition now poses less of a problem, since some years ago Dennis Bethell drew attention to the implications of the existence of a copy of the narrative of Abbot Stephen in a twelfth-century manuscript. BL, MS Additional 38816 clearly derives from the York abbey, and can be dated later than 1157 but before the end of the century; whether the text as it stands was the work of Abbot Stephen or not, the tale that it tells was accepted at York as the authentic version of events.[8]

Each of these sources tells its own story, and adds details which reflect the special interests of its compiler. Just as Symeon of Durham was occupied with the background out of which Durham emerged, so the Memorial concentrates its attention on the monk Reinfrid, the man behind the revival of monastic life at Whitby. But it tells also of Whitby's lay patrons, and especially of the Norman baron, William de Percy, who is credited with the foundation. Stephen, by contrast, was concerned to tell of the beginnings of the great abbey of York; and, as we shall see, there are good reasons why his account, or the emphasis in his account, should diverge in places from that of the Whitby narratives. I have not the space in this paper to do justice to the complexities of the sources; I am, however, inclined to accept as authentic the broad outlines of Stephen's account, and the sequence of events which I suggest is based on that judgement.

From these sources we can suggest the following narrative. Around 1073 or 1074 Reinfrid and his two companions left the Midland monasteries of Evesham and Winchcombe and journeyed to Jarrow, where they were granted the site of the Anglo-Saxon monastery by Bishop Walcher of Durham. They found the buildings in ruins, and covered the roofless walls with rough timbers and hay, and 'beneath the walls they erected a little hovel in which they slept, and took their food, and thus they sustained, by the alms of the religious, a life of poverty.'[9] They attracted

6 W. Dugdale, *Monasticon Anglicanum*, revised edn, J. Caley, H. Ellis, and B. Bandinel (London, 1817–30), III, 544–6. For comment see *Cart. Whit.*, I, xxxiv–xxxvii, li–lxxxvii; D. Knowles, *The Monastic Order in England* (2nd edn; Cambridge, 1963), pp. 166–71.

7 A. Hamilton Thompson, 'The Monastic Settlement at Hackness and its Relation to the Abbey of Whitby', *YAJ* 27 (1924), pp. 388–405, at p. 394; *Early Yorkshire Charters*, I–III, ed. W. Farrer (Edinburgh, 1914–16), II, 198–201.

8 Bethell, 'The Foundation of Fountains Abbey', pp. 1–27. Another twelfth-century copy survives in CCCC, 139, which also contains a copy of the longer letter of Archbishop Thurstan concerning the secession from St Mary's in 1132 (ibid., p. 24); on this manuscript and its Durham connections see the essay by Bernard Meehan, below, pp. 440–2.

9 *LDE*, bk. 3, ch. 21 (pp. 108–9); trans. *CHE*, p. 693.

considerable attention there, and, when the arrival of recruits had swelled the community, Aldwin, the 'one who most thoroughly despised the world', the 'most humble in dress and disposition', moved on to Melrose, a site associated with St Cuthbert. Reinfrid left Jarrow too, and around 1077 settled as a hermit among the ruins of St Hilda's monastery at Whitby. There he gathered around him a number of followers, and within a year or so authority over them passed to a man named Stephen, who had only recently joined the community, and who now received endowments from William de Percy. Stephen soon realised that the clifftop site of Whitby was vulnerable to attacks from pirates; he therefore approached the king for help and acquired from him the inland site of Lastingham as a secure retreat from raids. This is the first instance of that royal intervention which was so to alter the fortunes of the monks. Some time later, but probably not much later, part of the convent transferred to Lastingham, though not to escape raids but rather as a result of antagonism from their lay founder. This is a theme to which I shall return. Not all the monks moved with Stephen, and some remained with Reinfrid at Whitby. However, there they continued to be harrassed by robbers and pirates, and so, with the consent of William de Percy, removed not to the alternative site which was available to the Whitby community, that is, Lastingham, but to another location, Hackness. During their stay at Hackness Reinfrid was killed accidentally and was succeeded as prior by Serlo de Percy, brother of the lay founder, thus cementing the relationship between the monastery and its patron. The monks were still at Hackness in 1086, but subsequently returned to Whitby, possibly by c.1090 but certainly by 1096 when William de Percy departed for the Holy Land on crusade. Abbot Stephen and his monks remained only a few years at Lastingham, during which period they entered into confraternity with the monks of Durham.[10] By 1086 they had moved to York, initially to the church of St Olave in Marygate, just outside the city, which they had acquired from one of William I's leading northern settlers, Count Alan of Brittany and Richmond. Two years later, in 1088, while on a royal visit to York, King William II is said to have granted a more spacious site, adjacent to St Olave's, where the ruins of St Mary's Abbey now stand. He then formally assumed the patronage of the abbey.[11]

One feature to emerge from all these accounts is the importance of the Anglo-Saxon legacy in the geography of the monastic settlement of Yorkshire. Symeon of Durham tells us clearly that this was the inspiration behind the journey of those three men from Evesham. Aldwin, prior of Winchcombe, Symeon tells us,

> understood from the History of the Angles that the province of the Northumbrians had formerly been peopled with numerous bands of monks, and many troops of saints . . . These places, that is, the sites of these monasteries, he earnestly desired to visit, although he well knew that the monasteries

[10] *Liber Vitae*, fol. 48: 'Pro monacho Sancti Petri Lestingaensis, unusquisque sacerdos x missas, et alii cantent psalter' tres in conuentu autem sicut pro monacho nostro, hoc est xxx[ta] plenaria officia'.

[11] On the possibility that William II did indeed visit York in 1088 see Christopher Norton, 'The Buildings of St Mary's Abbey, York, and their Destruction', *Ant. J.* (forthcoming).

themselves were reduced to ruins; and he wished, in imitation of such persons, to lead a life of poverty.[12]

What Symeon does not tell us – perhaps did not know – is that another of the trio, Reinfrid, had first-hand acquaintance of one of those sites 'reduced to ruins'. It was the Whitby source, the Memorial of foundation and benefactions, which preserved at the abbey the tradition that Reinfrid had, as a soldier in the army of the Conqueror, visited and been moved by the sight of the ruined abbey of Whitby.[13] If, as is most likely, the occasion of his visit to Northumbria was the harrying of the North in the wake of rebellion, this reminder of the glorious Anglo-Saxon past may have been all the more poignant. The experience of seeing Whitby and all that it represented in the tradition of monasticism was apparently the first step in Reinfrid's conversion to the monastic life. He became a monk at Evesham, and when the opportunity came, through his meeting with Aldwin, to revisit the North, Whitby must have been much in his mind. And so to Whitby he returned some time around 1077, and settled in the ruins of the former monastery. According to the Memorial, 'there were then in that same vill, as old country people have told us, nearly forty monasteries or oratories, whose walls and altars remained empty and roofless on account of their destruction by pirate armies'.[14]

There is a strong evocation here of the Anglo-Saxon legacy. Pirate raids, it seems, were not a thing of the past. It is evident from all our accounts that they were a feature of life at eleventh-century Whitby, and led Abbot Stephen to contemplate, and Prior Reinfrid to effect, a dispersal from the exposed coastal site. Here again, the importance of the tradition of Anglo-Saxon sites is remarkable. When Stephen appealed to the king for assistance he was granted Lastingham 'now assuredly empty, but once outstanding for the great number and devotion of the monks who dwelt there' – a reference to the monastery of St Cedd.[15] Furthermore, when those brethren who remained at Whitby under Reinfrid found that they were still unable to sustain the attacks, the site to which they removed was also an Anglo-Saxon one, Hackness. The transfer is recorded in the Dodsworth transcript. Although this may be a late source, and on some matters is of dubious reliability, it may well preserve a kernel of truth in its statement that William de Percy, from whom the monks

---

[12] *LDE*, bk. 3, ch. 21 (p. 108); trans. *CHE*, pp. 692–3. The 'History of the Angles' referred to here is Bede's *Ecclesiastical History of the English People*. On the popularity of this work throughout the Middle Ages, see R.H.C. Davies, 'Bede after Bede', in *Studies in Medieval History presented to R. Allen Brown*, ed. C. Harper Bill, C.J. Holdsworth, and J.L. Nelson (Woodbridge, 1989), pp. 103–16; on the importance of Bede in the northern revival, see especially pp. 105–9.

[13] *Cart. Whit.*, I, 1–2. Reinfrid may well have been a knight of the baron William de Percy. His son, Fulk, on one occasion described as 'Fulk the steward, son of Reinfrid, prior of Whitby', became steward of Alan de Percy, and a benefactor of Whitby: see *Early Yorkshire Charters*, IV–XII, ed. C.T. Clay (Yorkshire Archaeological Society Record Series, extra series; 1935–65), XI, pp. 92–3; Farrer, *Early Yorkshire Charters*, I, nos. 529–30 (p. 410), II, no. 856 (p. 201) and no. 859 (p. 204).

[14] *Cart. Whit.*, I, 2.

[15] On Anglo-Saxon Lastingham, see *HE*, bk. 3, chs. 23 and 28.

sought help, was moved to grant them Hackness because of the fact that Abbess Hilda, the most famous occupant of Anglo-Saxon Whitby, had founded a monastery there, in other words, because of its Anglo-Saxon associations.[16] William de Percy evidently envisaged that the monks would remain at Hackness as a temporary expedient and that a return to Whitby would take place at some stage. However, the stay at Hackness was long enough for a community to become established. The Memorial speaks of 'the church of St Peter [Hackness] where our monks served God, died and were buried'. And it was at Hackness, in the churchyard of St Peter's, 'in the middle of the east wall, against the altar', that the monks chose to inter Prior Reinfrid.[17] Moreover, the existence of the community at Hackness is attested by an entry in the Durham *Liber Vitae*:

> Conuentio inter monachos Dunelm' et monachos de Hakenesse. Pro Serlone sicut pro monacho ecclesiae nostrae et hoc idem ipse pro nobis: pro aliis autem sicut pro fratribus de Glestinbiri.[18]

This indicates that the monks of Durham had promised to pray for Prior Serlo as they would for a monk of their own church, and for the other Hackness monks as for the monks of Glastonbury. Temporarily, then, the Anglo-Saxon monastery at Hackness was revived in the place of Anglo-Saxon Whitby.

My second theme is the importance of the eremitical tradition in the monastic resettlement of the North. It is perhaps worth reminding ourselves here that eremitical and cenobitical monasticism are not incompatible. Cenobitic monasticism stresses the importance of community. By eremitical we should understand an emphasis on withdrawal from the world, on solitude and poverty. Eremiticism does not necessarily imply individual solitude, or the lack of some kind of rule; it is not, therefore, inconsistent with the foundation of communities, either informal ones or monastic houses following the Rule of St Benedict. It is more a question of the emphasis within individual settlements. This is how we should understand the difference between the two in terms of the monastic climate of the eleventh century. It is quite clear, as has been pointed out many times, that the aims of the three men responsible for the 'northern revival', as described by Symeon of Durham, are to be understood in terms of a quest for solitude and poverty as well as a devotion to the holy places of the golden age of Northumbrian monasticism. Their aim was not necessarily – although this was the end product of their expedition – to introduce Benedictine monasticism to the region. The foundation of houses like Durham and York was far from their minds. We have no reason to doubt that the inspiration of Reinfrid to move on from Jarrow to Whitby was a search for that same solitude which characterized their initial venture north; indeed, the eremitical nature of his settlement there is reinforced by the language used by Abbot Stephen, who states that Reinfrid went to Whitby 'for the sake of living a solitary life', and that he himself found there 'brethren living the eremitical

---

[16] Ibid., bk. 4, ch. 23.
[17] *Cart. Whit.*, I, 2–3.
[18] *Liber Vitae*, fol. 48d.

life', or 'living as hermits'. It can be suggested that what we are thinking about at Whitby around the year 1077 is a community, quite informally organized, where Reinfrid's companions gave mutual support in their endeavours to live a life of poverty withdrawn from the secular world. We can find an analogy for the combination of solitary and communal life in the order of the Grande Chartreuse, or, at a less formal level, in the hermit communities of north-west France in this same period.[19]

A change came with the arrival of Abbot Stephen and with the beginning of a more formal organization of the hermit band. According to Stephen's account, he was chosen to be head of Reinfrid's community – with the prior's own consent – within a short time of his arrival at Whitby. Allowing for some telescoping of events, this is quite plausible. As numbers grew, Reinfrid might well have looked around for someone more suited than himself to be head of the house. Indeed, in his brief mention of Stephen as abbot of York, Symeon of Durham speaks of him as an energetic, or efficient, ruler. But, as we have seen, the handover of authority was not as simple as that, for when Abbot Stephen led his monks to Lastingham, Reinfrid and others evidently remained at Whitby, from where they removed to Hackness. There was a schism. The reasons for the split in the Whitby community are nowhere explained in our sources. Indeed, the Whitby narrative does not mention York; nor does Stephen tell us that a community continued to exist at Whitby. If we are to speculate, then I think we can see the schism, not necessarily as an acrimonious event, but as a parting of the ways between Reinfrid, the hermit, drawn to the eremitical side of the monastic life, and Stephen the efficient administrator, whose aims, as articulated in his own account, were to rebuild and restore, to acquire and improve.[20] There were two important results of this schism. One is demonstrated by an entry in Domesday Book, which is crucial to our understanding of the relationship between Whitby and York. In 'Prestebi' and Sowerby there were two carucates of land held of William de Percy by the abbot of York.[21] 'Prestebi' is the name accorded by the Memorial to the site of the abbey; and the same source states that William de Percy's initial endowment comprised two carucates of land. As Hamilton Thompson pointed out many years ago, this initial endowment may well have been made to Stephen at the formal foundation of the monastery rather than to the hermit Reinfrid.[22] In 1086 the abbot of York, Stephen, was apparently holding the initial endowment of Whitby; while six carucates in Hackness, Suffield and Everlay were part of 'the land of St Hilda' (there is no reference to the abbot or prior of Whitby, seeming to confirm that the convent was, in 1086, resident at Hackness).[23]

Domesday Book, therefore, suggests that the abbey newly established in York

---

[19] On this theme, see H. Leyser, *Hermits and the New Monasticism: a Study of Religious Communities in Western Europe, 1000–1150* (London, 1984).
[20] A point made by L.G.D. Baker, 'The Desert in the North', *Northern History* 5 (1970), pp. 1–11, at p. 6.
[21] *DB*, I, fol. 305a.
[22] Hamilton Thompson, 'Monastic Settlement at Hackness', p. 395.
[23] *DB*, I, fol. 323a.

may have enjoyed – or claimed – a constitutional relationship with Whitby/Hackness. Certainly it claimed the endowment of Whitby. There was a second result of the split between Stephen and Reinfrid: it was not until *c.*1109 that there was an abbot of Whitby, William de Percy, nephew of the lay founder of the house; both Reinfrid and Serlo de Percy are always referred to as prior. The Memorial specifically states that:

> after the death of the beloved prior, Reinfrid, Serlo, brother of William de Percy, took up his office, and remained in it until lord William, their nephew, was made abbot of Whitby.[24]

Symeon of Durham does not mention a schism between Stephen's convent and the rump which remained at Whitby, but seems to hit on the real problem when he states that Reinfrid

> went to *Streoneshalch*, which is now called Whitby, in which place he received such persons as came to him, and began to build a habitation for monks; who, after his death migrating to York, built a monastery in honour of St Mary, ever virgin, which at this time is under the efficient administration of Abbot Stephen.[25]

This suggests that Symeon, in some way, viewed the abbey of York as the successor of the community at Whitby, and it was presumably on these grounds that Stephen, in 1086, claimed what had been the initial endowment of Whitby.

But what fashioned monasticism in the North, as elsewhere, was not just the aims of monks themselves but of those persons, lay and ecclesiastical, who backed them. The narrative of the Memorial of foundation and benefactions lays stress, initially, on the part of William de Percy as founder of the house and on his endowment of the monks; and indeed the charters copied into the cartulary confirm his generosity. But can we reconcile this picture of William de Percy with the statement, in the account of Abbot Stephen, which receives some corroboration from the Dodsworth transcript, that the relationship between William and the monks deteriorated so much that the baron tried to eject them from his lands and reclaim his endowments? The alleged antagonism of the lay founder of Whitby is one of the more problematic features of the story. The Memorial tells of William's munificent grants to the community; Stephen and the Dodsworth fragment, on the other hand, record his hostility. Now, the failure of the Whitby source, the Memorial, to mention this conflict might be accounted for by the fact that it was compiled at the abbey; its author would presumably have been unwilling to offend a lay patron by resurrecting old quarrels. However, it perhaps makes sense if we think of the conflict occurring between William de Percy and Abbot Stephen.[26] It

[24] *Cart. Whit.*, I, 2; see *Heads of Religious Houses, England and Wales, 940–1216*, ed. D. Knowles, C.N.L. Brooke, and V.C.M. London (Cambridge, 1972), pp. 77–8.

[25] *LDE*, bk. 3, ch. 22 (p. 111); trans. *CHE*, p. 694.

[26] The authenticity of the Dodsworth fragment, or transcript, is difficult to assess. However, I am inclined to agree with Hamilton Thompson ('Monastic Settlement at Hackness', pp. 398–9)

was at the convent at Lastingham/York, and at Abbot Stephen, rather than at Hackness/Whitby and Priors Reinfrid and Serlo, that William de Percy's antagonism was probably directed. And I think we may be able to conjecture a reason for this discord, namely, the decision of Stephen to move away from the Percy site to Lastingham, and later still the claims of the York house to the endowments of Whitby. The transfer of the main body of the community from Percy lands at Whitby to the royal demesne threatened to remove – and indeed did remove – the monastery from baronial into royal patronage. Stephen's place in the power structure of the North was enhanced further when his community removed to York and was formally taken into royal patronage. William de Percy not only saw his monastic foundation slip away from him, but also take with it the endowments with which he had furnished it. The reason given by Stephen for the conflict with Whitby's founder was that when William de Percy saw that the lands he had given the monks had been improved and enriched by them he tried to resume the property.[27] A second, and perhaps more likely, interpretation is that he was trying to recover it from the convent which had moved away from his land, and to return it to the hermit Reinfrid whom he had first encouraged and sponsored at Whitby.

The time came when it was deemed safe for the convent at Hackness to return to Whitby. Either to mark the reoccupation of the Whitby site or his departure on crusade in 1096, William de Percy issued a charter confirming the monks in considerable possessions.[28] However, it was still not until c.1109 that Whitby was raised to the status of abbey, when Serlo resigned as prior and his nephew became abbot. The change in status cannot be linked to anything as definite as the death of Abbot Stephen, who may not have died until around 1112.[29] So we do not know why, by 1109, the Percy family, both Alan de Percy now patron, and William de Percy, abbot, felt able to make a gesture – the election of an abbot – which effectively freed the Whitby community from any kind of dependence on York, and confirmed this in the eyes of the world. Charters issued by Alan de Percy may coincide with the election of his cousin, William de Percy, as abbot. One of them includes among Alan's confirmations to the abbey, Sowerby, which had been held by the abbot of York in 1086.[30] This suggests that the affirmation of the independent status of Whitby was accompanied by the resumption of lands which had been claimed by the York abbey. And the grounds for this claim must have been that York was the legitimate successor of the community founded by Reinfrid and William de Percy at Whitby.

that although the account is garbled, and confuses Serlo with Stephen, its outlines, if not the detail, accord with Stephen's account.

[27] Hamilton Thompson accepts this ('Monastic Settlement at Hackness', p. 395), pointing out that of the 28 carucates and 6 bovates of land recorded in Domesday Book in the soke of Whitby, only 6 carucates in 'Prestebi' and Sowerby were under cultivation in 1086.

[28] *Cart. Whit.* I, 3, and no. 27 (pp. 31–3), *Early Yorkshire Charters*, II, no. 855 (pp. 197–8), and XI, no. 1 (p. 20).

[29] *Heads of Religious Houses*, ed. Knowles, Brooke, and London, p. 84.

[30] *Cart. Whit.*, I, nos. 27 (pp. 33–5), 279 (pp. 223–4), and 405 (pp. 362–4), also printed in *Early Yorkshire Charters*, II, nos. 856–7 (pp. 201–2), and XI, nos. 2–4 (pp. 21–2).

The evidence therefore suggests an unsettled occupation of the Whitby site throughout the late eleventh century and uneasy tenure of its endowments. One of the charters of Alan de Percy, probably dated to c.1109, refers to grants made for building. Another rather earlier grant of land, made by Gospatric in favour of Prior Serlo and therefore dating to before 1109, is witnessed by Godfrey, the 'master of the works'.[31] However, there is no evidence of any building activity on the Whitby site between 1079 and c.1100 – and here the contrast with Durham and with York is clear. 1109, thirty years after he left Jarrow, marks the beginning of the full development of Reinfrid's foundation, and the apogee of the Yorkshire part of the northern revival.

So by 1093, the year which we are celebrating, the northern revival which resulted in Durham in the creation of a Benedictine cathedral priory, led further south in Yorkshire to a number of distinctive religious establishments. In, or rather just outside, the city of York, lay an abbey fulfilling what had come to be all the expectations of a major Benedictine house: an urban site and a powerful, in this case a royal, lay patron. Domesday Book shows us that by 1086 the territorial growth of St Mary's was under way, and the abbey was soon to acquire landed endowments from the leading barons of the North.[32] Indeed, as a result of the Norman kings' need for loyal outposts in a part of their *conquête* which was the most troublesome, the abbey acquired privileges which exceeded the modest expectations of many religious houses.[33] St Mary's, like Durham, flourished as a direct result of its close connection with the Norman regime. Abbot Stephen appears to have been used more than once as an agent of the king.[34] And along with Abbot Hugh of Selby – but apparently not, it may be noted, Serlo of Whitby – Stephen attended the translation of the relics of St Cuthbert at Durham in 1104.[35] And what of Whitby where our story began? It seems to have retained some sense of its eremitical origins, for it became the focus of a group of hermitages.[36] But after 1109, when permanent occupation of the Whitby site was assured, it emerged as an abbey under baronial patronage, but one which came to enjoy as well royal

---

[31] *Cart. Whit.*, II, no. 508 (pp. 92–3).

[32] *DB*, I, fol. 314a, records the 'Abbot of York' as the holder of lands in Lastingham, Spaunton, Dalby, and Kirby Misperton; and he is included in the table of holders of land in Yorkshire (fol. 298b). See also the charter of William II in favour of St Mary's, issued between 1088 and 1093, in which the king refers to Count Alan, who initially brought the monks from Lastingham to York, as *post me et patrem meum hujus abbatie inceptor et institutor. Early Yorkshire Charters*, I, no. 350 (pp. 264–5).

[33] *Early Yorkshire Charters*, I, no. 350; see also A. Dawtry, 'The Benedictine Revival in the North: the Last Bulwark of Anglo-Saxon Monasticism', in *Religion and National Identity* (Studies in Church History 18; Oxford, 1982), pp. 87–99, at pp. 92–3.

[34] He was, for instance, sent by the king to arrest Abbot Benedict of Selby: *The Coucher Book of Selby*, ed. J.T. Fowler (Yorkshire Archaeological Society Record Series 87, 90; 1891–3), I, 20–1.

[35] *De miraculis*, ch. 7 (*Sym. Op.* I, 258).

[36] J. Burton, 'The Eremitical Tradition and the Development of post-Conquest Religious Life in Northern England', in *Eternal Values in Mediaeval Life*, ed. N. Crossley Holland, (*Trivium* 26; Lampeter, 1991), pp. 18–39, at pp. 27–30.

privilege and favour. The evidence of the sources I have discussed today indicates that Whitby's progress towards being an independent abbey was retarded by its ambiguous status with regard to York, and hampered by the conflict between William de Percy and Abbot Stephen and the York convent. But perhaps 'retarded' is not an appropriate term to use, at least in terms of the aspirations of the earliest hermits of Whitby. We can, I think, see in the tension between Reinfrid the monk-hermit and his colleague Stephen, and between Stephen the abbot and his lay patron William de Percy, the uneasy relationship between the desire of monks for solitude, poverty, and simplicity, and those who make those aspirations conform to their own ideals of the monastic life.

Custodians of St Cuthbert: The Durham Monks' Views of their Predecessors, 1083–*c*.1200

MERYL FOSTER

IN THE MANY STUDIES of the establishment in 1083 of a Benedictine monastic community in Durham, to serve as cathedral chapter in place of the essentially secular clerks who had filled that role hitherto, relatively little attention has been focused on the views which the newly-arrived monks expressed concerning their predecessors. The Benedictines have been seen either as simply hostile and scornful towards the clerks, or as anxious solely to stress the new community's continuity with the Northumbrian past.[1] Closer scrutiny suggests, however, that the attitudes which the monks articulated on this subject between 1083 and the 1190s were both ambivalent and variable, reflecting their hopes, fears, and beliefs about the standing of their community and its place in the history of their church.

The clerks of the *Congregatio*[2] which served the church of Durham and St Cuthbert's shrine within it down to 1083 constituted a wealthy and powerful corporation. They were seen, by themselves and those around them, as the corporeal and spiritual heirs of the monastic community of seventh-century Lindisfarne. In so far as it is possible to discern, the *Congregatio* proper consisted of a provost or dean and seven clerks,[3] who with their families held designated portions of the lands of their church; associated with them was an unspecified number of priests and clerks who participated in the life of the church and the shrine.[4]

---

[1] See R.B. Dobson, *Durham Priory 1400–1450* (Cambridge, 1973), p. 25; B. Meehan, 'A Reconsideration of the Historical Works associated with Symeon of Durham: Manuscripts, Texts and Influences' (unpublished Ph.D. thesis, University of Edinburgh, 1979), pp. 167–9, and 171; and cf. G.V. Scammell, *Hugh du Puiset, Bishop of Durham* (Cambridge, 1956), p. 128; A. Gransden, *Historical Writing in England c.550–c.1307* (London, 1974), pp. 115, and 119; and A.J. Piper, 'The First Generations of Durham Monks and the Cult of St Cuthbert', in *Cuthbert*, pp. 437–46. My thanks are due to Dr W.M. Aird and Dr B. Meehan for permission to cite their unpublished theses, and to Elizabeth Hallam, Alan Piper, Susan Ridyard and Sr. Catherine Wybourne O.S.B. for comments and suggestions on this paper. Responsibility for the views expressed is mine alone.

[2] The term first occurs in *HSC*, § 31 (p. 213)

[3] For 'provost' see: A.S.C. Ross, E.G. Stanley and T.J. Brown, 'Other Writings by Aldred', in *Evangeliorum Quatuor Codex Lindisfarnensis*, ed. T.D. Kendrick and others (2 vols.; Oltun and Lausanne, 1960), II, ii, 31–2; and G. Bonner, 'St Cuthbert at Chester-le-Street', in *Cuthbert*, p. 392 n. 21. For 'dean' see: *LDE*, bk. 4, ch. 3 (p. 122); cf. *HReg*, *s.a.* 1080 (p. 210).

[4] *LDE*, bk. 2, ch. 10 (pp. 61–2), ch. 12 (p. 65), and bk. 3, chs. 1–2 (pp. 78–81). See also

The monks who replaced them faced no easy task. In the face of Northern distrust of incomers, interference with St Cuthbert's church, especially by those brought in from outside, was potentially perilous.[5] In order to establish themselves successfully at Durham, the monks needed to assert their rights in the patrimony of St Cuthbert, and to ensure the continuing flow of pilgrim traffic to the shrine and benefactions to the church. In the process of appropriating the Cuthbertine heritage, the Benedictines could not avoid articulating some view of the events of 1083; however, the power of local tradition alone would have suggested that it might be unwise to proclaim vociferously that the establishment of the new community was a victory of righteousness over sin and evil, or the triumph of reform over unregenerate local custom. A more prudent approach would be to characterize the clerks as essential players in the long history of St Cuthbert's church, but players whose role had now come to an end.

Much of what the Durham Benedictines came to regard as their past was inherited from the *Congregatio*: the ancient *Liber Vitae*, probably begun on Lindisfarne, the Lindisfarne Gospels, two cartulary-chronicles, namely the tenth-century *Historia de Sancto Cuthberto*[6] and the eleventh-century *Cronica* later embedded in the Book of the High Altar,[7] and a variety of other written material.[8] Both communities were familiar with the early history of Lindisfarne and the life, death, and initial translation of St Cuthbert, as recounted by Bede. There was ample material for monastic writers to use.

The first work believed to have been produced in the new community was a collection of seven tales of miracles performed by St Cuthbert between the ninth century and the early 1080s. Bertram Colgrave showed that this small collection was assembled by a Durham monk after 1083, but before the completion of the great *Libellus de exordio atque procursu . . . Dunelmensis ecclesie* in the years between 1104 and 1107.[9] The first four were derived from the *Historia de Sancto Cuthberto*; the others related to more recent events. In substance, they rehearsed standard hagiographical themes. Their significance in the present context lies in their settings: all seven related to events before 1083, with no reference to the fact that there had since been an all-but-complete change in the organisation, and probably

---

H.H.E. Craster, 'The Patrimony of St Cuthbert', *EHR* 69 (1954), pp. 197–8; *DEC*, p. 121 and references. Cf. F. Barlow, *The English Church 1000–1066* (2nd edn.; London, 1979), p. 211 (Cornwall).

[5] W.E. Kapelle, *The Norman Conquest of the North: the Region and its Transformation, 1000–1135* (Chapel Hill and London, 1979), especially chs. 4 and 5.

[6] For the date, see L. Simpson, 'The King Alfred/St Cuthbert Episode in the *Historia de Sancto Cuthberto*: its Significance for mid-tenth-century English History', in *Cuthbert*, pp. 397–411.

[7] H.H.E. Craster, 'The Red Book of Durham', *EHR* 40 (1925), pp. 523–9.

[8] Bonner, 'St Cuthbert at Chester-le-Street', but cf. D. Rollason, 'St Cuthbert and Wessex: the Evidence of Cambridge, Corpus Christi College MS 183', both in *Cuthbert*, pp. 390–3 and 415–22.

[9] B. Colgrave, 'The Post-Bedan Miracles and Translations of St Cuthbert', in *The Early Cultures of North-West Europe*, ed. C. Fox and B. Dickins (Cambridge, 1950), pp. 305–32, especially pp. 326–7.

in the personnel, of St Cuthbert's church; moreover, the wording of certain passages suggested an unbroken tradition of monastic life around the shrine.

Allusions in the second tale to those 'of the monastic way of life' (*religiosae conuersationis*), who accompanied Bishop Eardwulf on the flight from Lindisfarne in 875, and to the brief spell in 'a monastery in the vill called Crayke' near York, were followed in the third by a reference to the sojourn at Chester-le-Street where 'those who serve God perpetually around the body of his most holy confessor [St Cuthbert] were settled under regular descipline.' No such 'monastic' passages were found in the *Historia*.[10] From the *Historia* came the notion of the bishop and the *Congregatio*, but a reference in the third tale to 'the bishop together with all the brothers' was also new.[11]

The monastic tone became more explicit in the fifth tale, where the writer described an event during Tostig's tenure of the earldom of Northumbria (1055–65) as having occurred 'in our time' (*nostris . . . temporibus*). The unlikely hero, a notorious bandit, fled 'to the monastery (*monasterium*) of the blessed St Cuthbert', arriving 'after Prime, when the brothers had left [the church]'. The tale concluded with a reference to lavish gifts, 'which are preserved in the monastery to this day, as a memorial of this episode'; the writer claimed to have learned the story from the bandit himself and 'from the brothers who witnessed it all'.[12] The sixth tale recounted the flight to Lindisfarne in 1069 of 'the bishop and the congregation', fearful of Norman wrath following the murder of Robert of Commines.[13] The compiler's informants were those who had carried St Cuthbert's coffin on this journey; then they had been military men of worldly stature, 'but now they have made their profession with us in the saint's own monastery in Durham, and they are true monks, both in dress and demeanour'. The seventh tale concerned a theft of goods which local inhabitants had deposited for safety in 'the monastery'; the thief, a Norman (*Francigena*) in the force sent to Durham in 1080 after the murder of Bishop Walcher, was punished by fever, and vainly sought mercy from St Cuthbert, rushing into the church to prostrate himself before the saint's shrine, just as the choir was singing the *Te Deum* at Matins.[14]

This unexpected use of monastic terminology may reflect a campaign to convince St Cuthbert's devotees that there had been no real change in his church, because no change was necessary. One possibility, incapable of proof, is that this miracle collection stemmed from a more personal interest in establishing continuity, and, indeed, in glossing over the events of 1083. The obvious candidates for authorship in these circumstances would be either the former dean of the *Congregatio*, its only member known to have become a monk in the house, or his son, already a monk in 1083 (presumably at Jarrow or Wearmouth).[15] Although it is

---

[10] *De miraculis*, chs. 2 and 3 (*Sym. Op.* I, 235, 237, and 238); cf. *HSC*, § 20 (pp. 207 and 208).

[11] *De miraculis*, ch. 3 (*Sym. Op.* I, 239).

[12] *De miraculis*, ch. 5 (*Sym. Op.* I, 243–5).

[13] *De miraculis*, ch. 6 (*Sym. Op.* I, 246 and 247). Cf. below, p. 58 and n. 33.

[14] *De miraculis*, ch. 8 (*Sym. Op.* II, 334 and 335).

[15] *LDE*, bk. 4, ch. 3 (pp. 122–3).

unlikely that they or any others in the new community fully believed in such continuity, the composition of these tales indicates that some among the Benedictines, far from seeking to denigrate their predecessors by drawing odious comparisons, were prepared to ignore the very real differences between the two communities, as a step in the appropriation of the heritage of St Cuthbert.

At some point between 1104 and 1107, a more realistic and more subtle view was articulated in the *Libellus de exordio atque procursu . . . Dunelmensis ecclesie*, a temperate and elegant composition with an integral preface (to be distinguished from the later prefatory summary),[16] composed by one of the monks at the behest of his superiors. This 'official history'[17] of St Cuthbert's church and community from the foundation of the episcopal see and monastery on Lindisfarne in 635 to the death of Bishop William of St Calais in 1096, may be accepted as representative of the attitude which, in the twenty years after the foundation of their house, the Durham monks chose to adopt towards their predecessors.

Unlike its older-established southern contemporaries, Durham priory required more from its chronicler than a straightforward defence of its traditions, rights and possessions against those who seemed to threaten them during the upheavals which followed the Norman Conquest.[18] The Durham chronicler recognized the need to demonstrate not only that the the power and influence of the patron saint should command respect, but also that the members of the monastic community were the rightful heirs to the church and shrine. The *Libellus de exordio* was composed to justify the introduction of the monks and to depict them as worthy custodians of St Cuthbert's shrine;[19] the deliberately moderate view expressed by its author is likely to be explained not by any large-scale continuity of personnel, but primarily by the monks' insecurity.[20]

The *Libellus de exordio* is traditionally attributed to the monk Symeon, said to have been cantor in 1104,[21] whose hand has now been tentatively but persuasively identified.[22] The author had certainly been present at the 1104 translation of St Cuthbert,[23] and had probably resided in the diocese of Durham before 1083, for he claimed to remember the clerks and their monastic liturgy, although he had not

---

[16] See below, pp. 61–2.

[17] H.S. Offler, *Medieval Historians of Durham* (Inaugural lecture; Durham, 1958), p. 7.

[18] Cf. R.W. Southern, 'Aspects of the European Tradition of Historical Writing: 4. The Sense of the Past', *TRHS*, 5th ser., 23 (1973), pp. 248–9, 251; S.J. Ridyard, '*Condigna veneratio*: Post-Conquest Attitudes to the Saints of the Anglo-Saxons', *AN* 9 (1987), pp. 180–9, 196–206.

[19] D. Rollason, 'Symeon of Durham and the Community of Durham in the Eleventh Century', in *England in the Eleventh Century*, ed. C. Hicks (Harlaxton Medieval Studies 2; Stamford, 1992), pp. 183–98; and W.M. Aird, 'The Origins and Development of the Church of St Cuthbert, 635–1153, with special reference to Durham in the period *c*.1071–1153' (unpublished Ph.D. thesis, University of Edinburgh, 1991), p. 139.

[20] See below, p. 59 and n. 37.

[21] For differing conclusions on the attribution, see Offler, *Medieval Historians*, pp. 8 and 20, nn. 7–8, and Meehan, 'Reconsideration', pp. 9–21, 60–3, and 80–3.

[22] See below, pp. 95–109.

[23] *LDE*, bk. 1, ch. 10 (p. 34).

been of their number.[24] He was sharply aware of the power of the past, gathering information from a variety of sources, oral and written, most of which he acknowledged explicitly in the course of his work.[25]

He used his material to present a particular view of the history of the church of Durham: the church which was established originally on Lindisfarne, and which held the holy relics of St Cuthbert, endured (although no longer in its original location), in the same steadfastness of faith, with the dignity and authority of an episcopal see, and the presence of a monastic community, just as at the time of its foundation by King Oswald and Aidan, its first bishop.[26] He saw the Benedictine monks of Durham cathedral priory as the true and legitimate successors of the monastic community of Lindisfarne; their regular life represented a return to the pristine observance established by the founders, which had reached its zenith in the time of St Cuthbert. He implied also that elements of the community described by Bede had survived, albeit in distorted form, until the time was ripe for the restoration in St Cuthbert's church of a unified body consisting of monastic bishop, prior and monks, serving God and guarding the shrine, the patrimony, and the people of St Cuthbert in perpetual harmony, as in the best years on Lindisfarne.

Symeon did not pretend that the community of St Cuthbert had remained monastic throughout its history, but he drew on written and oral tradition to compose his affecting, familiar but questionable picture of the bishop and the last oblates of Lindisfarne, wandering for seven years with St Cuthbert's corpse, to settle first at Chester-le-Street and later at Durham, maintaining throughout the original monastic liturgy.[27] He named four of St Cuthbert's seven porters, 'from whom many in Northumbria, both clergy and laity, are proud to be descended, since these their ancestors are recorded as such faithful servants of St Cuthbert'.[28] Grandsons of two of the original porters were among those who settled at Durham in 995: one lived to the age of 210 and spent the last forty years of his life as a monk (Symeon did not say where), the other for the last six years of his life was able to speak only in church, 'so that no frivolous or unpleasant word might defile his tongue, which was employed so assiduously in prayers and psalmody'.[29] More explicit still was the author's admiration for Alfred, son of Westou, a mid-eleventh century member of the *Congregatio*. From one of Alfred's former pupils, later a monk at Durham, he learned of the activities for which this paragon among the clerks was renowned locally: principally the care of St Cuthbert's corpse and the collection, often by

[24] *LDE*, bk. 2, ch. 6 (p. 58).
[25] *LDE*, bk. 1, ch. 1 (p. 19), bk. 1, ch. 3 (p. 23), bk. 1, ch. 6 (p. 26), bk. 1, ch. 9 (pp. 31–2), bk. 1, ch. 11 (p. 38), bk. 2, ch. 13 (pp. 70–1), bk. 2, ch. 16 (p. 72), bk. 2, ch. 18 (p. 75), bk. 3, ch. 3 (p. 82), bk. 3, ch. 4 (p. 83), bk. 3, ch. 6 (p. 86), bk. 3, ch. 7 (p. 88), bk. 3, ch. 10 (p. 94), and bk. 3, ch. 11 (p. 95). See also: Offler, *Medieval Historians*, pp. 7 and 20 n. 6.
[26] *LDE*, bk. 1, ch. 1 (pp. 17–18).
[27] *LDE*, bk. 2, ch. 6 (pp. 57–8). See also Piper, 'The First Generations of Durham Monks', in *Cuthbert*, pp. 440–1.
[28] *LDE*, bk. 2, ch. 12 (p. 65).
[29] *LDE*, bk. 3, ch. 1 (79–80).

covert means, of relics of other Northumbrian saints, to rest beside Cuthbert in Durham.[30]

Nonetheless, the monastic writer perceived cracks in the structure. The clerks, however admirable, were not monks. To sustain his claim that 'the corpse of [St] Cuthbert was never without the zeal and obedience of monks down to the time of Bishop Walcher,' Symeon was obliged to turn to the bishops. Yet the eleventh-century bishops, despite fulfilling the requirement that they should be or should become monks, had fallen away from the best practice of their illustrious and holy predecessor.[31] Concentrating on this domestic dislocation, the monastic writer could ignore the complex and potentially embarrassing political entanglements of the bishops[32] and the *Congregatio*,[33] while distancing the clerks from Bishop Aethelric and Bishop Aethelwine, the Benedictine siblings from Peterborough. The bishops had failed their church; by implication, they and not the clerks had in the end fallen furthest short of the standards of St Cuthbert.

Thus, the clerks served their narrative purpose as genuine, if misguided, guardians of the traditions of St Cuthbert's church. In the *Libellus de exordio*, Bishop Walcher's arrival in 1072 was presented as the start of the process of reunification and regeneration. The fact that Walcher was a secular clerk was mitigated by his 'praiseworthy manner of life, [which] gave him the appearance of a monk'.[34] Similarly, his misguided attempt to persuade the clerks to adopt liturgical forms appropriate to secular canons was outweighed by his part in the settlement at Jarrow and Wearmouth of the southern Benedictine monks whose communities would in due course form the kernel of the new establishment at Durham.[35] Inspired by their example – at least according to the *Libellus de exordio* – Walcher considered furnishing his cathedral with a monastic chapter, or in Symeon's words,

---

[30] *LDE*, bk. 3, ch. 7 (pp. 87–9).

[31] *LDE*, bk. 2, ch. 6 (p. 58); cf. bk. 1, ch. 2 (p. 20), bk. 2, ch. 20 (p. 78), bk. 3, ch. 6 (p. 86), and bk. 3, ch. 9 (p. 91).

[32] For Bishop Edmund: *LDE*, bk. 3, ch. 6 (pp. 85–6). For Bishop Aethelric: *LDE*, bk. 3, ch. 9 (pp. 91–2); Craster, 'Red Book of Durham', p. 528; *ASC* 'E', *s.a.* 1069–70 (pp. 149–53); and *Liber Eliensis*, ed. E.O. Blake (Camden Society, 3rd ser., 92; 1962), pp. lvi–vii and 175, n. 7. For Bishop Aethelwine: *LDE*, bk. 3, ch. 17; *ASC* 'D' and 'E', *s.a.* 1071 (p. 154); cf. *Fl. Wig.* II, 9, and *HReg*, *s.a.* 1071 (p. 195). See also Kappelle, *Norman Conquest of the North*, pp. 31–3, 89–90; Aird 'Origins and Development', pp. 52–4, 57, 59.

[33] The flight to Lindisfarne with St Cuthbert's relics in 1069 probably reflects the community's traditional attachment to the house of Bamburgh, while William I's demand to view the relics in Durham in 1072 suggests his fear lest the relics had remained within sight of Bamburgh, a potential rallying-point for northern rebellion; the monastic writer blamed the bishop and Cospatric for the flight, and related miraculous proofs of St Cuthbert's wrath at the earl's wickedness and the king's presumptuous doubts: *LDE*, bk. 3, chs. 15–16 (pp. 100–4), and bk. 3, ch. 19 (p. 106). The *Libellus de exordio* contains no hint that the clerks were implicated in Walcher's murder: *LDE*, bk. 3, ch. 24 (pp. 116–18); cf. Rollason, 'Symeon of Durham', pp. 95–7; and see below, p. 289.

[34] *LDE*, bk. 3, ch. 18 (pp. 105–6).

[35] *LDE*, bk. 3, chs. 21–2 (pp. 108–13).

'settling a monastic establishment around St Cuthbert's corpse', but he was murdered before he could give effect to this proposal.

His successor, the Benedictine William of St Calais, was remembered by his community as an heroic figure, second in importance only to St Cuthbert. In a rare expression of overt disapproval of the clerks, Symeon recounted that on his arrival in 1081 the new bishop found St Cuthbert's land laid waste, 'and the place which the saint illuminated with the presence of his holy corpse shamefully bereft (*despicabiliter destitutum*), attended more negligently than his sanctity deserved'. The bishop was dismayed that the clergy of his cathedral were neither monks nor canons regular; having sought divine guidance and local advice, he decided to restore in Durham the original manner of observance of St Cuthbert's church on Lindisfarne. With royal, archiepiscopal and papal support, he was able, in due course, to bring together the monks from Jarrow and Wearmouth to form a single new Benedictine community in Durham. The previous occupants of the church, 'who bore the name of canons, but who in no way followed a canons' rule', were given the option of entering the new house; the monastic chronicler reported that only their dean was persuaded to this course, by his son, himself a monk.[36]

There seems to be no reason to accept Dr Aird's recent challenge to this statement;[37] had more than one of the clerks chosen to enter the new community, the author of the *Libellus de exordio* would have made much of it, as a demonstration of St Cuthbert's power to transform and renew the lives of his followers. But to remain in the church of Durham after 1083, the canons would have had to abandon their homes, wives and families, for the cenobitic and celibate life prescribed by the Rule of St Benedict. Symeon showed little surprise or disapproval that most of them felt unable to remain 'on these terms' (*taliter*). Still less did he express loathing or disgust of their way of life.

Like many of his contemporaries in northern England and beyond, Symeon was caught between two views of clerical life. He disapproved in principle of the marriage of priests – forbidden by canon law, but now a specific target of ecclesiastical reformers. On the other hand, in common with many of his contemporaries, he accepted that priests could have wives (*uxores*), rather than mere concubines, although they should, of course, live with them only in fraternal chastity.[38] Significantly, the tales in which he expressed his disapproval of priestly marriage did not relate specifically to the clerks of St Cuthbert.

Symeon's picture of St Cuthbert's attitude to women is perhaps less closely related to the question of the clerks' marital status than some recent writers have suggested. He introduced the subject by (unusually for him) embroidering upon Bede's account of the burning of the double monastery at Coldingham, probably in

---

36 *LDE*, bk. 4, chs. 2–3 (pp. 120–3).

37 Aird, 'Origins and Development', pp. 156–7, 171–4, 391–3.

38 *LDE*, bk. 3, ch. 10 (pp. 93–4), and bk. 4, ch. 9 (p. 131). Cf. C.N.L. Brooke, 'Gregorian Reform in Action: Clerical Marriage in England 1050–1200', in *The Medieval Church and Society* (London, 1971), pp. 83–90; J.A. Brundage, *Law, Sex and Christian Society in Medieval Europe* (Chicago, 1987), pp. 151–2, 214–19.

the 680s.[39] He continued with tales of the dire fate which befell those who defied the alleged subsequent prohibition upon the entry of women into the saint's churches.[40] The stories have been seen as the monks' expression of disgusted hostility towards the married clerks, used as a means to strengthen their position by promoting the image of the saint as misogynist.[41] However, the articulation of the notion of St Cuthbert's exclusion zone does not appear to have been accompanied by any attempt to suggest that the saint himself had condemned the clerks for their family life. None of the three women punished for trespassing on St Cuthbert's ground was said to have been the wife of a member of the *Congregatio*, although the widower of one of them had later entered the Benedictine house. Moreover, Symeon did not portray St Cuthbert as a misogynist, but rather as a disciplinarian. Women who transgressed against the rules allegedly set down by the saint were chastised for their disobedience, but those who approached him correctly could expect to receive due reward.[42]

This unparalleled exclusion of women from the shrine has been seen as a means of breaking the clerks' hereditary hold on the church's estates,[43] although that problem may have been addressed by the establishment of prebends in churches which did not belong to the ancient patrimony of St Cuthbert.[44] Most probably, however, the ban was intended primarily to enforce the concept of the monastic enclosure, not known in Durham before 1083.[45] Whatever lay behind it, the author of the *Libellus de exordio* did not use it as an opportunity to vilify and denigrate the clerks' style of life.

Throughout his narrative, the priory's official historian refrained from sweeping condemnation of the clerical *Congregatio*. This moderation is explained in part by the nostalgic respect which Symeon and some of his fellow monks felt for their predecessors, who had striven to maintain their patron's relics and traditions and who had received so many manifestations of his miraculous powers. But there were also elements of fear, not merely of giving offence in a potentially hostile local environment, but also the more domestic concern that Bishop Ranulf Flambard, in the early years of the twelfth century, wished to subvert the supposedly natural constitution of monastic bishop and chapter which had flourished in the days of St Cuthbert and had been revived by Bishop William of St Calais.[46] The *apologia pro*

---

[39] *LDE*, bk. 2, ch. 7 (p. 59); cf. *HE*, pp. 420, 424, 426.

[40] *LDE*, bk. 2, chs. 8–9 (pp. 60–1), and bk. 3, ch. 11 (pp. 94–5).

[41] V.M. Tudor, 'The Misogyny of St Cuthbert', *Arch. Ael.*, 5th ser., 12 (1984), p. 159; and idem, 'The Cult of St Cuthbert in the Twelfth Century: the Evidence of Reginald of Durham', in *Cuthbert*, pp. 456–7.

[42] *LDE*, bk. 3, ch. 3 (pp. 81–2).

[43] Aird, 'Origins and development', p. 161.

[44] *LDE*, bk. 4, ch. 3 (pp. 122–3 and n.a); and Rollason, 'Symeon of Durham', p. 191 and n. 37. Cf. below, pp. 147–8, n. 22.

[45] See also Piper, 'The First Generations of Durham Monks', p. 443.

[46] *LDE*, bk. 1, ch. 10 (pp. 32–3); see also H.S. Offler, 'Ranulf Flambard as bishop of Durham (1099–1128)', *Durham University Journal* 64 (1971), pp. 14–25.

communitate sua doubled as a mirror for bishops. Preference and prudence alike dictated a magnanimous approach to the old regime.

A generation later, a less tolerant view prevailed within the community. The first dated indication of the change of outlook is the privilege which Pope Calixtus II issued in May 1123, confirming to Durham cathedral priory all its possessions and estates.[47] The preamble stated that he had learned from Archbishop William of Canterbury and Archbishop Thurstan of York how Bishop William of Durham had, with advice from the king and leading churchmen of England and by means of a precept of Pope Gregory VII, established a monastic community in his church, replacing the secular clerks who then dwelt there, 'because of their depraved and incorrigible way of life'; now, in response to the supplications set before him by Robert, monk of Durham, on behalf of the community, the pope was confirming Bishop William's settlement of 1083. It is not clear whether the sharp comments on the clerks were quoted from a document (no longer extant) which was presented to Calixtus as Pope Gregory's bull or originated as part of the case put forward by the monks' representative.

It is doubtful whether Gregory VII was involved in any way in the 1083 establishment.[48] The earliest surviving reference to his alleged precept, a paraphrase in the *Libellus de exordio, s.a.* 1083,[49] was utilised, with minimal alteration, as the basis for the fabrication of an alleged charter of Bishop William (with the opening words *Ego Willelmus*), inscribed in the Durham *Liber Vitae* not long after the completion of the *Libellus de exordio* itself.[50] Neither version ascribed to the pope any criticism of the clerks. The production of these texts reflects the belief, common among twelfth century ecclesiastical bodies, that such a document must have, or at least ought to have, existed. Furthermore, it ought to be confirmed. In Rome in May 1123, the prevailing atmosphere was conducive to a harsher approach to the clerks. The First Lateran Council, which had met in March, had reiterated the prohibitions on clerical marriage and concubinage.[51] The monks would lose nothing by speaking ill of their predecessors, attributing trenchant criticisms to Pope Gregory, that most vigorous champion of reform.

A change in outlook is indicated also by the addition of a preface to the *Libellus de exordio*. The 'epitome' is often assumed to be an integral part of the earlier work, and is quoted as a succinct expression of the views of the author and his contemporaries. In fact it differs radically in both tone and presentation of events.[52] In the earliest surviving manuscript of the *Libellus de exordio* the epitome was an addition

---

[47] *Papsturkunden in England*, ed. W. Holtzmann, II (Berlin, 1935), no. 5, pp. 138–40.

[48] M. Gibson, *Lanfranc of Bec* (Oxford, 1978), p. 182 and n. 3.

[49] *LDE*, bk.4, ch. 2 (p. 121).

[50] *DEC*, pp. 6–15.

[51] The canons of the Council were known in Durham by the mid-twelfth century: *HReg, s.a.* 1123 (pp. 269–73); see also M. Brett, 'The Canons of the First Lateran Council in English Manuscripts', in *Proceedings of the Sixth International Congress of Medieval Canon Law 1980*, ed. S. Kuttner and K. Pennington (*Monumenta Iuris Canonici*, series C, *Subsidia* 7; Vatican, 1985), pp. 16–17.

[52] *Sym. Op.* I, pp. 7–11.

in a hand of two or three decades later than that responsible for the main text.[53] This is almost certainly also the date of its composition, as a preface designed to prejudice the reader's interpretation of the *Libellus de exordio* itself.

Its author was determined to distinguish as sharply as possible between the clerks and the monks. He stated categorically that the monastic community established in 635 endured for 240 years and that with the raids on Lindisfarne in 875 'monastic life around St Cuthbert's corpse came to an end'. Both these points had been carefully blurred by the writer of the *Libellus de exordio*. Of those who had served the church between 875 and 1083, he had nothing good to say. The young clerics who had followed Bishop Eardwulf from Lindisfarne had abandoned the way of life in which they had been instructed, and had come 'to hate ecclesiastical discipline and to succumb to the charms of a looser manner of living'. With no-one to control them, 'they were slaves to flesh and blood, begetting sons and daughters'. Their use of the monastic office, which the author of the *Libellus de exordio* saw as a brave effort to maintain contact with the past, the epitomist dismissed as a derisory remnant of former splendour.[54] He asserted openly that when Walcher had found the clerks not amenable to reform, the arrival of the southern Benedictines had offered the means of making changes; the bishop had sent them to Jarrow and Wearmouth only for the meantime (*interim*), until he could undertake the building work essential to the establishment at Durham, later completed by William of St Calais.

The attachment of such a preface to the priory's official history suggests a deliberate change of tone. This might be supposed to reflect increased confidence within the now well-established community, yet the epitome was defensive, justifying the 1083 plantation by scathing criticism of the clerks. A similar defensive mood, this time in respect of the monks' stewardship of St Cuthbert's shrine, is noticeable in the account of the 1104 translation of St Cuthbert, also composed in Durham during the second quarter of the twelfth century, probably between 1123 and 1138.[55] Taken together, these texts suggest that the Benedictines of Durham now felt threatened in their turn by more innovative and reform-minded newcomers. Durham, hitherto the leading regular establishment north of York, was confronted in the 1130s by a growing number of potential rivals as centres of devotion and recipients of offerings and patronage – Augustinians, Tironensians, Savigniacs and Cistercians. The composition of a detailed account of the 1104 translation could be used to enhance the reputation of St Cuthbert's church and

---

[53] Meehan, 'Reconsideration', pp. 174–5.

[54] Cf. *LDE*, bk. 2, ch. 6 (p. 57).

[55] *De miraculis*, ch. 7 (*Sym. Op.* I, 247–61). See also Colgrave, 'The Post-Bedan Miracles and Translations', pp. 329–30; F.M. Powicke, 'Maurice of Rievaulx', *EHR* 36 (1921), pp. 17, 20. The cavalier treatment of Bishop Ranulf suggests composition after 1128. Two points indicate embellishment of the known details of 1104 to provide a more impressive text for the 1120s or 1130s: the doubt cast on St Cuthbert's incorruption (*De miraculis*, ch. 7 (*Sym. Op.* I, 247–8); cf. *LDE*, bk. 1, ch. 10 (p. 34)); and the unnamed, probably fictitious, 'neighbouring' abbot who impugned the monks' good faith (*De miraculis*, ch. 7 (*Sym. Op.* I, 255–6)).

shrine, while the Durham Benedictines' own zeal and holiness of life was emphasized by vilification of their forerunners.

For mid-twelfth-century writers in Durham, notably Laurence the poet, and the continuators of the *Libellus de exordio*, the clerks were of no interest in the face of turbulent current events. However, in the third quarter of the twelfth century, the monks came to regard them once again with a degree of tolerant nostalgia. This seems to have been due largely to the influence of Ailred, monk and abbot of the Cistercian house of Rievaulx, and a leading figure in the northern historiographical and hagiographical circles in which Durham priory moved.[56] Ailred was proud to be the great-grandson of the greatest of St Cuthbert's clerks, Alfred, son of Westou. Despite the somewhat chequered relations between Ailred's grandfather and father and the Benedictines of Durham,[57] and notwithstanding his own dedication to Cistercian austerity, he felt neither hostility nor indifference towards the ancient cults of his home region or the clergy who maintained them.[58] If, as seems probable, Ailred prompted one devotee of St Cuthbert to leave Durham for the stricter life at Rievaulx,[59] he nonetheless inspired another to compose the longest, most elaborate and most ambitious of all the accounts of St Cuthbert's miracles.

Reginald of Durham's lengthy 'tract on the miraculous proofs of St Cuthbert's powers given in recent times', composed in two parts, in the mid-1160s and the early 1170s,[60] depicted the pre-1083 clerks once again as the well-intentioned guardians of St Cuthbert's cult, who had witnessed numerous miraculous manifestations of their patron's power, details of which had been passed down through the family of Reginald's mentor Ailred.[61] This may explain why Reginald, otherwise the most forthright recorder of St Cuthbert's distrust of women,[62] made no adverse comment on the marital status of the clerks who had once guarded the shrine. Rather, he remarked that those who had borne St Cuthbert's coffin after the flight from Lindisfarne in 875 were happy indeed, for having carried so fine a burden, the hope of heaven was theirs.[63] Speaking of the initial settlement at Durham, Reginald noted that 'the body of clerks, who had retained from among monastic observances only their manner of singing, were privileged to serve the church, under the bishop'. His words, similar in form to those of the epitomist, were wholly different in tone. He went on to explain, without adverse comment, that

---

[56] Gransden, *Historical Writing*, pp. 286–90; Meehan, 'Reconsideration', pp. 250–67 and references. For improved relations between Durham and the Yorkshire Cistercians in the 1140s, see below, pp. 363–4.

[57] Richard of Hexham, *Brevis annotatio . . . de antiquo et moderno statu ejusdem ecclesiae*, and Ailred of Rievaulx, *De sanctis ecclesiae Haugustaldensis*, in *The Priory of Hexham* I, ed. J. Raine (SS 44; 1863), pp. 54–6, 191; *DEC*, pp. 120–1.

[58] *Priory of Hexham* I, 173–203. See also: A. Squire, *Aelred of Rievaulx: a Study* (paperback edn; London, 1973), pp. 112–15.

[59] Powicke, 'Maurice of Rievaulx', p. 17.

[60] Tudor, 'The Cult of St Cuthbert in the Twelfth Century', p. 449.

[61] *Cuth. virt.*, chs. 1–2 (pp. 1–4), ch. 16 (pp. 28–32), ch. 26 (pp. 57–60), and probably also ch. 16 (pp. 22–8).

[62] Tudor, 'Misogyny of St Cuthbert', pp. 157, 160–2.

[63] *Cuth. virt.*, ch. 14 (pp. 20–1).

the clerks had held prebends, 'in the manner of those who nowadays are called secular canons'.[64] One further tale, of a miraculous cure at the shrine before 1083, came not from Ailred, but from Turold, an aged Durham monk, who had heard it from the clerks (a veteranis canonicis) who had witnessed it.[65] Their primary concern, according to the traditions which reached Reginald, was the care of St Cuthbert's shrine.

The revival of a less censorious view of the clerks was not unique to Reginald. Among the numerous forged charters produced by the priory community to strengthen their position vis-à-vis the bishop,[66] eight texts datable to between the early 1160s and the late 1180s, and attributed to Bishop William of St Calais, Archbishop Lanfranc of Canterbury, Archbishop Thomas I of York, and King William I, took an entirely neutral tone when speaking of the clerics or 'canons' whom the monks had replaced.[67]

In the 1190s, however, the conventual forgers reopened the attack on the clerks' 'incorrigible' way of life, most notably in the texts which were presented as the original bull of Pope Gregory VII (Sacrosancta), and yet another grant of Bishop William of St Calais (Venerabilibus patribus). The purported bull was as vicious in tone as the epitome of the Libellus de exordio, and went considerably beyond the disapprobation noted by Pope Calixtus II from whatever had been presented to him in 1123 as his predecessor's act. Sacrosancta attributed to Pope Gregory a decision that 'the evil-doing clerks of the church of Durham, some of whom are even born of that same shameful and sacrilegious stock, shall be completely removed thence, on account of their incorrigible way of life'.[68] Venerabilibus patribus also described the clerks' way of life as 'incorrigible', although without further comment.[69] Passages in both documents bracketed together the lifestyle of the clerks and the murder of Bishop Walcher as reasons for reform, the implication being that the cathedral clergy were guilty of complicity in their bishop's death.

Both offensive and defensive considerations lay behind the production of these texts in the 1190s. On the one hand, they represented the culmination of forty years' sparring with Bishop Hugh of le Puiset over the rights and liberties of the monastic community. Under the vigorous leadership of Prior Bertram, appointed in 1189, the monks obtained from the dying Puiset in 1195 agreement to a degree of freedom and power greater than any permitted to them hitherto, based largely,

---

[64] Ibid., ch. 16 (pp. 28–9).

[65] Ibid., ch. 19 (pp. 38–41).

[66] FPD, pp. xxxi–lxxxi; cf. Scammell, Puiset, pp. 300–7.

[67] Forged acta of Archbishop Lanfranc and Archbishop Thomas, made in the 1160s: FPD, pp. lxxvi, lxxvii. Ego Willelmus, inflated in two separate versions, one before 1165, the other before 1174: DEC, pp. 15, 21–2. A more elaborate charter of Bishop William, In nomine patris, in two versions, datable respectively to before 1174 and before 1189: DEC, pp. 26, 30–3, 36. Two purported privileges of King William I, forged before 1189: FPD, pp. lxvii, lxix. See also Scammell, Puiset, pp. 303–4, 307.

[68] Papsturkunden in England II, no. 2, p. 134.

[69] DEC, p. 54.

although not exclusively, on the forgery *Venerabilibus patribus*.[70] After Puiset's death, but before the consecration of his successor, this key document appears to have been confirmed by King Richard I, in February 1196;[71] the bull *Sacrosancta* was confirmed by Pope Celestine III in May of the same year.[72] Prior Bertram and his supporters had revived the policy of blackguarding the clerks as one way to reaffirm for the benefit of bishop, king and pope the Durham Benedictines' impeccable credentials.

On the other hand, the monks also perceived threats, not merely to their detailed claims, but to their position in the diocese and to their very existence. Determination to maintain their position as the only major religious community between Tyne and Tees underpinned their vigorous and ultimately successful resistance to attempts by Puiset's son to establish a community of Augustinian canons close to Durham in the 1180s.[73] Moreover, an idea was then current that the English bishops wished to abolish monastic cathedral priories.[74] Although there is no evidence to suggest that Puiset had any such plan for Durham, fear of his intentions may have prompted the monks to revive the notion that their community had been brought to Durham in 1083 specifically to replace a group of secular clergy who were beyond hope of reform. The later forgeries' brief but telling passages about the clerks were calculated to deter any attack upon a Benedictine community so visibly conscious of its origins and duties.

Thereafter, the clerks ceased to be of active concern to the monastic community. The *Libellus de exordio* and *Sacrosancta* were the only sources concerning the clerks used in Prior Wessington's early fifteenth century history of the church of Durham,[75] or in the late sixteenth-century tract on the monuments, rites and customs of Durham Priory before the Dissolution, which spoke with nostalgic relish of their 'evill and nawghtie living', and their 'lewd and lazy lives'.[76] During the century after 1083, however, the views which the Durham monks had expressed about their predecessors reflected closely the picture which, often for defensive purposes, they wished to project of themselves. Initially, local opinion needed to be mollified; later, other churchmen needed to be convinced of the Durham monks' ecclesiastical credentials. The Benedictines' principal concern was not unthinkingly to denigrate their predecessors, but to depict them in the way which, at any given time, was calculated to enhance the monks' view of their own place in the history of St Cuthbert's church.

---

[70] Scammell, *Puiset*, pp. 135–6, 261–3.
[71] *DEC*, p. 59.
[72] *Papsturkunden in England* II, no. 278, pp. 470–4.
[73] The fullest account is still *The Priory of Finchale*, ed. J. Raine (SS 2; 1837), pp. x–xii, 8–19.
[74] Scammell, *Puiset*, pp. 137–8.
[75] Bodl.L, MS Laud misc. 748, fols. 15r/v, 19, 23v, 26v–27 and 28–29. See also R.B. Dobson, 'Contrasting Chronicles: Historical Writing at York and Durham at the Close of the Middle Ages', in *Church and Chronicle in the Middle Ages: Essays Presented to John Taylor*, ed. I. Wood and G. Loud (London, 1992), pp. 207–9.
[76] *Rites*, pp. 67, 72.

Durham Priory and its Hermits in the Twelfth Century

VICTORIA TUDOR

ALTHOUGH THE ESSENCE of Benedictine monasticism is the religious life spent in community, the Rule which embodies it demonstrates an awareness of, and indeed an admiration for, the more taxing existence of the hermit. In the first chapter of the Rule St Benedict describes the two kinds of monk of whom he approves: first 'the cenobites, that is those who live in monasteries, serving under a rule and an abbot', and then 'anchorites or hermits, . . . those who after long probation in a monastery . . . go out well-armed from the ranks of the community to the solitary combat of the desert.'[1] Whether Benedict believed that it was desirable in practice for cenobites, for whom he was writing, to mature into hermits is less certain,[2] but the fact remains that the eremitical ideal was presented to every Benedictine monk with each reading of the Rule. Thus it is not out of keeping with the general tenor of Benedictine life that hermits should have played a role in the history of Durham priory in this early period.

These hermits were of two kinds. Those to be found on the island of Inner Farne and elsewhere were Durham monks who had indeed exchanged the security of the monastery for harshness and solitude. Another hermit, who lived in upper Weardale, although not a monk, was likewise a product of the house. Other individuals, of whom the most important is St Godric of Finchale, were not members of the community in the strict sense but were linked to it in various ways. The history of solitaries of both kinds can shed light on the character of the priory in the twelfth century.

The Inner Farne, the largest of a group of islands situated off the coast of Northumberland seven miles south-east of Lindisfarne, must in terms of its discomfort and bleakness approach those environments where human life is unsustainable. At least five Durham monks are nevertheless known to have lived there at this period. The earliest was probably Aelric, who was living there alone at some point before, and probably not long before, 1150. This solitary was the uncle of

---

[1] Rule, ch. 1; ed. and trans. J. McCann (London, 1952), p. 15. Other comments by the saint, relevant to the eremitic life, are discussed by H. Leyser, *Hermits and the New Monasticism* (London, 1984), pp. 11–12.

[2] Interpretations of the practical implications of Benedict's admiration for hermits vary. See, for example, Leyser, *Hermits*, p. 12, and C. Phipps, 'Romuald – Model Hermit: Eremitical theory in St Peter Damian's *Vita Beati Romualdi* Chapters 16–27', in *Monks, Hermits and the Ascetic Tradition*, ed. W.J. Shiels (Studies in Church History, 22; Oxford, 1985), at p. 71, n. 21.

Bernard, the sacrist of the monastery.[3] The next occupant was a certain Aelwin, who was in residence when Bartholomew, the most famous Farne solitary in this period, arrived in 1150. Aelwin's reaction was not positive and, although the two men tried to live together, Aelwin ultimately withdrew.[4] Bartholomew remained on the island until his death in 1193 with one short break.[5] This was occasioned by the arrival about 1163 of Thomas, the former prior, after his spectacular defeat in the on-going dispute with the bishop. So great was the friction between the two hermits that Bartholomew went back to Durham, but returned after a year to find that all the difficulties had resolved themselves. The two lived together until Thomas's death[6] but Bartholomew seems to have been joined by at least one other companion in the years that followed. A Brother William appears on Farne both before[7] and at the time of Bartholomew's death in 1193.[8] He is also found ministering to the sick on the island afterwards[9] and he may be the monk Bartholomew's biographer had in mind when he referred to the hermit's successor.[10] If to speak, as Craster does, of 'the two Durham monks who made up the little monastic community on the Inner Farne',[11] suggests an institutional rigidity inappropriate to the twelfth century,[12] the statement of the same biographer that the island was always occupied[13] may well be true, once the first Durham monk had recolonized it.

D.H. Farmer has provided a sketch of the life of a monk who lived on Farne in

---

[3] Aelric is described by the hagiographer Reginald of Durham as being in charge of the island (*Cuth. virt.*, ch. 27 (p. 61)), with no reference to a companion. When the hermit Bartholomew arrived on Farne in 1150 he found another hermit, Aelwin, already there (see next note). Aelric's occupation of Farne must therefore pre-date 1150, but it cannot do so by a substantial number of years as Reginald, writing possibly in the 1150s and certainly in the 1160s, refers to Aelric's living on Farne 'lately' and 'at this time' (*temporibus istis* (loc. cit.; for the date of the relevant work by Reginald, see V.M. Tudor, 'The Cult of St Cuthbert in the Twelfth Century: the Evidence of Reginald of Durham', in *Cuthbert*, pp. 447–67, at p. 449)). For Aelric, see also *Cuth. virt.*, ch. 27 (pp. 61–3); ch. 28 (pp. 63–5); ch. 78 (p. 163).

[4] *V.Barth.*, ch. 8–9 (p. 300). For Aelwin, see also *Cuth. virt.*, ch. 29 (p. 66); ch. 30 (p. 69).

[5] For Bartholomew, see *V.Barth.* The saint is discussed in 'St Godric of Finchale and St Bartholomew of Farne', in *Benedict's Disciples*, ed. D.H. Farmer (Leominster, 1980), at pp. 207–11. For the dates of his occupancy of Farne, see *V.Barth.*, ch. 30 (p. 320); ch. 33 (p. 322) and *Sym. Op.* I, Introduction, pp. xl–xli.

[6] *V.Barth.*, ch. 14 (p. 307). For Thomas, see Geoffrey of Coldingham, *Liber de Statu Ecclesiae Dunelmensis*, ed. *Script. Tres*, ch. 3 (pp. 7–8) and *V.Barth.*, chs. 14–15 (pp. 307–8).

[7] *V.Barth.*, ch. 27 (p. 317).

[8] *V.Barth.*, ch. 33 (p. 323).

[9] *V.Barth.*, ch. 35 (p. 324); ch. 36 (p. 325).

[10] *V.Barth.*, ch. 2 (p. 296); ch. 16 (p. 309). Cf. op. cit., ch. 28 (p. 318): the *haeredem loci* ('the heir to the place').

[11] H.H.E. Craster, 'The Miracles of St Cuthbert at Farne', *Analecta Bollandiana* 70 (1952), pp. 5–19, at p. 6. A translation of this text is given in *idem*, 'The Miracles of Farne', *Arch. Ael.* 4th ser., 29 (1951), pp. 93–107.

[12] While we have a number of references (including those already quoted) which indicate that two monks were living together on the island, there are other passages which suggest that at various times during this period Farne provided a home for one hermit only (for example, *Cuth. virt.*, ch. 111 (pp. 247–8); ch. 119 (p. 265); 'Miracles at Farne', ch. 5 (p. 14)).

[13] *V.Barth.*, ch. 20 (p. 312): *uiros uirtutum semper habet* ('it always possesses men of virtue').

the fourteenth century,[14] and there is no reason to doubt that in essence this describes the existence of his predecessors two hundred years earlier. Thus, while the setting for this life was exceptionally harsh, its basic framework would have been provided by the familiar monastic occupations of prayer, meditation and manual work. The last item would have included fishing and the chopping of drift-wood brought by the sea. We know also that barley was grown on the island in the twelfth century[15] and a flock of sheep – no doubt small – maintained.[16] As was the case with other hermits in this period, one or more servants helped with mundane tasks.[17]

Visitors seem to have made little impression on the fourteenth-century sources but in the twelfth century many came to the island and the guesthouse was often in use.[18] A substantial proportion of these visitors were fishermen or traders who were forced to seek shelter in bad weather[19] and who placed a severe strain on the hermits' meagre resources.[20] Less welcome visitors at some point in the early 1150s were Aeistan and his Norwegian raiding company, who seem to have come to Farne to repair their ships and who treated the hermits' property in characteristically highhanded fashion.[21] But many of those who travelled out to Farne in the twelfth century came for religious reasons. Farne was a centre for the cult of St Cuthbert; indeed, for those who lived north of the Tyne it seems to have been more popular than Durham.[22] The island's associations with the saint, who had of course lived as a hermit there himself, were well known before the arrival of the Durham monks,[23] but it is likely that the number of visitors increased when there was someone to receive them. Even the sick were prepared to make the somewhat difficult journey,[24] with most of the cures that occurred apparently being attributed to Cuthbert rather than to the resident hermits.[25] Despite this, the sanctity of the

---

[14] *The Monk of Farne*, ed. H. Farmer (London, 1961), Introd., p. 14.

[15] *V.Barth.*, ch. 20 (p. 312).

[16] *Cuth. virt.*, ch. 29 (p. 66). Cf. *V.Barth.*, ch. 14 (p. 307); ch. 20 (p. 312).

[17] *Cuth. virt.*, ch. 27 (pp. 61–2); ch. 111 (pp. 247, 248). Cf. the servants who worked for Godric at Finchale (see V.M. Tudor, 'Reginald of Durham and St Godric of Finchale: a Study of a Twelfth-Century Hagiographer and his Major Subject' (unpublished Ph.D. thesis, University of Reading, 1979), pp. 268–9).

[18] For example, *Cuth. virt.*, ch. 33 (p. 75); ch. 62 (p. 122); ch. 102 (p. 228).

[19] *Cuth. virt.*, ch. 31 (pp. 70–1); ch. 33 (p. 74); ch. 34 (p. 76).

[20] For example, *Cuth. virt.*, ch. 28 (pp. 63–4); ch. 34 (pp. 76–7); *V.Barth.*, ch. 11 (p. 304).

[21] *Cuth. virt.*, ch. 29 (pp. 65–6). We can establish the date of their visit because it occurred in King Stephen's reign (1135–54) and while Bartholomew, who arrived in 1150, was living on the island.

[22] Tudor, 'Cult', at p. 465. Cf. op. cit., p. 461.

[23] St Godric visited Farne for devotional reasons on his trading journeys in about the 1090s (*V.Godr.*, ch. 5 (pp. 31-2)). For the date, see Tudor, 'Reginald', Appendix VI, p. 376.

[24] For example, *Cuth. virt.*, ch. 62 (pp. 122–3); ch. 118 (pp. 263–4); 'Miracles at Farne', ch. 13 (p. 19).

[25] Most of the cures that we know to have taken place on Farne come from two collections of Cuthbert's miracles, that by Reginald (cited here as *Cuth. virt.*), and the 'Miracles at Farne'. The *Life of Bartholomew* contains only three cures, all of which Bartholomew performed posthumously (*V.Barth.*, chs. 34–6 (pp. 323–5)).

monks, like that of solitaries everywhere, attracted visitors in its own right. The wide range of benefits that hermits conferred on society in twelfth-century England has come to be more fully appreciated recently,[26] and Bartholomew fits well into the general picture that has been drawn, as he outspokenly denounced the inhumanity and corruption of the rich, for example, and offered sympathy and counsel to the poor and sick.[27] Indeed so numerous were the visitors who came to Farne that at one point he was tempted to espouse the stricter isolation of the anchorite.[28] Bartholomew may have been especially popular, in part because of his lengthy occupation of the island, but no doubt the other hermits offered assistance of similar kinds. Certainly Aelric possessed a reputation for generosity among the needy.[29]

Further evidence confirms the existence of an ascetic strain within the convent. Perhaps in 1106,[30] somewhat earlier than the recolonization of Farne, another product of the monastery was living as a hermit at Wolsingham in upper Weardale. This solitary, another Aelric, under whom Godric of Finchale served his eremitical apprenticeship, had been brought up from early youth in the 'court of St Cuthbert', that is, in the priory. He cannot have become a monk, however, as he is described as being almost totally uneducated.[31] When Aelric died servants from the convent, who had been brought up with him there, carried his body back to Durham for interment in the cathedral burial ground.[32] This suggests that Aelric and his fellows, although educated within the monastery, were not deemed suitable for training as choir monks. His friends remained within the house in the capacity of servants; Aelric on the other hand chose the solitary life. A generation later he might have become a Cistercian lay brother. He reveals, nevertheless, that it was not merely the choir monks within the Durham community who felt the attraction of the desert. Aelric may also have had a successor at Wolsingham. About 1160 Bishop Hugh of le Puiset granted Landieu at Wolsingham in Weardale to a certain Brother Rannulf and his brethren. It is very likely that Rannulf was a monk of

---

[26] See H. Mayr-Harting, 'Functions of a Twelfth-Century Recluse', *History* 60 (1975), pp. 337–52, and C. Holdsworth, 'Hermits and the Powers of the Frontier', in *Saints and Saints' Lives*, ed. K. Bate *et al.* (Reading Medieval Studies, 16; Reading, 1990), pp. 55–76.

[27] *V.Barth.*, ch. 10 (p. 303).

[28] *V.Barth.*, ch. 11 (p. 304).

[29] *Cuth. virt.*, ch. 78 (p. 163).

[30] For this date, see Tudor, 'Reginald', Appendix VI, p. 376.

[31] *V.Godr.*, ch. 11 (p. 45).

[32] For Aelric of Wolsingham, see *V.Godr.*, chs. 11–12 (pp. 44–52). Our chief source for this hermit is *V.Godr.* and it is interesting to note that an early draft of this life calls him not Aelric but Godwin (op. cit., p. 51, n. 1). This could be merely the result of confusion between two names but it may be significant that two hermits called Aelric and Godwin respectively appear in a Durham obit list most of whose entries belong to the twelfth and thirteenth centuries (*Liber Vitae Ecclesiae Dunelmensis*, ed. J. Stevenson (SS 13; 1841), pp. 141, 146). Their presence in the list indicates that they were linked to the convent in some way. It is possible that Godwin had companions in his solitude (*V.Godr.*, p. 51, n. 1).

Durham but, although he may have occupied a site associated with a hermit, the word is never applied to him and we have no way of telling if he was one himself.[33]

Thus during the first century or so of its existence six – possibly seven – members of the Durham community became hermits. It is, however, virtually impossible to compare this record with that of other religious houses. Hermits existed on the fringes of the formal institutions of the Church and their somewhat unofficial status means that they are poorly represented in the sources. References to hermits are usually very brief, for example, while the biographies of solitaries often reveal additional individuals who would otherwise be unknown,[34] suggesting that there were yet more who failed to leave any mark on the records. But if hermits in general are elusive, the monastic variety is particularly so. Many religious houses are known to have had recluses associated with them in the twelfth century,[35] but former inmates are rarely identified as such. If we know of individuals such as Hugh de Burun, monk of Lenton priory in Lancashire who was living alone at some point before 1184,[36] such a figure is rare. Thus to a large extent the context in which to judge these Durham hermits is lacking. We must also bear in mind here the wealth of source material that has come down to us from the monastery of Durham, which has been more fortunate in this respect than many other religious houses. Thus while we know of no other English monastery in the twelfth century which produced as many hermits as Durham, our knowledge does not extend very far.

The Farne solitaries, however, possess a significance which extends beyond this period. Soon after the death of Bartholomew in 1193 the island appears to have become a formal cell of Durham. It was staffed by two monks, the master or keeper and his companion, and the names of the masters are known from 1255 to the Dissolution.[37] Thus the twelfth-century hermits on Farne laid the foundations of a structure which endured for almost four hundred years. This is certainly the longest-lasting arrangement of this kind known to us, but only a few similar traditions are well documented and it would be unwise to draw a firm conclusion.

We can nevertheless suggest a few reasons for this marked ascetic tendency within the convent. The most important factor may well have been the spiritual vitality of the community itself. It is of course difficult to find direct evidence for anything so intangible but two factors may well have predisposed the convent to a state of spiritual health. In this period, despite its determination to find its roots in

---

[33] For Rannulf and Landieu, see *Script. Tres*, Appendix, p. lxxi; *FPD*, pp. 241, 242, and 245; G.V. Scammell, 'Two Charters of Bishop Hugh du Puiset of Durham relating to Landieu in Weardale', *Arch. Ael.* 4th ser., 33 (1955), at pp. 66–9; and *idem, Hugh du Puiset, Bishop of Durham* (Cambridge, 1956), pp. 110 and 192.

[34] For example, John, Abbot of Ford's *Life of Wulfric of Haselbury*, ed. M. Bell (Somerset Record Society 47; 1933), Introd., pp. xxxvii–xxxviii.

[35] See R.M. Clay, *The Hermits and Anchorites of England* (London, 1914), Appendix C, passim.

[36] VCH *Lancashire*, ed. W. Farrer and J. Brownhill, II (London, 1908), 113. For the date, see Clay, *Hermits*, Appendix C, p. 225.

[37] J. Raine, *The History and Antiquities of North Durham* (London, 1852), pp. 341–2.

venerable antiquity,[38] the priory was a young institution and as such likely to be full of youthful enthusiasm. The circumstances of its origin, in addition, may well have promoted a high degree of spiritual zeal. The monastery derived ultimately from the expedition of the southern monks Aldwin and Aelfwig and the former knight Reinfrid who aimed to live a life of poverty in the abandoned sites of monasticism in the north.[39] These pioneers have been identified as examples of 'new hermits', who differed from traditional ones in various ways, being, for instance, more gregarious and regarding the eremitic life as a chance to experiment, rather than an end in itself.[40] Thus the project initiated by Reinfrid and his fellow monks, which was to lead to the creation of the Durham community, was in itself eremitic. It is far from surprising that a religious house that took its origin from a band of hermits should in turn produce solitaries and ultimately establish an 'eremitic cell'.

Almost as important in accounting for the convent's asceticism was the example of St Cuthbert, the most famous of all the occupants of the Inner Farne and, as patron of Durham priory, where his body still rested, a compelling model of which no Durham monk could have been unaware. The force of Cuthbert's example can be seen in the history of Godric of Finchale. A visit to Farne, made during the course of trading journeys in about the 1090s, caused Godric to consider the eremitic life as a possibility for himself for the first time.[41] For Durham monks, furthermore, the example of Cuthbert was reinforced by that of his early successors on the island, Felgild and Aethilwald, who had also been noted by Bede.[42]

No doubt the monks revered their patron from 1083 onwards but it was not until some decades later, as far as we can tell, that the first Durham monk followed him to Farne. The Durham settlement of Lindisfarne, in progress probably in the 1120s when the monk Edward was stationed there,[43] to be followed by the establishment of a fully-fledged cell, probably had a part to play here. Lindisfarne and the Inner Farne are within sight of one another,[44] so, once Durham monks found themselves on Lindisfarne, Farne could exert a physical influence of its own, adding to that conveyed by the materials associated with Cuthbert in Durham. Presumably the risk of Scandinavian raids, from which the monastery of Whitby on the coast suffered towards the end of the eleventh century,[45] decreased as time went on, thus making the resettlement of Farne possible. Even in the early 1150s, however, the inhabitants of the island were not totally immune from attentions of

---

[38] For the stress laid by the *History* attributed to Symeon on the role of monasticism in the history of St Cuthbert's church, see A. Piper, 'The First Generations of Durham Monks and the Cult of St Cuthbert', in *Cuthbert*, pp. 438–42.

[39] *LDE*, bk. 3, chs. 21–2 (pp. 108–13) and bk. 4, chs. 2–3 (pp. 120–4).

[40] Leyser, *Hermits*, pp. 18–28; Appendix II, pp. 115 and 118.

[41] *V.Godr.*, ch. 5 (pp. 31–2). For the date, see n. 23 above.

[42] *The [Prose] Life of St Cuthbert*, ch. 46, in *Two 'Lives' of St Cuthbert*, ed. and trans. B. Colgrave (Cambridge, 1940), pp. 300–6.

[43] *DEC*, pp. 90–1, 92, 93, and 95–6. Cf. *Cuth. virt.*, chs. 21, 22 (pp. 44–50).

[44] Cf. *Cuth. virt.*, ch. 23 (p. 53).

[45] D. Knowles, *The Monastic Order in England* (2nd edn., Cambridge, 1966), p. 168.

this sort, as we have seen.[46] It was convenient, furthermore, that the Farne Islands, though situated some way from the monastery of Durham, undoubtedly formed part of its endowment,[47] thus obviating any difficulties on that score.

Other solitaries who were not members of the community were associated with it to varying degrees. Some of those who appear in the records of the house are no more than names. We know nothing of Robert, the recluse of Stanhope,[48] nor of the anchorites Wulsi and Columbanus,[49] if these two belong to this period at all. All we can say of the hermit Godwin is that he may have been associated with the settlement at Wolsingham and may also have been joined by other solitaries.[50] Of others we know a little more. Burcwen, the sister of Godric of Finchale, came to join him, probably at an early date, and she lived a life of prayer and asceticism within earshot of his cell for many years.[51] At some point the hermit John, 'restored to health by God's grace and the merits of St Cuthbert', received land from Hugh of le Puiset, bishop from 1153 to 1195, at Satley between Wolsingham and Lanchester,[52] and another John, a descendant of Bishop Flambard, was given ninety acres at Yearhaugh, on the River Derwent near Ebchester, by the same donor. The site seems to have been occupied by hermits before this second John's time but his aim was nevertheless 'to build a certain religious cell . . . in honour of God and Blessed Mary.'[53] Finally there was St Godric who established himself at Finchale, probably in 1112 or 1113, and remained there until his death in 1170.[54] Of this individual, thanks to three biographies by Durham monks,[55] we know a great deal.

What, as far as we can tell, was the relationship between these solitaries and the convent? Of Burcwen we know merely that Godric began to feel uneasy about her proximity, perhaps at the suggestion of some third party, and Ralph, the almoner of

---

[46] See above, p. 69.

[47] See, for example, the confirmation of King Henry II of all the possessions of the prior and convent, including Farne, printed in *FPD*, Appendix, no. 2, pp. lxxxiii–lxxxvi. Farne appears on p. lxxxv.

[48] *Liber Vitae*, fol. 42v. Despite the impression given by the earlier edition of the *Liber Vitae*, ed. Stevenson (SS 13), p. 46, there is no reason to believe that he was a monk of Durham.

[49] Wulsi and Columbanus appear in one of the obit lists printed in the earlier edition of the *Liber Vitae* (SS 13), pp. 141, 145. The name Wulsi suggests an early rather than a later date.

[50] *Liber Vitae* (SS 13), p. 146. See n. 32 above.

[51] For Burcwen, see *V.Godr.*, ch. 2 (pp. 23–4); chs. 60–1 (pp. 139–41); ch. 63 (pp. 143–5); *V.Godr.Gal.*, ch. 29 (p. 77); Tudor, 'Reginald', Appendix VII, pp. 380–1.

[52] For John and Satley, see *Script. Tres*, Appendix, p. lxxi; *FPD*, pp. 217, 240; Scammell, *Puiset*, p. 106.

[53] For John and the rather confusing history of Yearhaugh, see *V.Godr.*, p. 192, n. 4; *Script. Tres*, Appendix, p. lxxi; *Boldon Buke*, ed. and trans. W. Greenwell (SS 25; 1852), p. 34; *FPD*, pp. 217, 240, 277, 279–80, 301; VCH *Durham*, ed. W. Page (3 vols., London, 1905–27), II, 130; Scammell, *Puiset*, pp. 95 and n. 6, 110 and n. 3. St Godric may have assisted one hermit who came to live there (*V.Godr.*, ch. 87 (pp. 192–3)).

[54] *V.Godr.*, ch. 20 (p. 66); ch. 170 (p. 331). For the date of his arrival at Finchale, see Tudor, 'Reginald', Appendix VI, p. 377.

[55] Reginald's life appears in *V.Godr.* and Geoffrey's in *V.Godr.Gal.* Geoffrey's life incorporates material from a lost life by Prior Germanus.

the monastery, moved her to the hospital of St Giles in Durham, where she spent the remainder of her life.[56] John of Satley, on the other hand, entered the priory almonry and, by way of payment, conferred his land on the monks.[57] The other John, of Yearhaugh, was apparently entitled by Bishop Hugh's grant to give his land to the religious house of his choice. The object of his generosity was the monastery of Durham and shortly before John's death the subprior, representing the convent, was put in physical possession of the hermit's land. After John's funeral, further-more, a monk remained at Yearhaugh 'in order to retain possession of that place'.[58] It is perhaps worth mentioning here that while the bishop ultimately asserted his right to Satley and Yearhaugh, he agreed that Landieu, at Wolsingham in Weardale, the land of Brother Rannulf and his fellows and possibly also of the hermit Aelric, should belong to the sacrist of the monastery.[59]

It is of course the relationship between Godric and the convent which is most fully documented. After settling at Finchale the hermit lived there for perhaps a quarter of a century, or more, without supervision.[60] Then, his biographers tell us, some unspecified individuals suggested to him that obedience was an indispensable element in the religious life and Godric submitted himself to the authority of Roger, prior of Durham, a close friend. After Roger's death in 1149 the hermit chose the priors of Durham as his superiors and this arrangement lasted for the remainder of his life.[61] Perhaps the relationship that came into being during Roger's lifetime was an informal one, to be placed on a more rigid footing in or after 1149. Certainly it seems reasonable to assume that those who taught Godric the value of obedience were the Durham monks themselves. The argument that it was of central importance in the religious life was a powerful one and it was used elsewhere. When the future abbot of Kirkstall approached Seleth and his fellow hermits in 1152 he warned them of the dangers of following their own wills.[62]

The forming of the association with Durham marked a change in the hermit's life. Members of the community gave him instruction[63] and under the influence of the Benedictine Rule he seems to have moderated his severe asceticism. Monks were sent out to Finchale on a regular basis to say Mass[64] and, as Godric became

---

[56] V.Godr.Gal., ch. 29 (p. 77).
[57] FPD, p. 240.
[58] FPD, pp. 240, 277, 279–80, 301. The quotation comes from p. 279.
[59] Script. Tres, Appendix, p. lxxi; FPD, pp. 216–17.
[60] If, as is probable, Godric settled at Finchale in 1112 or 1113 and then submitted to the authority of Prior Roger of Durham (?1138–49) he would have lived an independent existence for at least twenty five years.
[61] V.Godr., ch. 58 (pp. 135–6); V.Godr.Gal., ch. 35 (p. 78).
[62] H. Dauphin, 'L'érémitisme en Angleterre aux XIe et XIIe siècles', in L'Eremitismo in Occidente nei secoli XI e XII (Miscellanea del Centro di Studi Medioevali, 4; Università Cattolica del Sacro Cuore, Milan, 1965), at p. 283.
[63] V.Godr., ch. 58 (p. 135); William of Newburgh, Historia Rerum Anglicarum, bk. 2, ch. 20, in CR, I, 150.
[64] For example, V.Godr., ch. 71 (pp. 159–60); ch. 89 (p. 195); ch. 93 (p. 202).

increasingly infirm in old age, one monk or more came to live at the settlement.[65] It was almost certainly under the influence of the monks, furthermore, that the hermit adopted strict rules of silence and would converse only with those visitors who brought with them a wooden cross furnished by the prior.[66] When a monk was in residence at Finchale, in addition, his permission was necessary before a visitor could address the hermit.[67] These provisions, which reflect passages in Benedict's Rule,[68] made Godric's position comparable to that of a professed monk but they also had the effect of keeping both the hermit and his establishment firmly under conventual control. Their strictness encourages one to suggest that it was the monks who suggested to Godric that the closeness of his sister Burcwen was unacceptable and should be brought to an end. Godric's influence on the community is less easy to define. The educational process seems to have been reciprocal, however, as the hermit could speak authoritatively on religious matters[69] and it has been suggested that the visions that he experienced provided the monks with a 'window' into the world of the supernatural.[70] He could also criticize abuses within the convent and had no inhibitions about condemning one of the monks for his lax manner of living.[71]

Confusion as to Godric's precise status at this stage may have prompted Reginald, his chief biographer, to describe his position at length. Godric, he says, was a monk of Durham and, although he did not live in the monastery, he was subject to its authority, had worn the habit of its monks for many years and had been made their associate by a decree of the common chapter.[72] Godric had evidently made no act of profession and we should therefore probably see him as an 'associate monk' rather than a full member of the house. He was also as closely bound to the convent as was possible, short of being brought to live within the walls of the monastery in Durham, which would of course have been self-defeating.

Even before the hermit's death the idea of a biography had been mooted. Reginald tells us that he was ordered by Ailred of Rievaulx and other close friends to commit to writing what he already knew of the saint and to delve further.[73] These close friends no doubt included Prior Thomas of Durham, the future hermit, as it was at his command and that of Ailred that the biographer first set out for Finchale to obtain information from Godric himself.[74] It was, in fact, very much in the convent's interest that a life of the hermit should be written. A formal work of hagiography brought honour to the saint and edified the faithful but it also

---

[65] For example, *V.Godr.*, ch. 120 (p. 243); ch. 125 (p. 249); ch. 132 (p. 256).

[66] *V.Godr.*, ch. 58 (p. 136) and ch. 59 (pp. 137–8).

[67] *V.Godr*, ch. 149 (p. 283) and ch. 155 (p. 293).

[68] *Rule* ch. 6 (ed. McCann, pp. 34–6), ch. 7 (p. 46), ch. 42 (p. 100), ch. 53 (p. 122).

[69] *V.Godr.*, ch. 79 (pp. 179–80).

[70] The idea of Professor Donald Matthew, expressed in March 1979.

[71] *V.Godr.*, ch. 77 (p. 176).

[72] *V.Godr.*, ch. 169 (pp. 325–6).

[73] *V.Godr.*, *Proemium* (p. 19).

[74] *V.Godr.*, ch. 140 (p. 269).

conferred prestige on the religious house associated with him and could publicize any embryonic cult.

On 21 May 1170 Godric died.[75] Even before miracles began to occur there was a strong expectation that he would at some point reveal his supernatural powers.[76] Surprise was expressed in the school in Durham that Thomas of Canterbury, so quickly sanctified by his martyrdom, was performing 'infinite miracles', while Godric, who had endured so much for Christ through the austerities he practised, was not.[77] At the border abbey of Kelso iron rings from his coat of mail, worn as an ascetic exercise, were applied to a sick girl as a test and there was every confidence that they would pass with flying colours. The cure of the girl, which duly happened, represented Godric's first posthumous miracle,[78] to be followed by the first wonder to occur at Finchale itself, the healing of an epileptic child on 23 June 1172.[79] With this event the floodgates opened[80] and Reginald's life is rounded off with a collection of more than two hundred miracles.

It seems likely that the Durham monks were at least partly responsible for this air of expectancy. After Godric's death they continued to maintain a presence at Finchale and encouraged the veneration of the saint there. When Godfrey, the almoner of Kelso, visited the hermit's tomb in 1171, he found a Durham monk in attendance and was furnished with the iron rings which were to prove so efficacious after his return home.[81] On the day, furthermore, that Godric performed his first miracle at Finchale, which was the vigil of the feast of St John the Baptist, the visitors found there were particularly numerous.[82] This suggests that local people were encouraged to pay regular visits to the site, perhaps by the provision of Mass on feastdays.

It is curious to note that the first wonder performed at Godric's tomb coincided quite closely with the first miracle St Cuthbert is recorded as having performed after what appears to be a break of some years. A description of this event, which occurs in a collection of Cuthbert miracles also by the monk Reginald, includes the information that it took place on 30 April 1172,[83] less than two months before the cure of the epileptic child at Finchale. The miracle is also one of a number designed to prove Cuthbert's superiority to – or at least parity with – St Thomas of Canterbury.[84] Perhaps the community's encouragement of wonders at Finchale was but one aspect of Durham's attempt to hold its own against this successful and dangerous rival.

75 *V.Godr.*, ch. 170 (p. 331).
76 *V.Godr.*, Appendix I, ch. 23 (pp. 368–9), Appendix II, ch. 1 (p. 372).
77 *V.Godr.*, Appendix I, ch. 22 (p. 367).
78 *V.Godr.*, Appendix I, ch. 23 (p. 369).
79 *V.Godr.*, Appendix II, ch. 1 (pp. 372–3). For the year, see the reference in the next note.
80 *V.Godr.*, Appendix II, preface (p. 371).
81 *V.Godr.*, p. 368, n. 2 (from an earlier draft of Reginald's life).
82 *V.Godr.*, Appendix II, ch. 1 (p. 372).
83 *Cuth. virt.*, ch. 112 (p. 254). For the position of this story in the collection of which it forms part and the resumption of miracle-collecting which it represents, see Tudor, 'Cult', at p. 449.
84 *Cuth. virt.*, chs. 114–16 (pp. 255–62), chs. 125–6 (pp. 270–2).

The monks' final efforts concerned Godric's land. This had been granted to him by Bishop Rannulf Flambard but we do not know the exact terms on which it was given. We are also told nothing of what happened to Finchale on the hermit's death. Perhaps Godric had transferred the rights over his property to the monks just before he died, like John of Yearhaugh. But in the years immediately following Godric's death Bishop Hugh of le Puiset obviously felt that it was still his to dispose of. Between 1170 and 1174 he granted Finchale, not to the convent, but to the monks Reginald, probably the hagiographer, and Henry, who were living there, and to later monks whom the prior should appoint to succeed them.[85] A letter of 1171–81, solicited by the convent from Pope Alexander III, nevertheless confirmed the site to the community 'just as you canonically possess it' and forbade the unauthorized removal of the saint's body.[86] This may well have been intended to add weight to a conventual claim to Finchale, as was the case with a charter which the monks seem to have produced between 1181 and 1195. According to this document, which Professor Offler proved to be a forgery, Bishop Flambard had made Finchale over to Prior Algar and the convent not long after Godric's first settlement there.[87] We do not know if the letter and charter influenced Bishop Hugh but at some point towards the end of his pontificate and probably on his deathbed in 1195 he granted and confirmed the hermitage to the monks and their successors.[88] Finchale was now a conventual possession, soon to be elevated to the status of a dependent priory. The monks were in sole control of both cult and site.

The two hermits by the name of John, Godric and his sister were all protégés of the bishop, if only, in Burcwen's case, through her brother. Yet the convent is found having dealings with all of them and in the case of three demonstrating a significant claim to the hermit's land. Even the property of Brother Rannulf, at Landieu in Weardale, though it did not pass directly from Rannulf to the monks, came ultimately into the hands of the sacrist of the priory. How should this evidence be interpreted?

Relations between monasteries and once independent hermits were common and, as we have seen, could be beneficial to both parties, but when the hermit's land and mortal remains were involved, they could be serious affairs. The bodies of dead hermits, the potential basis for future cults, were highly valued at this time and arguments, not to say tussles, over them were not unknown. Thus force was needed to save the bodies of Wulfric of Haselbury and Robert of Knaresborough from the monks of Montacute and Fountains respectively.[89]

---

[85] *The Priory of Finchale*, ed. J. Raine (SS 6; 1837), no. 20, pp. 21–2. The date limits are provided by the death of Godric, who is not mentioned, and the presence among the witnesses of John, archdeacon of Northumberland. The latter probably last appeared in the autumn of 1174 (*John Le Neve, Fasti Ecclesiae Anglicanae, 1066–1300*, II, *Monastic Cathedrals*, ed. D.E. Greenway (London, 1971), p. 40).

[86] *Papsturkunden in England*, ed. W. Holtzmann (3 vols., Berlin and Göttingen, 1930–52), II, no. 211, pp. 405–6.

[87] The charter is printed as *DEC*, no. 10, p. 68, and discussed on pp. 68–72.

[88] See *Priory of Finchale*, ed. Raine, no. 19, p. 21. Cf. *DEC*, pp. 71–2.

[89] John of Ford, *Life of Wulfric*, ch. 101 (pp. 127–9) and P. Grosjean, 'Vitae S. Roberti Knaresburgensis', *Analecta Bollandiana* 57 (1939), p. 398.

It has been suggested, furthermore, that in the period from its foundation to the middle of the twelfth century, the legitimate pride of the Durham community in its traditions and privileged position acquired an aggressive edge. Growing used to having its own way, partly through political circumstances, it wished to extend its rights, possessions, and liberties, for example, in electing the prior, wherever possible. At the same time it wanted to exclude all rivals from what it regarded as its sphere of influence, its ultimate aim being to 'enjoy a monopoly, spiritual, secular, and financial, in as large an area as could be claimed for St Cuthbert.'[90] Those it saw as rivals included the monks of St Albans, whom it tried to oust from their cell of Tynemouth,[91] and the canons of Guisborough, who attempted to found a cell on the outskirts of Durham at Baxterwood.[92]

Given the importance which monasteries attached to their relations with hermits in this period, together with the convent's desire to extend its rights where possible and its sensitivity to outside intrusion, it seems likely that the community tried deliberately to form relationships with neighbouring hermits. Indeed one could almost say that it had a definite policy towards them. A major consideration was no doubt the fear that if it did not 'adopt' them, some other religious house would. Then, while no doubt assisting the hermits in various ways, it sought where possible to exploit the relationships that had been formed for its own benefit.

The monastic hermits of Farne and elsewhere reveal the strong and persistent ascetic strain within the convent at this period. While there was no doubt an important spiritual dimension to the relations between the monks and once-independent hermits, such associations should probably best be understood in terms of a less attractive, grasping side which the convent manifested at this time. It should not be thought, however, that most Durham monks found these two aspects of the community in any way incompatible. Both, in a sense, stemmed from the worthiest of motives and owed a great deal to the community's patron saint. The hermits of Farne and elsewhere, following Cuthbert's example, went out to a life of solitude and austerity. Those who sought to extend the convent's rights and possessions, however, would no doubt have declared themselves concerned merely to increase the prestige of their saint, even if their activities at times seem to us to fall rather short of saintliness.

---

[90] Scammell, *Puiset*, p. 160. See also, op. cit., pp. 129–31, 149, 157–8, 159–60, 165, and 167.
[91] See H.H.E. Craster, *A History of Northumberland*, VIII (Newcastle upon Tyne, 1907), pp. 44–6, 50–1, 57–8, and 63–6. In fairness to the Durham monks, they did regard Tynemouth as part of their early endowment.
[92] See VCH *Durham*, II, 109.

The Durham Cantor's Book
(Durham, Dean and Chapter Library, MS B.IV.24)

A. J. PIPER

H IGH AMONG THE good works of Bishop William of St Calais stands his gift of some forty books to the Benedictine cathedral community that he established in 1083 by bringing to Durham the monks who had recently revived monastic life at Jarrow and Wearmouth. A list of these books was entered at an early date in the Bible that he gave, and study of the manuscripts from the monastic library suggests that a very considerable number of Bishop William's books survive.[1] Among these DCL, MS B.IV.24 is generally taken to represent the *Martyrologium et regula* with which the list concludes. The contents of the manuscript do not make that description inappropriate, and the appearance of the handwriting would date it to the later eleventh century.

DCL B.IV.24 is an assemblage of sections, quite possibly from more than one source, some of which do not seem to have been made with the Durham monks in mind. On the other hand the different sections are very similar in size and this may be evidence that the book was built up deliberately in stages, rather than being assembled from existing materials; it is also the case that one section of the book was written by a Norman-trained scribe responsible for an Augustine manuscript given by Bishop William of St Calais to the monks and four later documents in their favour.[2] Obviously this has a bearing on the question of whether DCL B.IV.24 represents Bishop William's gift, or whether it came to the North in some other way, for instance with the monks who came from Evesham and Winchcombe with a donkey-load of essential books and vestments, and were settled at Jarrow by William of St Calais's immediate predecessor, Bishop Walcher.[3]

The four most substantial sections of the manuscript are copies of the Rule of St Benedict, of Bishop Aethelwold's translation of this Rule into Anglo-Saxon, of the martyrology compiled by Usuard, and of the directory drawn up by Lanfranc and known as his Constitutions. An outline of the full contents is given on page 94 below.

---

[1] A.C. Browne, 'Bishop William of St Carilef's Book Donations to Durham Cathedral Priory', *Scriptorium* 42 (1988), pp. 140–55, with facsimile of the book-list at pl. 15.
[2] Identified by Michael Gullick, see pp. 97–108 below.
[3] D. Knowles, *The Monastic Order in England* (2nd edn, Cambridge, 1963), pp. 159–71 gives a fine account of the northern revival. The donkey carried 'libri necessarii et uestimenta sacerdotalia ad diuinum celebrandum mysterium' (*LDE*, bk. 3, ch. 21); a copy of the Rule would have been a necessity if a monastic observance was to be maintained.

Lanfranc's Constitutions

The origin of the copy of Lanfranc's Constitutions is the most readily identifiable, being written in a form of the script used at Canterbury and Rochester during the latter part of the eleventh century. The modern editor of the Constitutions, Dom. David Knowles, took the Durham copy as his base text, observing 'that it may well have been a text sent down from Canterbury, possibly by Lanfranc himself, to serve as a norm for the newly-organized Durham community'.[4] Possibly it came separately, being put with the other sections at a later date, but the way in which the dimensions of the sections match does suggest that they were made to go together. If that is so, the identification of DCL B.IV.24 as Bishop William of St Calais's *Martyrologium et Regula* might seem to be weakened, for this description makes no mention of Lanfranc's Constitutions, but the omission may simply reflect the fact that the text has no title in the manuscript.[5]

The Latin Rule of St Benedict

The Latin text of the Rule is one of eleven surviving copies believed to have been written in England before 1100; one, Bodl.L, MS Hatton 48, which is the oldest of all surviving manuscripts of the Rule, contains the *textus interpolatus*, but the others are all copies of the *textus receptus*, widely disseminated from the middle of the ninth century onwards, in the wake of Benedict of Aniane's reforms. Attempts to establish a *stemma* for the transmission of the text are extremely problematic, but an analysis of shared variants suggests that the Durham copy can be associated with one of the other extant early copies, and that together these two may well be connected with two early copies of Canterbury provenance, one from St Augustine's, the other from Christ Church.[6]

The Durham copy has two peculiar features that may be significant as pointers to its origin. First, there are the feminine forms of some words in the chapter-list that follows the prologue, all then altered to masculine forms, and Chapter 62 is omitted; it concerns the ordination of monks as priests and so would not be appropriate to nuns. These features may simply reflect the exemplar from which the Durham copy was made, but it is possible that the copy was originally written for a female community.[7] Second, where the opening words of Chapter 60 normally read 'If anyone in priestly orders should ask that he be received in a monastery . . .', the Durham copy appears to have 'If anyone should ask an abbot or a prior that he be received from an order of canons in a monastery . . .', with a parallel

---

[4] *The Monastic Constitutions of Lanfranc*, ed. and trans. D. Knowles (Nelson's Medieval Classics; London, 1951), p. xxv; and Knowles, *Monastic Order*, pp. 123–4.

[5] *Monastic Constitutions*, ed. Knowles, p. xxii; the heading quoted by Knowles is early fifteenth-century. The late fourteenth-century catalogue entry for B.IV.24 refers to *Consuetudines Dorbornensis ecclesie* (*Catalogi Veteres Librorum Ecclesiae Cathedralis Dunelm*, ed. B. Botfield (SS 7; 1838), p. 30).

[6] M. Gretsch, 'Aethelwold's Translation of the *Regula Sancti Benedicti* and its Latin Exemplar', *Anglo-Saxon England* 3 (1975), pp. 125–51, esp. pp. 128–33.

[7] N.R. Ker, *Catalogue of Manuscripts containing Anglo-Saxon* (Oxford, 1957), p. 148. The chapter-list, fols. 75–76, does include ch. 62.

amendment to the entry in the chapter-list, though not in the heading to the text of the chapter.[8] Although this variant referring to canons and to a prior would have been directly relevant to the situation at Durham in 1083, when Bishop William of St Calais formed a new monastic community in his cathedral and gave the former 'canons' the choice of either joining it or taking their leave, it is hard to believe that a copy of the Rule written for Durham would have contained feminine forms.[9] In fact it is easier to suppose that the references to canons and a prior belong to an earlier stage in this copy's transmission than the feminine forms: these references were inconspicuous, and even if they were noticed it would not have been an entirely straightforward matter to restore the normal text, whereas the elimination of the feminine forms would have been quite simple. If this is right, the references to canons and a prior may have owed their presence to the changes brought about by Lanfranc's associate Bishop Gundulf of Rochester in his cathedral, where monks replaced secular canons, apparently in 1083.[10] This would fit well with the text's possible affiliations to Canterbury copies, while the feminine forms might have been introduced in the course of an abortive attempt to found a house of nuns in Kent, one of the few areas in late eleventh-century England to see much activity of this kind, most notably in Bishop Gundulf's foundation at Malling in c.1090.[11]

The Anglo-Saxon Rule of St Benedict

The copy of the Rule in Anglo-Saxon occupies a portion of the manuscript that is physically separable from the Latin copy, but it is uniform with it in terms of writing space and number of lines on the page, and was decorated by a single hand; the two were apparently intended to go together, but the Anglo-Saxon version perhaps represented an afterthought, for, unlike the other three copies that accompany the Latin text, it does not have the vernacular alternating with the Latin chapter by chapter. Noting that this copy 'has an astonishing number of unique readings while being almost completely free from mistakes', Mechthild

---

[8] The Latin of DCL B.IV.24, 'Si quis abbatem uel prepositum de ordine canonicorum in monasterio se suscipi rogauerit . . .', could also be translated, 'If anyone should ask an abbot or a provost from an order of canons that he be received in a monastery . . .', but it is hard to identify a situation in which a provost would have any standing on this point even if the word *monasterium* were still bearing its wider meaning of 'minster'. The amended chapter-heading, 'De abbatis uel prepositis canonicis qui monasterio habitare uoluerint', is an untranslatable muddle.

[9] P. Meyvaert, 'Towards a History of the Textual Transmission of the *Regula S. Benedicti*', *Scriptorium* 17 (1963), pp. 83–110, suggested that 'deletions in the *capitulatio* and in the text show an attempt to adapt the Rule to a non-monastic community' (p. 110).

[10] *John le Neve: Fasti Ecclesiae Anglicanae 1066–1300 II, Monastic Cathedrals*, compiled by D.E. Greenway (London, 1971), p. 78. For an amplification to the martyrology concerning Rochester, see n. 20 below.

[11] Knowles, *Monastic Order*, p. 139; for later eleventh-century developments at Malling, Newington, Minster in Sheppey, or perhaps Minster in Thanet, see D. Knowles and R.N. Hadcock, *Medieval Religious Houses: England and Wales* (2nd edn, London, 1971), pp. 261–2, 70, and at Canterbury, below n. 22. The presence in the Rule of initials in a Durham style (see Gullick pp. 95, 96 below), presumably reflects its originally unfinished state.

Gretsch concluded that it represents 'a carefully revised text'; she also noted 'a striking number of variants which are unique to' this copy and one other, a manuscript that may well be associated with Winchester.[12] The only evidence of a copy of the vernacular text from Canterbury is an extract from it found as one of the supplements to an independent interlinear gloss on the Latin text.[13] Whatever the source of the Durham copy it does seem unlikely that Bishop William of St Calais would have commissioned it for his newly established cathedral community: while there is evidence of monks using the vernacular version of the Rule as late as the twelfth century,[14] Bishop William's Norman loyalties suggest that he would not have promoted such a practice among the monks who replaced the irregular Anglo-Saxon congregation of St Cuthbert. Equally, had DCL B.IV.24 been one of the books that came to the north in the 1070s in the wake of the monastic pioneers from Winchcombe and Evesham, it is strange that neither the Latin nor the Anglo-Saxon text of the Rule is closely related to the Worcester copies.[15]

The Martyrology of Usuard

The fourth substantial section of the manuscript is very largely occupied by a copy of the martyrology compiled in the mid-ninth century by Usuard, a monk of St-Germain-des-Prés.[16] This text, comprising brief daily notices naming the martyrs and the places with which they were associated, was subject not only to accidental corruption, when scribes blundered over unfamiliar names, but also to deliberate augmentation, when saints of significance to the users of a particular copy were added; the Durham copy is also interesting for minor changes in wording and syntax that would have rendered the text more readily comprehensible when read aloud.[17] The process of augmentation has left important evidence for the ancestry of this copy. A number of the saints not originally included in Usuard's text belonged to the Loire valley, and there are also two extended entries, one concerning the reception of the holy sponge and relics of the cross at the Benedictine house of Fleury, the other with the acquisition by Fleury of the relics of St Benedict.[18] A second layer of additions was made in England (see Appendix, pp. 90–2 below). These have at least one clear local focus: the Fenland monastery of Ramsey. It is mentioned in the entries for Felix (8 March) and for the martyrs Ethelred and Ethelbert and the translation of Etheldreda (17 October), and there

---

[12] Gretsch, 'Aethelwold's Translation', p. 142.

[13] Ker, *Catalogue*, no. 186.

[14] Ibid., p. 195, describing BL, MS Cotton Faustina A.X, fols. 102–51.

[15] CCCC, MS 178. See Gretsch, 'Aethelwold's Translation', pp. 132–4, 140–1.

[16] J. Dubois, *Le martyrologe d'Usuard: texte et commentaire* (Brussels, 1965). DCL B.IV.24's copy appears to be a conflation of the first and second recensions; from the characteristic differences between the two noted by Dubois, pp. 33–7, it is not immediately obvious whether the primary text was of the first or of the second recensions.

[17] E.g. 16 (2), 19 (1) March; 10 (2), 21 (1) April; 5 (1) September.

[18] 24 February and 11 July; the wording of the former matches exactly what is quoted from the Fleury copy of Usuard, Orléans, Bibliothèque Municipale, MS 322, by H. Rochais, *Analyse critique de martyrologes manuscrits Latins* (Mémoire . . . du diplôme; Paris, 1972), p. 109.

are two Ramsey festivals, the translations of its founder Bishop Oswald (15 April) and of Bishop Ivo (10 June), the latter taking place in 1001.[19] In the context of the English monastic revival of the later tenth century the transmission of a text from Fleury to Ramsey would not be surprising.

How the text of the martyrology came to Durham is much more obscure. Two names were certainly interpolated during the eleventh century, Archbishop Elphege of Canterbury (d.19 April 1012) and Herbert archbishop of Cologne (d.16 March 1021), but there is no obvious pattern of augmentation pointing to an identifiable intervening stage in the transmission between Ramsey and Durham.[20] As already noted, the copy in DCL B.IV.24 was apparently made to measure, with leaves of a size to match those of the Rule. Possibly it was made after the copy of the Rule had reached Durham, with resources provided by Bishop William, but it is difficult to believe that the martyrology was copied in Durham, for no steps were taken to ensure that Durham's saints, Cuthbert and Oswald, were entered in the desired way, and the manuscript had to be altered.[21] Moreover, Durham offers no explanation for the fact that St Martin, on both his feasts, was honoured as highly as the Virgin Mary, Peter, Paul, and Benedict, with his name written entirely in capitals.[22]

---

[19] Ramsey acquired the remains of the two Kentish martyrs, Ethelbert and Ethelred, late in the tenth century; see *Chronicon Abbatiae Rameseiensis*, ed. W.D. Macray (RS 83; 1886), p. 55. The editor of the only copy of their *passio* noted that the manuscript in which it is found, Bodl.L, MS Bodley 285, has every appearance of being a Ramsey book, apart from material concerning Kenelm of Winchcombe; see D.W. Rollason, *The Mildrith Legend* (Leicester, 1982), pp. 89 and 159 n. 2 to introduction. The martyrology has the same peculiarity, with an entry on 17 July for Kenelm that mentions Winchcombe. Ramsey and Winchcombe were connected at a very early stage, *c*.970, in the persons of Bishop Oswald, and Germanus, a monk of Fleury; see D. Knowles, C.N.L. Brooke and V.C.M. London, *The Heads of Religious Houses, England and Wales 940–1216* (Cambridge, 1972), pp. 61, 78.

[20] The presence of an isolated modern Cologne saint is striking, but eleventh-century England had many contacts with Lotharingia. Bishop Ealdred of Worcester, later archbishop of York (d.1069), went to Cologne in 1054 as the king's ambassador, possibly accompanied by Abbot Aelfwine of Ramsey; see F. Barlow, *Edward the Confessor* (London, 1970), p. 215; also M. Lapidge, 'The origin of C[orpus] C[hristi] C[ollege] C[ambridge, MS] 163', *Transactions of the Cambridge Bibliographical Society* viii:i (1981), pp. 18–28. Equally, for a pilgrim from Cologne at Ramsey, see *Chronicon Abbatiae Rameseiensis*, pp. lxvii–iii. The question of the transmission of the martyrology to the north becomes all the more tantalizing when set beside the Ramsey attribution proposed by M. Lapidge, 'Byrhtferth of Ramsey and the Early Sections of the *Historia Regum* Attributed to Symeon of Durham', *Anglo-Saxon England* 10 (1982), pp. 97–121.

The possible Kentish connection suggested by the addition of Elphege may be reinforced by the correct interpolation of Rochester as the place where Archbishop Paulinus of York died (10 October); for a possible connection of the Rule with Rochester, see above p. 81.

[21] Erasures were made at 20 March and 4 September for Cuthbert, and at 5 August for Oswald. There are original entries for Benedict Biscop (12 January) and Bede (26 May), but these are not evidence for localizing the manuscript; for occurrences of the former, see *English Kalendars before A.D. 1100*, ed. F. Wormald (Henry Bradshaw Society 72; 1934), pp. 30, 44 (Glastonbury), 58 (St Augustine's Canterbury), 72, and 86 (Exeter).

[22] Among English Benedictine houses for men or women dedicated to Martin, only Battle existed by 1100. Between 1130 and 1140 the long-established house of secular canons at St

Apart from the connections of the scribe, there is no evidence that the martyrology was copied with the Durham monks in mind.

The leaves (fols. 39v-45) following the martyrology, written by the same scribe, contain brief *euangelia in capitulo pronuntianda*, for the temporal, starting with Christmas Eve, then individual saints and finally for the common of saints. No saints of local significance are included and there is no immediately obvious clue to the circumstances in which the text was copied.[23]

Although there is much to be said about each of the main sections of DCL B.IV.24, only the copy of Lanfranc's Constitutions discloses its origins; each of the other sections has features to suggest that it was not made in Durham. This does not undermine the identification of the book as the gift of Bishop William of St Calais, particularly as there is no reason to associate any part of it with the monasteries of the Severn Valley that gave birth to the northern Benedictine revival, the most obvious alternative source from which it might have come. What perhaps happened was that William acquired existing copies of the Rule in Latin and English through colleagues in King William I's government, such as Archbishop Lanfranc or Bishop Gundulf of Rochester, who supervised the construction of the king's new London fortress, the White Tower;[24] and then had added the copies of Lanfranc's Constitutions, and the martyrology, both from southern sources.

The origins of DCL B.IV.24 are not yet fully understood, but its history after reaching Durham is far clearer, for the additions that it received relate closely to the functions laid down in Lanfranc's Constitutions for the monk holding the office of cantor or precentor. As well as a rôle in the liturgy that could be described as master of ceremonies, the cantor was also:

Martin's, Dover, was converted to an Augustinian house and was then taken over by the Benedictines of Christ Church, Canterbury; there is no evidence of any previous move in this direction; see C.R. Haines, *Dover Priory* (Cambridge, 1930), pp. 60 ff., but the peculiarity in ch. 60 of the Rule does concern canons becoming monks, see above pp. 80–1. Even more speculatively, there may have been a scheme to establish a religious house at St Martin's, Canterbury, once it had ceased to be the seat of the archbishop's *chorepiscopus*; see *Visitation Articles and Injunctions of the Period of the Reformation*, ed. W.H. Frere (Alcuin Club collections 14; 1910), pp. 35–40. There were nuns holding land near Canterbury by 1087, perhaps later the community of St Sepulchre, a dedication that presumably postdates the capture of Jerusalem in 1099; see W. Urry, *Canterbury under the Angevin Kings* (London, 1967), p. 62, and the Rule is peculiar in having feminine forms, see above pp. 80–1.

[23] Here the gospel for the 26th Sunday after Pentecost (i.e. the Sunday before Advent) is John 6:5 ff., *Cum subleuasset* (fol. 42r/v). Through a muddle with 'the fourth Sunday in Advent', this has been seen as a diagnostic distinguishing what Lanfranc laid down, on the basis of Bec usage, from English secular use (*The Bec Missal*, ed. A. Hughes (Henry Bradshaw Society 94; 1961), pp. vii and 126), but this is not so (J.W. Legg, *The Sarum Missal* (Oxford, 1916), p. 196); and in fact the beginning of the *temporale*, Advent – Epiphany eve, is missing from the Bec missal.

[24] H.M. Colvin, *The History of the King's Works* I (London, 1963), pp. 28–31.

to supervise the letters sent out to ask for prayers for the dead brethren, and to keep count of the week's and month's mind. He takes care of all the books of the house, and has them in his keeping.[25]

The focus of these functions was the daily meeting of the monks in chapter,[26] and DCL B.IV.24 could be described either as the cantor's book or as the chapter-house book.

The reading of a chapter from the Rule lay at the heart of the chapter meeting, and indeed from it was named the room used for the purpose and the body corporate there assembled. The day's portion of the martyrology was also read in chapter.[27] In DCL B.IV.24 the copy of the Rule has added accents and marginal notes to facilitate reading aloud, likewise the martyrology, which is followed by the short gospel pericopes.

Calendar and obits

At an early date a fifth and final section was added to the manuscript. It comprises a single quire, now placed immediately before the martyrology, and containing a calendar, laid out in the normal way, but devoid of all entries for feasts and festivals, so leaving most of the line for each day of the year blank. Into the blanks a few names were added, recording obits, and so presumably the calendar was intended to be a register of obits, such as the cantor would need to ensure that anniversaries were observed. In the event it proved to be much less significant for this purpose than the margins of the martyrology, having a mere twenty-two obits.[28] Nine of the obits in the calendar were entered in a single hand, quite possibly the hand of the calendar itself; as well as all four obits for men described as *miles et monachus*, the entries include the father and mother of Thomas I, archbishop of York (1070–1100), and Countess Matilda of Mortain, who is to be identified as the daughter of Roger de Montgomery, first earl of Shrewsbury, the first wife of King William I's half-brother Robert.[29] The sparse scatter of later obits includes Henry I's chancellor Ranulf (d.1123); Archbishop Thurstan (d.1140) and his parents; members of the family of William of Ste Barbe, bishop of Durham (1143–52); and three mid-twelfth-century priors of Durham, Algar, Lawrence, and Absalom. William, prior of Radford, the Augustinian house at Worksop, dedicated to St Mary and St Cuthbert, was entered in red; his appears to be latest obit, for he seems to have been alive as late as 1171.[30] Why this particular selection of obits

[25] *Monastic Constitutions*, ed. Knowles, p. 82.

[26] *Customary of the Benedictine Monasteries of St Augustine Canterbury and St Peter Westminster*, ed. E.M. Thompson (Henry Bradshaw Society 23, 28; 1902, 1904), I, 352 and 369.

[27] Ibid., I, 223; II, 182.

[28] To those in *Liber vitae ecclesiae Dunelmensis*, ed. J. Stevenson (SS 13; 1841), pp. 139–40, add 'Hilduuinus' at v kal. Feb.

[29] G.E. Cockayne, *Complete Peerage* III (London, 1913), p. 428. What claim she or her husband had on the prayers of the monks of Durham is not clear, and so it is difficult to press the argument that the lack of an obit for him indicates a dating between her death and his in 1090, but such a dating is palaeographically quite possible.

[30] W. Farrer, *Early Yorkshire Charters* III (Edinburgh, 1916), no. 1269.

should be found in the calendar is far from obvious, their only significant feature perhaps being the absence of popes and kings. It is certainly not clear whether these obits were commemorated in some way different from those recorded in the margins of the martyrology.

With anniversaries observed at the chapter meeting, where a portion of the martyrology was read, it is not surprising that the entering of obits in the margins of the martyrology was a practice found in other houses.[31] At Durham, however, it appears that the marking of anniversaries may not have taken place daily. A striking feature of the martyrology is that a high proportion of the obits are in groups and that they are not evenly distributed across the 365 days of the year. At first sight the distribution of the groups of obits seems haphazard, but at certain points there are signs that groups were entered about a week apart, most noticeably in December.[32] Moreover the weekly pattern can be seen to have resulted in obits being entered at slightly different dates from the date of death: for example, King Henry I on 2 rather than 1 December, King Malcolm IV of Scotland on 8 rather than 9, and Pope Calixtus II on 15 rather than 13. This explains the discrepancies between the dates of death known from other sources and those derived from the margins of the martyrology, and means that the latter cannot be taken as exactly right.[33]

It is far from clear whether the grouping of the obits directly reflects the way in which they were commemorated. It is possible that the weekly pattern relates in some way to the *rota* or *tabula* on which were posted the names of the functionaries of the week, the *hebdomadarii*, who fulfilled a range of liturgical and other responsibilities for a single week at a time.[34] It is not, however, easy to suppose that all the obits of the week were tabulated, and that each was then commemorated on the exact day of death; first, because the pattern does not exhibit exact intervals of a week, and second, because another source of information would have been needed to identify the exact day on which each obit was to be kept. It seems simpler to conclude that the Durham monks observed commemorations in chapter at intervals, rather than daily, until about 1160.[35] Such a practice could have been prompted by Bishop William's letter of exhortation, which he directed to be read weekly in chapter;[36] the insertion of a copy of it into DCL B.IV.24 (fol. 74)

---

31 *Customary of St Augustine and St Peter*, ed. Thompson, I, 296, 352, 364 'nomen eius inter familiares in martilogio scribetur'.

32 Successive groups fall on 2, 8 and 15 December. Cf. also 1, 8 January; 1, 8 March; 11, 18, (22), 25 April; 14, 21 May; 1, 8 August; 6, 13, 21 November.

33 Le Neve, *Fasti: Monastic Cathedrals*, pp. 29–34; references to the Martyrology margins are fols. 12–39 of Durham obit I, and pp. 140–7 of Durham obit II.

34 *Monastic Constitutions*, pp. 95–6; *Dictionary of Medieval Latin from British Sources* IV (British Academy; London, 1989), pp. 1140–1, references under *hebdomadarius*, meaning (2).

35 The earliest obit conspicuously entered on the exact day of death, rather than being included in the closest group of obits, is that of Theobald, archbishop of Canterbury (d.1161), 18 April; then Robert de Gorron, abbot of St Albans (d.1166), 26 October; Godric (d.1170), 21 May; Alquin prior of Westminster (d.c.1175), 21 May; and John abbot of Kelso (d.1180), 5 May.

36 *LDE*, bk. 4, ch. 6.

suggests that the monks obeyed him, and the reading may well have been accompanied by some form of commemoration.

The groups of obits in the martyrology were not created randomly, as deaths occurred. As alteration shows, the groups were normally carefully arranged on hierarchical principles. Popes and kings precede bishops and abbots; they are followed by the brothers and monks of Durham, *nostra congregatio*, and then some lesser ecclesiastics and a few laymen, such as the early twelfth-century Scottish benefactor of the monks, Thor Longus.[37] Rather better served than the four kings of England, from William I to Stephen, were their Scottish counterparts: as well as Malcolm III (d.1093), each of his four sons, who reigned from 1094 to 1153, and Malcolm IV (d.1165), there are entries for Malcolm III's second wife Margaret (d. November 1093), his daughter Matilda, the first wife of Henry I (d.1118), and for Alexander I's wife Sybilla (d. July 1122), while the entry for the Countess Ingibiorg (d. February) may refer to Malcolm III's first wife and that for Queen Matilda (d. October) to David I's wife.[38] The place accorded to Scots in the Durham monks' prayers paid due regard to their proximity and capacity for doing harm. Journeys southwards brought Scots to Durham, and they added lustre to important occasions: according to one source Malcolm III, on his way to King William Rufus in Gloucester, joined Bishop William and Prior Turgot in laying the foundation stones of the cathedral in August 1093,[39] and in 1104 King Edgar's brother Alexander was present for the translation of St Cuthbert into the new building.[40] More than that, however, King Edgar was the monks' most generous benefactor, a generosity reciprocated by the stipulation entered in DCL B.IV.24 for the observance of his anniversary that made him the only individual to rank with Bishop William.[41]

[37] On Thor, see J. Raine, *History and Antiquities of North Durham* (London, 1852), Appendix, p. 38.

[38] A Queen Matilda is entered immediately after King Stephen (died 25 October 1154) and so the entry may refer to his wife, although she died on 3 May 1152; for a comparable case, see Amice, widow of Robert de Beaumont, earl of Leicester, who became a nun after his death on 5 April 1168, and is entered immediately after him.

[39] In *DIV*, p. 105, and *HReg, s.a.* 1093; the one perhaps dependent on the other. Symeon of Durham, writing some fifteen years after 1093, did not mention Malcolm's presence, preferring 'other brethren' instead (*LDE*, bk. 4, ch. 8, with no trace of alteration at this point in the oldest copy of the text, DUL, MS Cosin V.II.6). If this is suppression on Symeon's part, at least three considerations might have prompted it: Malcolm's persecution of Aldwin and Turgot when they sought to revive monastic life at Melrose *c.*1074 (*LDE*, bk. 3, ch. 22); Malcolm's death while raiding deep into Northumberland late in 1093; or the embarrassment caused by Scottish resistance to the archbishop of York consecrating Prior Turgot on his elevation by King Alexander to the see of St Andrews in 1107, a situation perhaps further aggravated by Bishop Flambard obstructing Turgot's replacement as prior of Durham (see William of Malmesbury, *De Gestis Pontificum Anglorum*, ed. N.E.S.A. Hamilton (RS 52; 1870), pp. 273–4). Since a visit to Durham in August 1093 fits well with Malcolm's other known movements and with the likelihood that Bishop William would have been involved in his visit to the English king, its invention would represent a particularly lucky lie.

[40] *De miraculis*, ch. 7 (*Sym. Op.* I, 258).

[41] *North Durham*, Appendix, pp. 1–7. *Liber vitae* (SS 13; 1841), p. 139.

Almost two hundred of the obits in the margins of the martyrology refer to Durham monks, identified by the phrase *nostre congregationis fratres et monachi*, or some variation of it. Virtually all the names also occur in the two lists of the early monks, and as corroboration this is all the stronger because the lists record the monks in the order in which they entered the community, and so presumably derive from sources created at that time,[42] not when they died. One of the lists was inserted at the front of the oldest copy of Symeon of Durham's *Libellus de exordio atque procursu . . . Dunelmensis ecclesie*;[43] the other is in the *Liber Vitae*, which the author of the *Rites of Durham*, writing late in the sixteenth century, remembered as lying on the high altar of the cathedral.[44] It had presumably always lain there, that the names of monks and benefactors which it contained might be implicitly commemorated at the daily conventual masses.

As well as names, there were added in the *Liber Vitae*, on a blank page in the oldest part of the book, copies of fourteen undertakings for the performance of specified liturgical observances when members of other monastic communities or named individuals died;[45] the communities were all English, apart from St Calais, and the individuals all monks, apart from a canon of St Paul's London. These undertakings were entered in the *Liber Vitae* at various dates between 1083 and *c*.1110,[46] yet the third and fourth of them refer to the terms of other undertakings which are not found there, but instead among those recorded in DCL B.IV.24,[47] while all four of those in the *Liber Vitae* for communities, rather than individuals, were also entered in DCL B.IV.24.[48] The first batch of undertakings in DCL B.IV.24 differs, however, from those in the *Liber Vitae*, for they were apparently entered by one scribe, at one sitting, most probably early in the twelfth century.[49] The source was clearly not the *Liber Vitae*; it may well have been a loose sheet or sheets kept in the chapter house. The copying of the undertakings into DCL B.IV.24 marked a change of policy, for almost at once they ceased to be entered in the *Liber Vitae*, and instead were added in DCL B.IV.24, down to the last quarter of the twelfth century.[50] It had presumably been found more convenient

---

[42] A file of profession-slips for instance; an example from the earlier fifteenth century is DCDCM, Misc. Ch. 7221, and loose slips from Prior Melsonby's time (1234–44) are DCDCM, Misc. Ch. 1ª and 6067ª.

[43] DUL, Cosin MS V.II.6, fols. 7–8v (ed. *Sym. Op.* I, 4–6).

[44] *Liber Vitae*, fols. (pencil) 45 ff.; *Rites of Durham*, ed. J. T. Fowler (SS 107; 1903), pp. 16–17.

[45] *Liber Vitae*, fol. (pencil) 33v.

[46] The penultimate undertaking is for *Wlfraucnus* canon of St Paul's, identifiable as Ulfran who occurs in 1104/5 and 1114/5; see *John le Neve: Fasti Ecclesiae Anglicanae 1066–1300 I St Paul's, London*, compiled by D.E. Greenway (London, 1968), p. 57.

[47] *Liber vitae* (SS 13; 1841), pp. 135–6, nos. (4), Westminster, and (10), Glastonbury.

[48] Ibid., pp. 136–7, nos. (9) St Calais, (7) Chertsey, (8) St Mary's York, and (12) Pershore.

[49] I owe this observation regarding *Liber Vitae* (SS 13; 1841), pp. 135–6 nos. (2)–(10) to Mr Michael Gullick, who finds the scribe again at *Liber Vitae*, fols. (pencil) 54v–55, where the final text was composed after the death of King William II in 1100.

[50] The undertaking for Gerard, prior of Norwich (*Liber Vitae* (SS 13; 1841), p. 139) can be no earlier than 1175.

for the cantor to have them in a book used in the chapter house, where liturgical observances were organized, rather than in the church itself.

At first inspection some undertakings, potentially important evidence for the network of connections developed by the Durham community during the first century of its existence, seem to be missing, notably those for Worcester and Evesham.[51] This may be explicable: their priors do appear among the undertakings in the *Liber Vitae*, but the entries were later erased, presumably when the names of the members of both communities were added on blank pages in the older part of the book, an honour rendering any other form of observance *de trop*.[52] This leaves Rochester and St Augustine's Canterbury as the most striking omissions, but neither is unduly incredible. The modest representation of Scotland, with agreements only for the brothers of Dunfermline, an abbot of Kelso and monks of Melrose and Newbattle,[53] reflects the fact that the great expansion of regular monasticism in Scotland took place under King David I (1124–53).

One function of the cantor mentioned by Lanfranc was to provide a novice with ink, parchment and, if need be, a scribe, to write his profession-slip, after the chapter meeting where his petition to profess had been accepted;[54] this was an obvious extension of the cantor's rôle in the monastic writing-office. Tangible evidence for the procedure at Durham is the form of profession added into DCL B.IV.24 (fol. 4v); presumably it served as an exemplar for the individual slips.[55]

The culminating addition to DCL B.IV.24 was a single bifolium (fols. 2–3) containing a long list of books compiled in the mid-twelfth century.[56] Rather than describing their contents in full, it identifies the books briefly, and so would have enabled the cantor to check the collection, the most fundamental of his tasks in

[51] The religious houses and persons represented (*Liber Vitae* (SS 13; 1841), pp. 135–9) are: Bardney, Bridlington (Augustinian), Christ Church Canterbury, abbot of Cerne, Chertsey, Crowland, Glastonbury, Gloucester, priors of Norwich, Pershore, Peterborough, abbot of Revesby (Cistercian), St Albans, Selby, Westminster, Whitby, Winchcombe, Winchester, prior of Holy Trinity [York], St Mary's York; Dunfermline, abbot of Kelso, monk of Melrose, monk of Newbattle; St Nicholas Angers, St Stephen Caen, St Taurin Évreux, Fécamp, and St Calais.

The English Benedictine houses in existence in 1100 not represented are Abbotsbury, Abingdon, Athelney, Bath, Battle, Burton, Bury, St Augustine's Canterbury, Chester, Colchester, Coventry, Ely, Evesham, Eynsham, Malmesbury, Milton, Muchelney, Ramsey, Reading, Rochester, St Benet of Hulme, Sherborne, Shrewsbury, Tavistock, Tewkesbury, Thorney, and Worcester.

[52] *Liber Vitae*, fols. (pencil) 24v–25. I. Atkins, 'The Church of Worcester from the Eighth to the Twelfth Century', *Antiquaries Journal* 20 (1940), pp. 1–38 and 203–29, at 212–20, where the lists are edited and dated to between 1099 and 1109.

[53] *Liber vitae* (SS 13; 1841), pp. 137–9.

[54] *Monastic Constitutions*, ed. Knowles, pp. 107–8. For surviving Durham profession-slips, see note 42 above.

[55] The form is as *Customary of St Augustine and St Peter*, ed. Thompson, I, 4, but with 'uel subdiaconus uel acolitus uel conuersus' omitted, and the penultimate phrase 'in honore Sancte Marie semper uirginis et Sancti Cuthberti presulis'.

[56] *Catalogi veteres*, ed. Botfield, pp. 1–10; a new edition is in preparation. A.J. Piper, 'The Libraries of the Monks of Durham', in *Medieval Scribes, Manuscripts and Libraries*, ed. M.B. Parkes and A.G. Watson (London, 1978), pp. 214–16.

undertaking the care of all the monastery's books, as Lanfranc put it. Subsequent accessions were added to the list during the later twelfth century, but this practice had evidently been abandoned by 1200. The adding of other material to the book also ceased at the same period. The use of DCL B.IV.24 as the comprehensive current record-book of the cantor was an Anglo-Norman phenomenon. Of the documents that replaced it nothing survives, apart from later book-lists, but it may well be that convenience, reinforced by a sharper sense of archival propriety, prompted the substitution of separate documents to serve different purposes, such as reciprocation of suffrages and the observance of obits.

In a sense DCL B.IV.24 exemplifies the Anglo-Norman impact on Durham's cathedral and its community. Like the monastic constitution bestowed on the cathedral in 1083, its older texts had Anglo-Saxon, not Norman, antecedents. But, just as this indigenous constitution was given a new setting, the great building founded in 1093, so the additions in DCL B.IV.24 equipped the monastery's cantor to function as prescribed in the directory drawn up by William the Conqueror's archbishop. Again, while the additions bear clear testimony, suggestive of regular discipline and orderliness, the witness of the older texts to their origins is obscure and incomplete, like the evidence for the life of the pre-monastic cathedral community, which may through its obscurity be viewed as undisciplined and disorderly. Equally, it may be no accident that DCL B.IV.24 was supplanted at a time when its compendiousness represented an intellectual tradition that was giving way to a more analytic approach, when the emphasis was shifting from the patristic texts that bulked so large in the books given by Bishop William of St Calais, towards new books from the schools of France, brought in by Bishop Hugh of le Puiset (1153–95) and the masters in his entourage.[57]

APPENDIX

Supplementary British entries in the text of Usuard's Martyrology, DCL, MS B.IV.24, fols. 12v–39

Entry-numbers in brackets ( ), are those of the edition by J. Dubois; where no indication is given, e.g. 3 February, the British material follows other supplementary material.

January
12　*After* (2): Apud monasterium beati petri apostoli quod nuncupatur Wiremuthe depositio Benedicti [*Biscop*] deo dilecti abbatis. qui idem monasterium a fundamentis erexit ac monachorum regulam ibidem instituit.

---

[57] *DCM*, pp. 78–88.

February
3   In Brittania sanctae Wereburgae uirginis.
13 In Brittania sanctae Eormenhildae abbatissae [*again at 7 August*].

March
2   *After* (2): In Brittania depositio sancti Ceaddae episcopi et confessoris.
8   *After* (3): Ipso die sancti Felicis orientalium qui fuit predicator et episcopus
    Anglorum quique nunc cum magna gloria honoratur in monasterio Hrame-
    syge. ubi et conditus iacet.
16 *After* (3): Coloniae. sancti Hereberti archiepiscopi eiusdem ciuitatis. cuius
    uitam inclitam miracula post obitum eius facta testantur.
18 Eodem die sancti Eadwardi martiris.
20 *Alteration, by erasure and rewriting, early 12th century, putting entry for* deposi-
    tio sancti Cuthberti *in first place.*

April
11 Eodem die beati Guthlaci presbiteri et anachorite.
15 *After* (2): Eodem die translatio sancti Oswaldi archiepiscopi [*founder of
    Ramsey; main feast 28 February, for death in 992*].
19 *After* (4): Eodem die passio sancti Elfeagi archiepiscopi [*d.1012, translated
    Canterbury 1023*].
30 *After* (2): In Brittanniis depositio beati Erconuualdi episcopi et confessoris.

May
1   *After* (6): In Brittania sancti Courentini episcopi [*feast at Exeter on 1 May*].
7   *Marginal addition, apparently replacing erased text, earlier 12th century:* In
    Brittanniis depositio beati Iohannis [*of Beverley, d.721*] episcopi cuius gloriosa
    miracula fulgent in gente Northanhymbrorum quam pontificali rexit digni-
    tate.
16 *After* (3): In Hibernia sancti Brendani abbatis et confessoris. cuius mirabiles
    actus habentur.
19 Ipso die depositio sancti Dunstani archiepiscopi Cantuarie ubi etiam sepultus
    usque hodie crebris refulget miraculis.
26 *After* (6): Eodem die depositio uenerabilis Bedae presbiteri.

June
10 *After* (4): Ipso die translatio sancti Yuonis episcopi et confessoris [*to Ramsey, in
    1001*].
17 In Brittanniis depositio beati Botulfi abbatis.
18 *After* (3): Ipso die sancti Adulfi fratris beati Botulfi abbatis.

July
2   *After* (4): In Brittannia ciuitate UUintoniae depositio sancti Suithuni episcopi
    et confessoris.
6   *After* (5): In Brittannia sanctae Sexburgae uirginis.
7   *Marginal addition, earlier 12th century, keyed in after* (2): In Brittannia deposi-
    tio beati Boisili presbiteri et confessoris.
15 *At the end of* (3): et translatio beati Suithuni episcopi.
17 *After* (1): In prouincia Merciorum monasterio quod uocatur Wincaelcum
    passio sancti Kenelmi martiris.

31   *After* (3): Eodem die depositio beatissimi Neoti sacerdotis. meritis ac miraculis gloriosi.

August
 1   *After* (9): Eodem die natalis sancti Atheluuoldi episcopi.
 5   *Alteration by erasure and rewriting of* (2), *mid-12th century:* In Brintanniis natalis Beati Oswaldi martyris et regis Northanhymbrorum cuius post mortem sanctitas crebris miraculorum patuit iudiciis.
 7   *At the end of* (3): Et sanctae Eormenhildae abbatissae [*commonly 13 February*].
20   *Marginal addition, mid-12th century:* In Brittannijs natalis sanctj Oswini regis et martiris.
25   *Marginal addition, c.1100:* Item festiuitas sancte Ebbe VIRGINIS.
31   *Marginal addition, early 12th century:* In Brittannia sancti Aidani primi Lindisfarnensis episcopi. Eodem die commemoratio sanctarum reliquiarum eiusdem ecclesie.

September
 4   *All entries erased and rewritten, early 12th century, putting between* (1) *and* (2): Eodem die translatio beatissimi patris CVTHBERTI Lindispharnensis ecclesiae episcopi. qui non solum in hac uita sed etiam post hanc in numeris et miris claruit miraculorum signis [*feast of translation*].
     After (4): Item BYRINI episcopi et confessoris [*feast of translation*].
11   *Marginal addition, early 12th century:* Eodem die octauae sancti Cuthberti.
21   *After* (3): In Brittannia sanctae UUerburgae uirginis.
25   *After* (6): In Hibernia sancti Barri confessoris [*i.e. Finbar*].

October
10   *Entry for Paulinus* (5), *d. Rochester, 644, supplemented:* ciuitate Rofensi.
12   *Marginal addition, early 12th century:* In Brittannia sancti Wilfridi episcopi.
17   *After* (3): In Ramesiensi coenobio sanctorum Ethelredi et Ethelbyrti martirum. et translatio sanctae Aethethrythae uirginis et reginae.
20   *After* (4): Eodem die sancti Neoti presbiteri et confessoris.

November
16   *Marginal addition, 14th century:* Et deposicio sancti Edmundi [*Rich*] Cant' archiepiscopi [*d.1240*].
17   *Marginal addition, early 12th century:* In Britannia depositio sanctae Hildae uirginis.
20   *After* (4): In Brittania sancti Eadmundi martiris atque regis orientalium anglorum.

December
12   *After* (5): In Hibernia sancti Finniani confessoris.
29   *Addition after alteration by erasure, late 12th century:* Eodem die passio Sancti Thome Cantuariensis archiepiscopi.

The Scribes of the Durham Cantor's Book (Durham, Dean and Chapter Library, MS B.IV.24) and the Durham Martyrology Scribe

MICHAEL GULLICK

T HE MANUSCRIPT B.IV.24 in the library at Durham Cathedral comprises five items of similar date. These are a Calendar, a Martyrology followed by short Gospel Pericopes, Lanfranc's *Constitutiones*, and the Rule of St Benedict, first in Latin and then an Anglo-Saxon translation. The identification of the manuscript with the *Martyrologium et Regula* given by Bishop William of St Calais (d.1096) to Durham can hardly be doubted. The manuscript has a number of additions on formerly blank leaves and in the margins, which are mostly of some importance for their content (fig. 2). Alan Piper has dubbed the manuscript the Durham Cantor's Book.[1]

The Calendar, Martyrology and Pericopes were written on identical parchment, which suggests that they were written in the same place. The Calendar was written by an English scribe who also worked in the Durham *Liber Vitae* and he appears to have been active from about the 1080s to the 1100s.[2] The Martyrology and Pericopes were written by a continental scribe who was active at Durham from about 1091 to 1128 and his work is the subject of the second part of this paper.

The two versions of the Rule had a different English scribe for each version, neither of whom has been identified elsewhere.[3] The *Constitutiones* was written by two scribes, almost certainly at Canterbury, as one of them wrote a script associated with Christ Church. It is unlikely that it was written earlier than the early 1090s and almost certainly not written much later.[4]

---

[1] *DCM*, no. 51. For the texts (and the additions and amendments) of the manuscript see A.J. Piper, 'The Durham Cantor's Book (Durham Cathedral, MS B.IV.24)', pp. 79–92 above.

[2] The scribe wrote a manumission in Anglo-Saxon (fol. 47, lines 22–23) and several *conuentiones* between Durham and others (fol. 52 lines 11–18). One *conuentio* is with St Peter's, Lastingham, which was monastic for only a few years from *c.*1080 to 1086. The scribe also wrote the purported diploma of William of St Calais concerning the foundation of the monastery at Durham (fols. 53–54v) for which see *DEC*, no. 3, where it is discussed and dated to after 1104–7.

[3] Reproduction of Anglo-Saxon in *DCM*, pl. 33b.

[4] The first scribe wrote fols. 47–67v, line 7 and the second, who wrote a more English looking hand, wrote fol. 67v, lines 8–71v. For a reproduction of the first scribe's hand see A.

	Folio	Contents	Date	Scribes	
				Core Texts	Corrections etc.
	ir	16 lines of verse 'Hic leo'	xii.med		
	iv	List of books read at *collatio*	xii.med		
	1r–2r	List of [main] book collection	xii.med		
	2*	Record of confraternity	1175		
	3v	Papal letter on ending of schism	1177		
	4v	A form of profession	xii		
	5r–v	Agreements for suffrages (*conuentio*)	xi.ex–xii.ex		A and others
	5v	Liturgical ordinance	xii¹		
1	6r–11v	**Kalendar without saints**		one	B and others
2	12r–39v	**Usuardus *Martyrologium***		A	B and C
		Obits added in the margins	xi.ex–xii.ex		A and others
2	39v–45r	**Lectionary of chapter gospels**		A	B, C and others
	46v	Liturgical ordinance	xii¹		
3	47r–71v	**Lanfranc *Constitutiones***		two	
	72r	Liturgical ordinance	xii¹		
	74r	Omitted portion of Prologue to			
		Benedict *Regula*	xi/xii		B
		Letter of William of St Calais	xi/xii		C
4	74v–95r	**Benedict *Regula***		one	C
	95v	Omitted chapter [62] of *Regula*	xi/xii		B
	95v–96r	Two Letters of Anselm	xii.in		A and B
	96r	On types of monks	xii¹		
		Letter of Bernard of Clairvaux	c.1143		
	96v	Maundy ordinance	1154 x 1159		
5	98v–123v	**Anglo-Saxon translation of *Regula***		one	
	124r	Letter of P [?abbot] of Cluny to			
		L keeper of Nottingham	xii.med		
	124r–v	Liturgical ordinances, etc.,			
		partially recopied from f.126r	xii.med		
	126r–v	Liturgical ordinances, etc.	xi/xii		A
	127r	Miscellaneous, including one *conuentio*	xi/xii		mostly A

Fig. 2   The Durham Cantor's Book (DCL, MS B.IV.24): contents and scribes
The core contents are five items, numbered 1–5 above, and printed in **bold type**, probably
written and assembled together s.xi.ex (by 1096, perhaps 1091–6). Items 4 and 5 were
written in the same place, almost certainly with the intention that they would follow one
another. There were a number of important additions made to the manuscript soon after
it had been assembled and throughout the twelfth century.

The number of scribes involved in writing each of the core texts is noted. One scribe
who wrote one of the core texts and made a large number of the additions is identified as
Scribe A, and two scribes who each made a number of corrections, amendments and
additions are identified as Scribes B and C. The careful description of the manuscript by
Thomas Rud in his *Codicum Manuscriptorum Ecclesiae Cathedralis Dunelmensis Catalogus
Classicus* (Durham, 1825), pp. 204–18 is of fundamental importance and there is a
summary description by R.A.B. Mynors in his *DCM*, no. 51 with reproductions of
fols. 5 and 116 on pl.33.

The Cantor's Book has little decoration except for a few modestly decorated initials. The KL monograms in the Calendar and several initials in the Latin Rule employed a similar decorative motif as a finial, dubbed here the flame motif, which occurs in many Durham-made manuscripts from the late eleventh century to about 1125 (fig. 3).

The possibility that all of the Cantor's Book except for the *Constitutiones* was made at Durham is appealing but unfortunately the scribal evidence does not fit easily with the textual evidence. The Pericopes have no local symptoms, the Martyrology can hardly have been written with the needs of the Durham monks in mind, and the same is true of the Latin Rule. It appears, from some of the corrections, amendments, and additions which were made to the manuscript soon after it had been completed, that an effort was made by at least two scribes to make the manuscript more useful for its intended home. To judge by their hands, both of these scribes were Normans and both can be associated with Durham.

One of the two scribes (fig 2, scribe B) wrote the earliest entries in the Calendar,[5] supplemented the Martyrology,[6] added to the Pericopes[7] and added two missing portions of the Latin Rule.[8] This scribe also added part of a letter of Anselm, completed by another (fig. 2, scribe A).[9] This is almost certainly a scribe named William who probably came to Durham in or soon after 1091, the year William of St Calais returned to England after three years of exile spent in Normandy.[10]

The second scribe (fig. 2, scribe C) supplemented and altered the Martyrology[11] and added to the Pericopes,[12] as well as amending the Latin Rule[13] and writing, on a formerly blank leaf, a copy of the famous letter of William of St Calais to his

Lawrence, 'The Influence of Canterbury on the Production of Manuscripts at Durham in the Anglo-Norman Period', in *The Vanishing Past. Studies in Medieval Art, Liturgy and Metrology Presented to Christopher Hohler*, ed. A. Borg and A. Martindale (British Archaeological Reports, International Series 111; Oxford, 1981), pl. 8.17.

[5] These entries are for *Rodbertus, Hilduuinus, Gotscelinus, Osbertus, Giraldus, Guerinus, Hamelinus, Muriel* and *Mathildis comitissa de Moretonio.* Osbert and Muriel were described as the father and mother respectively of Thomas archbishop of York (1070–1100), and the other men, except for Hildwin, as *miles et monachus.* Entries, without distinguishing the hands of different scribes, are printed in T. Rud, *Codicum Manuscriptorum Ecclesiae Cathedralis Dunelmensis Catalogus Classicus* (Durham, 1825), p. 214.

[6] For example, fol. 37 foot margin, for Catherine.

[7] Following the work of the text scribe, fol. 44v, line 30/5 to the end of the page. Note: in all future references line nos. are followed by word nos., cited as: line 22/5.

[8] An omitted portion of the Prologue is on fol. 74, lines 1–11 and ch. 62 is on fol. 95v, lines 1–13.

[9] The letter follows an omitted portion of the Latin Rule, see previous note, fol. 95v, lines 14–22. The scribe who completed the letter also wrote another following the first.

[10] M. Gullick, 'The Scribe of the Carilef Bible: A New Look at Some Late Eleventh-Century Durham Manuscripts', in *Medieval Book Production: Assessing the Evidence*, ed. L.L. Brownrigg (Los Altos Hills, 1990), at pp. 68–9 with references.

[11] For example, fol. 14, foot margin for Felix, fol. 18v, lines 35–9 for Cuthbert, and fol. 31, lines 32/6 to fol. 31v, line 1, also for Cuthbert.

[12] Following an addition by William, fol. 45, lines 1–3/8.

[13] For example, fol. 81v, lines 27–9 and fol. 90v, lines 32/2–33, both written over erasure.

Fig. 3.   Drawings (not to scale) of a one colour (rarely more) decorative finial to minor initials found in Durham manuscripts. The essential structure of the motif is always more or less the same, a tri-lobed or tri-petalled terminal with the outer two elements solid and the central element voided, usually slightly wavy and with one or two lines (veins) within it. The central element is sometimes terminated with three solid or voided disks.

Top row: The Durham Cantor's Book fol. 6r (Calendar), fol. 35v (Martyrology), and fol. 79v (Latin Rule).

Centre: Berne, Stadtbibliothek MS 392 (s.xii.in), Cambridge, Peterhouse 74 (s.xii.in) and DCL, MS B.II.6 (before 1096).

Bottom: DCL, MS B.III.4 (s.xii.in), DUL, Cosin MS V.ii.6 (s.xii.in, after 1104–07), and BL, Cotton MS Faust.A.v (s.xii.in, after 1104–07).

monks.[14] Stylistically, the hand is very close to that of the scribe who wrote the earliest extant manuscript of Symeon of Durham's *Libellus de exordio*, DUL, Cosin MS V.ii.6, datable between 1104 and 1109, and it is likely that these two scribes are one and the same.[15]

The association of these two Normans with the Cantor's Book probably extended into the first decade of the twelfth century, but not much later. A third scribe, of the Martyrology and Pericopes (fig. 2, scribe A), does not appear to have amended the original manuscript but he did write a large number of the additions, probably, as will be seen below, over a much longer period. This man may have been the junior member of a group of three continental scribes who outlived his two seniors. It is possible, if not probable, that all three came to Durham in the early 1090s, for there is no evidence to suggest that any of them were at Durham before 1091.

The scribe who wrote the Martyrology and Gospel Pericopes in the Cantor's Book has been dubbed here the Durham Martyrology scribe (fig. 2, scribe A). His hand has been found in more than a dozen manuscripts and he also wrote seven charters. His earliest datable work is 1093 and he was still alive in 1128. In the account of the scribe's work which follows, some of the earliest manuscripts attributable to him, including his work in the Cantor's Book, are discussed in some detail because of the problems they present. The other manuscripts and the charters are discussed in a more summary fashion.

Two of the early manuscripts contain the same text, Bede's Prose Life of St Cuthbert, Bodl.L, MS Bodley 596, fols. 175–214, which also contains the Verse Life, and Bodl.L, MS Digby 175. The Bodley manuscript was at St Augustine's Canterbury by the fourteenth century when an *ex libris* and pressmark were entered on the first leaf. The medieval provenance of the Digby manuscript, which has lost its first quire, is unknown.

Digby, to judge by the character of the hand, is the scribe's earliest extant work. The scribe wrote and rubricated the manuscript except for the present first quire which was rubricated by another. The Prose Life is followed by two extracts from the *Historia Ecclesiastica* (commonly found accompanying the Prose Life), a miracle story concerning Cuthbert, incomplete because of leaf loss, and three further extracts from the *Historia Ecclesiastica*, all incomplete.[16]

The miracle story is the first of a group of seven composed before the 1104

---

[14] The letter follows an omitted portion of the Latin Rule written by William, fol. 74, lines 13–30.

[15] For a reproduction of the Cosin manuscript see N.R. Ker, *English Manuscripts in the Century after the Norman Conquest* (Oxford, 1960), pl. 8b. The scribe also worked in the *Liber Vitae*, see, for example, *Alexander rex* (1107–24), the first addition to a list of Scottish kings fol. 15v, col. c; *Brianus*, the first addition to a list of Durham monks written earlier by William, perhaps about 1104 at the time of the translation of Cuthbert, fol. 45v, col. a; and the list of names *Eiric rex danorum* (1095–1103) – *Gerbrun*, fol. 55v, lines 1–4.

[16] *Two Lives of St Cuthbert*, ed. and trans. B. Colgrave (Cambridge, 1940), p. 22 for the manuscript.

translation of Cuthbert. The first two lines, except for the last two words of the second line, were written in a more compressed script than that found in the bulk of the manuscript (see pl. 2a and b) but found in the scribe's later work. The absence of an initial or title suggests that the story (presumably with the other six) was an addition to the manuscript.[17]

The Prose Life in Digby belongs to the large Durham family of the text, dubbed Bx by Colgrave, found in nineteen manuscripts, at least eight of which were written at Durham.[18] Digby might be the oldest member of the family and as there is no evidence of a Bx manuscript at Durham before 1093, the exemplar for Digby need not be presumed to have been a Durham book.[19]

Bodley, like Digby, has matter following the Prose Life, the Verse Life followed by a History of the saint (*Historia de sancto Cuthberto*), both incomplete.[20] The History was written in the scribe's more compressed hand and was probably an addition. Another, contemporary, scribe added a Life and Office of Julian of Le Mans in a small neat hand of continental type on leaves which are integral with the Bede material and it is certain that these additions never had an independent existence.[21]

The Prose Life in Bodley belongs to a small group of four manuscripts, dubbed By by Colgrave. None of the others has any connection with Durham. Colgrave stated that all four were English, but in fact one of the others is French.[22] The History of Cuthbert in Bodley has a final paragraph found in one other manuscript, which Colgrave thought English, but which is French.[23]

Bodley, like Digby, need not be presumed to have been copied from a Durham exemplar and there is a real possibility that at least part of the manuscript was written in France. Bodley might have been William of St Calais's own book, for the bishop, abbot of St Vincent at Le Mans before coming to Durham, is more likely to have had an interest in the Le Mans saint than had members of the Durham community.

Bodley was written and rubricated by the scribe and the hand of the original part

---

[17] B. Colgrave, 'The Post-Bedan Miracles and the Translation of St Cuthbert', in *The Early Culture of North-West Europe. H.M. Chadwick Memorial Studies*, ed. C. Fox and B. Dickins (Cambridge, 1950), at p. 327.

[18] *Two Lives*, ed. Colgrave, pp. 49–50 for the Bx family. To the list of manuscripts of certain Durham origin listed there should be added the following: Bodl.L, MS Digby 20, fols. 194–227 and Bodl.L, MS Laud misc. 491, and Oxford, University College, MS 165.

[19] The only manuscript known to have been available as an exemplar at Durham is CCCC, MS 183, dating from about 937, a member of Colgrave's A family.

[20] *Two Lives*, ed. Colgrave, p. 24 for the manuscript.

[21] For the Le Mans material see *Latin Liturgical Manuscripts* (Oxford, Bodleian Library, 1952), no. 63. The hand of the scribe is like, but not the same, as the hand of a scribe who supplied a quire to an earlier manuscript, Le Mans, Bibliothèque municipale, MS 99, which has a St Julian, Le Mans provenance, fols. 41–47v.

[22] *Two Lives*, ed. Colgrave, p. 48 for the By family. Paris, Bibliothèque nationale, MS lat. 2475 is French s.XII².

[23] *Two Lives*, ed. Colgrave, p. 24 n. 3. Paris, Bibliothèque nationale, MS lat. 5362 is probably Norman of s.xi/xii and contains an A version of the Prose Life.

pleatur· hoc aute̅ dicebat q̅a prefatuſ x̅p̅i famuluſ epiſcopatuſ
eum gradu ſignificabat eſſe functuru̅· cuiuſ perceptionem ipſe
non parum deſiderio uit̅g̅ ſecretioriſ horrebat· x̅ 1 1 1 · cap·
Quomodo ælfled abbatiſſa· & puella ei̅ p̅ zona̅ ipſiuſ

Neq̅ VERO ſanitatum miracula per homine̅ ſint ſanate · ꝰ
c̅i tam & ſi longe ab hominibuſ poſitum fieri ceſſabant· Siquidem
uenerabiliſ ancilla x̅p̅i elfled quę inter gaudia uirginitatiſ ñ
pauciſ famularum x̅p̅i agminibuſ maternę pietatiſ curam
adhibebat· ac regaliſ ſte̅mmata nobilitatiſ potiori nobilitate
ſumme uirtutiſ accumulabat· multo uiru̅ d̅i ſemper excolebat·

S omp̅ſ iuſte miſericorſ· miſerico̅rd̅i̅e̅ q̅ iuſtuſ gente̅ anglox̅ dum p̅
ſuiſ multiplicib; offenſiſ flagellare diſponer & · paganaru̅ g̅entiu̅
freſonu̅ crudelic & atq; danoru̅ immanitate̅ illi p̅miſit dn̅ar1· ſteꝗ gꝯ
ubba duce freſonu̅ & halfdene rege danoru̅ agentib; inbritanniam quę
nc̅ anglia dr̅ uenienteſ· interſ turmaſ max diuiſe · trib; imparib;
terra̅ p̅uaſerunt· Nam eboracę ciuitatiſ menia una exhiſ reſtaurauit·
regioneq; iicaiututū incolenſ· ibide̅ p̅auſauit· At u̅ reliquę duę mul
to abhac ferocioreſ regnu̅ merciorū tra̅mq; auſtraliu̅ ſaxonu̅ mox oc
cupabant· omia̅q; incendiiſ· rapiniſ· atq; homicidiiſ q̅q̅ uerſu̅ exciniꝰ
nanteſ· diuina ęque ut humana c̅tagione barbarica contaminabant·
Quanta tunc abeiſ nobileſ & uiclari ſacerdoteſ cura ipſa ab· dn̅ica corpo

VONIAM DECIVITATI
debitaſ finib; deinc
ſc̅ q̅ntu̅ opiſ hui̅ cu̅
ſibi ipſi beatitudine̅
ut ab eoꝰ reb; uant
reſ ipſa hoc · e̅ · uerab
diuina
fidele
bonoꝰ & maloꝰ· multa & multiplici̅ int̅ ſe phyloſ
tentione uerſantel· inuenire conati ſe̅ q̅d efficiat h

Plate 2.   a. Bodl.L, MS
Digby 175, fol. 9r (Bede's
Prose Life of St Cuthbert;
detail, actual size).
b. Bodl.L, MS Digby 175,
fol. 24r (*De miraculis*,
ch. 1; detail, actual size).

c. DCL., MS B.II.22, fol.
181r (St Augustine's *City
of God*; detail, actual size).

Plate 3.   a. Bodl.L, MS Bodley 596, fol. 175v (Bede's Prose Life of St Cuthbert; detail, actual size.

b. DCL, MS B.II.6, fol. 79r (sermon of St Augustine, *De decem chordis*; detail, actual size).
c. DCL, MS B.IV.12, fol. 121v (sermon of St Augustine; detail, actual size).

d. DCL, MS B.IV.12, fol. 39v (letter of Prosper to Rufinus; detail, actual size).

of the manuscript (pl. 3a) is very close to the hand of the Martyrology. This part of the Cantor's Book was also written and rubricated by the scribe.

The largest and most handsome of all the scribe's work is DCL, MS B.II.22, containing Augustine *De civitate dei*, given by William of St Calais to Durham. It is probably the latest of the manuscripts discussed so far and it was copied, directly or indirectly, from an exemplar in the orbit of Bec-Christ Church, as the margins have *nota* signs written by the scribe in the form *.a.*, a sign linked to Lanfranc's activities at Bec and found in a number of Christ Church manuscripts. At the end of the manuscript, also written by the scribe, are Lanfranc's notes on the work.[24]

Bodl.L Bodley 596 and DCL B.II.22 are the only manuscripts of the four discussed above to contain decorated initials; the striking similarity of their style, colouring, and execution suggests that these were almost certainly the work of the scribe himself (see pls. 2c and 3a). A common structural device in the initials is the use of panels within the bows of round letters (occasionally in stems as well), a device frequently found in contemporary initials. The scribe terminated the panels at their widest point with pronounced concave contours and thus the pairs of panels always used in round letters define a circular area, usually divided with a horizontal line. This refinement is apparently very rare, for contemporary initials usually have panels finished with either horizontal or shallow curved contours.[25]

The opening initial in DCL B.II.22 contains an author portrait. The colouring and execution are identical to the decorative initials in Bodley and DCL B.II.22, but the style is close to contemporary Canterbury initials. The powerful hints in DCL B.II.22 of a close dependence upon a Canterbury exemplar may mean either that the manuscript was copied at Durham from a borrowed exemplar or that the scribe copied the manuscript away from Durham, perhaps at Canterbury itself.[26]

The manuscripts discussed so far have minor initials with decorative finials. All but the Martyrology have *N*s with small x-like motifs on the left hand stem (pl. 2a). The motif occurs in virtually identical form, usually on *N*, occasionally on *M*, in seventeen other probable or certain Durham books, including the Rule in the Cantor's Book.[27] Like the flame motif (fig. 2), the x motif was probably not used

---

[24] *DCM* no. 33 and pl. 22. For the Bec *nota* see R.W. Southern, *Saint Anselm. A Portrait in a Landscape* (Cambridge, 1990), pp. 35–8. For reproduction of the scribe's hand in the martyrology see Lawrence, 'Manuscripts at Durham', pl. 8.19.

[25] For reproductions of the principal initial in Bodley see O. Pächt and J.J.G. Alexander, *Illuminated Manuscripts in the Bodleian Library*, I (Oxford, 1966), pl. 37 (their no. 451) and Lawrence, 'Manuscripts at Durham', pl. 8.23.

[26] The initial is reproduced in *DCM*, pl. 22 and reproduced and discussed in Lawrence, 'Manuscripts at Durham', at pp. 98–100 and pl. 8.20.

[27] The motif occurs in the following manuscripts of Durham origin: Cambridge, Jesus College, MS Q.B.6 (23), fols. 10–13 (*DCM*, no. 69), DCL, MSS B.II.6, fols. 1–80 (no. 46), B.II.18 (no. 56), B.II.21 (no. 34), B.III.9 (no. 41), B.III.14, fols. 1–58 (no. 58), B.IV.7 (no. 53), B.IV.12 (no. 59), B.IV.13 (no. 43), B.IV.14, fols. 1–111 and 170–200 (no. 55), B.IV.24, fols. 74–95 (no. 51), and Hunter 100, fols. 43–84 (no. 57 and pl. 36), and Glasgow, University Library, MS Hunterian, T.4.2 (85) (no. 71).

The motif also occurs in the following manuscripts of probable or certain Durham origin: Berne, Stadtsbibliothek, MS 392 (Bede); BL, Cotton MS Faustina A.V (Symeon of Durham);

much later than about 1125. Neither motif can be associated with Durham before 1091 and it appears that the Martyrology scribe may have been responsible for introducing both into the Durham scriptorium.

At the end of the second and only surviving volume of a large Bible given to Durham by William of St Calais, DCL, MS A.II.4, the Martyrology scribe added an anonymous and incomplete commentary on the Apocalypse.[28] The commentary was written very small in a hand very like the hand of the Miracle story added to Bodl.L Digby 175 (see pls. 4a and 2b). The commentary opens with a handsome initial *A* which is attributable to the scribe. Its clumsy qualities are comparable to the scribe's earlier initials (see pls. 2c and 3a), although otherwise the initial is not obviously like the earlier ones. The minimal veining of the leaf and petal elements is a common feature but the *A* is much closer to two other initials attributable to the scribe in DCL, MSS B.IV.12 and B.II.6 (see pls. 3b and c). Neither of these initials, which both occur adjacent to rubricated titles by the scribe, were as carefully executed as the *A*. The initials probably all date from about the mid-1090s.

The manuscripts discussed so far are crucial for establishing the essential character of the scribe's hand. In his earliest, immature, work he wrote letters rather square in proportion, whose execution was decidedly stiff (pl. 2a). Next, the hand became a little more fluid (pl. 3a) but with a tendency to make the letters more laterally compressed (pl. 2c). The scribe then appears to have developed (either by choice or from direction) a hand with letters distinctly rectangular in proportion (pls. 2b and 4c) and this was continued and more or less maintained by the scribe throughout the rest of his career, although the hand varies considerably in the degree of its formality (pls. 4b and c).

The chronology and development of the scribe's early work centres on his earliest datable writing, an elaborate *conuentio* between Malcolm, king of Scotland, his queen Margaret and their children, and the Durham community, entered in the *Liber Vitae*, fol. 52v, lines 7–20. Malcolm and Margaret both died in 1093 and it is unlikely that the *conuentio* was written after that year. It may even date from about the time of the laying of the foundation stone of the new cathedral, for Malcolm is mentioned in one source as having attended the ceremony.[29] Margaret, whose devotion to Cuthbert is well known, might well have attended the ceremony with her husband.

The *conuentio* was written in a compressed hand and its general aspect is prickly,

---

Bodl.L, MS Digby 20, fols. 194–227 (Bede); and Oxford, University College, MS 165 (Bede). The Berne manuscript contains Bede's Prose Life of Cuthbert and its major initials are of the early clove curl type associated with Durham, see B. Colgrave and I. Mason, 'The *Editio Princeps* of Bede's Prose Life of St Cuthbert and its Printer's s.xiith Century Copy', *The Library*, 4th ser., 19 (1938), pls. 1–4 for reproductions. The manuscript might be the Life of St Cuthbert left at St Victor in Paris s.xii.ex by Robert Addington, for it contains a St Victor *ex libris*. For the manuscripts Robert Addington left to Durham see *DCM*, p. 79.

[28] *DCM*, no. 30 (Carilef Bible).

[29] *HReg*, *s.a.* 1093 (p. 220). For Malcolm's presence at the laying of the foundation stone see Piper, 'The Durham Cantor's Book', p. 87 and n. 39 above.

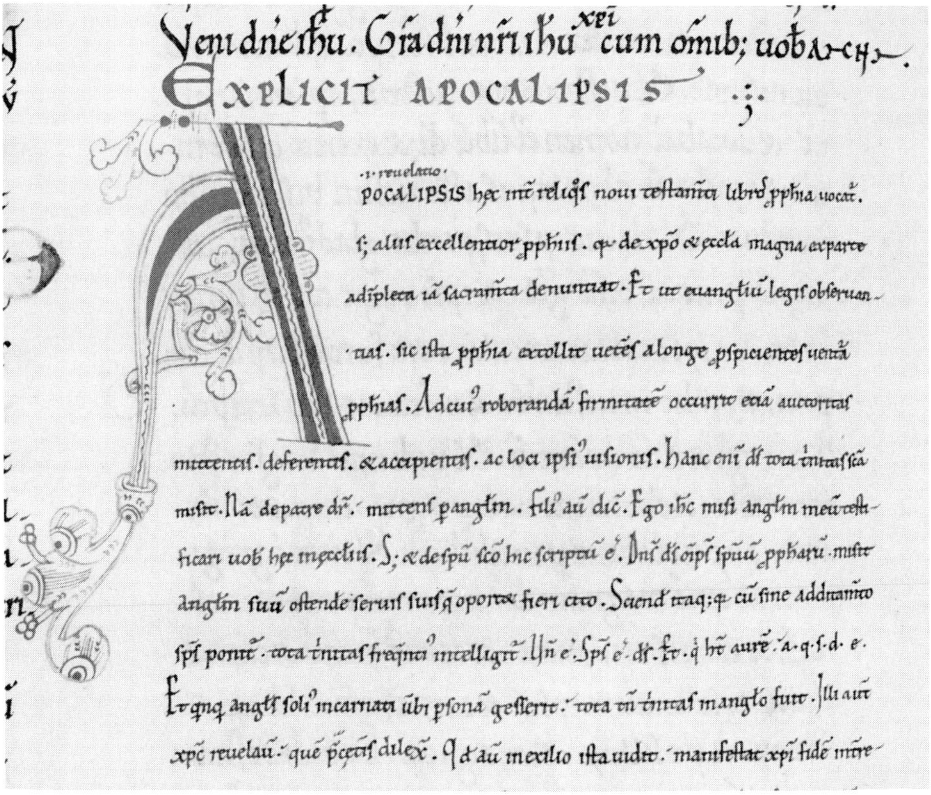

Plate 4. a. DCL, MS A.II.4, fol. 170v (the 'Carilef Bible'; detail, actual size).

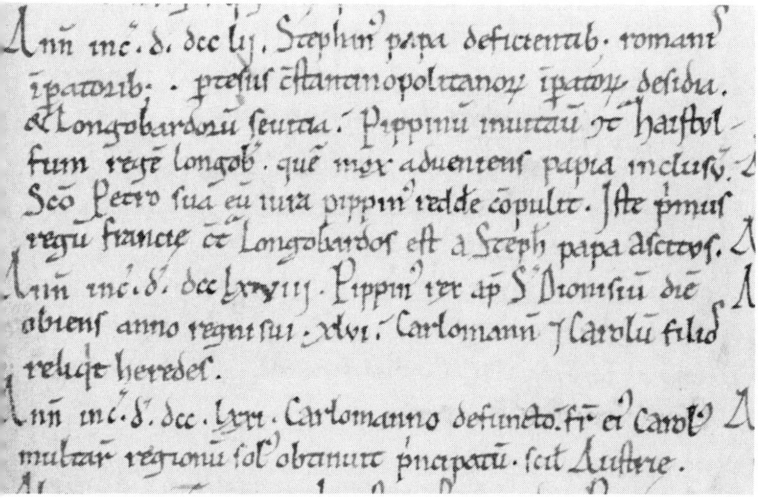

b. DCL, MS B.IV.22, fol. 4v (annals; detail, slightly enlarged).

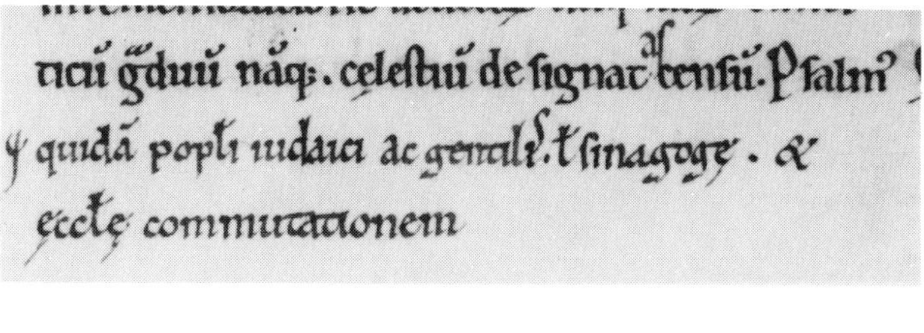

c. DCL, MS B.II.7, fol. 7v (Jerome, Commentary on Psalms; detail, actual size).

even sharp, and awkward. It may be an early example of the scribe's transition from the hand of Bodl.L Digby 175 to the hand of the Apocalypse commentary in DCL A.II.4. The writing is not entirely characteristic of the scribe, but this may be because it is transitional as well as because of the nature and importance of the document. However, the general impression which the hand makes on the eye and the occurrence of a number of idiosyncratic features found elsewhere in the scribe's work, make the attribution of the *conuentio* to the Martyrology scribe a safe one.

The hand of the Martyrology scribe also occurs in the following manuscripts, listed in roughly chronological order:

DCL, MS B.IV.13 (Gregory, Commentary on Ezechiel). Before 1096. The scribe corrected throughout. The two decorated initials are closely related to the scribe's style and technique and may have been executed either by him or under his direction.[30]

DCL, MS B.II.21 (Augustine, letters). Before 1096. The scribe rubricated part of the manuscript.[31]

DCL, MS B.II.6, fols 79–96 (Augustine, *De decem chordis*). Before 1096. The scribe rubricated the opening title and executed the opening initial (pl. 3b).[32]

DCL, MS B.IV.12 (Augustine, short works). Mid-1090s. The scribe wrote two short passages as models, rubricated part of the manuscript, and executed several initials (pl. 3c). The principal initial contains a rare structural device found in the scribe's work and must have been executed under his direction or influence (pl. 3d and pls. 2c and 3a).[33]

DCL, MS A.IV.16, fols. 66–109 (Augustine, *In Genesis ad litteram*). s.xi/xii. The scribe wrote the copy for the *incipits* and *explicits* in the margins and corrected throughout.[34]

BL, MS Harley 491 (*Gesta Normannorum*). After 1096 to 1100, perhaps in, or soon after, the first decade of the twelfth century. The scribe wrote the first eight lines, corrected throughout and probably wrote all of the quire signatures.[35]

BL, MS Harley 4688 (Bede, Commentary on Proverbs). Probably in or about the second decade of the twelfth century. The scribe wrote the opening six leaves.[36]

---

[30] *DCM*, no. 43 and Lawrence, 'Manuscripts at Durham', pl. 8.21.

[31] *DCM*, no. 34.

[32] *DCM*, no. 46.

[33] *DCM*, no. 59. The style and colouring of the principal initial are identical to the principal initial in another Durham manuscript, DCL, B.II.21, fol.12 (*DCM*, pl. 23 and Lawrence, 'Manuscripts at Durham', pl. 8.4). Both initials are adjacent to rubrication by the Martyrology scribe. In DCL, B.IV.12 the scribe wrote fol. 47, lines 1–15 and fol. 119, line 27/5 to the end of the page.

[34] *DCM*, no. 100.

[35] *DCM*, no. 84 and E.M.C. van Houts, *The Gesta Normannorum Ducum of William of Jumièges, Orderic Vitalis and Robert of Torigni*, I (Oxford, 1992), p. xcviii. The scribe wrote fol. 3, lines 1–10.

[36] *DCM*, no. 63. The scribe wrote fols. 1–7, line 7.

DCL, MS Hunter 100 (Treatises on the Calendar). After 1100, probably by 1110. The scribe wrote the opening leaves of a work by Robert of Lotharingia.[37]

Cambridge, Jesus College, MS Q.A.14 (14) (Bede, Commentary on Genesis and *De tabernaculo*). Probably in or about the second decade of the twelfth century. The scribe corrected throughout, wrote some, if not all, of the quire signatures and wrote the copy for the *incipits* and *explicits* for the second work in the margins.[38]

DCL, MS B.II.7 (Jerome, Commentary on Psalms). Probably in or about the second decade of the twelfth century. The scribe corrected the opening leaves (pl. 4c).[39]

DCL, MS B.IV.22, fols. 3–5 (Annals). In or soon after 1125. The scribe wrote and rubricated the leaves (pl. 4b).[40]

Glasgow, University Library, MS Hunterian T.4.2 (85) (Treatises on the Calendar). Probably some years either side of 1120. The scribe wrote the Annals in the margins for the years 532–1063.[41]

The scribe wrote the following single sheet documents:

DCDCM, Misc. Ch. 556. King Edgar (1097-1107) to Durham. The writing suggests a date nearer 1097 than 1107.[42]

DCDCM, Misc. Ch. 558. King Edgar to Durham. The writing suggests a date nearer 1107 than 1097 (pl. 5b).[43]

DCDCM, Misc. Ch. 722. A letter of Thor Longus to Earl David concerning a grant of the former to Durham. Perhaps between 1107 and 1117.[44]

DCDCM, 2.1.Pont.10. A precept of Bishop Ranulf Flambard. Between 1122 and 1128.[45]

DCDCM, 2.1.Pont.11. Another precept of Ranulf. Between *c.*1122 and 1127.[46]

DCDCM, 2.1.Pont.1. The important charter of Ranulf restoring to the monks all that he had taken away from them since his accession as bishop. *c.*1128.[47]

---

[37] *DCM*, no. 57 and W. Levison, 'Die *Annales Lindisfarnenses et Dunelmenses*, kritisch untersucht und neu herausgegeben', *Deutsches Archiv für Erforschung des Mittelalters* 17 (1961), at pp. 452–8. The scribe wrote fols. 17–19v, line 10.

[38] *DCM*, no. 69.

[39] *DCM*, no. 67. The psi used as an insertion sign preceding the correction reproduced here from this manuscript (pl. 4c) is the usual sign used by the scribe throughout his work.

[40] *DCM*, no. 117, where dated too early, as in or soon after 1115.

[41] *DCM*, no. 71 and Levison, '*Annales Lindisfarnenses et Dunelmenses*', at pp. 458–89. I know this MS only from microfilm. The scribe probably wrote not only the Annals on fols. 18–24v but also the Tables on the same leaves and also appears to have annotated and glossed several of the other works in the manuscript. (I am grateful to Jo Story for her help with this and the preceding manuscript.)

[42] *ESC*, no. 20. In line 3 the words 'cum diuissis sicut liulf habuit', with the following *punctus eleuatus*, were carefully writen over erasure by another scribe.

[43] *ESC*, no. 22. There are miserable facsimiles of this and the preceding charter in *Facsimiles of National Manuscripts of Scotland*, I (Southampton, 1867), pls. 3 and 4.

[44] *ESC*, no. 33.

[45] *DEC*, no. 17.

[46] *DEC*, no. 20.

[47] *DEC*, no. 24.

DCDCM, 2.1.Pont.2. Another important charter of Ranulf restoring to the monks the liberties they had enjoyed at his accession. 1128.[48]

The Martyrology scribe added material to the following manuscripts which had already been written:

DCL, MS A.II.4, fol. 1 (List of books given by William of St Calais to Durham). In or soon after 1096. The writing was influenced by the superb hand of the scribe of the manuscript itself, the Carilef Bible.[49]

DCL, MS B.IV.13. The scribe wrote, at different times, some short theological notes on a formerly blank endleaf.[50]

DCL, MS B.II.21. The scribe wrote two excerpts from letters of Augustine (the manuscript contains the saint's letters) and some other, unidentified, excerpts.[51]

In the Cantor's Book the scribe wrote several of the *conuentiones* between Durham and other houses and individuals, part of one and the whole of another of two letters of Anselm, a title to the Latin Rule, written in red, many of the earliest obits, including of members of the Durham community, in the margins of the Martyrology, and all of the earliest liturgical ordinances (fig. 2, scribe A).[52]

In the *Liber Vitae* the scribe wrote a considerable proportion of the twelfth-century matter which can be dated to about the first quarter of the century, including *conuentiones* and lists of names.[53]

Cambridge, Peterhouse, MS 74. Nearly all the pre-1130 additions to the manuscript, which are extensive, were written by the scribe over a period of time.[54] The additions have been characterized as 'disorderly' but are the only evidence in the surviving English-owned manuscripts of the *Collectio Lanfranci* of an attempt to

---

[48] *DEC*, no. 25. In his commentary Offler stated that this and the preceding charter were not written by the same scribe, which is certainly wrong.

[49] *DCM*, no. 30 and Gullick, 'The Scribe of the Carilef Bible', at p. 63 and fig. 1.

[50] *DCM*, no. 43.

[51] *DCM*, no. 34.

[52] For the *conuentiones* on fol. 5 see *DCM*, pl. 33. The scribe wrote lines 21–9 (including Bardney at the end of line 20) and line 34 to the end of the page. The one *conuentio* on fol. 127 was printed by Rud, *Codicum*, p. 210.

[53] For example, fol. 17v, col. a, last two names, and col. b, last four, fol. 25v, lines 1–5, archbishops and canons of Rouen, datable to after 1111 and probably before 1128, fol. 36, col. c, lines 1–16, fol. 36v, lines 1–15 and 20–4, fol. 52v, lines 20 and 25–9, the *conuentio* on lines 25–6, between Ilbert de Lacy and Durham, datable to before 1093–1100, by when Ilbert was dead, and fol. 55v most of the names in the lower half, from line 17, *herebertus* onward.

[54] *DCM*, no. 50. The additions are listed in M.R. James, *Descriptive Catalogue of the Manuscripts in the Library of Peterhouse*, (Cambridge, 1899), pp. 90–3, and the papal documents are listed in *Papsturkunden in England*, ed. W. Holtzman (3 vols., Berlin, 1930–52), III, 69–70.

The additions not written by the scribe are two letters of Pope Paschal and one of Henry I (fols. 117–18, line 4), three letter of Pope Innocent II (fol. 120r–v) and a letter of Thurstan archbishop of York (fol. 217). The papal letters on fol. 117r–v were written in a small, prickly continental hand by a scribe who probably also wrote a number of *conuentiones* in the Cantor's Book (fol. 5, lines 1–20, *DCM*, pl. 33) and copies of three royal charters and a list of lands held in Yorkshire by Durham in the *Liber Vitae* (fols. 54v–55). The letter of Henry I was probably written by the Norman scribe William.

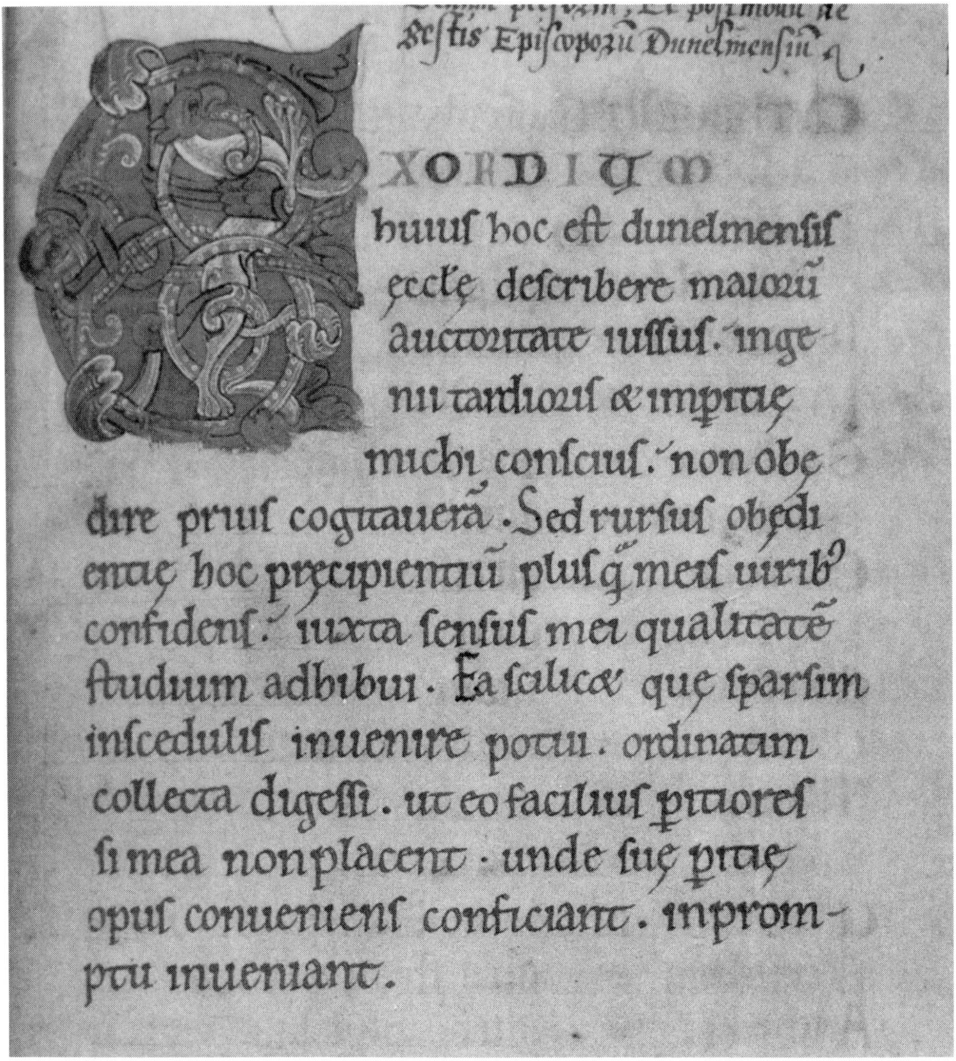

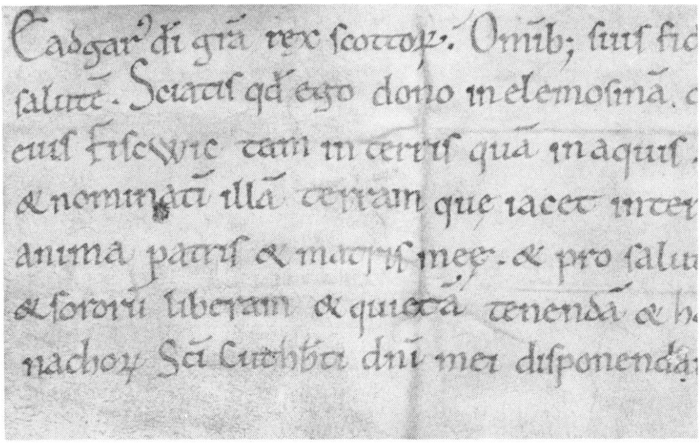

XORDIVM
huius hoc est dunelmensis
eccłę describere maioru̅
auctoritate iussus. inge
nii tardioris & impitię
michi conscius. non obe
dire prius cogitaueram. Sed rursus obedi
entię hoc precipientiu̅ plusq̄ meis uirib9
confidens. iuxta sensus mei qualitate̅
studium adhibui. Ea scilicet que sparsim
inscedulis inuenire potui. ordinatim
collecta digessi. ut eo facilius priores
si mea non placent. unde sue prtię
opus conueniens conficiant. inprom-
ptu inueniant.

Plate 5.   a. DUL, MS Cosin V.ii.6, fol. 6r (Symeon of Durham's *Libellus de exordio*: detail, actual size).

b. DCDM, Misc. Ch. 558 (charter of King Edgar of Scots for Durham; detail, actual size).

provide a 'continuous expansion' of the work.[55] These include extracts from papal decrees and councils, Jerome and Augustine, and a number of papal letters. The account of the first Lateran Council (1123) is the earliest English witness and may have been one of the last additions made by the scribe to the manuscript.[56]

The list of the Martyrology scribe's work is complete for the charters but perhaps not for the manuscripts. However, enough work has been firmly identified to outline the career of the scribe. He appears to have worked first for William of St Calais, perhaps even in Normandy before coming to England, but not necessarily based all the time in Durham. He was soon also working for the Durham community and it could only have been as a member of the community that he came to supervise the work of other scribes.

The material that the scribe added to earlier manuscripts reveals that he must have been a figure of considerable importance. No other contemporary Durham scribe can be compared to the Martyrology scribe in the range and extent of his work. Some of the material added by him to earlier manuscripts, such as the obits and liturgical ordinances in the Cantor's Book, would have been the responsibility of the cantor. At this date, the first quarter of the twelfth century, a monastic cantor is as likely to have been his own scribe as to have directed others to execute work for him. It is perfectly possible that the Martyrology scribe ended his career as cantor but if this were so it ought to be possible to name him. There is one obvious candidate: the historian Symeon of Durham.

To judge by his position in the lists of Durham monks in the *Liber Vitae* and the earliest manuscript of Symeon's own *Libellus de exordio*, the historian entered the Durham community in the early 1090s.[57] He is known to have been the cantor in, or soon after, 1126 and the coincidence of these dates with the career of the Martyrology scribe is striking.[58] Fortunately this coincidence is not all, for there is some palaeographical evidence which supports the identification of the scribe with the historian.

DUL, Cosin MS V.ii.6 is the earliest manuscript of Symeon's *Libellus de exordio*, datable between 1104 and 1109.[59] Soon after it was written (by one fine scribe)[60] and decorated, a number of substantial passages were thoroughly erased and a

[55] M. Brett, 'The *Collectio Lanfranci* and its competitors', in *Intellectual Life in the Middle Ages. Essays presented to Margaret Gibson*, ed. L. Smith and B. Ward (London, 1992), at p. 161 and n. 14.

[56] D. Whitelock, M. Brett and C.N.L. Brooke, *Councils and Synods with other documents relating to the English Church. I. AD 871–1204* (2 vols, Oxford, 1981), II, 728–30.

[57] Symeon is no. 42 in the *Liber Vitae* list (fol. 45) and no. 38 in the *Libellus de exordio* list (DUL, Cosin V.ii.6, fol. 7v). For Symeon's entry into the Durham community see B. Meehan, 'Outsiders, Insiders and Property in Durham around 1100', *Studies in Church History* 12 (1975), at pp. 57–8.

[58] H. Farmer, 'The Vision of Orm', *Analecta Bollandiana* 75 (1957), p. 76.

[59] *DCM*, no. 86.

[60] Fig. 2 (scribe C) and see pp. 95, 97 and n. 15 above.

second scribe wrote some alterations and additions of an authorial nature. The scribe of this matter is almost certainly the Martyrology scribe.

The second scribe altered or corrected in six places in the text (ranging in length from one to six words), rewrote the opening of the preface over erasure (see pl. 5a) and added two names to the list of Durham monks in a quire preceding the work.[61] The fundamental difference between the work of the scribe in the Cosin manuscript and the work attributed to the Martyrology scribe is its size. The writing in the Cosin manuscript is larger, and this, in combination with the nature and importance of the manuscript, led the scribe to write with unusual deliberation and formality. It is noticeable in the even proportion of the letters and their finish, in particular the serifs at the feet of minims. Despite this, the general impression of the hand in the Cosin manuscript, and many of its details also, are very close to the work of the Martyrology scribe.[62]

One piece of writing of the scribe close in date to the writing in the Cosin manuscript is DCDM, Misc. Ch. 558, datable between 1097 and 1107 (see pl. 5b).[63] The general aspect and proportion of the writing in the manuscript and charter are quite close. Despite the casual appearance of the writing of the charter, which was written quickly with little care taken in the finish of the letters, the similarities between the writing in the manuscript and charter are more pronounced than the differences. As with so much of the Martyrology scribe's work, it is necessary to see beyond the surface finish to the fundamental character of the hand. This is of crucial importance in the identification of the work in the Cosin manuscript with the work of the Martyrology scribe.

If the second scribe of the Cosin manuscript was Symeon, which appears likely, and if the scribe was the Martyrology scribe, which is virtually certain, the Martyrology scribe is likely to have been the Durham historian. If this is so, Symeon was responsible for a large body of scribal work, comparable in its extent to the work of his close contemporaries Eadmer of Canterbury, Orderic Vitalis, and William of Malmesbury, whose activities as scribes are well known.[64]

---

[61] The original scribe added one name, *Edmundus*, followed by two, *Alfredus* and *Normannus*, added by the second scribe in the same campaign as his work in the text. The second scribe later added further names to the list, *Thurstinus-Leuiat* (fol. 7v) and also attributable to the scribe are additions to the list of Durham monks in the *Liber Vitae*, *Thomas-Alanus* (fol. 45v cols. b–c).

[62] The similarities include the uneven texture or colour and horizontal alignment, and a distinct awkwardness in the execution. Common details include the long tail to the tailed *e*, the form and position of the *punctus eleuatus*, the (pointed) form of the 9 form of *-us*, and the forms of the (broad) ampersand, (narrow) *E* (so narrow that a later hand altered it in the Cosin manuscript, see pl. 5a, line 10), and *S*.

[63] See p. 105 and n. 43 above. The hand of the charter is very close to a *conuentio* written by the scribe in the *Liber Vitae* (fol. 36v, lines 20–24).

[64] I am deeply grateful to Alan Piper for his help, advice and encouragement during the preparation of this paper.

The Forged Charters of William the Conqueror and Bishop William of St Calais

DAVID BATES

WILLIAM GREENWELL was the first to recognise that the charters which are the subject of this paper were forgeries.[1] He attributed their production to between 1100 and 1125, a dating which has been subsequently and conclusively amended by H.S. Offler and G.V. Scammell, who both assign their compilation to the second half of the twelfth century. With a single exception, all the charters were printed by Canon Greenwell. The three supposed charters of Bishop William of St Calais were printed again according to the standards of twentieth-century charter scholarship and subjected to the most rigorous examination in Offler's edition of the *acta* of the first five Norman bishops of Durham.[2] The six royal *acta* will appear in my forthcoming edition of William the Conqueror's charters for the period between 1066 and 1087. This will include one previously unpublished Durham forgery.[3] It must also be made clear at the outset that these nine charters were part of a much more extensive campaign of fabrication. The monks of Durham also produced a bull of Pope Gregory VII and charters of King Henry I, Archbishops Lanfranc of Canterbury and Thomas and Thurstan of York to reinforce the claims which were being made in the forged royal and episcopal charters.[4] The earliest authentic Durham charters from the Norman period are a series of writs of William Rufus, of which five survive as originals.[5]

Conceptually – as is well known from a host of learned studies – medieval forgery can be very different from modern; the intention may well be neither to invent nor to deceive, but rather to authenticate in contemporary documentary

---

[1] *FPD*, pp.xxxi–lxxx.
[2] *DEC*, nos. 3a, 4, 7. Nos. 6 and 7 are also forged charters of Bishop William.
[3] *Regesta Regum Anglo-Normannorum: The Acta of William I, 1066–1087*, ed. D. Bates (Oxford, forthcoming), nos. 108–16. The previously unedited charter (no. 108) is taken from a late twelfth- or early thirteenth-century copy, DCDCM, 1.1. Reg., no. 18.
[4] The Gregory VII bull, of which the original does not survive, is published in *Papsturkunden in England*, ed. W. Holtzmann (3 vols.; Berlin, 1930–52), II, 132–6, no. 2. For the Henry I forgeries, see, most recently, *DEC*, nos. 3b and 4b. For the charters of the archbishops of York, see, most recently, *English Episcopal Acta: V, York 1070–1154*, ed. J.E. Burton (Oxford, 1988), nos. 3 and 43. For the Lanfranc diploma, *FPD*, pp. lxxv–lxxvi.
[5] *Facsimiles of English Royal Writs to A.D. 1100*, ed. T.A.M. Bishop and P. Chaplais (Oxford, 1957), plates VII–XI.

form rights and possessions which were already held, but for which appropriate written title was lacking. The Durham monastic community in the twelfth century should be seen as a self-perpetuating body, established in a politically unstable region and jealous of its status and privileges. Its activities in defence of these privileges are already well known and are the subject of several papers in this volume. The specific background to this set of forged charters was the persistent tensions between the bishop and the monks which were a feature of the episcopate of Hugh of le Puiset (1153–95).[6]

As far as charters are concerned, the story of fabrication begins before 1123. The *Liber Vitae* contains the text of what appears to be a diploma of Bishop William, which is apparently complete, except that there are no *signa*. As Offler recognised, its first part, a history of William of St Calais's establishment of a monastic community at Durham, is taken almost *verbatim* from the *Libellus de exordio atque procursu Dunelmensis ecclesie*, which was written at Durham between 1104 and 1107, and whose author is normally identified as Symeon of Durham. This unfinished diploma was another aspect of the process whereby the early history of the Durham monastic community was rewritten to convey an impression of religious improvement.[7] Its second part is an account of estates supposedly confirmed or granted by William the Conqueror. Offler's meticulous survey of these estates concluded 'in substance it probably represents pretty fairly what the monastery could have claimed to have acquired by the time of Bishop William's death in 1096.'[8] In detail, his observation is inaccurate – Hemingbrough in the East Riding of Yorkshire is, for example, not included, nor are William the Conqueror's gifts of Welton and Howden, which are both mentioned in the *Liber Vitae* and Domesday Book – but in its approach to the charter, it is spot on.[9]

This unfinished diploma belongs to a species of document of which understanding has deepened since Offler edited it, namely, the *pancartes* produced for a considerable number of religious communities in Normandy and England after 1066. The fundamental study is Lucien Musset's introduction to his edition of the *acta* of William the Conqueror and Queen Mathilda for the abbeys of St Étienne and La Trinité of Caen. This concluded that such documents evolved over time, that they were frequently edited versions of the grants and charters that they contained and that, as a result of this editing process, they can often contain chronological contradictions.[10] Musset's conclusions apply across a wider range of documents than were within his remit.[11] Some of these *pancartes* feature a short

<hr/>

[6] For a survey, based on a different view of the forged charters from the one taken here, G.V. Scammell, *Hugh du Puiset, Bishop of Durham* (Cambridge, 1956), pp.128–67.

[7] D. Rollason, 'Symeon of Durham and the Community of Durham in the Eleventh Century', in *England in the Eleventh Century*, ed. C. Hicks (Harlaxton Medieval Studies 2; Stamford, 1992), pp. 183–98.

[8] *DEC*, no. 3 and pp. 9–15.

[9] *Liber Vitae*, fol. 50v; and *DB*, I, fol. 304v.

[10] *Les actes de Guillaume le Conquérant et de la reine Mathilde pour les abbayes caennaises*, ed. L. Musset (Caen, 1967), pp. 25–35.

[11] See *Regesta*, ed. Bates, Introduction.

history of the religious community concerned and describe the properties it had acquired over a period of as much as thirty years. Some, like the Durham *pancarte*, were incomplete in the sense that *signa* were never added. It was possible for them to be carried round in search of additional *signa*, like the Lessay *pancarte*, which was certainly taken from Normandy to England and back to Normandy, almost after the manner of an obituary roll.[12] Such texts are known from post-Conquest England, most notably from newly founded or recently developed communities, such as the abbey of St Peter's Gloucester, or Lincoln cathedral.[13] The Durham diploma fits exactly into this scenario. The result of the documentary traditions of an era which was at its height in the late eleventh and early twelfth centuries, part administrative record and part literary text, it did not set out to pretend that the privileges of the cathedral and the monastic community were the product of a single great occasion. In these fundamental respects, it differs radically from the later fabrications for which it was a prime source.

The themes contained in the main forged charters of Bishop William and William the Conqueror are well known and need be rehearsed only briefly. They have been the subject of several studies.[14] The prior of Durham was to have tenure for life, his status was comparable to that of the dean of York and he was to have equivalent powers over the Durham archdeacons, he was to have an abbot's seat on the left side of the choir, the right to appoint and remove all monastic officials and the first say after the bishop in diocesan affairs and in episcopal elections. The prior and monks of Durham were to have absolute right to nominate incumbents to churches in their possession throughout England, with the bishop being specifically excluded from any role, and absolute right to dispose of their churches. The incumbents were to return all their revenues to the prior and the monks. With variations of wording, these liberties are hammered home in a series of charters. The main forged charters also describe properties supposedly granted by Bishop William and William the Conqueror. Others are devoted to the grant of a particular estate. The one unpublished forgery details the allowances which the prior and monks were to receive when they travelled to the royal court and deals with seating arrangements at royal, primatial and legatine councils.[15] The forged charters of the archbishops of York deal with the Durham community's possessions and franchises within the archbishopric.[16] The forged charter of Archbishop Lanfranc is a general confirmation of Durham's privileges and a confirmation of the status of the prior.[17]

Offler and Scammell suggested that the first stage in the production of this extensive range of forged charters was the interpolation and elaboration of the

---

[12] For a facsimile of this remarkable diploma, which was destroyed in 1944, *Musée des Archives Départementales* (Paris, 1878), planche XVIII; (for an edition, *Regesta*, ed. Bates, no. 175).
[13] *Regesta*, II, 410 (no. LXIa); *The Registrum Antiquissimum of the Cathedral Church of Lincoln*, I, ed. C.W. Foster (Lincoln Record Society; 1931), no. 3.
[14] *DEC*, passim; F. Barlow, *Durham Jurisdictional Peculiars* (Oxford, 1950), passim.
[15] DCDCM, 1.1. Reg. no. 18 (*Regesta*, ed. Bates, no. 108).
[16] *English Episcopal Acta: V, York*, ed. Burton, nos. 3, 43.
[17] *FPD*, pp. lxxv–lxxvi.

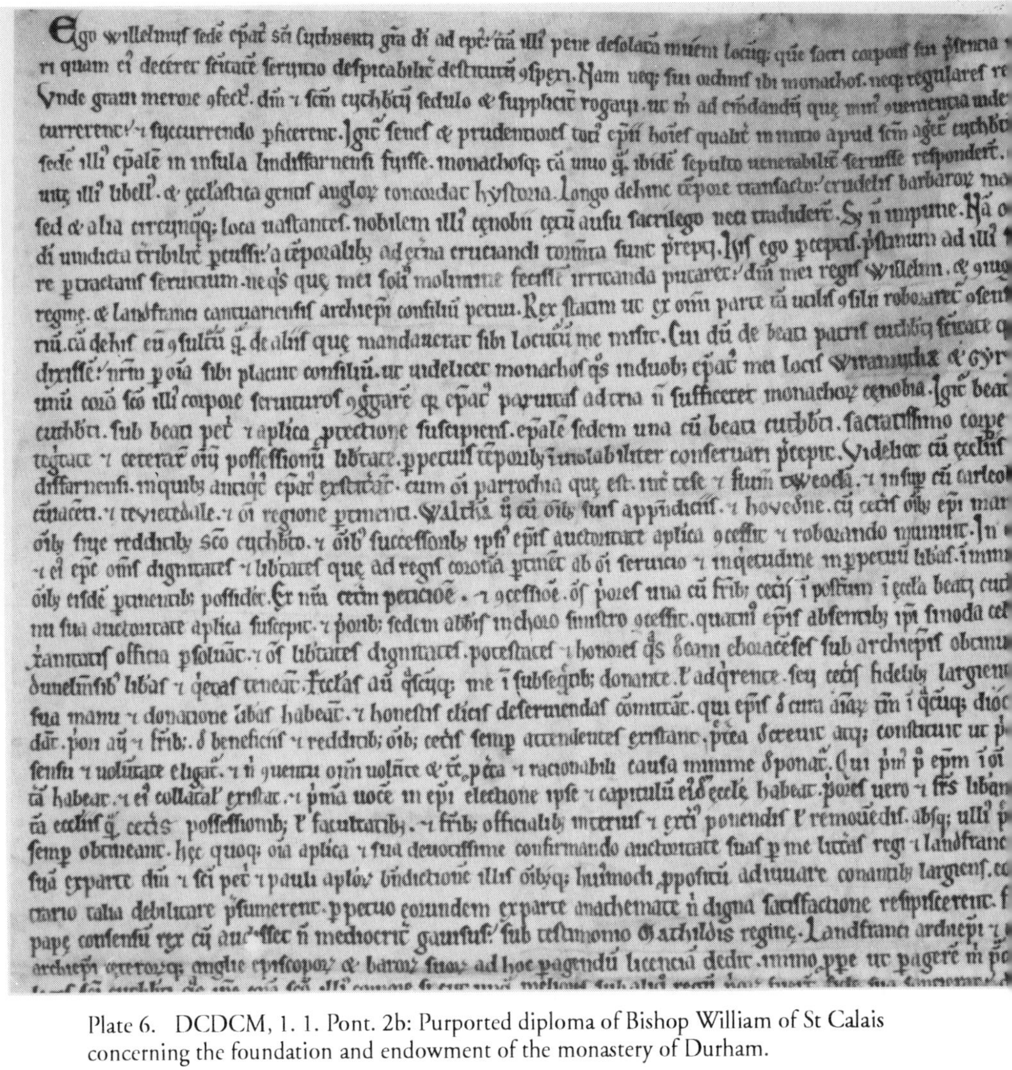

Plate 6. DCDCM, 1. 1. Pont. 2b: Purported diploma of Bishop William of St Calais concerning the foundation and endowment of the monastery of Durham.

unfinished *Liber Vitae* diploma in the 1160s.[18] Both argued that the resulting document, whose original survives, was probably the *authenticum scriptum* of Bishop William which Pope Alexander III confirmed in general terms in 1165 (pl. 6).[19] As Offler's edition shows, the new diploma was basically a version of the *Liber Vitae* text into which were inserted a statement that the bishopric should include Carlisle and Teviotdale and the list of the liberties of the priors and monks. The palaeographical evidence largely supports Offler's and Scammell's dating, although the hand could well belong to the first half of the twelfth century, rather than to the second. Offler was right to reject Scammell's suggestion that the same scribe wrote diplomas of Archbishops Lanfranc and Thomas, both of which are forgeries of a later date related to the main forged royal and episcopal charters.[20] The author of the forged diploma attributed the grant it contained to a meeting of the royal council which met in London in 1082 and added a long list of witnesses, several of whom were dead by 1082. His date of 1082 probably derives from Symeon's date of 1083 for the introduction of the monastic community at Durham and from his account of Bishop William's journeys to seek papal approval; the grants ought logically to precede the foundation of the community. It is not, however, entirely implausible, since Bishop William and the king were in each other's company in the south of England late in the year 1082.[21]

The production of this diploma was the prelude to an extensive campaign of charter-writing. Both Scammell and Offler did a great deal of work on the hands of the charters and made a number of identifications which are in general acceptable. They also examined the relationship between the various texts and showed how closely interdependent they all were. Neither, however, emphasised quite as forcefully as is, I think, necessary, the single-mindedness with which the production of forgeries was approached nor the role of a single scribe in the majority of the work. They also disagreed about the date at which the forgeries were produced. Offler argued that the majority should be dated to the 1170s and that the main text from which others were probably derived was written before 1174. Scammell favoured after *c*.1185.

Prima facie neither set of arguments is either conclusive or entirely convincing. Offler suggested the 1170s because his key forgery (1.1. Pont. 3a; pl. 7) mentions the Durham claim to Tynemouth priory, which was a live issue in the early 1170s, but which was settled against Durham in November 1174. He pointed out that a slightly later version of the same charter omitted Tynemouth, and that the former document ought therefore to have been composed while the dispute was going on and the latter after the settlement.[22] This may be right, but it is open to the

---

[18] Scammell, *Puiset*, p. 302; and *DEC*, p. 21.
[19] DCDCM, 1.1. Pont. 2b; *DEC*, no. 3a, and Holtzmann, *Papsturkunden*, II, 311, no. 120. The bull refers to 'libertates Dunelmensis ecclesie prioribus a bone memorie Willelmo quondam Dunelmensi episcopo canonice concessas'.
[20] *DEC*, p. 20.
[21] *Regesta*, I, no. 147 (*Regesta*, ed. Bates, no. 252).
[22] *DEC*, p. 31.

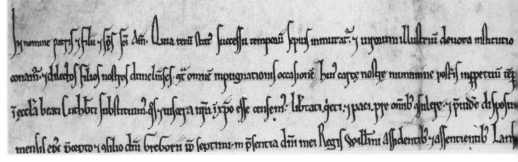

Plate 7.   DCDCM, 1. 1. Pont. 3a: Purported charter of Bishop William of St Calais
enumerating privileges and possessions granted to the prior and monks of Durham.

objection that the technique of producing a forged charter to aid recovery from a
set-back in a legal dispute was a very common one; it should also be noted that the
church of Tynemouth is mentioned in a further forged charter of Bishop William
of St Calais which both Scammell and Offler have dated to c.1190.[23] Scammell
built much of his case around his identification of the forger's hand in a charter of
Archbishop Roger of York confirming in general terms the liberties of the Durham
community (pl. 10). He believed the charter to be forged, that it must have been
written after the archbishop's death in 1181 and that it was part of a larger
campaign of forgery.[24] There is no doubt that he was right to suggest that this
document was written by the same scribe as the forged charters. There are, however, two problems with this line of reasoning. The first is that the charter might
not be forged, but might rather be a charter written on the archbishop's behalf by
its beneficiary's scribe. The second is that, even if it were a forgery, the charter
might be a later product intended to consolidate a case already built up in earlier
forged charters. Fortunately, there are alternative lines of attack on the whole
problem. Neither Offler nor Scammell apparently looked for other examples of the
forger's work in the Durham archive. As we shall see, the result of such an enquiry
confirms in all essentials Offler's dating.

Offler rightly identified 1.1. Pont. 3a (pl. 7) as the key text, since all the other
forgeries apparently derive from it in one way or another. It purports to be a
confirmation of the liberties and possessions of the prior and monks by Bishop
William in the fourth year of his episcopate in the king's presence at a council in
London. It is sealed with a specimen of Bishop William's forged seal.[25] As Offler
pointed out, the same scribe also wrote a second version of this same charter,[26] a
revised version of the earlier diploma based on the *Liber Vitae*,[27] and a supposed

---

23 *DEC*, no. 7.
24 Scammell, *Puiset*, p. 303.
25 *DEC*, no. 4, MS. A (1.1. Pont. 3a).
26 *DEC*, no. 4, MS. B (1.1. Pont. 3b).
27 *DEC*, no. 3a, MS. A (1.1. Pont. 2a).

Plate 8. DCDCM, 1. 1. Reg. 9: Purported diploma of William the Conqueror granting Hemingbrough to Durham.

grant by Bishop William of the churches in Allertonshire.[28] To this list can be added one of two texts of a revision of 1.1. Pont. 3a.[29] With the exception of a second revised version of 1.1. Pont. 3a (1.1. Pont. 4b), which was written by a scribe who also wrote a forged diploma of William the Conqueror,[30] and the supposed Bishop William diploma of the year 1093, which was certainly written at a later date,[31] a single scribe can therefore be shown to have been responsible for almost all the forged episcopal *acta*. Not only this, he also wrote the diploma by which William the Conqueror supposedly granted Hemingbrough to Durham (pl. 8),[32] and he was almost certainly the scribe of a William the Conqueror forgery (1.1. Reg. 11) which confirmed the liberties of the prior and monks of Durham, and included a list of estates which William had supposedly restored to the church and which also appears in the *Liber Vitae* diploma.[33] Many of the characteristic features of his script also appear on the forged charters of Archbishops Lanfranc and Thomas.

Offler also rightly suggested that 1.1. Pont. 3a was the source for a second William the Conqueror charter confirming the liberties of the prior and monks of Durham (1.1. Reg. 1),[34] and that this royal charter was the source for a forged charter of Henry I.[35] Pierre Chaplais has pointed out that this supposed Henry I charter is sealed with a forged exemplar of Henry I's third seal.[36] Both Greenwell and Offler correctly indicated that 1.1. Reg. 1 was written by the same scribe as

[28] *DEC*, no. 6 (4.1. Archiep. 1).
[29] *DEC*, no. 4a, MS. A (1.1. Pont. 4a). This identification is my own and does not appear in *DEC*.
[30] *DEC*, no. 4a, MS. B (1.1. Pont. 4b).
[31] *DEC*, no. 7.
[32] DCDCM, 1.1. Reg. 9 (*Regesta*, ed. Bates, no. 115).
[33] DCDCM, 1.1. Reg. 11 (*Regesta*, ed. Bates, no. 109).
[34] *DEC*, p. 33; see *Regesta*, ed. Bates no. 110.
[35] *DEC*, p. 33.
[36] P. Chaplais, 'The Seals and Original Charters of Henry I', *EHR*, 75 (1960), at p. 275; reprinted in idem, *Essays in Medieval Diplomacy and Administration* (London, 1981), ch. 20 at p. 275.

Plate 9. DCDCM, Misc. Ch. 602.

one of the two texts of the forged Bishop William charter, 1.1. Pont. 4b.[37] This second forger's work is clearly closely related to that of the main scribe of the forgeries. Not only did he produce a second text of a charter written by the main forger, but also the contents of his 1.1. Reg. 1 are very close to the main forger's William the Conqueror charter, 1.1. Reg. 11, differing only in including a passage placing the prior of Durham on the same level as the dean of York and in stating that the Durham monks had the right to dispose freely of their lands and churches. Otherwise it tends to express the material in 1.1. Reg. 11 more succinctly. Scammell commented that it was 'a more concise recension of earlier material'.[38] It is probable that this scribe worked either alongside or shortly after the main forger.

Two surviving originals of the same William the Conqueror charter stand some way outside this group (1.1. Reg. 2a and 1.1. Reg. 2b). The second of these carries a royal seal which Scammell wrongly suggested was Henry II's; it is in fact the second seal of King Stephen.[39] According to both Greenwell and Scammell, 1.1. Reg. 2a had the seal of Prior Bertram, appointed in 1189, attached to it. Although there are traces of red wax on the sealing cords, I have not been able to trace this seal.[40] The supposed presence of Prior Bertram's seal was one factor, along with his general views on the date of the forgeries, which led Scammell to date this particular forgery to the last decade of the twelfth century. Its close verbal parallels with 1.1. Reg. 1 and 1.1. Reg. 11 suggest, however, that if they are earlier, then it too ought to be earlier; Prior Bertram's seal could easily have been added later. It is most likely a shorter version of the same family of diplomas concerned with the liberties of the prior and the monks. Texts of two other forged William the Conqueror diplomas survive in later copies. One, available only in cartulary copies, is yet another statement of the liberties of the prior and the monks, with many verbal similarities to 1.1. Reg. 1, 1.1. Reg. 11, and 1.1. Reg. 2a/2b. The last one

---

[37] DEC, p. 36.
[38] Scammell, Puiset, pp. 303–4.
[39] Ibid., p. 305.
[40] Ibid., p. 305. Alan Piper has kindly confirmed that the seal cannot now be traced among the Durham muniments. Although the matter cannot at present be resolved, it is important to recognise that Greenwell was an exceptionally conscientious scholar.

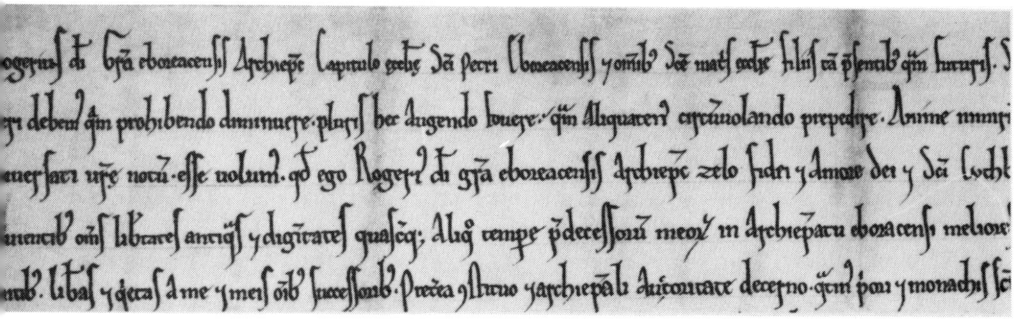

Plate 10. DCDCM, 1. 1. Archiep. 4.

deals with the Durham monks' allowances at the royal court and the seating arrangements for ecclesiastical councils. It is preserved in a copy on a late twelfth- or early thirteenth-century parchment, along with the incomplete text of a charter of Bishop Ranulf Flambard.[41] It draws on the same reservoir of phrases and claims.

The scribe who wrote the majority of the surviving original forged charters also wrote three charters for the Durham community on behalf of William the Lion, king of Scots. He also produced a fourth Scottish royal charter for the abbey of Jedburgh. All four documents can be located within the chronological period between 1165 and 1171 (pl. 9).[42] Geoffrey Barrow expressed no anxieties about the authenticity of these documents, and, although he did not say as much, because he did not have to notice the scribe's other work at Durham, it is clear that they are documents written outside the Scottish royal chancery, in three cases by a scribe supplied by the beneficiary. The scribe's hand also appears on two other Durham charters, a chirograph dated 1155 and a notification of the result of the hearing concerning Tynemouth priory, which must date from 1174.[43] This evidence is crucial for dating the main campaign of forgery. It shows that the career of the scribe responsible for the majority of the forged charters can be dated roughly to the period between the mid-1150s and the mid-1170s.

This evidence of twenty years of scribal activity suggests that the charter of Archbishop Roger of York, which Scammell believed to be a forgery of the 1180s, is an authentic charter dating from between 1154 and 1166 (pl. 10).[44] It was undoubtedly produced by the same scribe as all the other documents. It is notable for the absence of any echoes of the phraseology and language of the forged charters; Archbishop Robert confirmed to the prior and the monks 'omnes libertates antiquas et dignitates quascunque aliquo tempore predecessorum meorum in

[41] DCDCM, 1.1. Reg. 18; see further, *DEC*, no. 25.
[42] The Durham charters are Misc. Ch. 596, 602, and 609. All three have been edited in *RRS*, II, nos. 46, 66A, and 105B. For the Jedburgh charter and for a summary of the scribe's work, ibid., p. 86 and no. 62.
[43] DCDCM, 1.8. Spec. 34; and DCDCM, 2.2. Spec. 15.
[44] DCDCM, 1.1. Archiep. no. 4; printed, Scammell, *Puiset*, pp. 265–6, no. 14, who also suggests the dating limits.

archiepiscopatu Eboracensi meliores habuerunt' and that they should hold all their churches and chapels *secundum morem antiquum*. The incumbents were not obliged to attend the York diocesan synod and they were justiciable before St Cuthbert's court.[45] The charter's witnesses date it to between 1154 and 1166 and it was presumably written on the archbishop's behalf by the Durham scribe. Scammell argued that because a confirmation by Pope Lucius III of between 1182 and 1183 granted to Durham the liberties specified in the charters of Archbishops Thomas and Thurstan, and because Bishop Hugh and the monks sent attested copies of these charters for the pope's inspection between 1185 and 1187, Archbishop Roger's charter had not yet been compiled.[46] It is, however, much more likely that so loosely worded a document was kept in the background. The Thomas charter in particular refers to the other forgeries and is redolent of the forger's language.[47] The hand which wrote it has many similarities with that of the main forger. What had become vital to the Durham cause by the 1180s was not what had been granted or confirmed by a recent archbishop of York, but the range of grants supposedly made when monks were introduced at Durham, a collection of material which had been manufactured in an even more recent past.

The evidence therefore justifies Offler's basic suggestion that the majority of the forged charters were produced in the early 1170s. It is possible that the date should be a little earlier. The sheer scale of the material also confirms his remark that the Durham forgeries constituted a 'programme'.[48] This is demonstrated by the chronology that they sought to create, their contents and their attestations.

The chronology of the first main forged episcopal charter (1.1. Pont. 3a) and the three chief forged royal charters was purposefully coordinated. The first is dated to the fourth year of Bishop William's episcopate, that is to 1084. The three royal forgeries are dated to a council held at Westminster in the eighteenth year of the Conqueror's reign, that is to the period between 25 December 1083 and 25 December 1084. It is probable that our scribe chose this year for no better reason than that it was the closest one available to the magic year of 1083. He had after all already improved a forged diploma which bore the date of 1082. The new, better, ones had best be later in date, but they had also best be close to the year when monks had been introduced at Durham. As has long been recognised, the attestations to these diplomas are impossible ones for the year 1084.[49] It should also be noted that almost all the surviving evidence suggests that William was in Normandy throughout the year 1084.[50]

The use of similar phrases and language across the range of forged charters is

---

[45] For the Durham franchise within the archbishopric of York, Barlow, *Jurisdictional Peculiars*, pp. 53–69.
[46] *Papsturkunden*, ed. Holtzmann, II, no. 223.
[47] E.g., 'Nam post priuilegium Guillelmi fratris nostri Dun(elmensis) episcopi tam ego quam Lanfrancus Cantuariensis archiepiscopus litteris nostris subscripsimus et sigillis propriis concessimus et confirmauimus' (*English Episcopal Acta: V, York*, ed. Burton, no. 3).
[48] *DEC*, p. 33.
[49] *FPD*, pp.xxxvii–lxxiv; *Regesta*, I, nos. 195, 196, 197, 205.
[50] William was in Normandy on 18 July 1083 and presumably remained there during the fatal

obvious and striking. Thus, for example, on the prior's status as an abbot, the Bishop William charter written by the main forger has 'omnes futuri priores Dunelmensis ecclesie omnes libertates, dignitates et honores abbatis obtineant, et sedem abbatis in choro sinistro habeant', while a forged William the Conqueror charter has 'omnes priores Dunelmensis ecclesie qui futuri sunt, omnes dignitates et honores abbatis optineant, et sedem abbatis in choro sinistro habeant'.[51] The phrase 'et iure decani primum locum et uocem post episcopum et in episcopi sui electione cum capitulo suo teneant' occurs verbatim in both a Bishop William charter and the two main forged royal charters.[52] The scale of the interdependence is very great and the slavishness of the copying notable. It can only be fully appreciated once the new edition of the royal charters is available to set them alongside the episcopal. The variations from a common set of phrases tend to be minor ones. Thus, one royal charter has a passage which places the prior of Durham on the same level as the dean of York, whereas another does not.[53] In the same way that Offler suggested that one version of an episcopal charter was an abbreviation of another,[54] so the William I forgery which confines itself to the rights of the prior may well be an abbreviated version of the longer royal charters.[55] With the important exceptions of the Gregory VII bull and the supposed Bishop William diploma of 1093, I do not think that we should consider the Durham forgeries as a series of texts fabricated over a longish period of time. The borrowing is such as to suggest a concerted campaign of fabrication.

The charter compiled before 1165 on the basis of the *Liber Vitae* has a bank of *signa* on which all the other forged charters drew.[56] It has a list of fifteen archbishops and bishops, who include two Normans, Bishops Odo of Bayeux and Geoffrey of Coutances. All were in office during the period between 1072/3 and 1075.[57] The possibility that the list has been taken from a lost record of an ecclesiastical council or diploma of that period is increased by the description of Bishop Remigius as *Remigio Dorcensi vel Lincolniensi*, a title which reflects the usage

---

illness which killed his wife Mathilda on 2 November 1083 (*Regesta*, ed. Bates, no. 64). A charter whose dating-clause is internally contradictory should probably be interpreted in terms of his being in France on 9 January 1084, ibid., no. 251, and there are two charters which record a visit to Rouen during 1084, ibid., nos. 163, 247. It is generally thought that William also spent a considerable part of 1084 in Maine attending to the siege of Ste Suzanne, *Orderic*, IV, 48, n. 3. The only evidence to suggest a visit to England is the reference in *ASC*, 'E', *s.a.* 1083 to the six shilling geld, but this is not decisive.

[51] *DEC*, no. 4; *Regesta*, ed. Bates, no. 109. Another forged William I charter has 'omnes priores Dunelmensis ecclesie, qui futuri sunt, omnes libertates, consuetudines, et dignitates, et honores abbatis optineant, et sedem abbatis in choro sinistro habeant' (*Regesta*, ed. Bates, no. 110).

[52] *DEC*, no. 4; *Regesta*, ed. Bates, nos. 109, 110.

[53] *Regesta*, ed. Bates, nos. 109, 110.

[54] Offler describes *DEC*, no. 4a, as 'an abbreviated and rearranged version' of no. 4.

[55] Compare *Regesta*, ed. Bates, no. 111 to nos. 109 and 110.

[56] *DEC*, no. 3a.

[57] The limits are the appointment of Bishop Peter of Lichfield in 1072/3 and the death of Bishop William of London in 1075.

of the mid-1070s.[58] But the scribe lets himself down by calling Bishop Herfast the inaccurate *Hemeanensi episcopo uel Norwicensi*. The sophistication of his methods should not be over-estimated; it may be that he compiled a list from a variety of sources. The charter's list of eight abbots is a chronological nonsense, since it includes Abbot Aethelwig of Evesham, who died in 1077, and Abbot Thurstan of Glastonbury, who was appointed in 1081 or 1082; this collection suggests no more than random selection from lost sources. Eleven out of the twenty laymen and chaplains who appear among the *signa* have been taken from a record, which still survives in the Durham archives, of a dispute settled before King William II. They include names such as Richard de Couci, who had very little land in England under the Conqueror and who witnesses no known English charter of William I, Robert de Montfort, who did not succeed to his family's English lands until after the Conqueror's death and such familiar witnesses to Rufus's charters as Urse d'Abetôt, Haimo *dapifer* and Roger Bigod. The text of the William II settlement is preserved at Durham on an early twelfth-century single sheet of parchment, along with an unquestionably authentic writ of Henry I.[59] For his lay *signa*, the forger simply plundered a document in his own archives.

This same group of *signa* – sometimes referred to as *testes* – occur with additions and deletions in most of the other forgeries. The main forger, for example, selected eight of the bishops, six of the abbots, and eleven of the laymen from his exemplar to produce 1.1. Pont. 3a, the diploma which Offler identified as the key text.[60] He exchanged Thurstan for Edmund as abbot of Pershore and omitted Abbot Vitalis of Westminster and he selected eleven laymen and chaplains, to whom he added William Peverell and William the chancellor, the latter of whom appears on the William II settlement. Two of the forged royal charters have a small number of *testes*, but these have all been selected from the same group and are followed by the phrases *et aliis multis* and *cum aliis pluribus*.[61] The forged William the Conqueror charter with the most *signa* includes fourteen attestations which appear on the earliest episcopal forgery and eleven which appear on the William II settlement.[62] Two of the William I diplomas do contain more variations, but they also include some familiar names.[63] The sameness of the attestations surely proves beyond any doubt that we are dealing with a programme of forgery as Offler believed. The lay attestations to these diplomas also prove beyond any doubt that the monks of Durham had no authentic charter of either Bishop William or William the Conqueror on which to draw. It can finally be remarked that the forger knew little of eleventh-century diplomatic. In one case an attempt was made to scatter the attestations around the foot of the parchment and even to give the impression that

---

[58] D. Bates, *Bishop Remigius of Lincoln 1067–1092* (Lincoln, 1992), p. 11.
[59] DCDCM, 1.1. Reg. 17; *Regesta*, I, no. 349. For the original of the Henry I writ, DCDCM, 2.1. Reg. 5; *Regesta*, II, no. 918.
[60] *DEC*, no. 4.
[61] *Regesta*, ed. Bates, nos. 108 and 109.
[62] Ibid., no. 110.
[63] Ibid., nos. 114 and 115.

they had been written by different hands.[64] But the documents also produce examples of sealing by fold and tag and on cords.[65]

The forged Bishop William charter attributed to the year 1093 was discussed in depth by Offler.[66] He noted its close relationship to the other forgeries. The liberties granted by the king appear to derive from the two forged William the Conqueror diplomas (1. 1. Reg. 1 and 1. 1. Reg. 11); its attestators, six of whom were dead by 1093, were drawn from the same small group who appear on the other diplomas. Offler rightly placed this diploma in a separate category from most of the other forgeries. Not only was it written by a different scribe, its claims were in some respects less extreme than those made in the earlier forgeries; the equation of the prior's position with that of the dean of York no longer appears, nor does the assertion of superiority over the archdeacons. Offler also established the close relationship between this forged diploma and the forged Gregory VII bull. Both he and Scammell dated it to the last years of Hugh of le Puiset's episcopate. They also pointed out that it is on the basis of this diploma that the claims of the Durham monks were inserted into a bull of Celestine III of 1196 and a charter of King Richard I of the same year.[67] Although the diploma purports to have been drawn up at Gloucester, its date of 1093 is presumably based on another well-known date in Durham's history, the laying of the foundation-stone of the new cathedral. It and the Gregory VII bull marked the conclusion of the campaign of forgery associated with the forged diplomas of William the Conqueror and Bishop William of St Calais. The material in these documents was made official, not only in late twelfth-century royal and papal confirmations, but also through insertion of some of it into the earliest parts of the chronicle of Roger of Howden, which is now thought to have been written in the years 1192 and 1193.[68]

The charters discussed in this essay are connected with William of St Calais only in the sense that they must be an indirect reflection of his remarkable achievement in establishing a remodelled community and enlarged endowment in a difficult region. Their contents must also reflect the great powers and privileges which the Durham community apparently enjoyed from the beginning. They are also part of a long history at Durham of rearranging the past in order to suit the needs of the present. In this particular case, the background is undoubtedly the persistent tensions which existed between bishops and community throughout the century. A specific stimulus to forgery may well have been Bishop Hugh's removal of Prior Thomas in 1162.[69] These forged diplomas also reflect another important

[64] Ibid., no. 110.
[65] Ibid., no. 111 (two versions).
[66] *DEC*, no. 7.
[67] *DEC*, p. 59; Scammell, *Puiset*, p. 302.
[68] Roger of Howden, *Chronicon Magistri Rogerii de Houedene*, ed. W. Stubbs (4 vols., RS 51; 1868–71), I, 127, 137–8. For the date, D. Corner, 'The Earliest Surviving Manuscripts of Roger of Howden's *Chronica*', *EHR*, 98 (1983), pp. 303–10; idem, 'The *Gesta Regis Henrici Secundi* and *Chronicon* of Roger, Parson of Howden', *BIHR*, 56 (1983), pp. 129–30, 132–44.
[69] On this event, Scammell, *Puiset*, p. 133, n. 4, remarks: 'This important incident . . . had an obvious bearing on the content of the Durham forgeries.'

generalisation. Out of 351 surviving charters of William the Conqueror, sixty-one were either elaborated from an eleventh-century base or completely fabricated during the twelfth century. The statistic is even more remarkable when we note that fifty-nine out of 206 English charters were so written: that is, around a quarter. The most productive religious houses were Durham, Westminster, Battle, and Gloucester, all communities founded by, or owing a great deal to, the Normans and other newcomers. The Durham charters have their place in the history of determined medieval bishops and powerful, entrenched communities. They also have a secure place in a chronology of English medieval forgery. Viewed in this way, they are very much a product of their time.

The *De iniusta uexacione Willelmi episcopi primi* and Canon Law in Anglo-Norman Durham[1]

MARK PHILPOTT

H.S. OFFLER described the *De iniusta uexacione Willelmi episcopi primi* as 'a notable document in the cultural history of Anglo-Norman England.'[2] It is particularly appropriate to begin this paper with the dedicatee of the Anglo-Norman Durham conference, for his work has put the study of the tract on a wholly new footing. In his famous article of 1951 and in the preface and introduction to his unpublished edition of the text, Offler argued from an unrivalled knowledge of the tract and its manuscripts that it was not, as it purports to be, an eyewitness and verbatim account of the trial of William of St Calais, bishop of Durham, in the wake of the rebellion of 1088 which nearly cost William Rufus his throne. Offler's argument has recently been described as an 'unanswered case'.[3] In this paper we shall see that there are grounds for disagreeing with Offler, and that *De iniusta uexacione* gives us contemporary testimony of the utmost importance. Here we shall explore its evidence on the working of canon law in the English Church in the late eleventh century. It will be convenient to begin with a description of the tract and some of its contents.

The *De iniusta uexacione Willelmi episcopi primi* has two parts: the introduction and conclusion, which together form what has become known as 'the *uita*', and the central part, 'the *libellus*'.[4] The *uita* seems to have been composed later than the

---

[1] At the outset of this paper, it is my duty and pleasure to acknowledge three great debts of gratitude. Mrs Offler has kindly given me permission to use and quote from the unpublished critical edition of *De iniusta uexacione Willelmi episcopi primi per Willelmum regem fil<l>ium Willelmi magni regis* prepared by her late husband. Dr David Rollason has been extremely generous with ideas, kindness, practical help, and editorial forbearance. My former supervisor, the Reverend H.E.J. Cowdrey, encouraged me to work on the tract, discussed with me his Haskins Society paper, and kindly lent me a draft of it. In addition, I should like to record my gratitude to those who commented on two previous versions of this paper at seminars in Oxford, most especially the late Dr Margaret Gibson and Professor Leyser. Naturally all remaining errors, faults and inconsistencies are entirely my own responsibility.
[2] Offler, 'Introduction', p. ii.
[3] D. Rollason, 'Symeon of Durham and the Community of Durham in the Eleventh Century', in *England in the Eleventh Century: Proceedings of the 1990 Harlaxton Symposium*, ed. C. Hicks (Harlaxton Medieval Studies 2; Stamford, 1992), at p. 186.
[4] The distinction between *uita* and *libellus* was drawn by C.W. David, 'A Tract attributed to

libellus, and by a different hand. It draws almost exclusively and often very closely from *On the Origin and Progress of this Church of Durham* and amounts to a short biography of William of St Calais from his youth in Bayeux to his burial in Durham in January 1096.[5] This *uita* is, however, little more than a frame for the picture of the bishop's trial in 1088 presented by the *libellus*.

The *libellus* itself falls into three sections.[6] The first starts rather abruptly on 12 March 1088 with Rufus ordering the bishop's arrest and the disseisin of his lands and property. The bishop evades capture and reaches the safety of Durham castle. The background to these events is left unclear. The bishop presents himself as having acted as the perfect vassal during the early stages of the revolt, and never cares to explain his flight or to apologize for it. As far as we are allowed to see, the king seems to have viewed the bishop's desertion either as evidence of complicity in the plot against him or as in itself an act of treason, but this too is never spelt out. The first section of the *libellus* concerns itself with the negotiations initiated by the bishop from his stronghold. These are described in some considerable detail. Throughout the bishop insists that he is ready to offer the king *fidele seruicium* and that if the king will give him back his lands, he will offer him justice *secundum ordinem meum*.[7] He maintains that if the king will not restore the lands, he will take no part in any legal proceedings beyond perhaps defending himself by purgation. At an unsuccessful meeting, the king for his part requires that the bishop should be tried outside safe conduct and *laicaliter*.[8] Much pressure is put on the bishop; a show is made of giving away his lands and his messengers are harassed and imprisoned. But it is only with a royal army looting and burning his lands that he is forced to reach a *conuencio* with three of the king's *comites*.[9] This agreement was extremely favourable to the bishop. The king was to do him right *secundum legem episcopi*, and in the event of any dispute the bishop was to be conducted back to Durham. Even if a properly conducted trial went against him, the bishop and his men were to have safe conduct out of the kingdom.

The second part of the *libellus* describing the royal court at Salisbury on 2–3 November is the heart of *De iniusta uexacione*.[10] From the moment of his arrival in court, Bishop William misses no opportunity to stress his rights under canon law. His constant refrain is that he will accept no judgement that is not in accordance with the canons and the privileges of his episcopal order. His chief opponent in argument is Archbishop Lanfranc, who, in his late seventies, seems more than a

---

Symeon of Durham', *EHR* 32 (1917), pp. 382–7. The division falls at *DIV*, p. 91 ('Rex Willelmus iunior dissaisiuit . . .'), and p. 105 ('. . . rex permisit episcopo transitum').

[5] *LDE*, bk. 4, chs. 1–3 (pp. 119–24 and 127–9). As Offler pointed out in his edition, the *uita* must have had at least one other source, since the *LDE* does not supply the place of Bishop William's consecration, nor the date of Rufus's coronation.

[6] *DIV*, pp. 91–5, 95–103, and 103–5.

[7] *DIV*, pp. 91–4. Each of the bishop's three letters begins with the offer of service; the first two letters insist on him being tried according to his order.

[8] *DIV*, p. 93.

[9] *DIV*, pp. 94–5.

[10] *DIV*, pp. 95–103.

match for him. As the arguments continue, Rufus is heard demanding with increasing insistence the surrender of Durham castle. Finally, protesting that he has been compelled by necessity, Bishop William gives the king the sureties he demands and is given the promise that he will be allowed to leave England once the castle is firmly under royal control.

The final section of the *libellus* recounts the indignities inflicted on the bishop after the final surrender of his church, castle, and lands on 14 November.[11] Despite the promises of the *comites* and the king's safe-conduct, the bishop was not allowed to embark, as he claimed, to pursue his appeal to Rome.[12] Even when he was finally allowed to go to Southampton and although everything was ready for his departure, the king's servants prevented the bishop from boarding ship until after the wind had dropped. While he was waiting for the wind, the bishop was summoned back to the king's court to answer further allegations and placed under watch day and night. It was only through the pressing representations of the *comites* of the *conuencio*, whose good faith the bishop had called into question, that the king finally gave permission for the bishop to set sail.

On the face of it, then, 'There are very few stories which bring the men and the institutions of the latter part of the eleventh century before us in a more living way.'[13] Indeed, a whole host of historians have used the *De iniusta uexacione* as if it were a genuine source.[14] However, it cannot definitely be shown to have existed until shortly before 1375, when it was copied into the oldest (and best) of the surviving manuscripts, Oxford, Bodleian Library, Fairfax 6.[15] The Durham scribe of this manuscript was clearly copying a text that already existed, since he underestimated the space that it would require and had to squeeze the end into a margin. It may be that the *libellus* cited by the mid-twelfth-century Durham *Historia*

---

[11] *DIV*, pp. 103–5.

[12] Actually, as the *uita* shows (*DIV*, p. 105), the bishop got no further than Normandy, although Urban II did get to hear about his troubles, reprimanded Rufus, and ordered the matter to come to him for a proper trial. See *Epistolae Pontificum Romanorum Ineditae*, ed. S. Loewenfeld (Leipzig, 1885), p. 63, no. 129 (*Audivimus, te Dunelmensis* from the *Collectio Britannica*).

[13] E.A. Freeman, *The Reign of William Rufus and the Accession of Henry I* (2 vols., Oxford, 1882), II, 474.

[14] See, for example, F. Palgrave, *The History of Normandy and England* (4 vols., London, 1851–64), IV, 31; W. Stubbs, *The Constitutional History of England* (3 vols., 6th edn, Oxford, 1897), I, 476–7; F. Pollock and F.W. Maitland, *The History of English Law* (2 vols., Cambridge, 1895), I, 434; Z.N. Brooke, *The English Church and the Papacy from the Conquest to the Reign of John* (Cambridge, 1931), pp. 161–2; G.B. Adams, *Councils and Courts in Anglo-Norman England* (reprinted, New Haven, 1965), pp. 46–65; D. Knowles, *The Monastic Order in England* (Cambridge, 1950), p. 169; R.W. Southern, *St Anselm and his Biographer* (Cambridge, 1963), pp. 148–50; F. Barlow, *The English Church 1066–1154* (London, 1979), p. 281; A. Gransden, *Historical Writing in England c.550 to c.1307* (London, 1974), pp. 122–3; and M. Gibson, *Lanfranc of Bec* (Oxford, 1978), pp. 220–1.

[15] In these arguments, I rely heavily on Offler, 'Introduction', pp. 17–18.

Regum as its source for the events of 1088 was our *libellus*.[16] But this still leaves sufficient space for Offler's argument that the *libellus* was 'less a straightforward report of events made as they occurred or shortly afterwards than a piece of *ex post facto* pleading'.[17] He dated the *libellus* possibly as late as 1150 and saw it as an attempt by the monastic community at Durham to cover up an embarrassing blot on the reputation of one they considered founder and benefactor, and perhaps also to dispel the impression made by Eadmer's portrayal of Bishop William as the ringleader of Anselm's persecutors at the Council of Rockingham in 1095.[18]

It is possible to answer some of Offler's corroborative arguments in their own kind. For example, Offler pointed to 'anomalies and anachronisms' in the tract, including the numerous mistakes the *libellus* seems to make over names, as signs of later composition. He argued that the author of the tract wrote, for instance, about Roger Mowbray and Hugh Beaumont (when we would expect Robert and perhaps Henry) because he was writing at a time when the memory of details and personalities had blurred.[19] There is, however, an entirely satisfactory possible explanation of these anomalies as the result of an error by a later scribe. The original text certainly contained a number of abbreviations, since some have survived in our present manuscripts; for example, we meet *G. Constanciensis episcopus*.[20] It is altogether possible that there were once more abbreviations and that the expansions were made only in the 1370s by the scribe of Bodl.L, Fairfax 6, who seems unlikely to have been as well informed about Anglo-Norman prosopography as modern scholars. Even Offler admits that a careless expansion of an abbreviation by a later scribe might very well explain the curious transformation of Ralph Paynel into Roger Paynel, and perhaps also into Reginald Paynel.[21] Another problem in the text, which Offler sees as a sign of late composition, is that Roger le Poitevin is accorded the title *comes*, to which he does not seem strictly to have been entitled until 1091.[22] On each of the three occasions when it is definitely Roger le Poitevin who is referred to as Count Roger, he is mentioned in company with other *comites*.[23] On other occasions when he appears in the *libellus* he is not accorded the title, so it does not seem unlikely that he is given the title merely by association. In addition, as Barlow pointed out, the use of the title *comes* was not as rigidly restricted at this time as it later came to be.[24]

[16] As admitted by Offler, 'Tractate', pp. 325–6.

[17] Offler, 'Introduction', p. 5.

[18] Offler, 'Introduction', pp. 6–8. See Eadmer, *Historia Novorum in Anglia*, ed. M. Rule (RS, 81; 1884), pp. 53–66, especially pp. 59, 60, 62.

[19] Offler, 'Introduction', pp. 6, 9. Roger Mowbray occurs at *DIV*, p. 104 and Hugh Beaumont on three occasions pp. 97, 98, 99. Offler suggested ('Introduction', p. 9) that the author in fact intended Hugh Beauchamp.

[20] *DIV*, p. 97.

[21] *DIV*, pp. 91, 92 for Ralph; p. 96 for Roger who is definitely the same person; and p. 102 for Reginald who may well be.

[22] Offler, 'Introduction', pp. 9–10.

[23] *DIV*, p. 97 with Count Alan, p. 100 with Count Odo, and p. 105 with Counts Alan and Odo.

[24] F. Barlow, *William Rufus* (London, 1983), p. 85, n. 160.

Moreover, acceptance of Offler's arguments would create a number of problems, to which he offered no answer. It is far from clear why a mid-twelfth-century monk should have gone to the trouble of writing such a long document and *cui bono*. On the other hand, it is possible to suggest any number of reasons why a real eye-witness might have done so – in connection with proceedings in Rome; as self-justification; even perhaps as an occupation suitable to sharing the bishop's exile. For an attempt to clear Bishop William's name, the *libellus* had a remarkably tiny circulation. So far as Offler's studies could show, this amounted before *c.*1375 to the possible use in the *Historia Regum*, and perhaps the *Tractatus de Gestis Willielmi de Karilepho* in the now-lost manuscript 'O' of the 1395 Durham catalogue, which Offler dated to *c.*1200.[25] This would seem to constitute a rather silent reply to Eadmer.

However, these kinds of argument can only take us so far. None of them is conclusive and they can all be turned around. The names and titles might, after all, have been confused by a twelfth-century author rather than by a fourteenth-century scribe. It may be that a crisis arose in the affairs of Durham cathedral priory in the mid-twelfth century which precipitated a defence of Bishop William. The *libellus* might not have been used by Durham authors or copied by Durham scribes, because they knew it was suspicious; the history of medieval forgery is littered with fake or falsified documents which were hardly circulated or used even when opportunity arose.[26] In fact if such lines of argument are followed, it is virtually impossible to avoid concurring with Offler: 'Perhaps judgement about the "authenticity" of the *libellus* is fated to remain more a matter of temperament than of conviction on purely technical grounds. To some, anything as good as this must surely be true; to others it will always appear rather too good to be wholly true.'[27]

Yet, we shall see that this pessimism was ill founded. At the very centre of Offler's scepticism about the *libellus* lies his feeling that its author is too adroit in the canon law to have been a contemporary, and that Bishop William would not have known as much of the canons, nor have used them in the way the tract suggests. In short, he believed that the *libellus* must have been composed with reference books at a time 'when the new canon law was more freely current in England than was probable in 1088'.[28] Dr Gibson seems in part to share this view, suggesting that the *libellus* was written 'in Normandy, where more canon law and lawyers were

---

[25] Offler, 'Tractate', pp. 325–6 and 'Introduction', p. 18.
[26] A number of these are discussed by E.A.R. Brown, 'Medieval Forgers and their Intentions', in *Fälschungen im Mittelalter* (6 vols., M.G.H., Schriften 33; Hanover, 1988–90), I, 109–19. For example (p. 117) forgeries were created for the bishop of Le Mans in the ninth century, but rather than produce them in the royal court when necessary to the successful conclusion of his case, the bishop fled and never returned.
[27] Offler, 'Introduction', p. 11.
[28] Offler, 'Tractate', pp. 334–5. To avoid confusion, it is necessary to note that, from the context, by 'the new canon law' Offler seems to have meant 'the new canonical jurisprudence' he believed to have been mainly introduced into England by Lanfranc, that is to say pseudo-Isidorian texts.

available than in Durham.'[29] Certainly, it would be difficult to exaggerate the extent to which the *libellus* is saturated by canon law. The whole last section, for example, could have been written merely to show Rufus and his men transgressing the canonical requirements to put no hindrance in the way of those who appeal to the pope.[30] But more striking still is the extent to which the argument attributed to the bishop rests on the canons. From the beginning of the pleadings he says 'nichil se prorsus acturum ibi nisi canonice et secundum ordinem suum'.[31] He asks whether the bishops present should not robe as required by ecclesiastical custom. He requests the king to return to him his *episcopatus* which has been taken from him *sine iudicio*.[32] He rejects the judgement of the lay members of the court. He insists that he will make no answer to the charges against him until it is demonstrated justly that he ought to plead *dispoliatus* or he was invested with his bishopric *canonice*.[33] He urges the bishops to behave *ordinabiliter et canonice* and not to involve in their judgement those excluded by the canons.[34] When the mixed court pronounces that he must do the king right before having his bishopric returned, he demands to see *canonicam aliquam sentenciam* in support of this decision. He rejects the ruling

> quia contra canones et contra legem nostram factum est. Neque enim ego canonice uocatus sum, sed coactus ui regalis exercitus assum et dispoliatus episcopio extra prouinciam meam absentibus omnibus comprouincialibus meis in laicali conuentu causam meam dicere compellor, et inimici mei, qui michi consilium et colloquium suum et pacis osculum denegant, postpositis dictis meis, de hiis que non dixi me iudicant et accusatores sunt simul et iudices, et in lege nostra prohibitum inuenio ne tale iudicium suscipiam.[35]

This leads him to appeal to the pope 'cuius dispositioni maiores causas ecclesiasticas et episcoporum iudicia antiqua apostolorum eorumque successorum atque canonum auctoritas reseruauit.'[36] In all these major claims Bishop William is relying on the pseudo-Isidorian canon law, and the canons seep into even the smallest details of what he says. For example, when the bishop says that he will break his *conuencio* and give the king the sureties he demands *si necesse fuerit*,[37] it is a clear reference to the canonical maxim *necessitas legem non habet* which allowed for temporary waiving of the strict requirements of the canons.[38] *Pace* Offler, we

[29] Gibson, *Lanfranc of Bec*, p. 221.
[30] *DIV*, pp. 103–5. Compare, for example, Hinschius, p. 489, ch. XIV (CTC, MS B.16.44, fol. 38v, ch. XVIIII, and Cambridge, Peterhouse, MS 74, fol. 46, ch. XVIIII, which is marked in the manner described below).
[31] *DIV*, p. 95.
[32] *DIV*, p. 96.
[33] *DIV*, p. 97.
[34] *DIV*, p. 98.
[35] *DIV*, pp. 98–9.
[36] *DIV*, p. 99.
[37] *DIV*, p. 102.
[38] Hinschius, p. 700 (CTC, B.16.44, fol. 91). See also Hinschius, p. 550, ch. V (CTC, B.16.44, fol. 53), and for specific variations of normal provisions in cases of necessity,

shall see that it is precisely these references to the canons which tie the *libellus* to late eleventh-century Durham.

Among Bishop William's bequests to his cathedral was a book entitled *Decreta Pontificum*, which has been identified as the volume which is now Cambridge, Peterhouse, MS 74.[39] This is a copy of the series of extracts from the canons of the *Dionysio-Hadriana* and the canons and decretals of pseudo-Isidore, which is known to historians as the *Collectio Lanfranci*. 'Lanfranc's collection' owes its fame to Z.N. Brooke, who showed that letter 'a's written in the margin of Cambridge, Trinity College, MS B.16.44, the copy of the collection given by Archbishop Lanfranc to his cathedral, marked canonical authorities cited by the archbishop in his correspondence. Brooke was thus able to place the manuscript firmly in the archbishop's hands and to draw conclusions of the utmost importance from it.[40] We can do something similar for Bishop William's copy. Brooke pointed out that the Peterhouse volume copies some of the famous 'a'-marks from the Trinity manuscript, but he did not note another series of marginalia which is much more to our purpose.[41] Some thirty or so texts are marked in the margin with a symbol '9'. Almost all of the bishop's major appeals to the canons are marked in this way.[42] As Offler observed in a note to his edition, the wording of William's appeal to Rome is a direct quotation either from *Epistola I Sixti II*, ch. II or from *Epistola Iulii ad Eusebium cet.*, ch. XII (in Hinschius's division of the texts).[43] Both of these texts are marked in the margin of Peterhouse 74, on fol. 29v and fol. 41 respectively. In fact a number of texts reserving definitive sentence in episcopal or difficult or major cases to the pope are marked.[44] Bishop William's insistence that he could not be tried canonically while *dispoliatus* rests on the important canonical principle known as the *exceptio spolii*, which forbids anyone (especially a bishop) to be brought to trial while stripped of his possessions. This principle is marked.[45] Canons outlining the role of the comprovincial bishops in the preliminary

---

Hinschius, p. 521, ch. II (CTC, B.16.44, fol. 43r/v); Hinschius, p. 651, ch. IX (CTC, B.16.44, fol. 84v, ch. VI); Hinschius, p. 653, ch. XXVI (CTC, B.16.44, fol. 85v, ch. XXI); Hinschius, p. 728 (CTC, B.16.44, fol. 95); and Hinschius, p. 341, ch. XXXII (CTC, B.16.44, fol. 147v, ch. XXXII).

[39] C.H. Turner, 'The Earliest List of Durham Manuscripts', *JTS* 19 (1918), pp. 124 and 128; and *DCM*, no. 50.

[40] Brooke, *English Church and the Papacy*, ch. 5, especially pp. 58–73.

[41] Ibid., pp. 234–5.

[42] The one exception would seem to be his insistence on the exclusion of the lay members of the court, but this is so deeply engrained in the pseudo-Isidore and so frequently repeated as hardly to require extra emphasis.

[43] Hinschius, pp. 190 and 467.

[44] For example, Peterhouse 74, fol. 15v (Hinschius, p. 91, chs. VII–VIII); fol. 20, ch. III (Hinschius, p. 121, ch. IV); fol. 20v (Hinschius, p. 125, ch. II); fol. 21, ch. III (Hinschius, p. 128, ch. IV); fol. 21v (Hinschius, p. 132, chs. V–VI); fol. 38v, ch. IIII (Hinschius, p. 460, ch. VIII); fol. 41, ch. I (Hinschius, pp. 466–7, ch. XI); fol. 42, ch. XXVI (Hinschius, p. 470, ch. XII).

[45] Peterhouse 74, fol. 45v, ch. VIII (Hinschius, p. 486, ch. IX); fol. 46, ch. XVIII (Hinschius, p. 489, ch. XIV).

examination of episcopal cases and requiring this to be done within the province are marked.[46] Even Bishop William's insistence on acting according to his order seems to derive from a prohibition of acting *contra suum ordinem* which is marked twice.[47]

Since Bishop William owned a manuscript which contained all the authorities necessary to his case in the *libellus* and somebody has gone through marking almost all those texts, it would seem that we no longer need suppose that the tract was written at a time 'when the new canon law was more freely current in England than was probable in 1088.'[48] Rather it would seem that pseudo-Isidorian canon law was more current in England in 1088 than Offler supposed in 1951. When the Bishop proclaims his reliance on 'christianam legem quam hic scriptam habeo', we must surely imagine him with the Peterhouse manuscript in his hand.[49]

There is a possible objection to our argument, however. Since the marginalia are not even generally datable, we cannot definitely say that Offler's later author did not make the marks in the margins while preparing the fictitious arguments he put into the bishop's mouth.[50] Since the argument that the canons would not have been as well known in late eleventh-century Durham as they are in the *libellus* is at the heart of Offler's thesis, it does seem odd to try to keep that thesis alive without it. Bishop William was a very capable man: in the Durham tradition 'ecclesiasticis et secularibus litteris nobiliter eruditus', or in Eadmer's less than charitable view 'homo linguae uolubilitate facetus quam pura sapientia praeditus'.[51] Having such a weapon as the Peterhouse manuscript in his hand, would he have failed to use it? It is also assumed in Offler's argument that by the time his putative compiler was at work in Durham in the mid-twelfth century, there would have been other canon law books in the library. It is impossible to prove this beyond all doubt as, apart from a list of Bishop William's bequests, the earliest surviving catalogue belongs to the third quarter of the twelfth century.[52] But certainly by then there were collections of canon law available in Durham which would have been a great deal easier to use than 'Lanfranc's collection', which is extraordinarily unwieldy.[53] The Peterhouse manuscript is well over 200 folios long and, since the texts are arranged chronologically rather than systematically, it is quite a labour to discover what the collection says on any one issue. The burden of proof lies with the critics of the *libellus*, and we may consider ourselves free to use it as a contemporary source.

---

[46] Peterhouse 74, fol. 46, ch. XVIII (Hinschius, p. 488, ch. XIX); fol. 47 (Hinschius, p. 501, ch. [VII]).

[47] Peterhouse 74, fol. 30v, ch. IIII (Hinschius, p. 193, ch. VIII); fol. 43, ch. XXXV (Hinschius, p. 474, ch. XIX).

[48] Offler, 'Tractate', pp. 334–5.

[49] *DIV*, p. 101.

[50] I am extremely grateful to Dr David Rollason for pointing out this potential problem.

[51] *LDE*, bk. 4, ch. 1 (p. 119), and Eadmer, *Historia Novorum*, p. 59.

[52] *DCM*, p. 10.

[53] *Catalogi Veteres Librorum Ecclesiae Cathedralis Dunelm*, ed. B. Botfield (SS 7; 1838), pp. 1, 2, 4 includes a number of books on canon law, amongst them two copies of the systematically arranged Burchard's *Decretum*.

In fact the *libellus* provides all sorts of evidence of the utmost importance. For convenience we shall confine our consideration to some of what it has to tell us about the operation of canon law in Anglo-Norman England. Perhaps the most obvious point to stress is that Bishop William is not at all the sort of prelate whom previous scholars would otherwise have expected to have much to do with pseudo-Isidorian law. True, the *uita* described him as 'acerrimus ingenio, subtilis consilio, magne eloquencie simul et sapiencie' but it also made no bones about the fact that he owed his promotion to his usefulness to the king in difficult matters.[54] He was, in short, a thoroughly curial figure, yet he was perfectly willing and able to appeal to the canon law, and to advance opinions which, as Freeman put it, 'would have won him favour with Hildebrand'.[55] Indeed Lanfranc himself, although he had an excellent knowledge of the canons, could hardly have been described as a Gregorian in his rule over the English church. The pseudo-Isidorian corpus had no single *Tendenz*: it was open to any number of uses and large numbers of different interpretations.

The *De iniusta uexacione* gives further proof of this. Even through the tract's deep hostility to him, it seems possible to distinguish canonical elements in Lanfranc's arguments against Bishop William.[56] Most of the time Lanfranc is shown to be attempting to deny that the canons should be brought into the discussion. We might take as symbolic his reply to William's question about whether the bishops should not follow ecclesiastical custom by vesting: ' "Bene possumus" inquid "hoc modo uestiti de regalibus tuisque negociis disceptare. Vestes enim non impediunt ueritatem." '[57] Indeed the whole thrust of the primate's argument is summed up in his reply to William's impassioned appeal to the pope: 'Nos non de episcopio sed de tuo te feodo iudicamus, et hoc modo iudicauimus Baiocensem episcopum ante patrem huius regis de feodo suo, nec rex uocabat eum episcopum in placito illo sed fratrem et comitem.'[58] The matter under discussion is a feudal one, so feudal laws apply and the *curia regis* is competent to judge the king's man. However, just occasionally we hear an echo of canonical doctrine in his reported words. For example, when Bishop William asks for counsel from the bishops, Lanfranc retorts, 'Episcopi sunt iudices et eos ad consilium tuum habere non debes.'[59] The canons enjoined that accusers, judges and accused should all be separate people and required judges to pay equal attention to both sides.[60]

More importantly, Cowdrey suggests that Lanfranc bested Bishop William even

---

[54] *DIV*, p. 91.
[55] Freeman, *William Rufus*, I, 97.
[56] I owe this suggestion to the draft of H.E.J. Cowdrey, 'The Enigma of Archbishop Lanfranc' (A paper given to the Twelfth Conference of the Charles Homer Haskins Society in November 1993), p. 19.
[57] *DIV*, p. 96.
[58] *DIV*, p. 99.
[59] *DIV*, p. 98.
[60] Hinschius, p. 504, chs. XV–XVI (CTC, B.16.44, fol. 40v, ch. VII).

in his attempt to use the *exceptio spolii*.[61] For the *exceptio* to come into effect the accused had to be completely *nudatus*, he argues. As the bishop had only been deprived of his lands in Yorkshire and Lincolnshire and he continually offered to do the king suitable service, Lanfranc was able to maintain that the principle did not apply and the bishop had to make answer to the charges before restitution.[62] At the end of the trial, once William had been deprived of his castle and lands by sentence of the *curia* regis, according to Cowdrey, Lanfranc allowed that the rule now applied, insisting that it would be unjust for the king to implead him further 'cum de uobis nichil teneat'.[63] This may amount to an argument that the *exceptio* should come into effect, but it is cast in the same feudal language as Lanfranc is made to use throughout. Perhaps the discrepancy is to be explained by the fact that the *libellus* is so hostile a witness. The reason, Cowdrey argues, why Lanfranc was at this point prepared to concede the *exceptio spolii* and viewed the bishop's departure with equanimity is that its provisions meant that, even if Bishop William appeared in Rome to pursue his case, the pope could do nothing until his possessions had been restored. Certainly this is borne out by the terms of Urban II's letter to Rufus on the subject, which orders that the bishop be restored to his *episcopatus* first and only then be sent with legitimate accusers *si qui sunt* to a papal hearing.[64] At any rate we can see that the canons cut both ways and in the hands of clever pleaders like William and Lanfranc they could be made to stand for radically opposed positions.

The way in which Bishop William used the canons at his trial was similar in many respects to the ways in which Lanfranc used them elsewhere. Lanfranc had a tendency to quibble; for example, he claimed that Gregory I's constitution setting up two equal archbishops in England was not relevant to his primacy dispute with the archbishop of York, 'quod nec ego Londoniensis episcopus essem nec de Londoniensi aecclesia esset quaestio instituta'.[65] Bishop William puts real weight in argument on what look to us like mere debating points. He claimed that, contrary to the canons, he was being tried outside his province and in the absence of his comprovincials.[66] It is not at all clear that, as far as the canons concerning episcopal trials are concerned, this is true. In the pseudo-Isidore a *prouincia* is both the area

---

[61] Cowdrey, 'Enigma', draft, pp. 23–4.

[62] In suggesting that the accused had to be completely deprived of his possessions for the *exceptio* to come into effect, Cowdrey follows F. Ruffini, *L'actio spolii: studio storico-giuridico* (Turin, 1889), pp. 200–1. However, some of the canons seem to be drawn in a slightly different way: the bishop must have all of his property restored before being accused (see, for example, Hinschius, p. 133, ch. XII (CTC, B.16.44, fol. 18v)). Bishop William's case would certainly be covered by these provisions. It also seems hard to see Lanfranc's comment that the king had issued no writ by which the bishop had been disseised (*DIV*, p. 96) as a rejoinder that the *exceptio spolii* only applied when despoliation was complete (Cowdrey, 'Enigma', draft, p. 22).

[63] *DIV*, p. 103.

[64] Urban II, *Audivimus, te Dunelmensis*, in *Epistolae Pontificum Romanorum Ineditae*, p. 63, no. 129.

[65] *The Letters of Lanfranc, Archbishop of Canterbury*, eds. H. Clover and M. Gibson (Oxford Medieval Texts; Oxford, 1979), no. 4, p. 54.

[66] *DIV*, p. 99.

subject to a metropolitan and the area subject to a primate.[67] Many of the canons about episcopal trials reserve them to the jurisdiction of the bishops of the province and the primate, which suggests that the province within which a bishop was to be tried was of the primatial rather than metropolitan variety.[68] But William insists that he is outside his province, so he must have in mind the province subject to the archbishop of York. This makes his remark about the absence of his comprovincials rather curious, since it is not at all clear who they were. Apart from himself the only bishops who seem possibly to have acknowledged the authority of the archbishop of York were Ralph of Orkney, who had been consecrated by Archbishop Thomas in 1073, and Fothadh of St Andrews, who, according to a later York tradition, professed obedience to Thomas.[69] But these were not in any ordinary sense suffragans of York, or comprovincials of William's. William's objection to the absence of his comprovincials certainly seems to be of a piece with Lanfranc's rejection of the Gregorian constitution. The bishop promised to keep his *conuencio* with the 'comites sine omni malo ingenio, excepto ingenio placiti': he certainly made full use of this exception.[70]

Another striking feature of Bishop William's use of the canons is its selectiveness. If he had studied Peterhouse 74 with any attention, he would have known that he could not have afforded to let his case come to trial even under the canon law. Excommunication, or deposition and a life of penance in a monastery, awaited clergy who participated in rebellions against the king.[71] Given the attitude of the archbishops to him, despite his protestations that he had taken no part in the revolt, William can have had no very lively expectation of being found innocent. This raises the question of what William actually wanted to happen at the *curia regis*. This is by no means easy to discover from the *libellus* which, perhaps with a potential Roman audience in mind, gives few clues to any non-canonical aspects of William's case. However, he does avow himself ready to undergo purgation even while despoiled of his bishopric. In fact in one of his letters he seems to say that he will only insist on trial according to the canons if anyone attempts to oppress him in connection with the purgation.[72] He also says that he is prepared to make lawful amends, to offer the king service, and 'de meo, si placet, ei tribuam'.[73] So perhaps the bishop expected to be allowed to purge himself of guilt, pay a fine, and be restored to lands and favour. The king's hostility meant that this was not to be.

Nonetheless, it is striking that Bishop William, who was a man extremely used to the workings of the *curia regis*, should have thought that the canon law would have provided at least a weighty bargaining position. In fact, although the bishop

---

[67] See, for example, Hinschius, pp. 79–80, ch. XXVI (CTC, B.16.44, fol. 11r/v, ch. IIII).
[68] See, for example, Hinschius, p. 201, ch. IX (CTC, B.16.44, fol. 25v, ch. I).
[69] In *DIV*, Offler noted the York story, found in BL, MS Harley 433, fol. 260, but regarded it as 'very improbable'.
[70] *DIV*, p. 95.
[71] See, for example, Hinschius, p. 370, ch. XLIV (CTC, B.16.44, fol. 162v, ch. XLV) and Hinschius, pp. 380–1, ch. I (CTC, B.16.44, fols. 168–169, ch. I).
[72] *DIV*, pp. 93–4.
[73] *DIV*, pp. 101–2.

did not get the result he seems to have been hoping for, the church, its laws, and its views of the ways things should be done were surprisingly influential in the Anglo-Norman kingdom. The Conqueror especially seems to have been prepared to take a good deal of forthright criticism from bishops. Feeling himself wronged by the sheriff of York, Archbishop Ealdred vested in full pontificals, confronted the king, and threatened to curse him 'sicut ecclesiae Dei persecutori, et ministrorum Ejus oppressori, et promissionum atque juramentorum quae mihi coram altare Sancti Petri jurasti transgressori'. The king threw himself at the archbishop's feet and begged for mercy.[74] When *quidam scurra* proclaimed at one of William's solemn crown-wearings, 'Ecce Deum uideo', Lanfranc did not scruple to remind the king of the fate of Herod, who on being hailed as a god, not a man, had been smitten by an angel and died excruciatingly 'eaten of worms'.[75]

This is only one manifestation of the fact, so well-known as scarcely to require repeating, that the support of the church was absolutely fundamental to the whole regime. Historically speaking, the support of the papacy had played a role in legitimising William's conquest of England. The church was in practical ways one of the sinews of his power, with churchmen deeply involved in the running of government.[76] The church also contributed greatly to the theatre of power with the liturgy of the *laudes regiae* and great occasions like crown-wearings.[77] But, more than this, the whole structure of the state depended, in some sense, on being a hierarchy with God at its head. For one thing, the whole system was bound together with oaths. Just as the Conqueror was bound to Archbishop Ealdred and the church by oaths, so Earl Alan reminded Rufus that the king should not make him break his promise to Bishop William's *conuencio*, as the king would no longer be able to trust his word.[78] In these circumstances the law of the Church, which claimed continuity with the law of God, could be avoided, ignored, twisted, even broken, but not denied. Of course there was another side to royal authority, a matter of power and violence: we should not forget Rufus's reaction to Bishop William's subtle arguments: 'Dicas licet quicquid uelis, non tamen effugies manus meas nisi castellum prius michi reddas.'[79] In the face of implacable royal wrath, a despairing exclamation or the most sophisticated canonical argument had little weight.

Thus, even a brief examination of the *De iniusta uexacione Willelmi episcopi primi* has shown a great deal about the place and uses of the canon law in the Anglo-

---

[74] *Historians of the Church of York and its Archbishops*, ed. J. Raine (3 vols., RS, 71; 1879–94), II, 350–3, at p. 352.

[75] *Vita beati Lanfranci Cantuariensium archiepiscopi*, attributed to Milo Crispin, ch. 13, pr. *PL* 150, cols. 53–4.

[76] For example, Bishop William of Durham has been identified as 'the man behind the [Domesday] Survey'; see P. Chaplais, 'William of Saint-Calais and the Domesday Survey', in *Domesday Studies*, ed. J.C. Holt (Woodbridge, 1987), pp. 65–77.

[77] H.E.J. Cowdrey, 'The Anglo-Norman *Laudes Regiae*', *Viator* 12 (1981), pp. 37–78.

[78] *DIV*, p. 100.

[79] *DIV*, p. 101.

Norman kingdom. Canon law was more widely known than has been supposed; it is precisely Bishop William's references to the canons, which were once thought the chief obstacles to accepting the tract as contemporary, that actually tie the tract to late-eleventh-century Durham. The *libellus* allows us to see beyond the history of canon law collections, to glimpse canon law as it was actually used and enforced. It shows clearly that the canons were open to a number of different interpretations. Lanfranc and Bishop William both turned to the same collection of canon law for their authorities, and, in many ways, they approached those authorities in the same manner. They both tended to quote out of context and to quibble over the exact words, and, despite the lofty claims of the law Christian, they both twisted it to suit their own purposes. In William's case, he seems to have been trying to use the canon law as protection and as an instrument in his attempt to be received back into the king's favour. Both the attempt and its failure tell us much about the place of canon law in the Norman polity. The Church wielded real power and its laws were real and terrifying. Even an intelligent, perhaps wily, curial figure like Bishop William thought them worth relying on in an extremely tight spot. But in the face of determined royal power even the most exalted canonical authorities were only words. This was the space in which canon law had to operate in Anglo-Norman England, and its shape is shown most clearly in the mysterious *libellus* from Durham.

PART TWO

Church Architecture in
Anglo-Norman Durham

Early Romanesque Architecture in North-East England: A Style and its Patrons

ERIC CAMBRIDGE

I

THE ELEVENTH-CENTURY architecture of north-east England may at first sight seem comparatively uncontroversial territory. Previous work has tended to analyze buildings of this period in terms of a chronological development based essentially on stylistic and typological analysis, starting with a number of structures conventionally labelled 'late Saxon' or 'Saxo-Norman' and conventionally assigned either to the late pre-Conquest period or to the years immediately after the Conquest; these are followed by a small number of early post-Conquest Romanesque buildings, and the climax of the sequence is the arrival of the high Romanesque style with the start of work on the cathedral at Durham in 1093. In fact, recent work on comparable buildings elsewhere in Britain has questioned the generally accepted dates of many such buildings and has also raised important questions about the nature of the patronage which produced them. The present paper will review the evidence for the absolute and relative chronology of these buildings and will attempt to explain what processes underlay the choice of their particular architectural forms and how these may shed light on the regional context of the new cathedral.

II

A group of west towers in the North East, including Billingham (pl. 11) and Monkwearmouth in Co. Durham, and Ovingham and Bywell St Andrew in Northumberland, has generally been assigned to the pre-Conquest period, sometimes even as early as the late tenth or early eleventh centuries.[1] These towers are

[1] Monkwearmouth is dated early eleventh-century and Billingham to c.1000 in *ASA*, I, 443, 69; Bywell St Andrew and Ovingham are dated to period C (950–1100) in *ASA*, I, 121 and 478. These dates are followed by, for example, N. Pevsner, *County Durham* (The Buildings of England; revised E. Williamson et al., Harmondsworth, 1983), pp. 95 and 466; N. Pevsner and I. Richmond, *Northumberland* (The Buildings of England; revised N. Grundy et al., Harmondsworth, 1992), pp. 204, and 538. Dissenting voices advocating a later date have,

Plate 11.   Billingham church (Co. Durham), west tower from the south.

characterized by double belfry windows with mid-wall shafts and surrounding stripwork forming a super-arch. They are also generally of tall slender proportions without buttresses or offset courses (pl. 11). None of them is dated on documentary evidence, so this must be deduced from their form alone. Though these four towers have features in common which indicate their close relationship to each other (notably the comparatively squat belfry openings and the lack of offsets), it is important not to over-emphasize their regional distinctiveness, for they are not only comparable to towers in Yorkshire, notably Wharram-le-Street and St Mary Bishophill Junior in York, but also form part of a much wider phenomenon characteristic also of East Anglia and the East Midlands.[2]

What is the likely date-range for the north-eastern towers? The latest likely date for the type as a whole was established in an epoch-making paper published as long

however, been raised: S. Rigold, 'The Distribution of Early Romanesque Towers to Minor Churches', *Arch. J.* 136 (1979), p. 113; J. Bony, 'Durham et la Tradition Saxonne', in *Études d'art médiévale offertes à Louis Grodecki*, ed. S.M. Crosby, A. Chastel, A. Prache, and A. Chatelet (Paris, 1981), p. 82.

[2]   Rigold, 'Distribution', p. 116, fig. 1; and D.A. Stocker, 'Discussion: the Form and Date of the Pre-12th Century Church', in L.P. Wenham et al., *St Mary Bishophill Junior and St Mary Castlegate* (The Archaeology of York: Anglo-Scandinavian York, 8/2; York, 1987), pp. 143–4.

ago as 1923 by John Bilson, whose analysis of Wharram-le-Street church demonstrated that its tower was unlikely to date from before 1100.[3] This view has been challenged by the Taylors on the grounds that the features which pointed to an early twelfth-century date were later insertions in an earlier fabric, but their arguments are not convincing.[4] Unfortunately the form of the uppermost parts of the belfry openings at Wharram remains uncertain as they were altered in the later Middle Ages; but the likelihood is, as Bilson suggested, that the surviving stripwork surrounds originally supported a super-arch like those of the north-eastern towers.[5] And even if this were not so, the surviving lower parts are still sufficient to demonstrate that the form of its openings closely resembled the latter.

There are examples of towers of this general type where the mid-wall shafts of the twin belfry openings are surmounted by a capital, the style of which may allow an approximate date to be inferred. This is particularly characteristic of the Lincolnshire examples, which generally have capitals of Romanesque form almost certainly derived from the cathedral at Lincoln;[6] this was under construction from the mid 1070s to the early 1090s,[7] so the towers are unlikely to be earlier (but may well be later) than the 1080s. A major factor determining the presence of these Romanesque elements in the Lincolnshire towers must have been the increasing availability in the region of large numbers of masons trained to reproduce such forms, particularly as work on the cathedral neared completion. The dangers of inferring from the *absence* of overtly Romanesque forms that a tower dates from a period before these became generally current in England should, therefore, be immediately apparent. For example, it would be inappropriate to argue this in Yorkshire before the Romanesque cathedral of York was nearing completion in

---

[3] J. Bilson, 'Wharram-le-Street Church, Yorkshire, and St Rule's Church, St Andrews', *Arch.* 73 (1923), pp. 64, and 69–73. A date as late as the 1120s has been advanced for Wharram: see R.D.H. Gem, 'The English Parish Church in the 11th and early 12th Centuries: a Great Rebuilding?', in *Minsters and Parish Churches. The Local Church in Transition 950–1200*, ed. J. Blair (Oxford University Committee for Archaeology monograph no. 17; Oxford, 1988), p. 29. But this depends on inference from a hypothetical historical context, whereas Bilson's more cautious dating relies on a detailed analysis of the architectural forms which seems to me incontrovertible.

[4] *ASA*, II, 651–3. The Taylors' view depends essentially on the belief that the equivalent arches at St Rule's church at St Andrews, Fife (with which Bilson had compared Wharram) were insertions into an earlier fabric. Since Fernie has recently overturned the Taylors' structural analysis of St Rule's in favour of Bilson's (E.C. Fernie, 'Early Church Architecture in Scotland', *Proceedings of the Society of Antiquaries of Scotland* 116 (1986), pp. 404–5), their observations about Wharram are seriously weakened. Moreover, Gem ('Great Rebuilding', pp. 28–9) has recently (and convincingly) defended Bilson's view of the tower at Wharram at least as a single-phase structure.

[5] Bilson, 'Wharram-le-Street', pp. 60–1, pl. V.

[6] An exhaustive (but as yet unpublished) analysis of the Lincolnshire towers has been undertaken by David Stocker and Paul Everson.

[7] R. Gem, 'Lincoln Minster: ecclesia pulchra, ecclesia fortis', in *Medieval Art and Architecture at Lincoln Cathedral*, ed. T.A. Heslop and V.A. Sekules (BAACT for 1982; London, 1986), pp. 9–10.

*c.*1100,[8] and even less appropriate north of the Tees before work on Durham Cathedral (completed *c.*1133) was well advanced. Yet this is precisely the form of argument employed by the Taylors in dating the tower of Billingham to *c.*1000.[9] What is more, the Wharram evidence, where a form of Romanesque capital was used in the ground-floor openings yet is absent from the surviving mid-wall shafts of the belfry openings, suggests that the absence of such Romanesque forms in the latter context may sometimes reflect deliberate choice on the part of the designer and should therefore be used with even more caution as a chronological indicator.

The beginnings of this type of tower are much harder to determine precisely. There are two possible lines of argument. First, it has been suggested that the north-eastern towers are in some sense reflections of the west tower of the Anglo-Saxon cathedral of Durham, built between 1020 and 1042. As this was presumably an imposing monument in its day, the desire to emulate it may have been an important motive underlying the construction of the other west towers in the region.[10] There is, however, an important distinction between the Durham tower's functioning as a general precedent and its having been the source of specific architectural forms, still less the recruiting ground of the masons who constructed the other towers in the North East. In other words, it provides only a *terminus post quem*, and need not imply that these towers must have been built anything like as early as the 1030s or 1040s, a date which, as will be demonstrated below, is unlikely on other grounds. In this connection, it is worth bearing in mind that the west tower of the cathedral was probably not demolished until *c.*1104, and would therefore have been available to serve as a model (in the general sense defined above) throughout the eleventh century.[11] Second, Morris's recent analysis of church building in Yorkshire has argued convincingly that the widespread use of stone there dates only from *c.*1050.[12] It seems most unlikely that the pattern in the North East would be significantly at variance with that of the adjacent region to the south; indeed, there is one scrap of evidence to suggest that the development of

[8] D. Phillips, *The Cathedral of Archbishop Thomas of Bayeux. Excavations at York Minster, II* (Royal Commission on the Historical Monuments of England; London, 1985), 6–7. It is conceivable that the presbytery at Beverley built by Archbishop Ealdred (1060–9) introduced Romanesque forms into Yorkshire as early as the 1060s (R. Morris and E. Cambridge, 'Beverley Minster before the Early Thirteenth Century', in *Medieval Art and Architecture in the East Riding of Yorkshire*, ed. C. Wilson (BAACT for 1983; London, 1989), pp. 19–20). Even if so, however, this work was perhaps too small-scale to have made a lasting impact on its region, and I am now less confident that the early Romanesque arches at Kirkdale church should be seen as reflecting its influence, nor that they date from as early as *c.*1065, as suggested in ibid.

[9] *ASA*, I, 69.

[10] R.D.H. Gem, 'A Recession in English Architecture during the early Eleventh Century and its Effect on the Development of the Romanesque Style', *JBAA* 38 (1975), pp. 29–30.

[11] E. Cambridge, 'The Anglo-Saxon Cathedral at Durham', in H.D. Briggs, E. Cambridge and R.N. Bailey, 'A New Approach to Church Archaeology: Dowsing, Excavation and Documentary Work at Woodhorn, Ponteland and the pre-Norman Cathedral at Durham', *Arch. Ael.*, 5th ser., 11 (1983), pp. 91–7.

[12] R.K. Morris, 'Churches in York and its Hinterland: Building Patterns and Stone Sources in the 11th and 12th centuries', in Blair, *Minsters and Parish Churches*, pp. 191–9.

stone church building in Co. Durham did in fact conform in general terms to the model proposed by Morris for Yorkshire. It concerns the documented rebuilding of the church of Chester-le-Street in stone between 1042 and 1057.[13] This church, the resting place of St Cuthbert's relics between the late ninth and the late tenth centuries, was arguably (at least from the Cuthbert Community's point of view) the most important holy place in the region after Durham itself, so its reconstruction may be assumed to have been the Community's highest priority after the completion of their cathedral. If so, it may be argued that the provision of a stone church was, at this period, a prestigious (and presumably therefore, still a comparatively uncommon) exercise.[14] In that case, the immediate and direct architectural impact of the Anglo-Saxon cathedral should probably be seen as limited in scope, and the extension of stone building to other church sites in the region (including the western towers under consideration here) as representing a later and distinct development.

In conclusion, it seems most unlikely that any of the western towers in the North East dates from before the mid eleventh century, and there are one or two hints that they represent a later phase than the one documented work of that period at Chester-le-Street. In addition, the comparative architectural evidence indicates that closely related forms of western tower were popular in Lincolnshire in the late eleventh century and probably persisted in Yorkshire into the early twelfth, and that both should be seen as the earliest attempts by indigenous masons working at a local level to come to terms with the Romanesque style. There is no reason to suppose that the North East was particularly ahead of these developments (and some grounds for thinking that, if anything, it may have been some way behind), while the absence of overtly Romanesque forms in the northern towers need not imply that they are any earlier than those from other regions in which such forms are present. On the whole, therefore, a late eleventh- to early twelfth-century date range seems the most likely.

The other church in the North East of allegedly 'late Saxon' type is Norton, which has been dated as early as around the year 1000 (pl. 12).[15] Few chronologically diagnostic details survive with which to determine its date, but this may be inferred from the form of the plan. The precise original extent of the church remains in doubt, but the surviving remains demonstrate that it was cruciform with a central tower and three porticus, probably of equal size and certainly (as the surviving roof-lines demonstrate) of equal height, opening to north, south, and east (pl. 12).[16] Cruciform churches are not uncommon in parts of the south of England in eleventh- and twelfth-century contexts, where they seem to be

---

[13] *LDE*, bk. 3, ch. 9 (p. 92); see E. Cambridge, 'The Early Church in County Durham: a Reassessment', *JBAA* 137 (1984), p. 80.

[14] The absence of evidence that the mid-eleventh-century church at Chester-le-Street incorporated a west tower may also be significant.

[15] *ASA*, I, 469; Pevsner, *County Durham*, pp. 65 and 442.

[16] *ASA*, I, 466–7, fig. 223. The extent of the nave of this period remains uncertain. I am grateful to Barrie Singleton for reminding me that it may originally have been equal in size to the other three arms.

Plate 12.   Norton church (Co. Durham), from the south-west.

associated with churches staffed by communities of clergy.[17] The plan type is much rarer in the north, however, and even more unusual in the North East, where Norton is the only pre-twelfth-century example; and the fact that any form of cruciform plan remains unusual in post-Conquest contexts in the region strongly suggests that it must always have been uncommon, for one might otherwise have expected that traces of such plan-types would have survived fossilized in later medieval church fabrics.[18] The closest surviving parallel for the particular type of cruciform plan adopted at Norton, in which the angles of the tower form slight salients between four arms of equal height, is at Stow in Lincolnshire. This phase of Stow is not certainly dated, but has been most plausibly associated with a reorganization of the church as an episcopal minster under high-status secular patronage in the early 1050s.[19] What is more, Stow is the earliest dated example of this type; it thus provides a possible *terminus ad quem* for Norton. Detailed comparison between the two makes it immediately clear that they are not closely related in an architectural sense, however, for Norton is not only considerably

[17] J. Blair, 'Secular Minster Churches in Domesday Book', in *Domesday Book: a Reassessment*, ed. P.H. Sawyer (London, 1985), p. 137, fig. 7.2.
[18] St Cuthbert's Darlington is a possible example. See further below, n. 25.
[19] *ASA*, III, 1001–2, 1038 and 1040, fig. 746; Gem, 'Great Rebuilding', p. 26.

smaller but appreciably less monumental in conception. The surviving detail of the crossing arches at Norton is also much less elaborate than at Stow, and is comparable rather to Yorkshire examples such as the chancel arch of Kirk Hammerton, or the tower arch of St Mary Bishophill Junior in York.[20] The latter analogy is particularly significant for determining the likely date of Norton, since the Bishophill tower, which has been shown to be of a single build including the tower arch, has belfry openings closely similar to the Wharram-le-Street type; as has been seen, these most likely date from the later eleventh or even the early twelfth centuries.[21] In combination, then, the comparative evidence suggests a date in the second half of the eleventh century, and more likely towards the latter end of that period.

There is no known historical context which might explain the presence of such a remarkable building at Norton in the late pre-Conquest period; indeed, the dominance of the Cuthbert Community at Durham was such that the construction of a church of such unusual form elsewhere in the region at this time is difficult to account for. On the other hand, there is a possible context later in the eleventh century, for, according to a tradition first recorded in the early fourteenth century, Norton was one of the places at which clerks of the Cuthbert Community were resettled by Bishop William of St Calais following their replacement at Durham itself by Benedictine monks in 1083.[22] Could he have built Norton to house dispossessed clerks? If so, the choice of an architectural form which is as exotic in its local context as it is indicative of uncommonly high status in regional terms would then be more readily explicable. What is more, there are grounds for thinking that the cruciform plan may sometimes have had more specifically

---

[20] The resemblance would have been closer before the removal of the inner order of the arches at Norton (*ASA*, I, 467); on Kirk Hammerton, see Morris, 'Churches in York', p. 197, and idem, 'Kirk Hammerton Church: the Tower and the Fabric', *Arch. J.* 133 (1976), pp. 95–103; on St Mary Bishophill Junior, see Wenham, *St Mary Bishophill Junior*, pp. 97–8, pl. XVII.

[21] Wenham, *St Mary Bishophill Junior*, pp. 130–4. Stocker estimates that the Bishophill tower dates to *c*.1050–80 ('Discussion', p. 146).

[22] The others are Auckland, Darlington, and Easington: see D. Rollason, 'Symeon of Durham and the Community of Durham in the Eleventh Century', in *England in the Eleventh Century*, ed. C. Hicks (Harlaxton Medieval Studies, 2; Stamford, 1992), pp. 191–2, n. 37. The naming of Easington as one of the clerks' churches may tell in favour of the tradition's authenticity: like the other three, it was adjacent to a major episcopal manor; but it was annexed to the archdeaconry of Durham in 1256 (R. Surtees, *The History and Antiquities of the County Palatine of Durham*, I (London and Durham, 1816), part ii, p. 12) and so did not become collegiate with the others in the late thirteenth century, which implies that the addition to Symeon does not simply anachronistically reflect the situation when it was written down. Further, three of the four churches selected in 1083 would then be sited at or near the centres of their respective Wards (Stockton being within Norton parish). The exception is Auckland (in Darlington Ward), leaving Chester Ward without any settlement of clerks; but it is easy to see why Chester-le-Street church, with its long-standing Cuthbertine associations (see above, p. 145), might have been deliberately avoided at a time when the new Benedictine community needed to establish control over the cult. For the possible implications regarding the antiquity of the Ward boundaries, see below, p. 405.

episcopal associations in the North. Stow itself seems to have had quasi-cathedral status;[23] while Morris has recently drawn attention to the fact that several twelfth-century prebendal churches of York Minster are cruciform in plan.[24] Darlington is itself a late twelfth-century example of a similar phenomenon.[25]

If the context proposed above for Norton is accepted, it would be of particular importance in underpinning the chronological context already suggested on stylistic grounds for the group of western towers in the region. Unfortunately the upper parts of the tower at Norton itself were reconstructed in the later Middle Ages, so the original form of its belfry openings remains unknown (pl. 12). But comparison with St Mary Bishophill Junior has shown that the crossing arches at Norton could have been contemporary with belfry openings of the type which occur in the western towers of the region; indeed, it is not inconceivable that they and Norton are all the work of the same masons. Of course, some or all of the towers may have preceded the work at Norton, so associating them with it can only provide a *terminus ad quem*. Nevertheless, a date range for this group of buildings between about the 1080s and the early twelfth century accords with the conclusions reached above on the basis of comparative architectural analysis; and hazardous though arguments from general historical contexts undoubtedly are, this would also square with the political and economic situation in the region in the later eleventh century, for the immediately preceding period (from the sack of Durham in 1069 to the harrying of the region under Odo of Bayeux in 1080) seems to have been one of political disturbance and economic depredation, producing conditions generally unfavourable to building activity, whereas the years after 1080 seem to have been comparatively peaceful.[26] If such considerations do carry any weight, it is more likely that the group of western towers should be assigned to after 1080 rather than to the 1060s; it would also reinforce the suggestion that there is a hiatus between these and any building activity which may be directly associated with the period immediately following the completion of the Anglo-Saxon cathedral in the second quarter of the eleventh century.[27]

---

[23] Gem, 'Great Rebuilding', p. 26.

[24] R.K. Morris, *Churches in the Landscape* (London, 1989), p. 283.

[25] As Darlington was another of the churches at which the Cuthbert Community clerks were said to have been resettled in 1083, it may be that the plan of the existing church (cruciform with a central tower) has been determined by that of a predecessor which resembled Norton in form and date. The late thirteenth-century church at St Andrew Auckland is also cruciform, though lacking a central tower.

[26] W.E. Kapelle, *The Norman Conquest of the North. The Region and its Transformation 1000–1135* (Chapel Hill and London, 1979), pp. 120–46.

[27] See above, pp. 144–5.

III

The story of the revival of monastic life at Jarrow and Monkwearmouth in the late eleventh century is a familiar one.[28] Its architectural implications are of considerable importance, not least because they provide a closely dated context for the forms used in the buildings at both places which can be attributed to the monastic reoccupation. At Jarrow, this consists principally of the monastic buildings, which must have been erected between the arrival of the monk Aldwin and his companions on the site in *c.*1074 and the transfer of the community to Durham in 1083;[29] the circumstances of the monks' stay at Jarrow allow the likely date to be refined still further, however. Stone buildings intended to house a fully conventual community are unlikely to have been begun in the earliest years of the monks' presence at the site given the strongly eremitical motivation of Aldwin and his first companions;[30] further, building work may well have been suspended shortly before 1083, since the transfer of the monks to Durham was presumably being contemplated by Bishop St Calais from shortly after his appointment in 1080. The Jarrow buildings are therefore most probably the products of no more than four or five seasons' work beginning in *c.*1076;[31] and as the reoccupation of Monkwearmouth took place only after the community was securely established at Jarrow, the remains of the south respond of the chancel arch of Monkwearmouth church, which can probably be attributed to this phase because of their stylistic similarity to the bases at Jarrow, can be dated even more closely, to the very end of the 1070s.[32]

Today only the south and west perimeter walls of the cloister remain at Jarrow, but the evidence of engravings made when substantial parts of the east range still stood, combined with that of the recent excavations, demonstrates that the east range, together with most if not all of the cloister walks, are likely to have been completed in the building campaign of *c.*1076–*c.*1080.[33] The only architectural

[28] *LDE*, bk. 3, chs. 22–3 (pp. 108–13).
[29] It is uncertain how much (if any) of the church tower can be attributed to Aldwin, though substantial parts have been claimed to be of his time (*ASA*, I, 345–7; cf. the much more circumspect account in R.J. Cramp, 'Jarrow Church', *Arch. J.* 133 (1976), pp. 225–7). The top two stages (which I consider to be datable stylistically to *c.*1100) appear to be a heightening of an older structure (or perhaps a change of mind during construction), defined by corbel-tables on the north and south walls. To judge from the window in its north face (*ASA*, I, fig. 154), the upper parts of the latter at least are Romanesque also; if this window is really as early as Aldwin's time, it does not seem to be associated stylistically with the claustral buildings (see further below, n. 52).
[30] *LDE*, bk. 3, chs. 22–3 (pp. 108 and 112); E. Cambridge, 'The Re-founded Monastery of Jarrow, Co. Durham, and its Eleventh-century Remains' (unpublished M.A. dissertation, University of Durham 1977), pp. 4–6.
[31] Cambridge, 'Re-founded Monastery', p. 8.
[32] Ibid., p. 36, pl. XXII. A fragment of a similar *ex situ* base (perhaps from the destroyed north respond of the chancel arch) survives in the west porch (ibid., p. 41, pls. XXIII–XXIV).
[33] Cramp, 'Jarrow Church', pp. 227–8, fig. 31; Cambridge, 'Re-Founded Monastery', pp. 11–14.

Plate 13. Jarrow (Co. Durham), south jamb of
northern doorway, west cloister wall.

details of these buildings still *in situ* are the two doorways in the west wall; the
southern is a simple triangular-headed opening, but the northern is more elaborate
with a single order of shafts with cushion capitals and bulbous bases (pl. 13).[34] The
ex situ fragments consist entirely of one or other of these forms, strongly suggesting
that the demolished parts of the buildings used them exclusively.[35]

At first sight the forms used at Jarrow do not seem particularly diagnostic or
remarkable. Yet the presence of cushion capitals in the North East closely datable to
the second half of the 1070s is worthy of further analysis in view of what is known
of the origins and distribution of this form in England and the Continent in the

[34] Imposts with billet ornament survive in a doorway in the south cloister wall (Cambridge,
'Re-founded Monastery', pl. XVI).
[35] There are seven capitals, all comparable in dimensions to those surviving *in situ*; and seven
bases, of which five are like the *in situ* ones, the sixth being for twin and the seventh for triple
shafts (Cambridge, 'Re-founded Monastery', pp. 20–6, pls. II–III, V–X).

later eleventh century. There are no demonstrably pre-Conquest examples of cushion capitals surviving in England.[36] What is more, they never occur in eleventh-century Normandy, where the standard capital types are ultimately derived from classical Corinthian prototypes.[37] In contrast the cushion form (particularly the unmitred variety which is used consistently at Jarrow) is ubiquitous in the German Empire from the beginning of the eleventh century whence it spread to the Low Countries *c.*1040–50.[38] Now, Dr Gem has recently argued convincingly that the presence of cushion capitals at Canterbury from the early 1070s is due to the importation of pre-cut examples from Flemish quarries.[39] The question then arises as to how their presence at the other end of the country within a very few years of their arrival is to be accounted for. It is not inconceivable that the form was introduced at Canterbury and was then diffused very rapidly; on the other hand, there is no reason to suppose that there need have been only one introduction of the motif, and this seems unlikely on other grounds (see below).

The form of the bulbous base (pl. 13) is probably best understood as a derivative of the classical Attic type in which the upper torus has been eliminated and the lower enlarged and simplified. The general distribution of the form is less diagnostic than that of the cushion capital in the context of the later eleventh century, for it also occurs in early Romanesque contexts in Normandy, for example, at Ste Paix in Caen, probably of the 1070s, as well as in the Low Countries.[40] The closest English parallels for the bulbous bases at Jarrow are the capitals of Great Paxton church, Huntingdonshire (pl. 14). In making this comparison, however, one must allow for the difference in architectural register between the small-scale Jarrow bases and the Paxton capitals, which are larger and more complex in plan as befits their context as part of the main arcades of that church; the bases of the chancel arch at Monkwearmouth form a more appropriate parallel. Great Paxton was probably erected in the third quarter of the eleventh century under royal patronage.[41] Fernie's recent analysis of its design has demonstrated conclusively that it is closely associated with churches of the early to mid eleventh century in the Low Countries.[42] As noted above, the bulbous form is also found in that region used as a base, for example, in the crypt of the small collegiate church of Huy, where it also

[36] R.D.H. Gem, 'Canterbury and the Cushion Capital: a Commentary on Passages from Goscelin's De Miraculis Sancti Augustini', in *Romanesque and Gothic: Essays for George Zarnecki* (Woodbridge, 1987), pp. 95–6.

[37] G. Zarnecki, 'Romanesque Sculpture in Normandy and England in the Eleventh Century', *AN* 1 (1979), pp. 168–89, at pp. 177–8.

[38] See, for example, St Peter's in Utrecht of *c.*1040–50 (T. Hoekstra, 'The Early Topography of the City of Utrecht and its Cross of Churches', *JBAA* 141 (1988), pp. 9 and 13, pls. IVa–b). Examples in the southern Low Countries demonstrably earlier than the mid-eleventh century are hard to find, suggesting that it was a slightly later development there. For apparently the earliest dated example, at Huy, see further below, and n. 43.

[39] Gem, 'Cushion Capital', p. 96.

[40] I am grateful to Dr Baylé for drawing the Caen examples to my attention. For the Low Countries, see below, and n. 43.

[41] *ASA*, II, 484.

[42] Unpublished lecture to the British Archaeological Association conference in Utrecht, 1993.

Plate 14.   Great Paxton church (Huntingdonshire), capital of nave arcade.

occurs in combination with unmitred cushion capitals; Huy was rebuilt by a
bishop of nearby Liège as his burial church and is datable to c.1050–66.[43]

The architectural forms used at Jarrow thus appear to derive ultimately from
works of the immediately preceding generation (c.1050 onwards) in the Low
Countries. Despite the absence of surviving cushion capitals at Great Paxton, the
close association of that design with the same part of the continent, the use of
bulbous forms for capitals analogous to those of the bases at Jarrow, and the fact
that it is likely to predate the Jarrow buildings, combine to suggest that the
immediate source of the architectural vocabulary of the latter could have been an
English intermediary rather than a direct importation. This would then explain the
presence at Jarrow of features like the triangular-headed doorway at the south end
of the west cloister wall, a common form for minor doorways in England in the
mid to late eleventh century;[44] and at Monkwearmouth of a chancel arch respond
clearly not of standard continental Romanesque plan, but comparable rather to
indigenous examples at Wittering, Northamptonshire, or Clayton, Sussex.[45]

[43] X. Barral i Altet, *Belgique Romane* (La Pierre-qui-Vire, 1989), pp. 41 and 281, pls. 80–2.
[44] *ASA*, III, 807–8.
[45] Cambridge, 'Re-Founded Monastery', pp. 36–7. A comparable interpretation of Wittering

IV

The second structure relevant to the question of the introduction of Romanesque forms into the North East is the so-called 'Norman Chapel' in Durham Castle. Setting aside the problems relating to the possible archaeological context and function of this structure,[46] the present discussion will confine itself to its likely date and stylistic affinities. The most striking feature of the capitals is their close resemblance to northern French forms, both in terms of ornamental repertoire and iconography, particularly those current in the Duchy of Normandy itself in the second half of the eleventh century. The comparisons are familiar from the work of Professor Zarnecki and others and need only be summarized briefly here. All are of the Corinthian-derived type (pl. 15), the dominant form in Normandy itself throughout the Romanesque period. Motifs such as the use of chip-carved fields, portrait masks, profile animals, and a hunting scene, can all be paralleled within the duchy.[47] The exclusive use of a number of imported forms seems best explained as a reflection of the direct employment of carvers trained in Normandy. The chronological implications are less clear-cut, however. The only documentary evidence of relevance is the *terminus post quem* provided by the foundation of the castle in *c.*1072.[48] Though a date as early as the 1070s has been suggested, this seems to reflect an implicit assumption that the 'purity' of the importation must imply an early date.[49] But it is important to take the local context of the monument into account, and in the North East the likelihood that a team of imported masons could still be working in isolation later in the eleventh century must be taken seriously, and would not be incompatible with the stylistic character of the building.[50]

V

The Romanesque buildings erected at Jarrow and Durham Castle could hardly form a greater stylistic contrast with one another. The former are derived ultimately from Low Countries prototypes, but the immediate source of the masons was probably a building erected in that style in England in the third quarter of the

and Clayton as reflecting Romanesque influence at one remove has been advanced by Gem, 'Great Rebuilding', pp. 26–7.

[46] See below, pp. 414–15, 427–8.

[47] G. Zarnecki, *English Romanesque Sculpture 1066–1140* (London, 1951), pp. 12–13 and 25–6, pls. 1–10; idem, '1066 and Architectural Sculpture', *Proceedings of the British Academy* 52 (1966), pp. 96–7, pls. XV–XVI.

[48] *HReg, s.a.* 1072.

[49] Zarnecki, *English Romanesque Sculpture*, p. 12; '. . . the earliest work of Norman sculptors in England' (idem, 'Architectural Sculpture', p. 92); '*c.*1080' (idem, 'Normandy and England', p. 186). The early dating was first challenged by K. Galbraith, 'Notes on Sculpture in Durham' (unpublished; circulated at British Archaeological Association conference in Durham in 1977), pp. 20–2.

[50] I am grateful to Dr Baylé for her helpful discussion of this building.

Plate 15.   Durham Castle, 'Norman Chapel', from
the west.

eleventh century. But if the architecture of Aldwin's Jarrow speaks with a distinctly
Flemish accent, that of Durham Castle equally clearly speaks with a Norman-
French one. What is more, though the sample is admittedly small, each building
seems to be internally consistent in its use of distinctive architectural forms, in
marked contrast to the syncretism apparent in Yorkshire designs of the 1080s such
as the crypt of Lastingham or the gatehouse of Richmond Castle.[51] How are these
phenomena to be explained?

   One possible immediate recruiting ground for the masons who built Jarrow is
the west Midlands, the area around Winchcombe (where Aldwin had formerly

[51] The crypt at Lastingham must date to the brief monastic reoccupation of the site between
$c.1080$ and 1086 (see above, pp. 41, 45); the Richmond gateway is undated, but is likely to be
approximately contemporary. A mixture of Corinthian-derived and multi-scalloped capital
types apparently occurred in York Minster as rebuilt $c.1080-c.1100$ (Phillips, *Excavations*, pls.
83 and 126, figs. 26 and 34a–b).

been prior), and Evesham (where his two original companions had been monks). The earliest major Romanesque work in the region was presumably the reconstruction of Evesham, begun *c.*1077,[52] but nothing is now known of its details, and the dating of the two projects makes it an unlikely (though not impossible) source for Jarrow. A more plausible explanation is that the choice of masons reflects episcopal patronage. After all, it was due to Bishop Walcher (1071–80) that the monks were able to settle at Jarrow (for long a possession of the Community of St Cuthbert) at all.[53] And Walcher's influence was arguably also instrumental in persuading them to adopt the conventual form of organization presupposed by the construction of claustral buildings, for the impulse which originally inspired Aldwin and his companions, and which probably continued to inspire many of his community's early recruits, was eremitical rather than coenobitic.[54] What is more, Walcher, who had been a canon of Liège before becoming Bishop of Durham, had contacts with precisely the area of the continent with which the Jarrow buildings are most closely associated stylistically.[55] It was noted above, however, that the latter might equally well be derived from an English intermediary rather than directly from the continent. Walcher's patronage could still provide the explanation, however, for he also held the manor of Waltham in Essex. Immediately before the Conquest the collegiate church there had been under the patronage of earl Harold Godwinson who had undertaken a major rebuilding.[56] Nothing of the architectural forms of that church is known. As Dr Barrow has pointed out, however, the third quarter of the eleventh century was a period in which Lotharingian influence on the English church was at its height, and this supplies a likely context for comparable architectural contacts.[57] As has already been seen, it is likely that Great Paxton – itself probably a work of royal patronage – should be understood as belonging in such a context; might Waltham also have been another example? If Walcher had recruited

---

[52] Though planned under abbot Aegelwin (d.1077), work was only begun under his successor, Walter (1077–86), by whose death the eastern arm had been completed: see *Chronicon Abbatiae de Evesham, ad annum 1418*, ed. W.D. Macray (RS 29; London, 1863), pp. 96–7. While accepting that the continuous roll moulding around the window in the north face of the first stage of the tower at Jarrow may imply a connection with south-west English Romanesque (as suggested in C. Wilson, 'Abbot Serlo's Church at Gloucester (1089–1100): its Place in Romanesque Architecture', in *Medieval Art and Architecture at Gloucester and Tewkesbury*, ed. T.A. Heslop and V.A. Sekules (BAACT for 1981; London, 1985), n. 34, p. 77), this need not involve postulating a link with Evesham in Aldwin's time; a similar moulding frames a minor window at the base of the north transept stair turret (perhaps of *c.*1100) at Durham cathedral itself (*ASA*, III, fig. 683).

[53] *LDE*, III, 21.

[54] See above, p. 149, n. 30.

[55] *HReg, s.a.* 1071; see above, pp. 151–2, notes 42–3. Also above p. 33.

[56] *LDE*, bk. 3, ch. 23; *DEC*, p. 23; E.C. Fernie, 'The Romanesque Church of Waltham Abbey', *JBAA* 138 (1985), at pp. 50–1. For archaeological evidence allegedly associated with Harold's church, see P.J. Huggins and K.N. Bascombe, 'Excavations at Waltham Abbey, Essex, 1985–1991: Three pre-Conquest Churches and Norman Evidence', *Archaeological Journal* 149 (1992), pp. 282–343; cf., however, Fernie, 'Waltham Abbey', pp. 74–5.

[57] See above, pp. 33–4.

his masons in England rather than directly from his former home, it would still not be surprising to find that he had preferred to employ fellow countrymen; and if the argument that many of the buildings allegedly dating to the late pre-Conquest period in the North East were in fact erected contemporaneously with or (more likely) even later than those at Jarrow is accepted, there might have been very few masons of any kind available in the region during Walcher's episcopate, so that the importation of masons from further afield would then have been not merely desirable but essential.

Episcopal patronage can similarly be adduced to explain the stylistic character of the 'Norman Chapel' at Durham. Given the obviously continental-Norman character of its forms, and that these are at least as likely to date from after 1080 as before, the likelihood is that the designer and carvers were procured by Bishop St Calais (1080–96), himself from Maine, which borders on Normandy to the southeast. They may have been imported directly from Normandy or Maine; alternatively, as suggested in the case of Walcher, the choice may have been the result of giving preferment to fellow countrymen already in England; in view of the stylistic consistency of the work, however, the former is much the more probable. Since St Calais was in exile in Normandy from 1088 to 1091, the likelihood is that the building dates from between 1080 and 1088 (or, just conceivably, immediately after 1091).[58]

A general implication of the preceding discussion is that the architectural differences between the buildings under consideration cannot be adequately explained by assuming that they reflect different stages in a single sequence of stylistic development which only needs putting into order to be properly understood; these differences can in fact be more plausibly explained as a function of the ways in which patronage operated in the North East in the later eleventh century. Only the bishops seem to have had the contacts and the resources to procure masons from outside the north, let alone from across the Channel. If the Aldwinian works at Jarrow and Monkwearmouth do indeed represent the first evidence of a resumption of building activity in the region following a significant hiatus in the third quarter of the eleventh century, then Bishop Walcher presumably had no choice but to import masons from outside. But it is possible to argue that the patronage of his successor did involve choices for, if the association of Norton church and works at Durham Castle with Bishop St Calais is right, it suggests that he considered that masons presumably trained and recruited fairly locally, and with only a limited knowledge of Romanesque forms, were suitable for a church built to rehouse Durham clerks, whereas his own accommodation in Durham Castle (built either contemporaneously or only very shortly afterwards in an up-to-date and unequivocally Romanesque style) warranted the importation of masons from across the channel; this may have had something to do with the bishop's personal aesthetic preferences as well as his perceptions of what was appropriate to his own status compared to that of his clerks. What is more, since the new Romanesque cathedral

---

[58] An attribution to St Calais was first suggested by Galbraith, 'Notes on Sculpture', pp. 20–2.

at Durham is itself a product of St Calais's enterprise, the remarkable diversity of his patronage in response to a variety of contexts starts to become apparent.

The series of western towers in the region presumably reflects the activity of more local patrons. Though their identity remains uncertain, it may be ventured that one of them was the newly founded priory at Durham itself. It is greatly to be regretted that Monkwearmouth, the only church in the area with examples of building of both the imported and regional varieties,[59] is undocumented after the withdrawal of the Aldwinian monks to Durham in 1083, and that these two phases are not related stratigraphically. Nevertheless, the west tower seems at least as likely to date from *after* 1083 as to the period before the monks' arrival in the late 1070s;[60] and as the church seems always to have remained in Durham Priory's possession, the monks would presumably have been responsible for it. In this connection, it is interesting to speculate as to whether the similar tower at Billingham dates from before or after the priory regained possession of that church, apparently only in 1089–91;[61] the latter possibility would again suggest that it should be interpreted as due to the priory's patronage.

If there is any single common characteristic which emerges from the above analysis of building in the Durham region in the second half of the eleventh century it is the lack of connection between the various works even though the three principal projects, at Jarrow, Durham Castle, and Norton, were probably all erected within little more than a decade of one another. But a comparison with other regions of Britain which lacked a strong local tradition of stone church building at the advent of the Romanesque style suggests that an initial phase of isolated and episodic projects is precisely what one would then expect. Fernie has recently drawn attention to a similar situation in his analysis of the earliest examples of Romanesque architecture in Scotland.[62] The buildings vary enormously in the variety of their architectural sources, from Irish-influenced round towers on the one hand to a tower which is derived from the tall unbuttressed northern early Romanesque type and a mature high Romanesque great church design derived from the new cathedral at Durham itself. Of particular significance for present purposes is that these are all likely to date from the half-century or so between c.1090 and the 1140s. They observe no discernible typological sequence, take no account of each other, and have little subsequent regional impact. In effect, they form an unconnected series of *sui generis* and often (in their local contexts) prestigious projects. It is possible to see the early Romanesque buildings of northeast England as a comparable phenomenon dating from a generation earlier than their Scottish counterparts.

The phenomenon of discontinuity is a general characteristic of the peripheral

---

[59] See above, p. 149; and p. 141.
[60] The Taylors considered that the tower of Monkwearmouth dated from before the time of Aldwin (i.e. the late 1070s) and, indeed, to before the Conquest (*ASA*, I, 69); contrast, however, Bony, 'Tradition Saxonne', p. 82 ('au plus tôt de 1075').
[61] *DEC*, p. 10.
[62] E.C. Fernie, 'Early Church Architecture in Scotland'.

areas of Anglo-Norman England (that is, roughly speaking, those areas lying west of the Severn and north of the Trent) in the generation following the Conquest. The bishop's chapel at Hereford is perhaps the most obviously comparable west-country example.[63] The development of Romanesque architecture in these areas contrasts markedly with those parts of England lying east and south of this line, where most of the great abbeys and cathedrals were situated, and where, if a comparatively strong local building tradition was not already in existence before the Conquest, one developed very soon afterwards. What is more, it was in these southern and eastern parts of England that a broad consensus on what constituted the form of a great church became established comparatively quickly after the Conquest.[64] But it was precisely in the peripheral areas of the west and north, where such a consensus had not yet crystallized, that many of the most innovative architectural developments in the design of great churches in the late eleventh and early twelfth centuries – Gloucester and Tewkesbury in the South West, York and Durham in the North – were able to flourish.

From the perspective of its local architectural context, the commencement of Durham Cathedral in 1093 may be seen as yet another in a series of unconnected architectural episodes in the North East; in other respects, however, it marked a new development in the region, for the unprecedented increase in scale of that project and the length of time it took to complete alike imply the importation, in large numbers and on a long-term basis, of masons trained in the production of mature Romanesque forms.[65] The analysis of the immediately preceding period, moreover, demonstrates just how important active episcopal patronage must have been in procuring its designer. And it may well have been precisely the absence of any established regional tradition before 1093 which helped to make the adoption of a design as innovative as that of the new cathedral of Durham possible at all.

[63] R.D.H. Gem, 'The Bishop's Chapel at Hereford: the Roles of Patron and Craftsman', in *Art and Patronage in the English Romanesque*, ed. S. Macready and F.H. Thompson (Society of Antiquaries Occasional Paper (new series), VIII; London, 1986), pp. 87–96.

[64] B. Cherry, 'Romanesque Architecture in Eastern England', *JBAA* 131 (1978), pp. 1–29.

[65] The impact of the cathedral workshop on its region cannot be further discussed here, but it should be noted that its first fruits are, in my opinion, likely to include works (notably the lower parts of the tower at Jarrow and the nave of Tynemouth priory church) which others have argued *predate* 1093. For the former, see above notes 29 and 52; for the latter, see Appendix.

APPENDIX

A Note on Tynemouth Priory

One Romanesque building in the region for which a date preceding the start of work on Durham Cathedral has been claimed is Tynemouth.[66] Though the possibility cannot be ruled out completely, this view largely depends on a misunderstanding of the documentation of the site in the later eleventh century. The church there was granted to the Benedictines who had settled at Jarrow, probably shortly after their arrival in c.1074.[67] At this stage, building activity appears to have been confined to repairing an existing (and presumably pre-Conquest) church.[68] Ownership of Tynemouth would thus have passed to Durham priory with the transfer of the Jarrow monks in 1083. Later, however, it was granted by Robert Mowbray, Earl of Northumberland, to the monks of St Albans, who founded a dependent monastery there, a development bitterly resented by the Durham monks. As Professor Offler demonstrated, previous attempts to date the acquisition of the church by St Albans to the 1080s have depended on the acceptance as genuine of Durham charters which are clearly forgeries; Tynemouth is in fact unlikely to have been acquired before 1090 or 1091.[69] The first priority of the incoming St Albans monks would surely have been to construct a cloister and monastic buildings for themselves while retaining the existing church for the time being, exactly as happened at Jarrow.[70] The only fixed point in the chronology of the Romanesque church at Tynemouth is the translation of St Oswin's relics into it in 1110,[71] an event which must indicate that the eastern arm, and probably also the crossing and east end of the nave (which presumably housed the monks' choir) were complete by that time. The second half of the 1090s thus seems the most likely period in which work would have started on the church, since on the one hand this allows time for the cloister and monastic buildings to have been sufficiently advanced to accommodate the monks, while on the other the modest size of the Romanesque church implies that enough to enable a translation of relics to take place could have been built by the end of the first decade of the twelfth century.[72]

---

[66] See, for example, W.H. Knowles, 'The Priory Church of St. Mary and St. Oswin, Tynemouth, Northumberland', *Arch. J.*, 67 (1909), p. 3; A.W. Clapham, *English Romanesque Architecture After the Conquest* (Oxford, 1934), p. 36 (shortly after 1085); and Bony, 'Tradition Saxonne', p. 85, n. 7 ('peu d'anneés avant Durham même').

[67] Between 1075 and 1080 (*DEC*, p. 5).

[68] *LDE*, bk. 4, ch. 4 (p. 124).

[69] *DEC*, p. 5.

[70] See above, pp. 149–50. Traces survive at Tynemouth of the monastic buildings presumably of this period; they resemble the Aldwinian buildings at Jarrow in scale (R.N. Hadcock, *Tynemouth Priory* (London, 1952), plan at end).

[71] 'Vita Oswini Regis', in *Miscellanea Biographica* (SS 2; 1838), ch. 11 (p. 24).

[72] Knowles, 'Tynemouth', fig. on p. 6. The description by Matthew Paris (writing at St Albans in the mid-thirteenth century) of the burial in 1093 by Earl Robert Mowbray of the body of

To judge from its surviving remains, the design of the new church at Tynemouth was related stylistically to that of Durham in its use of cylindrical piers with octagonal scalloped capitals.[73] The chronology proposed above thus implies that Tynemouth should be seen as an early example of the architectural influence of Durham, but the fragmentary nature of the Romanesque remains there mean that it is now impossible to establish whether its design had been influenced by Durham from the beginning or whether this is merely an ad hoc borrowing.

Malcolm Canmore King of Scots 'in ecclesia de Thynemue, quam idem comes construxerat' (*Chronica Majora*, ed. H.R. Luard (6 vols., RS 57; 1882–86), VI, p. 372) can hardly be taken as reliable authority that the Romanesque church had been begun before 1093 (or, indeed, before Mowbray's death in 1095); it would have been all too easy to assume that the founder of the monastery had also been the builder of its church.

[73] Knowles, 'Tynemouth', pl. 5, no. 3.

The Roles of the Patron and the Master Mason in the First Design of the Romanesque Cathedral of Durham

MALCOLM THURLBY

S YMEON OF DURHAM relates that in 'the ninety-eighth year since it had been founded by Ealdhun, he [Bishop William of St Calais] ordered the church to be demolished and after he had laid the foundations in the following year, he began to construct another on a nobler and grander scale.'[1] On 11 August 1093 'the bishop and Prior Turgot, who was second in authority to him in the church, with the other brothers laid the first stones in the foundations. Shortly before, that is on Friday 29 July, the bishop and prior after saying prayers with the brothers and giving their blessing had begun to dig the foundations. While the monks were responsible for building the monastic buildings, the bishop carried out the work on the church at his own expense'.[2]

Payment for the work by Bishop William suggests that he was directly involved with the design of the building, not least for budgetary considerations, liturgical propriety, and the desire to ensure that his church was a worthy rival in scale and decoration to the grandest churches in Europe. He would therefore have formulated the brief in which the essential form of the building would have been determined. The situation may have been similar to the one suggested by Richard Gem for the Romanesque cathedral at Winchester, in which Bishop Walkelin's brief incorporated the most elaborate features of the new High Romanesque architecture of Europe, as well as reference to the pre-Conquest cathedral at Winchester, Edward the Confessor's Westminster Abbey, and the length of Old St Peter's Rome.[3] Gem observed, on the other hand, that the masonry technique, the system

[1] *LDE*, bk. 4, ch. 8 (pp. 128–9). I wish to thank many friends with whom I have discussed various aspects of this paper; Maylis Baylé, John Crook, Ian Curry, Eric Fernie, Richard Gem, Stuart Harrison, Fil Hearn, Hugh McCague, and Tom Russo. The Head Verger, Owen Rees, and his assistant, Reg Wright, have very kindly facilitated my access to all parts of the cathedral during the preparation of this study.

[2] *LDE*, bk. 4, ch. 8 (p. 129). On William's death the monks continued with the work of the church. Episcopal funding of the construction was not resumed under William's successor, Ranulf Flambard (1099–1128); see M.G. Snape, 'Documentary Evidence for the Building of Durham Cathedral and its Monastic Buildings', in *MAADC*, pp. 21–2.

[3] Richard Gem, 'The Romanesque Cathedral of Winchester: Patron and Design in the Eleventh Century', in *Medieval Art and Architecture at Winchester Cathedral* (BAACT 6 for 1980; London, 1983), pp. 1–12; see also, idem, 'The Bishop's Chapel at Hereford: the Roles

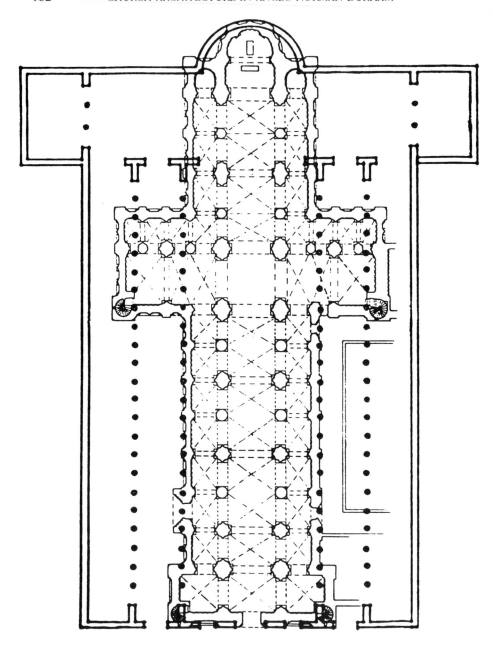

Fig. 4.   Durham Cathedral, plan of Romanesque church, superimposed on Rome, plan of Old St Peter's.

of construction, and individual forms, in other words, the 'grammar' of the architecture, indicated the work of a mason from the Anglo-Norman tradition established at Canterbury. There can be little doubt that, like Walkelin, William wished to emulate the greatest buildings in Europe, and to create a monumental display of Norman ecclesiastical order in the north as a sequel to the great symbol of secular authority of the castle. Sheer monumentality, however, would not suffice. The most progressive churches begun in England and Normandy in the decade or so before 1093 were increasingly elaborate in articulation and decoration. To create a suitable new setting for St Cuthbert, the cathedral had to have a richness appropriate for an architectural shrine, and, in the spirit of rivalry with Winchester and elsewhere, it had to suggest association with the shrine of St Peter in Rome. Examination of the salient features of the Romanesque fabric of Durham Cathedral will allow us to suggest the roles of Bishop William and his master mason in the design and execution of the church.

The great length of Romanesque Durham Cathedral is allied to Old St Peter's, Rome (fig. 4). The external length of Durham was 123.09 m; while that of Old St Peter's is estimated by Krautheimer to have been 122.38 m. The internal length at Durham was approximately 117.83 m; at Old St Peter's it was estimated to have been approximately 119.23 m.[4] Furthermore, the internal width of the choir and aisles at Durham is 23.52 m and the corresponding nave width 24.71 m; the width of the central aisle of the nave of St Peter's is given by Krautheimer as 23.65 m. The spiral piers in the presbytery and transept arcades at Durham (pl. 16) have been convincingly related to the spiral columns from the shrine of St Peter,[5] and it is possible that the ribs of the Durham vaults also reflect this source. It is universally accepted that the form of the fourth-century shrine of St Peter is faithfully represented on the Pola Casket.[6] On the other hand, the similar use of the spiral columns in the shrine on the Pola Casket and in Bernini's baldachin (1624–33) has been described as 'one of the strangest of coincidences – for he (Bernini) cannot possibly have had any idea of the original Constantinian canopy dismantled many centuries before.'[7] St Peter's shrine was rebuilt c.600 by Pope Gregory the Great, at

of Patron and Craftsman', in *Art and Patronage in the English Romanesque*, ed. Sarah Macready and F.H. Thompson (London, 1986), pp. 87–96; and Eric Fernie, *An Architectural History of Norwich Cathedral* (Oxford, 1993), pp. 59–61.

4   Richard Krautheimer, Spencer Corbett and Alfred K. Frazer, *Corpus Basilicarum Christianarum Romae: The Early Christian Basilicas of Rome (IV–IX Cent)* (5 vols., Vatican, 1937–77), V, 242–3 and 286, pl. V; Hugh George McCague, 'Durham Cathedral and Medieval Architecture: Manifestation of the Sacred through Number and Geometry' (unpublished M.A. thesis, York University, 1993), pp. 13–14.

5   Eric Fernie, 'The Spiral Piers of Durham Cathedral', in *MAADC*, pp. 50–8; for illustrations see Jocelyn Toynbee and John Ward Perkins, *The Shrine of St Peter* (London 1956), p. 202, fig. 20. See also, Eric Fernie, *Norwich Cathedral*, pp. 78–9 and 129–33.

6   On the Pola casket, see Richard Krautheimer, *Early Christian and Byzantine Architecture* (4th edn, revised by Richard Krautheimer and Slobodan Ćurčić, Harmondsworth, 1986), p. 56, ill. 23; and Toynbee and Ward Perkins, *Shrine of St Peter*, pp. 201–4, fig. 20.

7   Toynbee and Ward Perkins, *Shrine of St Peter*, p. 250. On Bernini's baldachin, see Howard Hibberd, *Bernini* (Harmondsworth, 1965), pp. 75–80, pl. 36. I should like to thank Professor

Plate 16. Durham Cathedral, north presbytery aisle
looking east.

which time the spiral columns were reused in a screen in front of the newly raised
presbytery. An outer screen of a further six spiral columns was added by Pope
Gregory III (731–41).[8] But there is also a remarkable similarity between the
openwork ribs in the canopy over St Peter's shrine represented on the Pola Casket
and those in Bernini's baldachin. Is this another coincidence or could it be that the
ribs from the Constantinian baldachin were either reused or copied in the one
created by Gregory the Great and therefore provided the exemplar for Bernini's
baldachin, as well as for the architectural canopy over the shrine of St Cuthbert?

Chandler Kirwin for discussing Bernini's baldachin with me and for sending me a typescript of
his forthcoming book, *Powers Matchless: Urban VIII, the Baldachin and Bernini.*
[8] Toynbee and Ward Perkins, *Shrine of St Peter*, p. 215, fig. 22, p. 216.

The presence of ribs in the St Peter's canopy throughout the Middle Ages would also help to explain the popularity of the rib as a signifier of an especially important place within a Romanesque church, such as a shrine or an altar – witness their use in the eastern bay of the presbytery at S. Abbondio at Como, at St-Martin-de-Boscherville, at Ewenny Priory, and formerly in the apse of Peterborough Cathedral – just as spiral piers often perform such an iconographic role.[9] In view of the similarity between certain dimensions of Durham Cathedral and Old St Peter's, there is reason to relate the spiral piers and the ribs at Durham to the shrine of St Peter. This iconographic parallel, which almost certainly would have been devised by Bishop William, associates St Cuthbert with the Prince of Apostles. Moreover, in translating the spiral column and the rib from the realm of church furniture at St Peter's to a truly monumental form integrated with the building at Durham, William has, in effect, created a great architectural shrine for St Cuthbert.

This association with the Constantinian basilica of St Peter's groups Durham with some of the most prestigious churches in Europe. In northern Europe the emulation of the huge scale of Old St Peter's commenced with the western transept of Abbot Ratger's church at Fulda (802–19), and was followed in Mainz Cathedral, commenced by Archbishop Willigis in 978, in the imperial cathedral of Speyer (c.1030) and Pisa Cathedral (1063), at the third Abbey Church of Cluny (1088), and at the great pilgrimage church of St Sernin, Toulouse (c.1080). The immediate precursors of the large scale of Durham, however, were the great post-Conquest churches in England, and for this reason Bishop William's new church had to be an especially worthy rival.

The tradition of large-scale churches in post-Conquest England was established at the abbey church of St Albans, begun by Abbot Paul of Caen in 1077, and was followed at Winchester Cathedral (1079), Ely Cathedral (c.1081), Bury St Edmunds Abbey (c.1081) and Old St Paul's in London (after 1087).[10] St Albans

[9] For S. Abbondio, Como, see Sandro Chierici, *Lombardie Romane* (La Pierre-qui-Vire, 1978), pp. 171–8, pl. 61. See also, Christopher Wilson, 'Abbot Serlo's Church at Gloucester, 1089–1100: Its Place in Romanesque Architecture', in *Medieval Art and Architecture at Gloucester and Tewkesbury*, ed. T.A. Heslop and V.A. Sekules (BAACT 11 for 1981; London, 1985), p. 64, pl. XI.F (Boscherville); Malcolm Thurlby, 'The Romanesque Priory Church of St Michael at Ewenny', *Journal of the Society of Architectural Historians* 47 (1988), p. 293; and idem, 'The Romanesque Apse Vault at Peterborough Cathedral', in *Studies in Medieval Art and Architecture presented to Peter Lasko*, ed. David Brickton and T.A. Heslop (Stroud, 1994), pp. 171–86. On the iconography of spiral columns, see Fernie, *Norwich Cathedral*, pp. 129–33.

[10] Eric Fernie, 'The Effect of the Conquest on Norman Architectural Patronage', *AN* 9 (1986), p. 85, refers to the 'near megalomania' of the new patrons, and suggests (idem, 'Observations on the Norman Plan of Ely Cathedral', in *Medieval Art and Architecture at Ely Cathedral*, ed. N. Coldstream and P. Draper (BAACT 2 for 1976; London, 1979), p. 4) 'that the great length of the more important Anglo-Norman churches is an attempt to emulate the size of the largest Early Christian basilicas in Rome'. See also, idem, *Norwich Cathedral*, pp. 135–6 and fig. 51, superimposing the plans of Bury St Edmunds Abbey and Old St Peter's. Richard Gem, 'The Romanesque Architecture of Old St Paul's Cathedral and its Late Eleventh-Century Context', in *Medieval Art, Architecture and Archaeology in London*, ed. L. Grant (BAACT 10 for 1984; London, 1990), pp. 53, 58.

Plate 17.   Winchester Cathedral, north transept, north aisle.

housed the shrine of St Alban, Winchester that of St Swithin; Ely had St Etheldreda, St Edmund was at Bury St Edmunds, and St Erkenwald at Old St Paul's. All these churches had long eastern arms: four bays at St Albans, Winchester, Ely, and Old St Paul's, five bays at Bury St Edmunds. This contrasts with the two-bay eastern arms in Normandy and in early Anglo-Norman England, such as St-Étienne at Caen (*c.*1064) and Lanfranc's Christ Church at Canterbury (1070), or the three-bay presbytery at Remigius's Lincoln (*c.*1072/5). Given the association of these long eastern arms, and long churches in general, with English saints, it is hardly surprising that Bishop William should have wanted the architectural shrine of St Cuthbert to rival these buildings. St Albans and Winchester seem to have been of particular interest in this connection.

The eastern arm of St Albans had a high groin-vault and may have had a three-apse east end with enclosed aisle apses.[11] Although normally regarded as a plain building, not least because of the use of flint and Roman brick as the primary building materials, St Albans in fact made significant contributions to the more elaborate articulation associated with the second generation of great post-Conquest churches. In the nave arcades and the arches from the nave aisles to the transepts three orders are used, rather than two as in earlier Norman buildings, with the concomitant stepped orders in the piers.[12] String courses are used between the main arcade, gallery and clerestories, while the painted groins of the extant Romanesque vaults of the presbytery aisles and the painted ribbons on the nave arcade arches are the typological forerunners respectively of the ribs and the moulded arches at Durham.[13] The proportions of the St Albans nave elevation, in which the main arcade is significantly taller than the gallery, presage Durham. While the proportions of the two buildings are not the same, the St Albans scheme comes significantly closer to Durham than the approximately one-to-one proportions of the main arcade and gallery in elevations of the St Étienne at Caen tradition, as at Christ Church at Canterbury, Winchester, and Ely (c.1081/3). The turrets at the corners of the transepts at Durham may also have been inspired by St Albans.[14]

The articulation of the piers and aisle walls at Durham betrays knowledge of Winchester Cathedral (pls. 16 and 17).[15] The alternation of compound and columnar piers reflects the Winchester presbytery and, in turn, the nave of Westminster Abbey.[16] The minor pier supporting the gallery at the end of each transept at Winchester is columnar and has a dosseret and half shaft towards the aisle. This is a forerunner of the minor piers of the presbytery and transept arcades at Durham with their stepped shafts towards the aisles. Similarly, the stepped aisle responds at Durham reflect Winchester.[17] The earliest extant example of a dado arcade in England is at Winchester where it takes the form of unmoulded round-headed arches on shafts with cushion capitals. At Durham the motif is more elaborate with intersecting arches on paired monolithic shafts and scalloped and multi-scalloped capitals.

[11] On the evidence for a high groin-vault in the St Albans presbytery, see *VCH, Hertfordshire*, II, ed. C.R. Peers and William Page (London, 1908), pp. 484 and 490. The form of the eastern termination at St Albans is not known for sure; see I.C. Buckler and C.A. Buckler, *A History of the Architecture of the Abbey Church of St. Alban, with especial reference to the Norman Structure* (London, 1847), p. 45.
[12] Lawrence Hoey, 'Pier Form and Vertical Wall Articulation in English Romanesque Architecture', *Journal of the Society of Architectural Historians* 48 (1989), pp. 262–3.
[13] Although the painted architectural decoration at St Albans is variously dated, that of the presbytery groin-vaults seems to be thirteenth-century but it covers a similar earlier scheme.
[14] On turrets and the grouping of towers, see Gem, 'Winchester', pp. 7–9.
[15] John Bilson, 'Durham Cathedral: The Chronology of its Vaults', *Arch. J.* 79 (1922), p. 108, suggested that the master mason of Durham may have worked at Winchester Cathedral.
[16] Gem, 'Winchester', p. 6; John Crook, 'The Romanesque East Arm and Crypt of Winchester Cathedral', *JBAA* 142 (1989), p. 25, fig. 5.
[17] John Bilson, 'The Beginnings of Gothic Architecture, II, Norman Vaulting in England', *Journal of the Royal Institute of British Architects*, 3rd ser., 6 (1899), pp. 291–3.

Plate 18. Durham Cathedral, north presbytery gallery looking east.

Of the features common to Durham, St Albans, and Winchester, many suggest
the choice of the patron, and further indicate his desire to surpass the architectural
achievements of his contemporaries. Thus, unlike St Albans, the high stone vaults
at Durham were not confined to the eastern arm.[18] Unmoulded arches and groin-
vaults at Winchester, and their painted counterparts at St Albans, become respectively moulded and ribbed at Durham.[19] The alternating pier system at Winchester
had plain minor columnar piers while at Durham they have incised spirals in the
presbytery and transepts, not purely for decoration, but to create a more visually
explicit link with Old St Peter's than had been achieved at either St Albans or
Winchester. For the proportions of the elevation the St Albans model may have
been preferred by Bishop William because Durham, like St Albans, adopted the
liturgy of the *Decreta Lanfranci* without altars in the galleries, as opposed to the

[18] For the view that high vaults were originally intended in the transepts, first expressed by
John Bilson, see Malcolm Thurlby, 'The Romanesque High Vaults of Durham Cathedral', in
Engineering a Cathedral, ed. Michael J. Jackson (London, 1993), pp. 47–55. The case for the
plan to roof the transepts in wood from the first is presented by Jean Bony, 'Le projet premier
de Durham: Voûtement partiel ou voûtement total?', in *Urbanisme et architecture. Études écrites
et publiées en l'honneur de Pierre Lavedan* (Paris, 1954), pp. 41–9; and E.C. Fernie, 'Design
Principles of Early Medieval Architecture as Exemplified at Durham Cathedral', in *Engineering
a Cathedral*, ed. Jackson, pp. 153–4.
[19] On the aesthetic aspect of the rib see Malcolm Thurlby, 'The Purpose of the Rib in the
Romanesque Vaults of Durham Cathedral', in *Engineering a Cathedral*, ed. Jackson, pp. 43–63.

Regularis Concordia which was followed at Winchester and required gallery altars.[20] Other parallels between Durham and Winchester, such as the similarity in the basic form of the piers and responds at Winchester and Durham, as well as the external articulation with pilaster buttresses and string courses, internal articulation with dosserets and half shafts, and the use of the cushion capital, were probably not determined by the patron, but rather indicate that the master mason of Durham was at work in England in the 1080s, a point to which we return below.

Recently it has been suggested that the Romanesque cathedral of Winchester may have had towers over the eastern bays of the presbytery aisles.[21] If this is correct, it would be another possible similarity between Winchester and Durham, since there is evidence for the former existence of eastern towers at Durham. The responds of the diaphragm arches across the galleries at the chord of the former Romanesque apses of Durham Cathedral are different from the responds of the other diaphragm arches in the choir and transept galleries there. Instead of projecting 15.2 cm from the wall in the south gallery and 26.7 cm in the north, they project some 1.22 m (pl. 18). They encase upward spiralling staircases, the lowest remnants of which are extant. It has been suggested that these staircases would have risen up as turrets.[22] As such they would only have given access to the gallery roof, in contrast, for example, to the turrets at Peterborough Cathedral which form the continuation of staircases on the inner angles of the apse chord and provide a link between the gallery and clerestory. Therefore, it seems more likely that these Durham staircases were connected with towers over the square enclosed apses. This interpretation is supported by fragments of Romanesque ashlar on both the north and south walls above the apse-chord diaphragm arches, and on the north wall by a break in the coursing of the stonework on the corresponding clerestory buttress (pls. 19 and 20).[23] This break can be explained by the removal of the west wall of the tower when the thirteenth-century extension of the presbytery was built.

Confirmation that the staircases in the responds of the apse-chord arches of the Durham galleries were connected with towers is found in the south nave gallery at Peterborough Cathedral (*c.*1150). Against the outer wall of the gallery opposite the penultimate pier of the Romanesque nave at Peterborough, a spiral stair starts up in the manner of those at Durham. The Peterborough stair is built against the east side respond rather than within the respond as at Durham, but otherwise the

---

[20] A.W. Klukas, 'The Architectural Implications of the *Decreta Lanfranci*', *AN* 6 (1983/4), pp. 151–3, 159 and 163–5, figs. 4, 7 and 11.

[21] Crook, 'Winchester', fig. 2.

[22] Ian Curry, 'Aspects of the Anglo-Norman Design of Durham Cathedral', *Arch. Ael.* 5th ser., 14 (1986), p. 45.

[23] Any such break in the corresponding section of the south clerestory will have been removed by its refacing. See Durham Dean and Chapter Minutes, III (April 1829–2 Feb. 1867), p. 817, 20 Nov. 1830: 'Ordered that a sum not exceeding £300 be granted towards the Restoration of the Clerestory, in the South side, between the West and East transepts, out of the General Fund . . .' On restorations in general, see Ian Curry, 'Continuity and Change: Masters, Surveyors and Architects to the Fabric of the Cathedral', in *Durham Cathedral: A Celebration*, ed. Douglas Pocock (Durham, 1993), pp. 36–54.

Plate 19.   Durham Cathedral, north presbytery gallery,
detail of masonry above south respond of apse-chord arch.

parallel is exact; and most importantly the Peterborough staircase was constructed
in connection with the planned western towers of the Romanesque fabric. The
main arcade and gallery piers at this point are bigger than those to the east, and
they are accompanied by broader transverse arches than in the other bays in the
aisles.[24] Also, the removal of the stonework above the transverse arch at Peterborough has left a mark like that on the walls above the transverse arches of the
apse chord at Durham (pl. 21).

Eastern towers were used in the Romanesque fabric of Hereford Cathedral
(c.1107–15) and above the north-east and south-east radiating chapels of Conrad's

[24] Sir Charles Peers, 'Peterborough Minster', in *VCH, Northamptonshire*, II, ed. W.D. Atkins
et al. (London, 1906), p. 440.

Plate 20.   Durham Cathedral, north presbytery clerestory,
detail of masonry at former junction of west wall of
north-east tower.

choir at Canterbury Cathedral (1096–1130).[25] They may derive from Lotharingia,
where they appeared before 942 at St Maximin at Trier, but seeing that staircases
seem to have flanked the apse of Old St Peter's, and that they may have been
carried up as towers, it is tempting, once again, to suggest that Bishop William had
in mind an iconographic association between Durham and the Vatican basilica, not
to mention the desire to rival the eastern towers at Winchester.[26] Furthermore, the
plan for paired towers at both the east and west ends of Durham may also have

[25] Royal Commission on Historical Monuments, *Herefordshire, Vol. 1, South-West* (London,
1931), p. 93; and Francis Woodman, *The Architectural History of Canterbury Cathedral* (London, 1981), p. 48, fig. 12.
[26] Krautheimer et al., *Corpus*, V, pl. 5. On eastern towers in general, see Pierre Heliot, 'Sur les

Plate 21. Peterborough Cathedral, south nave gallery
looking west.

been intended to represent a heavenly fortress, the ecclesiastical counterpart to the
secular castle on the other side of the peninsula.[27] This direct juxtaposition of
cathedral and castle is paralleled at Lincoln, and there is a further specific link
between the design of the cathedrals of Durham and Lincoln in the staircases. Both
are exceptionally wide in ecclesiastical terms; 1.7 m at Durham and 1.47 m at
Lincoln, as opposed to the approximately one-metre norm in large Anglo-Norman

tours jumelées au chevet des églises du moyen âge', in *Arte in Europa: Scritti di storia dell'arte
in onore di Edouardo Arslan* (Milan, 1967), pp. 249–70; and Charles B. McClendon, *The
Imperial Abbey of Farfa* (New Haven and London, 1987), pp. 86–90.
[27] E. Baldwin Smith, *Architectural Symbolism in Imperial Rome and the Middle Ages* (Princeton,
1956), pp. 74–106 esp. p. 85.

Plate 22.   Durham Cathedral, stair turret in west bay of
south nave aisle.

churches. Richard Gem has suggested that the need for miltary fortification was
one aspect of the design of Remigius's west block at Lincoln Cathedral.[28] The
possibility that such a military function existed at Durham is strengthened with
reference to the design of the staircases in the keep at Castle Hedingham (Essex).
The staircases in the western angles of the transepts and the western towers at
Durham project boldly into the church in the same way as the staircase does into
the keep at Castle Hedingham. The angle of the Castle Hedingham stair is even
articulated in the same manner as the western stairs at Durham (pls. 22 and 23).
Arnold Klukas has demonstrated that the galleries at Durham did not serve any

Plate 23. Castle Hedingham (Essex), Great Hall of the keep,
interior looking towards the stair turret.

liturgical purpose.[29] Therefore, the unusually large scale of the staircases cannot be
associated with processions of clergy but rather with the potential for the movement of troops to the upper reaches of the fabric.

The intersecting arches of the internal dado arcades are presaged in the canon
tables of pre-Conquest gospel books – specifically the Canterbury Gospels (BL,
MS Royal I.E.VI, fol. 4r) and the Bury Gospels (BL, MS Harley 76, fol. 8v)[30] –
and in Islamic architecture, as at San Cristo de la Luz at Toledo (999/1000).[31] The

[29] Klukas, 'Decreta Lanfranci', p. 165.
[30] Illustrated in David Wilson, Anglo-Saxon Art (London, 1984), figs. 103, 263.
[31] Marianne Barrucand and Achim Bednorz, Moorish Architecture in Andalusia (Cologne,
1992), illustration on p. 88.

Plate 24.   Durham Cathedral, south presbytery-aisle wall, detail of external dado arcade.

former analogy may indicate a conscious attempt by the patron to include an Anglo-Saxon motif in the new setting for the shrine of St Cuthbert.[32] On the other hand, the Islamic parallel may suggest William's desire for the exotic in the creation of a rich and varied aesthetic for his church which was to surpass the churches erected in honour of other English saints. Reference to San Cristo de la Luz and the mosque at Cordoba, may also be relevant for the use of ribs at Durham, for in addition to the rib itself, albeit of simple square profile, these Spanish buildings use pairs of divergent ribs which spring without transverse ribs in a manner that foreshadows the paired ribs in the first two bays of the transepts at Durham.[33] Moreover, the ribs in the dome over the bay in front of the *mihrab* (niche facing Mecca) of the mosque at Cordoba are articulated with short shafts on a ledge in the manner of the Durham presbytery and transept galleries. To assign precedent of one source over another is difficult and perhaps unnecessary. The design of Durham is eclectic and therefore there is nothing incompatible in seeing in the vault ribs, on the one hand, an iconographic reference to the shrine of St Peter in Rome, and, on the other hand, a motif, possibly inspired by Islamic architecture, which accords perfectly with the rich articulation of the building.

The complex stepped plinths beneath the external dado arcades (pl. 24) and the main arcade piers may have been requested by Bishop William as a pre-Conquest reference, as on the exterior of the presbytery at Repton (Derbs.), and in the

[32] Ibid., illustration on p. 79.
[33] Fernie, *Norwich Cathedral*, p. 144.

Plate 25.   Bradford-on-Avon (Wilts.), St Lawrence,
exterior, south-east.

crossing at Hadstock (Essex).[34] Other pre-Conquest analogies for specific motifs at Durham are 'grammatical' and seem to suggest the work of the mason rather than the patron. The use of single stones for the paired shafts of the Durham arcades is allied to the grouped shafts carved on monoliths in the gable of the south porticus and on the east front of St Lawrence at Bradford-on-Avon (Wilts.) (pl. 25). Furthermore, the setting of the latter looks forward to the grouped shafts above the minor piers in the presbytery and transept galleries at Durham (pl. 26). The design of the presbytery-gallery and transept-gallery windows with small paired apertures

[34] For Repton, see Eric Fernie, *Architecture of the Anglo-Saxons* (London, 1983), fig. 63; for Hadstock, idem, 'The Responds and the Dating of St Botolph's, Hadstock', *JBAA* 136 (1983), pp. 62–73.

Plate 26.   Durham Cathedral, presbytery, interior looking north-west.

beneath ample enclosing arches recalls the belfry openings of churches from the Anglo-Saxon/Norman 'overlap' period in the North East including Bywell St Andrew, Ovingham and Monkwearmouth (pl. 27).[35] The double-splay window in the north face of the north-west stair turret of the north transept and the same design in the former presbytery clerestory windows reflect a pre-Conquest rather than a Norman tradition. Here a post-Conquest intermediary in the North East may be the north aperture in the crossing tower at Jarrow.[36] A similar pre-Conquest link is suggested in one design detail in the aisle and clerestory windows. Here the hood mould of the windows continues as a string course between the windows. Rather than being contiguous with the abaci of the nook-shaft capitals, as is the practice in Normandy, the string is set immediately above the abaci in the manner of the north doorway at Laughton-en-le-Morthen (Yorks.) (pl. 28).

The rich arch mouldings at Durham (pls. 16 and 26) are not a single-step development from the painted arch ribbons at St Albans but rather reflect Norman precedent as well as developments on both sides of the Channel in the decade before work began on Durham in 1093. Soffit rolls appear in Normandy at Bernay, and in several English churches from the Anglo-Saxon/Norman 'overlap' period

[35] *ASA*, II, pl. 414 (Bywell St Andrew), pl. 531 (Monkwearmouth). For Ovingham, see Jean Bony, 'Durham et la tradition saxonne', *Études d'art medievale offertes à Louis Grodecki* (Paris, 1981), pp. 79–92, fig. 9.
[36] On the original form of the Durham presbytery clerestory windows, see Curry, 'Aspects', p. 34, fig. 2; *ASA*, III, fig. 623.

Plate 27.   Durham Cathedral, south transept, exterior
looking from the east.

such as Wittering (Northants.) and Clayton (Sussex).[37] Closer in style to Durham
are the mouldings of the crossing arches at St Étienne at Caen, and those of the
chancel arches at Bosham and Stoughton (Sussex) and the crossing at Stow
(Lincs.).[38] In the 1080s there was a tendency to multiply the number of orders in
major arches. As at St Albans, the nave arcade arches at Malvern Priory (c.1085)
have three plain orders. The arches from the nave aisles to the transepts at Shrewsbury Abbey (c.1080) have four orders of which orders one, two, and four are square
while order three has a heavy roll. Similar recessed rolls accompanied by soffit rolls

[37] Bony, 'La tradition saxonne', pp. 81–2.
[38] Fernie, *Architecture of the Anglo-Saxons*, pp. 164–8; Richard Gem, 'Holy Trinity Church,
Bosham', *Arch. J.* 142 (1985), pp. 32–6.

Plate 28.   Laughton-en-le-Morthern (Yorks.),
north doorway.

are used in the five-order transept-chapel arches at Worcester Cathedral (1084) and
the four-order western crossing arch at Blyth Priory (1088). In the meantime, angle
roll and hollow roll mouldings appear on the outer order of the three-order niches
in the west block of Remigius's Lincoln Minster, while in the east gallery arcades of
Ely Cathedral transepts roll and hollow mouldings and soffit rolls are introduced.[39]
     There are similar developments in Normandy. In the apse of St Nicholas at Caen
(1083) the lower range of windows has three orders both inside and out, of which
the outer order on the exterior and the middle and outer order on the interior have
roll and hollow mouldings (pl. 29). There is analogous enrichment of the interior

[39] The east gallery arcades of the Ely transepts belong to a second campaign of construction
starting c.1090.

Plate 29.   Caen, St Nicholas, apse, exterior looking from the
north-east.

of the lower range of three-order apse arches at Cérisy-la-Forêt (*c.*1085). The
external dado arcade at St Nicholas at Caen also provides precedent for this
motif, whose first appearance in England is at Durham (pls. 24 and 29). In
contrast to these Norman examples, however, Durham uses moulded arches
throughout the building to create, with the ribs, the intersecting dado arcades and
the incised columns, what Geoffrey Webb has called the all-over linear pattern.[40]
The closest conceptual precursor for this is at Milborne Port (Somerset), which
may have been commissioned by the royal clerk, Regenbald.[41] Here there are

[40] Geoffrey Webb, *Architecture in Britain: The Middle Ages* (Harmondsworth, 1956), pp. 38, 39.
[41] John Blair, 'Secular Minster Churches in Domesday Book', in *Domesday Book: A Reassessment*, ed. P.H. Sawyer (London, 1985), p. 134; and Richard Gem, 'The English Parish Church

three-order north and south crossing arches with quadrant roll mouldings like those in the aisles at Gloucester (1089), as well as heavy roll mouldings on the inner faces of the presbytery windows, upper external arcading on the presbytery walls, on the crossing tower, and formerly on the west front. The details are quite different from Durham but the idea of rich linear pattern is related. This is in keeping with the idea that Durham was informed by an indigenous aesthetic. Witness the multiple mouldings on the west doorway of the late Anglo-Saxon church at Earls Barton,[42] and the arch in the early Anglo-Saxon representation of the Sack of Jerusalem by the Emperor Titus on the Franks Casket (London, British Museum), on which object in the scene of Egil the Archer defending his home we also find incised decoration on the piers, stepped plinths and even chevron ornament in the arch.[43]

The consistent use of cushion and scalloped capitals throughout Durham Cathedral speaks of an immediate background for the master mason in England rather than in Normandy. Whether or not the cushion capitals were used in England before the Conquest, there are documented examples in the gatehouse of Exeter Castle (after 1068), at Christ Church and St Augustine's Canterbury (c.1073), and the motif is ubiquitous in English architecture thereafter.[44] The closest parallels for the Durham capitals are in the north of England. Double and triple scallop capitals are used in the presbytery aisle dado arcades. The multiplication of the scalloped form occurs in York Minster,[45] while the trumpet form of some of the capitals at Durham is presaged by the eastern responds of the nave arcades at Lastingham Priory (1078–85). Other details from churches in the north of England which were in building in the decade and a half before Durham suggest that William's master mason was recruited from the North. Fragments of roll mouldings were excavated from Thomas's church at York and these foreshadow developments at Durham,[46] while at Lastingham the form of the plinths presage those of the Durham presbytery arcade. The high groin-vault at Lastingham, although usually dismissed as a purely nineteenth-century creation, is in fact a restoration of the former 'ancient groining' and therefore an important precursor in northern England of the Durham high vaults (pl. 30).[47] At Tynemouth Priory

in the 11th and Early 12th Centuries: A Great Rebuilding?', in *Minsters and Parish Churches: The Local Church in Transition 950–1200*, ed. John Blair (Oxford, 1988), p. 27.

[42] Fernie, *Architecture of the Anglo-Saxons*, fig. 87.

[43] Wilson, *Anglo-Saxon Art*, figs. 34, 36.

[44] Richard Gem, 'Canterbury and the Cushion Capital: a Commentary on Passages from Goscelin's *De Miraculis Sancti Augustini*', in *Romanesque and Gothic: Essays for George Zarnecki*, ed. Neil Stratford (Woodbridge, 1987), pp. 83–101.

[45] Derek Phillips, in Royal Commission on the Historical Monuments of England: *The Cathedral of Archbishop Thomas of Bayeux: Excavations at York Minster*, II (London, 1985), p. 144, fig. 26),

[46] Ibid., p. 146, fig. 28.

[47] The present high vaults at Lastingham date from J.L. Pearson's restoration of 1879, but a citation and faculty of 1877, preserved in the Borthwick Institute, University of York (FAC 1877/2a, FAC 1877/2b), in which the language is very precise, refer to the proposal to 'restore the ancient groining of the nave (i.e. the square bay to the west of the presbytery) in place of

Plate 30.   Lastingham Priory, interior looking to the east.

(*c*.1085/90) the responds of the crossing piers presage the crossing piers and the major high-vault responds at Durham, and the parallel may be extended to a former crossing capital now in store on the abbey site at Tynemouth which is virtually identical to the Durham crossing and high-vault capitals. There are traces of a groin-vault in the eastern bay of the north nave aisle at Tynemouth and the nave arcade there is carried on columnar piers which have octagonal capitals like the minor piers of the main arcades at Durham. The east processional doorway at Tynemouth has three orders like the more elaborate arches of the 1080s and,

the present plaster ceiling', and to 'restore the ancient barrel vaulting of the chancel including the Apsidal East End'. I should like to thank Dr Christopher Norton for suggesting that I contact the Borthwick Institute in connection with documentation on Lastingham.

although the details are weathered away, the multiplication of mouldings in the Tynemouth nave gallery arches looks forward to Durham.[48]

To sum up: the vast scale of Durham Cathedral, which recreated the overall length and nave width of Old St Peter's, Rome, would have been determined by the patron. While we cannot be sure how the measurements were transmitted, the incised spiral decoration on the columnar piers of the presbytery and transept, the use of the rib, and possibly the towers flanking the apse, suggest that Bishop William wished to emulate Old St Peter's and to create monumental spiral piers and ribs fully integrated into the architectural shrine of St Cuthbert. The great length of the church, including the four-bay eastern arm, rivalled recent developments at St Albans and Winchester and other major post-Conquest churches housing English saints. These buildings also provided the inspiration for the height of the fabric, the structural system with thick walls, and articulation with pilasters, half shafts and string courses, which evolved from the tradition of Norman predecessors like St Étienne at Caen. The patron decided which parts of the building to vault and he would have been responsible for the military aspect of the eastern towers and the scale of the staircases. He would also have determined the degree of decoration and articulation of the surfaces and may be even the use of specific motifs. Thus the aisle and transept walls had both internal and external arcades, seemingly inspired by Winchester and St Nicholas at Caen respectively, while the intersecting arcading may have been specified by the patron as a detail appropriate to St Cuthbert's Anglo-Saxon heritage, or simply as an exotic element inspired by Islamic Spain.[49] The patron wanted to emulate the best of all buildings to date and especially to surpass those most recently undertaken by his fellow Norman abbots and bishops. In the former respect he followed the lead of Bishop Walkelin at Winchester, and his terms of stylistic and iconographic reference were geographically very broad. The articulation develops from and surpasses Anglo-Norman churches of the 1080s and early 1090s and provides a shrine-like richness for the setting of the body of St Cuthbert.

The master mason would have been responsible for the translation of this brief into reality, and this may well have involved him in visits to the major sites in both England and Normandy suggested by Bishop William. The spiral piers and the ribs, while iconographically reflecting Old St Peter's, were most likely translated into three-dimensional form from painted precursors like those preserved in the nave columns at St-Savin-sur-Gartempe (Vienne) and the painted groins in the presbytery aisles at St Albans.[50] Furthermore, while the idea for the ribs may have

---

[48] On Tynemouth Priory, see W.H. Knowles, 'The Priory Church of St Mary and St Oswin, Tynemouth, Northumberland', *Arch. J.* 67 (1910), pp. 7–12.

[49] On links between England, Normandy and Spain after the capture of Toledo in 1085, see Jean Bony, 'The Stonework Planning of the First Durham Master', in *Medieval Architecture and its Intellectual Context: Studies in Honour of Peter Kidson*, ed. Eric Fernie and Paul Crossley (London, 1990), pp. 33–4.

[50] David Park, 'The Interior Decoration of the Cathedral', in *Durham Cathedral*, ed. Pocock, p. 58, cites late eleventh-century columns from St Nicholas's Priory, Exeter, which were formerly painted with spirals, and lozenge and scale patterns, and, most interestingly, a

been to create a fully integrated architectural canopy in the apse above St Cuthbert, it may have been the mason who determined the use of the motif as an aesthetic device to complement the rich plastic articulation of the building. The rich articulation at Durham incorporates Norman and English developments of the 1080s to create an all-over linear pattern in keeping with the indigenous tradition. The consistent use of cushion, rather than volute, capitals speaks most clearly of an English, rather than Norman, origin of the master mason. This is reinforced by the use of the Anglo-Saxon motifs of paired shafts, complex plinths, double-splay windows, and especially the discoordinate abaci and string courses. Indeed, the detailed parallels with York Minster, Lastingham, and Tynemouth suggest that he was trained in the north of England. The inclusion of a high vault in the eastern arm of the small priory church of Lastingham strongly suggests that high vaults were used in the eastern arms of major buildings such as Remigius's Minster at Lincoln, Archbishop Thomas's York Minster, and St Mary's Abbey at York where the Lastingham monks moved after 1085, and starting in 1089 began construction of a larger church on land donated by the king.[51] Perhaps it was at York that the Durham master honed his skills in vault construction before entering the employ of Bishop William of St Calais. Whether or not that was the case, we must also remember the castle at Durham, begun in 1072, and the high quality of the masonry in the chapel there, an important factor given the excellent masoncraft at the cathedral.[52]

fragment of painted lozenge design of similar date from St Mary's Abbey, York, which was very like the lozenge pattern at Durham.
[51] John Bilson, 'The Plan of the First Cathedral Church of Lincoln', *Arch.* 62 (1911), pp. 543–64, recontructs Remigius's presbytery with a high groin-vault. Phillips, *York Minster*, p. 161, suggests that the eastern arm of Archbishop Thomas's Minster was barrel vaulted. William Dugdale, *Monasticon Anglicanum*, III (London, 1821), p. 529; John Bilson, 'The Eleventh Century East-Ends of St Augustine's, Canterbury, and St Mary's, York', *Arch. J.* 63 (1906), pp. 113–16.
[52] Bony, 'Stonework Planning', pp. 19–33.

The West Front of Durham Cathedral:
The Beginning of a British Tradition

J. PHILIP MCALEER

A S A TYPE, the twin-tower façade has most usually been associated with French Gothic architecture, particularly the Early and High phases of Île-de-France Gothic. So much is this case, that a British historian has suggested that the form of the early thirteenth-century Gothic twin-tower façade of Scotland's Elgin Cathedral is due to French influence.[1] French historians, of course, have rather taken the Frenchness of the type for granted, and constructed a family tree for it which begins with Romanesque Jumièges Abbey and St Étienne in Caen and includes almost all the major cathedrals (and other buildings of lesser rank) of the region erected between St Denis and the cathedral of Reims and St Nicaise in the same city, viz., Sens, Senlis, Noyon, Laon, Paris, Soissons, and Amiens.[2] The type has been dubbed 'la façade harmonique' by the French historians, the designation derived from and suggestive of the supposed relationship of the major vertical and horizontal divisions of the façade with the plan and elevation of the church behind it.[3] That is, towers rising over the west bays of the aisles flank the west bay of the nave, their buttresses emphasizing the triadic division, and elements such as portals and windows reflecting the interior horizontal divisions of nave arcade, clerestory and whatever happens in between. To be charitable, this designation is probably somewhat irrelevant, and not a little inaccurate or misleading. Most obviously, the horizontal divisions do not – or very seldom – accurately reflect the actual number and proportions of the storeys of the internal nave elevation, as in the case of Laon

---

[1] J.S. Richardson in H.B. Mackintosh and J.S. Richardson, *Elgin Cathedral: The Cathedral Kirk of Moray* (2nd edn, Edinburgh, 1980), p. 7: 'The west front of the Cathedral with its flanking towers is suggestive of French influence.'

Some of the research for the present paper was made possible by part of a grant from the Social Sciences and Humanities Research Council of Canada; attendance at the Anglo-Norman Durham conference was facilitated by a travel grant from the Faculty of Architecture, Technical University of Nova Scotia (SSHRCC: Direct Grants to Universities).
[2] M. Anfray, *L'architecture normande: Son influence dans le nord de la France au XIe et XIIe siècles* (Paris, 1939), pp. 285–91.
[3] Anfray, op. cit., pp. 233–6 (esp. p. 235), and pp. 260–2; C. Seymour, Jr., *Notre-Dame of Noyon in the Twelfth Century: A Study in the Early Development of Gothic Architecture* (New Haven, 1939), p. 144 n. 17: 'referring to the use of twin towers flanking the façade and an interrelation of interior to exterior design, especially in windows and portals.'

Plate 31.   Durham Cathedral, interior, view of the nave towards the
west towers.

Cathedral, for instance. Less obviously, but to my mind more importantly, the
interior design and spatial relationships of the parts of the west end are ignored
because the designation was primarily based upon external appearances – the
twin-towers as a façade-wall rather than as a façade-structure.[4]

For instance, if we look at a plan of the west end of Durham and compare it with
that of one of the latest Île-de-France façades, Reims Cathedral, we see no significant differences: in both churches the west towers are evident due to the enlarged
western piers of the arcade, and the extension of the bay under them beyond the
line of the aisle walls of the nave. In elevation, looking down the nave towards the
west (pl. 31), the presence of the towers is revealed only by the heavier mass of the

---

[4]   Anfray, loc. cit., for instance, never discussed the interiors of the buildings he examined.

piers expressed by the larger cluster of wall shafts which rise up the elevation. A look at the elevation of the west bay reveals an attempt to disguise the presence of the towers or to emphasize the unity and continuity of the nave elevation right to the west wall by mimicking the divisions in the nave, most significantly by including a clerestory-like opening into the adjoining stage of the towers (pl. 32). At Durham, this stage was originally relatively well lighted by large windows in the exterior walls of the tower; at Reims, as this stage of the tower is open to the elements, the openings to the nave are of necessity glazed, thereby becoming a true clerestory.

In other words, the structure of the towers has been as fully integrated into the design of the nave elevation as was possible. Reims shows no significant advance over Durham in this respect. By comparison, if we look at St Denis, which is usually regarded as the first Gothic façade-harmonique, even though Suger never constructed his nave, no integration of the towers with the interior was possible, for the two-bay depth of Suger's façade structure is filled by an upper level.[5] Thus, we enter into a low nave-like space above the vaults of which is a low chapel; the former is flanked by yet lower aisles over which there are taller chapels (if that be the proper term). St Denis on the inside is a kind of westwork structure, reflecting an older tradition, which had already been discarded in Normandy, at St Étienne, Caen, where the church of Duke William's Abbaye-aux-Hommes did not include a western gallery. Rather one entered directly into the nave space as at the remodelled version of the façade of Duchess Matilda's church (La Trinité) of the Abbaye-aux-Dames, Caen, and at later Durham. St Étienne was probably completed by 1100, La Trinité between 1100 and 1110, Durham by 1133.[6] All were complete – or nearly so – before the construction of St Denis, if not its planning, was begun some time between 1130 and 1137.

Durham itself relates back to the Norman Romanesque precedents, especially to St Étienne where the reduced westwork of Jumièges had undergone a further reduction as a result of the elimination of the western gallery.[7] At the same time, St Étienne introduced a significant new factor, by attempting to integrate the towers into the design and space of the nave by recalling the three stages of the nave in the elevation of tower bays: an arch imitating the nave arcade arches, but narrower; an arch above recalling the large gallery arches; and, at clerestory level, an arch

---

[5] S. McK. Crosby, 'The Plan of the Western Bays of Suger's New Church at St. Denis', *Journal of the Society of Architectural Historians* 27 (1968), pp. 39–43; idem, 'The Inside of Saint-Denis' West Façade', *Gedenkschrift Ernst Gall*, ed. M. Kühn and L. Grodecki (Berlin and Munich, 1965), pp. 60–6; idem, *The Royal Abbey of Saint-Denis from Its Beginnings to the Death of Suger: 475–1151*, ed. P.Z. Blum (New Haven and London, 1987), pp. 121–79.
[6] E.G. Carlson, 'The Abbey Church of Saint-Étienne at Caen in the Eleventh and Early Twelfth Centuries' (unpublished D.Phil. thesis, Yale University, New Haven, 1968), pp. 108–10, 115, and 264–93; M. Baylé, *La Trinité de Caen: Sa place dans l'histoire de l'architecture et du décor romans* (Bibliothèque de la Société française d'Archéologie, 10; Geneva, 1979), pp. 40–1, 49–51, and 68–9.
[7] M. Baylé, 'Les relations entre massif de façade et vaisseau de nef en Normandie avant 1080', *Cahiers de Civilisation médiévale* 34/3–4 (1991), pp. 227–30.

Plate 32. Durham Cathedral, interior, gallery and clerestory
levels of the south-west bay of the nave.

subdivided into two lights (pl. 33). This last formed the strongest contrast with the
bays to the east, where the clerestory design consisted of an arcade of four arches
spanning two bays below.[8] At the base of each tower, a solid wall (once) separated
the space under it from the space of the aisle. The pier under the corner of the
tower was more than simply an enlargement of the normal – heavy – pier of St
Étienne's alternating pier scheme; it was a segment of flat wall articulated at either
end by responds (shafts), with its flat surface towards the nave broken by

[8]   G. Bouet, 'Analyse architecturale de l'abbaye de Saint-Étienne de Caen', *Bulletin monumental* 31 (1865), esp. pp. 454–9, 473–4; and R. Liess, *Der früh-romanische Kirchenbau des 11.
Jahrhunderts in der Normandie* (Munich, 1967), pp. 183–201.

Plate 33. Caen, St Étienne, interior, view of the north-west
bay of the nave (now partly occupied by the eighteenth-century
organ loft).

wall-shafts rising the full height of the elevation. The integration of the tower bays
with the nave elevation was less complete than at later Durham.

Whether or not Durham was the first building in which the tower bay received
full integration is a problem I have considered elsewhere.[9] The conclusion that it
probably was can only be tentative, for the archaeological evidence is incomplete,
and will remain so. Three English buildings begun before Durham eventually
ended in twin-tower façades which may have been completed before Durham's,

[9] J.P. McAleer, 'Romanesque England and the Development of the *Façade Harmonique*',
Gesta 23/2 (1984), pp. 87–105 (with reference to the place of La Trinité, see Baylé, 'Relations',
pp. 231–3 and esp. p. 232 n. 24).

although in only one is it reasonably certain that the façade was completed before Durham was begun. That building is Christ Church, Canterbury, begun in 1070 by Archbishop Lanfranc and probably complete by the time of his death in 1089. Like the other two, it no longer exists. Of its Romanesque façade, only one tower survived the Perpendicular rebuilding of the nave in the fifteenth century, and it was demolished in 1834. Fortunately, it appeared in a number of views of the cathedral, and a section and two elevations were prepared by J.C. Buckler just before its destruction.[10] However, the Perpendicular remodelling of the base of the tower had removed all indication of how the tower originally related to the nave and aisles: whether, as at St Étienne, solid walls separated it from the aisles, with a smaller arch only opening to the nave, or whether it was fully open to nave and aisles, with a large arch like those of the arcades opening to the nave, creating a pier-like support at the angle. The treatment of the upper elevation is likewise unclear. That there may have been a western gallery, an episcopal loggia, has been suggested on the basis of precedent (the archbishop's throne was located in the western apse of the pre-Lanfranc building) and because of the presence of a small portal at first storey level on the west face which could have allowed entrance from the adjacent episcopal palace.[11] Yet, curiously, Buckler's section not only does not reveal any evidence of vaulting within the tower at the upper levels, but does not reveal evidence of any sockets for the joists of a series of timber floors.[12]

With St Augustine's Abbey, Canterbury we are on somewhat more secure ground, for the base of one tower still survives.[13] We have also numerous engravings of that north-west tower until its final collapse in 1822. The tower was begun after Wido (1087–99) became abbot, and I have argued that it was completed in the first decade of the twelfth century. From the remains, it is evident that the tower base opened into the nave and aisles, as at Durham, rather than being separated from them, as at St Étienne. From one of the engravings, it is clear that the tower also opened to the nave at the second stage through large arches imitating the gallery arcade. What none of the engravings record is if there was a false clerestory, or merely a blank wall. The evidence suggests that St Augustine's could have been the immediate model for Durham, the latter perhaps making a final refinement of the design by including a mock clerestory.

The third example is more problematic. It was perhaps the first Romanesque

[10] McAleer, op. cit., pp. 93–4, figs. 11–12; and F. Woodman, *The Architectural History of Canterbury Cathedral* (London, Boston and Henley, 1981), pp. 35–6, figs. 20–1.

[11] R. Gem, 'The Significance of the 11th-century Rebuilding of Christ Church and St Augustine's, Canterbury, in the Development of Romanesque Architecture', in *Medieval Art and Architecture at Canterbury before 1220*, ed. N. Coldstream and P. Draper (BAACT 5 for 1979; London, 1982), pp. 7 and 3; and J. Rady, T. Tatton-Brown, and J.A. Bowen, 'The Archbishop's Palace, Canterbury', *JBAA* 144 (1991), p. 4.

[12] Several later towers were built without internal floors or vaults: Chichester Cathedral, Arbroath Abbey (Tironensian), and Llanthony Priory (Augustinian).

[13] J.P. McAleer, 'The Ethelbert Tower of St Augustine's Abbey, Canterbury', *JBAA* 140 (1987), pp. 88–111; and T. Tatton-Brown, 'The Buildings and Topography of St Augustine's Abbey, Canterbury', *JBAA* 144 (1991), pp. 64, and 65–6.

Plate 34. Durham Cathedral, view of the north-west facade
tower from the north-east.

building in England: Edward the Confessor's church of Westminster Abbey.[14]
Excavations carried out in 1930 established that there were two west towers, which
were reconstructed on a plan identical to that of the towers at Durham or St
Augustine's, that is, with the towers' bases fully open to both nave and aisles. This I
feel, on the evidence of the Norman churches, Jumièges and St Étienne, is too
typologically advanced to have been part of the intended design at the time the
church was started some time between 1045 and 1060. As there is no clear

[14] L.E. Tanner and A.W. Clapham, 'Recent Discoveries in the Nave of Westminster Abbey',
Arch. 83 (1933), pp. 227–36; and R.D.H. Gem, 'The Romanesque Rebuilding of Westmin-
ster Abbey', *AN* 3 (1980), pp. 33–60, esp. pp. 40–4 and 55 (cf. McAleer, 'Romanesque
England', p. 102 n. 25).

Plate 35.   Durham Cathedral, the west front viewed from the
north side of the Galilee.

evidence as to when the church was finished, I have argued on the basis of
typological development, which may be risky, that the excavated remains reflect a
façade structure designed and executed *after* St Augustine's – and perhaps Durham
– were well under way.

There is no evidence that the façade of Durham *as built* was necessarily that in
the minds of the builders (or patron) when construction was begun in 1093. The
significant building break at the east end of the nave makes it impossible to be sure
that the design of the façade is any earlier than some time after the completion of
the choir in 1104 and of the work in the crossing *c.*1110.[15] That construction of

15 The break is clearly marked by a stylistic change, most obviously the adoption of the

the west front started as early as 1108, the date John James has assigned to the west portal chevron, is dubious.[16] But even a starting date as early as 1104, or 1108, rather than after 1110, allows the possibility that it was following the example of St Augustine's.

While we cannot be sure that Durham was the earliest to achieve the formula, in terms of internal arrangements, which became the norm among the later Île-de-France Gothic façades, the English buildings discussed above should form part of the pedigree, perhaps ousting or supplanting St Denis. Nonetheless it is obvious that, in several respects at least, the English buildings were not models for the later Île-de-France developments. This returns us to the exterior.

One could argue that Durham's is a truly harmonic façade, as the design of the towers is tightly related to the elevation of the nave (pl. 34), both by string courses and the levels of fenestration, and even the corbel table, much more emphatically than at St Étienne. Where Durham differs from the Île-de-France Gothic churches, however, and this may separate it from the kind of design logic emphasized by the French interpretation, is that the horizontal bands reflecting the interior three-storey elevation were not continued across the end wall of the nave; instead, there is a huge arch (pl. 35). The effect may be more extreme than intended, for with difficulty we have to disregard the late Perpendicular window, which fits so agreeably under the arch, and mentally substitute several smaller Romanesque windows, perhaps in two horizontal registers suggesting but not corresponding with the gallery and clerestory levels, for the presence of two internal wall passages reached by stairs descending from these levels means the west windows were 'displaced' downwards relative to them.[17] Nonetheless, the design concept was one that emphasized the three lower stages of the towers as terminating the aisles and flanking the volume of the nave space. This is an approach different from the French emphasis on continuous horizontal registers which tended to obliterate the verticality of the towers and downplay their flanking role.

A different attitude is also evident in the part of the Durham façade now least evident: the base or portal zone. Before the Galilee was constructed, and for several centuries afterwards, there was only a central portal, one which was not particularly large (pl. 36).[18] This is conspicuously different from the Île-de-France Gothic façades which seemingly taking their cue from St Étienne, and then St Denis,

---

chevron motif for the decoration of the archivolts: it occurs after the first two nave arcade bays (the first double bay), but after only one arch of the gallery level and none of the clerestory arcade. See J. Bilson, 'Durham Cathedral: the Chronology of Its Vaults', *Arch. J.* 79 (1922), pp. 101–60, esp. pp. 104, 110, 111, 113, 140, 141–3.

[16] J. James, 'The Rib Vaults of Durham Cathedral', *Gesta* 22/2 (1983), 144. According to James's chronology, only the choir aisles and apse were vaulted by 1104; the choir vaults were not constructed until 1104 to 1113, those of the nave aisles from 1115 to 1118.

[17] See I. Curry, 'Aspects of the Anglo-Norman Design of Durham Cathedral', *Arch. Ael.* 5th ser., 14 (1986), pp. 39–44.

[18] The west door remained functional until the construction of the tomb of Cardinal Bishop Thomas Langley (1406–37) and its accompanying altar (N. Pevsner, *County Durham* (Buildings of England; London, Melbourne and Baltimore, 1953), pp. 100, and 105–6).

Plate 36.   Durham Cathedral, the west portal as seen from
inside the Galilee.

always had three portals. Of course, much of early Gothic façade development in
north-eastern France centres on the increasing magnification of the portals through
the apparatus not just of sculpture but of projecting gabled porches. These expan-
ding portal zones created a broad horizontal base for the façade design rising above.
But this expansion of the portals was a matter for the future, well after Durham was
finished. Comparing Durham with St Denis in this respect, the difference is not
yet so considerable: certainly St Denis has three portals, but they are nevertheless
rather modest in scale and lacking porches. The significant difference is the sculptural embellishment which at St Denis is still restrained and subservient to the
larger architectural format but at Durham is totally absent.

The façade of Durham can be taken to represent the prototype for subsequent
developments in Britain. *Pace* J.S. Richardson, after these early examples the

Plate 37.   Lichfield Cathedral, interior, north-west bay
of the nave.

twin-tower façade did truly become at home in England, and also in Scotland,
many more being built in the twelfth century than now survive, with others
following in the several Gothic styles during succeeding centuries. Looking at those
façades which survive as more than foundations we can see that a number of factors
remain constant.[19]

[19] In England, twin-tower façades survive at (in approximate chronological order): Chichester
Cathedral, Castle Acre Priory, Southwell Minster, Dunfermline Cathedral, Wymondham and
Worksop Priories, Selby Abbey, Davington Priory, Melbourne, St German's and Reculver
parish churches, King's Lynn Priory, Llandaff Cathedral, Llanthony, Bridlington and Old
Malton Priories, Ripon collegiate church, Arbroath and Paisley Abbeys, Elgin and Lichfield
Cathedrals, St Mary's Scarborough, Bourne Abbey, York and Beverley Minsters, Westminster
Abbey, Canterbury and Aberdeen (St Machar's) Cathedrals.

In major buildings after Durham – and it perhaps would be unscholarly to lay the credit or blame directly on Durham – all twin-tower façades are integrated into the interior in a similar way. The tower bases open into the nave and aisles in such a way that the space of the aisle and the elevation of the nave read continuously, with only the merest of interruptions (especially in the later buildings) due to the bulkier tower piers or heavier arches across the aisles (as at Lichfield Cathedral, pl. 37).[20] The upper elevation mimics the second and third (clerestory) level designs, often even by glazing the clerestory openings. On the interior of the towers, there is only one level of vaults, continuous with those of the aisles, with the remainder of the tower being subdivided by wooden floors and covered by a wooden roof. Parenthetically, one may note that the lack of vaults above aisle level, characteristic of western towers in Britain right through the Perpendicular period, was in contrast once again to the Île-de-France buildings, where there are usually two or more levels of vaults in the towers. The only exceptions to these general principles are smaller churches which had only two-storey elevations: in these cases, the arcade arch was in some instances taller than the nave arcade, and there were neither aisle-level vaults (because these smaller buildings did not have vaulted aisles) nor false clerestories.[21]

On the exterior, despite stylistic changes of a fairly radical nature, the system tends to remain unchanged. The design of the towers generally continues to reflect the lateral elevations, although not always with the synchronized precision of Durham, and the nave end wall is seen as an 'independent' entity, that is expressing the reality of the nave space flanked by towers (as at Beverley Minster, pl. 38). In this respect, the portals continue to play a modest role by being most usually limited to one central one, and restrained in size with sculptural embellishment rare. That contrasts with the increasing immodesty of west windows which reached their zenith during the Perpendicular period which, in its zeal, replaced so many, if not absolutely all, earlier west windows, so that our sense of the balance of earlier pre-Perpendicular compositions is completely thrown off. They now create a dominating central emphasis although, in many cases, they must have replaced several smaller windows, perhaps placed in tiers, providing some horizontal linkage to the staged towers and internal elevation. Yet the great Perpendicular windows are not unfaithful to the British concept of the independence of the nave end wall.

This attitude can also be seen particularly strongly on the interior. In the design of the west wall, even in the Early English and Decorated styles, let alone the late Romanesque, there is seldom – one hesitates to say never – any attempt to carry the horizontal levels of the side elevations across the west front (as at Castle Acre Priory (Norfolk), pl. 39). Indeed, the opposite will happen, as not infrequently the string courses of the west wall which are present will jump a course or two above or below

---

[20] Ironically, because the bases of the towers are solid walls, pierced only by small doorways to the aisles, the west towers of Scotland's Elgin Cathedral do not fully belong to either the British or French tradition!

[21] Examples (included in the above list) are: Davington, Melbourne, St German's, King's Lynn, Scarborough, and Bourne.

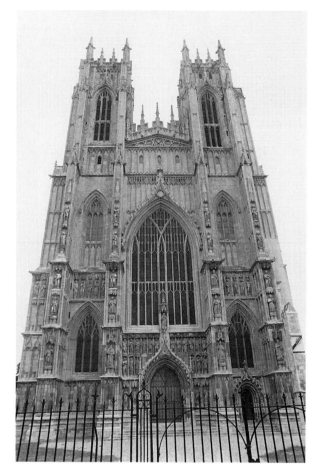

Plate 38. Beverley Minster, view of the west front from the west.

those of the adjoining second stage or clerestory, yet remain so close as to make it seem the avoidance of horizontal coordination was defiantly deliberate. Needless to say, the builders of the great Perpendicular windows, whether original (e.g., Beverley Minster, pl. 40) or introduced into an earlier context (e.g., Southwell Minster) made no attempt to coordinate their design with the levels of the nave elevation.[22]

---

[22] It is hoped that a forthcoming study will present the evidence for the generalizations in the above three paragraphs in considerable detail.

Plate 39.   Castle Acre Priory (Norfolk), interior, view of the
ruins of the south-west facade tower from the north-east.

The predictability of the later development, if it can be called that, and the
appearance of the twin-tower type in Britain, can be contrasted with Île-de-France
Gothic, for, despite their apparent uniformity on the exterior, their interior arrangements demonstrate more variety than was found in England, and in the few
Scottish examples. Western galleries did not disappear altogether, even if they were
incorporated into the design in a more integrated manner than at St Denis. The
form seems to have been particularly popular around Soissons, where, in addition
to the cathedral, versions were found at Mont Notre Dame (destroyed) and St Jean
des Vignes, all well into the thirteenth century.[23] That at the cathedral was created

23 E. Lefèvre-Pontalis, 'Cathédrale de Soissons', *Congrès archéologique* 78 (2 vols., Reims,
1911), I, 318–37; idem, 'Église du Mont-Notre-Dame', op. cit., I, 250–7; idem, 'Abbaye de

Plate 40.   Beverley Minster, interior, junction of the
north-west bays with the west wall.

by the continuation of the aisle-level vaults across the nave and the elimination of
the upper storeys of the elevation under the tower: as a result, the west gallery reads
as a kind of raised transept (pl. 41). Altars were placed against the east wall of the
towers at the upper level.[24] At Laon Cathedral, and at the collegiate church at
Mantes (pl. 42), there is no gallery, but here too the tower bays are open to the

Saint-Jean-des-Vignes', op. cit., I, 348–50 (348–54). P. Héliot, 'L'ancienne église abbatiale
Saint-Jean-des-Vignes à Soissons', *Ant. J.* 59 (1979), pp. 113–20, esp. pp. 115–18. J. Ancien,
Contribution à l'étude archéologique: Architecture de la cathédrale de Soissons (2nd edn, 1984),
does not deal with the western structure which he dated (pl. 19) to 1220–40.
[24] The cutting for an altar slab is preserved in both locations. Each altar was accompanied by a
niche: on the north side, there is one niche in the east wall; on the south side, there is one
niche in each of the east and south walls, the former with a double piscina.

Plate 41.   Soissons Cathedral, interior, view of the junction
of the west gallery ('raised transept') with the north nave
elevation.

nave above the level of the aisle vaults: the gallery, wall passage and clerestory
designs are not continued to the west front.[25] The towers are vaulted at the level of
the nave vaults. At Noyon Cathedral, a transept-like space surprises one behind a
conventional-appearing twin-tower 'harmonic' façade and this may well have been

[25] Courtauld Institute Illustration Archives: Archive 3. *Medieval Architecture and Sculpture in
Europe*, Pt. 6, *France: Laon Cathedral*, ed. L. Grant (London, 1978), pl. 3/6/98; Companion
Text 1, W.W. Clark and R. King, *Laon Cathedral: Architecture* (2 vols., London, 1983–7), I,
44–7, 52, and 54; II, 55, and 58–9, figs. 17, and 18. J. Bony, 'La collégiale de Mantes', *Congrès
archéologique* 104 (1946), pp. 184–6, and 202–6; R. Bailly, *La collégiale Notre-Dame à Mantes
la Jolie* (Mantes la Jolie, 1980), pl. on p. 175.

Plate 42. Mantes la Jolie, la Collégiale de Notre-Dame, interior, view of the south-west bay of the nave from the north-east.

the case at St Germer de Fly.[26] At Notre Dame in Paris, a gallery fills half of the depth of the west bay; however, the elevation design in this case continued to the west wall.[27] Thus, unlike Britain, a single exterior design formula was made to

[26] Seymour, *Notre-Dame of Noyon*, pp. 139–42 and 146–50; J. Henriet, 'Un édifice de la première génération gothique: l'abbatiale de Saint-Germer-de-Fly', *Bulletin monumental* 143 (1985), pp. 93–142, esp. 104–5, and 135–6; and P. Héliot, 'Remarques sur l'abbatiale de Saint-Germer et sur les blocs de façade du XIIe siècle', *Bulletin monumental* 104 (1956), pp. 81–114.

[27] M. Aubert, *La cathédrale Notre-Dame de Paris, sa place dans l'histoire de l'architecture du XIIe au XIVe siècle* (2nd edn, Paris, 1929), pp. 119–36, esp. 133–5 (the concern, as usual, is exclusively with the exterior design).

Plate 43. Melbourne (Derbyshire), Sts Michael and Mary,
interior, west gallery of the nave.

cover a variety of interior arrangements which have no parallels among surviving
British façades, except for the single example of Melbourne, a major 'minor'
(two-storey elevation) church, where a west gallery is present between the towers
(pl. 43), supported on vaults extending into the tower bays (the aisles were unvaulted).[28]

Chapels were mentioned as having existed at an upper level in the towers at
Soissons Cathedral. One other example of altars in towers is found at Sens

[28] R. Gem, 'Melbourne Church of St Michael and St Mary', *Arch. J.* 146 (1989), *Supplement:
The Nottingham Area* (Proceedings of the 135th Summer Meeting of the RAI, 1989, ed. N.H.
Cooper), pp. 24–9.

Cathedral,[29] one of the few straightforward Île-de-France twin-tower façades (Senlis, Sens, Amiens, Reims – a small group actually). In this respect one wonders if the large arched recess in the east wall of the gallery level of the north tower at Durham, now blocked up, could have been for an altar. There is no corresponding recess in the south tower. The *Rites of Durham* indicate that there was an altar of the Saviour at the end of the north aisle.[30] Supposedly, in the sixteenth century, part of the altar slab was still to be seen projecting from the *north* wall of this bay which is actually covered by intersecting arcading, appearing undisturbed and unrestored: no trace of any such slab is now visible.[31] If there was an altar in this vicinity, perhaps it was originally located at the gallery level, to be later repositioned (against the short east wall of the tower bay at aisle level?) when so many of the openings of the tower were blocked up, presumably at the time of, or as a consequence of, the construction of the freestanding stages of the towers or, more likely, of the spires.

Of the various aspects of the façade, the most interesting motif, which one is tempted to interpret as of special symbolic significance, had seemingly no imitators. Mention has already been made of the large but shallow arch which dominated the nave end wall. This was reflected or echoed by two large blind arches on the aisle ends (pls. 35 and 44). If one could wish away the Galilee, the presence of these arches would be more apparent. The giant arch recalls or anticipates the well-known, more emphatic arch at Tewkesbury Abbey, which has been called the triumphal arch *par excellence*,[32] with its roots, perhaps, in earlier medieval architecture, as in Charlemagne's Chapel (*c*.796–805) at Aachen. Was it the intention to express a somewhat similar idea – in a more modest way – at Durham, by erecting a façade with three, albeit shallow, arches rising triumphantly above the River Wear, this in an area where the Norman conquest had met with stiff resistance before the Conqueror's will and the new style were imposed? Or was the single order of the arches merely a consequence of the Romanesque tendency to layer the wall?

Another unusual feature is the scale of the stair vices at Durham (pl. 45). They are placed, as was the custom in Britain, at the western corners, as opposed to Normandy and the Île-de-France where they are always located at the east, and are, for Britain, unusually ample, the steps being nearly fifty-six inches wide. In this respect, they are more like the norm in north-eastern France, than the usually narrow ones in Britain. Those at the west, of course, repeat the unusual amplitude of the vices at the angles of the transept arms, and like them, intrude into the interior space of the tower bays, rather than being accommodated in the thickness

---

[29] The tall vaulted chambers, without east windows and with a solid wall towards the nave, were, on the south, the chapel of St Michael, and on the north (rebuilt in the thirteenth century) that of St Vincent.

[30] *Rites*, ch. 19. p. 38, and W. Hutchinson, *The History and Antiquities of the County Palatine of Durham* (2 vols., Newcastle, 1785 and 1787), II, 229 n. *.

[31] *Rites*, loc. cit.

[32] P. Verdier in his review of E.B. Smith, *Architectural Symbolism of Imperial Rome and the Middle Ages* (Princeton, 1956) in *American Journal of Archaeology* 64 (1960), p. 117.

Plate 44. Durham Cathedral, west face of the north-west tower.

of the wall. Their closest parallels in an ecclesiastical context are the stair vices of two non-twin-tower façades, those of Lindisfarne Priory, *c*.1120–30, and Rochester Cathedral, *c*.1150–60.[33] At both of these buildings, the stair turrets intrude into the space of the aisles. At Rochester, the stair vice, surviving only at the south-west angle, has an amplitude comparable to those of Durham; the stair vices at Lindisfarne, due to the smaller scale of the building, are of a more usual dimension. Because of their size, the stair vices at Durham result in extraordinary wide and

---

[33] M. Thurlby, 'The Building of the Cathedral: the Romanesque and Early Gothic Fabric', in *Durham Cathedral: A Celebration*, ed. D. Pocock (Durham, 1993), p. 25, pointed out parallels for the dimensions of the transept stair vices in fortified structures such as the late eleventh-century façade-block at Lincoln Cathedral, complete by 1092, and castle keeps, specifically Castle Hedingham (Essex), *c*.1140. See also above, pp. 172–4.

Plate 45. Durham Cathedral, interior of north-west stair vice.

massive exterior angle buttresses (pl. 44). Buttresses of a more normal dimension, like those found at the eastern exterior angles, which were introduced only at the clerestory level, define the angles of the towers towards the nave roof. (Such angle buttresses were missing not only at St Étienne, Caen, but also in the upper free-standing stages of the west towers of La Trinité, Caen).

When work on the nave ceased with the completion of the vaults in 1133, the towers were left incomplete and they were to remain so until the early decades of the next century.[34] But there is no doubt that the original design called for the westernmost bays to support towers extending one or two stages above the level of

[34] The free-standing stages of the towers are usually attributed to the period of Bishop Richard Marisco (1217–26): M.G. Snape, 'Documentary Evidence for the Building of Durham Cathedral and its Monastic Buildings', *MAADC*, p. 23. The spires survived until they were

the nave eaves, no doubt to be capped by pyramidal roofs, and that the builders anticipated the weight such upper stages would place on the lower walls.[35]

A number of features confirm that tall towers were foreseen right from the construction of the lowest levels of the west front. The structure of the west bay from floor to vault is in every way parallel to those (primarily later) examples where towers were raised well above nave roof level. Thus, the western bays are larger than the other aisle bays: this is not a necessary factor for the construction of western towers, as some later twin-towers were built over bays scarcely larger or even smaller than a normal aisle bay (e.g., Southwell Minster). At Durham, as at Chichester Cathedral, the enlargement of the west bay creates a square bay in contrast to the oblong ones of the aisles: the square may have been considered a more desirable base for a tower (although towers were sometimes erected over oblong bays, e.g., at Llanthony Priory where the long axis was west-east). Along with this increase in the dimensions of the west bays, we find that the westernmost pair of piers is considerably more massive than those of the remainder of the nave arcades and their bulk is expressed for the full height of the elevation by an increased number of wall shafts (or broad pilasters in some instances). These piers supported heavy arches springing from them to enlarged responds on the aisle walls which were increased in thickness in the tower bays. The western bays are vaulted at aisle level, but, at Durham, like all other British examples, there were only wooden floors at the upper levels. At gallery level, thick walls, pierced by an archway, separated the tower bay from the gallery: in later buildings it is usually a low broad arch, rather than a doorway-like opening, which separates the tower chamber from gallery or aisle roof space. Above, a division between the gallery and clerestory levels was lacking altogether, as was also not uncommon in later examples. In sum, all these features present in the west front of Durham up to the level of the nave's eaves, are characteristic of those later examples and also of St Augustine's Canterbury, where towers associated with the original period of construction were raised above the level of the nave eaves.

When work on the towers was resumed, the wide angle buttresses, themselves the consequence of the unusual dimensions of the stair vice within, gave the thirteenth-century builders some problems: at first they continued them upwards, but then it seems they were discontented with their massive width and they

---

removed in the 1650s: I. Curry, 'Continuity and Change: Masters, Surveyors and Architects to the Fabric of the Cathedral', in Pocock (ed.), op. cit., p. 37.

[35] M.F. Hearn has reminded me that in my 1963 Ph.D. thesis, *The Romanesque Church Façade in Britain* (New York and London, 1984), p. 523, I commented: 'The towers end exactly even with the level of the nave eaves, with corbel table and a low parapet above. This was as high as the Romanesque builders went, and *they may not have intended to go further* (emphasis added).' The implications of this, perhaps careless, observation, that a towerless façade-block might have been intended, were not, however, followed up by me either in the thesis chapter (I, 1–119, esp. 107–12) on twin-tower façades, or in my later article of 1984 (cited in n. 9 above); in both I assumed taller towers were intended, an assumption I believe now firmly confirmed by the evidence presented below.

Plate 46. Durham Cathedral, interior of north-west stair
vice, detail of rubble vault.

reduced the angle buttresses to a more normal dimension for the upper two stages
(pl. 44). The reasons they could do so are apparent on the interior.

Although the break between the early twelfth-century and the early thirteenth-
century work at Durham appears quite clearly on the exterior and occurs at the
level of the nave eaves (at the top of the clerestory), the break is less clear on the
interior. The clearest evidence of a building break is inside both of the angle stair
vices where a change in constructional technique occurs. From floor level up to a
point well above the eaves level, the construction of each vice is uniform, characterized by the use of a rubble barrel vault to support the stairtreads (pls. 45 and 46).
(The original mortar on the underside of both barrel vaults still exists, clearly
showing the imprint of the rough formwork which supported their erection;
indeed, pieces of the wood formwork are still embedded in the mortar in many

Plate 47.   Durham Cathedral, interior of north-west stair vice
showing change of construction.

places.) A change in construction, to a method typical of the thirteenth and later
centuries, which dispensed with the rubble vault, replacing it with a single stone for
both newel and the entire step, takes place twenty-two steps above the belfry floor
level (the east exit from the vice) in the north tower, forty steps in the south tower
(pl. 47). In addition, two smaller vices, with steps scarcely twenty-five inches wide,
were started at this same level (pl. 48). They flank the base of the west gable and
remain incomplete as they were abandoned when building was resumed: the north
vice stops after sixteen steps, the south one after an equivalent height, although
only nine steps are preserved.

   In both of the angle vices, the change in construction is followed by changes in
the location and dimensions of the vice. The axis of each vice was shifted to the
north- or south-west, and the steps were reduced to less than thirty-one inches in

Plate 48. Durham Cathedral, interior of west front,
beginning of abandoned stair vice flanking gable.

width; the north vice was also changed to a clockwise spiral. The beginning of the
reduced, repositioned vice occurs either just before or after a reduction in the
thickness of the tower walls which forms a setback or ledge on the interior just
above the pairs or triplets of lancets that, on the exterior, mark the first Early
English stage of the towers (the three semicircularly-arched openings in the tower
walls facing the nave roof are taller, so the setback occurs below their arches).[36] The
setback was probably intended to support the bell frame (pl. 49). The narrower
repositioned vice allowed a narrower external angle buttress.

For over seventy-five years, the west front of the cathedral must have presented a
rather unsatisfactory appearance, the upper stages of the west towers jaggedly

[36] The interior of the free-standing 'stages' of each tower is a single unsubdivided space.

Plate 49.   Durham Cathedral, belfry stage of the north-west
tower: mass of stair vice in north-west angle.

incomplete.[37] Actually, one wonders if more of an upper stage than now remains
was built in the twelfth century, work which was later removed by the thirteenth-
century builders, except for the core of the angle vices, in order to make a clean
beginning. Perhaps the ill-protected masonry had suffered from exposure to the
weather. Indeed, it would be expected that, in order to construct the nave roof over
the west bay, the walls of the tower over the nave elevation would have been raised
to some height. Perhaps this explains why the wall facing towards the roof in each
tower is distinct from the other three due to the use of semicircular arches and a

[37] It is unlikely that the towers were ever capped by pyramidal roofs at eaves level as is shown
on the cover of the exhibition booklet, *Monks and Masons: Durham Cathedral, Medieval to
Modern. The Archaeology of Durham Cathedral* (Durham, 1993).

Plate 50.   Durham Cathedral, south wall of belfry stage of
the north-west tower.

differing pattern of openings (pl. 50). These walls were retained because they were
– and are – essentially invisible in any general view of the cathedral from ground
level.

One can speculate that work on the towers slowed down, if it did not come to a
complete halt after 1133, during the period of the civil war between King Stephen
(1135–54) and the Empress Matilda (d.1167). Work may have resumed before the
thirteenth century, however. The evidence for this is the gable. The base of the
gable is pierced by seven tall, narrow lights, the outer jambs and surrounding
orders of which are decorated with vigorous chevron motifs which form, along
with slender shafts flanked by vertical bands of chevron, a continuous series of
arcades that flows over on to the buttresses at the inner angles of the towers – those
containing the small vices beginning at this same level which are each lit by two

narrow lights. The nature of the chevron decoration used accords ill with a date before 1133; rather, it seems close in style and spirit with work associated with Bishop Hugh of le Puiset (1154–95).[38] This suggests that Puiset may have had a scheme for completing the west towers which was subsequently overtaken by his decision to build the Galilee in the 1170s.

Although the west towers of Durham were not raised to their full intended height as a part of the initial continuous series of building campaigns, Durham's significance in the history of the twin-tower façade type in Britain and France is not thereby diminished, for its role as a potential model resided in the structure and design of the façade below the unexecuted free-standing stage or stages. The upper stages of towers did not present any particular problem to their designers or builders. It was at the lower levels that the potential for integrating the towers into the design of the west end of the nave lay and where the possibilities for giving them expression were present. Even incomplete, the intention and the achievement of the designer or designers of the Durham west front would have been clear to other twelfth-century builders. For these reasons, the west façade of Durham appears to stand at the beginning of a particularly British tradition of twin-tower façades.

POSTSCRIPT

(1) I have been informed that the recent excavations in the nave of Canterbury Cathedral uncovered the paving pattern of Lanfranc's building which extended into the tower bays, suggesting they were open to the nave and aisles by large arches.

(2) I have become convinced that the allegedly thirteenth-century stages of the Durham west towers are actually late twelfth-century, erected by Bishop Puiset.

---

[38] The chevron of the gable is much more three dimensional, bolder in relief than the few instances of the application of chevron as a continuous surround, on the doorway of the slype and on the north-facing aisle-level window (restored) and west-facing gallery-level window (redressed) of the north-west tower, pointed out by Curry, 'Aspects', pp. 42 and 48 n. 15: the comparison illustrates to my mind the difference in date (*pace* Curry who dated the gable to before 1133).

Observations on the Architecture of the Galilee Chapel

S. A. HARRISON

I. INTRODUCTION

T HE PURPOSE OF this paper is to reconsider the evidence for the form of the
Galilee Chapel (or porch) at Durham Cathedral and its place in the development of Early Gothic architecture in the North of England.[1] Contemporary
sources describe how Bishop Hugh of le Puiset (1153–95) began construction at
the east end of the cathedral but, following the failure of this first structure, he
abandoned the attempt to build at the east and started afresh at the west end.[2] The
Galilee, which was the result and is one of the most complete buildings patronized
by him to survive, is usually dated to 1175 but allowing for the extensive use of
chevron it may be as early as 1165, although not earlier than that since it seems on
stylistic grounds to be later than the North Hall doorway in Durham Castle.

Crammed in at the foot of the great Romanesque west towers of the cathedral,
the Galilee perches precariously on the edge of the cliff which forms the western
boundary of the cathedral precinct. In the middle ages it served a variety of
functions: site of the shrine of Bede, meeting place of the consistory court, the part
of the cathedral which could be entered by women, preaching station, location of
several chapels, and later on the location of the chantry of Cardinal Langley
(1406–37). Deprived of its usefulness after the dissolution of the cathedral priory,

[1] Society of Antiquaries of London, *Some Account of the Cathedral Church of Durham* (London, 1801), illustrated by detailed drawings of the cathedral by John Carter; R.W. Billings,
Architectural Illustrations and Description of the Cathedral Church at Durham (London, 1843),
pp. 31–4; G.M. Hills, 'The Cathedral and Monastery of St Cuthbert at Durham', *JBAA* 22
(1866), pp. 206–8; W. Greenwell, *Durham Cathedral* (Durham, 1881), pp. 32–6; N. Pevsner,
County Durham (Buildings of England; 2nd edn, Harmondsworth, 1983), pp. 20, 175–6,
187–9, 193–4; R. Halsey, 'The Galilee Chapel', in *MAADC*, pp. 59–69; and D. Park, 'The
Wall Paintings in the Galilee Chapel of Durham Cathedral', *Friends of Durham Cathedral* 57
(1990), pp. 21–34. I would like to thank: the vergers at Durham for their help whilst I was
measuring the Galilee; Ian Curry, the cathedral architect; and the works staff who provided
access and ladders to the Galilee roof. Special thanks are due to Eric Cambridge for his help
with the loose masonry and Malcolm Thurlby who initially persuaded me to prepare a study
of the Galilee Chapel and helped take measurements and gave sound advice during several
visits to Durham.
[2] *Script. Tres*, p. 11; cf. *Sym. Op.* I, 168.

Plate 51.   Durham Cathedral, Galilee chapel, general view across the interior from the north-west.

it was gradually abandoned and allowed to decay.[3] In the late eighteenth century an attempt at demolition was made but fortunately the Galilee was saved by the intervention of the antiquarian draughtsman and illustrator John Carter and the Society of Antiquaries. Subsequently it was extensively restored and brought back into use as a chapel.

The surviving twelfth-century core shows that the Galilee consisted of five aisles, virtually equal in width with arcades of four bays, the position of which was partially dictated by the desire to incorporate part of the existing shafted angle buttresses of the west front into the arcade responds (pl. 51). Because of the restricted area available for building, the chapel is wider than it is long. The problems of this restricted site were cleverly overcome, and though the division of the interior into five aisles was perhaps adopted in order to create spaces for several chapels, it also had the virtue of keeping the spans to be roofed narrow and therefore the height of the roofs relatively low above the tops of the walls. This meant that the height of the building could be maximized without unduly obscuring windows in the west front. The east wall was formed by the west front of the cathedral. As originally built, the central aisle must have been kept clear for access

3   Halsey, 'Galilee', pp. 60–3; Society of Antiquaries, *Some Account*, pl. 2, shows the consistory court sited in the third bay of the south aisle. The plan also shows the screen blocking the Cathedral west doorway and the blocking of the Galilee north doorway.

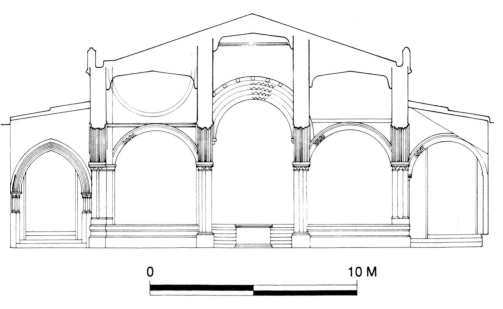

Fig. 5. Durham Cathedral, Galilee Chapel, schematic cross-section looking east showing the present arrangement of the high and side aisle roofs and the scar of the former roof across the south aisle.

to the great central doorway into the cathedral nave, so there was no central axial chapel (fig. 5). The other aisles had altars, apart from the first aisle to the south which housed Bede's shrine.[4]

Many changes have been made to the Galilee since it was built. Langley constructed an elaborate chantry chapel for his tomb,[5] which still survives built into the stairs in front of the central doorway, and partially blocked this doorway with a screen and pierced new doorways into the north and south aisles from the cathedral nave. He also constructed the present roofs and timber ceilings, consisting of a single, very shallow lead-covered span over the three central aisles and separate, lower sloping roofs over each outer aisle (fig. 5). The north and south walls were heavily restored in the Victorian period and the windows supplied with imitation Gothic tracery as were those in the west wall.

II. THE SURVIVING TWELFTH-CENTURY FABRIC

(a) *The South Aisle*

The south aisle was almost completely rebuilt in the fourteenth century. The aisle wall was rebuilt slightly out of line with the original wall, as indicated by the partial remains of an angle shaft, possibly of twelfth century date, high up in the south-

---

[4] *Rites*, p. 46.
[5] *Rites*, p. 44.

Plate 52.   Durham Cathedral, Galilee Chapel, east end of the south aisle
with the scar of the former roofline cutting across the hood-mould
framing the formers altar niche. This niche was pierced to form a
doorway during Cardinal Langley's remodelling of the chapel.

west corner. At the east end of the aisle is a recess with a segmental arch decorated
with chevron and enclosed with a hoodmould. The back of the recess was pierced
by Langley's masons to form a doorway.

Over the segmental arch is a sloping cut in the masonry for the lead flashing of a
roof (pl. 52, fig. 5). This indicates that the aisle wall was at one time considerably
lower than at present. At first sight, it appears that the hoodmould over the
segmental arch has been truncated on the south side to accommodate this roofline,
suggesting that the roof was later than the arch. In fact, however, above the arch in
its southern spandrel the masonry steps back and there is no sign that there were
ever voussoirs for the hoodmould here. It seems, therefore, that the hoodmould

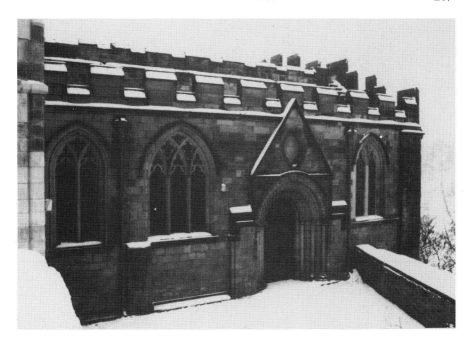

Plate 53. Durham Cathedral, Galilee Chapel, exterior of the north aisle showing the elaborate north doorway, erected in 1863 as a careful copy of the original doorway. The relationship of the side buttresses to the gablet shows that it is most unlikely that they ever rose higher and that the aisle was originally roofed with a series of transverse gables.

never extended over the whole of the arch, so that the roofline indicated by the sloping flashline may be an original feature.

(b) *The North Aisle*

The north aisle wall retains far more evidence for original masonry, although extensively restored in the nineteenth century. Internally it is divided into bays by broad pilasters which have moulded shafts on the angles. Only the lower section of the twelfth-century wall survives, the wall having been almost completely rebuilt above the stringcourse, which marked the baseline of the original window sills, and new windows having been introduced, in the thirteenth century. The aisle wall retains the principal entrance into the Galilee, a doorway of great magnificence, set externally and internally in a projecting frame with a gabled top decorated with an elongated quatrefoil (pl. 53). The whole of the external face of this wall dates from the nineteenth-century restoration, but restorers seem to have reproduced the original details of this door accurately, even going to the lengths of re-erecting the original stonework outside the Galilee to show how careful they had been.[6] Like

---

6 Hills, 'Cathedral and Monastery', p. 207. No remains of this doorway now survive amongst the collection of loose stonework from the Cathedral. See also I. Curry, *Sense and Sensibility: Durham Cathedral and its Architects* (Durham, 1985), p. 24.

Plate 54.   Durham Cathedral, Galilee Chapel, east end of
the north aisle with the thirteenth-century former altar
niche, pierced to form a doorway during Cardinal Langley's
remodelling of the chapel. The northern edge of the arch
cuts the twelfth-century corner pilaster of the north aisle
wall, showing that this was reduced to its present height
and remodelled at an early date.

the internal pilasters the external buttresses have been truncated by the later
windows except at the north-west corner where the restored buttress stands the full
height of the aisle wall.[7]

---

[7] This buttress has been heavily restored and its masonry is largely Victorian in date. In its
present form it has angle shafts which rise the full height of the buttress but Carter's drawing of
the north side of the Galilee does not show the shafts rising so high. This suggests that what
now exists is the product of restoration. See Society of Antiquaries, *Some Account*, pl. 4.

The east end of the north aisle has a wide, deeply recessed niche, like the south aisle, but instead of a twelfth-century segmental arch there is a thirteenth-century pointed arch which has shafted jambs with capitals and bases (pl. 54). This overlaps the truncated aisle wall internal pilaster at the north-east corner of the chapel and shows that the reduction in height and remodelling of the twelfth-century aisle wall occurred at an earlier date than the present windows would suggest. Presumably this scheme included a new series of windows which were subsequently replaced in the fourteenth century. Apart from a sloping marking on a single stone set high up, there is no sign of an earlier aisle roofline against the west front, though such evidence could have been removed when the present arch was inserted into the west front.

(c) *The Internal Arcades*

The piers of the internal arcades consist of a pair of monolithic Purbeck Marble shafts with matching base and capitals of waterleaf form. Between the bases, shafts and capitals are thick lead packings. Set between the marble shafts are added coursed freestone shafts with bases and capitals scribed and butted up to the originals. Even the lead packing at the base of the marble shafts is copied as a thin moulding. At first sight, the added shafts appear to give no support at all to the arcade which rest entirely upon the capital supported by the paired marble shafts and in several places the abaci of the added capitals are missing. For many years it was thought that the freestone shafts were added during Langley's alterations, but Halsey suggested that they were an afterthought to the original design and were introduced because the paired marble shafts were unsatisfactory in appearance.[8] It is certainly true that they vary considerably in their diameters and in the amount they taper, so that they may indeed have looked unsightly alone.[9]

Halsey's interpretation of the added shafts cannot, however, be correct.[10] The joints in the coursed shafts are level bedded at each side (pl. 55), which shows that they are built from throughstones, rather than being cut from two separate stones which were butted together. Had the coursed shafts been added immediately after the erection of the arcades they would surely have been cut in and butted together, behind the marble shafts. The use of single throughstones shows conclusively that the coursed shafts must have been built first and the marble shafts were then erected against them. The hypothesis that they have no structural function is therefore false. It may be true that they serve no useful purpose in supporting the arches, though the central part of each double capital may in fact be resting on these shafts, but they have an important function in stabilising the marble shafts,

---

[8] Halsey, 'Galilee', pp. 66–7.
[9] The diameter of the Purbeck Marble shafts ranges from 217mm to 280mm, the latter in the eastern respond of the south arcade. In total there are seventeen different diameters. The freestone shafts also show some variation between 237mm and 250mm but there is no logical pattern in their distribution, the majority being 240mm wide.
[10] Halsey, 'Galilee', p. 69.

Plate 55. Durham Cathedral, Galilee chapel, pier showing
the level bedding of the coursed pier core, against which the
Purbeck Marble monolithic shafts must have been erected.

preventing rotational displacement, by stopping them from twisting out of alignment and toppling over.

The fact that the freestone shafts cannot have been added once the arcade had
been erected has important implications for the design of the abandoned eastern
extension. It seems likely that the paired marble shafts, their bases and capitals, the
western responds,[11] and also the arcade which they support (since this takes no

---

[11] The western responds consist of paired shafts without the stone core of the freestanding
piers and must surely have been salvaged from the abandoned scheme. Some of the jointing of
the pilasters behind the western responds appear to lack proper bonding to the west wall and
this may be because they were also salvaged from that scheme.

Plate 56.   Durham Cathedral, Galilee chapel, detail of south arcade showing blocked outline of former clerestory window.

account of the added shafts) originally formed part of the failed eastern structure and were salvaged from that building. This suggests that the design of that structure must have been very similar to that of the Galilee, though just how it was attached to the Romanesque choir is unclear. The western responds did not receive added freestone shafts and their freestanding paired marble shafts give the best indication of what the original effect of the arcade piers may have been. The cause of the failure of the eastern design is readily apparent in the nature of the geology of the ground beneath the cathedral. At the west end the bedrock is relatively close to the surface but progressively drops towards the east until in the area of the Nine Altars Chapel it is around 4m below ground level. It seems clear that because of the small floor area covered by the pier bases the architects skimped the foundations which must have started to sink. They cannot have realised that with such a small pier base, supporting a large arcade, the point loading was very large.[12]

The arcade has paired keeled rolls separated and flanked by bold chevron mouldings, framed by a prominent hoodmould, the whole forming a rich and distinctive effect. Above the arches there are now no windows but in each of the outer arcades internally there are remains which look like windows which have been blocked up. In the south arcade these show in each bay, a small round headed

---

[12] The point loading of the pier bases must be quite large because of the small area each covers. The effect can be likened to that of the stiletto heel of a shoe, which can easily punch a hole in soft flooring materials because of its small area.

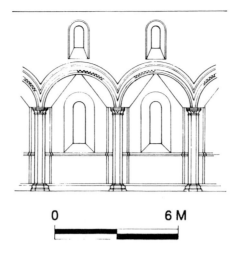

Fig. 6.   Durham Cathedral, Galilee
Chapel, bay design of main arcade
with small clerestory windows.

outline with a moulded frame on the angle (pl. 56, fig. 6), but in the north arcade
only the first few courses survive and that in the western bay is missing. Unfortunately no external trace of these features now survives, due on the south side to
nineteenth-century refacing and on the north to Langley's alterations. Halsey's
interpretation of these features is that if they are blocked clerestory windows they
formed part of a scheme which was never completed and was abandoned during
construction. He based this on the incomplete remains of the windows in the
north arcade, together with the allegedly twelfth-century nature of the blocking
material and the apparent lack of any external evidence for windows.[13] It seems
strange, however, that the architect, having presumably completed windows in one
arcade and half completed three out of four in the other, abandoned the whole
scheme and blocked up the openings. Now the north arcade leans more than the
others, particularly its western pier, and surely a more realistic interpretation is that
Langley, finding the Galilee in a dangerous condition, took down and rebuilt the
upper levels of the north arcade. In doing so his masons would have removed the
upper sections of the clerestory windows, destroying all trace of the westernmost
entirely, and have blocked up the openings in the south arcade as a precautionary
measure against further movement in the masonry and to conform with the new
arrangement of roofs. The absence of any trace of the clerestory windows externally
can be accounted for by the refacings of the walls during this reconstruction and
later restoration in the nineteenth century.

[13] Halsey, 'Galilee', p. 63.

Plate 57. Durham Cathedral, Galilee chapel, north central
aisle with elaborate altar niche, painted with sumptuous
hangings and figures of Sts Oswald and Cuthbert on the side
reveals. Above is a depiction of *c*.1300 of the Coronation of
the Virgin set in a circular frame. The remains of the circular
frame indicate that the original ceiling was of barrel form.

(d) *The End Walls*

Against the west wall of the Romanesque church the arcades were carefully bonded
to the existing early twelfth-century structure. This work now appears confusing
but in reality carefully employed several existing elements, such as the corner shafts
of the buttresses of the west front and the shafts of the west doorway as arcade pier
responds. The abutment of the two inner arcades partially masks the arch mouldings of the west doorway, which it overlaps (fig. 5). Between each of the arcades
and the aisle walls the west front was hollowed out to form wide, blind-arched,

recessed niches with segmental arches decorated with chevron mouldings and projecting hoodmoulds. Against the west wall of the Galilee internally the arcade responds were backed by wide pilasters which have keeled mouldings on the angles, similar in appearance to those employed to mark the bay divisions in the north aisle. These pilasters now extend to various heights and all were truncated during Langley's restoration of the Galilee.

(e) *Painted Decoration and the Principal Altar*

Large areas of walling which presumably must have been painted are now totally bare but much painting has survived, including substantial traces of red lining upon a white ground and red chevrons upon the keeled rolls of the arcades, which may have formed part of the original twelfth-century decoration.[14] The lack of a specific architectural feature to signify the position of the principal altar seems to have been compensated for in the decorative scheme. In the aisle to the north of the central doorway the wall-niche is sumptuously decorated with twelfth-century painting of draped hangings across the back wall and images of St Oswald and St Cuthbert on the side reveals (pl. 57), the soffit of the arch above being covered with a frieze of stylized leaves. David Park has argued convincingly that this was the site of the altar to the Virgin and on the wall above the niche is a much damaged panel of a later scheme of *c*.1300 which he has identified as depicting the Coronation of the Virgin. The figures of Christ and the Virgin seated upon a throne were set within a circular frame of which only the lower half survives, the upper section having been cut through by the alteration to the roofs undertaken during Langley's restoration.[15]

(f) *Ceilings and Roofs*

This wall painting has great significance for the form of the roofs which must have existed when it was executed. If the surviving lower part of the circular frame is projected to full circle it rises considerably above the level of the wallplate of the flanking arcades and strongly indicates that it was introduced as a painted architectural motif to echo the existing curve of a timber ceiling of barrel form (fig. 7). The introduction of such a ceiling could date from the renovation undertaken when the painting was executed, around 1300, but is far more likely to have been the design of the original twelfth-century ceiling, which was probably plastered and painted in imitation of a stone barrel vault.[16] This evidence for the former presence of a barrel ceiling suggests that all three central aisles were covered in this manner and therefore the outer roofs must have been formed by three separate steeply pitched roofs.

   The existence of such barrel ceilings over the three central aisles is further supported by Halsey's interpretation of the pilasters used to mark the internal bay

---

[14] Park, 'Wall Paintings', pp. 21–34.
[15] Ibid., p. 23.
[16] Barrel timber ceilings, because of their perishable nature, tend to leave little trace of their former presence.

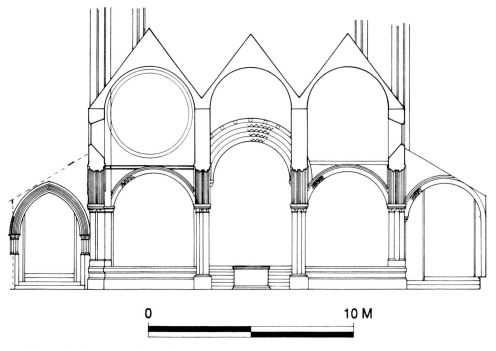

Fig. 7. Durham Cathedral, Galilee chapel, schematic cross-section looking east, showing the most likely arrangement of high and side aisle roofs and ceilings. The presence of barrel ceilings can be deduced by projecting the outline of the frame around the painting of the Coronation of the Virgin in the north central aisle. The use of separate gables over each high aisle kept the roofs relatively low.

divisions and to back the western responds as the remnants of a scheme of wall arches spanning each bay.[17] These arches would have provided a suitable architectural frame for the putative barrel ceilings over the three central aisles. On the west wall, these arches would have taken the form of blind arches which would have provided the perfect frame for rose windows above a series of lower round-headed windows (fig. 8).

Unfortunately the extensive recutting of the external masonry of the west front in the eighteenth century has removed any trace of the line of the original roofs of the three central aisles. The only thing which seems certain about these roofs is that, although the arcades below them rose nearly as high as the window sills of the Romanesque west front, the roofs cannot have intruded upon the windows. This is confirmed by the insertion in the late fourteenth century of a new west window which was apparently achieved without having to consider the Galilee roofs.[18] The conclusion must be that the roofs of the central aisles had thin east gable walls,

[17] Halsey, 'Galilee', p. 65.
[18] I. Curry, 'Aspects of the Anglo-Norman Design of Durham Cathedral', *Arch. Ael.*, 5th ser., 14 (1986), pp. 42–3, pl. 2, fig. 5, discusses the evidence for the original west windows and

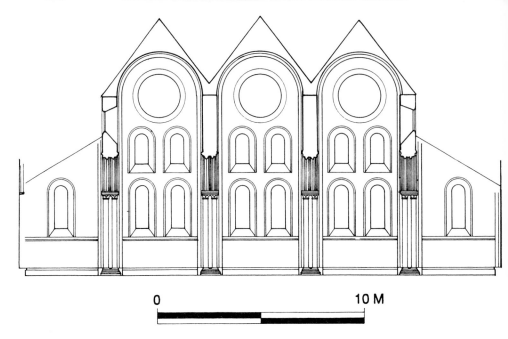

Fig. 8. Durham Cathedral, Galilee chapel, schematic cross-section looking west, showing a likely arrangement of twelfth-century windows, one of several which could have formerly existed. The presence of barrel ceilings is strongly suggestive of rose windows inspired by Cistercian examples such as Fountains.

spanning the space between the large flanking buttresses of the western towers, whilst still leaving a substantial space between themselves and the Romanesque west windows. This was possible because the central part of the west front was relatively deeply recessed between the flanking buttresses.

As for the roofs over the two outer aisles, neither the north nor south arcades, which are visible externally above the outer aisle roofs, retain their original twelfth-century masonry facings, although the north side does have some medieval, possibly twelfth-century, stonework much patched and altered. Towards the east end, at the level of the second ashlar course above the lead covering of the present outer aisle roof, there is visible the outline of what appears to have been a sloping hoodmould (fig. 9). Halsey interpreted this as the remains of a north-south transverse gable, and he considered that three such gables would have covered each of the outer aisles.[19] There are, however, serious objections to this. First it is not easy to explain why only this hoodmould remains from such a scheme. Secondly, my own measurements of this wall show that the gable reconstructed on the basis of the hoodmould cannot have been related to the original twelfth-century buttressing

reconstructs their most likely arrangement. All the indications are that the window sills were set as low as in the present arrangement.

[19] Halsey, 'Galilee', pp. 64–5.

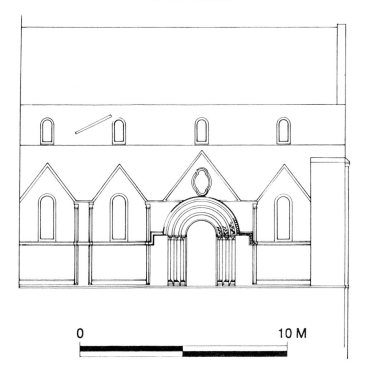

Fig. 9. Durham Cathedral, Galilee Chapel, reconstruction of the north aisle with separate transverse gables in each bay. The line above the aisle roof in the second bay from the east is a wall scar, possibly part of a later transverse gable roofing system connected with one of at least two remodellings of the aisle wall.

system, suggesting that if such a gable ever existed it must have been at a later date, possibly related to the later refurbishment of the Galilee. Thirdly, it is not clear that the masonry to the east of the gable is twelfth-century as Halsey maintains, since there is little difference between it and that to the west. There is certainly twelfth-century masonry in this part of the wall as a whole, but it is mixed in with larger blocks of Langley's work, suggesting that it has been salvaged from the earlier fabric in a radical rebuilding of the outer arcade wall, perhaps necessitated by its tendency to lean to the west.

Nevertheless there is evidence to suggest that the outer aisles were roofed with transverse gables, although smaller and more numerous than those postulated by Halsey. The principal doorway in the north wall is set within a projecting frame with moulded shafts worked up the angles (pl. 53). This doorway, as noted above, is an accurate nineteenth-century copy of the original, so its external framing is valid evidence for the former appearance of the aisle wall. The triangular pediment of this framing can be interpreted as the outer face of a small transverse gable. Moreover, since the flanking buttresses rise only as high as its base, each bay in the aisle may have had a similar transverse gable, perhaps combined with a low sloping

0   10 M

Fig. 10. Durham Cathedral, Galilee Chapel, schematic elevation of the west front, showing the immense height of the building and the various decorative tiers of arcading and trellis ornament. It is probable that the pilaster buttresses were carried up and finished with some form of turret pinnacles; possibly the internal pilaster mouldings were continued as angle features.

Plate 58. Durham Cathedral, Galilee chapel, interior of the north aisle
doorway with gabled frame. This indicates that this bay was once
covered by a transverse gabled roof.

roof like that indicated by the roofline at the east end of the south aisle (see above)
(fig. 10). This supposition is reinforced by the apparently less restored internal face
of the doorway which retains a truncated gabled top (pl. 58). This arrangement of
small transverse gables is all the more plausible since it would have reflected what is
thought to have been the system over the nave tribunes at the time when the
Galilee was built.[20]

---

[20] The best surviving evidence for this scheme is at the east end of the north aisle of the nave
where the slope of the gables can clearly be seen. Similar evidence for gables survived along the
south aisle wall until the nineteenth-century restoration. See Hills, 'Cathedral and Monastery',
p. 205, and Billings, *Architectural Illustrations*, pl. 8.

Plate 59.   Durham Cathedral, Galilee Chapel, edges of twelfth-century pilaster buttresses showing high up at the sides of Cardinal Langley's massive fifteenth-century additional buttresses.

(g)   *The West Wall Exterior*

The interior gives no hint of the precarious position of the Galilee. To gain sufficient floor space the west wall was built beyond the cliff edge and is therefore extremely high in relation to the aisle walls. This caused problems later when the west wall began to lean outwards and Langley built large buttresses against it to stabilize the building. Presumably the floor at the western end of the Galilee is made ground, backfilled between the western wall and the natural cliff edge. The original articulation consisted of shallow pilaster buttresses with shafts worked on the angles, and some sections of these can still be seen embedded in the upper parts of Langley's buttresses (pl. 59). Between the pilasters the wall was decorated by blind arcades in two tiers and a band of large trellis ornament set diagonally below the original windows. Much remains of this scheme and although it is sadly disfigured and partly obscured by the later reinforcements it is still possible to gain some idea of what the original must have looked like (fig. 10).[21]

---

[21] The present level of the path at the base of the west wall of the Galilee is much above the medieval level. This can be seen within an archway giving access to St Cuthbert's well, which is sited between two of Langley's buttresses. In John Carter's time more of Langley's base plinth and the archway were visible (Society of Antiquaries, *Some Account*, pl. 3).

Plate 60.   Fountains Abbey, transverse gables with an
arrangement of round-headed and circular windows in
the transepts. The infill masonry between the gables
was a later addition.

III. SOURCES OF INSPIRATION

Halsey suggested that Puiset obtained his masons from the York area because of similarities with work then being carried out at York Minster and at the adjoining episcopal palace by Archbishop Roger of Pont l'Évêque.[22] Whilst some features of this work, such as the use of marble, may have influenced Puiset, York's influence has probably been exaggerated. Puiset was a prolific builder who must have been as aware of the latest trends in architecture as Archbishop Roger, and study of his surviving works shows that the detail of the Galilee Chapel did not significantly depart from architectural trends which he had already established at Durham and elsewhere in the northern region. The vocabulary of architectural motifs, such as the extensive use of chevron, followed well-established traditions and the highly elaborate north doorway of the Galilee can be paralleled in his similarly sumptuous but earlier doorway in the North Hall of Durham Castle, and in the splendid new cloister doorway inserted into the east end of the south aisle of the cathedral nave. Romanesque motifs were mixed with the more modern Early Gothic waterleaf which gradually ousted the older forms of decoration. Such was the influence of Durham that motifs which occur upon the Castle North Hall doorway are also prominent features of doorways at Furness Abbey and Holm Cultram Abbey in Cumbria, both major Early Gothic churches, and of the cloister processional doorway of Chester Cathedral.[23] The use of barrel ceilings and transverse gables over aisles can be paralleled at a number of Cistercian sites, most notably in the transepts at Fountains Abbey, where stone barrel vaults over the chapels are combined with transverse gables, and the use of circular windows echoes the curve of the barrel vaults (pl. 60). Similar transverse gables combined with barrel vaulting can be reconstructed over the nave aisles at Rievaulx,[24] and high timber barrel ceilings combined with rose windows seem to have existed at Rievaulx, Fountains, Kirkstall, and Byland. In this connection, it should be noted that, although the barrel ceilings in the Galilee may have been inspired by Cistercian models, the idea of using transverse gables may originally have come from Durham, where their use in the nave tribunes of the cathedral was earlier than any Cistercian examples.

The corpus of surviving works by Puiset can be enlarged by reference to the extensive collection of architectural fragments which is stored at the west end of the undercroft of the Cathedral Library. Amongst them are considerable quantities of material which span the period of Puiset's episcopate, including several sumptuously decorated voussoirs, similar to those in the Castle North Hall doorway and the Galilee and cloister doorways. Measurement of their radii shows that they must

---

[22] Halsey, 'Galilee', pp. 67–8.

[23] P. Fergusson, *Architecture of Solitude: Cistercian Abbeys in Twelfth-Century England* (Princeton, 1984), pp. 56–62. To my knowledge the architectural connexions between Chester and Furness and Durham have never been explored. In addition to the cloister processional doorway at Chester, the vaulted west range looks very similar to the west range at Furness.

[24] *VCH Yorkshire, North Riding*, ed. W. Page (3 vols., London, 1914), I, 496.

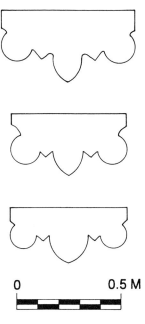

Fig. 11.   Early Gothic arch soffit
mouldings. From top to bottom:
Ripon, Byland, Durham.

represent at least two more doorways of this type. It has long been thought that the
nave arcade at Pittington, which features piers with elaborate chevron decoration,
was inspired by work at the cathedral,[25] and the fragments include parts of several
sumptuously decorated piers, which presumably formed the model for the Pittington designs. They probably originated from a now lost hall in the monastic
complex. There are also many pieces decorated with chevrons, including several
massive voussoirs with chevrons flanking a large roll which must have originated in
a building of substantial size. Some of the plainer elements are voussoirs from a
large arcade which employed the standard northern Early Gothic profile of a
central keeled roll flanked by roll mouldings, separated by arrises, such as was
employed at Byland Abbey and Ripon Cathedral (fig. 11).[26]

There are also the springers from a cloister arcade which featured gorged roll
mouldings. The latter can be partly reconstructed on paper (fig. 12) and show the
typical type of cloister arcade then common throughout the north of England,
with paired shafts supporting the arcading. The new processional doorway into the
cloister was mentioned above and it seems likely that it is all that survives of a

[25] Pevsner, *County Durham*, pp. 379–80.
[26] S.A. Harrison, 'The Architecture of Byland Abbey' (unpublished M.A. Thesis, University of
York, 1988), pp. 75–7, 118; C. Wilson, 'The Cistercians as Missionaries of Gothic', in
Cistercian Art and Architecture in the British Isles, ed. C. Norton and D. Park (Cambridge,
1986), pp. 96–7.

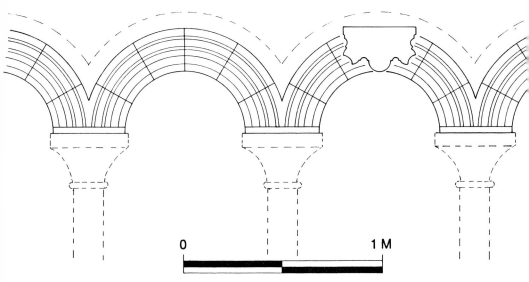

Fig. 12.   Durham Cathedral, schematic reconstruction of the late twelfth-century cloister arcade, based on surviving fragments.

much grander scheme to provide new cloister arcades as well. It seems certain that parts of this arcading were reused, after its replacement, in alterations to the Cathedral Library.[27] Substantial waterleaf and chalice-style capitals apparently from other lost buildings are also preserved. Such stylistic elements, together with the evidence from the surviving buildings such as the Galilee and the Castle North Hall show that the Durham masons kept pace with developments in the northern region and were probably in the forefront of architectural progress. Certainly the material indicates that they were not slow in adopting the latest Early Gothic motifs from France, but initially combined these with the large repertoire of late Romanesque forms which they had at their disposal. Whilst it cannot be proved that Puiset initiated or even provided any patronage towards this major group of lost buildings it seems clear that the same group of masons was involved in their construction. Even if Puiset was not directly involved, which considering his reputation as a great builder seems unlikely, he must surely in his position as bishop have given his tacit approval to any architectural schemes initiated by the Cathedral Priory.

[27] M. Johnson, 'Recent Work on the Refectory of Durham Cathedral', *TAASDN*, new series 1 (1968), pp. 92–3.

The Architectural Setting of the Cult of St Cuthbert in Durham Cathedral (1093–1200)

JOHN CROOK

I. INTRODUCTION

T HE TASK OF ASSESSING the influence of relic cults on English ecclesiastical architecture is not always easy, mainly as a result of the highly successful work of Henry VIII's Commissioners in eradicating the cult of 'the rotten bones that be called relics',[1] but also because of the more recent removal of archaeological evidence by restorers; in some cases even the exact site of the shrine has been forgotten. Thus at Worcester the position of the shrines of Sts Oswald and Wulfstan remains disputed, and at Winchester we have only recently been able to trace with some certainty the movements of St Swithun.[2]

Fortunately, in Durham, there can be little doubt over St Cuthbert's continued whereabouts. Though some still hold to the legend that his body lies hidden in a place known only to three Benedictines, it is more generally accepted that his bones reside, as they have done since 1104, within the former Romanesque apse of William of St Calais's cathedral, in the area known as the feretory. The body has been exhumed twice in recent times: in 1827, and again in 1899.[3]

This paper addresses three questions. Firstly, it considers the plan of Bishop William's original east end. Nearly a century has elapsed since John Bilson first discussed the subject.[4] The evidence is inaccessible, has not been illustrated at all adequately in the literature, and needs to be set out before investigating any

---

[1] Letter, Thomas Wriothesley to Cromwell, summarised in *Calendar of Letters and Papers, Foreign and Domestic, Henry VIII* (21 vols. and addenda, London, 1864–1932), XIII.ii, 155.
[2] J. Crook, 'St Swithun of Winchester', in *Winchester Cathedral – Nine Hundred Years*, ed. J. Crook (Chichester, 1993), pp. 57–68.
[3] For the 1827 excavation, see J. Raine, *Saint Cuthbert: with an Account of the State in which his Remains were Found upon the Opening of his Tomb in Durham Cathedral in the year MDCCCXXVII* (Durham, 1828), especially pp. 183–217. For the 1899 exhumation, see J.T. Fowler, 'On an Examination of the Grave of St Cuthbert in Durham Cathedral Church, in March, 1899', *Arch.* 57 (1900), pp. 11–28. The exhumations have been most recently discussed by Richard N. Bailey, 'St Cuthbert's Relics: Some Neglected Evidence', in *Cuthbert*, pp. 231–6.
[4] J. Bilson, 'On the Recent Discoveries at the East End of the Cathedral Church of Durham', *Arch. J.* 33 (1896), pp. 1–18; the paper was also published in *TAASDN* 4 (1896), pp. 261–80.

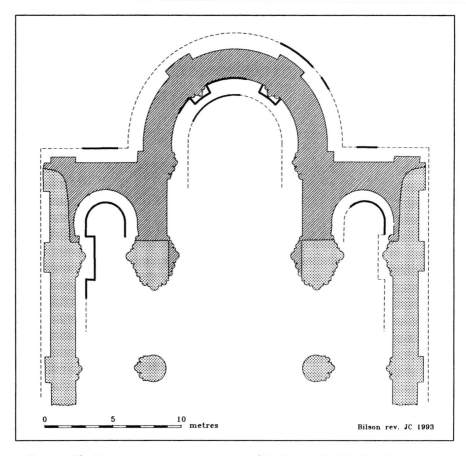

Fig. 13.   The Romanesque eastern termination of Durham Cathedral, after Bilson. Excavated areas are denoted by thick lines. Stippled: surviving; Hatched: evidenced by excavation.

possible influence that the cult of Cuthbert may have had on the design of the cathedral. Secondly, it discusses the date of various features evident in the feretory, which also shed light on the development of the eastern arm. Finally, some comments are offered on the form and appearance of the earliest shrine in the present cathedral.

II. THE PLAN OF THE EAST END
OF THE ROMANESQUE CATHEDRAL

The original plan of the east end of the Romanesque cathedral, begun by William of St Calais in 1093, was forgotten until the 1890s, and limited archaeological evidence discovered in 1827 and 1844 was wrongly interpreted by some historians

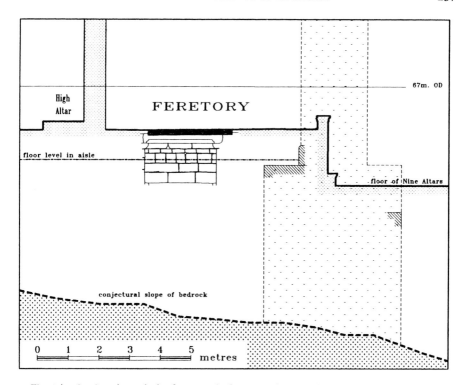

Fig. 14. Section through the feretory platform, Durham Cathedral, based on a new survey. The detail of Cuthbert's grave is after J. T. Fowler, 'The Grave of St Cuthbert', *Arch.* 57 (1900), fig. 2 (p. 13).

as proof of an apse-and-ambulatory structure.[5] In January 1895, however, the footings of the apse at the east end of the south aisle were discovered during heating work, confirming that the plan comprised a central apse flanked by two smaller apses (square externally) at the end of the aisles, and no ambulatory (fig.

[5] The foundation of the main apse was discovered during the examination of St Cuthbert's body in 1827, when James Raine observed that 'the foundation masonry was . . . ascertained to be in a perfect state a few feet below the level of the shrine': Raine, *St Cuthbert*, p. 131. The position of the outer face of the apse foundation was discovered in 1844, when part of it had to be removed to accommodate a grave: James Raine, 'On the Architectural History of the Cathedral Church of Durham', *Proceedings of the Archaeological Institute*, meeting held at Newcastle-on-Tyne, August 1852 (2 vols., London, 1858), I, 238, n. This was erroneously identified by Canon William Greenwell in 1883 as 'that of the Rev. James Townsend, who was buried in that year [1844], . . . on the platform, close to the east wall': W. Greenwell, 'Durham Cathedral', *TAASDN* 2 (1883), p. 201, n. James Raine originally believed, correctly, that the plan had three parallel apses: Raine, *St Cuthbert*, p. 94 (plan) and p. 104 (reference to 'the extreme eastern terminations of the three aisles, which were *coved* over their respective altars'), and idem, *A Brief Account of Durham Cathedral* (Newcastle, 1833), pp. 35–6: 'Each of the three aisles ends in a semi-circle.' Later, however, he proposed an apse-and-ambulatory structure, as shown in his plan of the east end: Raine, 'Architectural History of Durham', p. 224

13). Seven key areas were then excavated, and with remarkable consideration for future researchers they were left accessible.

Perhaps the most spectacular excavation was that of the deep, apsidal chamber formed by the foundation walls below the apse of the north aisle. Here, some 3.5 m of earth was removed, revealing the Romanesque footings built on solid rock. Presumably a similar chamber was created under the apse of the south aisle, but it was not fully excavated in 1895. It should be emphasized that as originally built these temporary chambers within the foundation walls were backfilled; there is no evidence that they ever formed any kind of crypt. Our section of the feretory (fig. 14) shows why such deep retaining foundations were necessary. The bedrock slopes away steeply towards the east, necessitating a large amount of building before pavement level was reached, some five metres above the bedrock.[6] Both the inner and outer faces of the foundations were investigated in 1895, when it was determined that the foundations are 4.43 m thick.

More relevant to the present paper was the excavation below the feretory pavement. The operation was recorded in a series of drawings by the cathedral architect, Charles Hodgson Fowler (fig. 15).[7] The massive foundation wall is formed of a core of sandstone rubble in lime mortar, with roughly tooled ashlar facing both externally and internally. It terminates in a flat surface 1.12 m below the present pavement. On top of the foundation wall two courses of well-jointed masonry survive beneath pavement level, forming the inner face of the apse wall (pl. 61). They terminate in a chamfer, thus identifying these courses as a plinth, similar to the plinth or wall-bench of the easternmost bays of the choir aisles.[8] The chamfer continues around a projecting element, 1370 mm wide and 550 mm deep. This was clearly one of two responds articulating the apse hemicycle into three bays.[9] The bases are similar to those of the responds of the choir aisles. The next course above the chamfered plinth is represented by one surviving block. Set back behind the plane of the chamfered face, this block is the moulded base of a dado arcade, showing that blind arcading, presumably interlaced, ran around the walls of the apse in a pattern similar to that surviving in the choir aisles. On this evidence, John Bilson was able to produce a conjectural plan of the east end of Durham cathedral, linking newly-discovered features to the Romanesque work that survived above ground level (fig. 13).[10]

and descriptive text, ibid., p. 228. Canon Greenwell followed Raine in this interpretation, until the excavations of 1895 revealed the true plan.

[6] The depth of the rock under the feretory was determined by the excavation of the apse to the north; further east the slope shown in fig. 14 is conjectural, based on the surface slope of this part of the Durham peninsula.

[7] DCDCM, Architectural Drawings 75/1–12. The excavation of the central apse was also illustrated by John Bilson, 'Recent Discoveries', p. 6.

[8] They lack the oversailing element visible further west in the choir aisles.

[9] Both respond bases were excavated, but only the north-east one remains accessible.

[10] Bilson, 'Recent Discoveries', plan facing p. 280. Some details remain obscure, and could be known only from a full excavation of the east end of the choir. Possible interpretations have been proposed by Ian Curry, 'Aspects of the Anglo-Norman design of Durham Cathedral', *Arch. Ael.* 5th ser., 14 (1986), pp. 44–7 and figs. 7–8.

Fig. 15.   Hodgson Fowler's drawing of the 1895 excavations in
Durham Cathedral, entitled 'Excavation showing foundation,
Norman apses of choir, from the East & looking N.E. Feb: 1895'
(DCDCM, Architectural Drawings 75/7).

This, then, was the apse into which Cuthbert's relics were carried in 1104.[11]
William of Malmesbury's story of the miraculous dismantling of the timber cen-
tring for the innovative vaulting over the choir, interpreted as Cuthbert's way of
showing that he was ready to be translated,[12] indicates that the vault was only just
complete. The translation of the saint's body into the new cathedral was preceded

[11] *De miraculis*, ch. 7 (*Sym. Op.* I, 248–9), translated in *The Relics of St Cuthbert*, ed. C.F.
Battiscombe (Durham, 1956), pp. 100–7, gives a near contemporary account of the translation of 1104. Arnold speculates (*Sym. Op.* I, 229, n.a.) that it was written by Symeon.
[12] William of Malmesbury, *De Gestis Pontificum Anglorum*, ed. N.E.S.A. Hamilton (RS 52;
1870), pp. 275–6.

Plate 61.   Durham Cathedral, excavation under the feretory, facing
south-south-east, showing the Romanesque foundation wall, cut through
by the thirteenth-century pier base, and the two surviving courses of the
apse, including the respond base.

by a formal examination of the relics, which is said to have taken place in the choir
of a church, being more spacious than the area behind the high altar where the
body normally resided.[13] In our view this church was the old cathedral, the eastern
end of which, at least, could have been left standing for use by the new monastic
community and to house the relics until the new church was ready for occupation.
True, Symeon mentions that in 1092 Bishop St Calais ordered the demolition of
the old cathedral;[14] but there is no reason to suppose that this took place until the

---

[13] *De miraculis*, ch. 7.
[14] *LDE*, bk. 4, ch. 8 (pp. 128–9).

Plate 62. Durham Cathedral, the feretory from the gallery.

main part of its successor, the east arm including the choir, was ready for use. It is possible that the monument described in the *Rites* as located on the east walk of the cloister marked not his temporary resting-place during building works, as was believed in the late sixteenth century,[15] but the actual site of the shrine in the pre-Conquest cathedral.[16]

One question which naturally arose at the time of the excavation of 1895 was that of the original floor level within the apse of Bishop William's cathedral. The presence of a chamfered wall-bench implies a floor level about 300–450 mm below

[15] *Rites*, pp. 74–5.
[16] A conclusion also reached by Eric Cambridge, in 'The Anglo-Saxon Cathedral at Durham', *Arch. Ael.* 11 (1983), pp. 91–7.

it; Hodgson Fowler and Bilson both believed that the pavement was originally set on top of the apse foundation, which would be consistent with the chamfer.[17] A new survey of the levels confirms Bilson's suggestion that this would give a floor at the same level as the nave, transepts and choir aisles: in other words, a cathedral paved at the same level throughout.[18]

However, it is questionable whether a floor was actually laid at this level within the apse. As we shall see, the present level of the feretory pavement had been established before the demolition of the Romanesque apse in the early thirteenth century, and parts of that early pavement may actually survive. If an even earlier floor had been laid immediately on top of the apse foundation wall, some evidence might perhaps be expected to have survived, such as bedding mortar. The medieval builders might have removed the paving slabs, but they would not have been expected to clear other material before importing infill; we cannot, however, be sure that Hodgson Fowler's workmen did not enthusiastically clear away important evidence. More convincingly, possibly, the facing masonry of the inside of the apse is clean, with crisp, undamaged tooling. None of the abrasion usually apparent in plinths is visible, nor is there any sign of any wall-plaster.

In short, the evidence provided by the Romanesque apse wall suggests that, although the cathedral was originally intended to be floored throughout at the same level, by the time of its consecration in 1104 requirements had changed, and the feretory platform had been laid at the higher level, covering over the plinth. This is a suggestion that might have been definitively substantiated by further excavation beneath the pavement, but unfortunately the brick side-wall of the excavation trench does not allow access to the section.

III. THE PAVEMENT OF THE FERETORY

At about the time of the 1895 excavation, Hodgson Fowler made a plan of the feretory pavement, a copy of which was published by J.T. Fowler.[19] I believe that the plan pre-dates the excavation of the feretory,[20] and that its purpose was to ensure that the paving slabs were correctly relaid; the small differences between the plan and the present layout may result from the re-laying process. A few more modern modifications to the pavement have evidently occurred since 1895.

The most obvious feature of the layout of the floor is the way in which it seems to preserve an apsidal structure (pl. 62 and fig. 16). This was previously noted both

[17] DCDCM, Architectural drawing 75/2; and Bilson, 'Recent Discoveries', pp. 266–7.

[18] The floor of the cathedral appears to have risen by approximately 150 mm. throughout.

[19] DCDCM, Architectural drawing 75/1, published in Fowler, 'The Grave of St Cuthbert', fig. 1. The latter art-work is preserved amongst the papers of Sir William St John Hope as 'Notes on Shrines', Canterbury, Cathedral Chapter Library, Additional MS 83.

[20] The trapdoor set in the pavement to give access to the excavation is not shown, and the outline of the Romanesque apse seems to have been added to the plan.

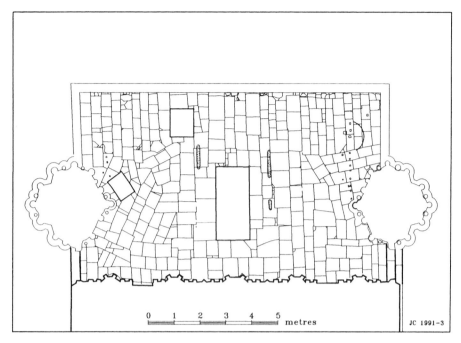

Fig. 16. Durham Cathedral, lay-out of the pavement of the feretory.

by the authors of the description of the cathedral in the *Victoria County History*,[21] and in 1828 by James Raine, who wrote, 'the curving direction of some of the flags designates the original semicircular termination of the middle aisle of the Cathedral'.[22]

Other differences apart from the layout are also apparent. A close examination of the paving stones reveals differences in the colour and texture of the stone. Though all seem to be from the same Carboniferous sandstone, a type known as the 'Lower Main Post',[23] two distinct varieties are visible in crucial areas, deriving presumably from different geological horizons or different quarries.

It is clear that there is a correspondence between the stone types and the position of the former apse (fig. 17). Leaving aside the large stones surrounding the grave, which date mainly from the Reformation but which may have been further altered during the two exhumations of the nineteenth century, two main types of stone are

[21] *VCH, Durham*, ed. William Page (3 vols., London, 1905–27), III, 96–122, 'Architectural Description', by John Quekett and F.H. Cheetham, at p. 100.
[22] Raine, *St Cuthbert*, p. 182; Raine reproduces (ibid.) a detail of the pavement taken from an engraving by de Guche published in Bede, *Historia ecclesiastica*, ed. J. Smith (Cambridge, 1722), facing p. 264.
[23] G.A.L. Johnson and Kingsley Dunham, 'The Stones of Durham Cathedral; a Preliminary Note', *TAASDN* new series, 6 (1982), pp. 53–6.

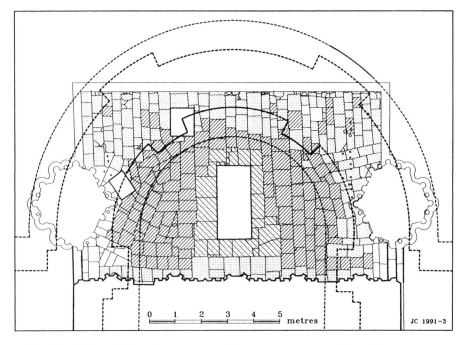

Fig. 17. Durham Cathedral, stone types of feretory pavement, and line of Romanesque apse determined by excavation.

apparent: the dark, very fine-grained stones within the line of the apse and the lighter, sandier stones outside the apse.

There is a further difference, and that is one of average size. The paving slabs of the central area have a mean area of 0.253 square metres; those outside the apse a mean area of 0.198 square metres: i.e. 22% smaller.[24] The standard deviation in both cases is almost the same (0.081 and 0.082 square metres respectively), suggesting that the quarries from which the two separate consignments of stone derived were aiming for similar consistency in the size of their product.

We conclude that the feretory platform is of two distinct phases (fig. 18). The first phase was a raised platform constructed within the Romanesque apse, possibly before 1104, as we have suggested. This platform was retained when the chapel of Nine Altars replaced the original east end; the chapel walls rose around the earlier east end, and eventually the central apse was taken down to just below the level of the feretory pavement. The thirteenth-century builders made use of the excellent foundations provided by William of St Calais's main apse. In order to set their new piers at a height consistent with the lower floor level of the Nine Altars, the Romanesque apse foundation was hacked away at either end of the platform.

[24] Only entire paving slabs were included in this analysis, those that had been cut down to accommodate a border being excluded.

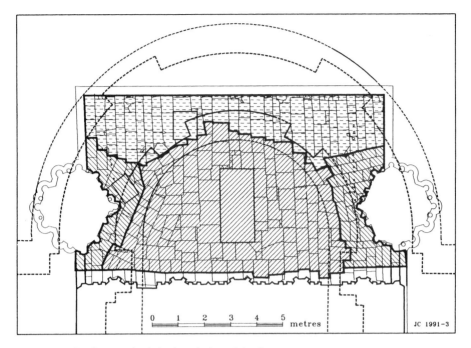

Fig. 18. Durham Cathedral, phased plan of the feretory pavement.

Interestingly, those piers are provided with bases all round which were subsequently submerged below the platform, so the initial intention may have been to do away with the platform altogether; and indeed the bases do show signs of uncertainty in design.[25] But the platform was retained; the floor was made good in two stages (suggesting further uncertainty about the design): first by the angled stones between the old apse and the piers, and finally by the straight rows of paving stones at the east end of the platform.

A few other features of the feretory platform should be mentioned at this point. Some are well-known, such as the line of square sockets on the north and south ends of the platform, some with lead matrices still in position, which have been identified as the fixing for the reliquary cupboards ('almeryes of fine wenscote') described in the *Rites of Durham*.[26] In fact their layout suggests that they are more likely to have supported a metal grille, perhaps part of an arrangement for displaying additional relics preceding that described in the *Rites*. The arc-shaped wear caused by a door is visible at the south end of the platform; from its

[25] The lowest moulded course shows provision for secondary shafts; this conception was abandoned, only to be taken up again when the Frosterley marble shafts were added, which merely rest on the feretory pavement, without bases.
[26] *Rites*, p. 5.

Plate 63.   Durham Cathedral, wear patterns in the feretory pavement.

relationship to the other marks this may be associated with the wooden 'almeryes' rather than the putative grille.

Less well-known are two deep channels worn into the original stones of pavement on either side of the grave (fig. 16). They are visible in a raking light (pl. 63), although partly covered by the marble plinth of the final shrine and by the large candlesticks. James Raine wrote in 1828 that they were 'by uniform tradition, said to have been produced by the devotional *scrapings* of the feet of pilgrims',[27] but five years later, he changed his mind: to suggest pilgrims were responsible was 'an improbable tale, as so humble a floor can scarcely be coeval with the times of popery'. He considered now that they were modern, attributable to Roman Catholics visiting the shrine in recent times, and wrote that, 'They become deeper every day, for now almost every visitor, in his turn draws his foot through their furrowed channel, for no better reason than that he must imitate those who have gone before him.'[28]

However, the evidence already discussed shows that the floor must indeed pre-date the destruction of Cuthbert's final shrine, and is in part Romanesque. Post-Reformation pilgrims may have contributed to the wear-pattern; but it is more likely that it was caused mainly by the scuffing of toes of pilgrims kneeling on the step of the final shrine as described in the *Rites*,[29] and that it thus provides

[27] Raine, *St Cuthbert*, p. 182.
[28] Raine, *Brief Account of Durham Cathedral*, pp. 65–6, n.
[29] *Rites*, p. 4: there were four niches under the shrine (presumably two each side) where people could kneel to make intercession.

evidence for the width of that structure, and also for its position: the wear-pattern suggests indeed that the present grave of Cuthbert is precisely located on the site of the shrine; so the body was buried in 1542 with the saint's head on the focus of the apse.

IV. THE INFLUENCE OF CUTHBERT'S CULT ON THE ARCHITECTURE OF THE CATHEDRAL

Let us sum up the findings so far. The cathedral was of three-apsed plan, and the shrine of Cuthbert was located, as William of Malmesbury's comment makes clear, within the apse. Though William of St Calais's original intention was to pave the cathedral on the same level throughout, during the Romanesque period – and probably before the cathedral came into use in 1104 – a platform 955 mm. above the general level of the rest of the church was created within the apse.

Compared with the elaborate arrangements found on the Continent for the display of saintly relics, or with those in the Anglo-Saxon period, for example at Winchester, Durham seems rather unambitious: little in the architecture would suggest the presence of a major cult. But this accords precisely with what is apparent throughout Anglo-Norman architecture; in the first phase relic cults had little or no influence on architectural planning. Crypts, for example – so closely linked to relic cults in Carolingian churches – had simply become a way of compensating for irregularities in the terrain, no longer specially prepared places for the display of shrines. Indeed, a crypt might have been expected at Durham, and could so easily have been provided; instead the empty spaces enclosed by the foundation walls were simply infilled.

It is interesting, too, that in three major English churches with major native saints' cults – St Albans Abbey, Canterbury and Durham Cathedrals – the apse-and-ambulatory formula, which was employed in the great continental pilgrimage churches going up at around the same time, was not employed. Indeed, there is no obvious correlation between apse-and-ambulatory plan and saints' cults in post-Conquest England; true, Winchester and Worcester Cathedrals and the abbey churches of St Augustine's, Canterbury and St Edmund's, Bury, were of apse-and-ambulatory plan; but then so was Norwich, which did not possess a major saint.

All this raises the question of just how much access to the shrine of St Cuthbert was given to lay pilgrims during the immediate post-Conquest period. Perhaps we see in its remote position an echo of Cuthbert's own injunctions to the Lindisfarne monks that his body should be buried there within the church so that they could control access to it.[30] Two of the miracles recounted by Reginald of Durham refer

---

[30] *Two Lives of St Cuthbert*, ed. and trans. B. Colgrave (Cambridge, 1940), pp. 278–81 (Bede, *Vita S. Cuthberti*, ch. 37). 'It seems best that you entomb it [my body] in the interior of your church, so that while you yourselves can visit my sepulchre when you wish, it may be in your power to decide whether any of those who come thither should approach it.'

to an inner enclosure and seem to emphasise the difficulties that pilgrims had in acceding to the shrine.[31]

Later in the twelfth century, a new interest in relic cults is evident in the architectural response elsewhere; at Winchester, for example, a feretory platform was created so that Swithun's relics could be raised up higher behind the high altar, within the apse; and there is documentary evidence for similar twelfth-century raising of relics at Westminster and St Albans, where taller shrine-bases were created to give greater prominence to the relics. At Durham, however, the shrine and high altar appear, as we have seen, to have been elevated in the first building campaign; there were no further alterations to the level of the feretory pavement, and only in the late fourteenth century was greater prominence given to the shrine by creating a taller shrine-base.

V. THE FORM OF ST CUTHBERT'S SHRINE IN THE ROMANESQUE PERIOD

By 'shrine' in the following discussion is meant the entire arrangement of reliquary and supporting base. Stones from the plinth of the final shrine of St Cuthbert were discovered within his grave in 1899. They now lie around the grave, on the feretory platform. This shrine-base probably dated from 1372, when a new shrine of alabaster and marble was provided by Lord John Neville.[32] This was the structure so well described in the *Rites of Durham*.[33]

Its presumably Romanesque predecessor is less well documented. Several illustrations of the shrine of Cuthbert occur in a manuscript of Bede's *Life of Cuthbert*, Oxford, University College, MS 165, now dated by Malcolm Baker to perhaps as early as the end of the eleventh century, i.e. before the translation of 1104.[34] Certainly the shrine depicted bears no relation to the documentary and comparative evidence discussed below, and the illustrations of the shrine in this manuscript are perhaps best regarded as the illustrator's idealised conception of what a major shrine ought to look like.

The most telling description of the Romanesque shrine occurs in the *Chapters concerning the Miracles and Translations of St Cuthbert*, in the account of the miraculous cure of Abbot Richard of St Albans, which is said to have occurred during the translation of 1104. We learn that 'the reliquary-coffin of the incorrupt body was to be lifted up higher behind the altar on a stone, diligently wrought by

---

[31] *Cuth. virt.*, chs. 79–80 (pp. 164–8).

[32] Raine, *St Cuthbert*, p. 110.

[33] *Rites*, pp. 3–6.

[34] M. Baker, 'Medieval Illustrations of Bede's *Life* of St. Cuthbert', *Journal of the Warburg and Courtauld Institute* 41 (1978), pp. 19–21. D.H. Farmer, 'A Note on the Origin, Purpose and Date of University College, Oxford, MS 165', ibid., pp. 46–9, argues an even earlier date, of *c.*1092, suggesting that it was created as a book of private devotion for St Margaret of Scotland.

the hand of craftsmen for the purpose of sustaining such a burden, which nine columns raise higher above the ground, as befits its size.' The Prior of Durham, Turgot, climbed on to the slab in order to set the coffin in place, and invited Abbot Richard to help him. He did so, and his paralysed left hand was miraculously cured.[35]

What seems to be described is a type of simple shrine-base of which a few examples survive or have been reinstated in France, such as at the church of Ste Radégonde, Poitiers.[36] It consisted of a raised slab supporting, in the case of Durham, the ancient reliquary-coffin of St Cuthbert, now enclosed in a new outer coffin. As at Ste Radégonde's, the chronicler's insistence on the diligent working of the slab by craftsmen suggests that it was decorated.

Such shrine-bases are known in England from documentary and iconographical evidence. A detail from one of the windows of the Trinity Chapel at Canterbury Cathedral shows that Becket's first shrine in that chapel was of this sort. Of this type, too, was probably the late twelfth-century shrine base at St Albans Abbey, set up by Abbot Simon (1166–83), depicted by Matthew Paris. A large portion of what has been identified as the finely decorated slab of this shrine survives.

The account in the *Miracles and Translations* is corroborated by Reginald of Durham, writing later in the twelfth century; he describes several miracles at the shrine from which we can infer: that pilgrims were able to crawl beneath it in order to receive the holy radiation from the reliquary;[37] that it was about three feet high (a man with toothache, kneeling down, was able to place his cheek against the slab);[38] that the slab was only a few inches wider than the coffin on top of it.[39] We learn, too, that the shrine was raised up on steps;[40] so we must envisage at least two steps on the feretory platform, then the slab on its nine columns. A Durham charter of 1128 refers to the 'Altar of St Cuthbert', implying the customary altar against the west side of the shrine.[41]

By the late twelfth century, the cult of Cuthbert was in full swing. Reginald records an increasing number of miracles from the 1170s onwards, and it would seem that Durham was trying to compete with the renewed interest in relic cults that followed the murder of Becket.[42] But serious architectural influence of the cult on the form of the cathedral was not apparent for another fifty years or so. It seems

---

[35] *De miraculis*, ch. 20 (*Sym. Op.* II, 359–61).
[36] Another very rustic example is the shrine of St Phalier at Chabris, about twenty miles west of Bourges.
[37] *Cuth. virt.*, ch. 114 (p. 259).
[38] *Cuth. virt.*, ch. 130 (p. 278).
[39] *Cuth. virt.*, ch. 45 (p. 92).
[40] Ibid.
[41] *DEC*, pp. 112–14. *Rites*, p. 4, describes the altar at the west end of the latest shrine, where mass was celebrated only on St Cuthbert's feast-day.
[42] A point made by Victoria Tudor, 'The Cult of St Cuthbert in the Twelfth Century: the Evidence of Reginald of Durham', in *Cuthbert*, pp. 455–6.

probable that the construction of the Nine Altars was in part a response to the increasing number of pilgrims flocking to the shrine of St Cuthbert,[43] and it provided them with the access that appears to have been lacking in the original design.

[43] An Indulgence dated 1235 speaks of the need to provide a more secure and suitable setting for the saint: *Rites*, p. 150. In 1334 Bishop Richard Poore issued an Indulgence in which he expressed a wish that 'the Church of Durham, in which is honourably placed the incorrupt body of our venerable Father Cuthbert, may be frequented with becoming honours, and the numerous access of people': DCL MS, published by Raine, *St Cuthbert*, pp. 103–4. Peter Draper has emphasised the important role of saints' cults in the remodelling of Romanesque east ends of so many English cathedrals from the thirteenth century: P. Draper, 'The Retro-choir of Winchester Cathedral', *Architectural History* 21 (1978), pp. 1–17, especially pp. 13–14.

The Romanesque Rood Screen of Durham Cathedral: Context and Form

THOMAS E. RUSSO

E XHIBITED IN the treasury of Durham Cathedral are two stone relief panels, dated 1155–60, whose damaged appearance belies their significance for our understanding of the liturgical division of space in twelfth-century cathedrals (pls. 64, 65).[1] Although easily overlooked, these panels belonged to what was perhaps the single most important piece of ecclesiastical furniture in the Romanesque cathedral of Durham: the rood screen. Like all Romanesque sculpture in our museums and treasuries today, these panels have been uprooted from their original, medieval context. Displacements like this often occurred centuries ago and we are fortunate for the mere preservation and continued conservation of such works of sculpture. But to some degree our full understanding of the function and meaning of these works is hampered by the loss of their original setting. The scarcity of evidence for the decorative elaboration of rood screens in the twelfth century makes the Durham panels important vestiges of a type of ecclesiastical furniture whose origin is still obscure to us. Through an examination of the evidence from the remains of other medieval rood screens, from literary sources, and from the fabric of Durham cathedral itself it is possible to reconstruct the original context of these relief panels. Such a reconstruction will augment our knowledge of the tradition of sculptural ornamentation on medieval rood screens and at the same time shed some light on the typology of these screens in the twelfth century, the period in which they seem to have taken on their mature form.[2]

---

[1] For the dating of these panels see E. Prior and A. Gardner, *An Account of Medieval Figure Sculpture in England* (Cambridge, 1912), p. 220 and more recently *English Romanesque Art 1066–1200* (Hayward Gallery Exhibition; London, 1984), pp. 188–9, cat. nos. 154a and 154b. The frank and informal discussions amongst colleagues which took place at the Anglo-Norman Durham Conference were invaluable to me while revising this article. In particular I would like to thank Eric Fernie, Jane Geddes, Richard Gem, Stuart Harrison, M.F. Hearn, J. Philip McAleer, and Malcolm Thurlby for their suggestions and criticisms. I would also like to express my gratitude to Jeff Barber for creating the computer-based illustrations which appear in this article.

[2] There is a serious lacuna in research on the variety of rood screen forms. The most thorough attempt at creating a rood screen typology is E. Doberer, 'Der Lettner, seine Bedeutung und Geschichte', *Mitteilungen der Gesellschaft für vergleichende Kunstforschung in Wien* 2 (December 1956), pp. 117–22. See also M. Hall, 'The Italian Rood Screen: Some Implications for Liturgy

Plate 64.   Durham Cathedral Treasury, relief panel, *c*.1155,
showing *Noli Me Tangere* and Christ Appearing to the Two
Marys.

The Durham relief panels have not survived the centuries unscathed. The panels
are made of sandstone and measure 83 cm in height, 53 cm in width, and 24 cm in
depth. According to the *Rites of Durham*, a late sixteenth-century source which
describes the interior arrangement of ecclesiastical furniture in Durham Cathedral,
the rood screen, along with its sculptural decoration, had already been dismantled
and removed from the cathedral by 1593.[3] The consistent and complete defacing
of the figures on both panels suggests deliberate mutilation and is indicative of

and Function', in *Essays presented to Myron P. Gilmore*, ed. S. Bertelli and G. Ramakus (2 vols.,
Florence, 1977–8), II, 213–18; and idem, 'The *Ponte* in S. Maria Novella: The Problem of the
Rood Screen in Italy', *Journal of the Warburg and Courtauld Institutes* 37 (1974), pp. 157–73.
[3] *Rites*, pp. 33–4.

Plate 65. Durham Cathedral Treasury, relief panel, c.1155, showing the Transfiguration.

iconoclastic spoliation during the period of the dissolution of the monasteries in the sixteenth century as well as that which occurred during the waves of Puritan demolition under Cromwell in the seventeenth century. Yet despite the extensive damage that the Durham panels have sustained, they still evoke a sense of their original splendour in the preservation of details, in the graceful gesticulation of the figures, and in the overall competence of their compositional design. The two panels depict four scenes which illustrate events from the life of Christ: the *Noli Me Tangere,* and Christ's Appearance to the Two Marys on one panel (pl. 64) and two scenes representing a distinctive type of Transfiguration which encompass both the upper and the lower pictorial zones of the other panel (pl. 65).[4]

4 Zarnecki was the first to propose that this second panel represented the Transfiguration; see

Plate 66.　Photograph by R.P. Hawgrave-Graham (early twentieth-century)
of Durham relief panels.

There is some mystery about where and when these panels were discovered. The
first notice of the panels in modern scholarship is in Prior and Gardner's 1912
publication on medieval sculpture, where the panels are described as having been
found 'in the walls of a canon's house reused as building material'.[5] Where Prior
and Gardner procured this information relating to the discovery of the panels is

G. Zarnecki, *Later English Romanesque Sculpture* (London, 1953), p. 33. Evidence from
contemporary Byzantine and western medieval sources supports Zarnecki's proposal and suggests that this panel represents a conflation of two scenes from an extended Transfiguration
narrative; see T.E. Russo, 'The Durham Relief Panels and the Medieval Rood Screen: Reconstructing A Romanesque Context' (unpublished Ph.D. dissertation, Indiana University, 1993),
ch. 3.
[5]　Prior and Gardner, *Medieval Figure Sculpture*, p. 220.

unknown and they did not document it. The Chapter minutes of Durham Cathedral from the nineteenth and early twentieth century are silent concerning any discovery of the panels.[6] But the tradition that the panels were found in the walls of a house in the cathedral precincts is supported by a photograph from the first half of this century which is attributed to R.P. Hawgrave-Graham (pl. 66). The photograph shows the panels displayed in an alcove of the cathedral library before they were moved to their present home in the treasury. On the wooden supports beneath the panels is written the phrase 'wall of house in college'; presumably this inscription relates to their place of discovery. That medieval spolia from Durham Cathedral were used as building material is well documented as early as the sixteenth century, so that it is entirely plausible that the Durham panels should have been reused in this manner in a wall of a house.[7]

Information about the panels between the time they were removed from the cathedral in the sixteenth century and their appearance in Prior and Gardner's survey is exceedingly sparse. A sketch of the Transfiguration panel appears in Samuel Grimm's eighteenth-century collection of drawings now in the British Library (pl. 67).[8] Grimm's Durham drawings are not dated, but his Northumberland series was executed in 1778 and it was perhaps on this trip to the North that Grimm also sketched his drawings of Durham.[9] Grimm's death in 1794 at least provides us with a *terminus ante quem* for the drawing of the Durham Transfiguration panel.

On the back of this drawing Grimm wrote 'Basso relievo in Durham College'. The 'College' refers to the geographical area constituted by the monastic precinct and buildings south of the cathedral, so the inscription is not helpful in pinpointing the exact location of this panel within the cathedral complex at the time Grimm drew it. However, it seems clear from the Grimm evidence and that provided by Prior and Gardner that these panels have always been in the vicinity of the cathedral and there is no reason to doubt their Durham provenance. No further evidence exists concerning the Durham panels in modern times.

In 1934 Alfred Clapham suggested that the original context of the panels was the twelfth-century rood screen of Durham cathedral.[10] Clapham based this

---

6 It was not unusual for the canons of Durham to record in the Chapter minutes the discovery of sculpture during renovation work. However, there is no such reference to the discovery of the Durham panels in the following volumes of Chapter minutes in the Dean and Chapter Library of Durham: '27 December 1847–2 October 1856', '20 July 1876–28 September 1890', '4 October 1890–5 November 1898', '19 November 1898–7 October 1905', '21 October 1905–4 January 1913'; the Chapter minutes from 11 January 1806–24 November 1810 found in 'Durham Dean and Chapter Minutes Extracts', vol. 2, '1 January 1726–28 March 1826' are likewise silent as concerns the panels.

7 See *Rites*, pp. 60–1 and 81–2 for the destruction and reuse of parts of the cathedral by the Puritan Dean Whittingham (1563–79).

8 BL, Additional MS 15538, fol. 174. I would like to thank Eric Cambridge and Jane Cunningham for bringing Samuel Grimm's collection of drawings to my attention.

9 See BL, Additional MSS 15542–3 for the dated drawings in the Northumberland collection.

10 A. Clapham, *English Romanesque Architecture after the Conquest* (Oxford, 1934), p. 149.

Plate 67.   BL, MS Additional 15538, fol. 174: drawing by
Samuel Grimm (*c*.1770–94) of Durham relief panel,
showing the Transfiguration.

opinion on a section of the *Rites of Durham* which describes the rood screen of the
cathedral prior to the dissolution of the monastery in 1539.[11] The author of the
Rites noted that the rood screen stood at the western side of the crossing and that
its sculptural decoration depicted 'the whole storie & passio of o[r] Lord wrowghte in
stone'.[12] The reference to the images on the rood screen as representing the life and
Passion of Christ agrees with the scenes we find depicted on the Durham panels.

---

[11] For the suppression of Durham Cathedral Priory see *VCH, Durham*, ed. William Page (3
vols., London, 1905–28), II, 30–3, and III, 28.
[12] For the complete description of the rood screeen, too lengthy to quote here, see *Rites*, pp.
33–4.

This iconographic correspondence is the principal evidence for Clapham's attribution of these panels to the twelfth-century rood screen in the cathedral.

It is legitimate to ask whether the twelfth-century rood screen could still have been in use in the sixteenth century or whether the author of the *Rites* might have been describing a later medieval screen. In fact, the survival of earlier medieval monuments in Durham cathedral up to the time of the Dissolution is well documented in the *Rites*. A late eleventh-century shrine of St Cuthbert erected by Bishop William of St Calais (1081–96) survived until the 1550s when it was destroyed by the iconoclast dean Robert Horne. Even then, an ancient image of St Cuthbert from the same shrine was left intact by Horne, until it was 'broken in pieces' by his successor William Whittingham.[13] In addition, the great paschal candlestick of Durham, a work attributed to the twelfth century, survived until 1579 when the Chapter ordered it to be defaced.[14] As the liturgical focal point for lay services in the nave of the cathedral, the rood screen and its attendant altar constituted an extremely important piece of ecclesiastical furniture. Such an ornately carved rood screen as described in the *Rites* and as reflected in the Durham panels would have been a highly esteemed possession for any cathedral or church in an age which sought the glorification of God through the sumptuous elaboration of His house; its preservation would have been a matter of pride for both lay and monastic worshippers alike. Thus, it is very likely that the twelfth-century rood screen of Durham Cathedral was still in use in the sixteenth century and was the very screen described by the author of the *Rites of Durham*.

Before proceeding to the reconstruction of this screen and its sculptural programme, it is essential to clarify the distinction between the better-known choir screen and the lesser-known rood screen. The choir screen, as its name suggests, sealed off the view of the choir from the transept and the eastern side-aisles, thereby providing the monks with a modicum of privacy during their daily services. One of the defining characteristics of the choir screen is its large, central door. Later medieval choir screens still standing at York Minster and Canterbury Cathedral demonstrate the considerable size and elaborate decoration of these screens.

In addition to the choir screen, monastic churches commonly possessed a second screen known as the rood screen. The rood screen takes its name from the fact that depicted above it was the image of the Rood, that is, Christ on the Cross, often with Mary and John to either side. The screen was placed to the west of the choir screen and its architectonic function was to separate the nave from the eastern end of the church, that is from both the choir and the transept. This division was completed by smaller secondary screens across the north and south nave aisles.

Distinct from the choir screen in design, the rood screen is characterized by its two doors which permitted ingress and egress to and from the eastern end of the church. On the west side of the screen the area between these two doors was

---

[13] See *Rites*, p. 74. Horne was dean 1551–53 and again 1559–61; for Whittingham's tenure see n. 7 above.
[14] J. Geddes, 'The Twelfth-Century Metalwork at Durham Cathedral', in *MAADC*, pp. 140–8.

Plate 68. Tynemouth Priory, west face of rood screen, late twelfth/early thirteenth-century.

reserved for the nave altar. This altar was typically dedicated to the Holy Cross, as at Canterbury, or to Jesus, as at Durham, and served as the main altar for the parish congregation.[15] Remains in the church of the Benedictine priory of Tynemouth (Northumberland) provide a fine example of a late twelfth/early thirteenth-century rood screen with its two lateral doors (pl. 68). Though the nave altar is no longer extant, it was this type of screen which would have stood in Durham Cathedral and of which the Durham panels would have formed part.

The combination of choir screen and rood screen in monastic cathedrals and priories forcefully underscored the division of interior space between the monks and the laity.[16] On a utilitarian level, the two screens allowed the nave altar to be used for lay services even while the monastic community performed its daily regimen of offices at canonical hours in the choir. In addition to prohibiting lay entrance into the eastern end of the church, the rood screen also barred secular intrusions into the cloister as the screen was typically placed to the west of the main

[15] Gervase notes the dedication of the nave altar at Canterbury to the Holy Cross in his twelfth-century description of the fire at Christ Church; see R. Willis, *The Architectural History of Canterbury Cathedral* (London, 1845), p. 37. For the dedication of the nave altar at Durham to Jesus see *Rites*, p. 32. The most comprehensive treatment of the Holy Cross altar is J. Braun, *Der christliche Altar in seiner geschichtlichen Entwicklung* (2 vols., Munich, 1924); see especially ch. 4, 'Der Heiligkreuzaltar'.

[16] The significance of choir and rood screens as fundamental threshold signs of ritualized space is being treated by the author in a forthcoming study on the iconography and meaning of screens in the Romanesque period.

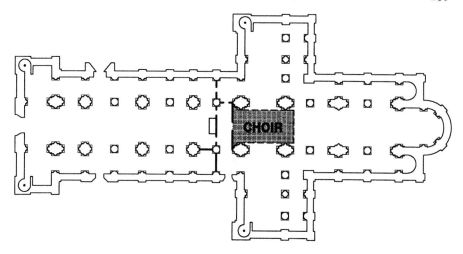

Fig. 19.   Durham Cathedral, plan showing the arangement of rood screen and choir screen as proposed by A. Klukas.

door which led from the nave or transept into the cloister. Thus the rood screen can be regarded as a physical, tangible sign of monastic enclosure.

The location of medieval rood screens varied, sometimes being placed at the western side of the crossing and at other times several bays into the nave when the choir area itself extended beneath the crossing. Where was the rood screen of Durham Cathedral placed? Arnold Klukas has suggested that the rood screen was placed one bay west of the crossing in the nave and the choir screen between the western crossing piers (fig. 19).[17] In this arrangement, the choir area would then have extended under the crossing, cutting off access to the north and south transept chapels via the crossing area.

The reasoning behind Klukas's suggestion is that 'the cloister door usually gave access to the passage between the rood screen and the pulpitum'.[18] Accordingly, because the eastern cloister door at Durham Cathedral is located in the wall of the southern side-aisle and one bay west of the western crossing piers, Klukas placed the rood screen one bay into the nave. However, this elaborate eastern cloister door is an insertion of Bishop Hugh of le Puiset (1153–95); the original Romanesque cloister door, now blocked up, was located at the northern end of the west wall of the south transept where it can still be seen. Thus, because the original cloister door did give the monks direct access to the area 'between the rood screen and the pulpitum', there would have been no need to place the rood screen one bay into the nave. No evidence exists in support of Klukas's plan, which runs counter to the evidence of the *Rites of Durham* and the fabric of the church itself. According to the

[17] See A. Klukas, 'The Architectural Implications of the *Decreta Lanfranci*', *AN* 6 (1983), pp. 137–71.
[18] Klukas, 'The Architectural Implications of the *Decreta Lanfranci*', p. 165; Klukas uses the term 'pulpitum' in specific reference to the choir screen.

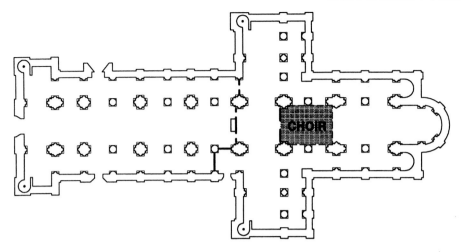

Fig. 20. Durham Cathedral, plan showing the arrangement of rood screen and choir screen as described in the *Rites of Durham*.

Rites, the rood screen was on the axis of the western crossing piers and the choir screen was on the axis of the eastern crossing piers (fig. 20).

The author of the *Rites* notes that the rood screen was located 'in the body of yᵉ churche betwixt two of yᵉ hiest pillors supportinge & holding vp yᵉ west syde of yᵉ Lanterne . . .'.[19]

An analysis of the church fabric in this area yields signs of damage which confirm the placing of the rood screen at the western crossing. In the north aisle of the nave, the north face of the crossing pier and the south face of the respond on the aisle wall opposite to it display a set of grooves and rectangular holes approximately the same size as each other and in direct alignment with each other across the aisle (fig. 21). These features are almost certainly the result of anchoring the secondary minor screen associated with the rood screen across the north aisle.

As for the position of the main section of the rood screen in the nave, where the relief panels would have been located, the south face of the north-western crossing pier exhibits a set of holes that correspond to a similar set found on the north face of the south-western crossing pier (pl. 69). No doubt these sets of holes are related to each other in function; the most likely explanation for them is that they once provided anchoring-points for the top of the rood screen.

Finally, an examination of the fabric in the south aisle shows a deep groove as well as shaved-off moulding on the west face of the plinth of the south-western crossing pier. The moulding is also partially shaved off the plinth on the first circular nave pier to the west, and on the corresponding half-column respond against the south aisle wall. These modifications of the fabric are consistent with the account in the *Rites* of the secondary screen across the south aisle as illustrated in figure 20. The right-angle arrangement of the south aisle screen is most likely an

---

19 *Rites*, p. 32.

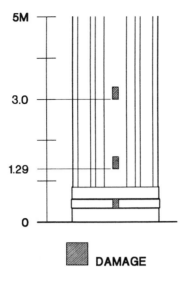

Fig. 21. Durham Cathedral,
diagram of damage areas on
north aisle respond opposite
the north-west crossing pier.

alteration to accommodate the insertion of the new cloister door in the south aisle
by Bishop Hugh. Taken as a whole, this evidence clearly substantiates the location
of the rood screen at the western side of the crossing.

There is additional evidence in the Romanesque design of Durham Cathedral
which provides definitive proof concerning the location of the rood screen in the
twelfth century in relation to the choir area. The present-day choir and its accompanying stalls are located in the first two bays east of the crossing. This area is
defined by the eastern piers of the crossing and the massive compound piers which
articulate the alternating arcade in the eastern arm of the cathedral. An examination of the design of these compound piers which delineate the eastern limit of the
choir show them to be articulated with a major half-column respond flanked by
two minor shafts which appear at first sight to extend from the clerestory to the
choir floor (an additional set of minor shafts is added at gallery level) (pl. 70). In
fact, the minor shafts to the west of the half-column responds do not continue to
the pier bases but terminate on scalloped corbels more than four meters above the
choir floor (pl. 71).[20] The same is also true for the easternmost minor shafts on the
eastern crossing piers which stand at the entrance into the choir. Because the choir
stalls abut this section of the eastern crossing piers it is not possible to examine the
fabric surface below the point at which the minor shafts terminate. Fortunately this

[20] The truncated minor shaft on the northern compound pier in the second bay of the choir
terminates approximately 4.81 m above the choir floor; that on the corresponding southern
compound pier terminates approximately 4.70 m above the choir floor.

Plate 69.   Durham Cathedral, interior looking east showing damage on western crossing piers.

is not the case at the eastern end of the choir and the masonry below the corbels here appears to be original twelfth-century ashlar.

This truncating of minor shafts is unique to these two sets of compound piers. Throughout the rest of the cathedral the minor shafts on all the compound piers run from the clerestory level to the pier bases. What is the significance of this design change and its restriction to these two sets of piers? Eric Fernie has convincingly demonstrated that in a number of medieval churches and cathedrals, both secular and monastic, such design changes in the complexity of piers signify a change in function of space.[21] In particular, he has noted how alterations in the composition of the piers at the cathedral of Laon, at Romsey and Peterborough Abbeys, and at Norwich Cathedral were meant to denote the extent of the choir areas in these churches. Such is almost certainly the case at Durham also. The abbreviated shafts on the compound piers at Durham would have physically designated the extent of the twelfth-century choir area. It would appear that the architects sought visually to distinguish the limits of the choir through a modification in the interior design of the architecture. Because the wall surface beneath these truncated shafts is in its original state, one can conclude that the original plan of Durham Cathedral called for a choir which began at the eastern crossing piers and extended two bays eastward toward the high altar. Such an arrangement would

[21] See E. Fernie, 'La fonction liturgique des piliers cantonnés dans la nef de la cathédrale de Laon', *Bulletin Monumental* 145/3 (1987), pp. 257–66.

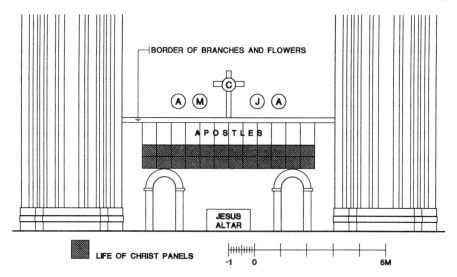

Fig. 22.   Durham Cathedral, reconstruction of the twelfth-century rood screen showing the distribution of sculptural ornamentation.

require the choir screen to be placed on the chord of the eastern crossing piers and the rood screen on the chord of the western crossing piers as the analysis of the fabric evidence has already implied. This being the case, the design of Durham Cathedral represents an early example of the choir area being relegated strictly to the eastern arm of the church, a disposition which was not to become common in secular cathedrals until the thirteenth century and later.[22] As for monastic churches, Durham may be the earliest instance of such an arrangement. Only after a late twelfth/early thirteenth-century renovation did the rood screen and choir arrangement at Tynemouth reflect that at Durham. Little evidence survives for screen locations in monastic cathedrals. Durham's plan may have been based on that of Christ Church, Canterbury. Gervase describes the Canterbury rood screen as being between the western crossing piers in the time of Anselm (1093–1109), but he makes no mention of the location of the choir screen.[23]

Standing on the chord of the western crossing, the twelfth-century rood screen in Durham marked the physical centre of the cathedral and represented both the means of segregation and the avenue of integration between lay and monastic space. What did the rood screen look like? This screen may be reconstructed with reference to: the description of the rood screen in the *Rites*; the dimensions of the nave of Durham Cathedral; and comparisons with other rood and choir screens from the twelfth century and later (fig. 22).

[22] For example, at Chartres, Soissons, Beauvais, Lincoln, Salisbury, and York. In the twelfth century, most choirs of secular cathedrals extended under the crossing as at Old Sarum, Chichester, Wells, Noyon, Lyon, and Reims; see Fernie, 'La fonction des piliers cantonnés', p. 265.
[23] See Willis, *Architectural History of Canterbury Cathedral*, p. 109.

Plate 70.   Durham Cathedral, north choir arcade, compound
pier two bays east of eastern crossing piers.

The width of the Durham rood screen is established by the distance between the
north-west and south-west crossing piers, which is 8.04 m. This is broadly in line
with the widths of other twelfth-century rood screens such as those at Ely (9.98 m)
and Tynemouth (6.56 m), and also the fourteenth-century rood screen at
Crowland Abbey (Lincolnshire) (8.61 m). What were the dimensions of the two
doors which would have led through the rood screen? When the twelfth-century
rood screen in Ely Cathedral was dismantled in 1770, the person responsible for its
demolition, James Essex, made a number of sketches of the screen which he
annotated with corresponding measurements.[24] He noted that the width of the two
Ely rood doors was 87 cm. That such a width can be accepted as within a standard

[24] For the Ely screen see W. St John Hope, 'Quire Screens in English Churches with Special

Plate 71. Durham Cathedral, north choir arcade, detail of truncated shaft on compound pier two bays east of eastern crossing piers.

range for rood doors is substantiated by the doors in the Tynemouth rood screen which are 85 cm wide and those in the fourteenth-century rood screen at Crowland which are 89 cm wide.[25] The distance of these doors from the crossing piers is conjectural. For the purpose of reconstructing the Durham screen, I have

Reference to the Twelfth-Century Quire Screen Formerly in the Cathedral of Ely', *Arch.* 68 (1917), pp. 85–8.

[25] I am obliged to the Dean and Chapter of Durham Cathedral for granting permission to take the measurements of the cathedral used in the reconstruction of the screen here. Also, I am very grateful for the kind assistance of Jane Geddes and Malcolm Thurlby in measuring the Tynemouth rood screen and of Caelan Mys for her help in measuring the Crowland rood screen.

used the equivalent measurement from the Crowland Abbey rood screen as a guide since it is the closest example in terms of width to the Durham screen, and have placed the doors approximately 86 cm from the north and south crossing piers.

A height of 2 m is proposed for the door openings in the Durham screen on the basis of the equivalent measurement from the Ely screen whose doors stood at 1.98 m and those of the Tynemouth screen which are 2.05 m in height. Round-headed arches above the rood doors would be expected on a Romanesque rood screen and the twelfth-century examples at Ely, Tynemouth, and Boxgrove Priory (Sussex) provide sufficient evidence to support the inclusion of such arches in the Durham screen.

The overall height of the screen itself depends greatly on the original layout of the sculptural elements on the screen. As no twelfth-century rood screen with its decorative features remains intact today, we must rely on the description of the screen in the *Rites* and on the dimensions of the relief panels in the treasury to determine the height of the screen. The author of the *Rites* describes the scenes of the life of Christ as extending 'frō piller to piller'; above these scenes was another register representing the apostles which also reached from 'yᵉ one piller to thother'; and above the apostles was a border of branches and flowers 'frome piller to piller'.[26] The emphasis placed on the length of the decorative elements as extending from 'piller to piller' suggests that the position of the relief panels was above the two rood doors. The height of the Transfiguration and Marys panels is 83 cm which, if the apostle panels were of the same dimensions, gives a total height of 1.66 m for the two superimposed registers. By adding to this height that of the door openings, the voussoirs on the door arches, and the border of branches and flowers, a total height of approximately 4.18 m for the Durham rood screen can be conservatively suggested. That the screen may even have been taller is not beyond the realm of possibility for the Ely screen is recorded as being 4.42 m in height and the screen at Crowland stands approximately 4.57 m high.[27]

In terms of the decorative elaboration of the Durham rood screen, the *Rites* informs us that on top of the screen stood the great rood depicting Christ on the Cross (fig. 22, 'C'), flanked by the Virgin Mary on the north side and John the Evangelist on the south side (fig. 22, 'M' and 'J'). Beside each of these figures there would have been placed an angel (fig. 22, 'A').[28] Gervase of Canterbury records a similar rood group above the early twelfth-century rood screen in Canterbury Cathedral.[29]

Beneath this rood group the series of apostle reliefs extended across the screen wall. The Gothic choir screens of Bourges, Bamberg, and possibly Chartres also

[26] *Rites*, p. 33.
[27] The fourteenth-century screen at St Albans rises to a height of about 6.57 m; see A. Vallance, *Greater English Church Screens* (London, 1947), p. 90.
[28] *Rites*, pp. 33, and 221.
[29] Though Gervase ascribed the rood screen and the choir screen to the period of Lanfranc, it is generally accepted that they belong to the time of Archbishop Anselm (1093–1109); see Willis, *Architectural History of Canterbury Cathedral*, p. 109.

possessed images of the apostles.[30] On the Durham screen, the apostles stood as witnesses to the crucifixion of Christ in the rood group above them. Extending from 'piller to piller', the apostles register (and that of the life of Christ as well) would have comprised a total of twelve panels, assuming a uniform width for all the panels. If the other panels on the screen were set off by a frame consistent with that found on the surviving Marys panel, then each panel width would have been approximately 60 cm, leaving a space of only approximately 40 cm between the shafts of the crossing piers which abutted the screen and the last panels in the registers; thus, only twelve panels could have fitted in each of the registers across the face of the rood screen. Whether each apostle panel was divided into two pictorial zones as in the surviving Transfiguration and Marys panels cannot be determined. Because of their relationship with the rood image above, however, and the fact that they extended across the full width of the screen, it is probable that each panel depicted a single, standing apostle, and were perhaps similar to those on the Bamberg choir screen.[31]

Below the images of the apostles extended the series of panels which depicted the life of Christ; it was to this register that the two surviving panels in the Durham treasury belonged. Durham was not the only cathedral to possess a screen decorated with Christological imagery in the twelfth century. An early thirteenth-century description of the choir entrance at Lincoln Cathedral informs us that during St Hugh's episcopal tenure (1186–1200) the rood screen had a single altar, as it is suggested there was at Durham, and that on the screen was depicted the 'progress' of Christ's life, presumably a reference to a Christological cycle such as that from which the Durham panels came.[32]

Sculptural evidence also demonstrates the use of Christological narrative on twelfth-century screens in England. The well-known reliefs from the choir screen of Chichester Cathedral depict two such scenes: Christ and the Sisters of Lazarus and the Raising of Lazarus.[33] But it is the great choir screens of the Gothic period which help us most in visualizing the magnitude of the Durham screen and its extensive sculptural program depicting the life of Christ. Earlier in this paper, a clear distinction between the form of the rood screen and that of the choir screen

---

[30] See E. Verheyen, 'The Choir Reliefs of Bamberg Cathedral', *Gesta* 4 (1965), pp. 12–14; and C. Gnudi, 'Le jubé de Bourges et l'apogée du "Classicisme" dans la sculpture de l'Île-de-France au milieu du XIIIe siècle', *Revue de l'art* 3 (1969), pp. 28–30. A number of fragments of standing, robed (apostle?) figures still exist from the Chartres screen; see H. Bunjes, 'Der gotische Lettner der Kathedrale von Chartres', *Westdeutsches Jahrbuch für Kunstgeschichte* 22–3 (1943), pp. 106–7, pls. 56–64.

[31] See E. Verheyen, 'The Choir Reliefs of Bamberg Cathedral', pl. 3.

[32] The reference in this metrical description to a single '*tabula aurea*' suggests that an altar of the Holy Cross was centred in the screen at Lincoln; typologically this implies a rood screen rather than a choir screen; for the full description of the screen see Gerald of Wales, *The Life of St Hugh of Avalon*, trans. R. Loomis (New York, 1985), pp. 83–95. See also St John Hope, 'Quire Screens in English Churches', p. 55 for his interpretation of this screen as a choir screen.

[33] See G. Zarnecki, 'The Chichester Reliefs', in his *Studies in Romanesque Sculpture* (London, 1979), pp. 106–20.

was established. However, in terms of iconography these screen types are easily confused with one another because of the similar imagery associated with them. In churches where no rood screen existed, such as Chartres, Bourges, or Notre-Dame, Paris, the rood group and its concomitant imagery were transferred to the choir screen. Because of this transference the images on Gothic choir screens become valuable clues to the narrative scenes which once adorned the monastic rood screens of the Middle Ages.

Large sculptural cycles depicting the life of Christ are known to have adorned the choir screens at the cathedrals of Chartres (1230–60),[34] Bourges (c.1250),[35] Amiens (c.1291),[36] and Notre Dame, Paris (1296–1350).[37] The figural panels which survive from these sites reveal that a considerable iconographic repertoire of the life of Christ was utilized in ornamenting Gothic choir screens.

The fourteenth-century screen from Notre-Dame most fully illuminates our understanding of how extensive these sculptural programmes were. Among the twenty-three events from the life of Christ completely or partially preserved from the Notre-Dame screen are scenes of the Visitation, the Nativity, the Massacre of the Innocents, the Baptism of Christ, the Last Supper, Christ in the Garden of Gethsemane, the Harrowing of Hell, the *Noli Me Tangere*, Christ Appearing to the Holy Women, the Journey to Emmaus, and the Incredulity of Thomas.[38] A forceful parallel between the Durham Marys panel and the Notre-Dame screen exists in the juxtaposition of the *Noli Me Tangere* immediately preceding Christ's Appearance to the Holy Women.

The vast narratives of the life of Christ from Gothic choir screens give us an idea of the other scenes which may have been included on the Durham rood screen, and which would have proclaimed the importance of this structure to the Durham community, both lay and monastic alike. The rood screen was much more than a physical barrier. With its extensive sculptural program, it was a visual statement of church doctrine writ in stone. As the vehicle which presented the rood, as well as the images of the life of Christ and his Passion to the faithful, the rood screen provided a concise, visual declaration of the redemptive theme of the mass. The physical centrality of the rood screen in the heart of the church, with the monumental, iconic rood above it, ensured that this message was proclaimed to all who entered.

---

[34] See Bunjes, 'Der gotische Lettner von Chartres', pp. 70–114.

[35] The arrangement of the sculptural components of the Bourges screen (Christological cycle, apostle figures, and foliage border) provides a striking similarity with that of the Durham screen. For the Bourges screen see Gnudi, 'Le jubé de Bourges', pp. 18–36; see also Bunjes, 'Der gotische Lettner von Chartres', pp. 93–4.

[36] Though no sculptural evidence now remains, it is known that the figural elaboration of the choir screen at Amiens Cathedral also illustrated the life of Christ; see Bunjes, 'Der gotische Lettner von Chartres', pp. 98–100.

[37] See D. Gillerman, *The Clôture of Notre-Dame and its Role in the Fourteenth Century Choir Program* (New York, 1977).

[38] For the other scenes represented in this cycle see Gillerman, *The Clôture of Notre-Dame*, pp. 28–48.

The Architectural Influence of Durham Cathedral

E. C. FERNIE

W E CAN ASSUME that those responsible for the building of the cathedral erected at Durham between 1093 and 1133 intended it to have a number of effects on those who worshipped in and visited it, either as a source of religious awe or, through its scale and the implied technological prowess and creative ability of its builders, as a reminder of secular power, or as the two inextricably intertwined. Where there are no relevant written accounts, as is the case with Durham, then the only evidence of either intention or response lies in the ways in which the building was copied or used in later structures. Examples of buildings which appear to show a debt to Durham can be divided between those of Norman character in England and Scotland on the one hand and those relevant to the origins of the Gothic style in northern France on the other.

I. DURHAM'S INFLUENCE IN ENGLAND AND SCOTLAND

The priory church at Lindisfarne has, like Durham, a three-storey elevation, an alternating system of compound and cylindrical piers, incised decoration, rib vaults, chevron and moulding profiles, all of a particular type more or less closely related to their equivalents at the cathedral (pl. 72). Chevron was introduced, apparently for the first time in northern Europe, part way through the building programme at Durham, while it is there throughout the church at Lindisfarne, suggesting that the smaller building is the later of the two. The cathedral was no doubt seen as a highly appropriate model because of the importance of Lindisfarne in the life of Cuthbert.[1]

The abbey church at Selby in the West Riding of Yorkshire was begun in the time of Hugh de Lacey, who was abbot from 1097 to 1123 (pl. 73). The surviving parts of this phase of building, the transept arms, the crossing, and easternmost bays of the nave, follow Durham even more closely than Lindisfarne does,

---

[1] E. Cambridge, *Lindisfarne Priory and Holy Island* (London, 1988); A.J. Piper, 'The First Generation of Durham Monks and the Cult of St Cuthbert', in *Cuthbert*, p. 444, links construction to the activities of Edward the monk in the early 1120s.

I am very grateful to Dr Malcolm Thurlby, Dr Barrie Singleton, and Professor Donald Matthew for helpful comments on a number of aspects of this paper.

Plate 72.   Lindisfarne Priory (Northumberland), north wall
of the nave, looking east.

including the overall layout, the elevation of the nave, alternating piers, incised
decoration and attached responds on the cylindrical supports, comparable moulding profiles, rib vaults, chevron, and an unusual plinth of two major elements. It is
noteworthy that the builders at Selby introduced chevron at a similar point in the
eastern bays of the nave to that at Durham, suggesting that Selby, although begun
later, was under construction at almost exactly the same time. Durham may have
recommended itself as a model to de Lacey in preference to Archbishop Thomas's
cathedral at York, begun in the early 1080s, because of the standing of St Cuthbert
and because of the new, rich decoration of Durham.[2]

2   E.C. Fernie, 'The Romanesque Church of Selby Abbey', in BAACT for 1988, on York, ed.
L. Hoey, forthcoming.

Plate 73. Selby Abbey (Yorks.), easternmost bays of the south wall of the nave.

Dunfermline Abbey in Fife was begun in 1128 and consecrated incomplete in 1150 (pl. 74). Only the nave of this building survives, but the north arm of the transept is known from a nineteenth-century drawing to have been decorated, like the nave, with motifs such as chevron and moulding profiles associated with Durham. The north aisle has rib vaults, the nave an elevation of three storeys, and four of the cylindrical piers have incised decoration in the same order as at Durham, that is, with zigzags to the west and spirals to the east. There is substantial evidence to support the view that these four supports marked the site of the tomb of St Margaret and of the nave altar, just as the spirals at Durham can be seen as marking the main sanctuary and the transept chapels. The project was supported by the king, David I (1124–53), whose mother is the Margaret (d.1093) buried in the nave, and whose father Malcolm (1058–93) was the only layman purportedly

Plate 74.   Dunfermline Abbey (Fife), north wall of the nave,
looking east.

present at the laying of the foundation stone of Durham in 1093. The fact that the
Scottish crown chose Durham Cathedral as a model for what was evidently intended to be its dynastic burial church indicates that Durham's architectural influence was in this case strongly political in character.[3]

Kirkwall Cathedral was begun in 1137 by Ronald, the Norse earl of Orkney (pl.
75). The east arm, transepts, and easternmost bays of the nave of this building
survive, and exhibit close links with Durham in both layout (such as the large spiral
staircase in the outer western corner of each transept arm) and detail (such as the

---

[3] E.C. Fernie, 'The Romanesque Churches of Dunfermline Abbey', in BAACT for 1986, on
the medieval diocese of St Andrews, ed. J. Higgitt, forthcoming. See also E. Fernie, 'The Spiral
Piers of Durham Cathedral', MAADC, pp. 49–58.

Plate 75. Kirkwall Cathedral (Orkney), aisle vault corbels in the eastern arm.

interlaced arcading, and the rib vaults supported on paired corbel heads). These and other aspects of the design indicate a knowledge on the part of the builders both of Dunfermline and of Durham. Ronald's choice of Durham as the model for his cathedral therefore indicates that, within only four or five years of its completion, the fame and importance of Durham had reached as far as the Scandinavian world.[4]

In addition to these four instances where whole buildings appear to have been influenced by the cathedral there are three where a single feature, namely the use of decorated columnar piers, may have been based on those at Durham. In the first phase of Norwich Cathedral, begun in 1096 and completed before 1119, the four cylindrical piers in the nave which at present mark the site of the nave altar are all decorated with spiral grooves (pl. 76). There is good evidence to suggest that these four supports were intended to be different from the remainder of the piers, and

---

[4] S. Cruden, 'The Founding and Building of the Twelfth-Century Cathedral of St Magnus'; R. Fawcett, 'Kirkwall Cathedral: An Architectural Analysis'; and E. Cambridge, 'The Architectural Context of the Romanesque Cathedral at Kirkwall', in *St Magnus Cathedral and Orkney's Twelfth-Century Renaissance*, ed. B. Crawford (Aberdeen, 1988), pp. 78–87, 88–97, and 111–26 respectively. It is of interest to note that when Archbishop Thurstan of York summoned churchmen to Selby in 1140 he included Radulph, bishop of Orkney, in their number; see W.W. Morrell, *The History and Antiquities of Selby* (Selby, 1867), pp. 53–4.

Plate 76. Norwich Cathedral (Norfolk), site of the nave altar, looking east.

that they would have marked the position of the altar of the Holy Cross to the west of the choir screen. As sanctuary markers they would therefore have had the same function as the spiral piers at Durham.[5]

The surviving nave of Waltham Abbey, probably of the second quarter of the twelfth century, has minor piers of cylindrical form decorated with the same patterns in the same order as those at Dunfermline and Durham, that is with zigzags to the west and spirals to the east (pl. 77). The original liturgical arrangements at Waltham are less apparent than at either Norwich or Dunfermline, but the raised floor level of the easternmost bays suggests that once again the spirals marked an important area such as the site of the nave altar.[6]

The undated church of Kirkby Lonsdale in Westmorland retains in the north arcade four alternating piers, the cylindrical ones with incised decoration of the Durham type, though rather crudely executed. By contrast the decorated cylindrical piers in the crypt of the 1150s in York Minster are of the highest quality, but because of their squat proportions and their location in the building they are less clearly linked with Durham.[7]

[5] E.C. Fernie, *An Architectural History of Norwich Cathedral* (Oxford, 1993), pp. 78–9.
[6] E.C. Fernie, 'The Romanesque Church of Waltham Abbey', *JBAA* 138 (1985), pp. 59–66.
[7] N. Pevsner, *Cumberland and Westmorland* (Buildings of England, Harmondsworth, 1967), pp. 260–2. R. Willis, *The Architectural History of York Minster* (London, 1848), reprinted in *Architectural History of Some English Gothic Cathedrals, by the Rev. Robert Willis, M.A., F.R.S.* (2 vols., Chicheley, 1972–3), I, fig. 2.

Plate 77. Waltham Abbey (Essex), south wall of the nave,
looking east.

There are also two respects in which Durham can be said to have had a general
influence on architecture in England and Scotland in the late eleventh and twelfth
centuries, namely in terms of decoration and of rib vaults. While there are one or
two earlier indications of a new interest in decoration (for example in Lanfranc's
dormitory at Canterbury of before 1089), Durham is the first large building since
the Conquest in which decoration plays a major part in the architectural effect. As
such it can be said to mark one of the main turning points in Norman architecture
in England, from the plainness of the first generation of buildings after 1066 to the
richness of buildings in the decades after 1093. Interlaced arcading, chevron, and
complex arch mouldings, all features of Durham, characterize buildings of all types
thereafter. The contrast can be gauged from a comparison of, for example, the

crypt of Walkelin's cathedral at Winchester, shortly after 1079, with that of Anselm's extension at Canterbury, after 1096.[8]

Durham can also be seen as the main influence on the development of rib vaulting in Anglo-Norman England. Apart from those already mentioned at Lindisfarne, Selby, and Dunfermline, there are early ribs in the transept aisles at Winchester Cathedral, after 1107, and in the aisles of Peterborough Abbey, begun after 1114. One should not, however, assume that vaulting was considered superior to a wooden ceiling. With the exception of Lindisfarne, none of the buildings discussed here had contemporary vaults over the main space, and the new east arm of Canterbury Cathedral, built between 1096 and 1130, had a wooden ceiling rather than a vault, which was described in the most glowing terms by William of Malmesbury.[9]

II. DURHAM AND THE SOURCES OF THE GOTHIC STYLE

The Gothic style, in Nikolaus Pevsner's classic statement, is constituted by

> the pointed arch, the flying buttress, and the rib vault. Not one of them is a Gothic invention. Pointed arches appear occasionally in Romanesque churches, e.g. in Burgundy and Provence, and at Durham. Flying buttresses were common in several parts of France and also used at Durham. They were not usually realized as such because they were kept under the roofs . . . the ribs of Durham [are probably the earliest rib-vaults of Europe] . . . What the Gothic style brought to these motifs was their combination for a new aesthetic purpose.[10]

In judging the accuracy of this assessment the function, relevance, and dating of these features, particularly the flying buttress and the rib, need to be reconsidered.

The origins of the flying buttress are unclear. The earliest examples of unequivocal function and date appear to be those in the nave of Notre Dame in Paris of 1178, while St Germer in the early 1160s has a similar type but placed under the gallery roof.[11] The main point which needs to be established here, however, is the

---

[8] For Lanfranc's undercroft and Anselm's crypt at Canterbury see D. Kahn, *Canterbury Cathedral and its Romanesque Sculpture* (London, 1991), pp. 30–1 and passim; and for the crypt at Winchester see *Winchester Cathedral: Nine Hundred Years, 1093–1993*, ed. J. Crook (Chichester, 1993), fig. 3.6.

[9] The rib vaults which survive and which have been argued for at Gloucester and Tewkesbury may form their own sequence. For Gloucester see C. Wilson, 'Abbot Serlo's church at Gloucester (1089–1100): Its Place in Romanesque Architecture', in *Medieval Art and Architecture at Gloucester and Tewkesbury*, ed. T.A. Heslop and V. Sekules (BAACT 7 for 1981; London, 1985), pp. 52–83, esp. pp. 63–4.

[10] N. Pevsner, *Outline of European Architecture* (Harmondsworth, 1958), p. 75.

[11] W. Clark, 'The Flying Buttress: a New Reconstruction of the Nave of N.D. de Paris', *Art Bulletin* 66 (1984), pp. 47–65. For an argument in favour of the original existence of flying buttresses in the east arm of St Denis, 1140–4, see C. Wilson, *The Gothic Cathedral: The Architecture of the Great Church* (London, 1990), pp. 39–43.

Plate 78.   Durham Cathedral, half arches of the nave galleries,
as in 1843 (from R.W. Billings, *Architectural Illustrations of the
Cathedral Church at Durham* (London, 1843)).

extent to which the half arches in the nave galleries at Durham had any buttressing
function at all. In their present form they consist of three rows of masonry with a
wall built up on their haunch, but originally they consisted of only one course of
masonry without any additional loading (pl. 78).[12] There are two reasons for

[12] The original form of the half arches with only one course is illustrated in an engraving in
R.W. Billings, *Architectural Illustrations of the Cathedral Church at Durham* (London, 1843).
The masonry shown on the haunch of each arch in the engraving must have been added when
the roof was changed from its original form with a row of gables to the unbroken run from east
to west. The evidence for the gables is clear in Billings's southern elevation and is still visible *in
situ* on the exterior of the north gallery. See S. Gardner, 'The Nave Galleries of Durham
Cathedral', *Art Bulletin* 64 (1982), pp. 564–79.

thinking that these half arches could not have acted as buttresses. First, they were a mere 40 cm thick, forming what would be a remarkably slight buttress for a building which is otherwise massively over-engineered. Secondly, their closest parallels, the half arches which can be reconstructed over the galleries at Norwich Cathedral, were built to abut an unvaulted main space. The point is clinched at Norwich by the fact that the one section of wall where there were no half arches, the ambulatory around the apse, is the one part of the building where there almost certainly was a high vault to buttress.[13] At both Durham and Norwich the most likely function for the half arches is that of joining the upper parts of the main wall to the wall of the aisle and gallery, thereby increasing the stability of the structure. It is of course necessary to distinguish between how we think these structures function and what the original architect thought he was doing, but there is no positive evidence to support the idea that he conceived of the half arches as buttresses.[14]

Turning to the rib vault, this is not the place to set out the arguments for whether Speyer Cathedral, Lessay Abbey, Durham Cathedral or any other candidate had the earliest examples in northern Europe; suffice it to say that the ribs in the east arm of Durham have an excellent claim to the title and that the place of Durham in the history of the rib vault is secure. There is also no doubt about the precocity of the nave vault at Durham, of between 1128 and 1133, which uses the rib in conjunction with the pointed arch and in which the webbing of the vaults was made progressively thinner as the bays were constructed from east to west, indicating that the builders were thinking in similar terms to those designing later buildings.

By the late 1130s, however, rib vaults in conjunction with pointed arches were being built right across northern France, as at St Étienne at Beauvais, providing ready models for the architect of the east arm of St Denis of 1140 to 1144, the structure which is usually considered to be the first example of the Gothic style.[15]

---

[13] Fernie, *Norwich*, pp. 38–9. The nave of Durham was also designed to be unvaulted, and it is likely that the half arches were designed before it was decided to erect a vault. There are, however, differences of opinion as to the point in the elevation at which this decision was taken.

[14] Although they are much later, the thin half arches rising just above the gallery roof of Canterbury Cathedral in the late 1170s or early 1180s may be relevant to this assessment. See Y. Kusaba, 'Some Observations on the Early Flying Buttress and Choir Triforium of Canterbury Cathedral', *Gesta* 28 (2) (1989), pp. 175–89.

[15] On the origins of Gothic see J. Bony, *French Gothic Architecture of the Twelfth and Thirteenth Centuries* (Berkeley, 1983), especially the sections on rib vaulting (pp. 7–17), on the pointed arch (pp. 17–21), and on the significance of the Romanesque, in particular that of Normandy and England, for the early Gothic style (pp. 21–39); and Wilson, *Gothic Cathedral*, pp. 7–43.

III. CONCLUSION

Durham Cathedral was one of the great buildings of western Europe in the eleventh and twelfth centuries, an assessment supported by the objective evidence of its immense scale, technological daring, and use of techniques and designs which imply an extensive knowledge of architectural forms from far-flung sources. Its patrons must have wanted a building which would impress and their architects provided them with one which did, from its immediate vicinity to Scotland and the Norse areas in the north, as well as to East Anglia, Essex, and elsewhere in the far south. Its importance for the invention of Gothic is less direct, since, while the builders of Durham were at the forefront of architectural technology, there was no need for the master of St Denis to have looked beyond northern France for the elements which enabled him to invent the new style.

The two forms of influence just discussed, that in England and Scotland on the one hand and that in France on the other, differ not only in the resulting assessment of the part played by Durham in the architecture of its time, but also in the kinds of historical investigation being conducted. The place of Durham in contemporary England and Scotland can be assessed by asking questions such as 'What was the status of the building when it was built?' and 'What was that status intended by its patrons to be?', questions which limit, as far as that is possible, the need for the wisdom of hindsight. Assessing the place of Durham in the rise of Gothic takes us into a very different sort of history, one which can *only* be written with the wisdom of hindsight, from a perspective which is strictly speaking only available to the modern historian. This is not to suggest that the sequence of events in question was predetermined in a Hegelian manner, only that it cannot be discussed without a knowledge of events well into the future. I do not wish to argue that one of these kinds of history is preferable to the other, only that the investigator should be aware of the fundamental differences between them.

PART THREE

The Prince Bishops

An Absent Friend:
The Career of Bishop William of St Calais

W. M. AIRD

BISHOP WILLIAM of St Calais (1081–96) holds a central position in the history of Anglo-Norman Durham for two main reasons.[1] In 1083 he introduced the Rule of St Benedict into the Community of St Cuthbert, thereby reconstituting the arcane, quasi-monastic, practices of the *congregatio sancti Cuthberti* along more orthodox lines. Secondly, soon after returning from a period of three years' exile in Normandy, Bishop William ordered that the 'White Church', the Anglo-Saxon minster, should be demolished 'in the ninety-eighth year after it had been founded by Aldhun'.[2] On 29 July 1093 he joined in prayer with the prior and monks of the church of St Cuthbert and began the the foundations for the magnificent cathedral which so dominates the skyline of the city of Durham today.[3] As a direct result of these achievements Bishop William has been considered the architect, though perhaps not in the literal sense, of what we have come to think of as Anglo-Norman Durham.

The career of Bishop William of St Calais has become so overshadowed by this establishment of the Benedictine convent and the foundation of the Cathedral that it is difficult to imagine the history of Anglo-Norman Durham without him. The basic premise from which this paper proceeds is, however, that the career of Bishop William is marked, characterized even, by his prolonged absences from the bishopric. Therefore St Calais was, in large measure, a stranger as far as the members of the Community of St Cuthbert were concerned. His duties at the *curia regis*, the king's

---

[1] The most recent study of the career of Bishop William of St Calais is: H.S. Offler, 'William of Saint-Calais, First Norman Bishop of Durham', *TAASDN* 10 (1950), pp. 258–79, resumé of earlier biographies at p. 258, n. 1a.

I would like to thank Dr David Rollason for inviting me to speak at the Conference. In preparing this paper for publication I am grateful to the Department of History at the University of Sheffield. In revising this study I have benefited greatly from discussions with members of the Anglo-Norman Durham Conference and, in particular, Dr David Bates, Dr Chris Lewis, Dr Paul Dalton, Mr Michael Gullick, Ms Valerie Wall and Ms Emma Cownie.

[2] *LDE*, bk. 4, ch. 8 (pp. 128–9). Aldhun had established the Community of St Cuthbert at Durham in 995 and so the commencement of the work on the new cathedral may be dated to 1092–3.

[3] The foundation stones were laid on Thursday 11 August 1093 and Symeon marks the occasion by an elaborate dating formula.

court, were so burdensome and occupied so much of his time that the affairs of the diocese of St Cuthbert and its inhabitants had to take a subordinate position in his list of priorities.[4] It might even be suggested that his relationship with the church of St Cuthbert and its patron saint was eclipsed by his devotion to St Calais and the religious house dedicated to him, where Bishop William had accepted his monastic vocation.[5]

Any study of the pontificate of William of St Calais, as with so many aspects of the history of Anglo-Norman Durham, must begin with the work of Professor H.S. Offler. His assessment of the career of Bishop William was published in 1950, the year before he launched an attack on the authenticity of the tractate, *De iniusta uexacione Willelmi episcopi primi*, one of the major sources for St Calais's life.[6] The tractate deals with the trial of Bishop William before the royal court at Old Sarum in November 1088. The author was very obviously a partisan of Bishop William, a fact somewhat indicated by the tractate's title, 'Of the unjust persecution of Bishop William I', and the piece defends St Calais against the charge that, during the rebellion of 1088 in favour of Robert Curthose against William Rufus, the bishop of Durham first of all failed to support the king against his enemies and then actively engaged in treasonable acts against the crown. The *De iniusta uexacione* provides such a vivid description of the proceedings of the bishop's trial that it is difficult to believe that it was, in Offler's words, 'an extraordinarily well-contrived piece of fiction' concocted in Durham at least forty years later to defend the defendant's reputation.[7] By 1125–50, to which period Professor Offler assigned the production of the tract, the relationship between the bishop and the convent had deteriorated, largely as a result of the predatory pontificate of Ranulf Flambard.[8] In these circumstances the scriptorium of the monastery would seem to have been an

---

[4] Dom Léon Guilloreau remarked: 'Les séjours de Guillaume de Saint-Calais à Durham furent intermittents' ('Guillaume de Saint-Calais, évêque de Durham (. . .?–1096)', *Revue Historique et Archéologique du Maine*, 74 (1913), pp. 209–32, 75 (1914), pp. 64–79, at 74, p. 222. *Haliwerfolc* was the name given to the inhabitants of the diocese and, by extension, to the land upon which they lived.

[5] See below, pp. 287–8. In dealing with Bishop William and the cult of St Calais I have benefited greatly from the advice of Mr Michael Gullick.

[6] See above, n. 1, and Offler, 'Tractate'. For authenticity and significance of the tract see H.E.J. Cowdrey, 'The Enigma of Archbishop Lanfranc', delivered to the Haskins Society at The University of Houston, November 1993. I am very grateful to Dr Cowdrey for allowing me to read a draft. See also W.M. Aird, 'The Bishop and the Bloodhound: The Trial of Bishop William of Saint-Calais, 1088' and Ms Cary Dier, 'The Proper Relationship between Lord and Vassal: Toward a Rationale for Anglo-Norman Litigation' also at the Haskins Conference. Cf. above pp. 125–37.

[7] Offler, 'Bishop William', p. 272. For text and translation, see *DIV*.

[8] The extent of Flambard's attack on the possessions of the monks may be judged from the charters of restitution issued to the convent at the end of his life (*DEC*, nos. 24, 25). See Offler, 'Rannulf Flambard as Bishop of Durham, 1099–1128', *Durham University Journal* 64 (1971), pp. 14–25. For the relationship between the convent and the Norman bishops, see W.M. Aird, 'The Origins and Development of the Church of St Cuthbert, 635–1153, with Special Reference to Durham in the Period, 1071–1153' (unpublished Ph.D. thesis, University of Edinburgh, 1991), pp. 193–259.

unlikely place to have found an episcopal partisan. In addition, during the 1090s, after his return from exile, St Calais was actively engaged in an ultimately unsuccessful attempt to recover his position within the king's familia. The tract may therefore have been part of an attempt to rehabilitate his reputation in Durham. For these reasons inter alia, I am reluctant to consign the tractate to the category of 'tendentious fiction' as Professor Offler did.[9]

The other sources for the career of Bishop William are rather disappointing, not so much in respect of their number, for St Calais, in comparison with other prelates of his generation, is well served by accounts of his pontificate, but rather with regard to their lack of detailed information.[10] There is one particularly hostile account provided by Eadmer of Canterbury, who described Bishop William's prosecution of Archbishop Anselm on Rufus's behalf at the Council of Rockingham in 1095.[11] Anselm was, of course, Eadmer's hero and so his appraisal of the man assigned by the king to the task of brow-beating the archbishop into submission must be judged in the light of this knowledge.[12]

The account of Bishop William produced in the first decade of the twelfth century here in Durham, probably by the monk Symeon, is rather disappointing. There are hints in Symeon's work that the monks were rather disgruntled with Bishop William's treatment of the convent and that he failed to fulfil the expectations which they had of their founder and first abbot. There are, for example, no authentic foundation charters surviving from St Calais's pontificate; this embarrassing lack of title and the difficulties attendant thereon prompted the monks to produce a series of detailed forgeries in the latter half of the twelfth century when the relationship between the bishop and convent had deteriorated further.[13] There are notices concerning William of St Calais in the *Anglo-Saxon Chronicle* and the southern chroniclers Florence of Worcester and William of Malmesbury. Finally, there are the references to Bishop William in a number of royal charters which give some indication of his position within the *curia regis*.

Leaving aside the problem of the authenticity of the *De iniusta uexacione*, the main source for the career of William of St Calais remains the account given by Symeon in his *Libellus de exordio et procursu istius, hoc est Dunelmensis ecclesie*, which was written between 1104 and 1107.[14] The concluding book of Symeon's

---

[9] See above, pp. 125–8 and following.
[10] Others of the Anglo-Norman episcopacy received more detailed attention than Bishop William. St Calais was not the subject of a dedicated biography unlike, for example, both Wulfstan of Worcester and Gundulf of Rochester. Offler drew attention to the fact that, despite St Calais's notoriety, Orderic had very little to say about him other than to record his death in 1096, Offler, 'Bishop William', p. 274, n. 51
[11] Eadmer, *Historia Novorum in Anglia*, ed. M. Rule (RS 81; 1884), pp. 59–60.
[12] R.W. Southern, *Saint Anselm and his Biographer* (Cambridge, 1966), pp. 344–54.
[13] For texts and discussion of the forgeries, see, *DEC*, nos. *3, *4, *4 (a), *5, *6, *7. The crucial problem with the forgeries is deciding how much of their texts was concocted and how much a genuine record of the arrangements made in 1083 (Offler, 'Bishop William', p. 259).
[14] *LDE*.

Libellus de exordio is devoted to the narrative of St Calais's episcopate.[15] The *Libellus de exordio* must, however, be treated with extreme caution. Symeon admits that he was writing on the orders of his superiors and in many respects his *Libellus* is a carefully crafted piece of monastic propaganda.[16] The purpose of his work was not only to demonstrate that the Benedictine monks introduced in 1083 were the appropriate guardians of the shrine of St Cuthbert, but also to remind Ranulf Flambard of his obligations as bishop towards the convent.[17] The description given of William of St Calais is, for the most part, concerned with his treatment of the monks. Given that St Calais was the founder of the Benedictine convent the opportunity was there for Symeon to compose a eulogy. However, his account of Bishop William is a rather low-key affair and whatever praise there is, is almost always to be found in association with a comment which contradicts, undermines, or tempers the force of the eulogising. For example, Symeon states that Bishop William:

> never abstracted anything from the church but rather he was anxious to add to its possessions and decorate it with valuable ornaments. With God's help and by his wisdom and efforts, he [Bishop William] defended the rights, laws and privileges of the Church so that during his lifetime they could be infringed or violated by no-one.[18]

This passage immediately follows the account of how the church of Tynemouth, which had been granted to the monks at Jarrow, had been lost to the abbey of St Albans.[19] Similarly, Bishop William made plans to ensure that the monks were sufficiently provided for in terms of food and clothing. He was on the point of implementing these plans when his death and that of King William I prevented the completion of his scheme.[20] It may be deduced from this that St Calais had made no firm arrangements for the provisioning of the convent during the years between its establishment in 1083 and his death in 1096.[21] Much of what Symeon has to

---

15 *LDE*, bk. 4 (pp. 119–35).

16 *LDE*, preface (p. 3).

17 See D. Rollason, 'Symeon of Durham and the Community of Durham in the Eleventh Century', in *England in the Eleventh Century*, ed. Carola Hicks (Harlaxton Medieval Studies 2; Stamford, 1992), pp. 183–98. Offler believed that there was an 'atmosphere of calculated fraud' surrounding the production of historical writing in Durham in the early twelfth century (Offler, 'Bishop William', p. 259).

18 *LDE*, bk. 4, ch. 5 (p. 125): 'episcopus Willelmus nihil unquam de ecclesia auferebat; quin potius semper inferre, et multis eam ac pretiosis ornamentorum speciebus studebat exornare.'

19 For the grant of Tynemouth and the dispute with St Albans, see *DEC*, no. 2 (c).

20 *LDE*, bk. 4, ch. 3 (p. 124): 'Episcopus quoque aliquantulum quidem terre monachis largitus est; ueruntamen ut sine indigentia et penuria Christo seruirent, sufficientes ad uictum illorum et uestitum terras eis una cum rege ipse prouiderat, et iam iamque daturus erat. Sed ne id ad effectum perueniret, primo regis ac postea episcopi mors impedimento fuerat.'

21 Symeon's ambivalent attitude towards Bishop William is demonstrated in his account of a dream experienced by Boso, one of the bishop's knights. St Calais was warned that his death was imminent and immediately took steps to amend his life (*LDE*, bk. 4, chs. 9–10 (pp. 132–3)): 'Cum ergo uisionis suae ordinem iubente retulisset, ille talia contremiscens

say about William of St Calais's achievements has this hollow ring to it. It is almost as though Symeon felt obliged to praise St Calais but there was something preventing his whole-hearted endorsement of his regime. That something was Bishop William's comparative neglect of his bishopric and the monastery at Durham.[22]

As has been noted, Bishop William's career is outlined by Symeon in Book 4 of his *Libellus de exordio*. St Calais's origins are, however, dealt with only very briefly. As a young man William was one of the clerks of the church of Bayeux, an ecclesiastical corporation which supplied a number of prelates to the English church after the Conquest. This association with Bayeux prompted Dom Leon Guilloreau to suggest that Bishop William was 'du Bessin probablement', but there is no evidence in the contemporary sources to support this.[23] It seems unlikely, however, that the future bishop of Durham owed advancement in his ecclesiastical career to the direct patronage of the Bishop Odo as St Calais's employment in the cathedral chapter at Bayeux seems to have been relatively short.[24] At an unknown date William's father became an inmate of the monastery of St Calais in the County of Maine. There is no information on the status of William's father but he may have been a knight who hoped to atone for his earlier misdemeanours by ending his days as a monk. The name of William's mother, Ascelina or Anselma appears in the Durham liturgical record, but, as yet, his father's name has not been identified.[25]

When describing Bishop William's adoption of the monastic vocation Symeon merely says that St Calais was following his father's example. This is, of course, entirely plausible as the motivation for making such a decision varied from individual to individual. For example, Gundulf of Rochester, a near contemporary of William of St Calais, entered the monastery of Bec after completing a pilgrimage to the Holy Land. By comparison William's decision seems to betray a distinct lack of originality or deep devotion. However, there is evidence to suggest that he may have had a pious attachment to the cult of St Calais.[26] St Calais or Carilefus was a companion of the early sixth-century ascetic Avitus. In his search for the eremitic

uehementer expauit, atque studiosus deinceps sue salutis curam gerere coepit, largiores uidelicet eleemosynas faciendo, prolixius et intentius orando, nullius negotii gratia priuata orationum quotidianarum statuta praetermittendo'.

22 Compare Gundulf of Rochester, cf. R.A.L. Smith, 'The Place of Gundulf in the Anglo-Norman Church', *EHR* 58 (1943), pp. 257–72. The *Vita Gundulfi* has been edited by R. Thomson, *The Life of Gundulf, Bishop of Rochester* (Toronto Medieval Latin Texts; Toronto, 1977) and translated by the nuns of Malling Abbey as *Vita Gundulfi: The Life of the Venerable Man, Gundulf, Bishop of Rochester* (Malling Abbey, 1968).

23 Guilloreau, 'Guillaume de Saint-Calais', p. 210. In view of the family's attachment to the monastery of St Calais it is equally likely that William's origins were in Maine.

24 See D. Bates, 'The Character and Career of Odo, Bishop of Bayeux (1049/50–1097)', *Speculum* 50 (1975), pp. 1–20. For the connections between members of the Anglo-Norman episcopacy and the church of Bayeux, see D. Nicholl, *Thurstan, Archbishop of York (1114–1140)* (York, 1964), pp. 6–7 and n. 18.

25 Offler, 'Bishop William', p. 261, n. 8 for the references in a Durham *Martyrologium* and *Obituarium*.

26 I am most grateful to Mr Michael Gullick for drawing my attention to the possibility of

life he finally settled in Maine where he became the abbot of a small monastic community. The cult which later developed seems to have been very localised.[27] As Guilloreau pointed out, there is a record of a confraternity agreement between the monks of Durham and those of St Calais, which it seems most appropriate to date to the pontificate of Bishop William.[28] Also Bishop William made arrangements for a grant of land in Lincolnshire to be made to the abbey of St Calais.[29] Bishop William seems to have brought his devotion to St Calais to Durham, for there is a *Missa sancti Karilephi abbatis* preserved in a Durham missal.[30] In addition, at Le Mans there survives a brief, incomplete *Life of St Karileph*. Perhaps, while he was abbot of the important abbey of St Vincent, William exploited his position to provide the cult of St Calais with a locally produced manuscript.[31] Finally, it is surely not insignificant that Bishop William is now known by the locative epithet St Calais, although it must be admitted that his biographer Symeon does not refer to him in this fashion.[32]

William's monastic career is the story of an inexorable rise through the ranks. Symeon has little to say other than that William was first prior of the cloister, then chief prior at St Calais before becoming abbot of the monastery of St Vincent.[33] William's advancement is attributed to his 'love and devotion for the monastic order', yet this devotion did not preclude leaving the cloister to participate in secular affairs at the highest level.[34]

Around 1078 William was elevated to the abbacy of the monastery of St Vincent at Le Mans but there is little indication of how he performed in this office. The only record from the abbey in which Abbot William is anything more than a name concerns his defence of the abbey's rights to a mill and his acknowledgement of a

Bishop William's promotion of the cult of St Calais, and in particular the information regarding the eleventh-century Life of St Calais in Le Mans, MS 10, fols. 1–8.

[27] St Calais's feast day was 1 July. See *Butler's Lives of the Saints*, edited, revised and supplemented by H.J. Thurston, S.J. and D. Attwater (3 vols., London, 1956), III, under 'St Carilefus' and *Dictionnaire d'Histoire et de Géographie Ecclésiastiques* (Paris, 1949) under 'Calais'.

[28] *Liber Vitae*, fol. 33v. See Offler, 'Bishop William', p. 261, n. 11, and Guilloreau, 'Guillaume de Saint-Calais', 75, pp. 78–9.

[29] Guilloreau, 'Guillaume de Saint-Calais', 75, p. 75 and Offler, 'Bishop William', p. 261 and n. 10.

[30] See Offler, 'Bishop William', p. 262 and n. 12.

[31] See above n. 26. Michael Gullick has suggested to me that it is just possible that the manuscript dates from the period 1078–80 when William was abbot of St Vincent. Thus it seems reasonable to suppose that William had commissioned the *Vita* and this may have been to express his devotion to the patron saint of the house where he had become a monk.

[32] Later in the twelfth century the appointment of William of St Barbe forced Durham historians to make a distinction between the two.

[33] Prior William has left no trace in the cartulary of St Calais; see L. Froger, *Cartulaire de l'Abbaye de St Calais* (Le Mans, 1888).

[34] *LDE*, bk. 4, ch. 1 (p. 119): 'suscepto habitu monachico, in monastici ordinis obseruantia singulariter pre ceteris amore ac studio strenuus habebatur, ideoque ad superiores gradus paulatim ascendens promouebatur.'

gift of some houses in Le Mans made under the auspices of William the Conqueror.[35] It is possible that it was on one of these occasions or on another visit by William the Conqueror to Le Mans that Abbot William's administrative acumen came to the attention of the king.

Professor Offler suggested that William of St Calais acted as a royal agent in Maine at a time when the Norman hold on the county was threatened by native resistance and the persistent territorial ambitions of the Angevins.[36] Matters were further complicated by William I's acrimonious dispute with his eldest son, Robert. Abbot William made himself useful to the Conqueror 'in certain very difficult matters', which, Offler reasoned, concerned the tense political situation in Le Mans.[37] Whereas it may be true that Abbot William's actions in Maine drew him to the attention of the king, it seems to be stretching a point to say that he was appointed to Durham in order to rectify the dangerous and disordered situation in the North-East of England.

Despite the successful suppression of the Northumbrian revolt in the early 1070s and the subsequent establishment of French barons in Yorkshire, the Norman hold on the land to the north of the River Tees was tenuous.[38] The native aristocracy retained much of its power, with political leadership focused on the ancient fortress of Bamburgh.[39] Within the bishopric of Durham the quasi-monastic *congregatio sancti Cuthberti* serving the shrine at Durham retained its close links with the *Haliwerfolc*, despite the appointment of the Lotharingian bishop Walcher in 1071.[40] Following the deposition and execution of Earl Waltheof of Northumbria in 1075, Walcher had assumed nominal control over the government of the earldom.[41] The bishop's household formed an uneasy partnership with the native Northumbrians which broke down with the murder of Walcher and his partisans at Gateshead in May 1080. In addition, the territorial ambitions of the Scots king Malcolm III 'Canmore' were expressed in the form of intermittent but devastating attacks on the North-East of England. In the 1070s and 1080s Malcolm III sought to reunite Lothian with the southern portion of the ancient Anglian kingdom of Bernicia, a dynastic aim which was achieved by his son David I and his grandson Earl Henry.[42]

In certain respects, therefore, the situation on the northern frontier of William

[35] R. Charles and M. d'Elbenne, *Cartulaire de l'Abbaye de Saint Vincent du Mans* (Mamers, Le Mans, 1886), nos. 99, 100, 621. See Offler, 'Bishop William', p. 262 and n. 13.

[36] Offler, 'Bishop William', pp. 262–3. For William I's difficulties in Maine during this period, see D.C. Douglas, *William the Conqueror* (London, 1964), pp. 235–9.

[37] *LDE*, bk. 4, ch. 1 (p. 119): 'in rebus saepe difficillimis'. See Offler, 'Bishop William', p. 262.

[38] On the political situation in the North-East of England see W.E. Kapelle, *The Norman Conquest of the North: The Region and its Transformation 1000–1135* (Chapel Hill and London, 1979).

[39] C.J. Morris, *Marriage and Murder in eleventh-century Northumbria: A Study of De Obsessione Dunelmi* (University of York, Borthwick Paper 82; 1992).

[40] See Aird, 'Origins', pp. 78–134.

[41] F.S. Scott, 'Earl Waltheof of Northumbria', *Arch. Ael.* 4th ser. 30 (1952).

[42] See W.M. Aird, 'St Cuthbert, the Scots and the Normans', in *AN* 16 (1994), pp. 1–20 and below, pp. 313, 339, 349–50.

I's kingdom resembled that in the southern marches of Normandy. It is not unreasonable, therefore, to suppose, as Offler did, that Bishop William of St Calais's appointment had a political dimension to it.[43] However, Bishop William's frequent and prolonged absences from Durham prevented him from acting effectively on the king's behalf as a Marcher lord in this volatile region. Far more important in this regard was the appointment of Aubrey de Courcy and that of his successor, Robert de Mowbray, to the earldom of Northumbria. It was under their direction that Norman settlement advanced beyond the Tyne and subdued those Northumbrians who had assassinated William of St Calais's predecessor.[44] For the most part, therefore, Bishop William's career was characterized by his administrative rather than his martial abilities.

William of St Calais was nominated for the see of Durham by William I in November 1080 and consecrated by Archbishop Thomas I of York at Gloucester in January 1081.[45] Symeon listed the qualities which had recommended St Calais to William I as an administrator. He was 'very well versed in sacred and secular learning, very conscientious in matters of divine and worldly business, and so remarkable for good conduct that he had no equal amongst his contemporaries. He had, moreover, such a keen understanding of matters that no-one could be found who could give sounder advice.'[46] Not unrelated to these qualities were his eloquence and his capacious and tenacious memory. This latter ability was prized above all others in any administration at this time, where being able to retain and disseminate information was fundamental in an age still learning the techniques of written government. Although it was by no means unusual for bishops to be employed at the royal court, it does seem that William of St Calais, more than most, was preoccupied with the diurnal administration of the *regnum*.[47] The study of Bishop William's administrative career is the one area which has challenged Professor Offler's gloomy prediction that to what was already known about William of St Calais in 1950, 'it seems unlikely that substantial additions will be made'.[48] The importance of St Calais to the governmental machinery of Anglo-Norman England has been underlined by Pierre Chaplais in his elucidation of Bishop William's part in the compilation of the Domesday Survey.[49] If Chaplais was correct, William of St Calais was the guiding hand, Galbraith's man behind the

[43] Offler, 'Bishop William', p. 265.

[44] The *nouum castrum* on the north bank of the Tyne built by Robert Curthose in 1080 was thus less a defensive measure against the Scots than a bridgehead into the region controlled by the regime at Bamburgh.

[45] *LDE*, bk. 4, ch. 1 (p. 119).

[46] Ibid.: 'ecclesiasticis et secularibus litteris nobiliter eruditus, in diuinis et humanis rebus multum industrius, morum honestate ita compositus ut per id temporis nemo in hac ei putaretur esse praeferendus. Inerat illi etiam tanta ingenii subtilitas, ut non facile quis occurreret, qui profundius consilium inueniret.'

[47] See D. Walker, 'Crown and Episcopacy under the Normans and Angevins', *AN* 5 (1983), pp. 220–33 and H.R. Loyn, 'William's Bishops: Some Further Thoughts', *AN* 10 (1988), pp. 223–35.

[48] Offler, 'Bishop William', p. 258.

[49] P. Chaplais 'William of Saint-Calais and the Domesday Survey', in *Domesday Studies*, ed.

compilation of the Survey.[50] Taking with him a team of scribes from Durham, St Calais visited the centres of the Domesday circuits where the returns were collated, in order to oversee the production of this important administrative document. By its very peripatetic nature this task kept William away from Durham for many months, from the inception of the project in 1085 until the death of the Conqueror in 1087.

There is further evidence of St Calais's central position in the government of William I. The surviving royal charters support the idea that Bishop William was the governmental factotum of the first Norman king. Although it is rarely possible to assign these documents to a specific year or place of production, an examination of the witness lists is instructive.[51] In a significant number of the *acta* of William I in which Bishop William's name appears, he is one of only three or four witnesses.[52] Where Bishop William appears with other witnesses he is invariably near the head of the list, taking second place only to members of the king's family or figures such as Lanfranc, Walchelin, bishop of Winchester, or Geoffrey of Coutances. This conjures up a picture of the king and his chief administrator working together with the most important ecclesiastical and secular magnates.[53]

St Calais's administrative skills, Symeon tells us, recommended him to the king of France and the pope as well as to the king of England. However, it was, perhaps, overstating the case to say that these leaders of Christendom were gratified to receive a visit from the bishop of Durham and listen to his wise and eloquent discourse.[54] It is suggested that within a year of his episcopal consecration, Bishop William was at the papal curia on the king's business and it was while he was there, probably in 1082, that he obtained, so Symeon claims, papal sanction for his project to introduce the Benedictine Rule to the church of St Cuthbert. The pope gave his full support and sent letters to the king and Lanfranc asking them to assist William in his plans.[55] Thus in the following year, William of St Calais established orthodox Benedictine monasticism in the church of St Cuthbert at the expense of the ancient liturgical practices of the *congregatio sancti Cuthberti*.[56]

What effect did Bishop William's absences from Durham have upon the running of his episcopal see and his relationship with the convent which he had established in 1083? First, there is no mention of William performing the quotidian duties of a diocesan, such as consecrating churches, investing priests, or making visitations. This is not exceptional in itself but even the notoriously worldly Ranulf Flambard

---

J.C. Holt (Winchester, 1986), pp. 65–77. See also C. Lewis, 'The Earldom of Surrey and the Date of Domesday', *Historical Research* 63 (1990), pp. 329–36.

[50] Chaplais, art. cit., p. 66.

[51] *Regesta*, I, nos. 143, 146a, 147, 148, 215, 216, 217, 220, 232, 233, 234, 235, 236, 274, 275, 278, 282, 284, 286.

[52] E.g. *Regesta*, I, nos. 215, 217, 235, 236, 274, 282 (sole witness), 284.

[53] Guilloreau suggested that St Calais was responsible for tempering William I's policy towards monasteries, 'Guillaume de Saint-Calais', 74, pp. 223–4.

[54] *LDE*, bk. 4, ch. 1 (p. 120).

[55] *LDE*, bk. 4, ch. 2 (p. 121).

[56] See Aird, 'Origins', pp. 135–92

is recorded as having preached at least one sermon – albeit an especially prolix and, fortunately, rain-interrupted one.[57] Symeon's silence on St Calais's performance of diocesan duties stands in stark contrast to his description of the role of Prior Turgot who, Symeon asserts, was given the status of an archdeacon in 1093 at the foundation of the cathedral.[58] The career of Prior Turgot provides an interesting comparison with that of Bishop William. Turgot was a Lincolnshire nobleman who was taken as a hostage by the Normans, presumably to ensure the good behaviour of his countrymen after 1066.[59] Turgot bribed his way out of captivity and fled to Norway where he became the confidant of King Olaf III. In the early 1070s Turgot returned to England, once more a wealthy man. His ship was wrecked, however, and he understood the reversal of his fortunes to be a call to a more spiritual life. He joined the revitalised monastic community at Jarrow, established by Aldwin of Winchcombe and his companions under the auspices of Bishop Walcher.[60] His succession to Aldwin as prior of Durham in 1087 began a career which was to result in Turgot administering the see of Durham during St Calais's absences and acting as bishop in all but name. The prominence of Prior Turgot in the affairs of the bishopric may be judged from the fact that an early twelfth-century collection of the miracles of St Cuthbert is dominated by his presence.[61] Needless to say there are no examples of Bishop William being associated with the performance of any late eleventh-century Cuthbertine miracles. During St Calais's exile, from 1088 to 1091, Turgot took charge of the bishopric and William Rufus is reported as having been uncharacteristically generous to the church of Durham in this period. Such was his respect for the authority and bearing of Turgot that, according to Symeon, when the prior came to him he would humbly stand in his presence and receive him kindly. Moreover, Rufus invited Turgot to administer the diocese as if he were its bishop.[62]

Bishop William's relationship with the Benedictine community was, therefore, necessarily remote. It is even to be doubted whether he played as major a part in its foundation as is usually believed.[63] Lanfranc's influence pervades the history of monasticism in this period. For example, he directed the introduction of a

[57] De miraculis, ch. 7 (Sym. Op. I, 260).

[58] LDE, bk. 4, ch. 8 (p. 129).

[59] Turgot's career in HReg, s.a. 1074 (Sym. Op. II, 202–5). See R.H. Forster, 'Turgot, Prior of Durham', JBAA 63 (1907), pp. 32–40. A Thorgautr appears in Lincolnshire Domesday holding estates TRE worth over £40. It is not clear if this Thorgautr is Thorgautr Lagr who was a man of some importance in Lincoln, on which see J.W.F. Hill, Medieval Lincoln (Cambridge, 1949), p. 45. I owe these references to Ms Mary Frances Smith and Dr David Roffe. I hope to examine the career of Prior Turgot in greater depth elsewhere.

[60] LDE, bk. 3, chs. 21–2 (pp. 108–13).

[61] W.M. Aird, 'The Making of a Medieval Miracle Collection: The Liber de Translationibus et Miraculis Sancti Cuthberti', Northern History 28 (1992), pp. 1–24.

[62] LDE, bk. 4, ch. 8 (p. 128).

[63] Professor Offler tentatively made the suggestion that 'the part of Lanfranc went beyond support. . . Can we suppose that something more than Lanfranc's example, that some positive act of promotion or suggestion on Lanfranc's part was here in play?' ('Bishop William', p. 268).

Benedictine community to the church of St Andrew at Rochester and may have played a similar role in the reorganisation of the church of St Cuthbert.[64] There is evidence in the matter of monastic reform and ecclesiastical affairs in general that Bishop William relied heavily upon Lanfranc. Not only did Canterbury supply the constitutions by which the convent was to be run, but one of the texts possessed by St Calais was the *Collectio Lanfranci*, a compilation of canon law probably produced at Canterbury.[65] That Bishop William should rely so heavily upon Archbishop Lanfranc in the establishment of a Benedictine convent is entirely understandable. Lanfranc was an acknowledged expert on monastic affairs and it would be natural to seek his advice. It was, perhaps, not only deference to a recognized authority on the subject which led Bishop William to seek the archbishop's guidance. If St Calais was as fully occupied on the king's business as I have suggested, then it is likely that he simply lacked the time to organise in meticulous detail the constitution of 1083. That was a task left largely to Prior Aldwin and his successor Turgot, who relied on materials supplied by Lanfranc.

Symeon does, however, insist that William was a devoted father to his monks, so devoted that he wrote to them constantly when he was away from them. Nonetheless, Symeon can produce only one letter from the bishop to his convent, and that a rather conventional epistle, stressing adherence to the monastic order and asking the monks to remember him in their prayers. The only pictorial representation of Bishop William has been described as 'conventional' and may reflect his unavailability for portraiture (pl. 79).[66] It is possible that this paucity of evidence for contact between the bishop and convent is due to the loss of a more substantial archive. However, St Calais mentions that the letter should be read once a week in the chapter, which rather suggests that it was to suffice in the absence of further communication.[67]

In 1088, William of St Calais became involved in the attempt by a cabal of Anglo-Norman magnates, led by Odo of Bayeux, to put Robert Curthose on the throne. The tractate discussed above gives the details of this rebellion and its aftermath. It is not clear why Bishop William joined the rebels. It is unlikely that he was acting out of loyalty to Odo of Bayeux, but it is possible that he considered the interests of the *regnum* to be best served by the reunification of Normandy and England under Robert. After the collapse of the rebellion and his retreat to Durham, St Calais was called to account for himself before the *curia regis* at Old Sarum in November 1088. Despite a masterly attempt to defend himself based on his status as an ecclesiastic, Bishop William went into exile from November 1088 until September 1091. Although he claimed that he would take his grievance to the

---

[64] For Rochester see R.A.L. Smith, 'The Early Community of St Andrew at Rochester', *EHR* 60 (1945), pp. 289–99.

[65] DCL, MS B.IV.24 contains, *inter alia*, Lanfranc's *Consuetudines*, together with the Rule of St Benedict in Latin and Old English. See *DCM*, no. 51, pp. 44–5, and above, pp. 79–97, esp. 80–2. The *collectio Lanfranci* is now Cambridge, Peterhouse College, MS 74.

[66] See DCL, MS B.II.13, fol. 102 and Offler, 'Bishop William', p. 277, n. 66.

[67] *LDE*, bk. 4, ch. 6 (p. 126).

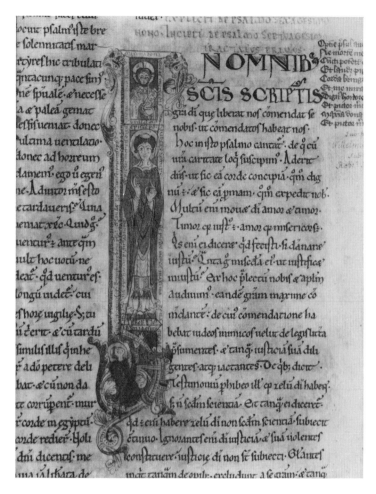

Plate 79. DCL, B.II.13, fol. 102r, St Augustine, 'Commentary on
Psalms', showing an initial containing a portrait of Bishop William
of St Calais, with at his feet a small kneeling monk, identified in the
inscription as Robert Benjamin. The poem around the initial indicated
that this monk was the artist (*pictor*) of the initials.

papal curia, St Calais assumed the role of chief administrator of Normandy on
behalf of Curthose.[68] This period of exile can have done nothing to deepen his
connections with Durham and it is to this period that the growth of Prior Turgot's
power should be assigned.

[68] A letter from Urban II to William Rufus dating from 1089 sets out the bishop's case and
asks that the king restore St Calais to his bishopric and only then bring his accusations against
him before the papal curia; see S. Loewenfeld, *Epistolae Pontificum Romanorum ineditae*
(Leipzig, 1885), no. 129, p. 63.

During Rufus's campaigns in Normandy Bishop William was able to recover his standing with the king. According to Symeon, St Calais arranged for the lifting of a siege and the release of Rufus's adherents.[69] C.W. David suggested that the bishop was responsible for the peace treaty between Robert and Rufus in 1091, although the sources are hardly conclusive on this point.[70] When St Calais returned to Durham in 1091, he was confronted by a very powerful monastic corporation which had asserted its rights in the diocese.[71] The elevation of Prior Turgot to the status of an archdeacon in 1093 was a formal recognition of the *de facto* ecclesiastical franchise which the convent had established.[72] St Calais's absences had, therefore, weakened his position within the diocese, to the extent that the monastic corporation of which he was *ex officio* abbot was able to pursue successfully an ecclesiastical policy which sought to establish a large measure of independence from the diocesan. This situation must not be exaggerated, however, as there is evidence to suggest that there was no lasting animosity or ill feeling between Bishop William and the convent.

St Calais's period of exile had been profitable and he returned laden with gifts for the church and enough wealth to undertake the building of a new cathedral.[73] It was agreed initially that the new cathedral should be the financial responsibility of the bishop, whilst the monks were to provide funds for their own conventual buildings.[74] Despite undertaking this huge capital project, William returned to the *curia regis* and the series of royal *acta* bearing his attestations resumes soon after his return from exile.[75] He regained royal favour sufficiently to be granted the privilege of holding his lands in alms rather than in fee.[76] It was during his last years as a royal counsellor that William's reputation suffered a blow which has largely tarnished assessments of his career ever since.[77] St Calais acted as Rufus's chief

---

[69] *LDE*, bk. 4, ch. 8 (p. 128).

[70] C.W. David, *Robert Curthose* (Cambridge, MA, 1920), p. 59, n. 79 and Offler, 'Bishop William', pp. 272–3.

[71] On the development of the conventual franchise within the bishopric, F. Barlow, *Durham Jurisdictional Peculiars* (Oxford, 1950), pp. 1–16 and Aird, 'Origins', pp. 193–259.

[72] *LDE*, bk. 4, ch. 8 (p. 129).

[73] *LDE*, bk. 4, ch. 8 (pp. 128–9). St Calais's gifts for the Church included a number of manuscripts which, presumably, he had collected during his stay in Normandy; see C.H. Turner, 'The Earliest List of Durham Manuscripts', *JTS* 19 (1918), pp. 121–32 and Michael Gullick, 'The Scribe of the Carilef Bible: A New Look at some Late Eleventh-Century Durham Cathedral Manuscripts', in *Medieval Book Production: Assessing the Evidence*, ed. L.L. Brownrigg (Los Altos Hills, 1990), pp. 61–83. I am grateful to Mr Gullick for supplying me with a copy of this article.

[74] *LDE*, bk. 4, ch. 8 (p. 129).

[75] For example, *Regesta*, I, nos. 330, 331, 332, 336, 337, 338, 340, 341.

[76] H.H.E. Craster, 'A Contemporary Record of the Pontificate of Rannulf Flambard', *Arch. Ael.* 4th ser. 18 (1930), pp. 33–56, no. I, pp. 35–6. Craster dates this document to Rufus's Christmas court at Gloucester, 1093.

[77] For example, Offler, 'Bishop William', p. 275: 'St Calais's later dealings with Anselm are beyond the power of apology to defend.' Cf. the article by M. Creighton in *Dictionary of*

prosecutor during the arraignment of Anselm in 1095 and, as we have seen, his abrasive and bullying attitude won him the condemnation of Anselm's biographer Eadmer, who accused Durham of having ambitions towards the archiepiscopal see itself. It was perhaps St Calais's failure at Rockingham which finally soured his relations with Rufus and when William died early in 1096, he was at the king's court, summoned on some unspecified charge which may, however, have been related to the rebellion in 1095 of Earl Robert de Mowbray.[78] Perhaps Rufus felt that St Calais had not properly represented his interests in the North-East of England. St Calais's body was returned to Durham and buried in the monastic chapter-house, as he felt that he was not worthy to be interred near St Cuthbert.[79]

There can be no doubt that William of St Calais was a prominent figure in the medieval history of the church of St Cuthbert, but, paradoxically, the significance of his influence was the direct result of his absences from Durham. There are signs that his foundation of the Benedictine convent was rather haphazard. Symeon, for example, states that the bishop made a division between episcopal and conventual lands but never completed the task of delimiting the convent's estate.[80] This was of little consequence during his own pontificate but a more rapacious prelate such as Flambard was able to exploit the ambiguity of the situation for his own ends. Once Bishop William had returned to the *curia regis* the supervision of the building of the cathedral fell to Prior Turgot. During the vacancy after St Calais's death the convent had to assume the financial burden of the project, despite the arrangement noted earlier. St Calais may well have been responsible for the establishment of the convent, but it was his continued absence which strengthened its position within the bishopric, to the detriment of that of the diocesan. It was a legacy which shaped the often volatile relationship between bishop and convent throughout the twelfth century.

In the light of this examination of William of St Calais's career it is difficult to see the bishop as taking a significant part in the development of Norman power in the North-East of England.[81] It may well be too harsh to say that St Calais neglected Durham, especially in view of the massive contribution which he made to the church's architectural remains and his gifts to the monastic library, but it is certainly true to say that the administration of the church of St Cuthbert took a second place to the administration of the kingdom. St Calais was an archetype of the curial bishop and his place was at the heart of the administration of the realm

National Biography, ed. L. Stephen (reprinted Oxford University Press, 1921–22), III, under *Carilef*, where the bishop is described as 'a man without principles in public matters'.

[78] See Offler, 'Bishop William', p. 276 regarding E.A. Freeman's suggestion that St Calais was implicated in the rebellion of Robert de Mowbray.

[79] On the excavation of the supposed grave of St Calais see, J. Raine, *A Brief Historical Account of the Episcopal Castle or Palace of Auckland* (Durham, 1852), p. 8, n. 1.

[80] See above, p. 286.

[81] Offler suggested that Bishop William was 'a proper representative to help teach a recalcitrant north the lessons of Norman organisation and of Norman order' ('Bishop William', p. 279).

rather than in the episcopal chair of the church of St Cuthbert. This is well illustrated by the fact that when, in 1082, St Calais won approval for his scheme to introduce monks to Durham, he was at the papal curia in Rome, on the king's business.[82]

[82] *LDE*, bk. 4, ch. 2 (p. 121).

The Career of Ranulf Flambard

J. O. PRESTWICH

RANULF FLAMBARD's career has been so fully and so admirably described and assessed by Sir Richard Southern, Professor Offler and Professor Barlow that it may seem superfluous to consider some aspects of it yet again.[1] Yet Flambard, bishop of Durham for almost three decades from 1099 to 1128, cannot be excluded from a volume commemorating the nine hundredth anniversary of Durham cathedral. As Offler justly observed, no other bishop of Durham, save Wolsey, has played anything like as prominent a part on the national stage as did Flambard. Here I propose to consider two very general questions: first, given the very differing judgements passed by contemporaries, what were the qualities which made Flambard so prominent? Second, what was his contribution to the structure and working of the institutions of central government?

In its barest outline Flambard's career was conventional. He was the son of a village priest in the diocese of Bayeux, born probably a few years before the battle of Hastings, rose in the service of Maurice, the Conqueror's chancellor in the latter part of the reign, achieved the highest eminence under Rufus, and was rewarded with the bishopric of Durham in 1099. Ranulf was an early member of a long line of royal clerks whose efficiency was similarly rewarded. By the time of the Conqueror's death over half the English bishoprics were filled with royal clerks; by the middle of Henry I's reign the proportion was over three-quarters.[2] Most of these men, however eminent as administrators or statesmen, have left few traces of their personalities in the surviving evidence. The biographer of Roger of Salisbury had to conclude that 'the complete individual eludes us,' and that 'until almost the end he was hidden by his success.'[3] The thoughts and personality of Henry II's great minister, Richard of Ilchester, bishop of Winchester from 1173 to 1186, remain obscure, despite the volume of evidence for his decisive influence.[4] And

[1] R.W. Southern, 'Ranulf Flambard', in *Medieval Humanism and Other Studies* (Oxford, 1970), pp. 183–205; H.S. Offler, 'Rannulf Flambard as Bishop of Durham (1099–1128)', *Durham University Journal* 64 (1971), pp. 14–25; and F. Barlow, *William Rufus* (London, 1983).
[2] F. Barlow, *The English Church, 1066–1154* (London, 1979), p. 218; and D. Walker, 'Crown and Episcopacy under the Normans and Angevins', *AN* 5 (1982), p. 220.
[3] E.J. Kealey, *Roger of Salisbury, Viceroy of England* (London, 1972), pp. 206–7.
[4] C. Duggan, 'Richard of Ilchester, Royal Servant and Bishop', *TRHS*, 5th ser. 16 (1966), p. 21.

Robert Burnell, despite his immense influence under Edward I, eluded even Powicke's power to conjure up a vivid image from unpromising material.

In sharp contrast to these industrious and discreet servants of the crown Flambard imposed himself on his contemporaries by his exuberant personality. He was still making his way in the Conqueror's court when he was nicknamed 'Flambard', torch-bearer, incendiary.[5] It is easy to underestimate the force of this: contemporaries knew that the torch was a more destructive weapon than the sword or lance, and it seems that Flambard earned his nickname because of his successes as a prosecuting counsel for the crown. All the sources agree that Flambard was an exceptionally fluent and forceful speaker. Dramatic and scandalous stories accumulated around him. It was presumably from Flambard himself that the Durham monks heard how, when he was at the height of his power under Rufus, he was entrapped on a ship in the Thames estuary by enemies who planned to kill him. By sheer force of personality he persuaded his captors to set him free.[6]

Perhaps this experience encouraged Flambard in his second escape. Ten days after the coronation of Henry I Flambard was arrested and imprisoned in the Tower of London, charged with embezzlement, an obvious scapegoat for the malpractices of Rufus's reign which Henry professed to renounce. But within six months, early in February 1101, Flambard escaped and made his way to Normandy. This required both nerve and careful planning: the smuggling in of a rope, the provision of a feast for the guards with enough wine to get them drunk, arrangements with friends and followers to have good horses ready at the foot of the Tower, and the provision of ships to take himself and his mother across the Channel.[7] It is a remarkable tribute to Flambard's abilities, energy and persuasiveness that Robert Curthose made him his chief of staff and that within six months Flambard had raised an invasion force which he guided to an unopposed landing at Portsmouth on 20 July 1101. Yet Robert Curthose lost his nerve, and it might have been expected that with the defeat and capture of Curthose at Tinchebray in 1106 Flambard had nothing more to hope for than a long and embittered exile from the reunited Anglo-Norman lands. But long before this Flambard had come to terms with Henry I and had been restored to his bishopric. This is puzzling. Perhaps Henry decided that he no longer needed a scapegoat; and perhaps he considered that Flambard's great abilities could be productively employed in the outpost at Durham.[8]

Flambard had still to meet charges that he was unfit to be a bishop. To Anselm Ranulf, though formally a priest, had been the chief oppressor of the church, conspicuous for his cruelty. In 1102 Pope Paschal II threatened to depose Flambard; and in 1125, according to a report which reached Winchester,

---

5 *Orderic*, IV, 172.
6 *Sym. Op.* I, 135–8.
7 *Orderic*, V, 310–12.
8 C.W. Hollister, 'The Anglo-Norman Civil War: 1101', *EHR* 88 (1973), pp. 315–34, reprinted in idem, *Monarchy, Magnates and Institutions in the Anglo-Norman World* (London, 1986), pp. 77–96. Page references below are to the latter volume.

numerous charges of immorality were brought against Ranulf, and he was again threatened with deposition.[9] We cannot check the truth of all the stories told of Ranulf while bishop; but it is nevertheless significant that the stories were circulated as plausible and that they came from different quarters. William of Malmesbury, writing while Flambard was still alive, alleged that he made his monks dine with him on food forbidden by the rule, and that he had them served by attractive girls in body-hugging dresses. If the monks kept their eyes modestly cast down, Flambard accused them of hypocrisy; if they did not, he rebuked them for impropriety.[10] According to the biographer of Christina of Markyate, niece of Flambard's former wife or mistress, Flambard once sought to seduce her but was outwitted by the girl, who prudently locked the door of the chamber, with the frustrated bishop on the inside and herself safely outside.[11] It was with the help of another niece that, as was believed at Winchester, he escaped from the threat of deposition by the papal legate, John of Crema, in 1125. For Flambard arranged for the legate to be caught with the girl in compromising circumstances and, as the report drily concludes, Flambard was troubled no more over the threatened loss of his bishopric.[12] Offler justly observed that the evidence for the story about Christina would hardly have convicted Flambard in any court of law, and all these stories tell us more about the bishop's reputation than about his conduct.

To critics such as Orderic Vitalis Flambard was the oppressive minister of an impious king, a social upstart, almost illiterate, cruel and avaricious, too fond of food, drink and women. But Orderic also singled out his sharp intelligence, handsome looks, readiness as a speaker, and generosity to his servants and supporters. When Orderic came to account for the friends and helpers who assisted Flambard in his escape from the Tower, he conceded that he could often be generous and affable and that he had made himself widely liked.[13] Nevertheless, when we consider the judgements passed on Flambard by those who had served under him at Durham, it is difficult to recognize him as the same man who had been so widely vilified as Rufus's minister. The poet Laurence of Durham who as a young novice had known Bishop Ranulf and who rose to become prior in 1149, remembered the bishop as a great man under whom Durham had enjoyed a golden age.[14] A tribute from Laurence was worth having, for Laurence was no mere sycophant trying his hand at complimentary verses: he had been chaplain to Bishop Geoffrey, had kept the accounts, and was a talented administrator well qualified to appreciate Flambard's legacy to Durham. A fuller account of Flambard was given in the mid-twelfth century by a Durham monk in a continuation of the

[9] M. Brett, *The English Church under Henry I* (Oxford, 1975), p. 93; 'Annales monasterii de Wintonia' (hereafter 'Ann. Wint.') in *Annales Monastici*, ed. H.R. Luard (4 vols., RS 36; 1864–9), II, 47–8.

[10] William of Malmesbury, *De Gestis Pontificum Anglorum*, ed. N.E.S.A. Hamilton (RS 52; 1870), p. 274, n. 5.

[11] *The Life of Christina of Markyate*, ed. C.H. Talbot (Oxford, 1959), pp. 40–2.

[12] 'Ann. Wint.', pp. 47–8.

[13] *Orderic*, IV, 170–4; V. 312.

[14] *Dialogi Laurentii Dunelmensis monachi ac prioris*, ed. J. Raine (SS 70; 1880), p. 22.

history of the church of Durham which goes under the name of Symeon. While this stresses the jealousy and hostility which Flambard aroused as Rufus's minister, its judgements on him as bishop are almost wholly favourable. He vigorously defended the rights and privileges of the see; he was a great builder, not only in driving on the work on the cathedral but in constructing Framwellgate bridge in stone, in linking cathedral and castle by a defensive wall, and in establishing Norham castle. Flambard was generous to the poor, and perhaps the writer was thinking of the bishop's foundation of St Giles's church and its hospital.[15]

To this account of Flambard as a rich, powerful and conscientious bishop its author added some perceptive observations on Flambard's character and personality. He stressed Flambard's remarkable energy of mind and body. The bishop was never ill until his last two years, and all the reports bring out the sheer animal vitality which does so much to account for his resourcefulness and resilience in crises. He could be stern and intimidating, though like Rufus he assumed an angry demeanour rather than allowing himself to be dominated by his emotions. He was a quick-witted and persuasive speaker, though his hearers were not always certain whether he was serious or jesting – doubts which clever and confident men often arouse in those with slower minds.

One of Flambard's more attractive qualities was a strong sense of loyalty. According to the report of the attempt to assassinate Flambard in the Thames estuary, he had been enticed into the boat by being told that his old master, Maurice bishop of London, was ill, nearing his end, and anxious to see Flambard. Flambard's immediate response was the more creditable since the same account tells us that Flambard had left the bishop's service when disappointed of a deanship and had hoped for better things in royal service. Not everyone would have responded with this generosity of spirit. Not everyone did. Late in 1160, when Archbishop Theobald was in his last illness, he repeatedly urged Becket, then royal chancellor, to see him before he died. Becket owed a very great deal to Theobald and had been his favourite clerk. Nevertheless he did not respond: there was nothing to be gained from a dying man, and, as Theobald put it in a bitterly reproachful letter, 'the favour of the dead is generally of little value, and the memory of their services is as transitory as themselves.'[16]

Flambard was also loyal to the cause of his metropolitans, the archbishops of York, in their resistance to the claims of Canterbury to the primacy. On one occasion he was prepared to back his loyalty with his money, offering Henry I a bribe of over £700 (1,000 marks and 100 for the queen). But Henry refused, and it was uncharitably supposed at York that he knew that Canterbury would offer more.[17] Despite Flambard's independence on this issue he was not driven by Henry

[15] *Sym. Op.* I, 135–41. Flambard's responsibility for the first Framwellgate bridge is commemorated by a plaque on the bridge; but it is unfortunate that the authorities responsible should have supposed that his first name was Ralph, and that his episcopate began in 1100.
[16] *The Letters of John of Salisbury*, vol. I, ed. W.J. Millor and H.E. Butler, revised by C.N.L. Brooke (Oxford, 1986), no. 129.
[17] Hugh the Chanter, *The History of the Church of York, 1066–1127*, ed. and trans. C. Johnson, revised by M. Brett, C.N.L. Brooke, and M. Winterbottom (Oxford, 1990), p. 46.

into an internal exile at Durham. He attended the royal council at Nottingham in 1109 when the see of Ely was created.[18] In December 1115 he was with Henry at St Albans and joined Robert Bloet, Roger of Salisbury, and Richard Belmeis in consecrating the new abbey church, making up a quartet of bishops with a varied and unrivalled record of service to the Norman monarchy.[19] In 1119 Flambard was in Normandy and was a member of the delegation sent by Henry to represent his interests at the papal council of Rheims, held in October.[20] Henry rightly suspected that Louis VI and the French would seek to recover by diplomacy what they had lost on the battlefield of Brémule two months previously. Even William of Malmesbury, who had been so severe on Flambard as Rufus's minister, conceded that his achievements as a bishop had won some glory for him; and he accordingly classed Flambard among those prelates of the day whose efficiency in secular affairs did something to compensate for their spiritual laxity.[21]

When G.V. Scammell in his biography of Hugh of le Puiset, bishop of Durham from 1153 to 1195, considered the institutions and methods of government which underlay Puiset's opulence and magnificence, he concluded that Flambard had been their main architect.[22] Similarly Offler's slightly more cautious judgement was that 'study of Rannulf's management of the temporal affairs of the bishopric leaves the impression of a dominant and designing intelligence.'[23] It is therefore worth while asking whether Flambard, as Rufus's minister, had made any decisive and enduring contribution to the structure and methods of central government. By the late twelfth century, in the age of Glanville and Hubert Walter, there were two centres of royal government. There was the itinerant headquarters staff with the king, primarily concerned with war, diplomacy, and the exercise of political management through the distribution of patronage and penalties; and in England there was a fixed central government, its routine supervised by the chief justiciar, remarkably effective in mobilizing men, materials and money, and, for most of the time, in preserving internal order. It was distinguished above all by its capacity to obtain and to exploit tested information, by the practice of despatching members of the central administration on circuit throughout the country as justices or commissioners, and by the use of the sworn inquest and the enforcement of the set rules and procedures familiar to readers of the *Dialogue of the Exchequer* and of the treatise which goes under Glanville's name.

What part did Flambard play in the evolution of this central government? Was he in effect chief justiciar in the sense of presiding over and directing the men controlling royal finance and justice? Were these men members of an institution which in the twelfth century became known as the exchequer? In raising money for Rufus was Flambard merely predatory and extortionate, or did he bring an

---

[18] *Regesta*, II, no. 919.
[19] Ibid., no. 1102.
[20] *Fl. Wig.*, II, 73.
[21] William of Malmesbury, *De Gestis Regum Anglorum*, ed. W. Stubbs (2 vols., RS 90; 1887–9), II, 517; and Malmesbury, *De Gestis Pontificum*, pp. 274–5.
[22] G.V. Scammell, *Hugh du Puiset, Bishop of Durham* (Cambridge, 1956), p. 219.
[23] Offler, 'Rannulf Flambard as Bishop of Durham', p. 20.

inventive and even reforming approach to the problems of finance? Was he indeed, as Sir Richard Southern concluded, 'the first outstandingly successful administrator in English history'?[24]

This claim requires qualification. No evidence has survived to indicate that Flambard had any part in any of the stages in the making of Domesday Book. The principles and methods of financial and judicial administration exemplified in the Domesday survey were already those which underlay so much of Angevin administration: the division of the country into manageable circuits; the assignment to each of a body of powerful commissioners provided with a searching questionnaire; the obtaining of answers by methods which included empanelling jurors on oath; the checking of the information and its reduction into, as far as possible, a uniform and usable digest. In all the work on Domesday, much of it occasioned by the novocentenary in 1986, not enough has been made of the great survey as a landmark in administration, though Galbraith had noted that it anticipated the general eyres of a later period.[25] Galbraith's hypothesis of 'a single mind' behind Domesday was accepted and elaborated by Pierre Chaplais who postulated an individual 'with vice-regal powers' who 'directed the whole Domesday campaign' and supervised the final compilation. Chaplais adduced strong palaeographical evidence identifying this individual as William of St Calais, bishop of Durham, the man we know to have headed the panel of Domesday commissioners for the southwestern counties. Chaplais also offered the plausible suggestion that the bishop's exile in 1088 would explain the failure to complete Great Domesday. He also noted that after the bishop's restoration to favour in 1091 every writ referring to Domesday Book was witnessed by William of St Calais, just as similar writs of Henry I were witnessed by Roger of Salisbury. This led Chaplais to surmise that William of St Calais had been granted the powers, though not the title, of the justiciarship in 1091 or shortly afterwards.[26]

If so, he was being restored to a position given to him by Rufus at the very outset of the reign. Several sources agree that Rufus then took Bishop William as his chief counsellor, and, according to William of Malmesbury, precisely the powers of the later justiciarship, the *administratio rerum publicarum*, were conferred on the bishop.[27] It was natural that Rufus should delegate the management of the central administration to the man who had planned and supervised the Domesday survey; it was natural that Odo of Bayeux, who had enjoyed viceregal powers before his arrest in 1082, should have resented being passed over and have led a rebellion; and when William of St Calais joined in that rebellion, or at least withdrew to the sidelines, it was natural that he should have been singled out for a state trial. Historians like to look for origins, and if we are looking for the origins of the twelfth-century justiciarship, there is a good case for dividing the credit between

[24] Southern, 'Ranulf Flambard', p. 188.
[25] V.H. Galbraith, *The Making of Domesday Book* (Oxford, 1961), p. 59.
[26] P. Chaplais, 'William of Saint-Calais and the Domesday Survey', in *Domesday Studies*, ed. J.C. Holt (Woodbridge, 1987), pp. 65–77.
[27] Malmesbury, *De Gestis Regum*, II, 360.

Rufus and William of St Calais: Rufus because he understood the need to delegate, and Bishop William because he had shown what one man could do in planning and carrying out an administrative operation along lines which Hubert Walter would have found familiar.

It cannot therefore be held that Flambard was the first man to see the possibilities of concentrating powers in a way which anticipated the chief justiciarship of the late twelfth century. A different line of argument is that Flambard cannot have made a major contribution to later methods of government since his practices were condemned and renounced by Henry I in his coronation charter, and since a fresh start was made with the emergence of Roger of Salisbury as chief minister and the simultaneous appearance of the exchequer. But the coronation charter was a hastily drafted bid for support, not a programme of action; and a glance at the surviving Pipe Roll of the reign shows that the charter had been forgotten once the initial crisis had been surmounted. Moreover Flambard was a convenient and isolated scapegoat. As Professor Hollister pointed out, Rufus's most active administrators who had worked closely with Flambard – Robert fitz Haimo, Roger Bigod, Haimo *dapifer*, Eudo *dapifer*, and Urse d'Abetot – passed readily and immediately into Henry's service.[28] So too did Robert Bloet, William Giffard, Hugh of Buckland, and William Warelwast. Long ago A.L. Poole called attention to the fact that in 1110 Henry I sent a writ to the barons of the exchequer witnessed by Roger of Salisbury. He held that the word 'exchequer', of which this is the first appearance, indicated a great advance in financial organization, and that the witness was the author of this development.[29] For Lady Stenton the exchequer, as both a permanent financial bureau and a court of justice, was a momentous innovation, the outstanding achievement of Henry's reign, primarily the creation of Roger of Salisbury.[30] Richardson and Sayles were independently to state this thesis with characteristic vigour and some inconsistency.[31]

Twelfth-century writers did not draw a sharp distinction between Flambard and Roger of Salisbury. Between 1123 and 1126, when Roger was acting as viceroy in England, he called himself *procurator* of England.[32] William of Malmesbury, writing while Flambard was still alive, referred to him as having been made *procurator* of the whole kingdom, while both the Durham monk and Orderic Vitalis mentioned Flambard's appointment as *procurator*.[33] For Henry of Huntingdon Roger of Salisbury was justiciar of all England and second after the king, while the

---

[28] J.C. Holt, *Magna Carta*, 2nd edn (Cambridge, 1992), pp. 37–8; Hollister, 'Anglo-Norman Civil War', p. 81.

[29] A.L. Poole, *From Domesday Book to Magna Carta, 1087–1216* (Oxford, 1951), p. 416.

[30] D.M. Stenton, *English Justice between the Norman Conquest and the Great Charter, 1066–1215* (London, 1965), pp. 59–60.

[31] H.G. Richardson and G.O. Sayles, *The Governance of Mediaeval England from the Conquest to Magna Carta* (Edinburgh, 1963), p. 159.

[32] Kealey, *Roger of Salisbury*, appendix 2, nos. 9 and 10; Malmesbury, *De Gestis Pontificum*, p. 274; *Sym. Op.* I, 135; *Orderic*, V, 310; David Bates, 'The Origins of the Justiciarship', *AN* 4 (1981), p. 11.

[33] Malmesbury, *De Gestis Pontificum*, p. 274; *Sym. Op.* I, 135; *Orderic*, V, 310.

biographer of Christina of Markyate applied almost the same words to Flambard – *totius Anglie iudex, secundus post regem*.[34] Just as the Battle Abbey chronicler described Roger as administering the royal rights throughout England, so the Anglo-Saxon chronicler had Flambard driving and managing the king's courts throughout England.[35] Those writers who described Flambard as holding a definite position as head of the administration, second to the king, were presumably thinking of the last few years of Rufus's reign. For when Rufus left for Normandy in November 1097 he appointed Flambard together with Bishop Walkelin of Winchester as regents.[36] Two months later Walkelin died, and in the summer of 1099 Flambard's pre-eminence was recognized and rewarded with the bishopric of Durham. It is not easy to explain away this evidence. A possible hypothesis is that the twelfth-century writers, knowing of Roger's authority and accepting Flambard as the villain of Rufus's reign, improperly assumed that what they knew to be true of Roger had also applied to Flambard. This is implausible. It is unlikely that both William of Malmesbury and Orderic Vitalis knew that Roger had been *procurator*, though they never said so, and applied the term to Flambard without justification.

The first appearance of the term 'exchequer' in the records in 1110 has long seemed to historians to mark a decisive stage in the history of English administration, to point to the contrast between the purely personal authority of Flambard dependent upon his bustling and imperious energy, and the quiet efficiency of the institution of which the elaborate structure and careful rules were described in the *Dialogue of the Exchequer*. One scrap of evidence seems to me to weaken the force of this contrast. The famous writ for the Worcester relief of 1095 was cited by Round as showing Flambard 'actually at work'. It imposed sums ranging from £40 to £1 on the tenants of the bishopric, to produce a total of £250. 'It is now my will', Rufus was made to say, 'that you should give me from your lands such a relief as I have determined by the agency of my barons (*per barones meos*)' and there immediately followed the list of names with the figure for which each was liable.[37] The natural explanation of the expression *per barones meos* is that it was shorthand for, or an anticipation of, *per barones meos de scaccario*, the members of the central board of audit, as they were termed in a writ of Henry I.[38] Flambard is commonly found acting together with such men as Bishop Walkelin, Bishop Robert Bloet, Robert fitz Haimo, Haimo *dapifer*, and Urse d'Abetot. Not even Flambard could hope to run finance and justice single-handedly, assisted only by a few junior clerks; and we should think of the exchequer of Henry I's reign not as a sudden creation but as the product of developments which began at least as early as Flambard's ministry.

---

[34] Henry of Huntingdon, *Historia Anglorum*, ed. T. Arnold (RS 74; 1879), p. 245; *Christina of Markyate*, p. 40.

[35] *The Chronicle of Battle Abbey*, ed. and trans. E. Searle (Oxford, 1980), p. 132; *ASC, s.a.* 1099.

[36] 'Ann. Wint.', pp. 39–40.

[37] J.H. Round, *Feudal England* (London, 1895), pp. 308–9.

[38] *Regesta*, II, no. 1538. I first made this suggestion in J.O. Prestwich, 'War and Finance in the Anglo-Norman State', *TRHS*, 5th ser. 4 (1954), p. 30.

The years from 1086 to 1106 were years of almost uninterrupted crises for the Anglo-Norman state, years marked by the rivalries between the Conqueror's three sons; the separation of Normandy from England for most of these years; the hostility of neighbouring powers; the frustrations of the second generation of the lay aristocracy who, like Roger of Hereford as early as 1075, inherited diminished powers and increasing dangers; the independent ambitions of reforming bishops and a reformed papacy; all combined to present almost insoluble problems to the rulers and their servants. Flambard's contribution to the survival of the Anglo-Norman monarchy was to provide the treasure with which to hire troops, to pay ransoms, to build and garrison castles, to secure allies, to bribe enemies, to reward supporters, and to impress subjects. Westminster Hall was just as much an instrument of power as was the Tower of London, and Rufus's much publicized extravagance and ostentation were as much the product of policy as of temperament. We never hear of Rufus's enterprises being impeded for lack of money as those of Edward I so frequently were. According to William of Malmesbury Rufus's reputation for wealth and extravagance spread throughout the western world and even reached the east.[39] To Suger Rufus was 'that wealthy man, a pourer out of English treasures', sharply contrasted with the impecunious Louis of France. Suger exaggerated when he claimed that Rufus could put at least twenty times as many knights into the field as could young Louis, who was thereby made to appear all the more valiant.[40] But Barlow's estimate that Rufus enjoyed an ordinary annual cash revenue of approximately £29,000, rising in his last four years to perhaps double this figure, indicates a formidable financial achievement.[41]

There are indications that Flambard did more than merely exploit existing sources of revenue to the limit. Some of his methods were ingenious but ephemeral, such as the reported mobilization of 20,000 English infantry at Hastings in 1094, when Flambard took 10s. from each, sending the men home and the money across the Channel to Rufus.[42] Similar ingenuity lay behind the Worcester relief of 1095, and again there is no good evidence that any attempt was made to repeat this. A more lucrative practice and one which later rulers were to value and to develop was that of the exploitation of regalian right, the seizure for the crown of vacant bishoprics and abbeys, diverting revenues into the hands of royal custodians after providing for the maintenance of the monks or cathedral chapter.[43] Both William of Malmesbury and Orderic Vitalis believed that Flambard was responsible for Rufus making this a regular policy. Certainly Flambard was active in this field from the beginning of the reign, taking control of Hyde abbey in Winchester in 1088, and of the archbishopric of Canterbury in 1089. By 1097 he was said, probably rightly, to have brought sixteen vacant monasteries and bishoprics under

---

[39] Malmesbury, *De Gestis Regum*, II, 368.
[40] Suger, *Vie de Louis VI le Gros*, ed. and trans. H. Waquet (Paris, 1964), p. 8.
[41] Barlow, *William Rufus*, p. 259.
[42] *ASC, s.a.* 1094.
[43] M. Howell, *Regalian Right in Medieval England* (London, 1961), pp. 5–19.

his control,[44] and it has been estimated that by the end of the reign he was producing about a fifth of Rufus's revenue from England from this source.[45] No doubt the anguished protests in many churches were justified: when annual auctions were held for the right to exploit estates during vacancies the successful bidders had every reason to be ruthless. But exploitation was not uniform. In the long vacancy at Durham after the death of William of St Calais Rufus took £300 p.a. from the temporalities but nothing from the monks, who were protected and treated generously.[46] It is tempting to suppose that Flambard had already been promised the bishopric.

Flambard showed how the great wealth of the church could be tapped for the monarchy, and the lesson was not forgotten. Regalian right remained an important source of revenue down to the fourteenth century. Moreover it was not the only, and perhaps not the most lucrative, method of exploiting the resources of the church. Flambard was held to be responsible for the policy of selling bishoprics and abbacies, and he himself paid £1,000 for Durham.[47] We are told that by 1097 he not only had sixteen bishoprics and monasteries in his hands during vacancies, but was also extracting between £200 and £300 from each of the others.[48] Sometimes there were legal grounds: the abbot of Abingdon owed £300 to the crown in 1095 as surety for an absconded tenant.[49] Sometimes the money was just demanded, as when Bishop Walkelin of Winchester was required to pay £200 at the end of 1097.[50]

Flambard was undoubtedly the main agent in the financial exploitation of the church, and probably, as William of Malmesbury believed, the author of the methods employed. Was he also the author of an attempt to reform the land tax, the levies of geld? Orderic Vitalis believed that he was, and his statement that Flambard successfully persuaded Rufus to revise the Domesday assessment and accordingly increased the burden of taxation deserves respect, even though the account of a fresh division of the land in the interests of the crown must be rejected.[51] It deserves respect because Orderic used the official term for the Domesday survey, *descriptio totius Anglie*, the term which appears in Domesday Book and in a writ of the Conqueror.[52] Flambard certainly relied on the geld in 1096 in order to raise the 10,000 marks which Rufus lent to Robert Curthose, Rufus receiving Normandy as security during Robert's absence on crusade. Some historians have supposed that in addition to the geld of 4s. on the hide there was also a feudal aid; but the *Leges Edwardi Confessoris* makes it clear that the levy was an aid granted in

---

[44] *Orderic*, IV, 174–6; Malmesbury, *De Gestis Regum* II, 369; 'Ann. Wint.', pp. 36–9.

[45] Barlow, *William Rufus*, p. 259.

[46] *Sym. Op.* I, 135.

[47] Malmesbury, *De Gestis Pontificum*, p. 274, n. 3.

[48] 'Ann. Wint.', p. 39.

[49] *Chronicon Monasterii de Abingdon*, ed. J. Stevenson (2 vols., RS 2; 1858), II, 38.

[50] 'Ann. Wint.', p. 37.

[51] *Orderic*, IV, 172.

[52] *DB* I, 3a, 164a, 252a, 269a; *DB* II, 450; and *Facsimiles of Royal Writs to A.D.1100*, ed. T.A.M. Bishop and P. Chaplais (Oxford, 1957), plate xxiv.

the form of the 4s. geld, just as the aid in 1110 for the marriage of Henry I's daughter, Matilda, to the emperor Henry V was levied in the form of a geld of 3s. on the hide.[53]

Moreover the Worcester chronicler makes it clear that the geld of 1096 was levied on the Domesday plan, making the greater tenants-in-chief responsible for its collection and payment, a method continued under Henry I.[54] As Maitland put it long ago, 'for one reason the king can not easily tax the rich; for another he can not easily tax the poor; so he gets at the poor through the rich.'[55] One argument against the view that the Domesday survey had been intended to lead to a reform of the geld is that no such reform, no systematic reassessment, ever occurred. It is however invalid to argue back from results to intentions, and in any case by 1130 there had been major reassessments in Berkshire, Surrey, and Hampshire, while some individuals were offering large sums to avoid reassessment.[56] Flambard may have made some experiments, but it is probable that he used the Domesday survey to enforce the collection of the geld in full, not to reform the system. That there was no general reform has recently been described as 'the greatest failure of Norman government'.[57] But this is to ignore the political dimension. To reform a land tax in which great landholders are politically strong is exceptionally difficult. It was attempted in 1198, but in county after county we read of compositions being paid in order that the reforming inquest should not be held; and it was not.[58] Elizabeth I complained of the notorious underassessment of so many of her richer subjects. But in the debate of 1593 Raleigh protested against the obvious remedy, saying that it would be 'inconvenient to have so many men's livings surveyed'; and they were not surveyed.[59]

What then were Flambard's achievements? As an administrator he did not possess the creative abilities of William of St Calais or Hubert Walter. But he demonstrated what could be achieved when the supervision of finance and justice

---

[53] For the disagreements over the nature of this levy see Barlow, *William Rufus*, p. 246, n. 139. The evidence of the *Leges Edwardi* combined with that of Henry of Huntingdon, *Historia Anglorum*, p. 237, on the aid of 1110 appears conclusive. On the latter see K.J. Leyser, *Medieval Germany and its Neighbours, 900–1250* (London, 1982), pp. 194–5 and 195, n. 2, where he notes with faint surprise that the first aid *pour fille marier* should have been levied as a geld and not on the knight's fee. Unlike most historians neither Flambard in 1096 nor Roger of Salisbury in 1110 was impeded by the concept of feudalism.

[54] *Fl. Wig.* II, 40. For the practice under Henry I see for example *Chron. Abingdon*, II, 125, and *Regesta*, II, no. 576.

[55] F.W. Maitland, *Domesday Book and Beyond* (Cambridge, 1897), pp. 121–2.

[56] J.A. Green, 'The Last Century of Danegeld', *EHR* 96 (1981), p. 253.

[57] W.L. Warren, 'The Myth of Norman Administrative Efficiency', *TRHS*, 5th ser. 34 (1984), p. 130.

[58] *Pipe Roll 1 John*, ed. D.M. Stenton (Pipe Roll Soc., 48, n.s. 10; London, 1933), pp. xix–xx.

[59] *Tudor Economic Documents*, ed. R.H. Tawney and E. Power (London, 1924), II, 233, 238. Sir Henry Knyvet had suggested 'a survey of all mens Lands and Goods in England, and so much to be yearly levied as to serve the Queen to maintain wars'. The Normans may have been inefficient, but they did at least carry out their survey, unlike their successors five centuries later.

was entrusted to a single man with Flambard's energy, resilience, and nerve, and he commanded Rufus's confidence as William of St Calais never did. Indeed William of St Calais was threatened with a second state trial in Rufus's court just before his death at the beginning of 1096, according to William of Malmesbury, and perhaps, like Hubert Walter a century later, he had been troubled by the mounting cost of war and the resulting political difficulties.[60] Flambard had no such doubts, and his unfailing ability to provide Rufus with the resources he required both enabled the Anglo-Norman state to survive the military, political, and ideological challenges of these years and made possible the reunion of England and Normandy in 1096. Moreover Flambard's achievements in the latter years of the reign must be measured against the economic distress caused by the succession of bad harvests from 1095 to 1098. He was an administrator, not a politician, without the breadth of vision possessed by Robert of Beaumont, count of Meulan. But of the two he had the more genial temperament. He was hospitable, generous to the poor, and devoted to the interests of the numerous members of his family, sometimes unwisely. Two great monuments to his financial ability and executive energy survive: Westminster Hall commemorating the minister and Durham cathedral the bishop.

---

[60] Malmesbury, *De Gestis Pontificum*, p. 273. Barlow rejects William of Malmesbury's report, partly because it wrongly places the Christmas court, to which William of St Calais was allegedly summoned, at Gloucester, but chiefly because, in Barlow's view, the imputation of treachery is unthinkable (Barlow, *William Rufus*, p. 354, n. 54). However, William of Malmesbury's mistake over the Christmas court is readily explicable, since he supposed that Rufus followed the Conqueror in invariably holding his Christmas court at Gloucester whenever he was in England, so for William, if it was Christmas, it must be Gloucester (Malmesbury, *De Gestis Regum*, II, 335). William of St Calais may well have remained loyal during the rebellion of 1095, but his name could nevertheless have been included in the second list of conspirators provided by Morel (*ASC, s.a.* 1095).

The Kings of Scotland and Durham

G. W. S. BARROW

I N THE WHOLE of Scotland there was only one known pre-Reformation dedication to St Wilfrid,[1] despite the friendly relations which existed in the earlier
Middle Ages between the church of Hexham and the kings and nobles of Scotland.
The dedication, appropriately enough, was at Abercorn in West Lothian, where
about 675 a bishopric for the Picts was established under Northumbrian auspices,[2]
clearly intended as a counterpoise to the Iona-based (or at least Scottish-based)
churches active in the Pictish kingdom from the Firth of Forth to Orkney and
Shetland.

A very different picture emerges if we turn to Scottish dedications to St
Cuthbert. In Scotland besouth Forth thirty-six pre-Reformation dedications to
Cuthbert are known,[3] three of which at least are relatively late (thirteenth-century
or later),[4] while a good many others may be not earlier than 1100 or 1150.[5] A
number of Cuthbert sites are unquestionably ancient, and there seems no reason to
doubt that the association with Cuthbert may go back to the ninth century or even
earlier. Among these eight sites we might list Channelkirk and Eccles in Berwickshire,[6] Maxton and Ednam in Roxburghshire,[7] St Cuthbert under the castle of
Edinburgh,[8] Dalmeny beside South Queensferry,[9] St Cuthbert of Desnesmor in

[1] J.M. Mackinlay, *Ancient Church Dedications in Scotland: Non-scriptural dedications* (Edinburgh, 1914), p. 264.
[2] *HE*, bk. 1, ch. 12 (pp. 42 and 428).
[3] Mackinlay, *Ancient Church Dedications*, pp. 247–58; and A. Hamilton Thompson, 'The
Manuscript List of Churches Dedicated to Saint Cuthbert Attributed to Prior Wessyngton',
TAASDN 7 (1936), pp. 172–3.
[4] Chapels in Moffat, Drummelzier, and Sorn (Mackinlay, *Ancient Church Dedications*, pp.
252 and 256–7).
[5] Information regarding Scottish church dedications is seldom available for the period before
c.1100 unless the dedication is embodied in a place-name. Mackinlay, *Ancient Church Dedications*, pp. 250–6, lists a number of churches whose dedications to Cuthbert may date from
their foundation in the twelfth century.
[6] Mackinlay, *Ancient Church Dedications*, pp. 247–8 and 250.
[7] Ibid., p. 251.
[8] Ibid., pp. 253–4.
[9] Ibid., p. 255.

eastern Galloway, better known as Kirkcudbright,[10] Kirkcudbright of Glencairn[11] and Kirkcudbright-Innertig, otherwise Ballantrae in south Ayrshire.[12]

Although dedications to Cuthbert are rare north of the Forth, his cult seems to have been observed in Strathtay[13] – where a number of saints of Lindisfarne are commemorated, e.g. at Fortingall and Logierait[14] – and the fact that the chaplain of Kilconquhar and dean of Christianity of Fife in the 1170s and 1180s bore the name Gillecuthbert[15] demonstrates that the cult was established in east Fife.

In the Jacksonian sense in which the Gododdin of Aneurin can be described as the 'oldest Scottish poem'[16] – and perhaps in a rather stronger sense – Cuthbert may be claimed as one of the greatest and most influential of Scottish saints. Brought up from the age of eight in a settlement on the edge of Lammermuir which was aligned west to east and had a name corruptly transmitted as 'Hruringa-ham'[17] – circumstances which might tempt us to identify it as Whittingehame[18] – Cuthbert received his training and promotion in the strongly Scottish-dominated monastery of Old Melrose. Neither the history of Melrose nor the Scottish dimension in the beginnings of the Northumbrian church were enough to dissuade Scottish kings from raiding and plundering right across the territory rich in factual and legendary associations with Aedán, Finán, Eata, Boisil, and Cuthbert. Assuming that the cult of Cuthbert in northern England and southern Scotland was established long before the twelfth century, it may also be inferred that the cult was genuinely popular and not fostered by secular rulers.

The surviving evidence, admittedly not abundant, gives no hint of any devotion to Cuthbert on the part of Scottish rulers of the Cenél nGabráin, who held sway in Alba from the mid-ninth century. In marked contrast, the house of Wessex adopted Cuthbert with enthusiasm at least from the time of Athelstan.[19] Moreover, a long tradition of Durham historians built up a picture of Cuthbert as the defender not merely of his own church and clergy but of the whole of Northumbria against the

[10] Ibid., pp. 247 and 256. For Desnesmor see *Wigtownshire Charters*, ed. R.C. Reid (Scottish History Society, 3rd ser. 51; Edinburgh, 1960), pp. xix–xxi.
[11] Mackinlay, *Ancient Church Dedications*, p. 256.
[12] Ibid.
[13] Ibid., p. 257. The church of Weem is said to have been dedicated to Cuthbert.
[14] Ibid., pp. 239–40 and 260. But W.J. Watson, *The History of the Celtic Place-names of Scotland* (Edinburgh, 1926), p. 314, attributes the dedication place-names in Fortingall and Logierait not to the brothers Cedd and Chad but to Coeddi, bishop at Iona, who died in 712. On general grounds this may be thought more probable.
[15] *Liber cartarum prioratus S. Andree in Scotia* (Bannatyne Club; Edinburgh, 1841), pp. 137, 175, 179–80 and 259–60; *Carte monialium de North Berwic* (Bannatyne Club; Edinburgh, 1847), no. 4.
[16] K.H. Jackson, *The Gododdin. The Oldest Scottish Poem* (Edinburgh, 1969).
[17] *Two Lives of Saint Cuthbert*, ed. and trans. B. Colgrave (Cambridge, 1940), pp. 90 and 323.
[18] If OE *wenn* following the initial h, and a subsequent t, were both misread as r, an original 'hwit(t)ingaham' underlying modern Whittingehame, E. Lothian, might have been copied as *Hruringaham*; but Whittingehame may be thought to lie too far from the valley of the Leader Water where Cuthbert's origins are probably to be located.
[19] *HSC*, § 26 (pp. 211–12).

Scots. From the mid-tenth century 'St Cuthbert's Land' or 'Haliweresfolc' had evidently lost its grip upon the territories benorth Tweed to which it had once laid claim – that is, the land between Whitadder and Leader Waters and even St Baldred's Land between Tynninghame and Inveresk.[20] Yet at the turn of the eleventh and twelfth centuries it must have been well understood that St Cuthbert did have claims upon parts of Berwickshire and Roxburghshire, e.g. Coldingham, Ednam, Edrom, and Earlston.[21] If Duncan II's charter of 1094 is authentic, the Scots recognised a Cuthbertine claim to Tynninghame in East Lothian,[22] and David I undoubtedly recognised a Durham claim to Old Melrose and Swinton as late as the 1130s.[23]

The first king of Scots to show any reverence towards St Cuthbert seems to have been Malcolm III, and that only at the very end of his life, after he had personally led four savagely destructive raids the length and breadth of English Northumbria. A Durham tradition, reported by the monk Reginald in his book of the saint's miracles, tells us that Cuthbert was one of the saints whom Margaret, Malcolm III's queen, held in special reverence.[24] How far we should attribute this to the influence of Turgot can only be speculation. He is known to have venerated the Bernician saints from the early 1070s,[25] and, before becoming prior of Durham, apparently served Margaret in the later years of her life as chaplain or confessor.[26] It may well have been Margaret who persuaded her husband to treat St Cuthbert with greater respect. At all events, on 11 August 1093 the only layman to take part in the laying of the foundation stones of the new cathedral at Durham was Malcolm, king of Scots.[27] It is surely to this occasion that we should date the bond of confraternity solemnized between the Durham community and the Scottish royal house, the text of which was copied into the *Liber Vitae*:

---

[20] G.W.S. Barrow, *The Kingdom of the Scots* (London, 1973), pp. 152–3; and *HSC*, § 4 (p. 199).

[21] For Coldingham, see below. Durham's claims on Ednam, Edrom and Earlston are demonstrated by documents edited by James Raine, *The History and Antiquities of North Durham* (London, 1852), Appendix, nos. 102, 161, and 162 (Ednam); 19, 20, 21, 40, 41, 111, and 112 (Edrom); 116, 164, and 165 (Earlston).

[22] *ESC*, no. 12; A.A.M. Duncan, 'The Earliest Scottish Charters', *Scottish Historical Review* 37 (1958), pp. 118–25; J. Donnelly, 'The Earliest Scottish Charters?', *Scot. Hist. Rev.* 68 (1989), pp. 1–22.

[23] *ESC*, nos. 99, 100, and 101. The choice of Holm Cultram in Cumberland as the site for a daughter house of Melrose Abbey in 1150 was probably influenced by a Durham tradition that this place had belonged to Lindisfarne from early times, if 'Culterham' is to be identified as Cultram (*HReg, s.a.* 854 (p. 101).

[24] *Cuth. virt.*, ch. 8 (pp. 217–18).

[25] *LDE*, bk. 3, chs. 21–2 (pp. 108–13).

[26] A.O. Anderson, *Early Sources of Scottish History* (Edinburgh, 1922), II, 59, 65, and 74–5.

[27] *HReg, s.a.* 1093 (p. 220), and *History of Northumberland*, VIII, ed. H.H.E. Craster (Newcastle upon Tyne, 1907), p. 120n. In the account given in the *LDE*, bk. 4, ch. 8 (*Sym. Op.* I, 129) Malcolm III's name is omitted. The propensity of the Durham writers to think ill of the Scots gives the positive statement greater weight here than the negative.

This is the covenant which the convent of Saint Cuthbert has promised to Malcolm, king of Scots, and to Queen Margaret, and to their sons and daughters, to keep for ever. Namely that, on behalf of the king and queen, while they are alive, one poor man shall be nourished daily, and likewise two poor men shall be maintained for them on Thursday in Holy Week at the common maundy, and a collect said at the litanies and at mass. Further, that they both, in this life and after, they and their sons and daughters, shall be partakers in all things that be to the service of God in the monastery of St Cuthbert, that is to say in masses, in psalms and alms, in vigils and prayers and in all things that are of this kind. And for the king and queen individually, from the day of their death there shall be thirty full offices of the dead in the convent, and *Verba mea* shall be done every day, and each priest shall sing thirty masses and each of the rest ten psalters; and their anniversary shall be celebrated as an annual festival like that of King Athelstan.[28]

What has not been noticed, as far as I am aware, is that the hand in which this quite elaborate covenant was copied into the *Liber Vitae*, presumably in August 1093 or not much later, appears to be identical with the hand of King Duncan II's famous but problematical charter of 1094, and also of one version of William Rufus's confirmation of King Edgar's extremely generous grant of 1095.[29] The scribe who wrote this distinctive hand was identified by Bishop and Chaplais as a favoured clerk of Bishop William of St Calais, also called William, who was responsible for the production of two manuscripts still extant in the library of the Dean and Chapter.[30] It looks very much as though under Bishop William, and closely associated with him, there was a determined drive by Durham to link the ruling dynasty of Scotland with St Cuthbert and his community. At first this link was forged with Malcolm and Margaret, but when within four months of the founding of the cathedral he had been ambushed and slain near Alnwick while she had died, grief-stricken, in Edinburgh, the ties had perforce to be renewed with Malcolm's first-born son Duncan 'constans hereditarie rex Scotie'. In Duncan's one and only charter it is Durham that is declaring the new king's legitimacy, Durham providing the trusted scribe, Durham doubtless fashioning the king's equestrian seal, and Durham making sure that it will receive a sizeable slice of Scottish territory.[31] The attempt to put Duncan II on the throne of his ancestors failed,

---

[28] *Liber Vitae*, fol. 48v; in the edition by J. Stevenson (SS 13; 1841), the *conuentio* appears on p. 73.

[29] I wrote this in the summer of 1993, still unaware that Mr Michael Gullick had identified the hand of the *conuentio* between Durham and the king and queen of Scots as that of the scribe who wrote the Durham Martyrology (DCL, MS B.IV.24), whom he identifies as Symeon of Durham. If Mr Gullick is right, the point made here, of a close connection between Bishop William of St Calais and the Scottish royal house in the persons of Malcolm, Margaret, Duncan II, and Edgar, remains valid, because William the scribe and Symeon were both in Bishop William's service, having been brought by him to Durham from Normandy. See pp. 102–4.

[30] *Facsimiles of English Royal Writs to A.D. 1100, presented to Vivian Hunter Galbraith*, ed. T.A.M. Bishop and P. Chaplais (Oxford, 1957), pl. VIII (*a*), note. DCDCM, Misc. Ch. 554.

[31] See above, n. 22.

fatally for him personally. Durham pressure, apparently with the backing of William Rufus, now centred upon Duncan's half-brother Edgar – passing over the presumably older Edmund (who had sided with his uncle Domhnall Bán) and Aethelred, perhaps in some way unsuitable for secular rule.[32]

We may accept that Duncan II's charter is authentic provided that we realise that King Duncan was not in the business of issuing or sealing charters. The document is a unique Durham production, authentic only in the sense that it records a gift which the king of Scots freely and willingly made. It is a different matter when we consider the charter which King Edgar issued – or which at least records the grant which King Edgar made – in the graveyard of St Cuthbert's church at Norham on Tweed on 29 August 1095.[33] The grant involved was the extremely liberal, indeed prodigal, one of Coldinghamshire *and* Berwickshire. While I would accept Joseph Donnelly's arguments for rejecting Edgar's own charter as a forgery, made possibly as late as the thirteenth century,[34] I also accept, with Donnelly,[35] that an authentic confirmation by William Rufus, surviving in duplicate originals,[36] proves that the two shires were given to St Cuthbert by Edgar before he had vindicated his claim to the Scottish throne.[37] Had not relations between the king of Scots and the see of Durham deteriorated sharply with the advent of Ranulf Flambard in 1099 Edgar's generous grant might have stood, with consequences for the Scottish Crown and Anglo-Scottish relations at which we can only guess. Instead, Edgar deprived Flambard of Berwick and took away from his diocese the large district of Teviotdale, which seems to have been allocated immediately to Glasgow.[38]

Although Berwickshire did not stay with Durham, the monks, perhaps as some kind of compensation, had charters from Edgar for Paxton, Fishwick, and Swinton.[39] It would be unsafe to attribute to Edgar the curious anomaly that Wester Upsettlington, just across the Tweed from Norham, belonged to the diocese of Durham till the fourteenth century – the only Scottish parish in an English

---

[32] I consider it most probable that Margaret's first four sons, in order of their birth, were named respectively after grandfather (Edward), great-grandfather (Edmund), great-great-grandfather (Aethelred) and great-great-great-grandfather (Edgar). But the order of names in the Durham *Liber Vitae*, fol. 43 (ed. Stevenson, p. 54, col. 3 at foot), is Edward, Edgar, Edmund, Aethelred (*Aeilredus*).

[33] *ESC*, no. 15, DCDCM, Misc. Ch. 559 (see Duncan, 'The Earliest Scottish Charters', pp. 103–18; and Donnelly, 'The Earliest Scottish Charters', pp. 1–22).

[34] Ibid., pp. 21–2.

[35] Ibid., pp. 3–5 and 13.

[36] *Facsimiles of English Royal Writs*, ed. Bishop and Chaplais, pls. VIII (a) and IX.

[37] The fourteenth-century historian John Fordun evidently knew of evidence (perhaps one or more of the charters mentioned here) that Edgar had granted Coldinghamshire to the priory of Durham and Berwickshire to the bishop: see *Johannis de Fordun Chronica Gentis Scotorum*, ed. W.F. Skene (Edinburgh, 1871), I, 225.

[38] Ibid. See also, for Teviotdale, J. Raine, *Historians of the Church of York* (3 vols., RS 71; 1879–94), III, 37; *HReg, s.a.* 1072 (p. 198); and *Sym. Op.* I, 139 (first continuation of *LDE*); and *ESC*, no. 50 (esp. p. 46).

[39] Ibid., nos. 20, 21, and 22, DCDCM, Misc. Chs. 556, 557, 558.

diocese,[40] although of course Whithorn was a Scottish diocese in an English province, at least until the Wars of Independence.

The building of Norham Castle, which was to be a thorn in the side of the Scots for many centuries, is enough to show that Ranulf Flambard was no friend of the northern kingdom. Relations with the Durham monks, however, were on a quite different footing. In 1104 a signal favour was conferred upon King Edgar's younger brother Alexander, afterwards King Alexander I, when he was the only layman invited to witness the opening up of St Cuthbert's coffin.[41] Alexander's name figures in the *Liber Vitae* with special prominence, curiously enough with greater prominence than that of David I or for that matter of those of any of the kings of England and Scotland from the time of Athelstan.[42] David I does at least enjoy the unique distinction of appearing three times. On the first occasion his name is followed by those of his two grandsons 'Melcolm rex' and 'Willelmus Rex',[43] on the second by needless repetition: 'King David, Earl Henry his son, the younger King Malcolm of Scotland son of Earl Henry who was the son of David king of Scotland' – the whole entry being followed somewhat inconsequentially by 'Alice de Vere, Adam and William monks of Wenlock'.[44] On a third occasion, David appears in a list of the children of Malcolm and St Margaret, in which interestingly the older of his two sisters, better known to us as Matilda or Maud ('Good Queen Maud'), is given her baptismal name of Eadgith (Edith).[45]

The *Liber Vitae* was also used as a safe repository for copies of two Scottish documents, one of which was judged sufficiently important to be copied twice. The less important document is surely the oddest, least expected entry in the whole manuscript. It is a little brieve or writ of David I commanding Edward (the monk in charge of Coldingham before the priory was established) to supply enough logs to replenish the royal log-pile at Berwick upon Tweed from an unidentified wood, the ownership of which was in dispute between Coldingham and a local laird, Liulf son of Uhtred.[46] Since the brieve conferred no benefit but rather imposed a burden on Durham, and since the operation involved was surely a short-term matter, there seems to have been no motive for copying it into the *Liber Vitae* save as a mark of respect for King David.

The more important of the two pieces of Scottish record is a narrative statement that on 17 July 1127 Robert, bishop of St Andrews, at the special request of King David, had exempted the church of Coldingham for all time coming from

---

[40] I.B. Cowan, *The Parishes of Medieval Scotland* (Scottish Record Society, 93; Edinburgh, 1967), pp. 204–5.

[41] *De miraculis*, ch. 7 (*Sym. Op.* I, 258).

[42] *Liber Vitae*, fol. 12v.

[43] Ibid.

[44] Ibid., fols 12v–13 (at foot).

[45] Ibid., fol. 43.

[46] Ibid., fol. 47; and *ESC*, no. 174 (Lawrie mistakenly took *calang'* to be a place-name, whereas it is Old French for 'dispute', 'challenge'. Interestingly, it is embodied in the Staffordshire place-name Callingwood. The place-date 'Pebles' has been misread by Stevenson as 'Peples', a mistake repeated by Lawrie.)

episcopal aids and other services and particularly from the immemorial burdens, due to the bishop as a great Scottish lord, of *cáin* and *conveth*, that is to say tribute in respect of lordship together with compulsory seasonal hospitality.[47] In the bishopric of Durham these burdens would still have been very familiar in 1127 as cornage and waiting.[48] This exemption, to which the bishop was urged by King David, may well have been the most valuable of the benefits conferred upon Durham by the king. The grant was certainly made solemnly and publicly. Bishop Robert announced it before the door of St John the Evangelist's church at Roxburgh in the presence of King David, Archbishop Thurstan of York, Bishop Ranulf of Durham, Bishop John of Glasgow, Geoffrey abbot of St Albans, the prior and sub-prior of Durham, a cross-section of the parish priests of East Lothian and Berwickshire, and 'many others who were witnesses and were present when the bishop said these things'.[49] King David himself issued a sealed notification of the bishop's concession. Although the archives at Durham contain the largest single collection of original charters and brieves of King David, not one of them provides evidence of a major benefaction for which the king himself was responsible. But the comparative lack of enthusiasm shown towards Durham by the king of Scots must be set against a wider background of Scottish royal policy towards the North of England as a whole. This policy was clearly intended to supply the place previously filled by English kings. Today, at site after site throughout English

---

[47] *Liber Vitae*, fols 44 and 47. Lawrie did not print this, but gives the text of Bishop Robert's charter of exemption (*ESC*, no. 73, with incorrect date of St Kentigern's day instead of St Kenelm the martyr's day), also printed by Raine, *North Durham*, Appendix no. 446. The narrative adds the word *clerico* after *Rodberto*, the first witness, and lists Orm priest of Hume and Osbern priest of Ednam among the witnesses, as against the charter's Orm priest of Ednam which is probably an error. The narrative also adds the name of Robert sub-prior of Durham as convened by Bishop Robert along with Prior Algar. The narrative omits explicit reference to *cáin* and *coinnmheadh*.

[48] G.W.S. Barrow, *Scotland and its Neighbours* (London, 1992), pp. 140–8. W. Kapelle, *The Norman Conquest of the North: The Region and its Transformation 1000–1135* (Chapel Hill and London, 1979), pp. 60–1, argues that the *cáin* of eastern Scotland cannot be equated with cornage, since it 'was a general food render, principally of grain, not a cow render like cornage', and that 'there is no sign of royal *cáin*, cornage, or even peasant grain renders in Lothian and the Merse.' But Malcolm IV confirmed to Scone Abbey grants of woolfells, cow and ox hides and tallow, fat etc. from north of Lammermuir, and David I did the same for Dunfermline Abbey (*RRS*, I, 36), while David I granted to Kelso Abbey half of the animals slaughtered for his kitchen together with half the hides, this coming from Lothian, Tweeddale, Teviotdale, and the Merse. There is no reason to doubt that this represented *cáin*, which was explicitly what Bishop Robert of St Andrews claimed to have from Coldinghamshire. As for *conveth* or waiting, the fact that royal clerks seem to have preferred, for the English-speaking South East, the terms 'waiting' or *conredium* (*ESC*, no. 178) while the episcopal clerks used the Gaelic expressions *cáin* and *coinnmheadh* (for which see the episcopal exemptions in Raine, *North Durham*, Appendix, nos. 446, 462, 473, and 484 and the bulls of Adrian IV (3 February 1157) and Alexander III (no date) printed in *Papsturkunden in England*, ed. W. Holtzmann (3 vols., Berlin, 1930–52), II, nos. 94 and 202) may simply have been due to differing fashions of nomenclature.

[49] *Liber Vitae*, fols 44 and 47.

Northumbria, the tourist literature tells us of the destruction wrought by the Scots upon monasteries, churches, castles, and other monuments of antiquity. It is salutary, therefore, to remind ourselves of what the tourist literature does not tell us, namely that between them David I and his son were benefactors, sometimes on a substantial scale, of the Benedictine monks at Tynemouth, Holy Island, St Bees and Wetheral, of the Cistercian monks of Newminster and Holm Cultram, of the nuns of St Bartholomew in Newcastle upon Tyne and of Holystone in upper Coquetdale, of the Augustinian canons of Carlisle, Hexham, and Brinkburn, and of the hospital of the Blessed Virgin Mary in the Westgate of Newcastle.[50]

Where Durham is concerned, it is hard to avoid the impression that by the middle of David I's reign the atmosphere had changed since the days of Malcolm Canmore, St Margaret and William of St Calais. The unsympathetic episcopate of Flambard was followed, after a five year vacancy, by the eight year occupation of the see by Geoffrey Rufus. Bishop Geoffrey could hardly prevent the Scots taking possession of Northumbria in 1139 but he resisted King David's attempt to obtain an oath of fealty and to treat him as a subordinate bishop of Northumbria.[51] It looks as though David, even before Geoffrey's death in 1141, was manoeuvring to get his chancellor William Cumin (formerly a clerk in Geoffrey Rufus's household) elected as Geoffrey's successor.[52] Cumin, as is well known, overplayed his hand woefully and was quickly disowned by a somewhat chastened Scottish king.[53] But the whole episode, coming as it did after David's unleashing of the Scottish host across the Northumbrian countryside, can only have soured relations between Durham and the Scots.

The mild but firm rule of King David's son Henry, a conscientious earl of Northumberland from 1139 till his untimely death in 1152, a year before his father's, may have gone some way to improving matters. Earl Henry took care to respect Durham's rights[54] and we have no record of any quarrel between the Scots and William de St Barbe, despite the fact that he was the convent's choice as bishop against William Cumin, the Scottish candidate.

It was not the bishop of Durham but the archbishop of York, Henry Murdac, who between 1149 and 1152 complained to King David at Carlisle that the Scots, in their haste to exploit the silver ore between Alston and Nenthead, were despoiling the archbishop's forests.[55] Presumably the German contractors working for David had been cutting timber in West Allendale, part of the archbishop's liberty of Hexhamshire.

---

[50] *ESC*, nos. 52, 119, 123, 140, 187, and 244–7; *RRS*, I, nos. 24–8, 30–2, 43, 83, 84, 93, 96, and 97; and H. Summerson, *Medieval Carlisle: the City and the Borders from the Late Eleventh to the Mid-Sixteenth Century* (Cumberland and Westmorland Antiquarian and Archaeological Society; Kendal, 1993), I, 41.

[51] Richard of Hexham, *De gestis Regis Stephani*, in *CR* III, 156–7.

[52] A. Young, *William Cumin: Border politics and the bishopric of Durham, 1141–1144* (Borthwick Papers no. 54; York, 1979), especially pp. 10–13.

[53] Ibid., pp. 18–19.

[54] Ibid., pp. 23–5; and *RRS*, I, no. 23.

[55] *Sym. Op.* II, 328 (continuation of *HReg* by John of Hexham).

It seems to have been in this period that the priory of Coldingham took shape, formed out of the community of monks already figuring in records of the late 1130s and early 1140s.[56] It may well have been King David and his son who were responsible for this development, who were keen to see a self contained daughter-house tidily established on Scottish soil. The priory of St Aebbe[57] (and St Mary)[58] at Coldingham may be evidence not of renewed warmth towards Durham but of a slight cooling of relations. Although a prior of Coldingham occurs in a record of 1147,[59] a papal privilege for Durham dated ten years later merely states that the appointment and removal of all St Cuthbert's monks at Coldingham, and of the prior 'if prior there be', were to be reserved to the church of Durham.[60] A further privilege, as late as 1162, does not even mention a prior at Coldingham, but perhaps significantly reserves appointment and removal of monks there to the prior of Durham.[61] King Malcolm IV's brieves, however, of the same period are addressed to the prior of Coldingham.[62] The Scottish Crown preferred to have a resident head of house with whom it could deal directly; and certainly before the death of Pope Alexander III papal letters were being addressed to the prior and monks of Coldingham.[63] The priors of Coldingham from the twelfth to the fourteenth century seem to have been Englishmen. The priory's lands, however, were tenanted by people who, at any rate by the end of the thirteenth century, saw themselves as Scots. In 1298 (or shortly afterwards) Edward I confiscated some sixty freeholders of Coldinghamshire because they had fought under the banner of Wallace at what was called the 'discomfiture' of Falkirk.[64]

The long pontificate of Hugh of le Puiset, coinciding with the reigns of Malcolm IV and William the Lion, saw relations between the royal house of Scotland and the see of St Cuthbert at their lowest ebb before the time of Anthony Bek. Much of the earliest work that can still be seen at Norham, including the first two storeys of the keep, was commissioned by Puiset and built under the direction of the bishop's engineer, Richard of Wolviston.[65] Even although the bishop was punished by Henry II for his disloyalty during the Young King's rebellion in 1173–4, his conduct was not due in any way to friendship towards William the Lion. On the contrary, his concern was directed entirely towards saving the territory of

[56] Raine, *North Durham*, Appendix, nos. 19 and 20; and *ESC*, no. 183.
[57] The dedication to St Mary is normal in twelfth-century documents, but the St Aebbe (Abb or Ebbe) dedication is found in the period 1182 × 1232 (Raine, *North Durham*, Appendix, no. 125) and was probably older than that to the Virgin.
[58] The earliest mention of St Mary's church of Coldingham occurs in King Edgar's charter of Swinton (*ESC*, no. 20; and Raine, *North Durham*, Appendix, no. 4). This seems to refer to a fresh dedication.
[59] *ESC*, no. 182.
[60] Holtzmann, *Papsturkunden in England*, II, no. 94 (p. 277).
[61] Ibid., no. 107.
[62] *RRS*, I, nos. 134 and 189.
[63] Holtzmann, *Papsturkunden in England*, II, no. 205.
[64] G.W.S. Barrow, *Scotland and its Neighbours*, pp. 160–1 and 192.
[65] *Norham Castle* (HM Stationery Office, 1966, repr. 1978), p. 6; and *Cuth. virt.*, ch. 47 (pp. 94–6).

Haliwerfolk from Scottish depredations. The going rate seems to have been about 57s. for one day's peace.[66]

The fact is that Hugh of le Puiset was too deeply set in the mould of his Blois origins and connections. Animosity was his natural, instinctive feeling towards the Scottish royal family which had such close ties with Henry I, the Empress Matilda and her son Henry of Anjou. The only evidence we have of unforced co-operation between Bishop Hugh and William the Lion is their agreement – which unfortunately does not survive in written record – to build a border bridge across the Tweed at Berwick, half of which would of course have been in Scotland, half in England – more particularly in Islandshire which belonged to the bishopric.[67] The bridge must have benefited both Scotland and St Cuthbert's Land, and it is therefore surprising to find that when, in the summer of 1199, a great spate in the Tweed swept the bridge away, Puiset's successor Philip of Poitiers at first refused to allow Earl Patrick of Dunbar, keeper of Berwick, to replace it.[68]

The persistent bone of contention between the Scots kings and Durham was the ill-defined but dignified and much-prized earldom of Northumbria or Northumberland. David I and William the Lion saw the earldom as theirs by hereditary right. St Cuthbert's Land, in their eyes, was no more than a special cluster of estates which had gradually accumulated *within* the earldom. After all, even as late as the reign of Richard I the wapentake of Sadberge, well to the south of Durham, was part of the earldom,[69] and villages in the valley of the River Skerne were still earldom estates in the 1140s.[70] Hart and Harterness may have become detached from the earldom at an early date, but they never formed part of the Patrimony of St Cuthbert.[71] Gainford also came late to the bishops' lordship.[72]

All this was surely seen quite differently by those prince bishops, such as Ranulf Flambard, Hugh of le Puiset and Anthony Bek, who really aimed to be princes. In their eyes it was the earldom which was the anomaly, in fact a nuisance unless it could be brought under the control of the bishopric. The Conqueror had shown the way by entrusting the earldom to Bishop Walcher, though the fate which befell him was not exactly a hopeful omen.[73] We can only imagine the bitterness felt by William the Lion when Hugh of le Puiset acquired the earldom from Richard I in 1189.[74] William had been put in possession by his grandfather when he was barely nine, only to be deprived five years later by Henry II. Until his dying day, William

[66] *Gesta Regis Henrici Secundi Benedicti Abbatis*, ed. W. Stubbs (2 vols., RS 49; 1867), I, 64.
[67] Roger of Howden, *Chronica Magistri Rogeri de Houedene*, ed. W. Stubbs (4 vols., RS 51; 1868–71), IV, 97–8.
[68] Ibid.
[69] VCH *Durham*, ed. W. Page (3 vols., London, 1905–27), II, 143; *Registrum Palatinum Dunelmense. The Register of Richard de Kellawe . . . bishop of Durham, 1311–1316*, ed. T.D. Hardy (RS 62; 1873), I, pp. lxix–lxxii, iii, pp. viii–xxv; and G.V. Scammell, *Hugh du Puiset, Bishop of Durham* (Cambridge, 1956), p. 49.
[70] *RRS*, I, no. 23.
[71] VCH *Durham*, II, 143–4 and n. 79.
[72] Ibid.; *Registrum Palatinum Dunelmense*, p. 1.
[73] Walcher was consecrated in 1071 and murdered in the bishop's hall (perhaps in the area of Bottle Bank?) at Gateshead on 14 May 1080.

strove obsessively to recover Northumberland, without success. Puiset, moreover, took over the shrievalty along with the earldom, giving him virtually monopolistic control over the whole territory between Tweed and Tees. The bishop seized his opportunity on Henry II's death to create a palatine earldom-bishopric (or bishopric-earldom) of a kind perhaps more familiar on the continent of Europe than in Britain or Ireland. But Hugh of le Puiset had left it too late. Easily toppled by William Longchamp, he was forced to abandon his ambitions shortly before his death in March 1195.[75] His successor, Philip of Poitiers, although an able administrator, never attempted to revive Puiset's palatine objectives, and the lengthy vacancy from 1208 to 1217 gave the Crown the opportunity to reassert direct royal authority in north-east England.[76]

Cuthbert, however devoutly the kings of Scotland may have revered him, proved a *sair sanct* for the Scottish crown. His cult was manipulated and exploited skilfully and quite ruthlessly by a line of bishops and a community of Benedictine monks numbering several individuals of outstanding ability and sometimes of overwhelming ambition. The political entity which they created enjoyed remarkable independence but it was invariably conceived within the context of a strong and relatively centralised Norman-Angevin kingdom of England. In this regard the baronage of the bishopric – I mean those families of Norman or other continental origin – saw eye to eye with their counterparts among the baronage of the earldom; their loyalty was given to a bishop who was loyal to the English Crown.

It is understandable that during the Anarchy the Scots were able to hold the loyalty of a significant number of Anglo-Norman barons of Northumbria – Merlay of Morpeth,[77] Bertram of Mitford,[78] Umfraville of Prudhoe and Redesdale,[79] Grenville of Ellingham,[80] Darreyns [de Arenis] of Callerton by Ponteland,[81] and a few more. These families may not have been disposed to favour the Scots, but equally they may not necessarily have been supporters of Stephen. At the death of Earl Henry the Norman baronage of Northumberland was reluctant to swear fealty to young William of Scotland.[82] By the time William the Lion was drawn into the Young King's rebellion in the mid 1170s the situation had altered profoundly, and the Muscamps of Wooler were almost the only Anglo-Norman family of note to take the Scottish king's side.[83] It may have been a rather different matter where the

[74] Scammell, *Puiset*, pp. 49–50.
[75] Ibid., pp. 51–2.
[76] Royal authority was exercised largely by Philip of Oldcoats, for whom see J.C. Holt, *The Northerners* (Oxford, 1961), pp. 47, 83–4, 100–1, and 223; *Pipe Roll 13 John* (Pipe Roll Soc., 2nd ser. 28; London, 1953), pp. 35–41.
[77] *ESC*, no. 247; and *RRS*, I, nos. 11, 23, and 32.
[78] *RRS*, I, nos. 11, 27, and 32.
[79] *ESC*, nos. 124, 130, 131, and 257; and *RRS*, I, nos. 11, 23, 25, 27, 28, 30–2, and 43.
[80] *ESC*, no. 131; *RRS*, I, no. 32; *Arch. Ael.* 45 (1967), pp. 181 ff.
[81] *RRS*, I, nos. 32 and 43.
[82] *Sym. Op.* II, 327 (continuation of *HReg* by John of Hexham).
[83] *History of Northumberland*, XI, ed. K.H. Vickers, (Newcastle upon Tyne, 1922), p. 306; and *RRS*, II, nos. 126, 135, 147, 148, 175, 175, 201, and 202.

thegns and drengs of Northumbria were concerned, families of Old English or Scandinavian origin. Their affinities, especially before the death of David I, often lay with the Scottish kings and nobility.

Some of these thegnly families were richly endowed. In Henry I's reign Liulf son of Uhtred owned a substantial estate in Northumberland, half of it north of the Coquet, half to the south.[84] His son Uhtred failed to retain the estate but appears as lord of Mow, south of Kelso, as well as being a tenant of the king of Scots at Scotby beside Carlisle.[85] Uhtred's heir was his daughter (or granddaughter?) Eschina, an only child, who married the first of the Scottish Stewarts,[86] Walter son of Alan; with him she became ancestor of all the sovereigns of Scotland from Robert II to Anne. A contemporary Old English heiress, Hextilda daughter of Uhtred son of Waltheof of Tynedale, having first of all been given in marriage by David I to Richard Cumin, nephew of his discredited chancellor William Cumin, subsequently married Malcolm earl of Atholl, descended from the Scottish royal house.[87] Hextilda had children by both her marriages, and at some time during her second marriage the entire double family seems to have come to Durham on a package pilgrimage. On folio 63 of the *Liber Vitae* fourteen names were duly entered, beginning with the earl and his wife and continuing with their three sons (Simon, Henry and Gilleithne), the earl's brother (Duncan) and nephew (Constantine) and his three sisters (Bethoc, Christina and Margaret), and concluding with members of Hextilda's first family, her son William Cumin and his sisters Christian, Edna and Ada.[88] The careers of Eschina of Mow and Hextilda of Tynedale remind us that Northumberland's loss could be Scotland's gain. But by the 1160s the thegns and drengs of Northumberland were mostly of small wealth and comparatively little consequence. Until 1152 King David's vision of a Scoto-Northumbrian realm may not have appeared altogether unrealistic to those who had experienced the Anarchy. If we seek the most effective single obstacle to the achievement of that vision we

---

[84] *Regesta*, III, no. 373a. We have seen above (p. 316) that Liulf son of Uhtred was a landowner on the boundaries of Coldinghamshire.

[85] *ESC*, nos. 196 and 197, and pp. 361 and 412.

[86] *Liber S. Marie de Calchou* (Bannatyne Club; Edinburgh, 1846), nos. 146 and 147 (referring to Eschina's two deceased husbands, Walter son of Alan and Henry). It is just possible that since Eschina used the surname de Londres and was living as late as 1198 she was granddaughter, not daughter, of Uhtred son of Liulf. In any case she was his heir.

[87] *RRS*, I, no. 103; *Calendar of Documents relating to Scotland*, ed. J. Bain, I (Edinburgh, 1881), no. 2287; *Scots Peerage*, ed. J. Balfour Paul, I (Edinburgh, 1904), 414–17. According to the genealogy produced for John Comyn of Badenoch in 1291, at the time of the competition for the Scottish throne, Hextilda's mother Bethoc was the daughter of Domhnall Bán, brother of Malcolm III and himself king of Scots 1094–97 (E.L.G. Stones and G.G. Simpson, *Edward I and the Throne of Scotland, 1290–1296* (2 vols., Oxford, 1978), II, 138). If this was true (and the claim does not seem to have been challenged by anyone in 1291), Hextilda was a Scot on her mother's side and second cousin to her second husband.

[88] *Liber Vitae*, fol. 63 (pencil foliation). I take 'Kelehathonin' to represent Gilleithne, 'St Eithne's servant'. My interpretation of the family relationships of Malcolm and Hextilda differs somewhat from that proposed in the *Scots Peerage*, p. 417 and n. 5.

must surely find it in the church, community and bishopric of Durham. It is supremely appropriate that at the heart of this politico-ecclesiastical entity stood, and still stands, the grandest monument to the Norman Conquest in the whole of England, whose nine hundredth anniversary this volume celebrates.

Malcolm III and the Foundation of Durham Cathedral

VALERIE WALL

O N 11 August 1093 Malcolm III laid one of the foundation stones of the new cathedral. His presence is overshadowed by the events at Gloucester on 24 August, his slaying at Alnwick on 13 November, and the subsequent Scottish succession crises. The purpose of this paper is to offer a reappraisal of his participation in the ceremony, but in the first instance I will consider the various ways in which the event was recorded by the Durham writers.

Malcolm is mentioned in two Durham sources, the *De iniusta uexacione Willelmi episcopi primi* and the *Historia Regum*. Although it was compiled after the *De iniusta uexacione*, I will take the *Historia Regum* first.[1] Its reporting is factual and laconic. 'The new church was commenced at Durham on Thursday 11 August by Bishop William and the first foundation stones were laid by Malcolm, king of the Scots, and Prior Turgot.'[2] The initiative is with the bishop, and Turgot and Malcolm are given equal, but secondary roles. The contemporary *De iniusta* is primarily a defence against accusations implicating Bishop William in the plot of 1088 to replace William Rufus as king with his brother Duke Robert of Normandy. It gives a sympathetic account of his trial and exile, but after his restoration to the king's favour in 1091, Bishop William returned to Durham and began work on the new church:

> On the third of the ides of September [11 September] in the second year of his return, he destroyed to the foundations the old church, which Aldhun, bishop at that time, built, and the following year, that is, 1093 from the Incarnation of the Lord, he began another better work, that is in the thirteenth year of his episcopate, and the eleventh year of the monks coming to Durham; and in that year on Thursday 11 August, he and Prior Turgot who was second to him in the church laid the first foundation stones. Malcolm, king of the Scots, who was visiting there at that time, joined with them in laying one of the foundation stones.[3]

[1] H.S. Offler, 'Hexham and the *Historia Regum*', *TAASDN*, n.s. 2 (1970), pp. 51–62.
[2] *HReg, s.a.* 1093 (p. 220).
[3] *DIV*, p. 105. Dr Philpott's paper (above, pp. 125–37) explored the question of the dating of the *DIV*. I would agree that this was a contemporary account of the arrest and trial of William of St Calais, and that the account of the foundation ceremony was part of an additional section concluded soon after the death of Bishop William in 1096.

Here the close harmony between Bishop William, Prior Turgot, and the monastic community is stressed, as is the position of Turgot as second in authority to the bishop. Malcolm's presence as a visiting layman is incidental to the proceedings. The total destruction of the old church and the construction of the new building is symbolic of the return to the ideals of a brotherhood of monks, and contrasts with the account in the *Libellus de exordio et procursuistius hoc est Dunelmensis ecclesie* (*Historia Dunelmensis ecclesie*) of Aldhun's work in 995 which was a community effort between himself, his son-in-law Uchtred, earl of Northumbria, and all the people of the Patrimony.[4]

The most detailed account of the ceremony is in the *Libellus de exordio*, composed between 1104 and 1107 by Symeon of Durham. The earliest extant manuscript is Durham University Library, Cosin MS V.ii.6, written soon after the text's composition in or before 1109.[5] The *Libellus de exordio* does not record Malcolm's presence. The usual explanations for this are threefold. Firstly, that he was not even present.[6] I think this hypothesis can be discounted. There is no reason why his presence should be faked in the *De iniusta uexacione* or in the *Historia Regum*. Indeed, in the *Historia Regum*, which specifically includes details of his armed incursions into Northumbria, one might assume logically that his participation would be passed over in silence.[7] This deals in part with the second point – that these raids were the reason for the omission in the *Libellus de exordio*, and more pertinently that he broke the *conuentio* drawn up between himself, his wife Margaret and his children, and the community at Durham.[8] In that case, he should have been omitted from the account in the later *Historia Regum*, and from the *De iniusta uexacione*. The third explanation is that his exclusion from the *Libellus de exordio* reflects the sensitive ecclesiastical issues at or soon after the time of its compilation.[9] If that were so, we might expect an erasure, but there is none on the

---

[4] *LDE*, bk. 2, ch. 2 (pp. 80–1).

[5] Michael Gullick, Dominic Marner, and Alan Piper, *A Catalogue for an Exhibition of Manuscripts in the Treasury, Durham Cathedral*, ed. David Rollason (Durham, 1993), pp. 18–20; and Symeon of Durham, *On the Origin and Progress of this the Church of Durham*, ed. and trans. David Rollason (Oxford, forthcoming).

[6] D. Baker, ' "A Nursery of saints": St Margaret of Scotland Reconsidered', in *Medieval Women*, ed. D. Baker (Studies in Church History, Subsidia 1; Oxford, 1978), p. 119; and J. Hodgson Hinde, *Symeonis Dunelmensis Opera et Collectanea* (SS 51; 1869), p. 104.

[7] *HReg, s.a.* 1093 (pp. 221–2).

[8] *Liber Vitae*, pp. xix–xx and fol. 48v. BL, Cotton MS Domitian A.VII has been consulted, but references to entries in the *Liber Vitae* will be taken from the facsimile edition. For the most recent examination of the *Liber Vitae*, see J. Gerchow, *Die Gedenküberlieferung der Angelsachsen, mit einem Katalog der libri vitae und Necrologien* (Berlin, 1988). The *conuentio* is discussed in detail below.

[9] The appointment of Turgot as bishop of St Andrews in 1107 and that of Eadmer in 1120 became embroiled in the chain of refusals to profess obedience of the bishops of Scotland to York, and of York to Canterbury. For a brief discussion, see A.A.M. Duncan, *Scotland; the Making of the Kingdom* (Edinburgh, 1975), pp. 128–31. The exchanges are usefully collected in A.O. Anderson, *Scottish Annals from English Chroniclers* (London, 1908, repr. Stamford, 1991), pp. 129–69.

Cosin MS V.ii.6 copy.[10] Whilst we cannot entirely dismiss the usual explanations for the omission, I would suggest that in using the account in the *Libellus de exordio* as a barometer for the monks' attitude to Malcolm, there is a danger of focusing incorrectly on the purpose of its composition, which is to stress the close and harmonious relationship between bishop, prior and the monastic community. In this respect it expands on the account given in the *De iniusta uexacione*:

> It was begun in the year one thousand and ninety three from the Incarnation of the Lord, in the thirteenth year of the pontificate of William and in the eleventh year of the monks coming to Durham on the third of the ides of August [Thursday 11 August]. On that day the bishop and Prior Turgot, who was second to him in the church, with the rest of the brothers, laid the first foundation stones. Not long before, that is on the fourth of the kalends of August [Friday 29 July] this bishop and prior, having prayed with the brothers and given blessing, began to dig the foundations.[11]

After recording the division of building duties, the *Libellus de exordio* relates that at that time ('quo tempore'), the bishop led Turgot out before all the people of the bishopric and appointed him archdeacon, decreeing (*statuens*) that 'all who should be his [Turgot's] successors in the office of prior should likewise succeed him in that of archdeacon.'[12] There are points here to note. One cannot fail to be struck by the repeated emphasis on the close monastic community of bishop, prior, and brothers. As in the *De iniusta* there is the detailed dating formula. In contrast to 995, the laity are now in a passive role – they are observers not participants in the new building work. The appointment of Turgot as archdeacon is clearly associated with the foundation ceremonies. The justification for the authoritative action of Bishop William is sought in the distant past. We are informed that he did not act without authority or example.[13] This was to be found in Bede and in the Rule of St Benedict. From Bede were taken the precedents of Boisil's and Cuthbert's preaching missions at Melrose.[14] There are incidentally four references to St Cuthbert in the *Libellus de exordio* account. The Rule of St Benedict is cited in the explanation of the use of the terms *praepositus* and prior.[15] Mr Piper has drawn attention to the strong monastic element of Symeon's *Libellus de exordio*.[16] This work was composed possibly against the feared exactions of Bishop

---

[10] I am grateful to Mr A.J. Piper for confirming in discussion with me that there is no erasure here.

[11] *LDE*, bk. 4, ch. 8 (p. 129).

[12] Ibid.: 'ut quicunque illi successores fuerint in prioratu, similiter succedant et in archidiaconatu.'

[13] Ibid.: 'quod non sine auctoritate uel exemplo fecit.'

[14] *HE*, bk. 4, ch. 27.

[15] For a discussion of these terms in connection with the Patrimony of St Cuthbert, see G. Bonner, 'St Cuthbert at Chester-le-Street', in *Cuthbert*, p. 394; and C. Stancliffe, 'Cuthbert and the Polarity between Pastor and Solitary', in *Cuthbert*, p. 30.

[16] A.J. Piper, 'The First Generations of Durham Monks and the Cult of St Cuthbert', in *Cuthbert*, pp. 437–46. He noted the elaborate dating formulae being reintroduced in 1083 to emphasise the return to the monastic community, pp. 439–40.

Ranulf Flambard.[17] Ranulf's efforts to curb the authority of Turgot reached to the extent of securing the latter's appointment as bishop of St Andrews and thereafter separating the dual role of prior-archdeacon at Durham.[18] The guiding hand of Turgot is surely behind this version of the ceremony and his prime concern is the defence of his own position as second in authority to the bishop.

A textually close version may be found in the *Liber Vitae*, but here the date of Turgot's appointment is firmly given as that of the foundation ceremony. The intervening sentence in the *Libellus de exordio* on the division of building duties, which leaves the date of the appointment unclear, is omitted from the *Liber Vitae*.[19] It is even here suggested that Bishop William had previously appointed Turgot's predecessor Aldwin, the first prior of the post 1083 monastic community, as archdeacon, although there is no other evidence for this.[20] The memorandum concludes, almost as it does in the *Libellus de exordio*:

> Wherefore, Bishop William, the founder of the same church, is known to have so appointed for ever that each successor of St Cuthbert in the office of prior in his church, should succeed him also in the office of preaching and in the exalted ministry of the archdeaconry, responsible for the spiritualities [spiritual jurisdiction] of the whole bishopric of the church of Durham.[21]

A common feature of the *Libellus de exordio* and the *Liber Vitae*, in addition to the importance given to Turgot, is the specific dates of 29 July and 11 August, between which we are expected to believe that the preparatory work could have been completed in time for the ceremony of stone laying. However, if one purpose of these versions is to place on record the appointment of Turgot as archdeacon by Bishop William, then I would suggest that the dates 29 July to 11 August represent those within which it was known that the bishop was in the North of England. It would be pointless to record the delegation of authority by William if it could be proved that he was not even present. Dr Aird points out that Bishop William was more absent from the bishopric than present. Although it is impossible to construct a detailed or entirely certain itinerary, the bishop was in the south of England with William Rufus for part of the summer. He accompanied the king to Dover, where he witnessed the treaty with Robert of Flanders.[22] He was at Rochester with Robert, count of Meulan, where together they acted as counsellors to the king in his

---

[17] Ibid., p. 442.

[18] For Turgot's appointment and the role of the archdeacon at Durham, see F. Barlow, *Durham Jurisdictional Peculiars* (London, 1950), pp. 3–4, 13–15, and 153–6. For the archdeacon in the wider context of the post-Conquest English church, see F. Barlow, *The English Church 1066–1154* (London, 1979), pp. 48–9 and 135–7.

[19] *Liber Vitae*, fol. 46v. On p. xxiii, there is an error in the transcription and translation where the date of Wednesday 10 August is suggested for the start of the digging of the foundations. The transcription should be *Nam paulo ante id est iiij Kal. augusti, feria vi*, i.e. Friday 29 July.

[20] *Liber Vitae*, fol. 46v. See Barlow, *Durham Jurisdictional Peculiars*, p. 153.

[21] *Liber Vitae*, fol. 46v; and *LDE*, bk. 4, ch. 8 (p. 129).

[22] F. Barlow, *William Rufus* (2nd edn, London, 1990), p. 309.

dispute with Anselm.[23] He travelled north possibly to act as escort for Malcolm, in the manner of 1059, continuing on with the Scottish king to Gloucester for the proposed meeting with William Rufus on 24 August.[24] In conclusion, I would suggest that there is no place for any layman in the account in the *Libellus de exordio* of the foundation ceremony. In any event, by 1104 Malcolm was no longer useful to the monks in terms of patronage and protection, and their attention was firmly focused on his children. It is in this connection and bearing in mind the criterion that the concern of the community of Durham was to create an impression of *renouatio* by seeking precedents in the distant past, that I wish now to turn to a continuity of a different kind – that of a dynasty, in an effort to understand Malcolm's participation in the foundation ceremony.

By 1093 we should not be referring to a system of succession in Scotland where a collateral took precedence over lineal descent if there were direct heirs of the king. Malcolm's brother Donald was surely chosen by the Scots in November 1093 to forestall English interference. The problem for Malcolm was how to accommodate the sons of his two marriages. There is no evidence that he was planning to disinherit Duncan, his son from his first marriage. However, some role within the kingdom of Scotland in its broadest territorial sense would have to be found for the six sons of his second marriage to Margaret, sister of Edgar the Aetheling. One son Aethelred was already lay abbot of Dunkeld.[25] It is feasible that Malcolm was planning to grant some authority in Lothian to Edward, the eldest son of the second marriage. This hypothesis could be borne out by the subsequent divisions. When Donald was restored in 1094 after Duncan's unsuccessful attempt to take the kingship, he seems to have shared the rule with Edmund, the third son of Malcolm's second marriage. When Edgar became king in 1097, his younger brother Alexander was given some subordinate authority. This situation was repeated on Alexander's own accession in 1107, when the youngest brother David held the subordinate role.[26] The latter reflects the terms of the childless Edgar's will in 1107.[27] If this were so, then the cultivation of a peaceful relationship with the Patrimony of St Cuthbert could be advantageous to both parties, since in terms of peace and security the community would take a great interest in the Scottish succession. Here again, the man behind the scenes is Turgot. The importance of the

[23] Ibid., p. 306.
[24] Ibid., p. 309; and F. Barlow, *Edward the Confessor* (2nd edn, London, 1979), p. 203.
[25] *ESC*, no. 14, pp. 11–12.
[26] William of Malmesbury, *De gestis regum Anglorum*, ed. W. Stubbs (2 vols., RS 90; 1887–9), II, 476; *HReg*, s.a. 1104 (p. 236) where Alexander is described as *comes*. These possible relationships are, however, complex and are discussed in depth in my thesis on the Scottish succession in the eleventh and twelfth centuries (in preparation). See also G.W.S. Barrow, *Kingship and Unity: Scotland 1000–1306* (Edinburgh, 1981, repr. 1989), p. 32; G.W.S. Barrow, 'The Anglo-Scottish Border', *Northern History* 1 (1966), pp. 32–3; and Duncan, *Scotland: the Making of the Kingdom*, p. 128.
[27] *RRS* I, no. 49, p. 163. Professor Barrow suggests that this represents Cumbria, Teviotdale and Lothian south of Lammermuir. See also his introduction to the *RRS* I, p. 37.

prior has on the whole been underestimated, although recent scholarship has gone some way to correcting this.[28] Hinde missed the point when he wrote:

> His tenure of the priorate was unmarked by any important events, if we except the rebuilding of the church of St Cuthbert, a work more immediately due to the bishop, but to which he contributed his assistance, and the translation of St Cuthbert's remains. His subsequent career as bishop of St Andrews was as unsatisfactory as his earlier experience of the same country during his residence at Melrose.[29]

In fact, this tells us all that was so significant about the career of Turgot, in particular the forty-year connection with both the Patrimony and the Scottish royal family from 1075 to 1115. Bishops came and went, and might have treasonable tendencies, but it was Turgot who gave a permanence to the relationship between Malcolm's family and the community. We know from his *Life of St Margaret* that he visited Scotland and had personal knowledge of the family.[30] He had not seen Margaret for more than six months before her death, but on that occasion she told him that it would be the last time they would meet. She requested of him that 'as long as you live you will remember my soul at the Mass and in your prayers; the other is that you will take care of my sons and daughters, pour out your love on them, above all, instruct them to fear and love God and never cease from teaching them.'[31] The supposed wishes of the queen closely resemble those in the *conuentio*, the agreement of spiritual friendship between Malcolm, king of the Scots, Queen Margaret and their sons and daughters, which the convent of St Cuthbert promised to keep for ever.[32] It must have been drawn up between 1083 and 1093, but if it were dated to the time of the foundation ceremony, it could be seen as a response to the earlier request of Margaret, since in part it echoes the same concern for the whole family. It promises that 'in this life and the next, both they and their sons and daughters will share in all things that are to the service of God in the monastery of St Cuthbert, that is in masses, psalms, alms, vigils, prayers, and in all things of this kind'.[33] The covenant is entered in the *Liber Vitae* within a group of agreements, which from their varied affiliations might be seen to represent some of

---

[28] See above, pp. 292, 294. See also W.M. Aird, 'The Making of a Medieval Miracle Collection: the *Liber de translationibus et miraculis sancti Cuthberti*', *Northern History* 28 (1992), pp. 1–24.

[29] *Symeonis Dunelmensis Opera et Collectanea*, ed. J. Hodgson Hinde (SS 51; 1869), p. lxi.

[30] I have used the version printed in *Symeonis Opera*, ed. Hinde (SS 51; 1869), pp. 234–54. The authorship of the work has been discussed by Baker, ' "A Nursery of Saints" ', pp. 119–41; Lois L. Huneycutt, 'The Idea of a Perfect Princess: The *Life of St Margaret* in the Reign of Matilda II (1100–1118)', *AN* 12, pp. 81–97. Taken together with the various scriptorial activities at Durham during the period 1104–1107 behind which can be detected the influence of Turgot, I believe that he is the author of the *Life*. In this respect, the longer version is, as Huneycutt suggests, the earlier version datable to that time.

[31] *Symeonis Opera*, ed. Hinde, p. 251.

[32] *Liber Vitae*, fol. 48v (translation on pp. xix–xx); and Anderson, *Scottish Annals from English Chroniclers*, pp. 110–11.

[33] *Liber Vitae*, fol. 48v.

the personal allegiances of the bishop and the prior.[34] It is the only one made with lay *confratres*. In this respect it differs from the confraternity agreement of Bishop Wulfstan of Worcester made *c.*1077 with seven local Benedictine houses. These houses were united in their veneration of God, the Blessed Virgin and St Benedict, but more importantly in their promise to be faithful to King William and Queen Matilda before God and the world.[35] There were close relationships between some of these houses and Durham. Aldwin, the first prior of the monastic community at Durham, had travelled from Winchcombe with two companions from Evesham to revive monasticism in Northumbria. It was he who accompanied Turgot to Melrose, where they had their first encounter with Malcolm III in 1074.[36] The *conuentio* could be considered in the light of Bishop Aethelwold's *Regularis Concordia*, drawn up in 964 under the auspices of King Edgar during the period of mid-tenth-century monastic revival. Aethelwold's adaptation of the Rule of St Benedict included extensive prayers, psalms and masses for the king, queen and the royal house.[37] If Durham were adapting this aspect of Wulfstan's agreement, or of the *Regularis Concordia*, it is significant that prayers are being offered for the Scottish king and his family rather than an expression of loyalty to the Norman kings of England. However, perhaps this comparison should not be overdrawn. The monastic community at Durham was making a personal covenant with the Scottish family and the emphasis is on the spiritual nature of the agreement. (Admittedly it is difficult to separate the hope of eternal reward from the expectations of worldly material benefits.) We should perhaps distinguish between regional and national interests, and interpret the *conuentio* as an insurance policy which placed a moral obligation on Malcolm that, in return for prayers for his family, he would protect the lands of St Cuthbert. In this context, it is worth asking why

[34] For a brief discussion on this and other aspects of post-Conquest confraternity agreements in England, see F. Barlow, *The English Church 1066–1154* (London, 1979), pp. 187–8.

[35] The seven houses were Worcester, Evesham, Chertsey, Bath, Pershore, Winchcombe, and Gloucester. This agreement has most recently been considered by E. Mason, *St Wulfstan of Worcester c.1008–1095* (Oxford, 1990), p. 197. A copy of Lanfranc's *Institutions* was at Durham in the late eleventh century. It makes provision for the admission of lay persons into monastic confraternities, but does not include prayers for the royal family. No one could doubt Lanfranc's loyalty to William I: *The Monastic Constitutions of Lanfranc*, ed. D. Knowles (London, 1951), p. xxv and pp. 114–15.

[36] *LDE*, bk. 3, ch. 21 (pp. 108–9); and bk. 3, ch. 22 (pp. 111–12). See I. Atkins, 'The Church of Worcester from the Eighth to the Twelfth Century' (part 2), *Ant. J.* 20 (1940), pp. 212–13 and 219. Atkins notes the names of Worcester and Evesham monks in the *Liber Vitae*, fols. 21v and 22, and suggests that they were entered there at the time of the Translation of St Cuthbert in 1104, at the instigation of Turgot. Mason, *St Wulfstan*, also notes the close ties.

[37] *Regularis concordia*, ed. and trans. T. Symons (London, 1952), p. xlvi, and pp. 5, 13, 14, 16, 21, and 22 for the prayers, psalms and masses for the royal house. Symons's reference to 'nationality' and prayers for 'king and country' (p. xlvi) might have some validity extended to Wulfstan's agreement, but not to the *conuentio* and 'king of Scots'. See also Mason, *St Wulfstan*, pp. 11–12 and 200. See above, p. 35, for the importance of the king to Aethelwold in the context of tenth-century monastic reform, and the possible influence of Aethelwold on Bishops Walcher and William of St Calais.

Malcolm did not lead armed incursions into England during the exile of Bishop William (1088–91) until the expulsion from Normandy and the return of Edgar the Aetheling led him to fear some act of aggression from William Rufus. During the three years I would suggest that the cultivation of a peaceful relationship with the Patrimony was under way, and it is even possible that the *conuentio* was agreed during that period.

Although I believe that one has to be careful about interpreting the presence in Northumbria of Malcolm as 'king of the Scots' on what might be claimed to be English soil, the dynastic connotations cannot be avoided. The final sentence of the *conuentio* is revealing. In referring to Malcolm and Margaret, it concludes 'and their anniversary shall be celebrated every year with festivity as is King Athelstan's.'[38] A theme of several papers at the St Cuthbert Conference in 1987 was the tenth-century association between the house of Wessex and the community at Chester-le-Street, set particularly in the context of political influence expressed through the cult of saints' relics. A significant aspect of the *Historia de sancto Cuthberto* is the familial continuity in terms of devotion to St Cuthbert from Alfred to his son Edward the Elder to his grandsons Athelstan and Edmund over the period 871 to 946. The implication is that the family owed its victory in annexing Northumbria to St Cuthbert, and no doubt the West Saxon kings saw the advantage of acknowledging such a powerful supplicant. Each generation instructs the next to repay the saint both spiritually and materially.[39] Taken from Durham's point of view and considered purely in terms of dynastic continuity, an association with Malcolm and his family could provide a similar long-term opportunity for the reclamation or reaffirmation of alienated rights north of the Tweed. The precedent of Athelstan as protector and benefactor could be interpreted as an appeal to Margaret's pride in her ancestry, which she expressed in the names given to four of her children, Edward, Edmund, Edgar and Aethelred.

The *conuentio* was obviously agreed whilst Malcolm and Margaret were alive, but if it is to be used as evidence for a rekindled interest in Athelstan in the eleventh century or at least up to 1093, then it should be noted that this group of agreements is entered in the *Liber Vitae* in hands of the late eleventh or early twelfth centuries, that is, possibly after their deaths.[40] Athelstan's name appears first in the *Liber Vitae* standing alone in a tenth-century hand, squeezed in at the top of folio 12, alongside the heading, in the original hand, of *nomina regum vel ducum*. Perhaps it was entered for future reference as a possible starting point if and when the book came to be brought up to date. On folios 12v and 43v are entered in a twelfth-century hand two lists of Anglo-Saxon names, which appear to represent

---

[38] *Liber Vitae*, fol. 48v.

[39] Luisella Simpson, 'The King Alfred/St Cuthbert Episode in the *Historia de sancto Cuthberto*, its Significance for Mid-Tenth-Century English History', in *Cuthbert*, pp. 397–411; G. Bonner, 'St Cuthbert at Chester-le-Street', ibid., pp. 387–95; and D. Rollason, 'St Cuthbert and Wessex: The Evidence of Cambridge, Corpus Christi College MS 183', ibid., pp. 413–24. See also D. Rollason, *Saints and Relics in Anglo-Saxon England* (Oxford, 1989), p. 146.

[40] I am grateful to Mr Michael Gullick for his help on the hand of the *conuentio*, which can be identified as that of a scribe active in 1093.

witnesses to two charters of Athelstan in favour of St Cuthbert, now lost to us.[41] It is suggested that the monks copied names from those charters because Athelstan's renown as a great benefactor was such that those who had attested his charters qualified in their own right as benefactors.[42] On folio 12v, after the original list of royal and noble benefactors in the ninth-century hand, a twelfth-century hand has added the names of kings and queens of England from Athelstan to Henry I and his wife Matilda, and of the kings of the Scots from Malcolm III to Alexander I. They must have been inserted after the accession of Alexander in 1107, since his successors are added in different hands.[43] This list represents a conscious effort by the monastic community to unite the house of Wessex with those of the Scottish and Norman kings, and again suggests dynastic continuity. It seems that during the early part of the twelfth century, the *Liber Vitae* was being brought up to date in readiness for placing on public display on the altar of the new cathedral at the time of the translation in 1104. Present on that occasion was Alexander.[44] The Athelstan connection may be the reason for the *conuentio* being copied into the *Liber Vitae*, his name providing the starting point for the continuity which the monastic community was constantly seeking.

However, that is in the future, and if we return to 1093 and make the Athelstan connection with Northumbria with the family of Malcolm and Margaret, it is possible to see how it could serve a further purpose. If Malcolm were planning to use his son Edward in Lothian, the association with the Patrimony of St Cuthbert, once synonymous with a united Northumbria, including Bernicia north of the Tweed, might give him and his heirs a foothold not just south of the Tweed, but south of the Tyne. The strategic position of Durham is obvious. Set in the wider context of the impressive building programme of cathedrals and churches, and the importance placed on the translation of saints' relics, Durham stood alone north of the Tees, and the potential for political influence could be considerable.[45] Northumbria could still be annexed to the house of Wessex, not as in the tenth century from the remote south, but from a different point of the compass, from Scotland, and through the descendants of those same ninth- and tenth-century kings of Wessex. It is significant that the desire for continuity and the seeking in the past for precedents within the family, both in the lay and monastic sense,

[41] E.E. Barker, 'Two Lost Documents of King Athelstan', *ASE* 5 (Cambridge, 1977), pp. 137–43.
[42] Ibid., p. 141.
[43] *Liber Vitae*, fol. 12v.
[44] *De miraculis*, ch. 7 (*Sym. Op.* I, 258); and *HReg, s.a.* 1104 (p. 236).
[45] See F. Barlow, *English Church*, p. 12, n. 53 for those churches and cathedrals which were being rebuilt in England at this time. Rollason, *Saints and Relics in Anglo-Saxon England*, pp. 230–3 for buildings and translations; figure 7.1 on p. 178 for the principal relic translations to English churches in the later Anglo-Saxon period; p. 212 for those saints north and south of the Tweed whose relics were at Durham, i.e. Acca and Alchmund from Hexham, Balthere and Bilfrith from Tyninghame, Boisil and Cuthbert from Melrose, King Oswine from Tynemouth, Bede from Jarrow, the abbesses Ebba and Aethelgitha from Coldingham. See also S.J. Ridyard, '*Condigna veneratio*: Post-Conquest attitudes to the saints of the Anglo-Saxons', *AN* 9 (1987), pp. 179–206.

should serve the purpose of both Malcolm and Durham. Opportunism is a powerful stimulant. However, all this must be considered from a third perspective: in other words how this intrusion south of the Tyne by Malcolm and his family might be viewed by William Rufus.

It is surely no coincidence that this apparent revival of the West Saxon pretensions in Northumbria, now through the Scottish royal house, and in an atmosphere of reciprocal friendship rather than violence, was taking place at a time when William was in a position to extend his own real authority over all England. Indeed he was the first English king capable of achieving this with a certainty of permanence, and not in terms of the temporary expedients of the military forays of his predecessors since the time of Athelstan.[46] William, like Malcolm, recognised that the one institution with the capacity for survival was the Patrimony. As the *Libellus de exordio* makes clear, he protected the monks like a father during the exile of Bishop William.[47] In 1091 he received the community's delegation and rose humbly to greet Turgot.[48] He treated Durham with more respect than he did other monasteries and churches, taking nothing from the monks and even giving them something of his own.[49] There is evidence that William Rufus well understood the importance of saints' relics, and concerned himself with dedications and translations.[50] It is worth setting this into the context of Rollason's question on the cult of non-royal saints as instruments of royal power, 'To what extent did that association enhance and reinforce royal power in the context of the unification of England?'[51] However, it appeared that in 1093 Malcolm, not the Norman king, would be the promoter of the cult of St Cuthbert. Two kings were vying peacefully for the patronage of St Cuthbert, but William would be anxious to limit the Scottish king's possible future influence south of the Tweed.

After laying one of the foundation stones on 11 August, Malcolm travelled to Gloucester for his expected meeting with William Rufus. The English king had made lavish arrangements. In particular he had sent Edgar the Aetheling to accompany Malcolm south.[52] It is likely that Malcolm had with him, in addition to his brother-in-law, some of his own sons, perhaps Edward, Edmund and Edgar. The West Saxon dynasty was well represented. The debate about what was to be discussed will never be resolved. Florence of Worcester refers to the desire for a renewal of peace and the establishment of a firm friendship, but records that William refused to meet or speak with Malcolm:

[46] Rollason, *Saints and Relics*, pp. 136–7.
[47] *LDE*, bk. 4, ch. 8.
[48] Ibid.
[49] Ibid.
[50] See, for example, *The Chronicle of Battle Abbey*, ed. and trans. E. Searle (Oxford, 1980), pp. 96–7. Barlow, *William Rufus*, p. 292. S.J. Ridyard, *The Royal Saints of Anglo-Saxon England* (Cambridge, 1988), p. 232.
[51] Rollason, *Saints and Relics*, p. 144.
[52] *ASC, s.a.* 1093.

Moreover he wished to compel him to make amends in his own court, according to the judgement of his own barons only; but Malcolm was in no way willing to do this, except on the confines of his own kingdom, where the kings of the Scots were accustomed to make amends to the kings of England and according to the judgement of the barons of both kingdoms.[53]

Dr Emma Mason, in an appraisal of the achievements of William Rufus, drew attention to his importance in the definition of the borders of his kingdom and the development of the legal system, and stated that 'effective royal justice was essential if there were to be a unified kingdom.'[54] But where were the legally defined confines within which William could insist on such a judgement? In 1092 he had annexed Cumbria south of the Solway. In 1093 he turned his attention to the North-East, and in this context I wish to refer to the charter of Duncan II of 1094 and that of Edgar of 1095, both in favour of St Cuthbert for lands north of the Tweed.[55] These were drawn up after the slaying of Malcolm and when the initiative, in terms of political influence in Northumbria, had passed temporarily from the Scots, and when the monks at Durham and the English king were able to exploit ruthlessly the Scottish succession crises.

In his grant, Duncan is by hereditary right king of the Scots. William Rufus is not mentioned and there is no claim to overlordship. Duncan is making his grant out of the possessions held south of the Forth by the late Bishop Fothad of St Andrews. To all intents and purposes this is a gift of the hereditary king of the Scots, made independently of the English king. There is nothing which could associate the grant with Lothian as part of the larger kingdom of Scotland. The issue of Lothian is not addressed, suggesting that it was being held back to be dealt with separately. Not one of the signatories could be clearly identified as a lay or ecclesiastical baron of William's court, but Duncan's brother Edgar supports his right.

Turning to Edgar's charter, this is a different matter. 'Edgar son of Malcolm, king of the Scots, holds all the land of Lothian and the kingdom of the Scots by gift of his lord William, king of the English, and by paternal inheritance.' Edgar's right is one of lineal descent against his uncle Donald and is protected by the witnesses who include his brothers Alexander and David, and one of Duncan's sons; also Constantine son of MacDuff, and if we accept that he was descended from the senior line of Dubh discarded in 1005, then his presence suggests his right to enkinging (i.e. installing a king on the throne).[56] Lothian now passed formally to

---

[53] *Fl. Wig.* II, 31. The problems of translating *rectitudinem facere* have been previously addressed. See for example, Barlow, *William Rufus*, p. 310.

[54] E. Mason, 'William Rufus: Myth and Reality?', *Journal of Medieval History* 3 (1977), pp. 6–7 and 11.

[55] *ESC*, no. 12, pp. 10–11 and no. 15, pp. 12–13. A.A.M. Duncan, 'The Earliest Scottish Charters', *Scottish Historical Review* 37 (1958), pp. 103–35. J. Donnelly, 'The Earliest Scottish Charters?', ibid. 68 (1989), pp. 1–22; see p. 2 for his definition of these charters (DCDCM, Misc. Ch. 554 and 559). I am aware of the difficulties of using the extant copy of Edgar's charter as historical evidence for 1095.

[56] Duncan, *Scotland: the Making of the Kingdom*, pp. 114–15.

the sons of the second marriage. Anyone who could challenge Edgar's rights to the kingdom of the Scots or Lothian, or indeed William Rufus's right to be involved, is seen to give assent. Edgar the Aetheling, representing the house of Wessex, is also a signatory. Equally important, it is the first written legal record that Lothian was part of the larger kingdom of Scotland.

In the context of Mason's argument, I would suggest that William is using this occasion to force the son to do what he could not force the father to do: to accept the border at the Tweed between the kingdoms according to the judgement of his own barons only. Whilst William's concern was to establish the parameters of his kingdom within which his own justice would prevail, Malcolm's acceptance of such a judgement on the issue of the border, or indeed of Lothian, would have reduced him to the status of a client king. Appended to some of the surviving copies of this charter is a confirmation drawn up at Norham, in the cemetery of the church of St Cuthbert, in the presence of Bishop William and Prior Turgot, and of leading named lay barons of England and of a great unnamed multitude of *Francorum et Anglorum*. Lawrie suggested that Edgar appeared to be holding some sort of court.[57] I would suggest that it was not Edgar who was holding a court, but that it represented one of William Rufus, in the presence of his own barons in his own court in his own kingdom. The *continuatio prima* of the *Libellus de exordio*, when recording the building of Norham castle by Bishop Ranulf in 1121, referred to the Tweed as the border between the English and Scottish kingdoms.[58] This is the first reference in Durham writings to the Tweed in these terms, rather than as a border between the two provinces of Lothian and Northumbria. In effect William had put a legal written line through the older Patrimony of St Cuthbert. He had limited a friendship forged outside the royal court and possible future Scottish influence south of the Tweed whilst leaving unhampered any claims which the Patrimony might have north of that river. Malcolm had seen the limitations in accepting such a judgement, and in his anger and humiliation he resorted to the old ploy. He led an armed expedition across the Tweed to draw William north to be forced to ratify, in the old style and at a military disadvantage, an alliance of friendship close to the confines of the kingdom of the Scots, i.e. at or near the Forth, and subject to the judgement of the men of both kingdoms. He lost the initiative, and paid with his life and that of his son Edward.[59]

Much of the written evidence on which this paper is based comes from the twelfth century, when the initiative for political exploitation of a spiritual friendship with Durham had passed from Malcolm. The brief contemporary record of Malcolm's presence in August 1093 was entered in the *De iniusta* and thereafter there seems to have been a decade or so during which no major written works were undertaken at Durham. When the Scottish-West Saxon association with Durham came to be set down in writing in the early- to mid-twelfth century following the

57 *ESC*, p. 248.
58 *Sym. Op.* I, 140 (first continuation of *LDE*): 'in confinio regni Anglorum et Scottorum'. This first reference is noted by Barrow, 'The Anglo-Scottish Border', p. 36.
59 *ASC, s.a.* 1093; and *Fl. Wig.* II, 31.

marriage of Henry I to Malcolm's daughter Edith-Matilda, it would be from a different perspective. I have already drawn attention to the entries in the *Liber Vitae*. When the familial continuity of devotion to St Cuthbert from Athelstan to Edmund in the *Historia de sancto Cuthberto* was copied into the *Libellus de exordio*, it was extended to include Eadred, the third son of Edward the Elder.[60] This is surely no coincidence. Taken together with the inclusion of miracle stories to demonstrate William I's eventual appreciation of the power of the saint, of William II's grants to, and protection of, the community, and his deference to Turgot, it is a lesson directed at Henry I, the third son of the Conqueror.[61] Malcolm did not live long enough after the foundation ceremony to be rehabilitated in writing in the manner of the first Norman king, but his family continued to play a part in the affairs of the Patrimony. It is Malcolm III whose name should be associated with the foundation of the new cathedral, and the possible political implications at that time should be borne in mind. He was a king capable of seeing all the advantages of associating his whole family as benefactors and protectors of the community at Durham.

---

[60] *HSC*, §§ 15, 16, 19, 21, and 25–8; and *LDE*, bk. 2, chs. 10, 15, 17, 18, and 20.
[61] *LDE*, bk. 3, chs. 15, 19, and 20.

Scottish Influence on Durham 1066–1214

PAUL DALTON

T HE MOST CONSPICUOUS influence exercised by the Scots on the land of St Cuthbert (that is, most of modern county Durham) was military. The Scots had posed a military threat to the community of St Cuthbert for centuries before the arrival of the Normans.[1] In the eleventh century we are told that the Scots besieged Durham in 1006 and 1039, violated the peace of St Cuthbert on Lindisfarne in 1061, and ravaged the land between the rivers Tyne and Tees in 1070 and 1091.[2] In the twelfth century they launched further plundering attacks on the land of St Cuthbert in 1136 and 1138.[3]

Despite their military power the Scots were never able to establish permanent control of Durham. Indeed, if we choose to believe Richard of Hexham's description of the Scottish defeat at the battle of the Standard in 1138, they never stood a chance, because wherever they went they could not escape the long arms of God and St Cuthbert which were bound to stop them:

> The ground on which the . . . battle was fought was alone the possession of St Cuthbert, the whole surrounding district being owned by others; and this occurred not by design of the combatants, but by the dispensation of Providence; for it may clearly be observed that divine justice would not allow to go unpunished the iniquity that had been perpetrated in the territory of this holy and beloved confessor and bishop, but would speedily visit it with wonted vengeance.[4]

[1] A.O. Anderson, *Scottish Annals from English Chroniclers A.D. 500 to 1286* (London, 1908; repr. Stamford, 1991), pp. 11, 36, 42–3, 47, 49–50, 55–6, 62–3, and 80–6.

My thanks are due to Mr A.J. Piper and Dr J.M. Fewster for their help and kindness during my visits to the Durham archives and special collections, and to Bill Aird, Geoffrey Barrow, and Alan Young for reading this paper in advance of publication. My gratitude is also due to the British Academy, the Liverpool Institute of Higher Education, and Sheffield University for financial support towards the research for this paper.

[2] *De obsessione Dunelmi*, in *Sym. Op.* I, 215–16; *LDE*, bk. 3, ch. 9; *HReg, s.a.* 1061, 1070; A.O. Anderson, *Early Sources of Scottish History* (2 vols; Edinburgh, 1922; repr. Stamford, 1990), II, 23 and notes; *De miraculis*, ch. 10 (*Sym. Op.* II, 338–41); and *ASC* 'E', *s.a.* 1091.

[3] *Sym. Op.* II, 287 and 291–3 (continuation of *HReg* by John of Hexham); *CR* III, 153, 155–6, and 159.

[4] *CR* III, 165.

The iniquity of which Richard speaks was the military devastation of the land of St Cuthbert carried out by the Scots while on their way to the Standard.[5] There is little doubt, in spite of the probable exaggeration of the chroniclers, that the Scottish attacks on the land of St Cuthbert involved widespread plunder and destruction. In 1070 King Malcolm is said to have 'savagely overrun the lands of St Cuthbert and robbed all men of everything, and several of their very lives also'.[6] In 1138 King David devastated 'the greatest part of the land of St Cuthbert, in the eastern district between Durham and the sea. . . Very many also of the farms of the monks who serve God and St Cuthbert day and night he destroyed in like manner . . . and with them their cultivators.'[7]

In the absence of estate surveys and pipe rolls the economic impact of these attacks on the land of St Cuthbert is difficult to determine with any sort of precision. However, it is likely that although extremely injurious at the time, the debilitating effects of the attacks were short-lived. This is the conclusion which has been reached by Dr Lomas in his recent study of border warfare in north-eastern England in the much better documented period between 1296 and 1603.[8] In the late eleventh and twelfth centuries individual Scottish campaigns in the land of St Cuthbert were brief in duration, probably rarely exceeding a period of a few weeks, and almost certainly never longer than a few months; and they were usually separated by periods of several years, during which time the devastated lands could recover. It is unlikely that the campaigns ever took in all of the settlements which lay between the rivers Tyne and Tees. In January or February 1138 King David's army is specifically stated to have ravaged only the land between Durham and the mountains, and to have returned in April to plunder that between Durham and the sea. Even after all this, David was still able to find crops, vills and churches which 'had been left untouched on the other occasion' when he invaded the region for the third time that year, probably in July or August.[9] The Scots were also prepared to exempt lands from destruction in return for payment. In 1138 the monastery of Tynemouth, 'paid to the king of Scotland and his followers twenty-seven marks of silver, to buy for itself and for those who resided there peace in the present need'.[10] In 1174 Bishop Puiset paid William the Lion 300 marks for the extension of a truce.[11]

If the suffering of the countryside around Durham may have been short-lived, the city itself probably escaped the worst of the devastation. Despite the fact that King David is reported on one occasion to have been planning to attack Durham, the only time in the Anglo-Norman period that the Scots besieged or gained access to the city appears to have been during the election dispute of the early

5   Op. cit., p. 159.
6   *HReg, s.a.* 1070.
7   *CR* III, 155.
8   R. Lomas, *North-East England in the Middle Ages* (Edinburgh, 1992), pp. 54–72.
9   *CR* III, 153, 155, and 159.
10 Op. cit., p. 153.
11 *Gesta Regis Henrici Secundi Benedicti Abbatis*, ed. W. Stubbs (2 vols., RS 49; 1867), I, 64; and *Chronica Magistri Rogeri de Houedene*, ed. W. Stubbs (4 vols., RS 51; 1868–71), II, 57.

1140s.[12] One chronicler, in describing the reaction of the people of Northumbria to King Malcolm's invasion of 1091, reveals that Durham was considered to be a safe haven from the Scots, and in doing so suggests a probable reason for the Scottish reluctance to attack the city: 'many, and especially those who are called peculiarly St Cuthbert's people, carried their goods to Durham; for here in times of danger they have ever a sure place of refuge, trusting in the protection not so much of the place as of the peace due to the presence of the holy body.'[13]

This description strongly suggests that the Scottish leadership held back from attacking Durham out of respect for the power of St Cuthbert. The suggestion is strengthened by the respect displayed by this leadership for the peace of the town of Hexham, the resting place of other Northumbrian saints. During his first invasion of 1138, for example, King David 'respected the dignity and age of the church of Hexham . . . preserved peace with it and all who had taken refuge at it; sending there five Scots, lest anyone dared to invade it with a hostile intention.'[14]

If the destructive influence of Scottish aggression on Durham and the lands attached to it was not as harmful as might be supposed, this was also true of its influence on the attitude of the Durham community towards the Scots. Dr Meehan has argued that the attitude of the Durham monks to outsiders was to some extent ambivalent; they had to balance their aggression towards outsiders with a protective attitude towards their bishops, and with a desire to maintain and expand the territorial basis of their community.[15] Meehan based his conclusions mainly on the relations between the Durham monks and the Normans. A similar ambivalence may be detected in the attitude of the monks to the Scots, and is to be explained in similar terms.

The monks of Durham were aware that although the Scots could be enemies of Durham, they could also enrich the community, as the donations made by Scottish kings and magnates in Lothian testified.[16] Thus, while the Durham writers were happy to record Scottish defeats, and to castigate the Scots as barbarians, their superiors were ready to make agreements with King Malcolm III and his queen concerning charitable acts at Durham and the celebration of their anniversaries and those of their children after their deaths, and to admit their names and the names of their relatives into the Durham *Liber Vitae* which commemorated the *confratres* of the church who were prayed for as members of the community.[17] Moreover, they

---

[12] *CR* III, 145; *Sym. Op.* II, 309; and A. Young, *William Cumin: Border Politics and the Bishopric of Durham 1141–1144* (Borthwick Paper, 54; York, 1979), p. 27.

[13] *De miraculis*, ch. 10 (*Sym. Op.* II, 338–41).

[14] *Sym. Op.* II, 290 (continuation of *HReg* by John of Hexham).

[15] B. Meehan, 'Outsiders, Insiders and Property in Durham around 1100', in *Church, Society and Politics*, ed. D. Baker (Studies in Church History 12; Oxford, 1975), pp. 50–6.

[16] Above, p. 313. See also W.M. Aird, 'St Cuthbert, the Scots, and the Normans', *AN* 16 (1994), pp. 1–20.

[17] See above, note 2; B. Colgrave, 'The Post-Bedan Miracles and Translations of St Cuthbert', in *The Early Cultures of North-West Europe: H.M. Chadwick Memorial Studies*, ed. C. Fox and B. Dickins (Cambridge, 1950), pp. 311 and 324; and *Liber vitae ecclesiae Dunelmensis nec non Obituaria duo ejusdem ecclesiae*, ed. J. Stevenson (SS 13; 1841), pp. 2–3 and 73.

appear to have allowed Malcolm to participate in the laying of the foundation stones of the new cathedral in 1093, and the future King Alexander I to be the only layman to attend the inspection of the body of St Cuthbert and its translation to this cathedral in 1104. The political significance of this has been examined by Valerie Wall.[18] The foundation and translation were doubtless intended in part to impress upon the Scottish royal dynasty that the political and spiritual power of Cuthbert was still very much intact and at Durham. The corollary of this is that Scottish military power and potential Scottish patronage should be counted among the complex range of factors which influenced the Durham monks to promote and develop the cult of St Cuthbert in the eleventh and twelfth centuries, and in doing so to construct a new cathedral and to translate the holy body there in 1104.

There were other forms of peaceful contacts between Scotland and Durham which served as channels or potential channels for feeding the growth of Scottish influence between the rivers Tyne and Tees: religious, familial, and tenurial. The tenurial ties of the community of St Cuthbert with Scotland stretched back centuries.[19] Although most of these ties had been severed by the mid-tenth century, in the Anglo-Norman period the community of Durham was determined to restore them. The most obvious example of this, which has been examined by Professor Barrow, is the establishment of a cell at Coldingham and its later development into a fully fledged priory.[20] Other connections began to be restored in the early 1070s when the future priors of Durham, Aldwin of Winchcombe and Turgot, went to Melrose to revive the religious life there.[21]

Although Aldwin and Turgot were persecuted by King Malcolm and soon returned to England, the convent of Durham maintained a claim to Melrose, and Turgot maintained his links with Scotland.[22] While prior of Durham, Turgot participated with Malcolm in laying the foundation stones of the new cathedral in 1093, and possibly wrote a *Life* of Malcolm's queen, Margaret. This *Life* indicates that the author was an intimate friend and confidant of the queen, had been entrusted by her with the custody of her children, and had been in regular contact with her, possibly throughout her life in Scotland. One version of the *Life* states that Turgot was Margaret's confessor and was summoned to hear her life story when she knew she was dying.[23] Turgot's relations with Margaret may provide part of the explanation for the presence of Alexander of Scotland in Durham in 1104, and Alexander's choice of Turgot to be bishop of St Andrews and head of the Scottish church in 1107. Although Turgot and Alexander subsequently quarrelled,

[18] *HReg, s.a.* 1093; *De miraculis*, ch. 7 (*Sym. Op.* I, 258); and above, pp. 325–37.

[19] H.H.E. Craster, 'The Patrimony of St Cuthbert', *EHR* 69 (1954), pp. 179–80.

[20] Above, p. 319.

[21] D. Knowles, *The Monastic Order in England* (2nd edn, Cambridge, 1966), pp. 167–8.

[22] *LDE*, bk. 3, ch. 22; and *ESC*, no. 99.

[23] L.L. Huneycutt, 'The Idea of the Perfect Princess: The *Life of St Margaret* in the Reign of Matilda II (1100–1118)', *AN* 12 (1990), p. 85. For the *Life*, see *Vita S. Margaretae Scotorum Reginae*, in *Symeonis Dunelmensis Opera et Collectanea*, ed. J. Hodgson Hinde (SS 51; 1868), pp. 234–54; D. Baker, ' "A Nursery of Saints": St Margaret of Scotland Reconsidered', in *Studies in Church History Subsidia: Medieval Women*, ed. D. Baker (Oxford, 1978), pp. 128–32.

and Turgot returned to England, eventually dying at Durham in 1115, his career and writings clearly illustrate the operation of Scottish influence on Durham.

An even more famous Northumbrian monk to have very close connections with both Scotland and Durham was Ailred of Rievaulx. Ailred's great-grandfather, Alfred son of Westou, was a Durham canon; his grandfather, Eilaf I, served as treasurer of the church of Durham; his father, Eilaf II, was a tenant and benefactor of the community of Durham, and retired to become a monk there in 1138; and his kinsman, William Havegrim, was an archdeacon of Durham and one of the men who inspected the body of St Cuthbert in 1104. Ailred almost certainly acquired part of his education at Durham, but was brought up with King David's son Henry at the Scottish royal court. He subsequently held a minor post in David's household, and was employed by the king on diplomatic missions before entering the abbey of Rievaulx; a move which Dr Dutton has recently argued was planned in advance by David and others as the logical fulfilment of a career directed from the first towards power and authority.

Whilst at Rievaulx, Ailred maintained close contacts with Scotland and Durham. In 1138 he appears to have stayed at Durham while accompanying Abbot William of Rievaulx north to the siege of Wark. In 1147 he was involved in the settlement at Durham of a dispute between the prior and archdeacon. At some point before 1154 he received a letter from Laurence, who became prior of Durham in 1143, which refers to Ailred as a friend.[24] Together with Prior Thomas of Durham he selected the Durham monk Reginald to write the *Life* of Godric of Finchale; and he encouraged and helped Reginald to compose his *Miracles of St Cuthbert*.[25] The miracle stories with which Ailred supplied Reginald had been collected while the abbot was journeying through Galloway; probably during his periodic excursions to the daughter houses of Rievaulx which had been established with the help of King David at Melrose in 1136 and at Dundrennan in 1142. We have no evidence that Ailred attended the Scottish court during these visits; but what we do know is that Ailred's writings in this period reveal a deep respect for King Edgar and King Alexander, and a strong devotion to King David. Moreover, as Sir Maurice Powicke suggested, these writings almost certainly reflect political ideas prevalent at the Scottish court. If, as Dr Foster suggests, Ailred was able to influence the attitude of the Durham monks to the pre-monastic community of Durham, he may also have been able to influence their attitude to the Scots;[26] and it is interesting that his friend Prior Laurence wrote verses in praise of King David.

Turgot and Ailred were not the only clergy connected with both Scotland and

---

[24] For the above details, see *The Life of Ailred of Rievaulx by Walter Daniel*, ed. and trans. F.M. Powicke (Oxford, 1978), pp. xxx, xxxv–xlviii, lxx, lxxv, xc–xciv, 3–4, 10, 13–16, and 33; Knowles, *Monastic Order*, pp. 241–5, 630; M.L. Dutton, 'The Conversion and Vocation of Aelred of Rievaulx: A Historical Hypothesis', in *England in the Twelfth Century*, ed. D. Williams (Woodbridge, 1990), pp. 31–49. I am grateful to Professor Barrow for his suggestion that Ailred's position in David's household was not as important as has hitherto been assumed.
[25] V. Tudor, 'The Cult of St Cuthbert in the Twelfth Century: the Evidence of Reginald of Durham', in *Cuthbert*, pp. 448–9 and 462.
[26] Above, p. 63.

Durham. We know that Samson and Alan 'monks of Durham' witnessed a charter of Robert bishop of St Andrews issued *c.*1148. It has been suggested that Samson may afterwards have become bishop of Brechin.[27] The appointment of Patrick, sub-prior of Durham, to the abbacy of Dunfermline in 1202 shows that Durham monks continued to be attracted by careers in Scotland.[28] This may also have been true of some of Durham's most prominent clerics in the time of Bishop Puiset, including Master William of Howden and his son Master John, Master William of Blois, Master Angerius, and Master Richard of Coldingham, who appear to have attested Scottish charters.[29] It is possible that Master Richard and two of his most influential contemporary Durham clerics who also possessed what are possibly Scottish toponymic surnames, Master Walter and Master Robert of Haddington (East Lothian?), originated in Scotland.[30]

More ecclesiastical ties between Durham and Scotland are illustrated by the Durham Cantor's Book (DCL, MS B.IV.24) which records that masses were to be said for Alan monk of Melrose and *Efrardus* monk of Newbattle after their deaths, and that the convents of Durham and Dunfermline had also made an agreement concerning the saying of masses for the souls of departed Dunfermline monks. Among the obits commemorated at Durham we find those of Richard, bishop of St Andrews (1165–78), Herbert, abbot of Kelso (*c.*1128–47), *Bricius* and Hugh monks of Kelso, and Adam monk of Dunfermline.[31] The Cantor's Book reveals that the relationship between Durham and John abbot of Kelso (1160–80) was even closer. We read that:

> Upon the death of lord John . . . there shall be one plenary service for him in the convent, as is usual in the case of a brother who dies outside the church. Thirty masses shall be given for him by the priests; and in the next *tricenna-rium* that is said after his death, it shall be done for him as for one of our brethren. Each person of lower rank shall chant for [him] fifty psalms . . . and his name shall be placed in the martyrology, among the names of our brethren.[32]

We should be wary of taking such arrangements at their face value. The favour shown by the Durham community to Abbot John of Kelso may have something to do with the fact that Durham and Kelso had engaged in a conflict in 1171 over possession of the chapel of Earlston in Berwickshire, which had ended with Kelso's surrender.[33] It is possible that what we are seeing here is the Durham community

27 *ESC*, no. 206 and p. 416.
28 Anderson, *Early Sources*, II, 349 n. 4.
29 G.V. Scammell, *Hugh du Puiset, Bishop of Durham* (Cambridge, 1956), pp. 100, 235–6, and 255; *RRS*, II, no. 161; and G.W.S. Barrow, *The Kingdom of the Scots* (London, 1973), p. 135 n. 267.
30 For the Haddingtons, see Scammell, *Puiset*, pp. 70, 101, 255, 260, and 262.
31 *Liber Vitae*, ed. Stevenson, pp. 139, 137, 143, 94, 95, and 105.
32 Ibid., p. 138.
33 Scammell, *Puiset*, pp. 119 and 159.

balancing its aggression towards ecclesiastical outsiders with a desire to preserve its lands and rights, in the same way that it balanced its aggression towards secular outsiders. However, it is probable that there was more to it than this. The twelfth century, arguably, was the great age of the cult of St Cuthbert, and it is clear that at this time Durham's development as a pilgrimage centre proceeded apace.[34] There was a great deal of genuine and strong devotion to St Cuthbert north of the border which the monks of Durham were keen to promote, and it would be a mistake to doubt that the commemoration of the names of Scottish ecclesiastics in the Durham Cantor's Book owed something to the expression of this devotion at Durham, and to heartfelt thanks of the Durham community.[35]

The religious, familial and tenurial ties between Scotland and Durham were not confined to clergy. As Professor Barrow has noted, the Durham *Liber Vitae* shows a steady stream of Scottish secular lords paying their respects to St Cuthbert in the twelfth century. They included Dugald son of Somerled lord of Argyll and his sons; Earl Duncan II of Fife with his brother Adam; Duncan's kinsman, Laurence of Abernethy, and his wife Dervorguilla; Earl Malcolm son of Madet of Atholl, his wife Hextilda the former wife of Richard Comyn, and several of their relatives; and representatives of the families of Louvetot, Ridel, Stewart, Brus, Comyn, Colville, del Bois, Vaux, Lindsay, and the earls of Dunbar.[36]

The ties between many of these families and Durham went beyond the occasional pilgrimage and seeking of confraternity. This can be seen in the case of the earls of Dunbar who were the descendants of Uhtred and Gospatric I, earls of Northumbria, and who were related to the Scottish royal family.[37] Uhtred was married for a time to the daughter of Bishop Aldhun of Durham, may have influenced the bishop's decision to establish the shrine of St Cuthbert at Durham in 995, and possibly played a vital role in lifting the Scottish siege of Durham in 1006.[38] Gospatric was implicated in the murder of Robert de Comines at Durham in 1069, and advised Bishop Aethelwine to flee to Lindisfarne when the Conqueror came north in the same year.[39]

It is possible that the relations between Gospatric I and his descendants with Durham remained close, if not always friendly, after his flight to Scotland in 1072.[40] It may have been Gospatric I who brought Aldwin and Turgot to settle at

---

[34] Tudor, 'Cult of St Cuthbert', pp. 447–67.

[35] R.B. Dobson, *Durham Priory 1400–1450* (Cambridge, 1973), pp. 18–19; and Tudor, 'Cult of St Cuthbert', pp. 457 and 462–6.

[36] G.W.S. Barrow, *The Anglo-Norman Era in Scottish History* (Oxford, 1980), p. 159, citing *Liber Vitae*, ed. Stevenson, pp. 4, 135, 37, 94, 112, and 100. See also *Liber Vitae*, ed. Stevenson, pp. 50, 53, 69, 83, 99, 102, and 109–10.

[37] See A.A.M. Duncan, *Scotland: The Making of the Kingdom* (Edinburgh, 1975), p. 118; *DEC*, p. 2; Anderson, *Early Sources*, II, 39–40, 91 n. 5; idem, *Scottish Annals*, p. 81 and n. 1, and p. 96. But see also A.O. Anderson, 'Anglo-Scottish Relations from Constantine II to William', *Scottish Historical Review* 42 (1963), p. 8 and n. 4; and B. Meehan, 'The Siege of Durham, the Battle of Carham and the Cession of Lothian', ibid., 55 (1976), p. 3.

[38] Dobson, *Durham Priory*, p. 23; above n. 2.

[39] *HReg*, *s.a.* 1072; and *LDE*, bk. 3, ch. 16.

[40] For Gospatric's career, see Duncan, *Scotland*, pp. 118–20, and 122.

Melrose, and he is also stated to have summoned them to hear his confession shortly before his death.[41] The Edward son of Gospatric and Waltheof son of Edward who are named in the Durham *Liber Vitae* may have been Gospatric I's son and grandson respectively.[42] Gospatric I's heir, Gospatric II (d.1135 x 1139), appears to have been a somewhat reluctant grantor of lands in Edrom and Nisbet (Berwickshire) to Durham; and his grandson, Gospatric III (d.1166), seized the properties which his father had bestowed on Durham.[43] Despite this it has been suggested that Gospatric III is the 'Cospatricius earl and monk' who appears in the Durham Cantor's Book, and the 'Earl Gospatric' whose inscribed tombstone has been found at Durham.[44]

A number of prominent families holding lands of the bishopric of Durham acquired lands or other associations north of the border in the course of the twelfth century. They included the Vescys,[45] the Muschamps,[46] the Percys,[47] the Brus, the Balliols,[48] the Colvilles,[49] the Farlingtons,[50] the Papedys,[51] the Nobles[52] and the Audreys,[53] most of whose connections with Scotland are well known. In addition a number of Scottish nobles acquired lands or other associations in the land of St Cuthbert. One of the earliest to do so was Thor Longus who, in or about 1105,

---

[41] Anderson, *Early Sources*, II, 38, and 59 n. 1.

[42] Op. cit., p. 38.

[43] Duncan, *Scotland*, p. 143.

[44] Anderson, *Early Sources*, II, 264 n. 1.

[45] *The Red Book of the Exchequer*, ed. H. Hall (3 vols., RS 99; 1896), I, 417. For Eustace Fitz John, the ancestor of the Vescys, see below, pp. 350–1; and *ESC*, nos. 115, 123, 133, 177, and 247; and *RRS*, I, nos. 17 and 21. Fitz John's grandson, Eustace of Vescy, married William the Lion's daughter Margaret, and fought with King Alexander II in 1216: *Rogeri de Wendover Liber qui dicitur Flores Historiarum, ed. H.G. Hewlett (3 vols., RS 84; 1886–9), II, 194; Anderson, Early Sources*, II, 410 and notes; idem, *Scottish Annals*, pp. 320, 331, and 334 and notes.

[46] A.M. Oliver, 'The Family of Muschamp, Barons of Wooler', *Arch. Ael.*, 4th ser. 14 (1937), pp. 243–7.

[47] *Early Yorkshire Charters* (vols. I–III, ed. W. Farrer, Edinburgh, 1914–16; vols. IV–XII, ed. C.T. Clay, Yorks. Arch. Soc. rec. ser. extra ser., 1935–65), XI, 2–3; and *Red Book*, I, 416.

[48] *ESC*, no. 54, pp. 307–8; C.M. Fraser and K. Emsley, 'Durham and the Wapentake of Sadberge', *TAASDN*, n.s. 13 (1970), pp. 71–82; G.W.S. Barrow, *Robert Bruce and the Community of the Realm of Scotland* (2nd edn, Edinburgh, 1976), pp. 28–38; K.J. Stringer, *Earl David of Huntingdon 1152–1219: A Study in Anglo-Scottish History* (Edinburgh, 1985), pp. 186–9; G. Stell, 'The Balliol Family and the Great Cause of 1291–2', in *Essays on the Nobility of Medieval Scotland*, ed. K.J. Stringer (Edinburgh, 1985), pp. 150–65; and VCH *Durham*, ed. W. Page (3 vols.; London, 1905–28), II, 144 n. 79 and pp. 145–7.

[49] Barrow, *Anglo-Norman Era*, pp. 31–2, 47, and 177; Scammell, *Puiset*, pp. 173 and 239 and notes; and *RRS*, II, no. 489.

[50] Scammell, *Puiset*, pp. 61, 188, 190, 226, 229, and 239.

[51] Op. cit., pp. 224, 232, and 239.

[52] *Red Book*, I, 416; and Barrow, *Anglo-Norman Era*, p. 96 n. 19.

[53] Roger de Audrey, a military tenant of the demesne of St Cuthbert in 1166, may have been related to the Audreys who were tenants of the honour of Huntingdon, and to the William de Audrey who attested charters of Malcolm IV and William the Lion. See *Red Book*, I, 417; *RRS*, I, 205, nos. 213–14; II, no. 39; and W. Farrer, *Honors and Knights' Fees* (3 vols.; London and Manchester, 1923–5), II, 386.

gave the church and land in the Roxburghshire vill of Ednam to the monks of Durham for the soul of King Edgar, whom Thor refers to as his lord; a gift which may have earned Thor his obit in the Durham Cantor's Book.[54] They may also have included Robert Corbet who was granted land at Hunstanworth by Bishop Puiset before 1183.[55] Jordan I Hairon, who was a tenant of the bishopric of Durham in Yorkshire by 1166 and married the heiress of Ralph of Worcester, a military tenant of the demesne of St Cuthbert, may also have begun his career in Scotland.[56] It is also possible that William of Lindsay, lord of Crawford and justiciar of Lothian, who died c.1205, may be the same William of Lindsay who appears to have held property of the bishopric of Durham in the vill of Barford.[57]

It remains to consider the extent to which the occasional military power exercised by the Scots in the land of St Cuthbert, and their religious, familial and tenurial ties with the region enabled them to command political support there. It is a question bound up with fact that, 'Until, and indeed well beyond, the date of the Norman Conquest, Saint Cuthbert's power and reputation was . . . entangled – in a way which still needs to be analysed in detail – with the political issue of "Northumbrian Separatism".'[58] One element in this separatism was political independence from the Scots; and the entanglement of St Cuthbert and his convent with it is illustrated, perhaps, in the miracle stories written at Durham before and during the Anglo-Norman period which depict Cuthbert intervening to foil Scottish attacks on his community.[59] By the 1140s the will of the Durham convent had 'hardened to a masterful independence';[60] reflected most graphically in the fierce resistance offered by the convent to the attempt of the Scottish chancellor, William Cumin, to establish himself as bishop of Durham between 1141 and 1144.[61]

Several of the bishops of Durham appear to have been as determined as the convent to maintain the political independence of the community from Scotland. Bishop Aethelwine appears not to have followed the drift of northern nobles who sought refuge from Norman aggression north of the border, and went to Scotland

---

[54] *ESC*, no. 24, and see nos. 33–4; J. Raine, *The History and Antiquities of North Durham* (London, 1852), Appendix, nos. 102, 161–2; and *Liber Vitae*, ed. Stevenson, p. 143.

[55] Scammell, *Puiset*, p. 228. Robert may have been a member of the Corbet family who were originally tenants of the lordship of Huntingdon before obtaining interests in Scotland. See Barrow, *Anglo-Norman Era*, p. 98; *ESC*, nos. 35, 46, 50, 74, 83, 94, and 103; and *RRS*, I, nos. 6, 7, and 131; and II, 41 and 64, nos. 63 and 246 and note.

[56] W. Percy Hedley, 'The Origin of the Families of Heron and Swinburne', *Arch. Ael.*, 4th ser. 37 (1959), pp. 291–301. Bishop Puiset granted additional lands to Jordan and to a Gilbert Hairon by 1183, and employed a Richard Hairon as one of his clerks: see Scammell, *Puiset*, p. 236.

[57] *FPD*, p. 53 n. 1.

[58] Dobson, *Durham Priory*, p. 24.

[59] *HSC*, § 33; *De miraculis*, ch. 10 (*Sym. Op.* II, 338–41); and Colgrave, 'Post-Bedan Miracles', pp. 313–14. For the motives behind the writing of the Durham miracle stories, see W.M. Aird, 'The Making of a Medieval Miracle Collection: The *Liber de Translationibus et Miraculis Sancti Cuthberti*', *Northern History* 28 (1992), pp. 1–24.

[60] Scammell, *Puiset*, p. 129.

[61] Young, *William Cumin*, pp. 11 and 14–25.

only after being driven there by an unfavourable wind during an attempt to sail to Cologne.[62] His independence or neutrality is possibly also reflected in his adoption of the role of mediator between King Malcolm and King William in 1068.[63] Bishop Walcher made his position clear in the early 1070s. When he heard that King Malcolm had demanded fealty from Aldwin and Turgot, who had settled at Melrose, Walcher 'threatened that he with the clergy and all the people would excommunicate [Aldwin and Turgot] in the presence of the most sacred body of St Cuthbert, unless they returned to him to dwell under St Cuthbert'.[64] Bishop Flambard's attitude to the Scots is probably best reflected in his construction of a castle at Norham and his improvement of the fortifications at Durham.[65] Bishop Geoffrey seems to have been reluctant to commit himself fully to either side in the conflict between the kings of England and Scotland in 1138; refusing to swear fealty to King David, but offering little resistance to Scottish incursions.[66] The same was true of Bishop Puiset during the rebellion of 1173–4 when he promised unopposed passage to King William of Scotland and his army through his lands, but never actively supported Scottish aggression.[67] Although all these bishops were undoubtedly trying to protect their bishopric from Scottish depredations, it is more than likely that their policies were also influenced by a determination to maintain the political independence of their community from Scotland.

With the exception of the unusual circumstances of the 1140s, there is little evidence that the Anglo-Norman tenants of the land of St Cuthbert owed or displayed any political allegiance to the Scots in this period. In the 1173–4 rebellion one of these tenants, William of Vescy, fought on the English side against the Scots.[68] The only nobleman connected with Durham who is known to have joined the Scots in the rebellion is Thomas of Muschamp.[69] In addition, Jukel of Smeaton, one of Bishop Puiset's *familia*, and the vill of Northallerton, were fined for communing with the enemies of Henry II. However, no tenants from the county of Durham appear among those amerced for this offence, suggesting that they did not side with the Scots.[70]

Although the Anglo-Norman tenants of the land of St Cuthbert appear to have been mostly opposed to Scottish penetration of the North, as Professor Barrow suggests it may have been a different matter where the indigenous northern thegns

---

[62] *HReg, s.a.* 1070; *LDE*, bk. 3, ch. 17.
[63] *Orderic*, II, 218.
[64] *LDE*, bk. 3, ch. 22.
[65] H.S. Offler, 'Rannulf Flambard as Bishop of Durham (1099–1128)', *Durham University Journal* n.s. 33 (1971–2), p. 20.
[66] *CR* III, 157. The banner of St Cuthbert was conspicuous by its absence at the battle of the Standard in 1138.
[67] *Radulfi de Diceto Decani Lundoniensis Opera Historica*, ed. W. Stubbs (2 vols., RS 68; 1876), I, 376; *Jordan Fantosme's Chronicle*, ed. R.C. Johnston (Oxford, 1981), p. 40; and Scammell, *Puiset*, pp. 37–43.
[68] *Red Book*, I, 417; and *Jordan Fantosme's Chronicle*, pp. 40, 42, 88, and 140.
[69] *Gesta Regis Henrici Secundi*, I, 48; Barrow, *Anglo-Norman Era*, p. 18; *RRS*, II, nos. 126, 135, 147–8, 175, 201–2; and *Pipe Roll 21 Henry II* (Pipe Roll Society; London, 1897), pp. 172–3.
[70] Scammell, *Puiset*, pp. 42–3.

and drengs were concerned.[71] This is illustrated by a famous agreement between Prior Algar of Durham and Dolfin son of Uhtred made in 1131. The agreement states that the prior and convent conceded to Dolfin and his heirs the important territory of Staindrop and Staindropshire, and that in return Dolfin was to become 'homo ligius Sancti Cuthberti et Prioris et monachorum, salua fidelitate Regis Angliae et Regis Scociae et Dunelm. Episcopi Domini nostri, et ligiorum dominorum suorum'.[72] This agreement indicates that the king of Scotland was one of several men to whom one of the most important tenants of Durham owed fealty. But it also implies either that the Durham monks may not have known to whom Dolfin owed ultimate allegiance, or that Dolfin may have been keeping his options open. It is just possible that on at least one occasion in the twelfth century some of Dolfin's relatives put their loyalty to Scotland before their loyalty to Durham and England. During one of the Scottish invasions of England in 1138 a group of warriors under the command of Edgar son of Earl Gospatric sallied from the camp of the king of Scotland, attempted to plunder the land of St Cuthbert, and having failed to do so proceeded to ravage lands belonging to the church of Hexham.[73] Accompanying Edgar, according to Richard of Hexham, were Robert and Uhtred sons of Meldred, men who were probably related to Dolfin, and who may have been his nephews or cousins.[74]

The only time in the period from 1066 to 1214 when the Scots appear to have been able to exercise considerable political influence within Durham was during the Durham election dispute from 1141 to 1144. Dr Young has shown that up until King David's desertion of his chancellor in 1142, William Cumin was able to secure control of the city and castle of Durham with the support of the episcopal chaplains, the keepers of Durham castle, Archdeacon Robert, some of Bishop Geoffrey's relatives, and a significant number of the most powerful barons of the bishopric of Durham, many of whom appear to have been in the Scottish king's following at this time.[75]

It is significant that during the election dispute Earl Henry appears to have been

---

[71] Above, pp. 321–2.

[72] *FPD*, p. 56 n. 1.

[73] *CR* III, 166–7; and *Sym. Op.* II, 298 (continuation of *HReg* by John of Hexham).

[74] Although Dolfin's son, Meldred, had a son named Robert, he cannot be the Robert named in 1138. Meldred occurs in the time of Bishop Geoffrey Rufus and Bishop Puiset, and his son Robert was alive in the early 1240s, aged about eighty. However, it is possible (although there is no evidence) that Meldred, the father of the Robert and Uhtred named in 1138, was either a younger brother of Uhtred (father of Dolfin), or a younger brother of Dolfin. The relationship between the Robert and Uhtred named in 1138 and Dolfin is strengthened marginally by the fact that several historians have assumed a family relationship between Dolfin and Earl Gospatric I. The assumption seems to be based on the fact that Dolfin's father or grandfather and Gospatric's brother shared the same name: Meldred. See *DEC*, p. 76, nos. 12, 29, and 31; *RRS*, II, 116; W.W. Gibson, 'The Manor of Winlaton', *Arch. Ael.*, 4th ser. 23 (1945), pp. 8–10; and J. Raine, *The Priory of Hexham* (2 vols., SS 44, 46; 1864–5), I, 95 n. c. I am grateful to Geoffrey Barrow and Alan Piper for advice on this family.

[75] Young, *William Cumin*, pp. 10–28.

more keen than his father to promote Scottish authority within Durham;[76] and it is possible, perhaps even probable, that in the early days of the dispute Henry was able to exploit Cumin's control of Durham to exercise direct administrative and judicial authority within the land of St Cuthbert. This is suggested by a charter issued at Newcastle upon Tyne by Henry in 1141. The charter commands William Cumin and Osbert the sheriff and all men of the land of St Cuthbert and Northumberland that certain lands in what was to become County Durham, 'which the monks of Saint Cuthbert hold of the earldom', shall be in peace; and that the monks were not to be impleaded in respect of this land save before the earl himself or his justice.[77] Whether Henry was claiming authority over the whole of the land of St Cuthbert, or just the comital vills named in the charter, is uncertain; but the quasi-royal style of the address clause, the absence of similar charters issued by Henry concerning the land of St Cuthbert, and the territorial jurisdiction claimed by him in Northumberland would seem to favour the former proposition.[78] What is certain is that Earl Henry was also seeking to use Cumin's position to assert claims to lands which had been in dispute between the families of the earls of Northumbria and the community of Durham since the early eleventh century.[79] And not only Cumin's position: Henry's charter also addresses Osbert the sheriff, who may have been sheriff of Durham, and who was certainly the Osbert nephew of Bishop Flambard (one of the most important military tenants of the bishopric of Durham) who served as sheriff before 1128. Professor Offler suggested that Osbert may have been restored to office by Earl Henry. Whether this is true or not, there is more than a suggestion in the earl's charter addressed to Osbert, that the Scots – albeit briefly – may have been exercising their influence over and through one of the most wealthy, well-connected and administratively experienced members of the magnate community of the land of St Cuthbert.[80]

The extent of Earl Henry's ambitions within the land of St Cuthbert in the early 1140s, and the methods he employed to achieve them, may also be reflected by a charter issued by Henry II (probably *c*.1157) confirming to William of Vescy the possessions of his father Eustace Fitz John, who is known to have supported the Scots in the late 1130s.[81] The possessions include the fee and service of Geoffrey Escolland whose descendant, Elias, held between two and three knights' fees *directly* of the land of St Cuthbert in 1166.[82] How Eustace acquired a claim to this

---

[76] See *Sym. Op.* II, 314 and 316–17 (continuation of *HReg* by John of Hexham); and Young, *William Cumin*, p. 24.

[77] *RRS*, I, no. 23.

[78] See P. Dalton, *Conquest, Anarchy and Lordship: Yorkshire 1066–1154* (Cambridge, 1994), pp. 203–7.

[79] See *DEC*, pp. 10–11.

[80] For Osbert, see *DEC*, nos. 15, 17, 20, 22–5, 26b, 27, 29–31, 35, 35a, 38–40, 42, and 45 and notes.

[81] London, Public Record Office, Chancery Miscellanea C 47 /9/5/2r, printed as an appendix to C.H. Hartshorne, *Memoirs Illustrative of the History and Antiquities of Northumberland*, Proceedings of the Archaeological Institute, Newcastle upon Tyne, 1852 (London, 1858), II, cx; *Sym. Op.* II, 291–2 (continuation of *HReg* by John of Hexham); and *CR* III, 158, 165.

[82] *Red Book*, I, 417.

overlordship is uncertain. However, his acquisition of extensive lands and overlord-ships within the honour of Huntingdon from Earl Henry at about the time of the Cumin dispute, to be held for no additional service, and his beneficial enfeoffment by Roger of Mowbray in another overlordship which later appears to have been revoked, invites the suspicion that Eustace owed his title to the Escolland fee to Scottish power in Durham in the early 1140s, and more specifically to the power of Earl Henry.[83]

In conclusion, the Scots exercised a variety of influences on Durham and the land of St Cuthbert in the period from 1066 to 1214. One of these influences was military, the real significance of which lies not so much in the devastation it caused but in the way it served to encourage the formation of more peaceful contacts between Scotland and Durham. The Scottish threat was probably one of the factors which led the monks of Durham to promote the cult of St Cuthbert in the late eleventh and twelfth centuries, and to involve the kings of Scotland in this promo-tion. There existed in this period a complex network of religious, familial and tenurial ties between Durham and Scotland, which indicate that the independence of the church and baronage of Durham was not as great as might be supposed. However, these ties do not usually appear to have been strong or abundant enough to have allowed the kings of Scotland to command substantial political support in the region between the rivers Tyne and Tees. This appears to have remained so to the end of our period when King John could still trust the prior of Durham to be a custodian of important Scottish hostages in 1213; and when outlaws from north of the border could still regard the land of St Cuthbert as a place of refuge and security from the authority of the kings of Scotland.[84] Durham, it seems, had maintained its political independence from Scotland largely intact.

This is not to argue that the multifarious ties which existed between Durham and Scotland were without political significance. During the early 1140s when the weakness of the English king and an election dispute at Durham gave the Scots the opportunity to extend their power in northern England, they were able to use and exploit their links with some of the most important political figures in the castle, church and territory of Durham to establish their chancellor in Durham, and possibly also to impose their supporter Eustace Fitz John on the Escolland fee, and their own administrative and judicial authority on the region between the rivers Tyne and Tees. Moreover, the significance of these ties is not confined to the unusual circumstances of the early 1140s. Dr Stringer has pointed out that England and Scotland were rarely at war between 1154 and 1217, and continu-ously at peace between 1217 and 1296, and that this stability was an important factor in the making of the territorial kingdom of Scotland. He has argued that in explaining these conditions the position and attitudes of magnates who had

---

[83] *RRS*, I, nos. 11–12, 14, and p. 103; and Dalton, *Conquest*, pp. 242–3. The suspicion is reinforced by Dr Young's suggestions concerning the role of Eustace in the election dispute: see below, pp. 357, 358, 361.
[84] *Calendar of Documents Relating to Scotland*, ed. J. Bain (4 vols; Edinburgh, 1881–8), I, nos. 574 and 342.

interests on both sides of the border, and whose views gained added strength from gentry families and churchmen who had established Anglo-Scottish concerns of their own, should not be discounted.[85] The evidence from Durham lends support to his argument. In mediating between Malcolm III and William I in 1068, in inviting Malcolm to help found their cathedral in 1093, in allowing the future Alexander I to be present at the translation of 1104, and in offering little or no military resistance to the Scottish incursions of the twelfth century, the community of Durham was seeking to promote peace with the Scots. Although relations between this community and the kings of Scotland may have cooled somewhat during the course of the twelfth century, other associations between Scotland and Durham were probably in the process of becoming closer and more friendly. It is highly significant, and not a little ironic, that in choosing William Scot, one of William Cumin's successors as archdeacon of Worcester, as their new bishop in 1226, the prior and convent of Durham did not share the fears of King Henry III who rejected the election on the grounds that it would be perilous to place the see of Durham in the charge of a Scotsman.[86]

[85] Stringer, *Earl David of Huntingdon*, pp. 210–11.
[86] *Calendar of Documents*, I, p. lix, nos. 942, 947, and 997.

The Bishopric of Durham in Stephen's Reign

A. YOUNG

THERE HAS BEEN a natural tendency for historians[1] to focus attention on the years 1141 to 1144 – the attempt by William Cumin, then chancellor of David I, king of Scotland, to usurp the bishopric – when discussing the bishopric of Durham in Stephen's reign. This reflects partly the preoccupations of the main primary sources, the Durham chroniclers[2] who were at the receiving end of the violence in these four years. It also reflects the fact that the episode was an unusually dramatic one[3] in the often turbulent history of northern England in the middle ages. Despite providing rich primary source material, the narratives of the Durham monks are closer to propaganda literature than analytical history. They do not adequately represent the complex interweaving of local, national and international pressures to which Durham was subjected in Stephen's reign as a whole.

The bishopric was exposed to the civil war in England, Anglo-Scottish warfare and two, not just one, disputed elections. The election controversy between 1152 and 1153 should be firmly placed alongside the more notorious dispute between 1141 and 1144. A third election dispute involving Durham's metropolitan, York, started in 1140 and continued to the end of Stephen's reign. This also had a bearing on matters in Durham. A number of other significant influences on the bishopric in this period have been relatively neglected in discussion. These include the expansion of papal jurisdiction, the growth of canon law, the influence of reformed monasticism and that of Bernard of Clairvaux. The fact that so many of these pressures were interrelated makes for a fascinating but complex mixture of political and ecclesiastical problems. The bishopric of Durham was vulnerable to a

---

[1] A. Young, *William Cumin: Border Politics and the Bishopric of Durham 1141–1144* (Borthwick Paper 54; York, 1979); R.A. Lomas, *North-East England in the Middle Ages* (Edinburgh, 1992), pp. 34–8; F. Barlow, *Durham Jurisdictional Peculiars* (Oxford, 1950), p. 16.

[2] Chiefly the unknown continuator of Symeon of Durham's chronicle, *Sym. Op.* I, 143–60, and Laurence of Durham, *Dialogi Laurentii Dunelmensis Monachi ac Prioris* (henceforth *Laurence of Durham*), ed. J. Raine (SS 70; 1870), pp. xxvii–xxviii; p. 5, bk. I lines 143–4; p. 12, bk. I, lines 429–30.

[3] For the detailed story including the infamous cover-up concerning Geoffrey Rufus's death, the forging of papal letters purporting to support Cumin's election, the torture of Cumin's opponents and the turning of the Cathedral into a barracks for Cumin's soldiery, see Young, *William Cumin.*

range of predators and pressure groups, both secular and religious. The issue was not merely one between the kings of the South and the kings of the North.

The problems of Stephen's reign exposed lack of definition in authority, jurisdiction, and territory in northern England. A number of ambiguities involved the bishopric of Durham. Stephen's reign, however, not only shed light on these ambiguities but clarified what was being competed for. The bishopric of Durham was a prize worth winning. The core of episcopal liberty was essentially the modern County Durham where the bishop, holding of the Crown, had a virtual monopoly of lordship. An important exception was the wapentake of Sadberge[4] in the south of the county and including most of the parishes on the north bank of the River Tees. The wapentake was, in fact, attached to the earldom of Northumberland. It contained two strategic tenancies of the Crown, that of the Balliols of Gainford, centred on Barnard Castle, and protecting the important route westward over Bowes Moor[5] and that of the Bruces, centred on Hart and Hartness and protecting the Tees estuary.[6] The wapentake's importance has not been fully represented in discussion about Durham in Stephen's reign. In addition to the virtual monopoly of lordship in Durham, there was important episcopal land in Northumberland centred on Norham. There was also a significant and deep enclave of episcopal land in Yorkshire with the hundreds of Northallerton, Howden, and Welton.[7] Control over this important northern lordship was made effective by the key castles of Norham, Durham, and Northallerton.[8] The bishopric of Durham was a wealthy see with an average annual income from all sources of over £3,000.[9] In addition it was lightly assessed for military service with a surplus enfeoffment of over sixty fees. It has been suggested that this light assessment was due to its particular responsibilities for border defence. If this was so, Bishop Geoffrey Rufus failed to fulfil his obligations at Norham in 1138.[10]

Stephen has usually been praised for decisive action in the first few years of his reign. This approval has been extended recently to include his policy towards the

[4] C.M. Fraser and K. Emsley, 'Durham and the Wapentake of Sadberge', *TAASDN* 2 (1970), pp. 71–82.

[5] *Early Yorkshire Families*, ed. C.T. Clay (Yorkshire Archaeological Society, Record Series, 135; 1977), p. 3; G.V. Scammell, *Hugh du Puiset, Bishop of Durham* (Cambridge, 1956), p. 187; Lomas, *North-East England in the Middle Ages*, p. 27.

[6] *DEC*, pp. 115–16; *DB*, 332, 332b, cited in *YAJ*, 22 (1913), p. 337, n. 1.

[7] Barlow, *Durham Jurisdictional Peculiars*, pp. 53–60; D. Nicholl, *Thurstan, Archbishop of York* (York, 1964), p. 20.

[8] Norham was built *c.*1121 (*Sym. Op.* I, 140; II, 260); Durham castle had been strengthened by successive bishops until by Stephen's reign it was an impregnable fortress (*Laurence of Durham*, pp. 8–9, bk. I, lines 271–302, 319–24); Northallerton castle was apparently built by William Cumin (*Sym. Op.* I, 148), but it is not clear whether this was a new castle or one from Geoffrey Rufus's time which was refortified; cf. J.L. Saywell, *The History and Annals of Northallerton* (Northallerton, 1885), pp. 8, 17.

[9] Scammell, *Puiset*, pp. 193–4.

[10] Richard of Hexham, *CR*, III, 157.

northern border.[11] According to J. Bradbury 'Stephen's activities on the northern border were successful' and after the battle of the Standard in 1138 'there was no great threat from the Scots through the rest of the reign'. Certainly he reacted swiftly to Scottish threats on Durham in 1136 and 1138 and paid his only visits to Durham in these years.[12] As was customary with royal visits, Stephen marked his short stay in the North with the usual display of patronage to religious houses in the area. It is noticeable however that there are relatively few recorded grants to religious houses north of the Tees[13] – three grants to the monks at Durham, including a general protection and four grants to Tynemouth Priory – compared with those made with Yorkshire houses.[14]

Stephen seemed to be relying very heavily in the early years of his reign on the northern officials of Henry I, chiefly Archbishop Thurstan of York, Geoffrey Rufus, bishop of Durham, Eustace fitz John, lord of Malton and Alnwick and Walter Espec, lord of Helmsley and Wark.[15] In 1136 he clearly expected Eustace fitz John to continue to represent English royal administration and justice in Durham and Northumberland. Eustace, incidentally, was the only royal official to be enfeoffed in the bishopric of Durham. A royal act issued between 1136 and 1138 ordered Rainer de Muschamp and Cecily his sister to honour a gift of their brother to the bishopric of Durham; it was added that Eustace fitz John would see to it if this was not done.[16] The task, it seemed, remained undone as Henry II in 1155 also had to insist that they honour the gift.[17] Eustace fitz John was, in fact, in the Scottish king's following by 1138.[18] Bishop Geoffrey Rufus remained loyal to Stephen in 1138 despite pressure from David, king of Scotland to change allegiance. He was, nevertheless, criticized by northern chroniclers for his poor defence of Norham castle which was taken by the Scots in that year.[19] Some responsibility for northern defence also seems to have been given to Bernard de Balliol in 1138. Bernard, who held five fees in chief in the wapentake of Sadberge, was sent with a special detachment from the king's household to strengthen resistance against the Scots.[20] He was, however, on the Scottish side briefly in 1141.

The only effective linchpin for English northern government in the early years of

[11] J. Bradbury, 'The Early Years of the Reign of Stephen 1135–39', in *England in the Twelfth Century*, ed. D. Williams (Woodbridge, 1990), p. 26.

[12] Richard of Hexham, *CR*, III, 145–6, 152–3.

[13] *Regesta*, III, nos. 255–7, 904–7; *Script. Tres*, app. no. xxvi.

[14] Particularly York houses and Bridlington Priory, but also Kirkham Priory, Beverley Minster, Fountains Abbey, Ripon Cathedral, Selby Abbey, Whitby Abbey; *Regesta*, III, nos. 99, 119–20, 335, 717, 816, 942, 975–80, 985, 989–91, 995.

[15] J.A. Green, *The Government of England under Henry I* (Cambridge, 1986), pp. 245–6, 250–2.

[16] *Regesta*, III, no. 256.

[17] G.W.S. Barrow, 'Northern English Society in the Twelfth and Thirteenth Centuries', in his *Scotland and its Neighbours in the Middle Ages* (London, 1992).

[18] Richard of Hexham, in *CR*, III, 158; Young, *William Cumin*, p. 13; and P. Dalton, 'William Earl of York and Royal Authority in Yorkshire', *Haskins Society Journal* 2 (1990), p. 157.

[19] Richard of Hexham, in *CR*, *III*, 158.

[20] Ibid., pp. 160–1.

Stephen's reign appears to have been Thurstan, archbishop of York. By 1137 he, rather than Geoffrey, bishop of Durham, had assumed responsibility for border defence, negotiating a truce with David at Roxburgh.[21] In 1138 he was an effective focus for baronial loyalties to Stephen. According to Richard of Hexham, 'it appeared as if they would actually have abandoned the defence of themselves and the country had not their archbishop, Thurstan, animated them by his counsel and exhortation'.[22] Loyalty to country was only one, and perhaps at this time not the pre-eminent, loyalty for the barons of northern England. Thurstan's loyalty to Stephen, almost certainly a personal loyalty, maintained Stephen's interests in the North but there were signs that he was failing in health by 1138 and with his influence decreasing royal authority seriously declined in the North.

The Scots were the most obvious ones to take advantage of this decline as their influence in the North-East was already great before Stephen's reign. The ease with which Northumberland castles, including the episcopal castle at Norham, surrendered to Scottish military pressure suggests *de facto* control over this area before the Second Treaty of Durham in 1139.[23] This treaty, which granted Henry, David's son, the earldom of Northumberland[24] excluding the castles of Newcastle and Bamburgh and specifically excluding the lands of St Cuthbert has been seen as a largely successful attempt to contain the Scottish threat and confine it to north of the Tyne.[25] The implications of the treaty for the nobility of the North in general and for royal authority in the North as a whole have been underestimated. The treaty did not take into account the familial and territorial aspirations of the northern nobility which often stretched from southern Scotland to Yorkshire. Thurstan had only with difficulty persuaded the bulk of the northern baronage to support Stephen's cause at the battle of the Standard. By 1138 there had already been some drift of northern nobility from Stephen. Eustace fitz John and members of the Bruce and Percy families were in David I's following at the battle of the Standard. The terms of the treaty of Durham in 1139 could only increase this trend as a number of prominent Yorkshire and south Durham families also held land in Northumberland, now more formally under Scottish control. The Balliols and Bruces in particular were placed in an impossible position. It is here that the attachment of the wapentake of Sadberge to the earldom of Northumberland becomes significant. It meant that in south Durham the Balliol fee based on Barnard Castle and the Bruce fee based on Hart and Hartness were now under Scottish control. The Balliols held two important lordships in the north, Bywell on the Tyne and Gainford (centred on Barnard Castle) on the Tees. Bernard de Balliol had been active on Stephen's behalf in 1138 when he was sent with a detachment from the king's household to bolster northern defences. With Robert Bruce, Bernard had tried to use his influence with David to dissuade him from attacking

[21] Nicholl, *Thurstan*, p. 218.
[22] Richard of Hexham, in *CR*, III, 159.
[23] John of Hexham, in *Scottish Annals from English Chroniclers, 500–1286*, ed. A.O. Anderson (London, 1908), p. 170.
[24] Richard of Hexham, in *CR*, III, 177.
[25] Bradbury, 'The Early Years of the Reign of Stephen', p. 26.

the North.[26] It is hardly surprising that Bernard was supporting the Scottish cause in Durham in 1141. In addition Walter Espec, lord of Helmsley and Wark and, like Eustace fitz John, an important northern official of Henry I, does not appear to have been in the English royal following after 1138.[27] Given Stephen's preoccupation with Empress Matilda's opposition in the South from the summer of 1138, there was clearly a big gap in English royal influence north of the Tees from 1139.

The Treaty of Durham of 1139 did not stop further Scottish aggression south of the Tyne. Having tried unsuccessfully to win over Bishop Geoffrey Rufus to Scottish allegiance in 1138, David I gave strong initial support for the attempt by his chancellor, William Cumin, to gain the bishopric of Durham on Rufus's death.[28] Cumin had been his chancellor since about 1136 and had fought for the Scottish king at the battle of the Standard in 1138.[29] Both he and his three nephews were well established at the Scottish court and, what is more, Cumin had been a pupil and protégé of Geoffrey Rufus in the English chancery of Henry I since about 1126. Important members of the northern nobility who were regularly in the Scottish king's following – Robert de Brus, Hugh de Moreville and by 1138 Eustace fitz John – knew Cumin and supported his plan because it had David I's approval.[30] In 1141, Bernard de Balliol supported this scheme also. David I himself came to Durham in 1141, claimed all things in the name of the Empress Matilda and formally placed the management of affairs in Durham in Cumin's hands.[31] Taking advantage of Stephen's capture at the battle of Lincoln on 2 February 1141, David accompanied a pro-Cumin delegation from Durham seeking Matilda's support for his candidate. The political importance of the bishopric of Durham in the north was recognized by both David and the Empress Matilda. Matilda's support was gained but Cumin's failure to win over the Durham chapter, a decline in Matilda's fortunes and his own near capture in the South caused David to distance himself from Cumin's struggle to be elected bishop of Durham.[32]

The Durham chroniclers' concentration from this point, 1142, on Cumin's forceful determination to maintain his challenge[33] obscures the Scottish position somewhat. It masks the continuing reality of Scottish military control over northeast England. Firm administrative control over Northumberland and the increasing prominence of Earl Henry is apparent from 1139 onwards. The question of

[26] John of Hexham, *Priory of Hexham*, I, ed. J. Raine (SS 44; 1864), p. 119. It seems that Robert Bruce and Bernard de Balliol were sent because of their Durham landholding. The Scots were attacking Durham at the time.
[27] Dalton, 'William earl of York', p. 157.
[28] *Laurence of Durham*, pp. 4–5, bk. I, lines 135–40; p. 12, bk. I, line 424; *Sym. Op.* I, 143.
[29] Young, *William Cumin*, pp. 2–9.
[30] Ibid., pp. 12–14; *Sym. Op.* I, 144; *ESC*, pp. 89, 91, 94, 96; *The History and Antiquities of North Durham*, ed. J. Raine (London, 1852), Appendix, pp. 24–5.
[31] *Sym. Op.* II, 309; see Young, *William Cumin*, pp. 15–17.
[32] In 1142 David I sent Herbert abbot of Kelso (not Roxburgh as stated in Young, *William Cumin*, p. 18) to Durham to inquire into Cumin's acceptability to the Durham monks, and probably put forward his own candidacy as an alternative; *Sym. Op.* I, 146–7.
[33] *Sym. Op.* I, 148; II, 312–13.

Scottish administrative control over Durham is more difficult to gauge although control over the wapentake of Sadberge must now be taken into account. The number of grants and protections by Earl Henry to St Cuthbert's monks between 1140 and 1152 seems to indicate a good deal of influence.[34] There is, however, evidence of only one issued at Durham.[35] Newcastle, despite the terms of the 1139 treaty, appears to have been Earl Henry's main administrative base. One charter of 1141 does indicate that Earl Henry was planning to exercise some administrative control in Durham through William Cumin and Osbert, sheriff of Durham.[36] It is interesting to speculate further that Eustace fitz John's administrative and judicial expertise in Durham under Henry I was now being used in Scottish interests. Eustace appeared prominently in Earl Henry's following and also played an important role in arranging a truce with Cumin in 1143.[37] What is more certain is that William de Ste Barbe, the canonically elected bishop of Durham in 1143, turned to Earl Henry of Scotland to help him gain his rightful place at Durham.[38] Earl Henry eventually brought Ste Barbe to Durham after being bought off for a while by Cumin. It was to Earl Henry that Cumin surrendered the castle of Thornley. The Durham chroniclers noted that this castle was returned to the bishop of Durham's care only at Earl Henry's convenience. To the monks of Durham, Earl Henry and his men were poor allies in that they caused much destruction around Durham and made 'unjust exactions'.[39]

As for David I, he did not fully abandon Cumin in his attempt on the bishopric until 1144.[40] There seems, in practice, to have been an agreed neutrality between Cumin and David. If Cumin had succeeded in being formally elected bishop, David might have adopted a more prominent role. Even after Cumin had abandoned his claim, his nephew Richard benefited from the patronage of David and Earl Henry to establish the first secular base of the Cumin family in Tynedale.[41] The Scottish position of strength in the North was confirmed by an agreement between David and Henry of Anjou in 1149 and contemporary chroniclers recognised that David and Earl Henry exercised general control over England north of the Tees.[42]

William Cumin's individual role as predator in the bishopric of Durham needs to be set in context. He was not quite the independent adventurer he appears in the Durham chronicles. Having lost direct Scottish support in 1142, he sought to confirm his hold over the temporalities of the see by gaining other secular support.[43] North of the Tyne and in the wapentake of Sadberge in the south of

[34] *ESC*, pp. 98–9, 138–9, 206–7.
[35] Ibid., pp. 100–1.
[36] *RRS*, I, 146–7.
[37] *ESC*, pp. 64–5, 89, 95, 101, 138–9, 199–200; *Sym. Op.* I, 154–5.
[38] *Sym. Op.* I, 157–8.
[39] *Sym. Op.* I, 159.
[40] Ibid.
[41] *Calendar of Charter Rolls*, II (*1259–1300*), pp. 40–1.
[42] *CR*, I, 70; *RRS*, I, 5.
[43] See Young, *William Cumin*, pp. 20–3.

Durham, Earl Henry was the dominant power and Cumin did, for a time, make a special truce with him. South of the Tees, Cumin made a marriage alliance between his nephew, another William, established at the key episcopal castle in north Yorkshire, Northallerton and a niece of William, earl of York. William, earl of York was, with some justification, described as more a king in the North than Stephen.[44] Cumin also induced Alan, earl of Richmond with promises of reward to come to his aid in 1143 and drive away his enemies, who were beginning to threaten him at Durham. The reward of marriage between another of Cumin's nephews and the daughter of Hugh fitz Pinceon, the steward of William of Ste Barbe, gained William Cumin another important ally. It also gained him William of Ste Barbe's new castle at Thornley, which was threatening Cumin's position at Durham. Even when Cumin abandoned his claim to the bishopric, his loyalty to the Angevin cause (an underestimated motivation for the actions of both the Scottish king and Cumin) won him reward in the south of England.[45] Cumin appears to have regained his archdeaconry of Worcester by 1157 and received the support of Theobald of Canterbury, the papal legate. With Angevin support in the South and Scottish loyal support in the North, both Cumin and his one remaining nephew Richard emerged from the failed usurpation in Durham with some success.

As Cumin's alliances have shown, other individuals in the North, including William, earl of York, Alan, earl of Richmond and Hugh fitz Pinceon, were prepared to take advantage of the problems in Stephen's reign. In practice, the bishopric of Durham's lands in Northumberland, Durham and Yorkshire provided three theatres for local politics and opportunism. In Northumberland, Earl Henry had no rival, but south of the Tees there was much rivalry between Alan, earl of Richmond and William, earl of York, to extend jurisdiction within episcopal lands in Yorkshire. Northallerton seemed to be the chief focus for competition though Howden and Welton were also affected. Local circumstances rather than national politics seemed to dominate policy not only during the Cumin usurpation but also after 1144. Though invested with much authority in York and Yorkshire by Stephen, the earl of York took an increasingly independent line after 1138.[46] He even allied with the Angevin supporter, Cumin, in order to acquire interests at Northallerton. His acquisitions at the expense of the bishopric of Durham continued after Cumin had given up his claims in 1144. The earl seized Howden and other episcopal lands from William of Ste Barbe and in 1147 even prevented him from appearing at Richmond to elect a new archbishop of York.[47] The fierce territorial rivalry between the earl of Richmond and the earl of York in Northallerton and other areas caused Stephen to make a rare visit to Yorkshire in 1142 to put an end to a dispute between two of his supposed supporters.[48]

[44] *CR*, I, 103.
[45] *The Letters and Charters of Gilbert Foliot*, ed. A. Morey and C.N.L. Brooke (Cambridge, 1967), p. 540; *Regesta*, III, 48, 117, 121, 172, 309–10.
[46] Dalton, 'William Earl of York', pp. 158, 162.
[47] *Sym. Op.* I, 148; II, 320.
[48] *Sym. Op.* II, 312; Dalton, 'William earl of York', p. 162. The earl of Richmond had encroached upon episcopal lands at East Cowton in the Northallerton area; *Regesta*, III, no.

Plate 80. Castle Hill, Bishopton (Co. Durham), earthworks.

It is interesting to note that Stephen did not attempt to intervene north of the
Tees. English royal influence was increasingly slight outside York. Within Durham,
the major theatre of conflict, William Cumin was opposed chiefly by Roger de
Conyers,[49] the constable who sought to return the legally elected bishop, William
of Ste Barbe, to his rightful place. While he owned much land in north Yorkshire,
Roger's special position as constable at Durham, a position inherited by his son,
dictated his political stance. Undoubtedly there were privileges and benefits attached to the office. Roger de Conyers' castle and centre for opposition to Cumin
was Bishopton, about twelve miles south of Durham.[50] The castle (pl. 80) with its
substantial motte, some thirty feet high, was encircled by a deep circular ditch and
its defensive position was strengthened by surrounding marshland.[51] While Roger's
policy was one of consistent loyalty to the bishopric, his son, another Roger, took
more forceful advantage of the office of constable.[52] In the vacancy following the

122. He also set up fortifications on the bishop of Durham's lands at Hutton Conyers from
which he terrorized the citizens of Ripon (*Priory of Hexham*, ed. Raine, p. 132). He was also
known to have had the right to the churches which belonged to the socages of Welton, either
as a gift from Cumin or as a usurpation (*Early Yorkshire Charters*, II, 298).
[49] *Sym. Op.* II, 314.
[50] *Durham History from the Air*, ed. N. McCord (Durham County Local History Society,
Newcastle upon Tyne, 1971).
[51] *Sym. Op.* II, 314.
[52] Scammell, *Puiset*, p. 12. Roger was later involved in a dispute over the church of Rounton
(*Early Yorkshire Charters*, II, no. 948).

death of Bishop William of Ste Barbe in 1152, this Roger taxed the men of the bishopric 'to add to the pomp of his military array'.[53]

While Roger de Conyers seemed to have acted independently of either the Scottish or of the English king, a complex mixture of local interests and personal loyalties affected two major nobles involved in Durham in the 1130s and 1140s. Eustace fitz John had changed to the Scottish side after 1136 and was probably acting for Earl Henry in Durham from 1141 to 1144. It is difficult, however, to tell whether he was acting to safeguard his local interests or on behalf of the Scottish royal family when he helped to arrange a truce with Cumin in 1143. Bernard de Balliol, a firm supporter of Stephen in 1138 and taken prisoner with the king on 2 February 1141, had succumbed to the reality of Scottish military dominance in Durham and Northumberland by supporting William Cumin's candidacy in 1141. Yet by 1143, he was a bitter enemy of Cumin who attacked his Durham lands.[54] Was he acting again on behalf of the English king or was he acting out of local self-interest between 1142 and 1144?

Secular pressure on Durham from the north and south was not confined to the period 1138–44. It continued to trouble the bishopric after Cumin abandoned his bid in 1144. Symeon of Durham's Continuator commented: 'Bishop William of Ste Barbe lived nine years in the bishopric suffering during his tenure many evils as well on account of the unjust exactions of the King of Scotland [probably Earl Henry was meant here] as because of the depredations of his neighbours and their plunderings, not frequent as much as almost incessant.'[55]

The political struggle in Durham was not only a secular struggle for power involving the kings of the North and the South with further complications caused by local power politics. Wider issues, international issues, were involved. As Sir Richard Southern has noted, 'It was in the decade 1140–50 that papal jurisdiction emerged as a perceptible fact in everyday life.'[56] The principal barrier to William Cumin's election in 1141 had been not secular opponents but canon law. Church reform against lay investiture and intrusion received expression through appeals to the papal curia, through the influence of papal legates and through the influence of reformed monasticism. Behind the pope and Cistercian monasticism lay the dominant figure of Bernard of Clairvaux.

The papal legate Alberic had already intervened in the tense political situation in the north in 1138.[57] Appeals to the pope, to canon law and the papal legate occur throughout the Cumin dispute, from 1141 to 1144. The insistence on a canonical election with proper procedures, after due notice, by the proper persons with the assent of the papal legate and the archbishop of York stopped Cumin in his bid.[58] A

---

[53] *Priory of Hexham*, ed. Raine, p. 167.
[54] *Sym. Op.* I, 155.
[55] *Sym. Op.* I, 167.
[56] R.W. Southern *Western Society and the Church in the Middle Ages* (Harmondsworth, 1970), p. 115.
[57] *CR*, III, 167–9; *Chronicle of Melrose*, ed. A.O. Anderson and others (London, 1936), p. 33.
[58] *Sym. Op.* I, 144; see Young, *William Cumin*, pp. 14, 20–1.

canonical election did take place in 1143 and William of Ste Barbe was consecrated at Winchester by the papal legate, Henry of Winchester.

Even Cumin's plotting recognised the power of papal jurisdiction. He drew a vagrant Cistercian monk into a plot which involved two forged papal letters.[59] One letter was addressed to the monks at Durham expressing the pope's joy at Cumin's election and saying that Henry of Winchester should not stand in his way; the other was addressed to King David asking him to support Cumin and the Empress Matilda in their respective claims. Knowledge of canon law and its implementation by the papal legate gave the Durham chapter, and especially the prior, considerable political influence in Stephen's reign. In 1152 when the Durham electors unanimously elected Hugh of le Puiset as successor to William of Ste Barbe,[60] Henry Murdac, archbishop of York, rejected Puiset's candidature. Again, the chapter appealed to the pope. With the help of the papal legate, Theobald of Canterbury, Hugh of le Puiset was elected and consecrated in 1153.[61]

The refusal of Henry Murdac to sanction the choice of the Durham chapter in 1153 raises two further issues. The first is Durham's ecclesiastical and political relationship with its metropolitan, York. The second issue is Durham's relationship with the reformed monastic movement, especially with the Cistercians and Augustinians at a time when both the archbishop of York, from 1147 Henry Murdac, and the pope, from 1145 Eugenius III, were Cistercians.

Who or what influenced the canonically elected choices in Durham of William of Ste Barbe in 1143 and Hugh of le Puiset in 1153? What did they represent as bishops of Durham? In 1139 the Lateran Council re-emphasized that episcopal chapters were not to exclude 'men of religion' from helping to elect a successor whenever their see became vacant, and that if the canons did exclude them then the election would automatically become null and void.[62] There is little doubting Cistercian political influence and especially the influence of Bernard of Clairvaux in the 1140s. Bernard had campaigned against the election of a Cluniac bishop of Langres in 1138 – the canons of Langres were ordered to take heed of the 'men of religion' and as a result Godfrey, prior of Clairvaux, was elected.[63]

In the north of England Richard, Cistercian abbot of Fountains, was involved in the legation of Alberic in 1138.[64] From this date onwards, papal legates participated in both the secular and the ecclesiastical politics of the North. During the prolonged election dispute at York[65] between William fitz Herbert, the royal

[59] *Sym. Op.* I, 147–8. The pope's advice was taken at all stages of the dispute, including the truce arranged with Cumin in 1144 (*Sym. Op.* I, 155).

[60] 'Vno animo, una uoce', *Script. Tres*, p. 4.

[61] Ibid., pp. 4–7.

[62] Nicholl, *Thurstan*, p. 240.

[63] Bruno Scott James, *The Letters of St Bernard of Clairvaux* (London, 1953), pp. 249–56.

[64] D. Baker, ' "Viri Religiosi" and the York Election Dispute', *Councils and Assemblies*, ed. G.J. Cuming (Studies in Church History, 7; 1971), p. 88.

[65] *Historians of the Church of York and its Archbishops*, ed. J. Raine (3 vols., RS 71; 1879–84), II, 220–7. Scott James, *Letters of St Bernard*, pp. 259–62, 265, 267–84. For discussion of this

candidate, and Henry Murdac, the reformers' candidate, representatives of Rievaulx and Fountains and their Augustinian allies at Kirkham and Guisborough priories forcefully represented their grievances against fitz Herbert at Rome. The traditionally accepted model of the York election dispute features two sides. On one side were the reformers, those against the royal candidate in York's chapter, the reformed religious orders in Yorkshire represented by the Cistercians at Rievaulx and Fountains and the Augustinian canons of Kirkham and Guisborough. This side had the strong backing of Bernard of Clairvaux. On the other side were the traditionalists, members and supporters of the royal family within the York chapter, such as Hugh of le Puiset and Robert de Gant, and the traditional religious orders represented by the Benedictines of Whitby and St Mary's, York.

Is this model relevant to the Durham elections of 1143 and 1153? At first sight it would appear that the degree of reformed monastic influence in Yorkshire could not be repeated in Durham. The diocese of Durham, dominated by one monastery, and that a Benedictine one, would seem to be an area immune from Cistercian or Augustinian influence and out of reach of Bernard of Clairvaux. Yet in 1143 Bernard of Clairvaux and William, abbot of Rievaulx, the mission centre for the spread of Cistercian influence in England, recommended to Prior Roger and the convent of Durham that Master Laurence of Durham would be a suitable candidate.[66] Henry Murdac may still have had Master Laurence in mind in 1153 when he objected to Durham's choice of Hugh of le Puiset. In Durham the influence of the reformers and that of the reformed monastic orders may have carried more weight than is usually supposed. The Cistercians' candidate at Durham, Master Laurence, was a Durham man and a protégé of Bernard. The letter from Bernard and William implies that while studying abroad he had discussed the affairs of the bishopric with Bernard and was bringing Bernard's letter of support with him to England.[67] Laurence was a relative of Ailred of Rievaulx, a friend of Maurice of Rievaulx and obviously well known in Cistercian circles in the North.[68] Maurice of Rievaulx himself had been brought up in the cloister of Durham before transferring to Rievaulx in 1140.[69] Ailred of Rievaulx had family connections with Durham which he maintained. He was in contact with Reginald of Durham. Ailred and William, abbot of Rievaulx, were at Durham in 1138.[70] William had played an important diplomatic role with regard to the surrender of his patron Walter Espec's castle of Wark to the Scots in 1138. Robert, abbot of Newminster, the first Cistercian house to be established in Northumberland and first daughter

dispute, D. Knowles, 'The Case of St. William of York', in idem, *The Historian and Character* (Cambridge, 1963), pp. 76–97.

[66] DCL., MS B.IV.24, fol. 96.

[67] F.E. Croydon, 'Abbot Lawrence of Westminster and Hugh of St. Victor', *Medieval and Renaissance Studies* 2 (1950), pp. 10–12.

[68] Ibid.; F.M. Powicke, *The Life of Ailred of Rievaulx by Walter Daniel* (Oxford, 1978), pp. xxxvi–viii; *Sym. Op.* I, 168; II, 330.

[69] *Priory of Hexham*, ed. Raine, pp. 149–50.

[70] Ibid., pp. 100, 108; Powicke, *Life of Ailred*, p. xlvi, n. 1; *DEC*, p. 120.

house of Fountains Abbey, was another friend of Bernard of Clairvaux. In 1147, Ailred of Rievaulx and Robert of Newminster acted as assessors to Durham to decide whether the prior or the archdeacon should have priority in Durham's chapter.[71] There was also strong feeling concerning the York election dispute in the area north of Yorkshire. In 1141, the prior of Hexham, a peculiar of York, felt so strongly against the election of William fitz Herbert as archbishop that he abandoned his Augustinian brethren to join Bernard at Clairvaux.[72]

The presence of the reformed monastic orders in southern Scotland and northeastern England was encouraged by the patronage of King David and Earl Henry of Scotland.[73] Melrose, the first daughter house of Rievaulx, was founded in 1136 and another, Dundrennan, was established in 1142. The Scottish royal family supported Newminster Abbey near Morpeth and the Augustinian priories at Brinkburn and Hexham.[74] Cistercian and Augustinian influence grew in and around Durham in the episcopate of William of Ste Barbe.[75] The chief beneficiaries were the abbey of Newminster and the Augustinian priory of Guisborough in north Yorkshire. The direct influence of the Cistercian pope, Eugenius III, on William of Ste Barbe's episcopacy is seen when Bishop William granted to the Cistercians at Newminster and the Augustinian canons at Guisborough land at Wolsingham and Trimdon in county Durham specifically 'at the intervention' of Eugenius.[76] Eugenius also issued confirmations of Durham's lands in 1146 and when William of Ste Barbe was suspended for failing to attend the Council of Rheims in 1148, a further grant in favour of Newminster was issued by Bishop William in 1149, seemingly to make satisfaction for this.[77]

Durham's choice of Hugh of le Puiset as the successor to William of Ste Barbe in 1153 and Henry Murdac's objection appear on the surface to be another 'Reformers' versus 'Traditionalists' debate, this time in Durham, not York. This is, however, slightly too simple an explanation. Durham's choice of Hugh of le Puiset can be interpreted in a number of ways. It could be seen as a reaction against Henry Murdac as archbishop of York and his reassertion of the metropolitan authority over Durham which had been dormant since Thurstan's death in 1140.[78] It could, alternatively, be seen as a reaction against Scottish royal influence which had been dominant during the episcopate of Geoffrey Rufus, the Cumin usurpation and throughout William of Ste Barbe's period of office. Puiset, although not a

---

[71] *DEC*, pp. 142–51.
[72] *Priory of Hexham*, ed. Raine, p. 139.
[73] G.W.S. Barrow, 'David I of Scotland', in *Scotland and its Neighbours int he Middle Ages*, pp. 48, 55.
[74] *ESC*, pp. 198–200; *RRS*, I, 148, 168–9.
[75] *DEC*, pp. 155–62, 176.
[76] *FPD*, pp. lxiii–lxiv; *Newminster Cartulary*, ed. J. Fowler (SS 66; 1878), p. 47; *DEC*, pp. 155–61, 176.
[77] *DEC*, pp. 14, 160.
[78] *Script. Tres*, p. 4; *Prior of Hexham*, pp. 170–1; Scammell, *Puiset*, pp. 12–14; Nicholl, *Thurstan*, p. 242.

direct royal nominee, was related to the English royal family and had been the most prominent supporter of the royal candidate, fitz Herbert, in the York election dispute and the most bitter opponent of Henry Murdac in York. The choice of Puiset could be viewed as reaction to the increasingly close contact between Murdac and the Scottish king.[79] It is probable that Henry Murdac was a supporter of the Scottish king's plans in 1149 to join forces with Ranulf of Chester and Henry of Anjou and capture York. Murdac had been elected archbishop of York at Richmond, rather than York, in 1147 and had been excluded from York by Hugh of le Puiset and the citizens of that city who identified closely with English royal interests. David had shown determination to resist the metropolitan authority of Thurstan over the Scottish bishops and he was in a strong position to use his links with the reform party in Yorkshire to influence the archbishopric of York itself. York was an increasingly isolated area of English royal influence in the North. Durham's unanimous choice of Hugh of le Puiset, the most fervent upholder of royal interests in York, should be set in this context. Durham, it seems, was trying to re-establish links, in effect lost since 1138, with the English royal house. It is interesting to note in 1153 the re-emergence of English royal interest in proceedings at Durham. Both Stephen and his son, Eustace, tried to intervene on Puiset's behalf when Henry Murdac objected to the Durham chapter's choice.[80]

The choice of Hugh of le Puiset by the Durham chapter could also have been a Benedictine reaction to the growing influence of reformed monasticism in Northumberland and Yorkshire. Was the Cistercian archbishop of York hoping to revive once more the candidacy of Master Laurence, the favoured candidate of Bernard of Clairvaux and William of Rievaulx in 1143?[81] The successful candidate in 1143, William of Ste Barbe, has also been classified as a reformer.[82] It is in practice, however, rather difficult to detect exactly what William de Ste Barbe represented. The Durham and Hexham chroniclers were not critical of Ste Barbe,[83] but his actions showed him to be an ineffective, unpolitical figure.[84] He was elected at York in his absence and was very reluctant even to accept his election. As seen from York, the bishopric of Durham was a vulnerable, isolated post with little prospect of English royal support. Perhaps Ste Barbe's reaction indicated not so much lack of resolve as realism! He was, in fact, unable to assert his influence over Cumin in Durham without the secular power of Earl Henry of Scotland. It is difficult to

---

[79] P. Dalton, *Conquest, Anarchy and Lordship in Yorkshire 1066–1154* (Cambridge, 1994), pp. 225–7.

[80] *Script. Tres*, p. 5; Scammell, *Puiset*, p. 15. Northern chroniclers clearly did not have much faith in the effectiveness of this support: 'the clergy of Durham, seeing that the archbishop enjoyed the pope's favour, did not venture to call to their support either the king or anyone else' (John of Hexham, *CHE*, IV, pt. 1, p. 31).

[81] A. Saltman, *Theobald Archbishop of Canterbury* (London, 1956), p. 121.

[82] Scammell, *Puiset*, pp. 8, 20.

[83] *Priory of Hexham*, ed. Raine, p. 142.

[84] *Sym. Op.* I, 149–51; *Laurence of Durham*, p. 7, bk. 1, lines 241–4; *Sym. Op.* II, 314; *DEC*, pp. 164–5 – his uncertainty is shown about the extent of his powers at Durham.

categorize him as a supporter of David I or Stephen. Though he was consecrated by Henry of Winchester as papal legate and with the approval of Stephen, he received no support from Stephen against Cumin. In an ecclesiastical sense, his stance is also not clear cut. He did not appear among William fitz Herbert's named opponents in the York election and was in fact supported by William fitz Herbert in his attempt to gain the bishopric of Durham in 1143–44.[85] As a crucial witness in the continuing election dispute at York, William of Ste Barbe prevaricated as to whether or not fitz Herbert's election had been canonical.[86] Yet later he was certainly seen to be a supporter of Henry Murdac as archbishop of York.[87] He received Murdac with due respect in Durham when York refused to accept him. Ste Barbe appears to have been influenced by the Cistercian pope, Eugenius III, and by the Cistercian archbishop Murdac in ecclesiastical matters as much as he was dominated by the Scots, especially Earl Henry in secular matters.

To see ecclesiastical politics in York and Durham in Stephen's reign as a matter between 'Reformers' and 'Traditionalists' is as misleading as is an interpretation of secular politics in the North as an issue between the kings of Scotland and the kings of England. Both 'models' give too little weight to local personalities and local power politics.[88] Northern churchmen were not divided into hostile and mutually exclusive factions. It was possible, for instance, for a close adherent of William fitz Herbert at York to become a Cistercian.[89] In Durham, Nicholas, prior of Brinkburn, a reformed priory of Augustinian canons, supported the nomination of Hugh of le Puiset in 1153.[90] Master Laurence, Bernard's candidate for Durham in 1143, was among those who objected to Murdac's excommunication of the prior and archdeacons of Durham in the disputed Durham election in 1153.[91] Only if local ecclesiastical affiliations are taken into account can the Durham chapter's appeal to the pope in 1153 be understood. The appeal was, after all, made to a Cistercian pope against the decision of a Cistercian archbishop of York. Yet Murdac needed to forbid support from the York chapter for the Durham appeal. The appeal also had the active support of the papal legate.[92] The issue would probably not have been resolved so easily in favour of the Durham chapter and Hugh of le Puiset if it had not been for the deaths of Pope Eugenius III, Henry Murdac, and Bernard of Clairvaux within a short period in 1153.

The Durham chapter supported Hugh of le Puiset above all as a strong character, with proven military and political capacity to defend the church and monks of

[85] Baker, ' "Viri religiosi" and the York Election Dispute', p. 97.

[86] *Historians of the Church of York*, II, 222, 224; D. Knowles, 'The Case of St William of York', p. 86 – Bernard gives the impression that Ste Barbe was a stronger opponent of fitz Herbert.

[87] *Priory of Hexham*, ed. Raine, p. 163; Knowles, 'The Case of St William of York', p. 90.

[88] Cf. Baker, ' "Viri religiosi" and the York Election Dispute', p. 98; Nicholl, *Thurstan*, p. 245, n. 24.

[89] *CR*, I, 81.

[90] *Sym. Op.* II, 329; *Priory of Hexham*, p. 167; Scammell, *Puiset*, pp. 19–20.

[91] *Sym. Op.* II, 330; Scammell, *Puiset*, p. 15.

[92] Scammell, *Puiset*, pp. 18–19; Saltman, *Theobald*, p. 121.

Durham from the secular and ecclesiastical pressures to which they had been subject from 1138 to 1153.[93] Murdac's active exertion of his metropolitan authority over Durham was resented. This seemed to be of greater concern, in fact, than the encroachment of the reformed monastic orders, although this still remained an issue, as Hugh of le Puiset was a supporter and benefactor of the reformed monastic orders,[94] especially the Cistercians at Rievaulx and Newminster and Augustinians at Brinkburn. The Durham monks reacted strongly when Hugh supported his son, Henry, in introducing the Augustinians of Guisborough into a cell at Haswell and later at Baxterwood, almost a suburb of Durham.[95] This was too close for the Durham monks and the move was quashed.

This episode introduces an issue which, unlike others, had largely been obscured because of the problems of Stephen's reign. The relationship between bishop and chapter could be tense. These tensions had surfaced briefly in the early years of Geoffrey Rufus's episcopate[96] but had largely been removed by the need for cooperation in the crisis of Stephen's reign. The bishopric of Durham had been subjected to a vast range of pressures in that reign. The choice of Hugh of le Puiset was an attempt to alleviate some, if not all, of them. Hugh of le Puiset made a determined attempt to strengthen his own position as bishop of Durham and reduce the pressures faced by bishops of Durham for much of Stephen's reign.[97] He was, for instance, to purchase the earldom of Northumberland and the wapentake of Sadberge both so influential in the northern political scene of Stephen's reign. He acquired the mines of Weardale from the crown just before Stephen's death. He tried to strengthen his hold over land in Yorkshire and even acquire an interest in the York chapter. Henry II also took steps to strengthen royal authority in the north with much expenditure on key castles at Newcastle, Wark and Norham.[98] He saw, too, the importance of having northern lords loyal to the English crown; he tried to ensure that key lordships went to his loyal followers.[99]

Solutions to the pressures so clearly revealed in Stephen's reign were not easy to find. The crisis of 1173–74 once more emphasized the key role of the bishopric of Durham and the importance of its castles of Norham, Durham and Northallerton in Anglo-Scottish relations as well as in the effective English government of the North.[100] Durham's role in Anglo-Scottish relations was to be a continuing theme

[93] *Script. Tres*, pp. 4–6, 9, 12.
[94] *Early Yorkshire Charters*, ed. Farrer, II, no. 958.
[95] Scammell, *Puiset*, pp. 96, 111.
[96] *CHE*, III, part ii, 717.
[97] For what follows see Scammell, *Puiset*, esp. pp. 101, 104, 154, 171–4, 181–6, 204, 240; for the wapentake of Sadberge, Fraser and Emsley, 'Durham and the Wapentake of Sadberge', p. 71.
[98] M. Strickland, 'Securing the North: Invasion and the Strategy of Defence in Twelfth-Century Anglo-Scottish Warfare', in *Anglo-Norman Warfare*, ed. M. Strickland (Woodbridge, 1992), p. 214.
[99] J. Green, 'Aristocratic Loyalties in the Northern Frontier of England c.1100–1174', in *England in the Twelfth Century*, ed. D. Williams (Proceedings of the 1988 Harlaxton Symposium; Woodbridge, 1990), pp. 98–9.
[100] Strickland, op. cit., pp. 211–12.

in the thirteenth century.[101] Durham's relationship with York was another recurring source of tension.[102] These and other problems continued but Stephen's reign remains remarkable for the unique blend of local, national, international pressures of both secular and ecclesiastical kinds to which it was subjected.

[101] C.M. Fraser, *A History of Antony Bek, Bishop of Durham 1283–1311* (Oxford, 1957), pp. 22–3, 176.
[102] Scammell, *Puiset*, pp. 17, 176–182; Robert Brentano, *York Metropolitan Jurisdiction and Papal Judges Delegate (1279–1296)* (University of California Publications in History vol. 58; Berkeley and Los Angeles, 1959), pp. 109–78.

Old and New Bishoprics: Durham and Carlisle

HENRY SUMMERSON

A MONG THE observations on the state of Britain which Gervase of Tilbury recorded early in the thirteenth century for his imperial patron Otto IV, we find this comment on the metropolitan province of York: 'The Archbishop of York has only these two suffragans: Durham, which enjoys so many privileges from the Roman church that it has now withdrawn into complete independence; and Carlisle, which is so very often and for so long a time vacant, that it is rather given to oblivion than to subjection.'[1] The purpose of this paper is to try to rescue the diocese of Carlisle from some of the oblivion into which Gervase cast it. Its aim is less, however, to discuss its links with its privileged neighbour to the east, than to trace the early fortunes, to follow the initial development, of the new bishopric, in the hope of shedding an oblique light on some of the factors which gave stability and permanence to the old one. For Carlisle was indeed, to men of Gervase's generation, a new diocese, created in 1133, that is, forty years *after* work began on Durham cathedral, and one hindered in its development, moreover, by its position in a remote and inaccessible region, which made it an appropriate setting for tall stories and Arthurian legends.[2] With difficulty of access went uncertainty of status, for in 1093 the overall standing of Carlisle and its hinterland – for the purposes of this article Cumbria south of the Solway, the old counties of Cumberland and Westmorland – had still to be resolved, both politically and ecclesiastically.

In the early summer of 1092 King William II had occupied Carlisle, then probably a thinly-populated estate centre, and annexed its region, taking under his rule lands which until then had with very little doubt formed part of the realm of the kings of the Scots, who for well over a century would remain unreconciled to their loss.[3] They were, indeed, only part of a larger Cumbrian region, in essence the old kingdom of Strathclyde, and in social, economic and linguistic terms the border which William Rufus created in 1092 was an artificial one. Much effort and expense on the part of successive English kings would be needed to keep it in place.

---

[1] Gervase of Tilbury, *Otia Imperialia*, in *Scriptores Rerum Brunswicensium*, ed. G. Leibnitz (Hanover, 1707), p. 917.
[2] H. Summerson, *Medieval Carlisle: the City and the Borders from the late Eleventh to the Mid-Sixteenth century* (Cumberland and Westmorland Antiquarian and Archaeological Society, Extra Series 25; 1993), p. 43. In the early twelfth century Carlisle was chosen by St Godric as an appropriately remote site for a spiritual retreat (*V.Godr.*, p. 41).
[3] Summerson, *Medieval Carlisle*, pp. 47–9.

For its secular government English Cumbria would be entrusted to a sheriff, for its spiritual direction to an archdeacon. At first the region appears to have been intended to have its own archdeacon, a charter of Thomas I of York referring specifically to 'archidiaconatum de Carleon'.[4] But the same charter gave ecclesiastical control of Cumberland and Westmorland to the bishop of Durham, and the latter may have acted quickly to try to bring them under his own control, since successive writs of William Rufus ordered the men of Carlisle first to obey the bishop of Durham and *his* archdeacon, and then, during the vacancy following the death of St Calais, the archdeacon of Durham alone.[5] In the second case the king ordered that rival claims were to be heard in the *Curia Regis*, suggesting that there had been local opposition to Durham's claims. But the source of such recalcitrance, if indeed there was any, remains obscure.

Durham's rights in Carlisle, as in much else, originated with St Cuthbert, who was plausibly said to have been given an estate in and around the city by King Ecgfrith in 685, and was subsequently recorded as performing episcopal functions there.[6] But although the *Historia Regum* records Carlisle as still part of Cuthbert's old see in 854, and in spite of the existence of a church dedicated to St Cuthbert at Carlisle, with very little doubt antedating the annexation of 1092, it is difficult to feel that Durham and Carlisle were ever very closely linked, not least because Durham sources have remarkably little to say about Cumbrian affairs.[7] Perhaps only in Gilsland, where Upper Denton, the site of one of Cumberland's oldest churches, long remained part of the diocese of Durham, did the successors of St Cuthbert wield real authority in English Cumbria.[8] Overall, the situation at the end of the eleventh century seems to have been one in which Durham, if active at all west of the Pennines – and Rufus's two writs suggest that the bishops and their representatives were active – was more concerned to establish new ties than to revive old ones. But all in vain. For in 1101, following Flambard's escape from the Tower of London, Cumbria was detached from the diocese of Durham by Henry I and entrusted to the archdeacon of Richmond, within the diocese of York.[9]

The steps by which the bishopric of Carlisle came into existence between 1101 and 1133 do not need to be related here.[10] Of greater relevance to this study are the forces whose interaction brought the new diocese into being. On the secular side there was royal power, on both sides of the border, as represented by Henry I,

---

[4] London, Lincoln's Inn Library, MS Hale 114, fol. 55.
[5] *Regesta*, I, nos. 463, 478.
[6] *LDE*, bk. 1, ch. 9 (p. 32); *Two Lives of St Cuthbert*, ed. and trans. B. Colgrave (Cambridge, 1940), p. 249.
[7] *LDE*, bk. 2, ch. 5 (p. 53); Summerson, *Medieval Carlisle*, p. 31.
[8] J.M. Todd, 'The Lanercost Cartulary' (unpublished Ph.D. thesis, University of Lancaster, 1991), I, 8. A link between Durham and Gilsland may also be indicated by the appearance of the name Bueth, which is found recurring in the ruling family of Gilsland, in Durham's *Liber Vitae* at a point suggesting a date around 1100 (*Liber Vitae Ecclesiae Dunelmensis*, ed. J. Stevenson (SS 13; 1841), p. 53).
[9] *Sym. Op.* I, 138–9 (first continuation of *LDE*).
[10] Summerson, *Medieval Carlisle*, pp. 30–8, and the works cited ibid., p. 52 n. 149.

determined to keep the Anglo-Scottish border where William Rufus had left it, and by Scottish kings, notably David I, who were anxious to recover the ground lost in 1092. On the ecclesiastical front there was Archbishop Thurstan of York, who, having fended off Canterbury's claim to primacy over York, aimed to establish York's superiority over the bishops of Scotland, while the latter, and above all John of Glasgow, resisted those claims quite as firmly and persistently as Thurstan made them. There were successive popes, anxious to break the ring fence which royal power had set around the *ecclesia anglicana*, for whom such disputes offered a means of exerting influence in Britain, both directly and through legates. And there was what can only be called 'The Church', the totality of the age's ecclesiastical organization and spiritual aspiration, above all as manifested in the favour shown to monasticism in north-west England as elsewhere. It was principally through monastic foundations that, in the early twelfth century, English Cumbria was tied in to the rest of Henry I's realm, and so to the rest of Christendom. In this process some of the other factors mentioned above can be seen at work. Thus Wetheral Priory was founded by Ranulf le Meschin, until 1120 Henry I's principal secular lieutenant in the North West, as a daughter-house of St Mary of York, and received no less than four charters of gift or confirmation from the English king, one of them addressed to Thurstan.[11] And Ranulf's brother William founded St Bees Priory as another daughter-house of St Mary's, explicitly on Thurstan's advice.[12]

Any residual links Cumbria may have had with Durham were increasingly superseded by connections with York. Even the influence of Durham cathedral clearly visible in the nave pillars of Kirkby Lonsdale church, datable to around 1115, seems to have been mediatized through York, the church having been given to St Mary's by Ivo Taillebois, lord of Kendal, shortly before 1100.[13] In or around 1122 Henry I, with or without the assistance of Walter the Priest, but certainly with Thurstan's approval, founded a house of Austin canons at Carlisle, in a move which may have been recognized at the time as a step on the road towards the establishment of a bishop's see at Carlisle. Such a progression was certainly resented at Durham, on the evidence of an anonymous tract, preserved in York, Minster Library, MS XVI.I.12 and Lincoln's Inn, Hale 114, which insisted on the bishop of Durham's superior right to Carlisle, and poured scorn on the pretensions of York.[14] But all Durham could actually do was put its resentment down on parchment and then, for the most part, rub it out again. The creation of the diocese of Carlisle was at bottom a considered act of royal policy, and ancient episcopal rights, real or only

---

[11] *The Register of the Priory of Wetherhal*, ed. J.E. Prescott (London and Kendal, 1897), nos. 5, 7–9 (pp. 14–19, 22–7).

[12] *The Register of the Priory of St Bees*, ed. J. Wilson (SS 126; 1915), no. 2 (pp. 28–30).

[13] N. Pevsner, *Cumberland and Westmorland* (Buildings of England; Harmondsworth, 1967), pp. 260–2; *Register of Wetherhal*, ed. Prescott, Illustrative Document XVI (p. 412).

[14] I owe my knowledge of this tract to the kindness of Dr Richard Sharpe, who will shortly publish an edition of it in *Symeon of Durham*, ed. David Rollason (forthcoming, 1995). The deletion of a passage from the earliest manuscript of *LDE* (DUL, Cosins V.ii.6) immediately following mention of Carlisle may also be significant. See *LDE*, bk. 2, ch. 5 (*Sym. Op.* I, 53 and n.).

claimed, were not, in the circumstances, likely to cut much ice with Henry I or even with Archbishop Thurstan.

That royal policy was the maintenance of the border established in 1092, and involved, among other things, the establishment of a relationship of proper superiority with the king of Scots and with such other powers in Scotland as might be able to affect the issue. This was more easily achieved with laymen than with ecclesiastics, since lords like Robert de Brus, whose barony of Annandale was specifically modelled on Ranulf le Meschin's at Carlisle,[15] often had estates in England as well as Scotland, and so were more readily amenable to English pressure. A prelate like Bishop John of Glasgow, with no such hostages in England, was harder for Henry I to control, but not much less important. His importance lay in the uncertainty of the ecclesiastical boundaries of what may be called Greater Cumbria, which made it impossible to give a clear answer to the question, where was the southern border of the diocese of Glasgow? That diocese had been revived, after a long vacancy, by the future David I, when he was ruling in southern Scotland as heir-apparent to his brother Alexander I.[16] A bishop had been chosen, one Michael, who was sent to Thomas II of York to be ordained. Michael had professed obedience to Thomas, and had then ordained priests and dedicated churches in English Cumbria.[17] There is no certain evidence that he acted as bishop north of the Solway (and no certain evidence that he did not, either).

A later source plausibly records that Michael's successor, John, although resolutely refusing to profess obedience to York, nevertheless also acted as bishop south, as well as north, of the Solway, dedicating churches and performing other *officia pontificalia* in Cumberland, greatly to Henry I's disgust.[18] It is easy to see why the English king should have been both affronted and alarmed. When Thurstan of York and John of Glasgow confronted one another in Rome in 1126, Hugh the Chanter reports that among the arguments deployed by the archbishop in the hope of forcing John's submission was that 'Scotland was part of the realm of England, and that the king of Scots was the king's man for Scotland', while on the Scottish side it was argued that 'Scotland was no part of the realm of England'.[19] From the Scottish point of view it followed inevitably that the whole see of Glasgow owed no allegiance to the king of England. And in the 1120s that see could be represented as including Cumbria south of the Solway – as, indeed, one eccentric bishop of Glasgow was still prepared to argue as late as the 1250s.[20] As long as the Scots remained unreconciled to the loss of Cumberland and Westmorland, this threat of

[15] *ESC*, no. 54 (pp. 48–9).

[16] *ESC*, no. 50 (pp. 44–7); N.F. Shead, 'The Origins of the Medieval Diocese of Glasgow', *Scottish Historical Review* 48 (1969), pp. 220–5.

[17] Hugh the Chanter, *The History of the Church of York 1066–1127*, ed. and trans. C. Johnson, revised by M. Brett, C.N.L. Brooke and M. Winterbottom (Oxford, 1990), p. 53.

[18] J.C. Dickinson, *The Origins of the Austin Canons and their Introduction into England* (London, 1950), p. 249 n. 1 (quoting Fordun).

[19] Hugh the Chanter, *History of the Church of York*, p. 213.

[20] *Chronicon de Lanercost*, ed. J. Stevenson (Bannatyne and Maitland Clubs, Edinburgh, 1839), p. 65.

episcopal encroachment across the border established by Rufus had to be taken seriously.

From the English point of view, the best solution to this problem was the creation of a new diocese for north-west England. This was not something to be undertaken lightly, although in an age of ecclesiastical expansion and reform there were precedents – there was a massive reorganisation of the Irish church, for instance, following the synod of Rathbreasail in 1111, when the whole island was divided into dioceses and provinces.[21] There were interests to be appeased, and interests to be created, and the process involved most of the forces listed above. For Thurstan there was the task of compensating the archdeacon of Richmond for the loss of his rights in the North West – he was given the right of institution to and guardianship of vacant churches in his archdeaconry.[22] There was the approval of the papacy to be obtained, again by Thurstan, whose own diocese was to be dismembered. The schism of 1130, and Innocent II's need for English support, must have made it more likely that such approval would be obtained. Yet it is significant, in the context of the expansion of papal authority in western Europe at this time, that Innocent first made it clear that only the Roman see could divide and unite dioceses, or create new ones, before he licensed Thurstan to form new bishoprics within his province. From the English king, on the evidence of a later letter to his successor, Innocent required an adequate endowment for the new bishopric, or at any rate the promise of one.[23] And though the object of the exercise was the containment of the Scots, some thought had to be given as to how the creation of the new diocese would be received north of that border which Henry I was so determined to maintain.

The solution to this last problem, in so far as it was solved, lay in the choice of the first bishop. In fact he was already at Carlisle, in the person of Athelwold, the king's confessor and occasional agent in ecclesiastical affairs.[24] Prior of Carlisle probably since that house's foundation, he was also prior of Nostell, an office he was licensed to retain. This last, unusual, privilege may have been given in part for financial reasons, but it was probably also granted because Nostell, a Yorkshire house of Austin canons, was much patronized by the Scottish royal family. It was through Athelwold and Nostell that the Augustinian order was introduced into Scotland in the 1120s. A canon of Nostell became bishop of St Andrews, the premier see in Scotland, in 1127, and Athelwold himself is very likely to have been *persona grata* at the Scottish court.[25] The elevation of the prior of Nostell to be

[21] F. Barlow, *The English Church 1066–1154* (London, 1979), p. 36.

[22] Roger of Howden, *Chronica Magistri Rogeri de Houedene*, ed. W. Stubbs (4 vols., RS 51; 1868–71), IV, 178.

[23] *The Historians of the Church of York and its Archbishops*, ed. J. Raine (3 vols., RS 71; 1879–94), III, 57–8, 60–1.

[24] *The Chronicle of Robert of Torigni*, in *CR*, IV, 123; Hugh the Chanter, *History of the Church of York*, p. 185; *Councils and Synods*, ed. D. Whitelock, M. Brett and C.N.L. Brooke (Oxford, 1981), I Part II, p. 757. Athelwold's name is spelt in a remarkably wide variety of different ways, even in his own *acta*. I have used one of its commoner forms.

[25] J. Wilson, 'The Foundation of the Austin Priories of Nostell and Scone', *Scottish Historical*

bishop of Carlisle was the nearest thing to a conciliatory gesture that Henry I could have made. So it was that in August 1133 Athelwold was consecrated bishop of Carlisle by Thurstan at York.[26] His endowment was tiny, made up almost entirely of spiritual revenues, but as he was still prior of both Carlisle and Nostell, and also, it seems, lord of the soke of Pocklington in Yorkshire, doubtless it was felt that adding to his revenues could wait.[27] Athelwold may have thrown himself into his episcopal duties with some energy, judging by a letter to him from Osbert of Clare, claiming that 'our friends rejoice and are glad over the vigour – *strenuitas* – of the new bishop'.[28] But in the short term all the new bishop's energy was to no avail. In 1135 Henry I died, almost at once the dreaded Scottish *revanche* took place, and the diocese of Carlisle passed under the rule of David I.

Nothing is known of the fortunes of the bishopric in the next three years, when Athelwold seems to have waited on King Stephen, even accompanying that monarch to Normandy.[29] Yet the interlude shows perfectly how quickly ecclesiastical lines hardened once they were laid down, in that although its bishop became an absentee only two or three years after his installation, no attempt was made to suppress the new diocese. Its survival may have been helped by the support which John of Glasgow gave to the antipope Anacletus, to his own discrediting, and by his departure in a mood of disgruntlement for the Continent.[30] Yet even if he had been on hand, it is hard to see what John could have done to engineer the disappearance of the see of Carlisle. Bishoprics were very hardy institutions. Glasgow had itself been long vacant, and the same was true of several other Scottish dioceses in the early twelfth century, but that had not prevented their resuscitation.[31] Probably the only thing the Scots could have done at Carlisle was to have kept Athelwold out of his cathedral city until he died or resigned, and then appointed a Scottish successor.

Perhaps this was what David I planned to do, but if so, he was frustrated. Other powers had an interest in the survival of the diocese, not least the papacy. Bishops were expected to reside. John of Glasgow, in his self-imposed exile at Tiron, was harried on this point, among others.[32] So when the papal legate Alberic came to Carlisle in 1138, he reinstalled both Athelwold at Carlisle and John at Glasgow,

Review 7 (1910), pp. 141–59; D. Nicholl, *Thurstan, Archbishop of York (1114–1140)* (York, 1964), pp. 147–8.

[26] *The Priory of Hexham: Its Chronicles, Endowments and Annals*, ed. J. Raine (SS 44; 1863), I, 109–10.

[27] *Calendar of Entries in the Papal Registers relating to Great Britain and Ireland, Papal Letters*, I, 1198–1304 (London, 1893), p. 91; *Early Yorkshire Charters*, I, ed. W. Farrer (Edinburgh, 1914), p. 337.

[28] *Epistolae Herberti de Losinga, Osberti de Clara et Elmeri*, ed. R. Anstruther (Caxton Society 5; Brussels, 1846), pp. 145–6.

[29] *Regesta*, III, nos. 280–2, 598, 608.

[30] Nicholl, *Thurstan*, p. 107; G.W.S. Barrow, *The Kingdom of the Scots* (London, 1973), p. 176.

[31] G. Donaldson, 'Scottish Bishops' Sees before the reign of David I', *Proceedings of the Society of Antiquaries of Scotland* 87 (1955 for 1952–53), pp. 106–17.

[32] *Priory of Hexham*, I, 121.

reconciling Athelwold and David so completely that the bishop secured for Nostell
– and himself witnessed – a grant of three marks yearly from the Carlisle silver
mines, to replace an identical sum once paid from the Scottish king's honour of
Huntingdon.[33] Politically his position remained slightly ambiguous, in that for
some time he continued – at intervals – to attend King Stephen's court, witnessing
for the last time for the latter at Peterborough in 1143, and also concerned himself
with ecclesiastical affairs in those parts of northern England not under Scottish
rule, above all in the great dispute over the archbishopric of York, when he was a
staunch supporter of Henry Murdac.[34] Yet he also attested charters for King David
and prince Henry, at least twice doing so at Edinburgh.[35] Once back in his diocese,
Athelwold's standing as bishop was probably such that it would have been difficult
to dislodge him even had anyone felt minded to do so – neither the pious David
nor his God-fearing son was very likely to try.

He was in fact above all active as a bishop, so much so that after its late start
Carlisle was quick to develop along the lines of other dioceses – by the time
Athelwold died, there was an archdeacon, rural deans (more to start with than later,
it would seem), apparently with quarterly chapters, and administration had advanced sufficiently to start to bring in the usual revenues, a charter for Wetheral
referring to *synodalia* and *archidiaconalia*.[36] He showed a fitting concern for the
maintenance of vicars by ordering the monks of St Mary's at York to make over a
sufficient proportion of their income from their Cumbrian churches to the priests
who served them.[37] It was almost certainly Athelwold who founded the school
whose issues were included among the revenues of the bishopric in the late 1180s.[38]
A Carlisle tradition would also ascribe to him the foundation of the hospital of St
Nicholas in the city's southern suburbs.[39] Perhaps there was indeed something in
Osbert of Clare's praise for Athelwold's *strenuitas*. By about 1150, however, the
bishop may have been feeling his years. The appearance of one Walter as prior of
Carlisle shows that Athelwold had resigned that office, and then he resigned as
prior of Nostell as well, referring to *debilitatem corporis mei* by way of justifica-
tion.[40]

It may be that another reason for Athelwold's resignation from Nostell was a
desire to keep out of the way of William FitzHerbert, Henry Murdac's old rival, in
1153 reinstated as archbishop of York.[41] Changing circumstances in the last years
of his life required Athelwold to show himself politically discreet in other directions

[33] *RRS*, I, pp. 111–12 and nos. 39–40.
[34] *Regesta*, 3, no. 655; *Priory of Hexham*, I, 155.
[35] *ESC*, nos. 146–7 (pp. 112–13).
[36] *Cartularium Abbathiae de Whiteby*, ed. J.C. Atkinson (SS 69; 1878), I, no. 32 (p. 38);
Register of Wetherhal, ed. Prescott, nos. 15, 48 (pp. 44–5, 109–10); *Early Yorkshire Charters*, V,
ed. C.T. Clay (Yorkshire Record Society, Extra Series, 2, 1936), pp. 72–3.
[37] *Register of Wetherhal*, ed. Prescott, no. 16 (pp. 45–7).
[38] *Pipe Roll 34 Henry II* (Pipe Roll Society 38; London, 1925), pp. 7–8.
[39] London, Public Record Office, SC8/322 no. E517.
[40] *RRS*, I, no. 244 (pp. 196–7); BL, Cotton MS Vespasian E. XIX, fol. 76v.
[41] Nicholl, *Thurstan*, p. 245.

as well. Predeceased by his son, King David died at Carlisle in 1153, and the bishop witnessed at least one charter for David's successor and grandson, the young Malcolm IV.[42] In the following year King Stephen died, and Athelwold attended the coronation of *his* successor, the not quite so young Henry II, and was with Henry at York in the following year.[43] Yet he does not appear to have suffered for his apparently double allegiance, and when the bishop of Carlisle himself died in 1156, he left his diocese intact and, it would appear, in good order.

Athelwold's demise was probably an important additional inducement to Henry II to recover the northern shires of England, lost early in Stephen's reign, since the way would otherwise have been left open for a tightening of Scottish control over the region by the appointment of a Scottish bishop. That was what seems to have happened during the next Scottish occupation of Carlisle, in 1216/17. The diocese was vacant at the time, and the cathedral canons were induced to elect a bishop chosen by, or at least acceptable to, Alexander II.[44] On that occasion the election was quickly quashed, and an English bishop was appointed shortly afterwards. But on the death of Athelwold, although his diocese passed back under English rule in 1157, nobody was found to succeed him. The bishopric, still effectively unendowed, was extremely poor, and there was no likelihood of the diocesan being able to hold several offices simultaneously as Athelwold had done. But the diocese never looked like disappearing. This may have caused disappointment at Durham, where the refurbishment of forged charters carried out at around this time included what may have been intended to be speculative references to Carlisle as part of the see of St Cuthbert.[45] But a satisfactory substitute for a bishop was found in the form of a series of archdeacons, who could be maintained from the much greater endowment of the cathedral priory, and ecclesiastical life in the diocese of Carlisle went on under their direction.

Then and always there was just one archdeacon for the whole diocese, as there was at this time for the diocese of Glasgow also. As at Glasgow an archdeacon may have been first appointed in order to provide a deputy for the unpredictable John, during his frequent absences,[46] so at Carlisle an archdeacon may initially have been found necessary to stand in for a bishop not always resident in his diocese – apart from his exile betwen 1135 and 1138, and his attendances at Stephen's court up to 1143, Athelwold is also recorded at Durham, Bamburgh and Edinburgh, and he seems to have attended the second Lateran council of 1139 as well (so providing further evidence for the growing impact of the papacy even upon far-flung parts of Christendom like Cumbria).[47] There were certain functions which only a bishop was entitled to perform, the consecration of churches, for instance. Hence the

---

[42] *RRS*, I, no. 115 (pp. 180–1).

[43] R.W. Eyton, *Court, Household and Itinerary of King Henry II* (London, 1878), p. 1; *Cartae Antiquae II*, ed. J.C. Davies (Pipe Roll Society, New Series 33; London, 1957), no. 455.

[44] *Calendar of Papal Letters*, I, 48.

[45] *DEC*, no. 3a (pp. 15–25).

[46] N.F. Shead, 'The Administration of the Diocese of Glasgow in the Twelfth and Thirteenth Centuries', *Scottish Historical Review* 55 (1976), pp. 137–8.

[47] *DEC*, no. 34 (pp. 135–8); Barrow, *Kingdom of the Scots*, pp. 181–2.

presence of Christian, bishop of Whithorn in Galloway, who was briefly on Henry II's payroll in the late 1150s, and who showed his Cumbrian sympathies by choosing to be buried in Holmcultram priory, at the head of the list of witnesses to the foundation charter of Lanercost priory in the late 1160s.[48]

But it was the archdeacon who ran the diocese. It was in that capacity that he received mandates from the archbishop of York, while a charter for Whitby abbey by Robert, 'by God's grace Archdeacon of Carlisle', is composed in a style that can only be called episcopal.[49] By the 1180s the archdeacon was calling himself *custos episcopatus Karleoli*, and well before then, in about 1163, Uctred of Galloway, in a charter giving the church of Torpenhow in Cumberland to Holyrood abbey in Scotland, willed that it be held as freely and quietly as any church *in toto episcopatu Karleolensi*.[50] There might not be an *episcopus*, but the *episcopatus* remained in being. The situation appears to have been accepted even in Rome. The papacy was inevitably kept informed on the point by York's persistence in its efforts to secure the obedience of the bishops of Scotland – since York's need for additional suffragans was one of the factors behind its campaign, the vacancy of Carlisle was bound to be a consideration in the dispute. Indeed, Pope Clement III, when he instructed the bishops of Durham, Glasgow and Galloway to consecrate Geoffrey Plantagenet as archbishop of York in 1190, showed by his failure to include the bishop of Carlisle in his mandate that he knew that the see was vacant.[51] It would seem that it had been tacitly decided that the vacancy should be treated as a problem which was sure to be solved in the fullness of time, and could therefore be left alone. In the event, it went unsolved for nearly half a century, but in the meantime the diocese of Carlisle, far from languishing for want of a bishop, continued to develop without one, much like other bishoprics. By the 1180s it had an official, and the revenues of the see during that decade included pentecostal offerings, pleas and perquisites – indicating the holding of church courts – and the issues of two synods each year.[52] Procurations are first recorded shortly afterwards.[53]

By that time a first attempt had been made to fill the vacancy at Carlisle. The initiative was said to have come from the cathedral canons, but as with the original foundation of the diocese, the man in command was the English king.[54] In 1186

---

[48] *Pipe Roll 5 Henry II* (Pipe Roll Society 1; London, 1884), p. 33; *Pipe Roll 6 Henry II* (Pipe Roll Society 2; London, 1884), p. 40; *The Register and Records of Holm Cultram*, ed. F. Grainger and W.G. Collingwood (Cumberland and Westmorland Antiquarian and Archaeological Soc., Record Series 7, 1929), no. 141 (p. 54); Todd, 'The Lanercost Cartulary', II, nos. 1, 180 (pp. 1–6, 216–17).

[49] *Early Yorkshire Charters*, I, 160–1; *Cartularium Abbathiae de Whiteby*, ed. Atkinson, I, no. 33 (pp. 38–9).

[50] *Register of Wetherhal*, ed. Prescott, nos. 120, 123 (pp. 216–17, 219); *Register of St Bees*, ed. Wilson, p. ix.

[51] *Scotia Pontificalia: Papal Letters to Scotland before the Pontificate of Innocent III*, ed. R. Somerville (Oxford, 1982), no. 155 (also nos. 40, 46, 54, 68, 80).

[52] *Register of Wetherhal*, ed. Prescott, no. 120 (pp. 216–17); *Pipe Roll 34 Henry II* (Pipe Roll Society; London, 1925), pp. 7–8.

[53] Todd, 'The Lanercost Cartulary', II, no. 173 (pp. 207–9).

[54] For details see Summerson, *Medieval Carlisle*, p. 70.

Henry II came to Carlisle, to deal with affairs in Galloway. At a time when he was increasingly concerned to extend royal authority in the north of England, Henry was likely to look with favour on the establishment of a power in the North West which could be amenable to control by himself rather than by the great local families whom he wished to restrict. Asked now for licence to elect a bishop, he gave it. The canons chose Paulinus of Leeds, master of the hospital of St Leonard of York (his house had property in Carlisle, and he may have been well known there), and when Paulinus demurred, Henry offered an endowment of rents worth £200 *per annum*. As bishop, Paulinus would still have been very poor, and he continued to refuse promotion. But although the bishopric remained without a diocesan, the episode was a turning point nevertheless, precisely because of the royal involvement in it. Once the king had decided that Carlisle needed a bishop, it was only a matter of time before the see received an occupant. Meanwhile the archdeacons largely ceased to be purely local figures, and tended to be royal servants as well. Peter de Ros, archdeacon in the years round 1190, acted as a royal justice.[55] His successor but one, Aimeric Thebert, was directly appointed to his office by Richard I in 1196. Since he was also archdeacon of Durham, Aimeric must have been a force to be reckoned with in the North, surely wielding his powers in the king's interest.[56]

In the end it was John who ended a vacancy of nearly fifty years, when he secured the installation at Carlisle of Bernard, the ex-archbishop of Ragusa (present-day Dubrovnik), who after being driven from his see took refuge with Richard I and came to England. Again, there were other interests to be taken into account – the canons of Carlisle, who in 1201 obtained an order from Innocent III that they should not have a bishop whom they had not canonically elected, and the archbishop of York, who was reluctant to have another archbishop, even an archbishop-in-exile, at large in his province. In both these cases the papacy was invoked, showing that Rome, too, needed to be consulted. But John's need to strengthen his position in the North – ultimately the centre of opposition to his rule – is likely to have been the determining factor, and early in 1204 Bernard was installed, with an annual pension of twenty marks from the king.[57] He may seem an odd choice for Carlisle, but such had been the development of the diocese, matching that of the church in western Christendom as a whole, that he would have found little there that he could not have understood.

In material terms Bernard was poor compared with nearly all the other English bishops – destitute by comparison with Durham – but in terms of functions there was little to distinguish him from them. His surviving *acta* certainly suggest a diocese very much like others. Provision is made for a vicar, *onera episcopalia* are secured in one charter, *sinodalia et archidiaconalia* in another, whereby a decision by judges delegate is also confirmed, the right of St Peter's hospital at York to a render of grain which it had enjoyed *ab antiquis temporibus* is upheld – it is all the

---

[55] *Register and Records of Holm Cultram*, ed. Grainger and Collingwood, nos. 70a, 71 (p. 28).
[56] *Chronica Rogeri de Howedene*, ed. Stubbs, IV, 14.
[57] Summerson, *Medieval Carlisle*, p. 93.

sort of thing which could have been happening anywhere.[58] The problems facing the bishop, like that of abolishing a hereditary priesthood, were likewise the same as those found elsewhere, though they might be solved by unconventional means.[59] Among the prodigies recorded of Cumberland by Gervase of Tilbury was a gigantic whelp, seen one night in a wood near Penrith with fire flashing from its mouth. This terrifying brute was being pursued by St Simeon, but before the saint could catch up with it, it had entered a priest's house and incinerated it, together with the priest's illegitimate offspring within.[60]

This bizarre fable has a scarcity value going beyond any interest it may have to the student of folklore, for the story of the early development of the diocese of Carlisle is one in which supernatural forces were seldom either active or invoked. Carlisle, it has been observed, was the only medieval English diocese unable to boast the burial place of a local saint.[61] The contrast with Durham is obvious. A great saint like Cuthbert, both as a focus for devotion and as a source of prestige, was a spiritual asset without a rival in the North. When Waldef of Melrose died, perhaps it was inevitable that Jocelin of Furness, in summing up his account of Waldeve's life, should have tried to compare him with St Cuthbert (they were equals at all points, he decided), the patron of Durham being the yardstick by which sanctity was judged within what had once been Northumbria.[62] On this level Carlisle could not compete. The cathedral developed what became a notable cult of the Virgin, but in the diocese as a whole Cuthbert was revered as he was elsewhere in the North, with fifteen churches dedicated to him, far more than to any other English saint.[63]

Many of those dedications have been shown to postdate the severance of Cumbria from Cuthbert's diocese. But the development implicit in such dedications, though interesting in itself, had little to do with the circumstances which first brought the diocese of Carlisle into being. The value of an analysis of those circumstances lies in that it shows what could be achieved *without* a saint for a bishopric to crystallize around, and the light it sheds on the agencies which lay behind such an achievement. Whereas Durham in the twelfth century can be seen as the splendid product of an earlier age, an age of saints, Carlisle was the much less glamorous product of a new age, an age of government. By then there were other forces active in Christendom which were able to create a diocese and keep it in

---

[58] *Cartularium Abbathiae de Whiteby*, ed. Atkinson, I, no. 35 (pp. 40–1); BL, MS Egerton 2827, fol. 300; BL, Cotton MS Nero D. III, fol. 48v; *Register of Wetherhal*, ed. Prescott, no. 117 (pp. 210–12).

[59] *Calendar of Papal Letters*, I, 91.

[60] *Otia Imperialia*, in *Scriptores Rerum Brunswicensium*, ed. Leibnitz, pp. 983–4.

[61] R.K. Rose, 'Cumbrian Society and the Anglo-Norman Church', in *Religion and National Identity*, ed. S. Mews (Studies in Church History 18; Oxford, 1982), p. 131.

[62] *Acta Sanctorum*, ed. J. Bollandus et al., August, I (Antwerp, 1733), p. 276.

[63] V. Tudor, 'St Cuthbert and Cumbria', in *Transactions of the Cumberland and Westmorland Antiquarian and Archaeological Soc*, 2nd ser. 84 (1984), p. 71; T.H.B. Graham and W.G. Collingwood, 'Patron Saints of the Diocese of Carlisle', ibid., 2nd ser. 25 (1925), pp. 12–14.

place, as contemporaries were aware. In his remarks on the suffragans of York,
Gervase of Tilbury said nothing about St Cuthbert: what impressed him about
Durham was its papal privileges. At Carlisle it is possible to see how a diocese could
be principally created and sustained by custom and the weight of a speedily
developing tradition, by the dictates of royal policy, and by the plenitude of papal
power.

The Durham Mint before Boldon Book

MARTIN ALLEN

I N 1183/4, when Bishop Hugh of le Puiset commissioned the Boldon Book
survey of his bishopric, there was no mint in Durham. Boldon Book asserted
that 'Cunei monete solebant reddere x marcas. Set dominus Rex Henricus Secundus per cuneos quos in Nouo Castello primum posuit redditus x marcarum
usque ad tres marcas diminuit et ad ultimum cuneos a multis retro temporibus
habitos abstulit.'[1] William Greenwell provided the first published translation of this
passage in his 1852 edition of Boldon Book: 'The dies of the mint used to render 10
marcs, but the Lord King Henry the Second, by means of the dies which he placed in
Newcastle for the first time, reduced the rent of 10 marcs to 3 marcs, and in the
end took away the dies which had been in use for many years before that time.'[2]

At the time of Boldon Book coins were struck by first placing a blank 'flan' of
silver between a lower die (the 'pile' or 'standard') having the obverse design, and
an upper die (the 'trussel') for the reverse, and then hammering the upper die to
produce impressions of the dies on the flan.[3] Dies for the English coinage had
nationally standardized designs or 'types' (except in some cases in the reign of
Stephen), changed at intervals of a few years until a reform of the coinage in 1158
achieved a permanent change of the system. The dies were almost always supplied

---

[1] *Boldon Book*, ed. and trans. D. Austin (Chichester, 1982), p. 10.

    I would like to thank the Harris Museum and Art Gallery, Preston, Nottingham City
Museums, Sunderland Museums, A.H. Baldwin and Sons Ltd, Mr Joseph Bispham, and Dr
Ian H. Taylor for allowing the illustration of their coins listed in the appendix. Nine of the
illustrated coins are reproduced by permission of the Trustees of the British Museum. Miss
Marion M. Archibald, Dr Mark A.S. Blackburn, Dr James Booth, Dr David Crook, Dr Robin
J. Eaglen, Mr Jeffrey J. North, Dr Veronica J. Smart and the Rt Hon. Lord Stewartby have
given invaluable assistance with various aspects of this paper, and Miss Archibald, Dr Blackburn and Lord Stewartby have been particularly generous in providing unpublished information. I owe the greatest debt of gratitude to Mr Christopher R. Wren, whose unfailing advice
and technical assistance have made this paper possible.

[2] *Boldon Buke*, ed. and trans. W. Greenwell (SS 25; 1852), p. 43.

[3] The appendix lists combinations of obverse and reverse dies used to produce coins in
Durham in the Anglo-Norman period. The known dies are distinct pairs, with the exception
of some of the dies used by the moneyer Fobund (plate 81, nos. 9–11), but the numbers of
coins surviving from some of the earlier die-combinations are too few to permit the assumption that only pairs of dies were originally supplied.

from London or some other single centre of die production,[4] although the dies used by the Durham moneyer Fobund seem to have been made locally (see below, pp. 382–91, and pl. 81, nos. 8–13).

The only coins produced in Durham in the Anglo-Norman period were silver pennies.[5] 240 pennies (with a face value of one pound) may have been intended to be struck from a pound weight of silver alloy,[6] although there is no direct documentary evidence for this; slightly more than 240 pennies were struck from a Tower pound of silver of sterling fineness from no later than 1234.[7] Mint customers offering silver to be exchanged for new coins were charged for the transaction: from 1158 the deductions seem to have been sixpence from each pound of silver as 'seignorage' (a profit ultimately at the disposal of the king), and a further sixpence for the minting charges, kept by the moneyer.[8] The seignorage from some of the English mints was wholly or partly granted by the king to an archbishop, bishop or abbot:[9] Boldon Book refers to dies working for the profit of the bishop of Durham. The 'rent' (*redditus*) of the Durham dies in Boldon Book would have been a 'farm' in lieu of seignorage, probably negotiated between the bishop and his moneyer.

Moneyers were usually men of relatively high social status in urban communities (such as prominent merchants and burgesses), responsible in the Anglo-Norman period for supervising the minting and (until 1180) the exchanging of the coinage,

---

[4] *Domesday Book* (*DB* I.172) refers to a payment *ad Londoniam pro cuneis monetae accipiendis*, and it is generally assumed that dies were usually supplied from London in the Anglo-Norman period. However, *Pipe Roll 26 Henry II* (Pipe Roll Soc. 29; London, 1908), p. 136, refers to the carrying of dies from Winchester to Oxford and Northampton, and back to Winchester, apparently as part of the preparations for the recoinage started in 1180. It is possible that dies were regularly supplied from Winchester at this time and, conceivably, at other times.

[5] W.J. Conte and M.M. Archibald, 'Five Round Halfpennies of Henry I: A Further Case for Reappraisal of the Chronology of Types', *Spink Numismatic Circular* (September 1990), pp. 232–6, discuss halfpennies produced at other mints.

[6] P. Nightingale, 'The Evolution of Weight Standards and the Creation of New Monetary and Commercial Links in Northern Europe from the Tenth Century to the Twelfth Century', *Economic History Review* 38 (1985), pp. 205–6, has argued that the Tower pound was introduced in 1158, superseding a Roman weight standard, with a consequent increase in weight of the penny at 240 to the pound.

[7] J.D. Brand, 'The English Coinage 1180–1247: Money, Mint and Exchange' (unpublished M.A. thesis, University of Kent, 1981), pp. 120–1, suggests that the production of more than 240 pennies from a pound of silver indicated by exchanging profits made in 1234–8 *de cremento denariorum receptorum per pondus et numeratorum per numerum* began either in 1234, or at an uncertain earlier date.

[8] P. Nightingale, ' "The King's Profit": Trends in English Mint and Monetary Policy in the Eleventh and Twelfth Centuries', in *Later Medieval Mints: Organisation, Administration and Techniques*, ed. N.J. Mayhew and P. Spufford (British Archaeological Reports, Internat. Series 389; Oxford, 1988), pp. 61–75 (especially pp. 67 and 70).

[9] An authoritative survey of royal grants of dies to ecclesiastics is provided by C.E. Blunt, 'Ecclesiastical Coinage in England; Part I: To the Norman Conquest', *NC* 6th ser. 20 (1960), pp. i–xviii, and 'Part II: After the Norman Conquest', *NC* 7th ser. 1 (1961), pp. i–xxi.

and for its weight and fineness.[10] The quality and intrinsic value of the coinage was guaranteed by the appearance of the moneyer's name on the reverse of his coins, linked by the conjunction 'ON' (i.e. 'in' or 'at') with a predominantly abbreviated form of the name of the mint. Sixty-five mints produced the *Paxs* type of William I or William II, with from one to eight moneyers at each,[11] but the number of mints fluctuated and declined to eleven by the 1170s.[12] The essential components of these mints were a workshop or workshops for the production of coins, and facilities for exchanging; not necessarily all in the same building or locality.[13] The Durham mint seems to have had only one moneyer at any one time in the Anglo-Norman period, whose output was generally relatively small,[14] and consequently there may have been only one mint premises in Durham. The mint may have been in one place throughout the period, or it may have moved on one or more occasions, and it may well have been in the castle or its vicinity. There was a 'moneyour hous' on the east side of Palace Green in the late fourteenth century,[15] and mint documents of the 1470s refer to the 'Castell of Duresme'.[16]

The removal of the Durham dies reported by Boldon Book provides the earliest documented example of the temporary closure of the Durham mint, which was to be repeated many times before the mint's final closure in the 1540s.[17] The chronicler Roger of Howden recorded the restoration of minting rights (*licentiam fabricandi monetam*) to Bishop Philip of Poitiers *sub anno* 1196 (i.e. in

[10] I. Stewart, 'The English and Norman Mints, c.600–1158', in *A New History of the Royal Mint*, ed. C.E. Challis (Cambridge, 1992), at pp. 68–75, provides a valuable summary of the evidence for the status and function of moneyers before 1158.

[11] D.M. Metcalf, 'Notes on the 'PAXS' Type of William I', *Yorkshire Numismatist* 1 (1988), pp. 19–23.

[12] D.F. Allen, *A Catalogue of Coins in the British Museum: The Cross-and-Crosslets ('Tealby') Type of Henry II* (London, 1951), pp. clxxviii, clxxxiii.

[13] Stewart, 'The English and Norman Mints', pp. 59–66, defines and analyses Anglo-Saxon and Anglo-Norman mints.

[14] Metcalf, 'Notes on the 'PAXS' Type of William I', pp. 20–3, tabulates a minimum of 6,472 surviving coins of the *Paxs* type (including 'mules'), only four of which (i.e. 0.06% of the total) are from the Durham mint. Idem, 'A Survey of Numismatic Research into the Pennies of the First Three Edwards (1279–1344), in *Edwardian Monetary Affairs (1279–1344): A Symposium held in Oxford, August 1976*, ed. N.J. Mayhew (British Archaeological Reports 36, Oxford, 1977), at pp. 26–31, speculatively estimates that the Durham mint used only six obverse dies of the *Cross-and-Crosslets* ('Tealby') type (I estimate four, p. 394 below), equivalent to 0.6% of his estimated national total of 1,044 obverse dies.

[15] J.T. Fowler, 'On the Distinctive Marks of the Coins of the Bishopric of Durham', *TAASDN* 6 (1912), pp. 101–2.

[16] M. Noble, *Two Dissertations Upon the Mint and Coins of the Episcopal-Palatines of Durham* (Birmingham, 1780), pp. 86–9.

[17] Fowler, op. cit., pp. 81–102, is outdated in many of its details, but its summary of the activity of the Durham mint is still useful. C.E. Challis, 'The Ecclesiastical Mints of the Early Tudor Period: Their Organization and Possible Date of Closure', *Northern History* 10 (1975), pp. 91–5, 97, 101–1, tabulates and discusses the mint rental evidence for the final closure of the Durham mint in the early 1540s, after intermittent periods of activity in the reign of Henry VIII.

1195/6).[18] However, there is no documentary evidence for the original grant of such rights.[19]

Coins are the only surviving source of evidence for the origins of minting in Durham. W.J. Andrew thought that an Aethelred II *Last Small Cross* type penny with a mint-signature supposedly reading 'DVNII', and a Cnut *Quatrefoil* type penny of 'DVM' (*recte* 'DVH'), might be coins of Durham.[20] H.A. Parsons attempted to attribute these coins to a mint at Dunwich,[21] but the evidence of die-comparison and die style supports their reattribution to London and Huntingdon or Buckingham, respectively.[22] William I pennies of BMC (*British Museum Catalogue*) type II said to have a 'DVRRI' mint-signature were tentatively attributed to Durham by Rogers Ruding,[23] but G.C. Brooke identified them as coins of Derby reading 'DVRBI'.[24] Thus the earliest known coins of Durham are the four pennies of the *Paxs* type (BMC William I type VIII) found in the 1833 Beauworth (Beaworth) hoard (plate 81, no. 1).[25]

Marion Archibald's suggestion that the *Paxs* type might refer to the proclamation of the King's Peace at William II's coronation[26] (which took place on 26 September 1087)[27] is very persuasive. It is certainly a remarkable coincidence that the first

---

[18] Roger of Howden, *Chronica Magistri Rogeri de Houedene*, ed. W. Stubbs (4 vols., RS 51; 1868–71), IV, 13. The ostensible date of the reference to the grant is 1196, but Stubbs deduced that years were reckoned from Christmas day in this chronicle (IV, xxx).

[19] W.J. Andrew. 'A Numismatic History of the Reign of Henry I, 1100–1135', *NC* 4th ser. 1 (1901), pp. 177–8, 182–3, suggested that a version of the '1082' charter *Ego Willelmus* (*Script. Tres*, pp. i–v), which allegedly recorded the bishop's claim to enjoy 'omnes dignitates et libertates que ad regis coronam pertinent', implied a grant of minting rights not actually mentioned. Andrew did not know that *FPD*, pp. xliii–xlv, had already demonstrated the spurious nature of *Ego Willelmus*.

[20] Andrew, op. cit., p. 181.

[21] H.A. Parsons, 'The Dunwich Mint', *BNJ* 9 (1912), pp. 124–7.

[22] G. Van Der Meer, 'Some Corrections to and Comments on B.E. Hildebrand's Catalogue of the Anglo-Saxon Coins in the Swedish Royal Coin Cabinet', in *Anglo-Saxon Coins: Studies Presented to F.M. Stenton on the Occasion of his 80th Birthday 17 May 1960*, ed. R.H.M. Dolley (London, 1961), pp. 169–87 and especially pp. 173 and 177, with the works cited by Van Der Meer; R.H.M. Dolley, D.J. Elliott and F. Elmore Jones, 'The Buckingham Mint', *BNJ* 24 (1965), p. 50.

[23] R. Ruding, *Annals of the Coinage of Great Britain and its Dependencies* (3 vols., 3rd edn, London, 1840), I, 149 and II, 164.

[24] G.C. Brooke, *A Catalogue of English Coins in the British Museum: The Norman Kings* (2 vols., London, 1916), I, ccviii and II, 17.

[25] E. Hawkins, 'Description of a Large Collection of Coins of William the Conqueror, Discovered at Beaworth, in Hampshire; With an Attempt at a Chronological Arrangement of the Coins of William I and II', *Arch.* 26 (1836), p. 10.

[26] M.M. Archibald, 'Coins', in *English Romanesque Art 1066–1200*, ed. G. Zarnecki (London, 1984), pp. 324, 328. S. Keynes, 'An Interpretation of the Pacx, Pax and Paxs Pennies', *ASE* 7 (1978), pp. 165–73, suggests that the letters 'PACX' and 'PAXS' on the types named after them may have been intended as chrismons, invoking Christ. Keynes's reasoning is ingenious, but his theory does not explain the pattern of incidence of PAX types.

[27] F. Barlow, *William Rufus* (London, 1983), pp. 57–8.

substantive type of Edward the Confessor, and the first (and only) type of Harold II, prominently feature versions of the word PAX. However, evidence authoritatively reviewed by Mark Blackburn tends to support Brooke's belief that Henry I's *Pax* type (BMC type III) was the third of his reign.[28] There does not seem to be any satisfactory explanation for this anomaly, but this does not necessarily invalidate Archibald's interpretation of the earlier PAX types.

The *Paxs* dies used in Durham could have been supplied for the use of Bishop William of St Calais between William II's accession in September 1087 and March 1088, when 'Rex Willelmus junior dissaisiuit Dunelmensem episcopum de suis et ecclesiae suae terris . . . et omnes res suas', according to the author of *De iniusta uexacione*.[29] However, it cannot be proved conclusively that the Durham *Paxs* pennies were struck for the profit of the bishop. The later use of Durham dies for royal profit, in periods of *sede uacante* (first documented, in 1195/6),[30] and during confiscations of Bishop Anthony Bek's temporalities by Edward I,[31] may have had undocumented precedents in the Anglo-Norman period.[32] P.W.P. Carlyon-Britton thought that the episcopal character of the *Paxs* pennies of Durham was indicated by the unusual large 'pellet' to the left of the king's portrait,[33] but Archibald has suggested that a similar mark on a BMC type IV/V 'mule' of William II, and other coins, may have been intended to cancel the dies before their withdrawal.[34] It is possible that the Durham die was cancelled, and brought back into use either during Bishop William's dispute with the king in 1088, or for royal profit after the bishop's November 1088 trial and sentence to exile.[35]

There is an apparent gap in the issues of the Durham mint between the *Paxs* type and BMC types II and III of William II (plate 81, nos. 2 and 3). Types II and III are known at Durham from only one specimen each, the coin of the former type being first published as recently as 1980,[36] and specimens of other types might conceivably be found at any time. Nevertheless, a tentative interpretation of the available evidence can be attempted. BMC type I of William II may have been

[28] M. Blackburn, 'Coinage and Currency Under Henry I: A Review', *AN* 13 (1990), pp. 57–8, 61–2.

[29] *DIV*, p. 91.

[30] M.R. Allen, 'The Carlisle and Durham Mints in the Short Cross Period', *BNJ* 49 (1979), p. 45.

[31] I. Stewart, 'Bishop Bek and the Durham Coins of Edward I and II', *BNJ* 54 (1984), pp. 81–5.

[32] Stewart, op. cit., pp. 83–4, has suggested that episcopal and royal dies were operated concurrently in Durham on at least one occasion in the reign of Edward I, but there is no reason to believe that this, if it occurred, had eleventh- or twelfth-century precedents.

[33] P.W.P. Carlyon-Britton, 'A Numismatic History of the Reigns of William I and II (1066–1100). Part II: The Histories of the Mints', *BNJ* 5 (1908), p. 114.

[34] M.M. Archibald, 'Dating Stephen's First Type', *BNJ* 61 (1991), p. 19 and pls. 2, 14.

[35] Barlow, *William Rufus*, pp. 85–9, describes the trial and its aftermath.

[36] A.J.H. Gunstone, 'Recent Chance Finds of Celtic, Anglo-Saxon and Norman Coins from Lincolnshire and South Humberside', *Lincolnshire History and Archaeology* 15 (1980), pp. 90–1.

introduced, and possibly superseded, in the course of Bishop William's exile, if it can be assumed that dies were not supplied for royal use during the exile. Carlyon-Britton correctly predicted the discovery of Durham coins of types II and III that, according to his chronology of the coinages of William I and II, could have been struck between Bishop William's return to Durham from exile in September 1091 and his death on 'New Year's day' (*recte* 2 January)[37] 1096.[38] The bishop's dies could have been restored in 1091 or later, by which time type II may have been in issue, and type III may have been current in January 1096, at the time of the bishop's death. No incontrovertible evidence for the chronology of the coinage of William II is available to test these essentially speculative inferences, but they do not conflict with G.C. Boon's proposed attribution of a coin of type II from local dies to a mint at Rhyd-y-gors *c.*1093–6.[39]

On the *Paxs* reverse die of Durham the moneyer's name is the impeccably local 'CVTÐBRHT' (i.e. Cutthb(e)rht), but on the William II type II reverse die it has changed to 'ORDPI' (i.e. Ordwi). The moneyer's name on the type III reverse die seems to read 'ORDRI', with two further indeterminate uprights. This has generally been read as 'ORDRIC',[40] but it could be a blundered version of 'ORDPI', which reappears on the Henry I coins of Durham (BMC types X and XIV). It can be suggested that only two moneyers, operating successively, were responsible for the production of coinage in Durham from its inception to the period of Henry I type XIV.

There is a long gap in the recorded activity of the Durham mint between William II type III and type X of Henry I. Type X was unknown for Durham before the discovery of a single specimen in the 1971/2 Lincoln (Malandry) hoard (plate 81, no. 4).[41] Despite recent hoards, and frequent single finds, our knowledge of the coinage of Henry I is still relatively incomplete, and it is quite possible that there will be additions to the list of Henry I types known to have been struck in Durham.

The order of Henry I's coin types before BMC type XII has been a matter of considerable controversy, but Blackburn's analysis of the evidence has firmly established type X as the eleventh type of the reign.[42] The absolute chronology of the types is much harder to establish. Blackburn has very tentatively allocated approximately two years each to types VI to XIV, between *c.*1107 and 1125, but he is undoubtedly correct to believe that the actual duration of individual types must remain uncertain.[43] His advocacy of the theory that type XIV ended at, or soon

---

[37] Barlow, *William Rufus*, p. 356 n. 61.
[38] Carlyon-Britton, 'A Numismatic History of the Reigns of William I and II', p. 114.
[39] G.C. Boon, *Welsh Hoards 1979–1981* (Cardiff, 1986), p. 65 n. 11.
[40] P.W.P. Carlyon-Britton, 'On a Penny of William Rufus struck at Durham', *Spink Numismatic Curcular* 29 (January–February 1921), col. 15, transcribed the name as 'ORDRDIC'
[41] *Coin Hoards* 1 (1975), p. 90.
[42] Blackburn, 'Coinage and Currency Under Henry I', pp. 58–9.
[43] Ibid., p. 72.

after, the Christmas-tide 1124/5 Assize of Moneyers is relatively convincing,[44] although Lord Stewartby has rightly cautioned that it is not certain that the introduction of type XV was a necessary or an immediate consequence of the Assize.[45] Blackburn's dating of type XIV, which is the latest type known for the Durham moneyer Ordwi (plate 81, no. 5),[46] to between c.1123 and 1125[47] is no more than a reasonable hypothesis.

It is possible that the apparent absence of coins of Ordwi later than type XIV was a direct result of the 1124/5 Assize of Moneyers. Ordwi almost certainly worked for the profit of the bishop, but he made the king's money and would not have been automatically exempt from royal justice in the Assize. The abbot of Bury St Edmunds was allowed to keep his mint only 'after justice has been done upon his moneyer',[48] and Peter Seaby may have been correct to suggest that 'some moneyers were remanded to the courts of their ecclesiastical lords for sentencing.'[49] Ordwi could have been remanded to the court of Bishop Ranulf Flambard, losing his office of moneyer.

Twenty-eight of the mints of type XIV, including Durham, are not known to have produced type XV, indicating a widespread closure of mints.[50] Unfortunately, the Pipe Roll accounts for the custody of the bishopric in the first two years after Bishop Ranulf's death on 5 September 1128, which include the remainder of the farm of the bishopric 'de tempore episcopi',[51] cannot be used to determine whether the Durham mint was closed before or after the bishop's death. Profits from the mint, if any were received, would probably have been included without comment in the 'de tempore episcopi' or *sede uacante* totals for the farm of the bishopric.

Various undocumented grants or usurpations of minting rights in the first few years after King Stephen's accession in December 1135 resulted in a significant increase in the number of mints during his first coinage type (BMC type I). At Durham ('DVNhO', plate 81, no. 6), and at a mint named as 'DVN' (no. 7), a moneyer or moneyers named H(en)ri struck coins of this type from regular

[44] Ibid., pp. 64–71, 74. The estimate of over 90 moneyers disappearing between types XIV and XV, provided by J.D. Gomm, 'Henry I Chronology: The Case for Reappraisal', *Seaby Coin and Medal Bulletin* (April 1985), p. 105, has been revised to 80–85 by Blackburn, but the correspondence with the figure of 94 said by the Margam annals to have been mutilated in the Assize is still persuasive.

[45] I. Stewart, 'Type XV of Henry I', *Seaby Coin and Medal Bulletin* (November 1989), pp. 259–64.

[46] J. Rashleigh, 'Descriptive List of a Collection of Coins of Henry I and Stephen, Discovered in Hertfordshire, in 1818', *NC* 1st ser. 12 (1849–50), p. 151, lists two type XIV pennies of Durham found in the Watford hoard. One of these coins is in the BM collection; it is possible that the other coin is the specimen in the collection of Dr I.H. Taylor (no. 5).

[47] Blackburn, 'Coinage and Currency Under Henry I', p. 72.

[48] *Regesta*, II, no. 1430.

[49] P. Seaby, 'Henry I Coin Types: Design Characteristics and Chronology', *Yorkshire Numismatist* 1 (1988), p. 35.

[50] Blackburn, 'Coinage and Currency Under Henry I', p. 68.

[51] *Magnum Rotulum Scaccarii vel magnum rotulum pipae de anno tricesimo-primo regni Henrici Primi*, ed. J. Hunter (Record Commission; 1833), pp. xvi–xvii, 130–3.

'metropolitan' dies almost certainly made in London.[52] Another Durham moneyer, Fobund, used unofficial dies imitating the type (nos. 8–13).

Archibald's recent elucidation of the relative chronology of type I obverse dies is generally convincing, although the absolute chronology of the type must remain a matter of probability and not certainty.[53] The two principal, chronologically distinct, series of metropolitan obverse dies identified by Archibald are both represented at Durham or 'DVN': plate 81, no. 6 has a 'better-style' die and no. 7 shows a 'poorer-style' die, with the presence of an inner circle and the letter 'R' of the king's title on the latter die probably placing it relatively early in the 'poorer-style' series. The dating of these two obverse dies is dependant upon the dating of the PERERIC(M) dies used elsewhere, if it is accepted that the 'poorer-style' obverse dies represent a restoration of Stephen's name to dies after the brief production of PERERIC(M) dies. Archibald's argument that the PERERIC(M) dies were produced in the summer of 1141 on behalf of the Empress Matilda, bearing a version of the Anglo-Norman *Empereric*, is persuasive, but not conclusive. Production of the 'poorer-style' dies could have begun shortly after Matilda's entry into London in June 1141, as Archibald suggests, but it is also possible that it began at some time after her departure the following month.[54] The Durham 'better-style' obverse die, which has a STIEFNERE: legend probably placing it relatively early in the 'better-style' series,[55] almost certainly was made and supplied before the death of Bishop Geoffrey Rufus on 6 May 1141,[56] but the 'poorer-style' die probably was not.

It is possible that the 'DVN' mint-signature on the reverse die used with the 'poorer-style' obverse die was intended to indicate Dunwich. There is ample evidence for the production of Stephen's types II, VI and VII at Dunwich (see below, pp. 391–2), and these later East Anglian issues include type VI coins of a moneyer named 'Hinri', who might possibly be identified with the 'Henri' of the type I 'DVN' coins.

Fobund's unofficial type I obverse dies have legends apparently copying the 'better-style' series. It need not be assumed that Fobund's dies were actually produced in the period of the official 'better-style' dies but, if they were, it is conceivable that Fobund preceded H(en)ri as the Durham moneyer. The possibility that the 'poorer-style' coins of 'Henri' were struck at Dunwich allows the alternative suggestion that Fobund permanently superseded H(en)ri at Durham, at a time when either 'better-style' or 'poorer-style' dies were being supplied to other mints. The 'better-style' coin of H(en)ri for which a weight is available exceeds the approximate 22 grains standard postulated by Blackburn for early issues of type I, but the recorded weights of coins of Fobund (from 15.2 grains to 20.2 grains, with

52 See note 4.
53 Archibald, 'Dating Stephen's First Type', pp. 11–17.
54 R.H.C. Davis, *King Stephen 1135–1154* (3rd edn, London, 1990), pp. 57–8.
55 Archibald, 'Dating Stephen's First Type', pp. 10–14; Archibald rightly cautions that the apparently cumulative abbreviations of the king's title were not necessarily chronologically mutually exclusive.
56 J. Le Neve, *Fasti Ecclesiae Anglicanae 1066–1300: II Monastic Cathedrals (Northern and Southern Provinces)*, comp. D.E. Greenway (London 1971), p. 30.

an average of 17.1 grains) are within the range of reduced weights of some late type I variants and non-metropolitan issues.[57]

The 1880 Nottingham hoard, which Andrew associated with the burning of Nottingham in September '1141' (recte 1140),[58] contained six coins of Fobund. This might seem to provide a terminus ante quem for Fobund's issues, but the hoard could have been damaged by a fire recorded in 1153,[59] and it is also possible that the apparent traces of fire damage on some of the coins from the hoard (e.g. plate 81, nos. 8 and 10) are normal corrosion products.[60] The presence in the hoard of an Oxford coin of Matilda,[61] produced no earlier than July 1141,[62] is consistent with the dating of the hoard to the early or mid 1140s.[63]

The coins of Fobund available for study[64] are from four obverse dies and six reverse dies. Three of the obverse dies (plate 81, nos. 8, 9–11 and 12) have a distinctive form of the letter 'R' otherwise only found on non-metropolitan dies thought to have been used in Newcastle and another place in the region not certainly identified. Archibald has argued that there was a die-cutter serving more than one northern mint, and that Fobund's coins were struck for Bishop Geoffrey Rufus c.1139–41.[65] The latter suggestion would be consistent with Archibald's chronology of type I, if it is assumed that Fobund's dies were contemporary with official 'better-style' dies. However, Brooke concluded that the associated north-eastern mints probably all worked for Earl Henry, son of King David I of Scotland, with the Durham coins probably being struck c.1141, at the time of William

[57] M. Blackburn, 'Coinage and Currency', in The Anarchy of King Stephen's Reign, ed. E. King (Oxford, 1994), pp. 167–73.

[58] W.J. Andrew, 'Buried Treasure: Some Traditions, Records and Facts', BNJ 1 (1903–4), pp. 30–1. Boon, Welsh Hoards, p. 71 n. 85, has corrected Andrew's dating of the fire from 1141 to 1140, using evidence also discussed by Davis, King Stephen 1135–1154, pp. 42–3.

[59] Boon, op. cit., p. 55.

[60] R.P. Mack, 'Stephen and the Anarchy, 1135–1154', BNJ 35 (1966), p. 71, attributed the appearance of no. 10 to the presence of base silver; Brooke, Catalogue . . . The Norman Kings, I, civ, believed that all of the coins of Fobund were 'apparently' base. However, D.M. Metcalf, 'The Quality of Scottish Sterling Silver 1136–1280', in Coinage in Medieval Scotland (1100–1600): The Second Oxford Symposium on Coinage and Monetary History (British Archaeological Reports 45; Oxford, 1977), pp. 73–84 (especially p. 81) tabulates X-ray fluorescence analyses indicating that the Ashmolean Museum coin of Fobund from the same dies as no. 10 is not relatively base: its measured silver content is 92.15%; three Oxford and two York coins of type I have measured silver contents ranging from 87.66% to 92.54%.

[61] E.W. Danson, 'The Nottingham Find of 1880: A Stephen Hoard Re-examined', BNJ 37 (1968), p. 63 (coin no. 173).

[62] Archibald, 'Dating Stephen's First Type', pp. 13, 17.

[63] Archibald, op. cit., p. 21, dates the Nottingham hoard to c.1142, and Blackburn, 'Coinage and Currency [King Stephen]', p. 201 suggests c.1145. I am grateful to Dr Blackburn for his advice on the interpretation of this hoard.

[64] A penny of Fobund formerly in the collection of the late G.C. Drabble, sold by Glendining and Co., 4 July 1939, lot 679 (part) is not available for study.

[65] Archibald, 'Coins', pp. 336–7. Miss Archibald now believes that an attribution to the time of William Cumin (1141–4) would be more probable, in view of the evidence discussed below, p. 390 (letter to the author 18 November 1993).

Cumin's intrusion into the bishopric.[66] Cumin's usurpation of the see from *c*.11 May 1141 to 18 October 1144,[67] begun with Scottish backing, would certainly have been a possible occasion for the use of dies not supplied by King Stephen's government.[68]

The possible association of Fobund's coins with William Cumin and his Scottish connections receives some support from Lord Stewartby's suggestion that Fobund might be identified with a moneyer of David I and William I of Scotland, having a name variously rendered as Folbold, Fobalt, Folpalt, Folpart, Fulpol(d?), Folpold and Folpolt.[69] The moneyer responsible for striking the Fobund coins, probably in the early 1140s, could have subsequently become a Roxburgh moneyer producing the earliest of the Scottish coins in question, which belongs to a phase of David I's coinage tentatively dated to the mid or late 1140s.[70] There are later coins of Roxburgh, Berwick, and a mint very implausibly identified as Durham and much more likely to be Newcastle.[71] There are also documentary references to debts owed by 'Folbold' Monetarius' in the 1160s,[72] and finally coins from the Perth mint, which was probably opened after the loss of Scottish minting places through the Treaty of Falaise of December 1174.[73]

The eight-pointed mullet by the sceptre on one of Fobund's obverse dies (plate 81, nos. 9–11), and the larger six-pointed mullets in the legend of one of the reverse dies (no. 9), are difficult to interpret. Seaby suggested that a similar symbol on the obverse of a coin attributed to Pevensey might be a feudal 'mark of difference',[74] but this very speculative explanation cannot apply to the Durham coins, unless it is improbably assumed that the 'mark' was intended as a reference to Earl Henry. Mullets or stars are prominently displayed on the obverses of various 'irregular' issues of the reign of Stephen, and there are six-pointed mullets in the quarters of the *Voided Cross* of BMC type II of Stephen. Mullets and stars may simply have been common decorative devices.

[66] Brooke, *Catalogue . . . The Norman Kings*, I, ciii–civ.

[67] Le Neve, *Fasti Ecclesiae Anglicanae 1066–1154*, p. 30.

[68] The circumstances of Cumin's usurpation have been comprehensively discussed by A. Young, *William Cumin: Border Politics and the Bishopric of Durham 1141–1144* (Borthwick Papers 54; York, 1978).

[69] I am extremely grateful to Lord Stewartby for allowing me to use material provided by 'Three Durham Notes: 1. Fobund', in advance of its publication in *BNJ* 63 (1993).

[70] I. Stewart, 'Scottish Mints', in *Mints, Dies and Currency: Essays Dedicated to the Memory of Albert Baldwin*, ed. R.A.G. Carson (London, 1971), pp. 192, 195 and 267.

[71] Stewart, op. cit., p. 189, suggested that a coin of the Scottish *Crescent and Pellet* type with a reverse legend that could be read as 'FO[..]ALT.O:NI.'V[T?]' might possibly be attributable to Newcastle. This tentative attribution is strengthened by a documentary reference discussed in idem, 'Three Durham Notes' (see note 72), connecting 'Folbold' monetarius' with 'nouo castello super tinam'. Mrs J.E.L. Murray's suggestion (cited ibid.) that the coin might be attributable to Cumin's Durham, with 'O:NI.'VT' representing 'on I(sola) (?) Cut(berti)', is improbable.

[72] H. Jenkinson and M.T. Stead, 'William Cade, a Financier of the Twelfth Century', *EHR* 28 (1913), pp. 224–5.

[73] Stewart, 'Scottish Mints', pp. 197, 199 and 201.

[74] P. Seaby, 'A Stephen "Star" Variant of Pevensey', *BNJ* 54 (1984), pp. 291–2.

One of the reverse dies that I attribute to Fobund (plate 81, no. 12) was known to Brooke from two coins (*BMC* 253 and a specimen from the Nottingham hoard), which together provided the reading '+[.]INDINEDON:EI'. Brooke noted the similarity between these coins and the issues of Fobund, but he was unable to identify the moneyer or the mint.[75] R.P. Mack tentatively interpreted 'EI' as a York mint-signature.[76] However, the 1972 Prestwich hoard has supplied two new specimens, which seem to provide 'F' as the missing first letter of the legend, allowing the suggestion that 'FINDINED' might be an extremely blundered version of 'FOBVND' (using letters that all occur on more coherent Fobund reverse dies). The 'EI' mint-signature could have been derived from other dies of Fobund: 'DVN:E:' on no. 11 and 'DVNI:' on no. 10 are possible prototypes. The proposed attribution of no. 12 to Fobund and Durham is strengthened by the fact that the only known parallels for the display of added annulets on the reverse of no. 12 are provided by nos. 9–11. The obverse of no. 12 has the same version of the king's name and titles as nos. 8–11, with the same distinctive north-eastern letter 'R', and the portrait of no. 12 is particularly close in style to the portrait of nos. 9–11.

The annulets on the reverse dies of plate 81, nos. 9–12 might have been intended as a mark of an ecclesiastical issue, as Archibald suggests.[77] However, although evidence reviewed by Lord Stewartby supports the conjectural identification of annulets as ecclesiastical marks on some coins before the Conquest, he was right to express caution about the post-Conquest evidence.[78] The annulets on the Durham coins might have been inspired by the curved ornaments at the four cross-ends on metropolitan dies, which can resemble annulets.

There are no known Durham coins of the reign of Stephen from metropolitan or local dies of types later than type I. Michael Dolley attributed a type II penny reading '+TVRSTAN:ON:DVN' to Durham[79] but the finding of type II, VI and VII coins of 'DVN(E)' in the 1989 Wicklewood hoard has provided Miss Archibald with the evidence to attribute them all to Dunwich.[80] She has very generously allowed me to summarize her unpublished arguments here. The hoard is from Norfolk and has a strong East Anglian bias, consistent with the attribution to Dunwich. Types II and VI seem to have been produced at mints confined to the South East, East Anglia and immediately adjacent areas. Finally, one of the hoard's type VI moneyer's names for 'DVN(E)' (Roger) is also known at Ipswich in types I and II, and another (Walter) is known at Norwich in the same types. The moneyer of a previously discovered type VII cut halfpenny reading '[ ]OL:ON:DV[ ]' is probably

---

[75] Brooke, *Catalogue . . . The Norman Kings*, I, c, ci, civ, and II, 386.
[76] Mack, 'Stephen and the Anarchy 1135–1154', p. 72. G. Alliss and P.J. Seaby, 'King Stephen's Mint of "Eie" ', *Seaby Coin and Medal Bulletin* (July 1984), pp. 182–4, suggested that 'EIE' or 'EI' on other coins might indicate Eye in Suffolk.
[77] Archibald, 'Coins', p. 336.
[78] B.H.I.H. Stewart, 'Stefanus R', *NC* 7th ser. 12 (1972), pp. 168-75.
[79] M. Dolley, 'The Anglo-Norman Coins in the Uppsala University Cabinet', *BNJ* 37 (1968), pp. 31–2.
[80] M.M. Archibald, 'The Wicklewood, Norfolk, Hoard of Coins of Stephen and Henry II', read to the British Numismatic Society, 25 September 1990.

Nicol, a name recorded at Ipswich and Norwich in later issues, and it may be significant that this coin was found at Thetford in Norfolk.[81]

It is possible that some of Fobund's type I coins might have been produced after the introduction of type II at mints receiving official metropolitan dies, which probably occurred either c.1142 or slightly later in the 1140s.[82] However, Fobund's period of office as the Durham moneyer may have ended at or before the October 1144 submission of William Cumin to Bishop William of Ste Barbe.

After a period of apparent closure, the Durham mint seems to have reopened for the production of Henry II's Cross-and-Crosslets (or Tealby) type, which began in 1158.[83] This is the only type known to have been struck in Durham between Bishop Hugh of le Puiset's election in 1153 and the compilation of Boldon Book, and the Boldon Book account of the bishop's income from dies evidently relates to it. It might be argued that Boldon Book has preserved some memory of the yield of the dies used in Stephen's reign, but that use probably ended approximately forty years before the composition of Boldon Book, which seems to be referring to one, uninterrupted tenure of dies terminated by their removal.

It can be assumed that the three Cross-and-Crosslets moneyers of Durham worked in succession. Waltier, Iohan and Cristien produced coins of classes (or busts) A, B and C respectively (plate 81, nos. 14–17), possibly in that order. However, at the analogous one-moneyer mint of Bury St Edmunds class B seems to have been struck after class C,[84] and some doubt must remain about the order of the Durham moneyers.

Carlyon-Britton's association of Waltier with the evidently deceased father of the 'Fil[ius] Walt[er]i Monet[arii]' recorded as a ward in the Pipe Roll of 11 Henry II (1164/5)[85] is possible but not entirely convincing. The Pipe Roll entries appear under Tickhill in Yorkshire, and the name is found at other mints in the reigns of Stephen and Henry II.

The end of the production of class A, the class produced by Waltier, was dated to c.1161 by D.F. Allen,[86] but this can only be accepted with reservations. It is quite possible that the initial burst of activity represented by class A lasted two or three years, a typical duration for comparable full or partial recoinages in the next one and a half centuries,[87] but Allen was wrong to suppose that there is conclusive documentary evidence for this.[88] It is true that the minting rights of the abbot of St

[81] M.M. Archibald and B. Green, in 'Coin Register', ed. C.E. Challis and B.J. Cook, BNJ 58 (1988), p. 162 (coin no. 232).

[82] Archibald, 'Dating King Stephen's First Type', pp. 19–21, has tentatively dated the introduction of type II to 1142, but evidence reviewed by Blackburn, 'Coinage and Currency [King Stephen]', pp. 195–9, seems to be more consistent with the later date he suggests (c.1145).

[83] Allen, Catalogue . . . Henry II, pp. lxiv–lxv.

[84] Ibid., pp. lxi–lxii and cxvii.

[85] Pipe Roll 11 Henry II (Pipe Roll Soc. 11; London, 1887), p. 55; P.W.P. Carlyon-Britton, 'Historical Notes on the First Coinage of Henry II', BNJ 2 (1905), p. 190.

[86] Allen, Catalogue . . . Henry II, p. lxxiv.

[87] I. Stewart, 'King John's Recoinage and the Conference of Moneyers in 1208', BNJ 59 (1989), pp. 41–2.

[88] Allen, op. cit., p. lxi.

Augustine's Abbey, Canterbury, ended in 1161,[89] but his moneyer Elverdus Porrere ('ALFERG' on the coins) could have continued striking his class A coins for the king after that date, or ceased activity before it.

A tentative *terminus ante quem* of *c.*1169 for the Durham dies of classes B and C can be derived from evidence provided by Pipe Rolls.[90] Class D was produced by the London moneyer Achard ('AC(C)ARD' on the coins), who was noted as having gone to Jerusalem in the Roll compiled after Michaelmas (29 September) 1169.[91] It is possible that Achard produced his coins of class D after his subsequent return, which can be inferred from the partial erasure of a reference to his absence, and the recording of a new debt, in the next year's Roll.[92] However, another London moneyer, Ioh(anne)s Pealcier (or Peucier; 'IOHAN' on the coins), who struck class E, was reported to be dead in the Roll prepared after Michaelmas 1172.[93] Thus it is probable that class E began *c.*1172 or earlier, and that class D superseded earlier varieties no later than *c.*1169.

D.F. Allen suggested that the pair of dies used by Cristien appeared to have been produced locally.[94] He noted a lack of uniformity in dies of class C, but the irregular 'local' dies he described as having 'lettering with reduced serifs' were used at Canterbury, Carlisle, Lincoln, London, Newcastle, Northampton, Norwich, Stafford and Wallingford, as well as at Durham.[95] It is possible that some or all of these dies were produced by an auxiliary die-cutter in London or some other centre of die-supply.

Reginald of Durham's *Libellus* provides an invaluable reference to Cristien as 'quidam Christianus Monetarius in Dunelmo . . . qui quondam minarium Episcopi sub debito conditionis accepit.' Having thus taken the bishop's mine at farm, Cristien apprehends 'quendam miserum', who is said to have found 'thesaurum aliquem' (probably mineral wealth claimed on behalf of the bishop).[96] In 1153/4 King Stephen had given Bishop Hugh a grant of a Weardale mine 'ut faciat in ea operari quantum uoluerit',[97] which has been plausibly interpreted as recognizing the bishop's right to extract silver from Weardale lead ores,[98] but that right seems to have been exercised before 1153/4. The *Dialogues* of Prior Laurence, composed in

---

[89] *William Thorne's Chronicles of St Augustine's Abbey, Canterbury*, trans. A.H. Davis (Oxford, 1934), p. 94.

[90] Allen, *Catalogue . . . Henry II*, pp. lxv–lxxii, provides an invaluable summary of the Pipe Roll evidence for the chronology of the *Cross-and-Crosslets* coinage, but some of this evidence can be usefully re-examined.

[91] *Pipe Roll 15 Henry II* (Pipe Roll Soc. 13; London, 1890), p. 172 and Allen, *Catalogue . . . Henry II*, pp. lxviii–lxx.

[92] *Pipe Roll 16 Henry II* (Pipe Roll Soc. 15; London, 1892), pp. 18 and 144.

[93] *Pipe Roll 18 Henry II* (Pipe Roll Soc. 18; London, 1894), p. 146 and Allen, *Catalogue . . . Henry II*, pp. lxix–lxx.

[94] Allen, op. cit., p. cxxxii.

[95] Ibid., pp. xxvi–xxvii, xxxviii, cxiii, cli and plates XI–XVIII. D.F. Allen's references to mints using 'reduced serif' dies do not entirely correspond with the evidence provided by his plates.

[96] *Cuth. virt.*, ch. 95 (p. 210).

[97] *Regesta*, III, no. 258.

[98] VCH *Durham*, ed. W. Page (3 vols., London, 1907), II, 348.

the 1140s, assert that the bishop took 'argenti tria magna talenta quotannis . . . a sterili . . . humo.'[99] G.V. Scammell may have been right to describe this annual yield of three great talents of silver as a farm,[100] but any silver mined by Cristien in the 1160s could have been coined to pay a money-farm or to provide the moneyer with a profit. It is possible that Bishop Hugh's other moneyers, Waltier and Iohan, also leased the mine. From 1157/8 to 1179/80 William FitzErembald similarly seems to have combined the farming of the 'Carlisle' mines with the office of moneyer at Carlisle and Newcastle.[101]

Victoria Tudor has convincingly argued that the first 111 chapters of Reginald's *Libellus*, which include the reference to Cristien, were probably completed by January 1167.[102] This provides a *terminus ante quem* for Cristien's appointment as the Durham moneyer, consistent with the proposed dating of his class C dies to no later than *c*.1169.

It is impossible to assess the profitability of Cristien's farm of the bishop's mine from the available evidence, but it may be possible speculatively to assess the profitability of the Durham dies during the production of the *Cross-and-Crosslets* coinage. The four pairs of *Cross-and-Crosslets* dies known to have been used in Durham are so well represented[103] (by a total of thirty-five coins studied) that it is almost certain that no more dies remain to be found.[104] The output of these die-pairs would generally be limited by the endurance of the reverse dies, which might possibly strike up to about 20,000 coins each.[105] Thus a hypothetical maximum of about 80,000 pennies or £333 could have been produced in perhaps five or ten years, providing a possible total of about eight pounds or twelve marks seignorage, at a rate of sixpence in the pound. These are extremely speculative estimates, based upon a series of assumptions, but they seem to indicate that Boldon Book's original farm of ten marks per year (equivalent to fifty marks in five

---

[99] *Dialogi Laurentii Dunelmensis monachi ac Prioris*, ed. J. Raine (SS 70; 1880), lines 169–70, pp. xxxii and 20.

[100] G.V. Scammell, *Hugh du Puiset, Bishop of Durham* (Cambridge, 1956), p. 217.

[101] Allen, *Catalogue . . . Henry II*, pp. xcviii and cxxiii–cxxvi.

[102] V. Tudor, 'The Cult of St. Cuthbert in the Twelfth Century: The Evidence of Reginald of Durham', in *Cuthbert*, p. 449.

[103] The *Cross-and-Crosslets* coins of Durham, Carlisle and Newcastle are often round and relatively well-struck, unlike most contemporary English coins, and consequently they may be over-represented in some hoards and modern collections. I am indebted to Lord Stewartby for the suggestion that the black patina of many of the surviving *Cross-and-Crosslets* coins of Durham may indicate that they came from the 1817 Outchester, Northumberland, hoard (discussed by Allen, *Catalogue . . . Henry II*, pp. xlix–lii).

[104] Allen, op. cit., p. 47n. refers to an unillustrated reverse die of Waltier which would increase the total of reverse dies to five, but die-study of the specimens examined during the preparation of this paper indicates that it does not exist.

[105] J.D. Brand, 'The Shrewsbury Mint, 1249–50', in *Mints, Dies and Currency*, pp. 129–50 (especially p. 139) shows that reverse dies used at Shrewsbury in 1249–50 produced about 20,000 coins each. Records for eight mints in 1299–1300 tabulated by M. Mate, 'Coin Dies Under Edward I and II', *NC* 7th ser. 9 (1969), p. 211, seem to indicate average outputs between 10,875 and 17,303 coins per reverse die.

years) may not have been sustainable from seignorage alone. It is also possible that any profit that might be made from the residue after expenses of the moneyer's own minting charges of sixpence in the pound, the possible inducement of the associated lease of a mine, and any undocumented privileges that the Durham moneyer might have enjoyed,[106] may not have provided sufficient extra incentives to justify the payment of ten marks. This could explain the reduction of the farm to three marks, and the appointment of three moneyers in a relatively short period.

Boldon Book seems to provide evidence of a belief that the Durham mint's profitability was reduced by the competition of the Newcastle mint. The Newcastle dies could have competed for mined silver, as D.F. Allen suggested.[107] Certainly, the estimated maximum output of Bishop Hugh's mint for the entire period of its existence (about £333) would not have been sufficient to coin the annual yield of three great talents (or 360 pounds weight)[108] of mined silver depicted by Prior Laurence in the 1140s. However, it is possible that Laurence overestimated the silver received by the bishop, or that the yield had declined by the 1160s. Furthermore, it should not be supposed that the output of the Durham mint consisted only of mined silver, even if it can be assumed that some or all of the bishop's mined silver was converted into coin. The Durham and Newcastle dies probably competed for the exchanging of silver not directly derived from mining.

It might be conjectured that the possible commercial difficulties of the Durham mint contributed to its closure, but Boldon Book unambiguously states that the king took away (*abstulit*) the dies. D.F. Allen was probably correct to see this as part of a royal policy of elimination of granted minting rights, progressively pursued during the production of the *Cross-and-Crosslets* coinage.[109] The supply of dies to Durham evidently ceased in the mid or late 1160s, and they were probably taken away before the end of the decade, although it cannot be proved that they did not survive longer.

There is still much to be learnt about the early history of the Durham mint, although it is unlikely that there will be significant additions to the documentary evidence. Progress will probably be achieved through increased understanding of the English coinage, and by the discovery of presently unknown coins. If finds of new coins continue at the rate of recent years, important advances in our knowledge of the Durham mint can be confidently expected.

---

[106] P. Nightingale, 'Some London Moneyers and Reflections on the Organization of English Mints in the Eleventh and Twelfth Centuries', *NC* 8th ser. 2 (1982), pp. 47–8, suggests that before the introduction of the *Cross-and-Crosslets* coinage some moneyers may have derived extra profit from money lending. Moneyers were often exempted from taxation, or taxed on a special basis (see Allen, *Catalogue . . . Henry II*, pp. lxxiv–clxxiv passim).

[107] Allen, *Catalogue . . . Henry II*, pp. cxxxi.

[108] The medieval English use of the great talent as a unit of 120 pounds weight is illustrated by an eleventh- or early twelfth-century MS in the British Library (MS Reg. 13A.XI, fol. 141b–142) published in *Select Tracts and Tables Relating to English Weights and Measures (1100–1742)*, ed. H. Hall and F.J. Nicholas, *Camden Miscellany* 15 (Camden Society, 3rd ser. 41; 1929), p. 3.

[109] Allen, *Catalogue . . . Henry II*, pp. lxxvi–lxxvii, c–ci and cxxiii.

APPENDIX

Coins Illustrated or Available for Study

The illustrated coins (pl. 81, numbered as below) are used here as the principal source of descriptions of the die-combinations known to me, with transcriptions of obverse (O.) and reverse (R.) legends. Illegible letters supplied by another coin or coins from the same die as the illustrated specimen are given in brackets. A letter, punctuation mark or symbol not visible is indicated by a stop. It should be noted that the precise details of letters and symbols cannot be accurately represented using a modern typeface, and some letters may be malformed, inverted, retrograde or ligated on the coins. A lower case letter 'm' has been used here to represent the peculiar letter 'R' seen on some obverse dies of Stephen. Weights are recorded in grammes (g.) and grains (gr.), when known. References are given to relevant volumes of the *British Museum Catalogue* (*BMC*) and the *Sylloge of Coins of the British Isles* (*SCBI*).

'William I' (William II?) BMC type VIII: *Paxs* (1087/8 at Durham?)
No. 1   O. +PILLELMREX   R. +CVTÐBRHTONDVNE
BM (*BMC* 653), ex Beauworth (Beaworth) hoard, 1.39g. (21.4gr.)
Four die-duplicates: Dr W.J. Conte, 1.42g (21.9 gr); Spink and Son Ltd., 1.42g. (21.9gr.); Sunderland Museums, 1.40g (21.6gr.) and Dr I.H. Taylor

William II BMC type II: *Cross in Quatrefoil* (1091x6 at Durham?)
No. 2   O. +PILLELMRE   R. +ORDPIONDVN
Sunderland Museums, 1.15g. (17.7gr.)

William II BMC type III: *Cross Voided* (1091x6 at Durham?)
No. 3   O. +PILLELMRE   R. +ORDRIIIONDVNL
BM (*BMC*-), 1.38g. (21.3gr.)

Henry I BMC type X: *Full Face-Cross Fleury* (c.1117–19?)
No. 4   O. [   ]N: R. +ORDPIOND[..]hA
BM (*BMC*-), ex Lincoln (Malandry) hoard, 1.18g. (18.2gr.)

Henry I BMC type XIV: *Pellets in Quatrefoil* (c.1123–5?)
No. 5   O. +hENRICVS: R. +ORDPI[:]ON:DVRhAN
Dr I.H. Taylor (ex Watford hoard?)
one die-duplicate: BM (*BMC*-), ex Watford hoard, 1.44g. (22.2gr.)

Stephen BMC type I: *Cross Moline* or *Watford*, 'Better-Style' (1135/6–1141?)
No. 6   O. +STIE[.NER]E: R. +h..[RI]:ON:DVN[h]O:
Dr I.H. Taylor, ex Linton hoard
one die-duplicate: BM (*BMC*-), ex Prestwich hoard, 1.49g. (23.0gr.)

Stephen BMC type I: 'Poorer-Style' (1141–c.1142 or later?; Dunwich or Durham?)
No. 7   O.   +S[.]I[E]FNER   R.   [+]h[E]NRI[....]DVN
Mr J. Bispham, ex Nottingham hoard
one die-duplicate: ex R.C. Lockett sale (cut halfpenny, lot 3935, part)

Stephen BMC type I: North Eastern Area Variants (c.1141–4 at Durham?)
No. 8   O.   [.....]ENEmE: R.   [....]VND:ON:DVN
Nottingham City Museums (SCBI 17, 836), ex Nottingham hoard, 1.31g. (20.2gr.)
No. 9   O.   +STIFENEmE   R.   +F[...]ND:*OND*VNh*
BM (BMC-), ex Prestwich hoard, 1.05g. (16.2gr.)
No. 10   O.   +STIF[E]NEmE   R.   +FOBVND:[OND]VNI:
Nottingham City Museums (SCBI 17, 835), ex Nottingham hoard, 1.14g.
(17.6gr.)
one die-duplicate: Ashmolean Museum, Oxford (SCBI 12, 280), ex Nottingham
hoard, 0.98g. (15.2gr.)
No. 11   O.   +ST[I]FENEmE   R.   +FO[BVND:O]NDVNI:[E:]
BM (BMC 252), ex Nottingham hoard, 1.00g. (15.5gr)
one die-duplicate: Mrs K. Ballingal, ex Nottingham hoard
No. 12   O.   +[STIF]E[N.]mE: R.   +FINDIN[EDO]N:[E]I
Harris Museum and Art Gallery, Preston, ex Prestwich hoard, 1.15g. (17.7gr.)
two die-duplicates: Blackburn Museum and Art Gallery, ex Prestwich hoard,
1.13g. (17.4gr.); Nottingham City Museums (SCBI 17, 837), ex Nottingham
hoard, 1.13g. (17.5gr.)
one coin from the same reverse die and (probably) the same obverse die: BM (BMC
253), 1.21g. (18.6gr.)
No. 13   O.   +STIFNE[.]LI: R.   +FOB[..]D:ON:DVNI.Cm
BM (BMC-), 0.98g. (15.2gr.)
N.B. Nos. 9–11 are from the same obverse die

Henry II: Cross-and-Crosslets or Tealby coinage

Class A2 (1158–c.1161?)
No. 14   O.   +hENRIREXANGL   R.   +WALTIE[R:O]N:DVN:
BM (BMC 254), 1.37g. (21.2gr.)
three die-duplicates: BMC 255, ex Leicester hoard, 1.40g. (21.6gr.); BMC 256, ex
Lark Hill hoard (cut halfpenny); Dr I.H. Taylor
No. 15   O.   +hENRIREXANGL   R.   +WALT[I]ER:ON:DVN:
A.H. Baldwin & Sons Ltd., 1.35g. (20.9gr.)
seventeen die-duplicates

Class B1 or B2 (c.1161–5x9?)
No. 16   O.   +hENR[IREXANG]   R.   [+IO]h[A]N:O[N:]DVNhO[L]
BM (BMC 252), 1.52g. (23.4gr.)
four die-duplicates

Class C1 (c.1161–5x9?)
No. 17   O.   +hENRI:R:AG   R.   +CRISTIE[N:]ON:DVN
BM (BMC 250), 1.45g. (22.4gr.)
seven die-duplicates

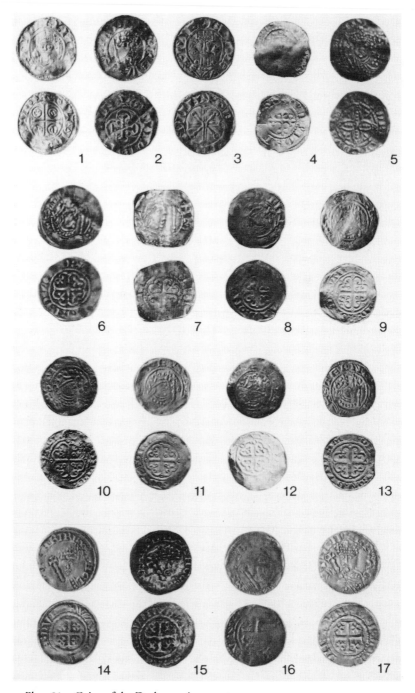

Plate 81. Coins of the Durham mint.

Boldon Book and the Wards between Tyne and Tees

P. D. A. HARVEY

BOLDON BOOK is a survey of the estates of the bishop of Durham. Its opening words tell how Bishop Hugh of le Puiset had it drawn up in his presence on the feast of St Cuthbert in Lent – 20 March – in the year 1183; but as we do not know whether the year began on 1 January or 25 March this may have been either 1183 or 1184 by our reckoning. The estates of the cathedral priory had been separated from those of the bishop nearly a century before,[1] and we have no contemporary survey of the estates of the Durham monks. Almost certainly none was made. Two of the four surviving medieval texts of Boldon Book come from the records of the cathedral priory, and it would be an odd mischance if the monks, in their remarkably well-managed archives, had kept copies of the early survey of the bishop's estates but had preserved not even a reference to their own.

In fact there seem to be only twelve other estates from which we have such manorial surveys dating from the twelfth century;[2] no doubt others have failed to survive, but it is unlikely that it was yet the normal practice for large estate-owners to compile records of this sort. Among these surviving surveys Boldon Book has long been considered especially important. Partly this is because it is the only one to come from a wholly northern estate, though the Templars' survey of 1185 has a substantial section on their Yorkshire properties. But even more it is because it covers an area excluded from Domesday Book, so that it is our earliest systematic record of any part of Britain north of Lancashire or Yorkshire. The particular significance that historians have attached to Boldon Book is reflected in the publication of these twelfth-century surveys. Of one of the others, from Burton Abbey, there have been two editions, but all the rest have been printed only once or not at all. In contrast, the Latin text of Boldon Book has been printed three times and there are three published translations.[3] There has been more historical research on

---

[1] *FPD*, pp. xxvii–xxxii (the possible division of estates with the pre-monastic convent is discussed on pp. xiv–xxv); VCH *Durham*, ed. W. Page (3 vols.; 1905–28), II, 86.

[2] To those listed in P.D.A. Harvey, 'Non-Agrarian Activities in Twelfth-Century English Estate Surveys', in *England in the Twelfth Century*, ed. D. Williams (Woodbridge, 1990), p. 101n, should be added the survey of Abingdon Abbey's properties in the time of Henry II: *Chronicon monasterii de Abingdon*, ed. J. Stevenson (2 vols.; RS 2, London, 1858), II, 296–334.

[3] *Libri censualis, vocati Domesday-Book, additamenta*, [ed. H. Ellis] (Record Commission; 1816), pp. 565–87, text; *Boldon Buke*, ed. W. Greenwell (SS 25; 1852), text and translation;

Boldon Book than on any of the other surveys, but it probably remains the least understood and it certainly still presents a formidable range of unsolved problems. This is partly for want of comparable documents from this region; in some ways, being a craggier, less polished record, it offers more footholds for research than most of the rest.

One serious difficulty is that none of the four surviving texts of Boldon Book is contemporary with the survey itself. The earliest may have been copied 150 years later, and all four incorporate changes made at some time or another to bring parts of it up to date. Some of these additions and alterations can be plainly identified and others we can guess at, but there are probably others too that are impossible to detect. The late Professor H.S. Offler has placed all future workers on Boldon Book greatly in his debt by the article, to be posthumously published, in which he definitively sets out the relationship of the four copies to each other and to the survey as first written.[4] The discussion that follows accepts his arguments and simply builds a little on the foundations that he has laid.

In three of the manuscripts of Boldon Book the text is badly disarranged: its last sections have been moved to an earlier part of the survey and the second quarter has been moved to the end. One or other of these three manuscripts is the basis of all editions and translations except Greenwell's in 1852, though the latest editor, Mr David Austin in 1982, sets out the correct arrangement in a note. Offler convincingly suggests that these three copies all derive from one written on four small quires that were put together in the wrong order, perhaps after having been dropped. The fourth manuscript, printed by Greenwell, presents the text in a different order; that this was the original and correct arrangement is clear from its sequence of places.

Most of the correctly ordered text forms a more-or-less straightforward itinerary through the bishop's estates between the Tyne and the Tees, the historic County Durham. It begins at Durham itself, and passes first to the nearby property at Newton, then north to Plawsworth and Gateshead, returning to Chester-le-Street before moving decisively north-east to Washington and Boldon. It was from Boldon that the survey took its name – it was already known as Boldon Book in the late fourteenth century[5] – because nineteen later entries refer back to the customs and services there set out in full: 'the holdings, rents and works are as at Boldon'. From Boldon, the survey proceeds clockwise round the county – Wearmouth, Houghton-le-Spring, Easington, Sedgefield, Stockton, Darlington, Bishop Auckland, Stanhope, and Lanchester are among successive places entered – and the itinerary concludes with the bishop's properties on the Tyne above Newcastle: Ryton, Crawcrook, Winlaton, and Barlow along with (as Offler shows) four properties elsewhere that were administratively connected with Winlaton.

VCH *Durham*, I, 327–41, translation; *Boldon Book: Northumberland and Durham*, ed. D. Austin (Chichester, 1982), text and translation.
[4] 'Re-reading Boldon Book', to be published in a forthcoming collection of essays by H.S. Offler. I am grateful to the late Professor Offler for letting me read a draft of this article.
[5] *Bishop Hatfield's Survey*, ed. W. Greenwell (SS 32; 1857), pp. 8, 11, 20, etc.

There follow entries for eight places held by the form of tenure called drengage; and the survey ends with an account of the bishop's properties in Northumberland that were centred on Bedlington and Norham.

Two hundred years after Boldon Book another survey of the bishop's estates was compiled, this time for Bishop Thomas Hatfield. The Hatfield Survey was probably drawn up between 1377 and 1380, but in its surviving form it incorporates revisions down to 1382, the year after Hatfield's death.[6] It is much fuller than Boldon Book – it is about five times as long – and is in four sections, one for each of the four wards into which the county palatine was now divided for administrative purposes: Darlington, Chester-le-Street, Easington, and Stockton. Boldon Book does not name places in at all the same order as the Hatfield Survey. All the same, if we assign the places named in Boldon Book to the wards of the Hatfield Survey, Boldon Book likewise divides neatly into blocks corresponding to these wards. Setting aside Durham City as a special case (the Hatfield Survey places it in Easington Ward), we find that every place entered in Boldon Book from Newton-by-Durham to Whitburn is in Chester Ward, every place from Wearmouth to Tursdale is in Easington Ward, every place from Sedgefield to Grindon is in Stockton Ward, every place from Ricknall to Frosterley is in Darlington Ward and every place from Lanchester to Winlaton and Barlow is again in Chester Ward. At first sight this might seem no more than one would expect: the wards, closely defined by the Hatfield Survey, formed compact quarterings of the palatinate and a systematic itinerary around the bishop's estates would naturally pass through each in turn. But in fact at the local level the itinerary represented by the succession of places in Boldon Book follows a quite intricate route, passing to and fro, doubling back on itself, and so on. It cannot be through mere chance that at no point does it move back and forth across the ward boundaries that existed two centuries later.

Why, however, does the survey divide Chester Ward in two, describing part of it at the start of the itinerary, part at the end? A likely explanation is that this itinerary was the route followed by the palatinate's steward or sheriff in making a tour of inspection. He would start from Durham itself and, though for much of the tour Boldon Book's itinerary would not be the quickest way to cover the ground, the route could well have been determined by historical precedent or administrative needs and we can certainly see that it might well be practical to divide the area that formed Chester Ward between the east parts visited at the beginning and the west parts visited at the end. Whether this itinerary was recorded by tradition or in writing, using it as the basis of Boldon Book would mean that no place was omitted, something that would otherwise be difficult to ensure if there was no existing survey either of the estate as a whole or of its component parts.

Whatever the origin of the route followed in Boldon Book, it is clearly related to the wards as recorded about 1382. Either the wards were created after the time of Boldon Book, but on the basis of the survey itself or of the itinerary that it follows, or else the wards were already in existence by 1184. That they did exist already and

6   Ibid., p. vii.

that they played a part in the bishop's administration of his estate is confirmed by the content of the entries in Boldon Book. A pattern of differences between the wards emerges if we take the wards of 1183–4 to be identical with those of about 1382. It emerges even more clearly, however, if a small adjustment is made to the ward boundaries in the north-east, placing Boldon, Newton-by-Boldon, Cleadon, and Whitburn not in Chester Ward as in the Hatfield Survey, but in Easington. In describing below the differences between the wards that appear in Boldon Book, all references to Chester and Easington Wards take this alteration into account. It is not unreasonable to assume that such a change was made in the course of the intervening two hundred years; it will have involved simply moving the northern limit of Easington Ward southward from the mouth of the Tyne to the mouth of the Wear (fig. 23).

It is the more reasonable to postulate this adjustment of the boundary in that some changes seem to have been made to the overall structure of the wards before the late fourteenth century. The register of Bishop Richard de Bury in 1344 lists four wards under the same names as the Hatfield Survey, but earlier in the fourteenth century there are references to Lanchester Ward as a forest area distinct from Chester Ward.[7] In 1293 there seem to have been neither four nor five wards but three: there was a coroner for each of the three wards in the liberty of Durham.[8] We shall see that in Boldon Book, though there are some features peculiar to a single ward, there are others that are common either to Easington and Stockton Wards on the one hand or to Darlington and Chester Wards on the other, perhaps pointing to division at some time into two wards only. It looks very much as if the wards, while fixed in broad outline, were subdivided or recombined from time to time in the course of the twelfth, thirteenth, and fourteenth centuries.

That the information in Boldon Book was collected ward by ward is suggested by some tiny verbal differences in the entries. These are not strikingly obvious; however it was assembled, the text of the survey must, as Offler points out, have undergone some degree of editing to iron out inconsistencies. However, he himself notes that one (perhaps the original) version of the text uses the phrase *e contra* in defining obligations of week-work at different times of year, but uses it only in Darlington Ward. Other differences can be found. In Easington and Stockton Wards entries of places where there are tenants of standard holdings always begin with the number of tenants: 'In Carlton there are 23 rent-payers who hold 46 bovates'. In Darlington and Chester Wards on the other hand they often begin with the number of holdings: 'In Blackwell there are 47 bovates which villeins hold'.[9] Again, in Chester Ward hamlets that return only a money rent mostly do

---

[7] *Registrum palatinum Dunelmense*, ed. T.D. Hardy (4 vols.; RS 62, 1873–8), II, 1134, 1161, 1162, 1216; IV, 271, 273–7; *Richard d'Aungerville, of Bury: Fragments of his Register, and other Documents*, [ed. G.W. Kitchin] (SS 119; 1910), p. 131.

[8] *Placita de quo warranto*, [ed. W. Illingworth] (Record Commission; 1818), p. 604.

[9] *Boldon Buke*, pp. 15, 17.

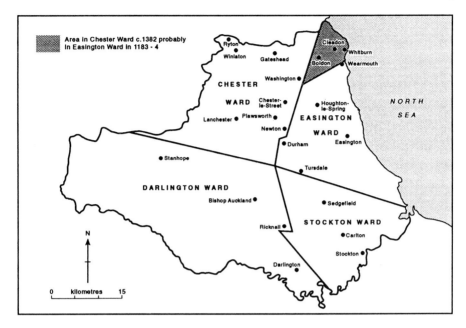

Fig. 23. Boldon Book and the wards.

not name the tenant: 'Medomsley renders 22s.' In the other wards the tenant is usually named: 'William holds Hardwick and renders 10s.'[10]

This last suggests that the information supplied for the survey differed from ward to ward. We may suspect that some apparent differences in custom from one area to another reflect inconsistencies in the collection of data rather than real differences in fact. Thus all the places where it is stated that tenants are required to work on the mill or mill-pond are in Darlington and Chester Wards;[11] there is no obvious reason for this, and it could well be that the same service was required in Easington and Stockton Wards too, but was either overlooked or thought too obvious to be worth mentioning.

Alternatively it may point to different practice. Some other differences between the wards certainly result from actual differences in management. This appears clearly in the entries of demesnes that have been farmed out. Thus, in Chester Ward, but nowhere else, all demesnes at farm are let out along with the entire vill, its services, rents, and mill.[12] Again, in Darlington Ward four of the five demesnes at farm have been let out by charter (*in cyrografo*).[13] This does not occur elsewhere, and it is unlikely that it was the general practice but recorded only in this one ward, as it would be such an obvious inconsistency to remove on editing. Leasing by

[10] Ibid., pp. 11, 32.
[11] E.g. ibid., pp. 26, 31.
[12] E.g. ibid., pp. 3 (Chester-le-Street), 34 (Whickham, Ryton).
[13] Ibid., pp. 18 (Darlington), 19 (Great Haughton), 20 (Ketton), 29 (Wolsingham with Rogerley).

written charter was anyway unusual in the twelfth century, and the survey's phraseology here seems to echo the wording of the charters themselves.[14] Then again, in Easington Ward four demesnes are farmed for 8 chalders of wheat, 8 of oats, and 4 of barley for each of some of the ploughs, plus (in three cases) 5 marks in cash for each of the rest of the ploughs. Elsewhere this pattern occurs only at Heighington, the one demesne at farm in Darlington Ward that is not said to be leased by charter.[15]

But differences between the wards appear in other aspects of management too. In Easington Ward there are seven entries of smiths who have service holdings, doing whatever smith's work was needed on the demesne in return for their land. Elsewhere smiths with service holdings are mentioned only twice, once each in Stockton and Darlington Wards.[16] By the 1180s this form of tenure was becoming a little old-fashioned; more often a smith would hold his land by normal rents and services and would be paid for whatever work he did.[17] Perhaps these service holdings had been more or less phased out in three of the wards but not in the fourth. The tenants of Boldon and the other manors with the same services all render each year two hens and ten eggs if they are villeins, twelve hens and sixty eggs if they are cotters.[18] Renders of hens and eggs are stipulated elsewhere too, but this ratio of one to five otherwise occurs only in Easington Ward, and it is only at some of the places in Darlington Ward that there is an obligation to render hens but no eggs.[19]

Some of these differences may well arise from older local custom rather than from managerial decisions in one or other ward. But it is a different matter when we come to the Boldon-type vills themselves – Boldon and the nineteen places where tenants held by the same customs and services 'as those of Boldon'. For the villeins, these services included heavy works, three days a week on the bishop's demesne lands. Other twelfth-century estate surveys offer no parallel to a long series of manors sharing exactly the same set of customs and services and, as Dr Brian Roberts points out,[20] such total uniformity can only have been imposed from above, though not necessarily on a single occasion.

In 1979 Dr William E. Kapelle argued that the Boldon-type vills, all in the east of County Durham, were places devastated by William the Conqueror's punitive expeditions of 1069–70: the harrying of the north. When he reconstructed them and reinstated the peasantry the bishop was able to dictate his own terms, and the

[14] In the references to enclosed yards, barns, and other buildings: ibid., pp. 18–20.

[15] Ibid., pp. 4 (Boldon), 5 (Cleadon with Whitburn), 6 (Ryhope with Burdon: 3 ploughs plus ½ ploughland), 9 (Shotton), 21 (Heighington).

[16] Ibid., pp. 5 (Tunstall), 7 (Newbottle, Houghton), 8 (Easington with Thorpe, Shotton), 10 (South Sherburn, Quarrington), 11 (Sedgefield), 16 (Darlington).

[17] Harvey, 'Non-Agrarian Activities', pp. 108, 111.

[18] *Boldon Buke*, pp. 3–4.

[19] E.g. ibid., pp. 6 (Newbottle), 22 (Middridge, Thickley).

[20] In an important forthcoming article: B.K. Roberts, ' "And They Work as They of Boldon": Tenure and Settlement on the Cuthbertine Estates in County Durham in the Eleventh and Twelfth Centuries'. I am grateful to Dr Roberts for allowing me to read this before publication.

heavy labour-services of the Boldon-type vills were the result.[21] This is an interesting suggestion. However, it raises some difficulties. The bishop was not the only property-holder in the area and it seems unlikely that his vills would have been particularly singled out for destruction; we thus have to assume the total devastation of half the lowland area of the modern county – a possible but not very probable hypothesis. It is noteworthy that all twenty of the Boldon-type vills are in Easington and Stockton Wards – and are all the places in those two wards where there were tenants that Boldon Book calls villeins (*villani*). This does not explain why the Boldon-type services were imposed, but at least it suggests strongly that it was a simple decision of the estate – or ward – management, unrelated to outside events. It also suggests that they do not pre-date the creation of the wards between Tyne and Tees; but in any case their complete uniformity in Boldon Book implies that they did not originate in the distant past.

What conclusions can be drawn from this discussion? The most obvious are that the administrative wards of the palatinate were already in existence by 1183–4 and that it was through them that the bishop's estates were managed.[22] But we may suppose that it was not only the management of the bishop's own lands that was based on them, and that the official in charge of each ward served as the representative of the bishop – or of the palatinate's steward or its sheriff – for all kinds of business there. Indeed, it would be anachronistic to draw a distinction in the late twelfth century between the management of landed property and the exercise of judicial rights over a wider area. In the other counties of England the sheriff served as the king's representative for all kinds of business, including managing the royal demesnes. The differences between the wards revealed by Boldon Book suggest that the bishop's officials were allowed some degree of initiative and independence. We know so little of twelfth-century estate management in general that this is of interest beyond the local history of Durham.

Many problems remain. Why does the survey omit parts of the estates outside County Durham? What, indeed, was the purpose of Boldon Book? Was it meant primarily to bring together information on the whole estate between Tyne and Tees with a view to making practice more uniform? We can only guess. Why were the entries of the eight places with drengage tenure placed together at the end of the lands between Tyne and Tees?[23] This is one of the most puzzling features of Boldon Book. They must have been extracted from the survey and placed together at quite a late stage of compilation, for their sequence is that of the main itinerary. Offler suggests that changes to these archaic tenures may have been contemplated, indeed, perhaps as part of a new policy of uniformity; but if so, as the Hatfield Survey shows and as he himself points out, it was not implemented. In all this, however, Boldon Book does not stand alone: we do not know precisely why any surviving estate survey of the twelfth century was compiled.

---

[21] W.E. Kapelle, *The Norman Conquest of the North: the Region and its Transformation, 1000–1135* (London, 1979), pp. 181–8.

[22] For the possible connection with episcopal churches, see p. 147 n. 22.

[23] *Boldon Buke*, pp. 35–8.

The Origins and Development of Durham Castle

MARTIN LEYLAND

DURHAM CASTLE is a very complex structure. Its buildings date from many different periods, and the fact that it is still occupied makes clear identification of the early buildings difficult. The documentary evidence is all too often ambiguous. The conclusions drawn in this paper are based on a study over six years, and are of necessity, preliminary.[1]

The early development of the town and its archaeological remains are discussed in a number of articles.[2] While the way the early town was defended is not entirely clear, it seems likely that there was a simple earth rampart and timber palisade enclosing the settlement. Since the neck of the peninsula is the weakest point, the main thrust of the defences was probably concentrated at this point.

The evidence of what was seen in 1904 beneath the North Hall of the castle is important here:

> an inspection shows that . . . when the adhering soil was removed it was found to have no particular face, no courses and no regular overhang of the stones, and the impression given is that it is the rough rubble backing of a wall built upon a sloping sandy surface.
>
> . . . It is to be noted that this building . . . is filled solid with a sandy soil from the level of the courtyard up to the underside of the joists of the Common Room.[3]

The first part of the description suggests the form of a rough retaining wall to an earthwork defence. It is possible that a fragment of the late Saxon defences to the peninsula was sealed within the construction of the North Hall basement which does not appear to be utilised in any way in the early period. Parts of the basement are still full of this material.

The castle is now of the motte and bailey type (fig. 24). It is not necessarily the case, however, that it always took this form; was the motte a primary feature? The

---

[1] M. Leyland, 'The Origins and Development of Durham Castle to AD 1217' (unpublished Ph.D. thesis, University of Durham, 1994).
[2] M. Bonney, *Lordship and the Urban Community* (Cambridge, 1990); M.O.H.Carver, 'Three Saxo-Norman Tenements in Durham City', *Medieval Archaeology* 23 (1979), pp. 25–6; M.O.H. Carver, 'Early Medieval Durham: the Archaeological Evidence', in *MAADC*, p. 16.
[3] VCH *Durham*, ed. W. Page (3 vols., London, 1905–27), III, 79.

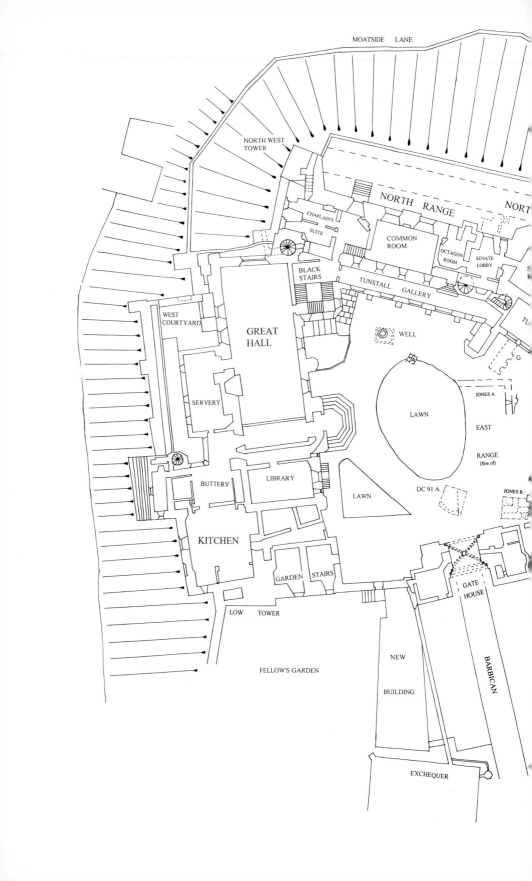

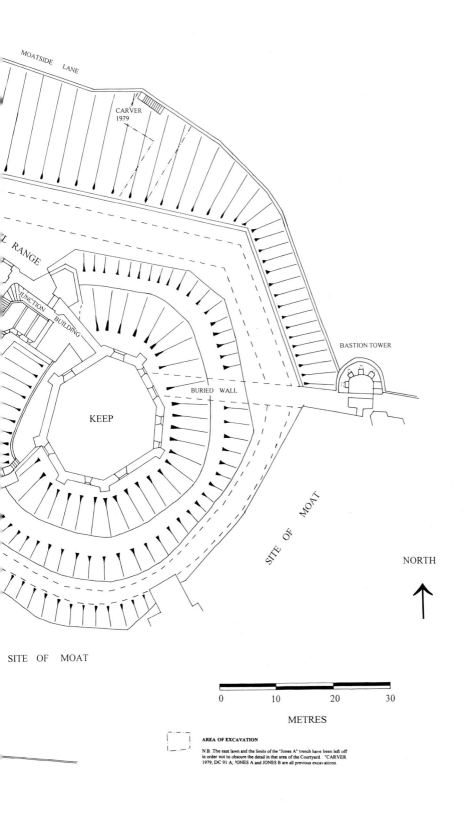

MOATSIDE LANE

CARVER
1979

L RANGE

JUNCTION BUILDING

BASTION TOWER

BURIED WALL

KEEP

SITE OF MOAT

NORTH

SITE OF MOAT

0   10   20   30

METRES

AREA OF EXCAVATION

N.B. The east lawn and the limits of the "Jones A" trench have been left off
in order not to obscure the detail in that area of the Courtyard. "CARVER
1979; DC 91 A; 'ONES A and JONES B are all previous excavations.

Conqueror himself, when he arrived in Durham, would have appreciated the strategic position of the old defence. Dover, London, Exeter, Hastings, Winchester and Pevensey were all placed within pre-existing fortifications and it is clear that William used these wherever possible. The geology must also have played its part. Corfe and Nottingham were placed on headland sites as were Tillières, Falaise and Ivry in Normandy. It may be notable that only Nottingham out of these has a motte and this is a natural rock outcrop. A motte was not the obvious form to employ at Durham.

Of noble castles, Chepstow and Okehampton, both early foundations, have no motte but both are on rocky spurs. Richmond occupies a cliff above the Swale river and here also there is no motte. Although Hereford, another early foundation, does have a motte, now only vestigial, its date is not known, nor is it clear whether it is a primary feature. It should also be noted that Durham Castle is not at the head of its peninsula but at the neck, and artificial height may have been thought better at this weaker point.

In this early period, it appears that the passage of what was later to become the North Gate was thought to be the main point needing strengthening. This is logical for it was the natural ingress into the town area and the early fortified settlement. At this time, of course, Palace Green did not exist as an open area and the bulk of the settlement must have been adjacent to the cathedral. When Flambard cleared these dwellings in the early twelfth century, it was a logical step to throw a wall around the peninsula and thus form a large outer bailey as well as placing the important shrine of St Cuthbert within a better defence.

No other Bishop had a castle nor such secular power as was given to Walcher and his Norman successors. The castle must have been an imposition on the town in an area previously dominated by the church. Yet the town was used to being fortified and had been so since its earliest days; indeed it would seem that Uchtred had designed it as a military refuge. The fortifying of essentially secular buildings would not therefore be so surprising or unexpected, and the question must be asked as to whether this work amounted to a true castle? This question is answered by the *Historia Regum*. This gives the Conqueror's reason for placing a castle here as: 'that it might be a place to keep the bishop and his household safe from the attacks of assailants'.[4] William clearly had in mind the massacre of Robert Cumin and his men by the townsfolk; Durham castle's watchful eye was at first turned inwards.

The word 'castle' conjures up a certain image. Most people today would have a hazy conception of a prominent or central tower-like keep, surrounded by strong buildings of stone. The buildings would be contained within a stone curtain wall, thick and high, and bristling with mural towers. There would also be a strong gate and perhaps a moat. Yet in the medieval period the word 'castle', applied to a group of buildings, could describe a much broad range of structures. At one extreme were royal castles such as Dover and London, complexes of defensive walls and towers, but also comfortable residences. The word could also be used to describe much

---

[4]   *HReg, s.a.* 1072 (*Sym. Op.* II, 199–200).

simpler buildings, little more than manors with crenellated walls. It seems it is the more popular definition of a castle that has influenced the development of castellology. Buildings considered castles have been examined in largely military terms. Development has been defined in terms of military evolution; by the addition and/or refinement of any of the features described above. It is only in the last ten years that the other part of a castle's function – that a castle is also a residence – has been closely examined.

Most of the early works seem to have been in stone. *In situ* fragments of outer walls can be seen on the north side of the Norman Chapel and the south side of the Low Tower and these are extremely thick – two metres or more in thickness. They give every impression of being massive defensive walls. There are clear military features in the primary building – towers on the curtain wall, such as the Low Tower, a sally-port survives in the early curtain wall on the north side of the Norman Chapel and last but not least is the keep on its motte. It is not known whether the moat was primary but it was certainly in place by the days of Prior Laurence (*c.*1149–1154). This is a clear military feature defending the castle from attack from the flat area on the south side, i.e. Palace Green. The keep, however, was of wood and there is no clear evidence that it was converted to stone until the days of Bishop Hatfield (1345–1381). Armitage pointed out that in the English climate it takes about ten years for soil to settle to the point where it provides a firm foundation for stone footings and therefore concludes that the first keeps were of wood and that Laurence's statement that 'from its gate the stubborn wall rises with the rising mound' does not suppose that the wall was constructed of stone.[5] She therefore did not consider Durham as a stone-built castle of the eleventh century and believed that Flambard's castle at Norham was also of wood.

The archaeological evidence does not favour this view. Details of the Great Hall's undercroft suggest it was constructed in the eleventh century. In addition evidence recovered from the courtyard excavation of the East Range suggests that it was built at a similar date. At the east end of the North Range a number of stone buildings were demolished to make way for the construction of the North Hall. The pottery recovered from the demolition fill beneath the North Range has been linked with kilns at Newcastle and given a preliminary date of not later than the early twelfth century.[6] All this evidence suggests substantial stone building at Durham before the end of the eleventh century.

Most discussions of the castle's early appearance have been based on the poem by Laurence of Durham. While authors have disagreed on exactly what the poem's description of the keep represents, there is a general consensus that the main tower is of wood and the description suggests that the tower was indeed carried at least part of the way into the mound or contained the topmost portion of the mound within it.[7]

---

[5] E.S. Armitage, *Early Norman Castles of the British Isles* (London, 1912), p. 82, n. 2; *Dialogi Laurentii Dunelmensis Monachi ac Prioris*, ed. J. Raine (SS 70; 1880), pp. 9–11.
[6] I am grateful to S. Mills for this information.
[7] *Dialogii Laurentii*, ed. Raine, pp. 9–11.

Undoubtedly many early keeps were of wood; Durham is not unusual in this respect. What marks it out as uncommon is that it is of wood in a castle that is predominantly built of stone from the first. Even if this construction was a temporary measure to save time in the first instance it is odd that it was not replaced in the more durable material, thus bringing it in line with the other buildings of the enclosure. It should be noted, however, that the keep at Shrewsbury was also of wood until its collapse around 1270.[8] Armitage believed that history demonstrated that the keep was not a refuge but the permanent residence of the noble. Again it seems highly unlikely at Durham that given the choice between two comfortable stone-built accommodation blocks in the court and the (probably damp) wooden tower on the motte that the bishops would have opted for the latter. It is difficult to determine what exactly the wooden keep at Durham was used for. The documentary sources are almost silent on the matter. The one exception is Reginald, who says that at Hugh of le Puiset's accession in 1153 the prison or dungeon was in the keep.[9]

In many contemporary castles such as Ongar, Berkhamsted, Hertford, and Oxford, the motte was encircled by a ditch. It is certain that the southern side of the motte at Durham was ditched. It is unlikely, however, that the motte was fully encircled. The deposits on the north terrace suggest a much steeper profile to the northern slope, in fact almost a cliff-like appearance. This would render the addition of a moat also on the north side a superfluous and unnecessary expenditure.

Due to the underlying geology of sandstone and glacial deposits and the water table, the moat was very probably dry. The aforementioned examples might suggest by parallel that the moat originally carried around the motte into the present courtyard area but there is no archaeological confirmation of this. Whether the ditch was also primarily along the south front is a matter for speculation – clearly from the recent excavations, it was dug here at some point. It cannot, however, be firmly stated to be primary.

The evidence recovered in the excavation of the East Range suggests that the original gate was located elsewhere from its present site.[10] I believe it may have been to the west near to the position of the present Garden Stairs building. The entrance would have been flush with the outer wall and taken the form of two blockhouses projecting back into the courtyard of which only part of the western block remains in the lower part of the east and south walls of the Garden Stairs building.

Bishop Walcher's building campaign appears to have been extensive. In the first instance the concern would have been the curtain wall and mound around/ supporting the keep, that is the primary defences: 'to keep the bishop and his household safe from the attacks of assailants'.[11] From the evidence of the excavations in the Fellows' Garden the moat can be estimated as at least 17.5 m wide,

8   R. Higham, 'Timber Castles – a Reassessment', *Fortress* 1 (1989), p. 52.
9   *Cuth. virt.*, ch. 50 (p. 105).
10 M. Leyland, 'The Origins and Development of Durham Castle to AD 1217'.
11 See above, n. 4.

150 m long, and in excess of 6 m deep.[12] This gives a minimum volume of 8000 cubic metres of soil. Given an approximate base of 30 x 40 m (although this is only a suggestion; the real figures are unknown) one could achieve a reasonable height on the motte of perhaps 8 m or more depending on slope. This is not to state the moat/motte relationship as primary, only to indicate that the motte could have been constructed from the excavated moat material if desired.

Since some of the accommodation must be primary, it can be assumed that some wooden buildings were quickly erected in the enclosure. When the enclosure was complete, possibly including the west range, Walcher was free to turn his mind to the East Range. This seems of a higher quality than the surviving work in the West Range, suggesting that time and expense was expended in its construction. The latter was not necessarily a problem since it is known that William gave the estate of Waltham to the bishop of Durham. It is known from a royal charter that the revenues from Waltham were used, at least by William of St Calais, to assist with the expense of constructing the castle.[13]

At the end of Walcher's episcopate the castle may have looked something like Phase Plan I (fig. 25). The appearance of the kitchen area is unknown but may have housed preliminary domestic arrangements – a simple oven house or service area adjacent to the West Hall. The north and north-west corner is also not clear. Apart from a fragmentary foundation at the north-west corner of the North Hall there is no substantial evidence for early structures in this area. On the north-east of the enclosure was the enclosure wall. The fact that this wall zig-zags begs a question. Was it built this way or has the northern defence been altered at this point? The northern enclosure wall may originally have been carried further to the north, prior to the construction of the North Range. Certainly such an extension would solve the problem of the awkward triangular space left between the west end of the south building and the northern enclosure wall as it exists at present. It has been stated, with reference to the Norman Chapel in the castle, that: 'Excavations have proved that the range extended further north-west.'[14] On the Jones plan of 1904 there are a number of dotted foundations shown in this area (marked on fig. 24). These, however, are on various alignments and do not give the impression of being part of an integral plan. Without details it cannot be assumed that these foundations belong to the eleventh century.

Bishop William of St Calais may have added the chamber block to the south of the chapel building and possibly the splendid garderobe that adjoins the south building on its south side. Whether there was any provision to link the south building and the garderobe to the East Range is at present unknown – the pipe trenches shown on the 1904 plan do not quite extend far enough. The present

[12] Information from R. Fraser, from excavations in the Fellows' Garden, Durham Castle, 1991.
[13] *The Early Charters of the Augustinian Canons of Waltham Abbey Essex 1062–1230*, ed. R. Ransford (Woodbridge, 1989), p. 5.
[14] N. Pevsner, *County Durham* (Buildings of England, 2nd edn; Harmondsworth, 1983), pp. 217–18.

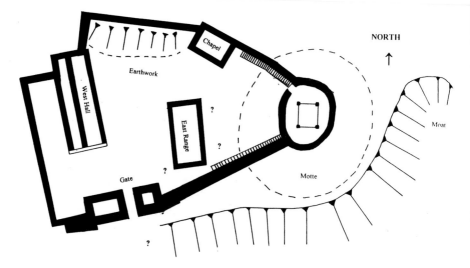

Fig. 25.   Durham Castle, Phase Plan I. Reconstructed layout in the time of Bishop
Walcher (1071–80).

archaeological evidence is not specific enough to choose between Bishops Walcher
(1071–80) and St Calais (1080–96) as the builder of the Norman Chapel. According to a recent study by Dr Eric Cambridge, stylistically the chapel strongly
suggests the work of St Calais. The problem here is the addition of the small
accommodation block which is immediately adjacent to the south of the building.
It seems slightly odd for St Calais to go to so much trouble over his chapel and then
dump a rather ordinary accommodation block right in front of it. Not only does it
prevent the chapel from being seen; it makes access to it that much more difficult.

   The chapel building is often suggested as a double chapel, with the surviving
Norman Chapel as a crypt for a relic which the bishops expected but never
received. Hereford is often cited as the parallel here and through that, Aachen. This
last parallel is rather dubious. The only real parallel with Aachen is the fact of
having one chapel over the other. The form of the two buildings and their internal
layout is quite different, reflecting their different liturgies and function.

   Hereford also presents a problem. It is most often cited as the English parallel to
Durham, either by arguing that the Durham Chapel is similar to Hereford in its
axial layout, and that therefore Durham must also be a double chapel as Hereford
is, or by suggesting that as Durham resembles a crypt, albeit a rather tall ornate
one, there must have been a chapel over it; therefore it must be a double chapel
building, a type of which can be seen at Hereford.

   Unfortunately, Hereford is the only surviving double chapel building in England
which distorts the argument. There was a double chapel at Bishop Auckland but its
form and layout are not known. The main development at Bishop Auckland
appears to have been from the days of Bishop Puiset (1154–95) – long after the
primary period of construction at Durham. It could be argued that Auckland was

imitating the existing situation at Durham Castle but this returns to the whole problem of the castle chapel's construction.

There is no archaeological evidence at present which answers the question either way, as to whether the chapel was single or double storey to begin with. With the addition of the south building a stairway was created from the first floor of this accommodation block down to the ground floor of the chapel. The access from the upper floor of the chapel to the upper floor of the accommodation block is provided by a very narrow plain door and there is no structural evidence of a larger or grander entrance in the past. The whole arrangement suggests that at this period, whether the chapel building was two storey or not, the focus of attention appears to have been the ground floor, in what is still thought of as the 'Norman Chapel'. The chapel may have begun as a single storey building, later elevated in order to place a chapel on the same level as Flambard's first floor hall. If the Chapel was two storey from the first, there is no archaeological or historical evidence at present, as to how access was gained to the upper floor. Unlike Hereford there is no internal stair and the external walls have been obscured by later overlays.

In the days of Bishop William of St Calais the focal interest of those living in the attached accommodation block to the south of the chapel was the lower floor. This does not preclude the existence of an upper floor at this time but the evidence suggests that the main functional part of the building was at ground level. The major problems here are the placing of the chapel lodgings to the south and the awkward join between the chapel and the North Hall The sequence described ascribes the construction of the chapel lodgings to Bishop William after the construction of the Chapel. Bishop Flambard would be the demolisher of the lodgings, prior to the construction of the North Hall.

The connection between the North Hall and the chapel range is haphazard to say the least. The bishops left themselves with an awkwardly angled, splayed entrance, which came through into the south-west corner of their chapel. The evidence of the natural deposits on the North Terrace shows, I think, that they clearly had room to extend to the north a little. If the hall and chapel were built together and with respect to each other, it seems to me that there would clearly be room to make the whole arrangement more conventional and satisfactory. The layout at this point gives every impression of being thrown together, of an organic growth in which the later bishops made the best of a disordered beginning.

The castle at this point would look something like Phase Plan II (fig. 26) with or without the chamber block to the south of the Chapel building. A comparison between Phase Plans II and III (fig. 27) and the overwhelming differences that appear between them illustrate the massiveness of Flambard's changes. There was not only a change of degree but also of emphasis and conception. The extensive nature of Flambard's building works are all the more extraordinary given the evidence of the document of Queen Mathilda.[15] This charter was a release of the canons of Waltham Abbey from the annual payment to the bishop of Durham

---

[15] *Early Charters of Waltham Abbey*, ed. Ransford, p. 5.

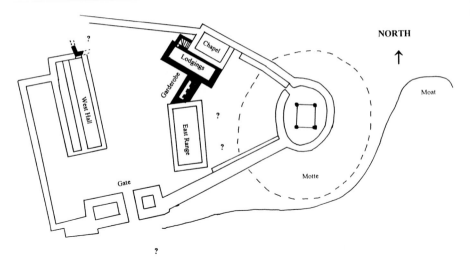

Fig. 26. Durham Castle, Phase Plan II. Reconstructed layout in the time of Bishop St Calais (1080–96).

which was made explicitly 'for the building of the castle'. This would suggest that the castle was considered complete by Flambard's day – his additions no doubt greatly strengthened the castle and city but were not perhaps perceived as necessary by the royal authority.

The changes within the castle itself must be seen in the light of the overall changes in the city layout and structure. The main thrust of defence was thrown outwards to the peninsula walls, the gates, and the bridge towers. Flambard's work in the castle is both domestic and defensive but perhaps with an overall eye to his own sense of self-grandeur. His defensive works are difficult to pin down with certainty. Symeon's continuator tells us that he cleared Palace Green, 'that the church might be neither polluted by filth nor endangered by fire.'[16] Perhaps also in his mind was the idea of clearing a large space whereby men might be better able to admire the new cathedral, and especially the nave, for most of which he was responsible. The *Historia Regum* also says that he constructed a wall between the church and the castle: 'Ranulf the bishop of Durham began a wall leading from the east part of the chancel of the church and as far as the citadel/fortress of the castle', and this is echoed by Symeon's continuator.[17] This is the wall that ran from the keep, down the mound through the site of the present master's house, along the east side of Palace Green and joined on to the old apse of the Norman cathedral, before the addition of the Nine Altars Chapel in the thirteenth century.

The north wall was built by Flambard with towers.[18] These are the towers

[16] *Sym. Op.* I, 140 (first continuation of *LDE*).

[17] *HReg, s.a.* 1099 (*Sym. Op.* II, 260) and text cited in n. 16.

[18] W. Hutchinson, *A History of the County Palatine of Durham* (3 vols., 1785), II, 284; W.T. Jones, 'The Walls and Towers of Durham', *Durham University Journal* 22 (1921), p. 242.

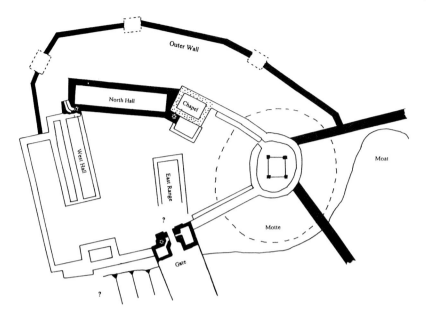

Fig. 27.   Durham Castle, Phase Plan III. Reconstructed layout in the time of
Bishop Flambard (1099–1128).

mentioned by Hutchinson as surviving in his day. The east walls of the peninsula
were similarly studded with towers and defensive look-outs. The building of these
extra walls attached to the castle must have occasioned some alteration to the keep
which was still presumably of wood at this time. Laurence's description has suggested to a number of writers the idea of a stone cylinder to which the walls
attach.[19] Contained within this cylinder, the old wooden tower rose above the
stone wall. It is a reasonable idea and also one which recalls the idea of Toy who has
suggested that Bishop Hatfield rebuilt the keep in the fourteenth century as an
octagon, following the original plan.[20] By relocating the gate and building an
approach to it from the Green, Flambard not only strengthened the weaker side of
the castle but also created for himself an open processional way from his cathedral
to his castle.

Flambard built the gatehouse in the new position where it survives to the present
day and this was surely a part of his conception of how the castle should be
developed. His intention was to build a new prestigious Hall on the north side of
the enclosure. To this end he also demolished the west end of the south building
attached to the chapel to give himself enough length. He may have been the
builder of this odd adjunct. This suggestion does no violence to the archaeological
evidence but as with the St Calais alternative (above) it is somewhat odd. To create
this block with its stair to the ground floor and then demolish a half of it,

[19] Ibid., p. 245.
[20] S. Toy, *The Castles of Great Britain* (4th edn, London, 1966), p. 56.

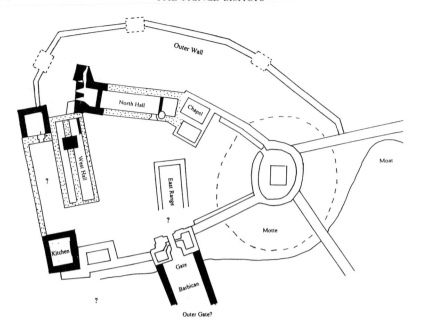

Fig. 28. Durham Castle, Phase Plan IV. Reconstructed layout in the time of Bishop Puiset (1153–95).

relocating the chapel as well, suggests a sudden and dramatic change in his building scheme and indeed what might be called his 'vision for Durham'.

The chapel was placed at first floor level and an access created to it from the North Hall. Assuming the chapel building was already two storey (which is not certain), it is not known what the upper chamber was originally used for. The old single storey accommodation on the east side of the enclosure was in the way of the new entrance. By clearing it and perhaps other structures in the courtyard Flambard may have echoed his clearance of the Palace Green area and perhaps from similar motives. In the castle it would leave a clear view of the new arrangements so that a visitor entering via the Barbican under the new decorated gate arch could look across an unobstructed courtyard and appreciate the new hall on the north side. It was certainly a strong defensive scheme. It should not be discounted that it must also have had a great visual effect.

Flambard's sweeping changes and the end of his episcopate are a punctuation in the castle's development, a full stop. Thereafter changes took place within the scheme and design that Flambard had created, and it is not mere romanticism to say that the later history is of maintenance of the scheme followed by its eventual collapse and decay.

Whether Bishop Puiset would have made any changes to the castle if there had not been a fire in the early years of his episcopate remains a moot point. It is an inescapable fact that the fire forced him to carry out extensive rebuilding and repair (fig. 28). Once again it must be noted that this rebuilding is within the existing

Plate 82. Durham Castle, view of the Norman Gallery level of the North Hall, looking south-east.

scheme of Flambard's layout but it did enable the addition of much decorative and sculptured stone work. The fire probably started in Silver Street and, fanned by a north wind as Reginald describes, swept through the West Range and gutted it completely. The damage to the North Range was not so extensive. The west end of the range must have been largely destroyed like the West Range itself. The central section and ground floor probably survived largely as a shell protected by the old internal earthen bank which Flambard in his wisdom (or luck) had built across. Puiset very probably built the kitchen tower as indicated by the surviving window on the west side of the building. Whether this was a construction *ab initio* replacing earlier domestic structures, or a rebuilding is not known. He must have rebuilt virtually all of the West Range. Here, perhaps, his architect saved the shell of Walcher's or St Calais's undercroft. The arches of the main arcade were probably demolished to the stone pads, which were left standing proud of the floor by about a metre, and the new arches were constructed on these bases.

Plate 83.   Durham Castle, Bishop Puiset's first-floor entrance doorway
to the North Hall.

The west end of the North Range was rebuilt although not quite on the same
alignment and there is still a visible kink in the building at this point. The upper
level of the North Hall was entirely rebuilt, installing the splendid arcading, still
admired today (pl. 82). It is not clear that the fire damaged the entrance to the
North Hall. Puiset may have taken advantage of the general rebuilding to aggran-
dise the hall in general and the entrance in particular (pl. 83). Mason's marks on
the upper part of the doorway suggest the same team were responsible for the
sculptural work in the Norman Gallery, that is, the rebuilt upper part of the Hall.

The arcade of relieving arches which runs along the base of the North Hall on its
south side is uncertain in date. As the arches survive they are finely pointed and
probably the work of Bishop Hatfield in the fourteenth century. A closer examination, however, reveals that all the tops have been rebuilt and this may originally

have been a Romanesque arcade. This may have been part of Flambard's original build but it is more likely to be an insertion by Puiset to strengthen the south wall. The building was certainly visibly moving by King John's tenure of the castle (1208–17) and may have been cracking in Puiset's day. It may also have been thought propitious to underpin a wall, perhaps weakened by fire.

The form of the North Hall is difficult to determine and relies on a complex set of evidence. This paper will merely point out that there are two possibilities. In the first, there is a main hall area with chamber blocks to either side (fig. 29). Alternatively the hall is divided horizontally into a reception chamber and upper audience hall, with a chamber block to the west (fig. 30). Although the latter reconstruction is a more comfortable model, there are problems with both interpretations.

The barbican, so largely destroyed, is difficult to pin down in date. Laurence's poem mentions a bridge leading across the moat but does not seem to describe any outworks. Puiset may have added the barbican and outer gate as part of the general rebuilding and to strengthen the gate approach.

When castles were discussed from the military viewpoint it was assumed that the lord of the castle would live in the highest and strongest point – that is the keep. His household would be accommodated in the buildings below in the courtyard. I have discussed above the detail of the early keep at Durham, as described by Laurence in his twelfth-century poem.[21] Laurence's words suggest Durham's keep as a timber building, appearing little more than a watchtower within a stone shell. Care is needed here. The recent excavations at Hen Domen have revealed the potential complexity of a timber monument and the degree of quality to which it could aspire.[22] The description of the timber keep created for Arnould, lord of Ardres, also demonstrates that the use of wood did not preclude quality or comfort.[23] These wooden buildings also have a certain longevity. Durham's timber tower was only replaced in the fourteenth century by Bishop Hatfield;[24] Shrewsbury's keep was left until it collapsed in 1270.[25] These presume fairly enduring structures rather than ephemeral buildings. The examples of Durham and Shrewsbury, however, suggest that these buildings did not always have the primary residential function ascribed to them by castellologists. Certainly these two keeps were renewed less often and had less attention than buildings in their enclosures which were presumably more central to the castle's daily activities.

At Durham there were two magnificent stone buildings in the enclosure: the West Hall, a ceremonial setting of some pretension, and the North Hall, a more compact comfortable room with well-appointed chamber blocks to either side. Here also was a large well-constructed garderobe and, in the early period, the East

[21] *Dialogii Laurentii*, ed. Raine, pp. 9–11.
[22] P.A. Barker and R. Higham, *Hen Domen, Montomery: A Timber Castle on the English-Welsh Border. Excavations 1960–88: A Summary Report* (Worcester, 1988).
[23] A. Hamilton Thompson, *Military Architecture in England during the Middle Ages* (Oxford, 1912), p. 54.
[24] *Script. Tres*, p. 138.
[25] Higham, 'Timber Castles – a Reassessment', p. 52.

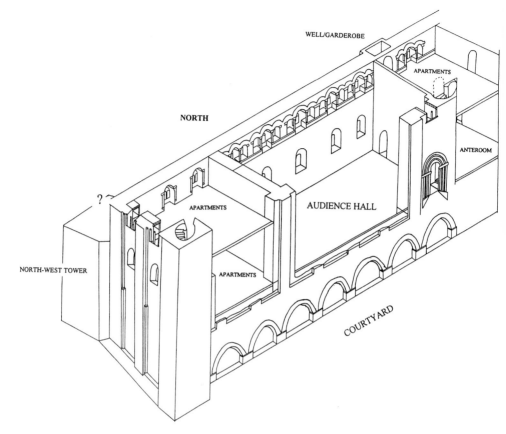

Fig. 29.   Suggested reconstruction of the North Hall in the time of Puiset, viewed from the south side, showing the proposed vertical division.

Range. This was another well-made chamber block with high quality stone work and richly painted plaster.

All this suggests that the focus of activity and daily life was in the courtyard in and around the two stone halls and their attendant structures. The building on the motte may therefore have served truly as a watch tower and as a place of last refuge in the event of attack. Durham was in a strong position and the fortifying of the peninsula with stone walls undoubtedly rendered it impregnable against all but the most serious assailants. Thus the timber keep as a last refuge may not have required the constant maintenance, renewal, and evolution, concomitant to the two halls which were the foci of the castle's daily life. Nor is Durham necessarily an eccentric castle. Founded by royal decree and occupied by a noble ecclesiastic, prominent in the English court, it might be expected to exhibit the common features of the day. An examination of other castles might support the widespread use of keeps as a last refuge, rather than a daily residence.

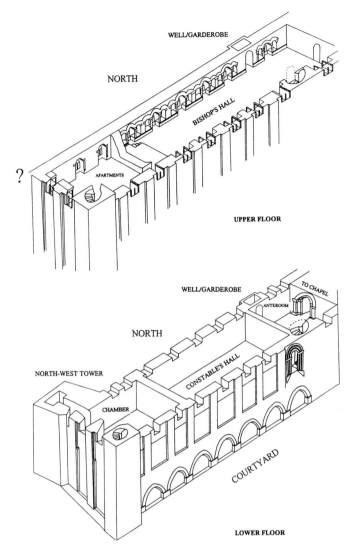

Fig. 30. Suggested reconstruction of the North Hall in the time
of Puiset, viewed from the south side, showing the proposed
horizontal division.

Laurence describes the two halls at Durham in his poem as 'duo magna palatia'.[26]
This is usually translated as 'two great/vast palaces'. Did Laurence, however, see
palaces in the same way as the present age perceives them? M.W. Thompson might
well agree that these buildings were part of a palace: that the building on the motte
was forgotten about *because* the bishops were more concerned with building a

26 *Dialogii Laurentii* ed. Raine, loc. cit.

palace than fortifying a castle.[27] Norham Castle is often cited in this respect as Durham's antithesis: Norham the castle, Durham the palace. Standing on the Scots border, Norham appears to be the quintessential square stone keep within a bailey, typical of its class. A recent study, however, has shown that this is not so.[28] The 'keep' at Norham demonstrates a complex history, starting life as a free standing two-storey hall, built by Bishop Flambard and only attaining its present shape in the fifteenth century. In the early period there appears to have been a rectangular layout with two halls facing each other, not unlike the appearance of Durham under Bishops Walcher and William of St Calais.

The problem lies in approach and terminology. Durham and Norham demonstrate that medieval buildings cannot always be slotted under a convenient label, however desirable. The labels themselves also bear examination. Approach Durham as a 'castle' or only as a 'palace' and only a part-picture is gained. Durham Cathedral challenges our senses with its splendid architecture. On the other side of Palace Green, too long taken for granted, the castle may challenge our complacency.

POSTCRIPT

The only archaeological section across the East Range suggests that it may have been left standing until the mid-fourteenth century. It is difficult to reconcile this with Flambard's placing of the new gatehouse.

---

[27] See below, pp. 425–36.
[28] P. Dixon and P. Marshall, 'The Great Tower in the Twelfth Century: the Case of Norham Castle', *Arch. J.* 150 (1993) pp. 410–32. I am very grateful to Dr Dixon for allowing me to see a draft of this article.

The Place of Durham among Norman Episcopal Palaces and Castles

M. W. THOMPSON

A SHARP DISTINCTION must be drawn between what bishops built at their residences, *sedes episcopales*, within the close by the cathedral, and what they built for themselves on manors that formed part of the episcopal estates. Durham might at first sight appear an exception but closer study suggests this was hardly so. The former type of residence may be considered first.

For obvious reasons the bishop's palace was an element of the close, so that its fortification against the rest of the close, including the cathedral which housed his throne, would be anomalous. Furthermore a certain legal status and dignity belonged to a palace that a castle did not possess. One need only think of the Tower of London and the Palace of Westminster to see the point. Of the seventeen English dioceses created by the reign of Henry I not one had a bishop's palace in the close that took the form of a castle founded by a bishop. A possible exception was at Rochester where Bishop Gundulph had built himself a tower by the north transept and even that may have been a belfry.[1] Among the great abbeys only at Peterborough (to be a cathedral at the Reformation) had the abbot, somewhat scandalously, thrown up a motte and bailey to the north-east of the church, the site normally reserved for the monks' cemetery.[2] At Ely the bishop had acquired the royal castle, when it was already disused,[3] while at Old Sarum the bishop had installed himself in the former royal castle at the cathedral, although when the cathedral was moved down to the river at Salisbury the new bishop's palace was in the close in the normal way.[4] Only at Durham did the bishop acquire a castle founded by the king or local earl and retain it throughout the middle ages and beyond.

Lichfield, Bath, Wells and the later Salisbury had no castle in the town, but at the majority of the episcopal seats there was a castle, usually royal and built

---

[1] W. St J. Hope, 'Gundulph's Tower at Rochester and the first Norman Cathedral there', *Arch.* 49 (1886), pp. 323–34.
[2] *The Peterborough Chronicle of Hugh Candidus*, ed. C. and W.T. Mellows (Peterborough, 1966), pp. 44–5.
[3] VCH *Cambridge and the Isle of Ely*, IV, ed. R.B. Pugh (London, 1953), pp. 28–9.
[4] Royal Commission on Historical Monuments, Inventories, *City of Salisbury*, I (London, 1980), 1–13.

Plate 84. Aerial view of Durham Castle and Cathedral showing intervening 'Green', formerly built over.

immediately after the Conquest. Such were Canterbury, Rochester, London, York, Winchester, Worcester, Exeter, Lincoln, Carlisle, Norwich and Ely. At Chichester and Hereford the castles were baronial, the latter probably of pre-Conquest origin.[5] As a rule the royal foundation was at the opposite end of the town to the cathedral as at London, York, Norwich, Lincoln, but Worcester was an unusual exception which impinged on the monks' graveyard.[6] Whether it was the king, as the *Historia Regum* said, or Earl Waltheof who chose the site for Durham castle, it was evidently intended to follow the usual pattern and place the castle at the opposite end of the town to the cathedral (pl. 84).[7]

The execution of the earl and the transference of the castle to the bishop created an entirely new situation.[8] The former palace may have been at the west end of the earlier monastic church but now the palace was outside the close and separated from the cathedral by the town.[9] The demolition of the intervening houses and the

5 E.S. Armitage, *The Early Norman Castles of the British Isles* (London, 1912), p. 161.
6 VCH *Worcestershire*, II, ed. J.W. Willis-Bund and W. Page (London, 1906), p. 204.
7 *HReg, s.a.* 1072 (*Sym. Op.* II, 199–200).
8 *HReg, s.a.* 1075 (*Sym. Op.* II, 207–8).
9 W. Greenwell, 'The Early History of Durham Castle', *TAASDN* 7i (1934), pp. 56–92, especially pp. 60–1.

construction of an enclosing wall linking the east end of the cathedral to the castle by Bishop Flambard regularized the position by extending the close forward northwards and creating the Green that we know today.[10]

The distance between castle and church is still considerable. Actual contiguity (as at Norwich or Paris), or at least close proximity, was preferred. Nevertheless the highly decorated doorway of Bishop Puiset on the south side of the Constable's hall was no doubt intended to allow him to emerge in full pontificals and move in majestic procession to the north door of the cathedral, a useful compensation.

A plan or air photograph (pl. 84) of Durham castle shows its general shape and the great mound which betrays its origins as a motte and bailey castle, but the classic castle features, curtain wall with flanking towers and double-towered gatehouse, are absent (fig. 24); the two great ranges are free-standing, not even interlocked at the end. The kitchen at the south-west corner is probably within part of an intended twelfth-century curtain wall, but the general impression is more of a bishop's palace than a castle and must have been from an early date. There are four main elements which bear particular comparison with their counterparts elsewhere.[11]

The poem of Prior Laurence written in c.1140, in spite of its tortured Latin, provides unique information on the *domus* within the *arx* on top of the motte, which it may be assumed served as a private apartment or solar for the bishop.[12] We have to go to the Continent to have comparable information about superstructures on mottes and their occupation.[13] There is much else of interest in the description, like the four posts on which the building rested or how the ground had been made up and compacted, perhaps after enlargement or the subsidence almost inevitable on made-up ground.

Returning to ground level the chapel and two palaces are mentioned by Laurence.[14] The present north range was probably built by Puiset and the present west range in the next century so we are not looking at the actual 'palaces' of Laurence. The present chapel (fig. 31) with its six columns then supporting the main chapel on the vault above is really a crypt, the building no doubt serving an adjoining two-storeyed range. Assuming that the east range, of which traces have been found by Martin Leyland (see pp. 412–13 above), had been demolished by the time of Laurence then the two ranges in their present position, two-storeyed and narrow on the north and over the present undercroft with a spinal arcade on the west, constituted the 'palaces' of Laurence.

The chapel, even in its truncated form, is one of the most interesting buildings in Durham. The bishop had another two-storeyed chapel, of uncertain date, at

---

[10] *Sym. Op.* I, 140 (first continuation of *LDE*).

[11] For detailed plan and history of the castle see VCH *Durham* III, ed. W. Page (London, 1928), pp. 64–90.

[12] *Dialogi Laurentii Dunelmensis Monachi ac Prioris*, ed. J. Raine (SS 70; 1880), lines 370–80.

[13] V. Mortet, *Textes relatifs à l'histoire de l'architecture . . . XI–XIIme siècles* (Paris, 1911), pp. 10, 50, 113, 181–5, 314–15.

[14] *Dialogi Laurentii*, ed. Raine, lines 399–402.

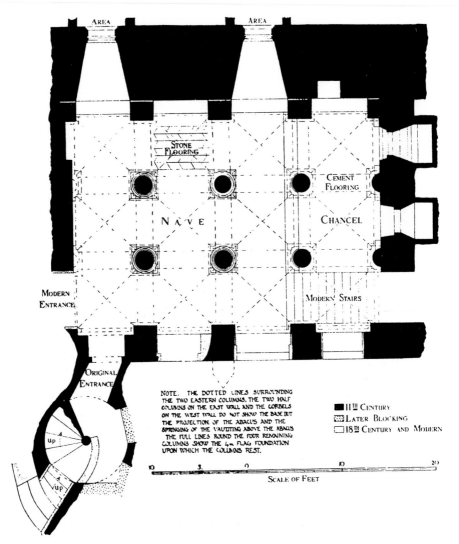

Fig. 31.   Plan of surviving crypt of Durham Castle chapel from *Victoria County History*.

Bishop Auckland palace, which was destroyed during the Commonwealth.[15] More to the point is the almost exactly contemporary two-storeyed chapel in the bishop's palace at Hereford, modelled according to William of Malmesbury on the royal chapel of Charlemagne at Aachen.[16] Albeit only surviving fragmentarily it was of

[15] J. Raine, *A Brief Historical Account of the Episcopal Castle or Palace of Auckland* (Durham, 1852), pp. 7, 81.
[16] William of Malmesbury, *De Gestis Pontificum Anglorum*, ed. N.E.S.A. Hamilton (RS 52; 1870), p. 300.

Fig. 32. Archbishop Sully's palace in Paris with Notre Dame in the background, showing the two-storeyed apsidal chapel at the east end (reconstruction drawing by Viollet-le-Duc).

almost square form with a square apse and spiral staircases at the west end.[17] The ground floor had a groined vault resting on four columns; it had therefore only three bays as opposed to the four at Durham, where the staircase was external at the south-west corner. The eastern windows at Durham would hardly allow an apse. This was perhaps precluded in any case by the ditch of the motte, but the matter deserves further investigation.

[17] A.W. Clapham, *English Romanesque Architecture* (2 vols., Oxford, 1934), II, 112.

Two-storeyed palace chapels, vaulted at both levels, are a well-known feature of the Middle Ages going back to very early times. At our period the inspiration was the palace chapel at Aachen, while in the thirteenth century St Louis's Sainte Chapelle in Paris was the Gothic climax of the series.[18] The Hereford chapel is closely similar to German examples, square and with intercommunication between the floors, while Durham is more elongated and could be entered from an adjoining building, recalling Archbishop Sully's late twelfth-century palace at Notre-Dame in Paris (fig. 32).[19] Durham and Hereford are very early, and for the elongated shape of the former we have to go back to the rather different double-storeyed, barrel-vaulted *Camera Santa* of the Visigothic royal house at Oviedo.[20]

The original inspiration for Aachen or Sainte Chapelle was the receipt of gifts of very special relics, the crown of thorns in the case of Sainte Chapelle;[21] if there was any equivalent motive for the construction of the Durham chapel it must be a matter for guesswork. If this chapel was built by Bishop William of St Calais (the real date is unknown) it is tempting to suggest that it was to house St Cuthbert's corpse during the time before the place in the new cathedral was ready for it.

The two principal ranges, the Bishop's Hall and Constable's Hall, have had these names since at least 1345,[22] an important point in view of the current discussion about halls. This kind of double range, not normally at right angles, is a recurrent feature of bishops' palaces; the 'palaces' seen by Prior Laurence evidently represent the earliest known English examples of this. Not being ruined like the ranges of Lincoln or Wolvesey, Winchester, those at Durham provide valuable information about their original use.

The Bishop's Hall underwent transformation not only in the thirteenth century for which the record is architectural, but also at later periods by Bishops Hatfield, who extended it southward, and Fox.[23] In 1494 there were thrones at the upper and lower end (*regalitatis sedes*) from which the bishop exercised his regalities when the hall was used as a courtroom. The facilities suggest that courts could be held simultaneously at either end of the hall, so it had a formal function, apart from its normal use. For the Constable's Hall there is no specific information on use except that as early as 1345 it bore this name. From the thirteenth century it may be inferred that the bishop lived mainly at Bishop Auckland and so the permanent resident officer gave the hall its name. The splendidly decorated upper floor, presumably Puiset's work, makes one think of a chapter house, a room for meetings or conferences, the *salle synodale* on the upper floor of a French bishop's palace.

[18] I. Hacker-Suck, 'La Sainte Chapelle de Paris et les chapelles palatins du moyen âge en France', *Cahiers Archéologiques* 13 (1962), pp. 217–57.
[19] E. Viollet-le-Duc, *Dictionnaire raisonné de l'architecture française du XI–XVIme siècle* (10 vols., Paris, 1875), VII, 14–17.
[20] V. Lamperez y Romea, *Historia de la arquitectura cristiana española en la Edad Media* (3 vols., Madrid, 1930), I, 335–9.
[21] A. Grabar, *Martyrium: Recherches sur la culte des reliques et l'art chrétien antique* (2 vols., Paris, 1946).
[22] *Script. Tres*, p. 150.
[23] Ibid., pp. 138, 150.

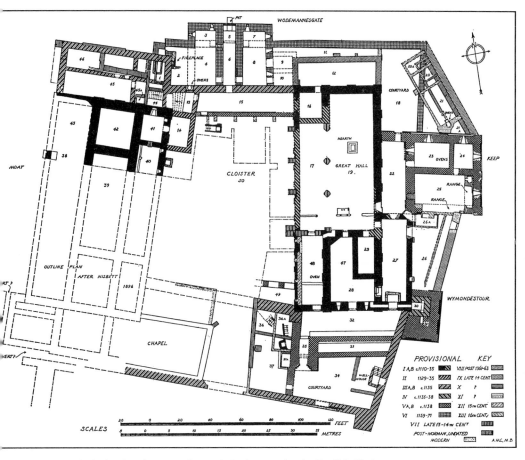

Fig. 33. The bishop's palace atWolvesey, Winchester, plan by English Heritage.

This range had then more of an ecclesiastical function and was certainly more of a private range than the western one. The *domus* on the motte top probably continued to be a private retreat throughout the Middle Ages, to judge by the works carried out there.[24] Bishop Fox was intending to create a suite with hall and appurtenances there when he was translated to Winchester, where he found for his use just such a suite on the motte top at Farnham castle, Surrey.[25]

The occurrence of two halls in bishops' palaces, an earlier two-storeyed one followed by a ground-floor example, usually aisled, has been described elsewhere.[26] Conspicuous examples are to be found at Wolvesey, Winchester (fig. 33),[27] and

[24] Ibid., p. 150.
[25] M.W. Thompson, *Farnham Castle Keep, Surrey* (HM Stationery Office; London, 1960).
[26] M.W. Thompson, *The Rise of the Castle* (Cambridge, 1991), pp. 179–80.
[27] M. Biddle, *Wolvesey Bishop's Palace* (London, 1986).

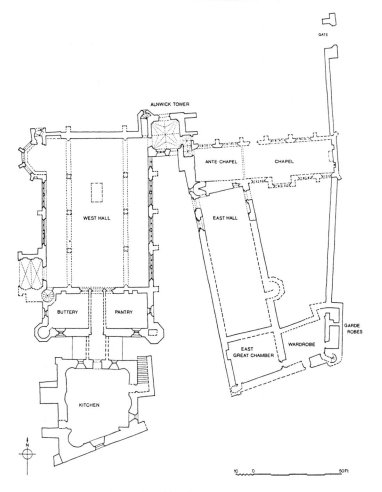

Fig. 34.   Plan of Lincoln Old Palace.

Lincoln (fig. 34),[28] with the second hall much later at Wells,[29] and Norwich.[30] These are now ruinous, although originally they were fine buildings, especially Wolvesey as revealed by Biddle's excavations. The first halls date from the first half of the twelfth century, a little later than the 'palaces' seen by Prior Laurence. The earlier halls at both Wolvesey and Durham (the northern) were set over earthern banks presumably belonging to preceding earthern defences. At Lincoln there is a huge vaulted undercroft below the earlier hall. The internal span of the Bishop's Hall at Durham might suggest the need for internal support perhaps resolved

28 P.A. Faulkner, 'Lincoln Old Bishop's Palace', *Arch. J.* 131 (1974), pp. 340–4.
29 M. Wood, *The English Medieval House* (London, 1965), p. 24.
30 A.B. Whittingham, *Norwich Cathedral Priory of the Holy Trinity: A Plan* (Norwich, revised, 1975).

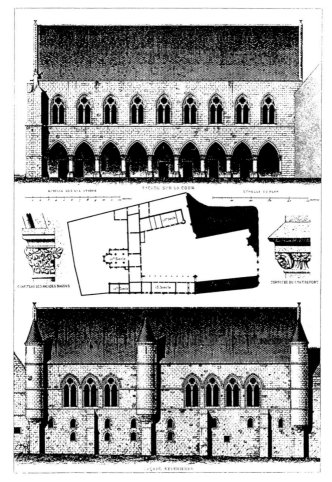

Fig. 35. Nineteenth-century plan and elevations of the
bishop's palace at Laon, Aisne (Verdier and Cattois).

originally as in its undercroft by a spinal arcade. In other cases the later hall is
aisled, albeit with single aisle at Wolvesey. There and at Lincoln the halls were set
slightly askew, while at Wells and Norwich there is no fixed relationship. Presumably the full development of the plan is seen at Laon, where two parallel ranges
(both two-storeyed) are linked at their west ends by another range with the earlier
twelfth-century, two-storeyed chapel set in the middle of it (fig. 35).[31]

Sufficient has been said to show that the principal buildings at Durham Castle
conform to the plan of English bishops' palaces of the twelfth century, and that this
plan must have been adopted at an early date. It is not a castle plan with single hall

[31] Viollet-le-Duc, *Dictionnaire raisonné*, VII, 18–20.

and subordinate buildings but a palace plan with double range, acknowledging the castle context only by the disposition of the halls at right angles.

If there were serious objections to a bishop building himself a castle as his residence in the close these did not apply to the episcopal manors. Bishop Gundulph of Rochester was something of a master-builder of castles in the eleventh century,[32] but it is in the second quarter of the twelfth century that there was an outburst of episcopal castle-building in the Midlands and South. Bishop Roger of Salisbury led the way with a remarkable courtyard inserted within the former royal castle at Old Sarum, and an even more remarkable one at Sherborne, Dorset. Bishop Alexander of Lincoln erected castles at Banbury, Newark and Sleaford. Bishop Henry of Blois in 1138 built a *domus quasi-palatium* at Wolvesey, Winchester, and castles on five manors: Farnham, Merdon, Downton, Bishop's Waltham and Taunton.[33] The distinction made by the chronicler between the *domus* at the episcopal seat and the castles on the manors neatly demonstrates the point made already. We might regard the *turris fortissima* with which the *domus* was furnished as implying a euphemism for castle were it not that the surviving ruin shows that this was not so.

The prince-bishops of Durham surprisingly were not castle builders of the first rank. Puiset, the nephew and protégé of Henry of Blois,[34] whom we might have expected to excel in this field, in fact is better known for his ecclesiastical and domestic buildings. The reason for this no doubt is that the times were much more propitious for castle-building in the 1130s than in the second half of the twelfth century, at least for everyone except the king.

The three castles rendered to the king by Puiset in 1174, Durham, Northallerton and Norham,[35] are, so far as we know, the only castles that Puiset possessed. There are vestigial remains of two mottes and baileys at Northallerton and it is possible that the confusing record is due to the fact that two different sites are referred to.[36] The first castle was erected in 1142 not by the bishop but by the claimant to the see, Cumin.[37] This was possibly refurbished or a new castle erected by Puiset which was demolished in 1176.[38] The bishop had a residence in Northallerton in the later Middle Ages which was definitely on the eastern site although not regarded as a castle.[39]

The other and much better known castle of Norham (pl. 85) is much further north on the banks of the River Tweed where it forms the border with Scotland, which is sufficient justification for its construction. As might be expected it has had a stormy history with many consequent alterations in its construction, none out of

---

[32] Armitage, *Early Norman Castles*, pp. 197, 198, 200.

[33] *Annales Monastici*, ed. H.R. Luard (3 vols., RS 36; 1864–9), II, 51.

[34] G.V. Scammell, *Hugh du Puiset, Bishop of Durham* (Cambridge, 1956), pp. 5–7, 43.

[35] Roger of Howden, *Chronica Magistri Rogeri de Houedene*, ed. W. Stubbs (4 vols., RS 51; 1868–71), II, 64–5.

[36] Plans of the two earthworks in VCH *Yorkshire*, ed. W. Page (3 vols.; London, 1912), II, 34.

[37] *Sym. Op.* I, p. 148 (first continuation of *LDE*).

[38] *Chronica Rogeri de Houedene*, ed. Stubbs, II, pp. 57, 63–5, 101.

[39] VCH *Yorks., North Riding*, ed. W. Page (2 vols.; London, 1914), I, p. 418.

Plate 85.   Norham Castle, aerial view of keep and inner
and outer wards.

line with work elsewhere, except possibly the adaptation for the use of firearms in
Tudor times. The natural strength of its situation first caught the attention of
Bishop Flambard who erected the first castle there in 1121.[40] This probably took
the form of an earthen motte and bailey. The fortifications were subsequently
destroyed by the Scots, but the castle was restored to the bishops of Durham.

The replacement of the earthwork defences in stone, curtain walls and its two
gates, together with construction of the great keep (*turris ualidissima*) was carried
out by Bishop Hugh of le Puiset, presumably in the 1160s.[41] There has been

[40] C.H. Hunter Blair and H.L. Honeyman, *Norham Castle, Northumberland* (HM Stationery
Office; London, 1960); recent revision in *Arch. J.* 150 (1993), pp. 410–32.
[41] *Script. Tres*, p. 12.

massive reconstruction at later dates but so far as one can judge the curtain wall did not have flanking towers and the gates were single square towers with the gate passage in the ground floor. The keep erected no doubt under the supervision of Puiset's chief mason, Richard of Wolveston,[42] was of a fairly standard pattern. It is divided into two unequal parts by a wall 1.5 m. thick which rose the full height of the building and divided each storey into two rooms 17 m. x 6 m. and 17 m. x 5 m. respectively. The rooms on the ground floor were vaulted and the external entry up stone steps led into the larger compartment on the first floor. Unlike the *Official Guide* I regard both the cross wall and the steps on the north as original, and would see the opening on the south-west corner as leading to a latrine, subsequently converted to a staircase.

The design of a cross wall placed off-centre to support floors and roof but intended to create a larger and smaller room at each level was usual in large keeps from the late eleventh to twelfth century, from the Tower of London to Dover Castle. The larger room on the first floor reached by external steps evidently served as a hall, while the inner room was a private chamber.[43] This type of 'hall keep' was also being erected at about this time at Bamburgh or Bowes and may be contrasted with the smaller 'solar keeps' being erected by the king at Newcastle, Scarborough and Orford along the east coast. The keep at Dover castle is one of the last and finest of the 'hall keeps' built on a grander scale of course than that at Norham.[44]

The contrast between Durham and Norham castles is the contrast between a castle converted to a bishop's palace and a normal secular castle, the work carried out by Puiset on the two sites strikingly displaying their different purposes. At Durham the castle's dramatic situation above the river and the great mound were not the choice of the bishops but taken over when the castle passed into their hands. No doubt in the Middle Ages walls and ditches which have long since disappeared gave it a more bellicose appearance than today, but the inside with its great ranges must always have had the feeling of a palace. At Norham the impression is always of the need for defence in the outer walls and in the great tower; the domestic buildings do not dominate but are huddled within for protection. The castle's position right on the Border determined all.

[42] J. Harvey, *English Mediaeval Architects* (2nd edn, Gloucester, 1987), p. 345.

[43] M.W. Thompson, 'A Suggested Dual Origin for Keeps', *Fortress* No. 15 (1992), pp. 3–15.

[44] R.A. Brown, *Dover Castle, Kent* (HM Stationery Office; London, 1966), p. 19.

PART FOUR

Scholarship and Manuscripts

Durham Twelfth-Century Manuscripts in Cistercian Houses

BERNARD MEEHAN

I. INTRODUCTION

S TRONG TIES between Durham Cathedral Priory and its Cistercian neighbours
have long been recognized. Ailred of Rievaulx exemplifies these ties on a
personal level as the great-grandson of the Durham sacristan and relic collector
Alfred Westou and as a prominent Cistercian in close contact with several members
of the Durham community.[1] His predecessor as abbot of Rievaulx was Maurice, a
former subprior of Durham who went on to become abbot of Fountains for a short
time.[2] It has also been established that texts were transmitted from Durham to the
new monastic houses. Mynors made several allusions to textual connections such as
those between eleventh-century Durham manuscripts presented to the community
by Bishop William of St Calais and twelfth-century copies at Rievaulx, linking
DCL, MS B.II.11 (minor works of Jerome) and DCL, MS B.III.16 (Raban Maur's
commentary on Matthew) with the Rievaulx manuscripts now York, Minster
Library, MS XVI.I.8 and CCCC, MS 86.[3] It was natural that in their early years
the new houses should have looked to the established library of Durham Cathedral
Priory for works of this kind, especially given the weakness of York as a centre of
learning. Early in the twelfth century, Dean Hugh of York found it necessary to
look to Durham for historical information on his own bishops. The reply, by
Symeon of Durham, was little more than a sketch, bearing witness to York's
historiographical weakness.[4]

It was characteristic of the traditions they had inherited that the Durham monks
should have sought to enlighten their neighbours about Durham's history and
hagiography. Fountains, for example, obtained from Durham an exemplar of

---

[1] A. Gransden, *Historical Writing in England c.550–c.1307* (London, 1974), p. 308.
[2] *The Heads of Religious Houses: England and Wales 940–1216*, ed. D. Knowles, C.N.L.
Brooke and V.C.M. London (Cambridge, 1972), p. 140.
[3] *DCM*, pp. 38, 40.
[4] *Sym. Op.* I, 222–8. For a comment on York, see Martin Brett, *The English Church under
Henry I* (Oxford, 1975), p. 72. York had few credentials as a cult centre: see Bernard Meehan,
'A Reconsideration of the Historical Works associated with Symeon of Durham: Manuscripts,
Texts and Influences' (unpublished Ph.D. thesis, University of Edinburgh, 1979), pp. 258–63.

Reginald's life of St Godric,[5] and owned an early copy of the *Libellus de exordio* attributed to Symeon.[6] The works of Bede circulated widely, certain manuscripts being used more than once as exemplars. DCL, MS B.II.35, fols. 38–150, contains among other works a copy of Bede's *Historia Ecclesiastica*, also presented by Bishop William of St Calais. This was used to produce three surviving twelfth-century copies, all of which passed to other houses: Newminster, the first daughter of Fountains (BL, Additional MS 25014); the Augustinian priory of Worksop (BL, Harley MS 4124); and Tynemouth (Cambridge, Pembroke College MS 82).[7]

CCCC, MS 139, CUL, MS Ff.1.27 and CCCC, MS 66, manuscripts associated with the Cistercian house of Sawley, a daughter of Newminster, fit well into this overall picture, since, it will be argued, sections of CCCC 139 and CUL Ff.1.27 were written at Durham, and perhaps also CCCC 66, although this is more doubtful.

II. CCCC 139

CCCC 139 is an important manuscript for the unique copies it contains of a number of texts, principally of the *Historia Regum* attributed to Symeon of Durham, and its provenance has stimulated considerable debate. Arnold suggested that it was written at the Augustinian canons' house of Hexham,[8] while Mommsen favoured Sawley.[9] James agreed with Arnold,[10] but Hunter Blair agreed with Mommsen, and the question was apparently closed by his discovery of an erased Sawley *ex libris* from the late twelfth or early thirteenth century on fol. 2r.[11] Despite this, Offler warned that 'it is not certain' that CCCC 139 was written at Sawley, since 'it may have come to Sawley as the result of gift or purchase'.[12] Dumville regarded this as no more than a 'formal caveat', and asserted vigorously that CCCC 139 was the work of Sawley scribes.[13]

5 *V. Godr.*, pp. 466–9. See below, p. 448.
6 This copy, BL, Cotton MS Faustina A.V, has a Fountains *ex libris* of the late twelfth or early thirteenth century on fol. 25r. There are also puzzling fourteenth-century ownership marks of one William de Coutton on fols 97v and 98v: see Meehan, 'Symeon' pp. 47, 250, and 267.
7 *HE*, ed. and trans. B. Colgrave and R.A.B. Mynors, p. xlix. Colgrave and Mynors also drew attention to a group of manuscripts of Bede from Yorkshire, including twelfth-century manuscripts from Selby, Jervaulx, and Kirkham. The parent manuscript of these was not identified, but here again the trail may lead back to Durham.
8 *Sym. Op.* II, x.
9 *Chronica minora saec. IV, V, VI, VII*, III ed. T. Mommsen (MGH Auctores Antiquissimi 13; Berlin 1898), 124.
10 M.R. James, *A Descriptive Catalogue of the Manuscripts in the Library of Corpus Christi College, Cambridge* (2 vols., Cambridge, 1912), I, 323.
11 P.H. Blair, 'Some Observations on the "Historia Regum" attributed to Symeon of Durham', in *Celt and Saxon*, ed. N.K. Chadwick (Cambridge, 1963), pp. 63–118 at pp. 74–76, and 118.
12 H.S. Offler, 'Hexham and the Historia Regum', *TAASDN* new ser. 2 (1970), p. 52.
13 D.N. Dumville, 'The Corpus Christi "Nennius" ', *Bulletin of the Board of Celtic Studies* 25 (1972–4), p. 372 n. 3; idem, 'Celtic-Latin Texts in Northern England c.1150–c.1250', *Celtica*

It has become clear that the manuscript is not a homogeneous one and that study of it must take this into account. Dumville disagreed with the view of James and Hunter Blair that CCCC 139 divides into two separate sections, gatherings 1–20 (fols. 1–167) comprising one section and gatherings 21–2 (fols. 168–82) comprising another.[14] While Dumville preferred to regard the manuscript as demonstrating 'diversity within unity',[15] Baker demonstrated that CCCC 139 should be viewed not as a unity but as a collection of four main sections written separately and combined at an early date to form a single volume, as gathering numbers of the late twelfth or early thirteenth century indicate.[16] Baker argued that CCCC 139 was written by the Cistercians of Fountains, his evidence being the fact that its text of the 'letter of Thurstan' (describing the foundation of Fountains after the secession from St Mary's York) seems to have been copied directly into the Fountains manuscript Oxford, Corpus Christi College, MS D 209. As Baker himself emphasised, however, this evidence applies only to the section of the manuscript which contains the 'letter of Thurstan' (gatherings 19–20; fols. 152–67). A strong case can be made that other sections were written at Durham. Textual study has demonstrated that the version of the *Historia Brittonum* in fols. 168v–78v and the life of Gildas in fols. 178v–182v were used to improve and revise the copies of those texts in the Durham manuscript, DCL B.II.35. The version of the *Historia Brittonum* in CCCC 139 has been shown to be from the same exemplar as that in Liège, University Library, MS 369 C, fols. 130r–142r, a manuscript which has a partially erased late twelfth- or early thirteenth-century *ex libris* of Kirkstall, a daughter house of Fountains. It was moreover used to produce 'a copy, with amplifications' of the *Historia Brittonum* in CUL Ff.1.27, fols. 11r–20v. Dumville drew the conclusion that CCCC 139 was sent to Durham from Sawley so that DCL B.II.35 might be 'improved' thereby.[17] This deduction seems to have little validity and derives from the assumption that CCCC 139 and CUL Ff.1.27 were produced by Sawley scribes. Baker has shown that this is an untenable assumption for CCCC 139. It is suggested below that CUL Ff.1.27 was written at Durham. I argued in 1978 that Liège 369C was also written there.[18] DCL B.II.35 itself has always been at Durham. Thus, of the four manuscripts known to have been involved in the revision of the text of the *Historia Brittonum*, three – Liège 369 C, CUL Ff.1.27 and DCL B.II.35 – can be attributed to Durham with a reasonable degree of conviction. Perhaps the rough, annotated copy of the *Historia Brittonum*

12 (1977), pp. 19–49. In a further study, 'The Sixteenth-Century History of Two Cambridge Books from Sawley', *Transactions of the Cambridge Bibliographical Society* 7 (1980), p. 440, n. 9, Dumville remained insistent on a Sawley origin.
[14] James, *A Descriptive Catalogue of the Manuscripts of Corpus Christi College*, I, 321; and Blair, 'Observations', p. 63.
[15] Dumville, 'Corpus Christi "Nennius" ', p. 370.
[16] Derek Baker, 'Scissors and Paste: Corpus Christi, Cambridge, MS 139 Again', *Studies in Church History* 11 (1975), pp. 85–6.
[17] Dumville, 'Corpus Christi "Nennius" ', p. 372.
[18] Bernard Meehan, 'Geoffrey of Monmouth, *Prophecies of Merlin*: New Manuscript Evidence', *Bulletin of the Board of Celtic Studies* 28 (1978), pp. 37–46.

contained in CCCC 139 was considered expendable in Durham once its readings had been transferred to DCL B.II.35 and later to CUL Ff.1.27. It was consequently given to Sawley, or perhaps first to Fountains, the copy in DCL B.II.35 being retained at Durham. This proposition seems preferable to Dumville's conviction that the text in CCCC 139 was written and corrected at Sawley and then sent to improve a Durham copy of the work. In view of the relative resources of the two houses, such a conjecture is both unlikely and unnecessary.

A Durham origin can be demonstrated for other sections of CCCC 139. The chronicle of Regino of Prüm in the earlier twelfth-century DCL, MS C.IV.15 was the exemplar for CCCC 139, fols. 19r–37v.[19] This text occurs in the second main section of CCCC 139 (gatherings 3–18, fols. 19–151), the section which makes up the bulk of the manuscript. The hand is similar to the major hand of CUL Ff.1.27 and the hand of BL, Cotton MS Caligula A.VIII fols. 25–58, which Mynors regarded as a Durham book.[20]

Copious annotations, in a variety of late twelfth- and early thirteenth-century hands, have been made to CCCC 139. Marginalia in section 2 of the manuscript demonstrate access to information on the bishops of Durham. For example, the text of the *Historia Regum* on fol. 96v records Bishop Aldhun's death before the battle of Carham in 1018, while a footnote places the event after the battle. This may be an attempt to conform to Symeon's *Libellus de exordio*, where Aldhun's death is presented as a dramatic result of the loss of Northumbrian lives in the battle.[21] A note on fol. 98v refers to the accusation made in the *Libellus de exordio* that Eadred had bought the bishopric from King Harthacnut in 1042 with money taken from the church.[22] The annotator's source may have been a copy of that work, perhaps even the copy in CUL Ff.1.27, since connections between the two manuscripts have long been noted,[23] though it is not possible to conclude whether the marginalia were added at Durham, at Fountains or at Sawley.

III. CUL Ff.1.27 and CCCC 66

Cambridge University Library Ff.1.27 contains Symeon's *Libellus de exordio* as well as an assortment of other pieces copied late in the twelfth century.[24] The accepted view of its provenance is derived from M.R. James's contention that it originally formed one book with CCCC 66. According to James, Archbishop Parker split this

---

[19] W.-R. Schneidgen, *Die Überlieferungsgeschichte der Chronik des Regino von Prüm* (Mainz, 1977), pp. 38–41. This suggestion was made to me first by Dr Meryl Foster.
[20] *DCM*, pp. 7–8. CCCC 139 is the subject of a major forthcoming study edited by M. Budny and T. Graham.
[21] Bernard Meehan, 'The Siege of Durham, the Battle of Carham and the Cession of Lothian', *Scottish Historical Review* 55 (1976), p. 14, n. 1.
[22] *LDE*, bk. 3, ch. 9 (*Sym. Op.* I, 91) and *HReg, s.a.* 1042 (*Sym. Op.* II, 162).
[23] See Dumville, 'Corpus Christi "Nennius" ', p. 371, n. 4; also Meehan, 'Symeon', p. 83.
[24] For a description of the contents, see *A Catalogue of the Manuscripts Preserved in the Library of the University of Cambridge* (5 vols., Cambridge, 1856–67), II, 318–29. A date early in the

book in two, took a fourteenth-century book from Bury St Edmunds, divided this as well, shuffled the pieces and fabricated two composite volumes, each containing a twelfth-century section and a fourteenth-century section. Parker gave one volume to the University Library, where it became CUL Ff.1.27, and gave the other to Corpus Christi College, where it became CCCC 66.[25] Dumville argued that it was possible to re-establish the structure of the original twelfth-century volume on the basis of an early modern pagination which survives in part, but this argument does not necessarily have any validity for the twelfth century.[26] The Sawley *ex libris* on p. 2 of the twelfth-century section of CCCC 66 has been taken to prove that both it and the twelfth-century section of CUL Ff.1.27 were written at Sawley, on the assumption that they originally formed a single book, and Dumville has claimed that there is 'no doubt' of this.[27] Even if we were to accept that the two sections did indeed form one book, the *ex libris* proves only that the book was in the Sawley library in the late twelfth or early thirteenth century. As to where it was written, earlier judgements seem preferable to those of Blair and Dumville. Mynors expressed his belief that CUL Ff.1.27 was a 'Durham product',[28] and Stevenson in 1838 noted that it was 'once, apparently, the property of the monks of Durham, if not transcribed in that monastery'.[29] The grounds for supporting Stevenson and Mynors in their emphasis on Durham are as follows: CUL Ff.1.27 divides into three main sections written, like CCCC 139, in a variety of broadly similar hands.[30] The first section (gatherings I–II, pp. 1–40), containing Gildas, *De excidio* and the *Historia Brittonum*, can be associated with Durham for reasons, described above, connected with its relationship to CCCC 139. The second section comprises the bulk of the manuscript: gatherings III–XI (pp. 73–220), written substantially in a single hand. It contains a great deal of material with a Durham orientation: works by Bede; Symeon's *Libellus de exordio* and its various continuations;[31] a charter on the privileges of the church of Lindisfarne; the *Historia de Sancto Cuthberto*; a list of relics contained in the church of Durham; the poem De *situ Dunelmi*; and Aethelwulf's *De Abbatibus*, which in this manuscript contains a modification of the text giving the misleading impression that the monastery in

thirteenth century has been suggested by Dumville, 'Corpus Christi "Nennius" ', p. 377, a conclusion contradicted in Meehan, 'Symeon', pp. 74–5.

[25] James, *A Descriptive Catalogue of the Manuscripts of Corpus Christi College*, I, 138 and 145.

[26] Dumville, 'Two Cambridge Books', pp. 434–6.

[27] Dumville, 'Corpus Christi "Nennius" ', p. 371.

[28] *DCM*, p. 8.

[29] *Gildas de excidio Britanniae*, ed J. Stevenson (English Historical Society, London, 1838), p. xvi.

[30] The collation of CUL Ff.1.27 is: I[8] (pp. 1–16); II[12] (pp. 17–40); the fourteenth-century section of the manuscript is intruded at this point; III[8]–V[8] (pp. 73–120); VI[6] (lacks 6) (pp. 121–130); VII[8]–IX[8] (pp. 131–78); X[14] (lacks 6, 10) (pp. 179–202); XI[10] (lacks 2) (pp. 203–20); XII[8]–XIII[8] (pp. 221–52). The collation of CCCC 66 is: I[1+8] (pp. 1–18; pp. 1/2 single leaf); II[8]–IV[8] (pp. 19–64); V[10] (lacks 10) (pp. 65–82); VI[8]–VII[8] (pp. 83–113).

[31] Some work remains to be done on the continuations to the *De exordio* on William Cumin, William of Ste Barbe and Hugh of le Puiset in CUL Ff.1.27. These seem to be in an earlier hand than the versions in DUL, MS Cosin's V.ii.6.

question was Lindisfarne.[32] It is difficult to imagine that these copies, or at least their exemplars, originated anywhere other than Durham. The third section (gatherings XII–XIII, pp. 221–252) can be linked with Durham through its relationship with the Gilbert of Limerick text in DCL B.II.35, fols. 36r–8r.[33]

The situation with regard to the twelfth-century section of CCCC 66 is more problematic. In the first place, it is not certain that the twelfth-century sections in it and CUL Ff.1.27 really formed one book as James supposed. It is true that a fifteenth-century list of contents in CCCC 66, p. 1, includes the contents of the twelfth-century sections of both volumes; but this evidence is not necessarily applicable to the twelfth century. It is also true that its twelfth-century section shares striking similarities with CUL Ff.1.27: in its main text hands; in its style of rubrication; in its uniformly well-prepared parchment; and in some aspects of its artistic style, the wheel of fortune in CCCC 66, p. 66, resembling closely the style of the church diagram in CUL Ff.1.27, p. 238, with its animal roundels and gold lines bounded with black.

Objections can nonetheless be raised to the assumption that CUL Ff.1.27 and CCCC 66 constitute a single manuscript. They should instead be regarded, like CCCC 139, as having been conceived in sections which were combined at an early date into a single volume. The two volumes vary internally and in comparison with each other in the number of lines to the page and in the dimensions of their ruled space. Several main scribes were involved, and several artists were responsible for the minor initials of the two manuscripts. Notably, CCCC 66 contains smaller, neater work than Ff.1.27, with the decorated initials of a number of pages of CCCC 66 making use of dots as space-fillers (pp. 6, 70, 71, 72, 73, 74, 77, 80, 82, 102). Significantly, there are serious differences between the list of the bishops of Lindisfarne, Chester-le-Street and Durham in CCCC 66, p. 97, and the succession detailed in the text of Symeon's *De exordio* which appears in CUL Ff.1.27 and which is consistent with lists in other twelfth-century manuscripts such as DUL, Cosin MS V.ii.6, fol. 6r/v, or Cambridge, Trinity College MS 1227, fol. 1v, or DCL B.II.35, fol. 149v. CCCC 66 omits the names of several bishops: Heathured, Ecgred, Eanbert, Wigred, Uhtred, Sexhelm and Aldred, and errs on Eardulf ('Edmundus') and Tilred ('Alfredus'). The name of William of St Calais is an interlinear addition, and probably not one made by the main scribe. The earlier bishops may conceivably have been omitted as a result of the scribe's missing a line of his exemplar, but such an exemplar must itself have been a very defective one. It is hard to believe that so many errors of this kind could have been made in a scriptorium which had knowledge of the Durham succession, and especially that a scribe working on another gathering of a manuscript containing a copy of the *Libellus de exordio* could have been so ignorant of the contents of this work.

Other difficulties relate to Gilbert of Limerick's *De statu ecclesiae*. The complete

---

[32] *Aethelwulf De Abbatibus*, ed. A. Campbell (Oxford, 1967), pp. x–xi. The author is mistakenly described as being 'lindisfarnensis'. It is not clear whether this modification was original to CUL Ff.1.27 or at what point in its textual history it occurred.
[33] See below, p. 445.

work appears in CUL Ff.1.27 pp. 237–42, and in DCL B.II.35, fols. 36r–8r. The CUL Ff.1.27 copy is based either on that in DCL B.II.35, as Mynors proposed, or more probably on a common exemplar, as Dumville decided.[34] The prologue occurs both in CUL Ff.1.27, p. 237, and in CCCC 66, p. 98, where it occupies the top two-thirds of column b. Neither appears to have been copied from the other. The *incipit* in both is the same, but whereas CUL Ff.1.27 reads simply *Explicit prologus*, CCCC 66 reads *Explicit prologus libelli Gille lumnicensis episcopi de usu ecclesiastico*. There are also minor differences in the text. Where CUL Ff.1.27 has *in corpore iungitur*, CCCC 66 has *corpore iungitur*. In CCCC 66, *peragendo* (which appears in CUL Ff.1.27) originally had an *n*, which was partially erased, intruded between the final two letters. Dumville regarded the prologue in CCCC 66 as a 'duplicate',[35] resulting from the blunder of a scribe who had intended to enter it in DCL B.II.35, which has a copy of Gilbert's work without a prologue at all, but this seems improbable if only because DCL B.II.35 is a substantially larger volume than CCCC 66 and a scribe is unlikely to have confused the two.[36] If we do not begin with the assumption that CUL Ff.1.27 and CCCC 66 form a single book, other conjectures may explain the double prologue. Perhaps a separate copy of Gilbert, now lost, once faced the prologue in CCCC 66. Perhaps it was planned that such a separate copy of the text should be made but it was never executed. From the fifteenth-century list of contents, it appears that, then at least, the two prologues faced each other as an opening (CCCC 66, p. 98 and CUL Ff.1.27, p. 237). When the twelfth-century sections of CCCC 66 and CUL Ff.1.27 were put together – and it is not clear when this occurred – the prologues may have been placed in this position simply because the texts coincided, giving a context to the stray prologue on CCCC 66, p. 98.

If, as it appears, the twelfth-century section of CCCC 66 was in origin a separate manuscript, consideration must be given to where it was written. The richness of its decoration makes it unlikely that it was written at a Cistercian monastery. Indeed, CCCC 66 is the only book associated with a Cistercian house to find a place in Kauffmann's survey of illuminated Romanesque manuscripts, though Kauffmann did not comment on this anomaly.[37] Despite its early *ex libris*, it is

---

[34] *DCM*, p. 8; Dumville, 'Celtic Latin Texts', p. 44.

[35] Dumville, 'Two Cambridge Books', p. 436.

[36] Dumville, 'Celtic Latin Texts', p. 44, n. 120. A conjecture which allows the two prologues to form part of the same manuscript is that the prologue appeared first in CCCC 66, then was copied into a hitherto blank leaf of CUL Ff.1.27 for the reason that CCCC 66, p. 98, is the last of its gathering and CUL Ff.1.27, pp. 237/8, is the first leaf of the gathering containing the work itself. The programme of copying went wrong, and it was realised that the prologue in what is now CCCC 66 was separated from the work itself. This argument presupposes that the twelfth-century sections of CCCC 66 and CUL Ff.1.27 constitute a single manuscript which was unbound at that stage. The prologue in CUL Ff.1.27 became an improved version, accommodating the correction to *peragendo*, and adding *in* before *corpore*. The *explicit* was contracted, perhaps indicating that it was added later, as were most of the rubrics in the manuscript.

[37] C.M. Kauffmann, *Romanesque Manuscripts 1066–1190* (London, 1975) p. 123.

particularly unlikely that such an expensively decorated volume could have been produced at Sawley, which was a house of only meagre resources. Founded in 1148 by William de Percy (1136–75), Sawley faced a struggle over a number of years until it was saved in 1189 by the intervention of the founder's daughter, Matilda, countess of Warwick.[38] CCCC 66 is of about the same date as Matilda's grants to the house and may have been a donation from her. This suggests a possible connection with Durham. There was a close family and personal link between the Percy family and that of Hugh of le Puiset, bishop of Durham (1153–95). Both were benefactors of Sawley, and Hugh of le Puiset is known to have had a son by Matilda's sister Alice.[39] Puiset had a collection of books, which he bequeathed to the monks at Durham. Some of his manuscripts, such as DCL, MS A.II.1 and DCL, MS A.II.19, have stylistic resemblances to the wheel of fortune in CCCC 66, p. 66, as Kauffmann observed. A *mappa mundi* is listed in Puiset's bequest,[40] recalling the map of the world on p. 1 of CCCC 66. This suggests the possibility that CCCC 66 is the very manuscript bequeathed by Puiset to Durham and that it was passed on by the Durham monks to Sawley. This of course is by no means certain. If CCCC 66 is not to be identified with Puiset's *mappa mundi*, it may perhaps be seen as a companion to this volume, commissioned by Matilda from the same source, or obtained by her from Puiset for donation to Sawley.

Other evidence points towards a Durham origin for CCCC 66. There are textual links between CCCC 66 and the Durham manuscript DCL B.II.35. The version of the *De Primo Saxonum Adventu* in CCCC 66, pp. 67–98, has close similarities to the copy in DCL B.II.35, fols. 131r–41v, and Christopher Norton has pointed out that CCCC 66, p. 69, appears to have been derived from DCL B.II.35, fol. 140r.[41] The lists of bishops in these two manuscripts are both placed under arcades and were composed around the same time, though they are not identical; and the account of the archbishops of York, ending with the burial of Thurstan in 1140, is the same in both manuscripts. Yet considerable difficulties remain in assigning the twelfth-century section of CCCC 66 to the Durham scriptorium, given that it lacks the extended account of the bishops of Durham which appears in B.II.35, fols. 139r–41v, and contains the strange errors, noted above, in the list of Durham bishops on p. 97.

[38] *The Chartulary of the Cistercian Abbey of St. Mary of Sallay in Craven*, 2 vols., ed. J. McNulty (Yorkshire Archaeological Society Record Series 87 and 90; 2 vols., 1933–4), II, 128–9.

[39] G.V. Scammell, *Hugh du Puiset, Bishop of Durham* (Cambridge, 1956), p. 227, n. 311. I should like to express thanks to Dr Nigel Wilkins for kindly depositing CCCC 66 in Cambridge University Library for consultation along with CUL Ff.1.27, to Dr P.N.R. Zutshi for accommodating this arrangement and for most obligingly checking my collation of CUL Ff.1.27, and to Dr Christopher Norton for stimulating and generous discussion of the problems involved. I have also benefited from conversations with Alan Piper on the subject. None of these is of course responsible for any of the views expressed here.

[40] *Catalogi veteres librorum ecclesiae cathedralis Dunelm*, ed. B. Botfield (SS 7; 1838), p. 119.

[41] Christopher Norton, unpublished paper delivered to the 'Anglo-Norman Durham' conference, September 1993.

IV. FURTHER INVESTIGATIONS

Clearly further work is needed in several areas. The structure, dating, hands and texts of CUL Ff.1.27 and CCCC 66 require fuller study along with CCCC 139 and will continue to provoke discussion. Further investigations are needed on northern twelfth-century hands, in particular on whether the hands of CCCC 139 and 66 and CUL Ff.1.27 can be related more closely to the hands of manuscripts whose origin is known with certainty. In a broader context, the place of Hexham in these manuscripts and in the historical and literary traditions of the twelfth-century north of England needs closer examination. Further comparisons might be made with the library of a house such as Byland, from which over a dozen twelfth-century books are known to survive.[42] The glossed Genesis in DCL, MS A.III.1 might be compared with the text in Dublin, Trinity College, MS 45, which has a Byland *ex libris*. The early twelfth-century texts of Gregory Nazianzen in DCL, MS B.IV.1 and in BL, MS Royal 5.E.XXII, which again has a Byland *ex libris*, might be examined. The manuscripts of popular authors like Hugh of St Victor may repay scrutiny, though frequently the absence of adequate modern editions is a handicap. Copies of his *De sacramentis* (written *c.*1134), for example, were in Durham, Whitby, and Tynemouth by the end of the twelfth century.[43] We should look to Durham for the line of transmission, since Hugh was well represented in the medieval Durham catalogues,[44] and connections existed between Durham and St Victor. Robert of Adington, whose books reached the Durham library, is known to have studied there,[45] and Laurence, prior of Durham between 1149 and 1154, may have corresponded with Hugh himself.[46] The Tynemouth copy of *De sacramentis*, BL, MS Harley 3847, was the gift of one *domnus henricus*, who was prior of Tynemouth late in the twelfth century and may earlier have been a monk of Durham.[47] It might be worth investigating whether a manuscript of the *De sacramentis* such as Bodl.L, MS Laud misc. 310, which is almost certainly the work

---

[42] N.R. Ker, *Medieval Libraries of Great Britain* (2nd edn, London, 1964) pp. 22–3; and *Supplement to the Second Edition*, ed. A.G. Watson (London, 1987), p. 7.

[43] G.E. Croydon, 'Abbot Laurence of Westminster and Hugh of St Victor', *Medieval and Renaissance Studies* 2 (1950), p. 171; *Cartularium Abbathiae de Whiteby*, ed. J.C. Atkinson (SS 69 and 72; 2 vols., 1878–9), I, 341.

[44] *Cat. vet. Dunelm.*, ed. Botfield, pp. 3, 8, 21, and 67.

[45] *DCM*, pp. 78–82.

[46] Croydon, op. cit.

[47] W.S. Gibson, *The History of the Monastery founded at Tynemouth* (2 vols., London, 1846–7), II, 20 identified him with the *Henricus de Tynemue noster professus* who appears in the Durham *Liber Vitae*, fol. 54r. In Cosin MS V.ii.6, fol. 8r/v, the name Henricus, though of course not necessarily the Tynemouth prior, appears in the lists of Durham monks at numbers 103, 159, and 183 in a later twelfth-century hand. The names of the early priors of Tynemouth are uncertain. *The Heads of Religious Houses*, ed. Knowles et al., pp. 96–7 has no Henry. H.H.E. Craster found plausible grounds for including him before 1189: see *The Parish of Tynemouth. A History of Northumberland*, VIII (Northumberland County History Committee; Newcastle-upon-Tyne, 1907), p. 122, n. 3, and the evidence of the *ex libris* in Harley 3847 seems compelling.

of Fountains scribes and has an *ex libris* of that house on fol. 1r, has a textual link with a Durham copy of the second part of the work, Cambridge, King's College, MS 22.[48] A Durham copy of Hugh's *Summa sententiarum* is in Bodl.L, MS Laud misc. 392, while the same text in Dublin, Trinity College, MS 279, fols. 34–81, has a contemporary Rievaulx *ex libris* on the opening page. It might be fruitful to determine whether the Rievaulx manuscript derived from the Durham exemplar. The same exercise might be attempted on CUL, MS Ff.4.41, a Durham copy of the *Panormia* of Ivo of Chartres, another popular author, and on a Fountains copy of the same work now at Clongowes Wood College, County Kildare.[49]

Other important questions remain concerning the proportion of books copied and decorated in Durham and the proportion executed in the recipient house from exemplars sent from Durham and returned after copying. Reference has been made to a Tynemouth manuscript of Bede's *Historia Ecclesiastica*, now Cambridge, Pembroke College, MS 82, which was copied from a Durham exemplar. Tynemouth had been a cell of St Albans since *c*.1090. This possession was disputed by Durham, and Pembroke 82 may, conjecturally, have been an offering designed to resolve divided loyalties. Its initials are coloured with a rough purple and yellow wash which may have been Tynemouth work, since it is markedly different from contemporary styles at Durham.

That manuscripts written at Durham might be decorated elsewhere is shown by an episode in Reginald of Durham's *Life of St Godric of Finchale* occurring in the late 1170s or early 1180s.[50] According to this, the monks of Fountains borrowed a copy of Godric's life from Durham in order to transcribe it, and found that the *exemplar* (that is, the Durham copy) had not yet been decorated.[51] The cantor set out to adorn the exemplar with *diversis . . . coloribus*. Before long he was called to vespers. During the service, a storm blew up and the leaves were scattered and soaked. The cantor fell into a worried sleep. In his sleep, he was led to Finchale, where Godric praised his endeavours and repaired the storm damage, leaving the book *sicca, integra et illaesa*. Reginald ends with the comment that the *libellus* which took the place of the exemplar still awaited decoration.[52] He expresses no surprise at the idea that a Durham manuscript should be decorated in Fountains. It may be that a cross-current of artistic influence went back and forwards between

---

[48] No critical edition exists of the *De sacramentis*, and no manuscripts are cited in the English translation: *Hugh of St Victor on the Sacraments of the Christian Faith*, trans. Roy Deferrari (Cambridge, Mass., 1951).

[49] Ker, *Medieval Libraries*, p. 88.

[50] I am grateful to Dr Victoria Tudor for advice regarding this date.

[51] 'Fratres de Fontibus Deo deuoti uitam Beati Godrici transcribendam de Dunelmensibus perquisierant; cujus exemplar quia nec dum illuminatum fuerat, illud pro ipsius honore et amore coloribus adornare decentius satagebant' (*V. Godr.*, p. 466).

[52] 'Ipse quidem libellus a fratribus Dunelmensibus eis accommodatus pro exemplari exstitit, qui et ibi, prout praemisimus, illuminandus fuit' (*V. Godr.*, p. 468). Anne Lawrence, 'English Cistercian Manuscripts of the Twelfth Century', in *Cistercian Art and Architecture in the British Isles*, ed. Christopher Norton and David Park (Cambridge, 1986), p. 288 appears to suggest that it was the Fountains copy which was not decorated and became the subject of the miracle.

Durham and the Cistercian houses. Mynors's identification of several abstract motifs as characteristic of Durham manuscripts is relevant here.[53] His 'clove-curl' ornament appears in many other manuscripts, including CUL, MS Gg.3.33 and CUL, MS Kk.4.15, manuscripts with the *ex libris* of, respectively, Roche and Louth Park, Cistercian houses established in a direct line of descent from Fountains. A particular form of initial *I*, with a 'pipette' protruding from the shaft of the letter, which Mynors noticed in Durham manuscripts, appears also in CCCC 66 and CUL Ff.1.27, and in the manuscript of Bede mentioned above, Harley 4124. It is used too in Cambridge, Emmanuel College, MS 17, a manuscript with the *ex libris* of the Premonstratensian house of Barlings in Lincolnshire. This is related textually to DCL, MS B.II.26, an early twelfth-century copy of St Augustine's *De Trinitate* which was observed by Mynors to have acted as an exemplar for DCL, MS B.II.28, written at Durham in the fourteenth century. It is significant too that Lawrence has identified Durham ornamental styles of the late eleventh century in twelfth-century Rievaulx manuscripts.[54]

The routes travelled by particular manuscripts are not always clear. A twelfth-century copy of Ennodius (now Berlin, Deutsche Staatsbibliothek, MS Phillipps 1715) has an *ex libris* on fol. 92r in a late twelfth- or early thirteenth-century hand indicating that the volume was the gift of one *Magister Atenulfus medicus* to Fountains abbey.[55] The text was copied from a ninth-century Corbie manuscript (now London, Lambeth Palace, MS 325) which is known to have been in Durham by the fourteenth century,[56] and probably as early as the twelfth century, since it may be that the Berlin copy was commissioned by Atenulfus for the Cistercians from Durham.[57] While many such questions of detail remain unresolved, it seems certain that in time more twelfth-century northern manuscripts will be seen to derive from Durham exemplars. It is hard to escape the impression that manuscripts left Durham, both permanently and as exemplars to be returned, on a large scale and that their influence matched the wide architectural influence of the cathedral whose foundation in 1093 constituted such visible evidence of Durham's ambition and cultural dominance in the North.

[53] *DCM*, pp. 6–9. Further work on such ornament has been done by J.J.G. Alexander, 'Scribes as Artists: the Arabesque Initial in Twelfth-Century English Manuscripts', in *Medieval Scribes, Manuscripts and Libraries. Essays Presented to N.R. Ker*, ed. M.B. Parkes and A. Watson (London, 1978), pp. 87–116.

[54] Lawrence, 'Cistercian Manuscripts', pp. 292–3.

[55] The *ex libris* reads in full 'Liber sancte marie de fontanis quem dedit ei pro redemptione anime sue magister atenulfus medicus. Anima eius requiescat in pace. Amen.' See *Magni Felicis Ennodi opera*, ed. F. Vogel, MGH Auctores Antiquissimi 7; 1885, p. xxxviii; and V. Rose, *Verzeichnis der lateinischen Handschriften der königlichen Bibliothek zu Berlin. Erster band. Die Meerman-Handschriften des Sir Thomas Phillipps* (Berlin, 1893), pp. 387–9. This parallels the gift of books to the twelfth-century Durham community by 'Magister Herebertus medicus' (*Cat. vet. Dunelm*, ed. Botfield, pp. 7–8).

[56] *DCM*, p. 26.

[57] R.M. Thomson, *Manuscripts from St Albans Abbey 1066–1235* (2 vols., Bury St Edmunds, 1982), I, 5–6, suggests that this was the practice at St Albans in the twelfth century.

The Artistic Influence of Durham Manuscripts

ANNE LAWRENCE

THIS PAPER is an enquiry into the degree and geographical extent of the artistic influence exerted by the manuscripts of Durham cathedral priory during the twelfth century. First, however, some comment is necessary as to why there should be sufficient suggestion that such influence is likely, to justify the enquiry. What is important here is Durham's unique position in northern England, in carrying into the twelfth century a library which was both extensive and long established. The manuscripts transferred to the possession of the new Benedictine priory in 1083 included both books of great age and importance, and the recent products of Bishop William of St Calais's patronage and of the scriptorium which seems to have been established at Durham by the late eleventh century.[1] There can also be no doubt that the large numbers of new monastic houses founded in the region would produce a demand for books for the liturgy, for teaching and for the *lectio diuina*.[2] In these circumstances, not only might Durham's scriptorium be a source of completed books, but its library might also supply exemplars for those houses able to have copies made. In both ways, the styles of decoration of Durham manuscripts would be made available at other centres, in conditions which may well have conferred prestige upon them.

The suggestion that Durham books might have had such prestige can perhaps be supported by looking at Durham's intellectual prominence, and at the impact of the cult of St Cuthbert. On the first point, Victoria Tudor has suggested that boys educated in the priory were accepted as full monks only if they reached certain standards.[3] It would seem that these standards were largely intellectual. This is further corroborated by Reginald of Durham's story of Robert de St Martin, a knight who became a monk at Durham, and who experienced considerable humiliation because of his slowness in learning Latin and in memorizing the required liturgical material. Indeed, he seems to have felt himself a laughing-stock, until the

---

[1] For a list of Bishop St Calais's books, see *Catalogi Veteres Librorum Dunelm.*, ed. B. Botfield (SS 7; 1838), pp. 117–18. For discussion of the existence of a scriptorium see above, pp. 93–109; also, A. Lawrence, 'The Influence of Canterbury on the Collection and Production of Manuscripts at Durham', in *The Vanishing Past*, ed. A. Borg and A. Martindale (British Archaeological Reports, Internat. Series 111; Oxford, 1981), pp. 95–103.

[2] For locations and dates of foundations, see L. Butler and C. Given-Wilson, *Medieval Monasteries of Great Britain* (London, 1979), passim.

[3] See V. Tudor, above, p. 70.

miraculous intervention of St Cuthbert enabled him to read the book with which he was struggling.[4]

That the education available at Durham was impressive is suggested by the mid-twelfth-century library list which survives in DCL, MS B.IV.24, and which records the presence at the cathedral priory of some 450 volumes.[5] As well as multiple copies of fundamental grammatical works, these included several books on rhetoric, on arithmetic and on the astrolabe, and one volume on geometry. There was also a group of works which appear to be for the instruction of novices, as well as an extensive collection of treatises on the monastic life. The listing of patristic works, biblical commentaries, and glossed books of the Bible is also impressive. Finally, given the fame of Durham's historical writers, it is not surprising to find at least twelve historical works, including three in Old English; but even more impressive are the gifts of medical and scientific works recorded as having been made to the priory, totalling nearly forty volumes, and the collection of nearly seventy volumes of classical works.

The book-list also demonstrates that the acquisition of books by individual members of the community, and their donation to the priory, were well established at Durham. Besides the more extensive listing of books attributed to named scholars, teachers or medical experts, at least two monks had copies of the *Life* of St Cuthbert, while no fewer than thirty-nine had their own copies of the Psalter, some in up to four versions.[6] Finally, there is evidence of interest in the study of canon law and in more recent theological works.[7]

It is well known that Durham's writers had a considerable influence upon other twelfth-century scholars. Master Laurence came to Durham from Harold's foundation of Waltham, and was the author of an historical work and at least one other composition, besides his *Dialogues*.[8] That he undertook some teaching at Durham seems likely, and it has been suggested that he played some part in the education of Ailred of Rievaulx.[9] Maurice, rather younger, was educated from childhood at Durham, and Walter Daniel states that he was regarded as a 'second Bede'.[10] Certainly his scholarly and spiritual qualities seem to have been appreciated not only at Durham but also at Rievaulx and Fountains, after he had become a Cistercian. Indeed, this movement would perhaps help to spread knowledge of Durham's scholarship and library further.

The influential status of the Durham library is demonstrated by the demand for

---

[4] *Cuth. virt.*, ch. 76.
[5] See *Cat. Vet.*, ed. Botfield, pp. 1–10.
[6] Ibid., pp. 6–9.
[7] See, for instance, the books listed as having belonged to individual scholars; ibid., pp. 8–9.
[8] For what may be a list of his books, see ibid., p. 8. DUL, MS Cosin V.iii.1 is a later twelfth-century edition of his 'collected works'.
[9] F.M. Powicke, 'Ailred of Rievaulx and his biographer Walter Daniel', in his *Ways of Medieval Life and Thought* (London, 1950), pp. 7–26; and M. Dutton, 'The Conversion and Vocation of Aelred of Rievaulx', in *England in the Twelfth Century*, ed. D. Williams (Woodbridge, 1990), pp. 37–8.
[10] F.M. Powicke, 'Maurice of Rievaulx', *EHR* 36 (1921), p. 19.

Durham exemplars of the works of Bede. A striking example is the copy of the *Historia ecclesiastica* which was made by a Norman scribe and presented by Bishop St Calais to Durham; this seems to have been the exemplar for copies made in the twelfth century for Tynemouth, Worksop, Sawley, and Newminster.[11] Kirkham and Selby also had copies of this work, but whether they descend from the Durham volume is not known. Equally influential, however, were the Durham versions of Bede's *Lives* of St Cuthbert. Of the twenty surviving copies of the *Prose Life* dating from the late eleventh and twelfth centuries, no fewer than nine were probably produced at Durham.[12]

Further evidence for the links between the cult of St Cuthbert and the prestige of Durham books comes from the writings of both Symeon and Reginald of Durham. Already in the early twelfth century, Symeon of Durham had associated at least two books with St Cuthbert. The better known is perhaps the gospel book, identifiable as the Lindisfarne Gospels, which fell into the sea, and was miraculously recovered by the bearers of St Cuthbert's coffin.[13] But Symeon also mentions another book, this time stressing Cuthbert's own scholarship, when he proudly states that Durham possesses the very book from which Boisil taught Cuthbert at Melrose.[14] Reginald contributes an account of a book found in St Cuthbert's coffin, and of how it was shown to distinguished visitors to the shrine, even being hung by a cord round their necks.[15] As this was a copy of the Gospel of St John, the text which Boisil and Cuthbert read together, it was very likely the same book.[16] Moreover, Reginald also stresses the theme of education, telling how the saint intervened to prevent disruption to a school held in the church at Norham.[17]

It is also striking that several of Reginald's stories suggest that painting was carried out within the priory, and that pictures of St Cuthbert in particular were made. The monks possessed a slab of Italian marble, the gift of the lord of Thornley; and it was upon this slab, Reginald states, that the monks ground their colours.[18] Moreover, Robert de St Martin, the ex-knight already mentioned, had the saint's image painted upon the margin of his book; and there is no suggestion of difficulty in finding an artist to do this.[19] Again, a monk of the priory is said to have worn a 'little book' about St Cuthbert hung round his neck; and his friend, the 'engineer' of Norham Castle, seems to have had another booklet, with an image

---

[11] *DCM*, p. 41.
[12] *Two Lives of St Cuthbert*, ed. and trans. B. Colgrave (Cambridge, 1940), pp. 20–39.
[13] *LDE*, bk. 2, ch. 12 (trans. *CHE*, pp. 662–3).
[14] *LDE*, bk. 1, ch. 3 (trans. *CHE*, p. 629).
[15] *Cuth. virt.*, ch. 91.
[16] This is also suggested by Symeon's description of the Cuthbert/Boisil volume's 'remarkable freshness and beauty', terms associated with St Cuthbert's own miraculous state of preservation. However, the content of the book described by Symeon is not specified, and, as a fourteenth-century relic list included a 'Liber sancti Boisili magistri sancti Cuthberti', it is possible that it is this other volume which is meant (DCL, MS B.II.35, fols. 192–8).
[17] *Cuth. virt.*, ch. 73.
[18] *Cuth. virt.*, ch. 75.
[19] *Cuth. virt.*, ch. 76.

 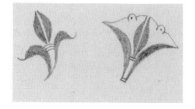

Forms of the 'clove-curl'   Forms of the 'split-petal'

Fig. 36.   Drawings of 'clove-curl' and 'split-petal' decoration in manuscripts.

of St Cuthbert.[20] Further evidence for the link between the cult and books is provided by the copy of the *Life* now at Oxford, which has a complete set of narrative illustrations, and was almost certainly made at Durham in the early twelfth century for an unknown patron.[21]

If Durham books enjoyed such prestige and influence, the next problem is whether it is possible to identify motifs or types of decoration which can be regarded as characteristic of the products of the Durham scriptorium, and can thus be used as indices of its artistic influence. For this purpose figure-drawings must sadly be excluded, since they do not occur in surviving twelfth-century books from other northern houses. Recurring decorative motifs, however, offer possibilities. Mynors listed a number in his analysis of Durham manuscripts, and gave them names which will also be used here.[22] Several of these are widely distributed in manuscripts of *c.*1100 and are therefore unhelpful; but two, Mynor's 'clove-curls' and 'split-petals', not only occur frequently in Durham books, but do so *before* they appear elsewhere (fig. 36).

Mynors himself suggested that the prototype of the 'clove-curl' was already to be found in a late eleventh-century manuscript of the *Register* of St Gregory, which was possibly part of Bishop St Calais's gift of books.[23] The motif then recurs in a number of Durham books with scripts of the first half of the twelfth century, developing in complexity of form. The case of the 'split-petal' is a little more complex. Mynors identified this motif in a group of Durham manuscripts of the third quarter of the twelfth century, in which it already occurs in complex and developed forms. However, simple versions of the 'split-petal' do in fact occur in BL, MS Harley 4688 and DCL, MS B.IV.15, a copy of Isidore's *Etymologies* (pl. 86), both dated by Ker to the early twelfth century.[24] The latter has a fourteenth-

[20] *Cuth. virt.*, chs. 47 and 54; however, there is some confusion, as the story is given in two different versions.

[21] For a discussion of this volume see M. Baker, 'Bede's "Life of St Cuthbert" ', *Journal of the Warburg and courtauld Institutes* 41 (1978), pp. 16–49.

[22] *DCM*, p. 7.

[23] *DCM*, p. 30.

[24] Elzbieta Temple also argued that this motif appeared in early twelfth-century Durham manuscripts, but did not list the books concerned. See 'The Twelfth-century Psalter in the Bodleian Library, MS Douce 293' (unpublished Ph.D. thesis, University of London, 1971), pp. 197–200, 238–41.

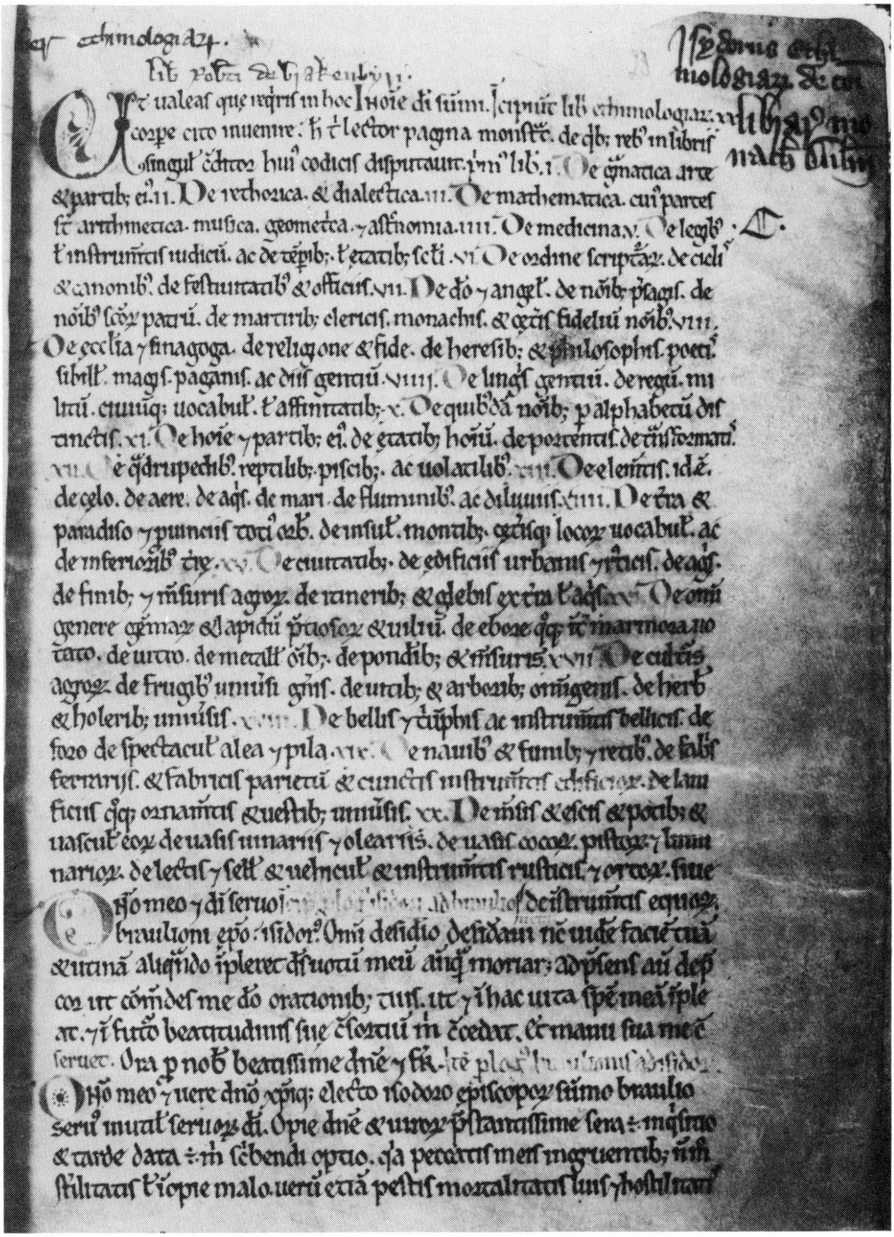

Plate 86. DCL, MS B.IV.15, fol. 23r (Isidore of Seville's Etymologies; from Durham).

century inscription, stating that it was then in the possession of *Robertus de Brakebyri*, but this does not mean that he had acquired it from elsewhere, since he is also recorded as having been granted possession of several books which had been in the Durham library for some time, one of them having originally been the gift of Bishop Hugh of le Puiset.[25] Moreover, the script of the copy of Isidore is of a Durham type.

Both these distinctive motifs therefore appeared first at Durham, in the early twelfth century. Their occurrence in later manuscripts from other centres can thus be used as evidence of the artistic influence of Durham. The next problems then are to discover over what geographical area such motifs occur, and what may be deduced from the contexts in which they appear. The most difficult obstacle here is simple lack of evidence. This is perhaps most severe in the case of Scotland, since only eight Scottish houses have any surviving twelfth-century manuscripts, and of these six have only one such book each, of a meagre total of some ten volumes. Of these, none yet examined shows evidence of direct influence from Durham; moreover, the Scottish houses with some recorded twelfth-century link with Durham, such as St Andrews, have no identified manuscripts from the period.[26] In these circumstances, Durham artistic influence can be neither proved nor disproved.

In the case of Cumbria, the problem of lack of evidence is only slightly less severe. This is particularly unfortunate, as other evidence suggests interest in Durham and its saints on the part of the Cumbrian houses. Wetheral and St Bees, both cells of St Mary's, York, and the Augustinian priories of Lanercost, Conishead, and Cartmel have no surviving twelfth-century books. From St Mary's, Carlisle, however, there is one relevant volume, a copy of the *Istoria Clementis*; this has no signs of Durham influence.[27] More complex is the case of Furness, which was founded as a Savigniac abbey by Stephen in 1124, before he became king, and which became Cistercian in 1147–50. Reginald of Durham records how a twelfth-century abbot of Furness erected an altar to St Cuthbert and travelled to Durham to tell of the saint's miraculous aid.[28] Indeed, further interest in the saints of Durham is suggested by Jocelin of Furness's *Lives* of northern saints and British bishops, written in the late twelfth century. These interests might well have led to the acquisition of books or exemplars from Durham, but neither Furness nor its daughter-house at Calder have left any identified twelfth-century manuscripts. Equally complex, though for different reasons, is the Cistercian house of Holm Cultram, a daughter of Melrose and member of the 'family' of Rievaulx. There are four surviving twelfth-century books from Holm Cultram, one of which appears to show Durham influence; but Holm Cultram's connection with Rievaulx makes it likely that Durham influence came via the mother house. These books will

[25] For a complete list of surviving, identified Durham manuscripts, see *Medieval Libraries of Great Britain: Supplement to the Second Edition*, ed. N.R. Ker and A.G. Watson (London, 1987), pp. 16–34.
[26] Attributions throughout this paper are based on N.R. Ker, *Medieval Libraries of Great Britain* (2nd edn, London, 1964), and on the *Supplement* (see above, n. 25).
[27] Ker, *Medieval Libraries*, p. 48.
[28] *Cuth. virt.*, ch. 55.

therefore be discussed together with those of Rievaulx. For Cumbria, the conclusion must be that, whilst Durham influence is very likely, it is impossible to prove.

It is hardly surprising that Northumberland and County Durham show much clearer signs of Durham influence, although here also the evidence is sparse. There were four twelfth-century foundations in the area from which books survive, and which were not simply cells of Durham. These are the Augustinian priories of Hexham and Newcastle, the Cistercian abbey of Newminster, founded from Fountains, and the Benedictine priory of Tynemouth.

Tynemouth was first refounded in the late eleventh century by the monks who were resettling Jarrow, together, according to the 'History of the Kings', with a canon of Durham.[29] However, it was subsequently given to St Albans by Roger de Mowbray and colonised from there. The ensuing dispute between Durham and St Albans dragged on until the 1170s, but Durham failed to regain possession. It is interesting that its mixed heritage is apparently reflected in Tynemouth's twelfth-century manuscripts. The link with St Albans is represented by BL, MS Harley 3847, a copy of Hugh of St Victor, of the second half of the twelfth century. The text was probably available at Durham, but this copy shows no sign of Durham influence. Moreover, St Albans was going to some trouble to build up a complete set of the works of Hugh of St Victor, and the inscription which notes that this book was the gift of Prior Henry is in a form standard in St Albans manuscripts.[30] However, an interest in more local figures is suggested by Cambridge, Pembroke College, MS 82, a copy of Bede's *Historia ecclesiastica* derived from DCL B.II.35, Bishop St Calais's copy of this work, and by BL, Cotton MS Julius A.X, fols. 2–43, a copy of the *Lives* of Sts Oswin and Oswiu. Particularly interesting for this enquiry is Bodl.L, MS Laud. misc. 4, a pocket-sized Processional. Its opening initial has a distinctive form of the 'split-petal', too different from those found in Durham manuscripts to be the work of a Durham artist (fig. 37). Possibly it was produced at Tynemouth itself, and is thus evidence for the artistic influence of Durham on that priory.

The evidence from the Augustinian houses again shows some Durham influence. Hexham had been granted to Alfred Larwa, the early eleventh-century sacrist of Durham, and his descendant, Eilaf, moved there from Durham in 1083.[31] However, this direct link with Durham was broken when, in 1112, Archbishop Thomas of York established the Augustinian priory at Hexham. In 1114 Archbishop Thurstan introduced Prior Aschatil from the influential house at Huntingdon, and made the community's link with York permanent. He is also recorded as having given relics, candlesticks and books to the community.[32] It would thus seem that Hexham's traditional links with Durham were broken at this time, and replaced by a link with York Minster. Five twelfth-century Hexham

[29] *HReg, s.a.* 1121 (trans. *CHE*, p. 602).
[30] Ker, *Medieval Libraries*, p. 165.
[31] See Richard of Hexham, 'Chronicle', bk. 2, ch. 9, in *The Priory of Hexham*, ed. J. Raine (SS 150; 1864).
[32] See D. Nicholl, *Thurstan, Archbishop of York* (York, 1964), p. 129.

Fig. 37. Bodl.L, MS Laud misc. 4, fol. 1
(mid-twelfth-century; from Tynemouth).

books have been identified, and these suggest the presence of a library at Hexham, as they all have early *ex libris* inscriptions. They include three volumes of the works of St Augustine and a copy of the Sermons of Gregory Nazianzenus. The copies of Augustine were standard works, but that of Gregory Nazianzenus is less common, making an exemplar more difficult to track down. It does, however, occur in the mid-twelfth-century Durham library-list. Moreover, DCL, MS B.IV.1, a Durham product of the early twelfth century, which has 'clove-curl' initials, may be the exemplar for the Hexham copy. Of the Hexham copies of Augustine, Bodl.L, MS Bodley 236, a copy of the *Contra Faustum*, has a 'split-petal' initial on fol. lv, which suggests Durham influence. There is no evidence for a Durham exemplar, but the Hexham book cannot be one of those given by Archbishop Thurstan, as it is from the mid twelfth century. This book, with its combination of Durham motifs with colours, such as grey, not used at Durham, therefore suggests the presence of a scriptorium at Hexham itself; moreover, one which was, presumably, in contact with York, but which was artistically influenced by Durham.

Of the books of the Augustinian priory of Newcastle, BL, MS Additional 35110 is a compound volume containing saints' *Lives* as well as short works by Ailred of Rievaulx. The selection of texts suggests an interest in the history of the church in northern England, especially as the saints include Cuthbert. In these circumstances it is unsurprising that its initials show Durham influence, most particularly an 'I' on fol. 35, which is of a distinctive Durham form noted by Mynors.[33]

This type of 'I' is also found in a manuscript from the Cistercian house of Newminster. It is now BL, MS Additional 25014, and contains Bede's *Historia ecclesiastica*. The evidence of the one other relevant Newminster manuscript is, however, more difficult to interpret. This is BL, MS Harley 3013, containing a Hymn to the Virgin and short works by Aldhelm. The contents of the volume, together with an epitaph for a 'Magister Petrus' on fol. 2, suggest the presence of at

[33] *DCM*, p. 7.

least one scholar at Newminster. No copy of this text is known to have been at Durham, but Durham books may have influenced this manuscript, as it has restrained initials in red and green, some of which use the 'split-petal'. However, this manuscript is of the later twelfth century, when the motif had become a very popular one in the manuscripts of Newminster's mother-house, Fountains.[34] Its presence here may therefore only indicate influence from Fountains.

This raises the important and complex question of contacts between Durham and the great Cistercian abbeys. Substantial groups of manuscripts survive from the Yorkshire houses of Rievaulx, Fountains and Byland.[35] These demonstrate that production and decoration of manuscripts was carried on at all three, as would be expected from the twelfth-century Cistercian legislation.[36] Moreover, links with Durham appear to have been strong, despite the geographical distance, and the ostensible tensions between Cistercian and traditional monastic houses in this period. It would, however, be an over-simplification to posit a general dependence of the newly-founded Cistercian houses on the established library of Durham; the pattern is more complex.

Intellectual contacts were strongest between Durham and Rievaulx, and this must have been related to the move of the respected scholar Maurice from Durham to Rievaulx, possibly, as in other recorded cases, taking books with him.[37] There was also the family link between Ailred of Rievaulx and Durham, the possible contact between Ailred and Laurence of Durham, and Ailred's continuing contact with the hagiographer, Reginald.[38] Mynors has already noted that the Rievaulx copies of works by Jerome, Rabanus Maurus, and Ennodius, may be textually based on Durham exemplars.[39] That artistic links were also strong is suggested by several manuscripts. Especially interesting is BL, MS Royal 8.D.XXII, the Rievaulx copy of the *Sermons* of Petrus Chrysologus, made at Rievaulx in the later twelfth century. Its main initial is based on a type found in a group of late-eleventh-century Durham manuscripts (pls. 87 and 88).[40] Unfortunately, a Durham exemplar cannot be proven, but the main initial of the Rievaulx book may be compared with initials in DCL, MS B.III.9, a copy of Gregory the Great's *Register*. Moreover, the same Rievaulx book has, on fol. 9v, a small 'split-petal' initial, handled in a simple way reminiscent of DCL, MS B.IV.15. The same motif, used in more complex

---

[34] For discussion of these, and illustrations, see A. Lawrence, 'English Cistercian Manuscripts of the Twelfth Century', in *Cistercian Art and Architecture in the British Isles*, ed. C. Norton and D. Park (Cambridge, 1986), pp. 290–6.

[35] Ker, *Medieval Libraries*, pp. 22–3, 88–9, 159.

[36] See Norton, 'Table of Cistercian Legislation on Art and Architecture', in *Cistercian Art and Architecture in the British Isles*, ed. Norton and Park, pp. 318–97.

[37] It is interesting that, whilst there is a list of the books of Master Laurence in the Durham book-list, there is none for Master Maurice.

[38] This contact is clearly demonstrated in Reginald's Preface, addressed to Aelred, and in the attribution of several of Reginald's stories to Aelred.

[39] *DCM*, cat. nos. 17, 39, 44.

[40] For further discussion of this group of manuscripts, see A. Lawrence, 'Influence of Canterbury'; and see above, p. 454.

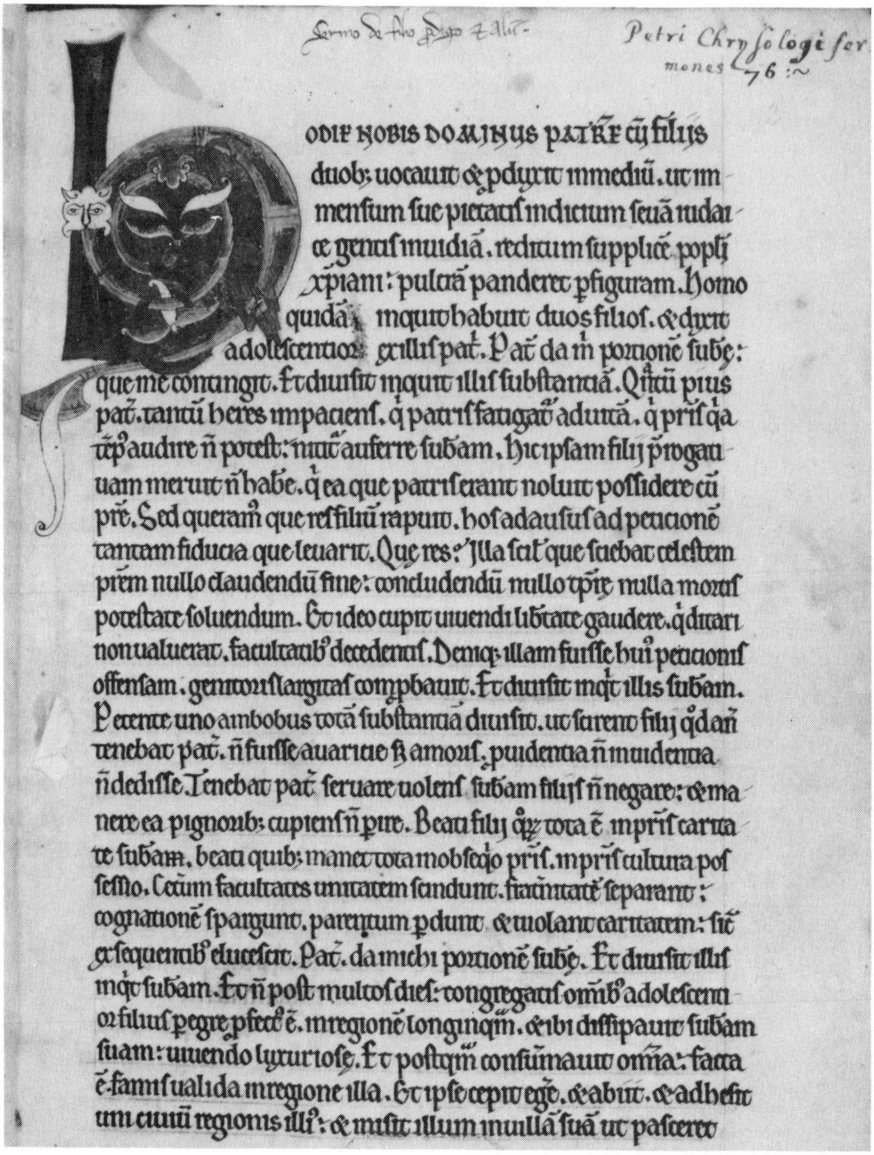

Sermo de filio [...] z aliis   Petri Chrysologi sermones 76 :~

ODIE NOBIS DOMINUS PATREM cum filiis
duobus: uocauit & pdixit in medium. ut im
mensum sue pietatis indictum seua rudar
ce gentis inuidia. redicum supplice poptj
xpianm: pulcra panderet pfiguram. Homo
quidam mquit habuit duos filios. & dixit
adolescentios gcillis pat. Pat da michi porcione sube:
que me contingit. Et diuisit mquit illis substanciam. O stulti pius
pat. tantum heres impaciens. q patris fatigat aduna. q pris qa
tepaudire non potest: tuuc auferre sueam. Hic ipsam filii progau
uam meruit n habe. q ea que patris erant nolunt possidere cu
pre. Sed queram que resfilium rapuit. hos adausis ad peticione
tantam fiducia que leuarit. Que res? Illa scit que suebat celestem
prem nullo claudendu fine: concludendu nullo tpe: nulla mors
potestate soluendum. Et ideo cupit uiuendi libtate gaudere. q ditari
non ualuerat. facultatib decederat. Denique illam fuisse hui peticionis
offensam. gentou largitas compbauit. Et diuisit mquit illis sueam.
Pecente uno ambobus tota substancia diuisit. ut sciret filii qdam
tenebat pat. n fuisse auaricie s amoris. pudencia n muidencia
n dedisse. Tenebat pat. seruare uolens sueam filiis n negare: & ma
nere ea pignoribus cupiens in pre. Beati filii q tota e inpris carita
te sueam. beati quibus manet tota mobseqo pris. inpris cultura pos
sessio. Cum facultates unitatem scindunt. fragilitate separant:
cognatione spargunt. parentum pdunt. & uiolant caritatem: sic
q sequentibus elucescit. Pat. da michi porcione sube. Et diuisit illis
mquit sueam. Et n post multos dies: congregatis omnibus adolesceni
or filius pegre pfectus e. in regione longinquam. & ibi dissipauit sueam
suam: uiuendo lyxuriose. Et postquam consumauit omnia: facta
e fames ualida in regione illa. Et ipse cepit egere. & abiit. & adhesit
uni ciuium regionis illi: & misit illum in uilla sua ut pasceret

Plate 87.   BL, MS Royal 8 D.XXII, fol. 2r (*Sermons* of Petrus Chrysologus; from Rievaulx).

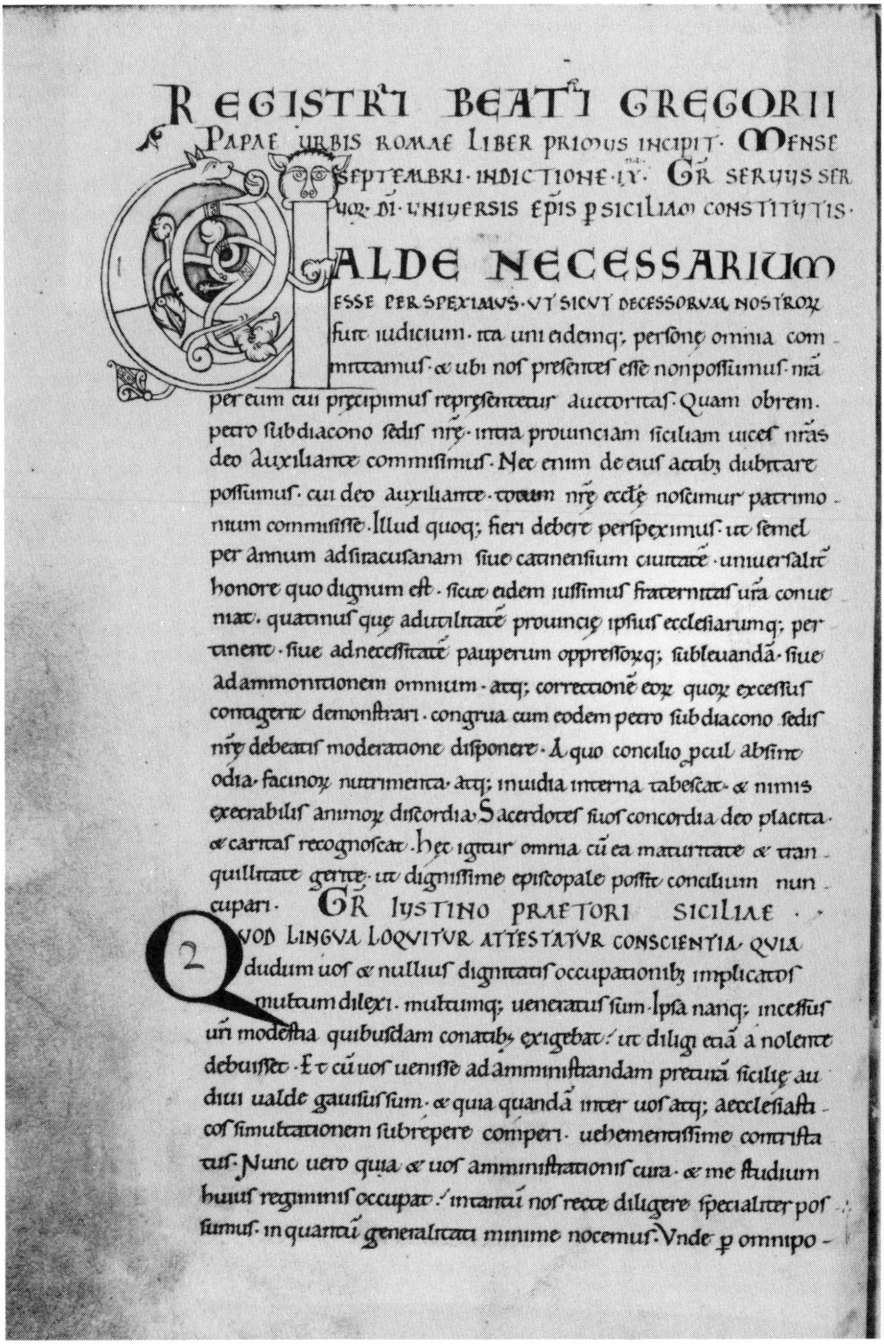

REGISTRI BEATI GREGORII
PAPAE URBIS ROMAE LIBER PRIMUS INCIPIT· MENSE
SEPTEMBRI· INDICTIONE·IX· GR· SERVVS SER·
VOR· DI· VNIVERSIS EPIS P SICILIAM CONSTITVTIS·

ALDE NECESSARIUM
ESSE PERSPEXIMVS·VT SICVT DECESSORVM NOSTROR
fuit iudicium· ita uni eidemq; persone omnia committamus· & ubi nos presentes esse nonpossumus· nra
per eum cui precipimus representetur auctoritas· Quam obrem·
petro subdiacono sedis nre· intra prouinciam siciliam uices nras
deo auxiliante commisimus· Nec enim de eius actibz dubitare
possumus· cui deo auxiliante·totam nre eccle noscimur patrimonium commisisse. Illud quoq; fieri debere perspeximus· ut semel
per annum ad siracusanam siue catinensium ciuitate·uniuersalit
honore quo dignum est· sicut eidem iussimus fraternitas ura conueniat· quatinus que aduilitate prouincie ipsius ecclesiarumq; pertinent·siue ad necessitate pauperum oppressorq; subleuanda·siue
ad ammonitionem omnium·atq; correctione eor quor excessus
contingere demonstrari·congrua cum eodem petro subdiacono sedis
nre debeatis moderatione disponere·A quo concilio pcul absint
odia·facinor nutrimenta·atq; inuidia interna tabescat·& nimis
execrabilis animor discordia·Sacerdotes suos concordia deo placita
& caritas recognoscat·hec igitur omnia cu ea maturitate & tranquillitate gerite·ut dignissime episcopale possit concilium nuncupari· GR IVSTINO PRAETORI SICILIAE··
VOD LINGVA LOQVITVR ATTESTATVR CONSCIENTIA· QVIA
dudum uos & nullius dignitatis occupationibz implicatos
multum dilexi· multumq; ueneratus sum·Ipsa nanq; incessus
uri modestia quibusdam conatibz exigebat·ut diligi etia a nolente
debuisset·Et cu uos uenisse ad amministrandam preturam sicilie au
diui ualde gauisus sum·& quia quanda inter uos atq; aecclesiasticos simultationem subrepere comperi· uehementissime contrista
tus·Nunc uero quia & uos amministrationis cura·& me studium
huius regiminis occupat·incantu nos recte diligere specialiter pos·;
sumus·in quantu generalitati minime nocemus·Vnde p omnipo

Plate 88. DCL, MS B.III.9, fol. 1v (*Registers* of Pope Gregory I; from Durham).

ways, is found in BL, MS Royal 6.C.VIII (pl. 89). This is the Rievaulx copy of Orosius, a work which is listed in the mid-twelfth-century Durham library-list. In this case, the similarity to fully-developed uses of the motif in contemporary Durham manuscripts, such as DCL, MS A.III.4, a glossed copy of I–IV Kings (fig. 38), is so close that they could almost be by the same designer.

That contacts were both close and reciprocal is suggested by DUL, Cosin MS V.ii.2, a Durham manuscript which contains an early copy of a short work by Ailred of Rievaulx, in a hand which is, as Mynors noted, similar to that of the portion of DCL B.II.35 which is datable to 1166.[41] Moreover, this latter contains genealogical texts which appear to be related to the sources used by Ailred in compiling his open letter to Henry II, on the Anglo-Saxon kings.

Fountains also borrowed exemplars from Durham. Reginald of Durham describes how the Fountains monks borrowed a *Life* of St Godric of Finchale, to copy it. In gratitude, and respect for the saint, the prior of Fountains asked the cantor to illuminate the book (apparently the Durham exemplar) with bright colours.[42] However, this story dates from late in the twelfth century. Its difficult early history suggests that the library of Fountains would have remained limited to basics, perhaps supplied by Clairvaux and Archbishop Thurstan, until the arrival of Hugh, dean of York, with his book-collection, in 1134–5. A scriptorium was active at Fountains by the middle of the twelfth century, and it might be expected that either St Mary's or York Minster would provide a geographically convenient source of exemplars. However, some hostility seems to have existed between St Mary's and the Cistercian abbeys at least until the 1160s.[43] This, together with the probable absence of a communal library at York Minster, would make it necessary for the Cistercians to look further afield. That Fountains might look to Rievaulx, and perhaps through that house to Durham, is made more likely by the fact that Fountains took two abbots from Rievaulx. These were Maurice of Rievaulx (though only for three months) and Thorold, another scholarly monk.[44]

This hypothesis is supported by the fact that, besides the *Life* of St Godric already mentioned, Fountains also seems to have looked to Durham for historical works.[45] Moreover, copies of patristic works made at Fountains were given complex 'split-petal' initials, closer to those of Durham than of Rievaulx in being executed in several colours. Examples include BL, MS Arundel 217, a copy of the *Letters* of St Cyprian, and Bodl.L, MS Laud. misc. 310, a copy of Hugh of St Victor. Durham may have provided exemplars, as it had copies of both works. That these

---

[41] *DCM*, p. 72.

[42] *V. Godr.*, pp. 466–8.

[43] Such hostility might be expected, given the hostility of the St Mary's community towards those who left to found Fountains; its continuation is suggested by the absence of all Cistercian houses, except Byland, from the very extensive set of confraternity agreements entered into by St Mary's, and recorded in BL, MS Additional 38816, fols. 21–39.

[44] See Powicke, 'Maurice', p. 18.

[45] For more detailed discussion see above, pp. 439–40ff. Mynors points out that BL, Cotton MS Faustina A.V, the Fountains copy of the *Libellus de exordio*, may have been written at Durham. See *DCM*, p. 61.

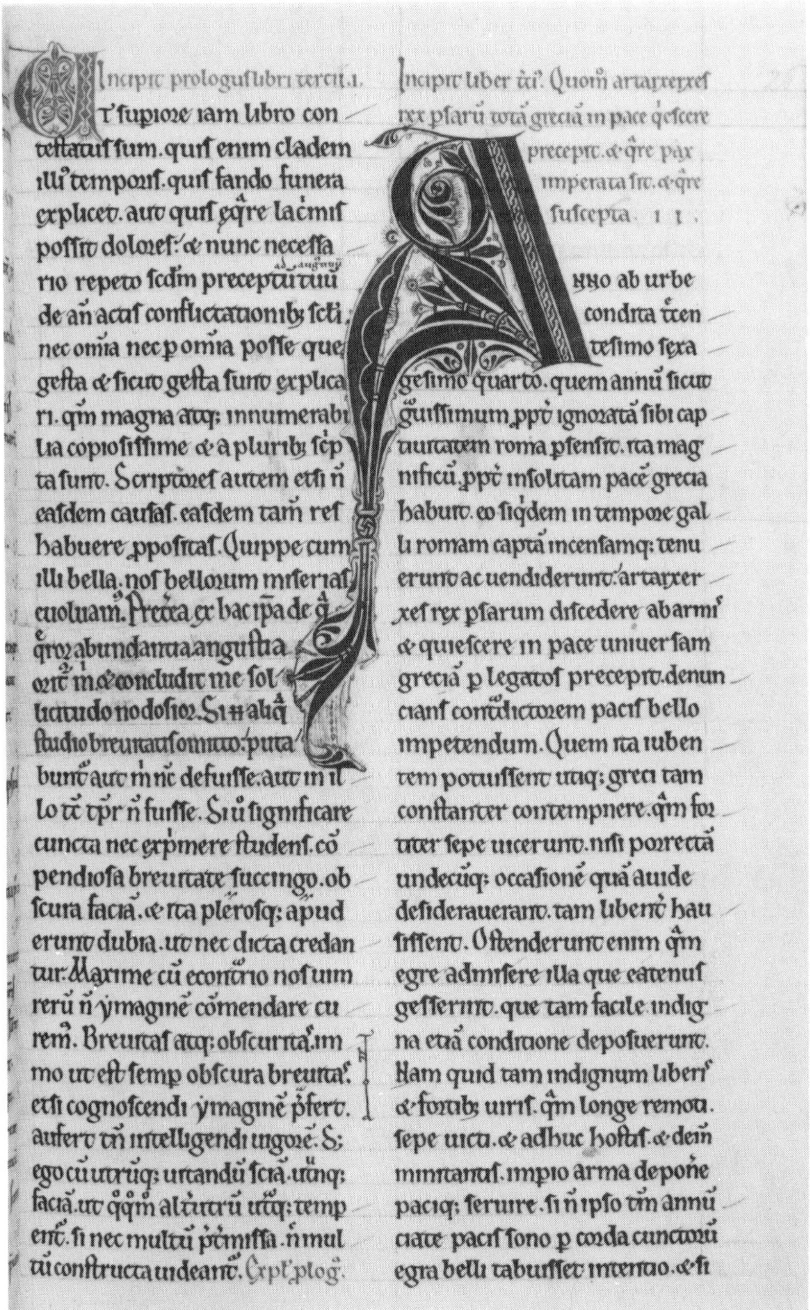

Incipit prologus libri tercii. Incipit liber tercii. Quom artaxerxes
T superiore iam libro con- rex psarum tota grecia in pace descere
testatus sum. quis enim cladem precepit. et qre pax
illius temporis. quis fando funera imperata sit. et qre
explicet. aut quis egre lacrimis suscepta. 1 1.
possit dolores. et nunc necessa-
rio repeto secundum preceptum tuum UNO ab urbe
de an actus conflictationibus scti. condita tren-
nec omnia nec p omnia posse que tesimo sexa-
gesta et sicut gesta sunt explica gesimo quarto. quem annum sicut
ri. qm magna atque innumerabi guissimum ppt ignorata sibi cap-
lia copiosissime et a pluribus sep tiurcatem roma psensit. ita mag-
ta sunt. Scriptores autem etsi n nificu. ppt insolitam pace grecia
easdem causas. easdem tamen res habuit. eo siquidem in tempore gal-
habuere ppositas. Quippe cum li romam capta incensamque tenu-
illi bella. nos bellorum miserias erunt ac uendiderunt. artaxer-
euoluam. Pretera ex hac ipsa de q- xes rex psarum discedere ab armis
gror abundantia angustia et quiescere in pace uniuersam
ortt in me concludit me sol- grecia p legatos precepit. denun-
tiatudo nodosior. Si in aliqu cians contradictorem pacis bello
studio breuitati somitto. puta- impetendum. Quem ita iuben-
burit aut in ne defuisse. aut in il- tem potuissent utiq: greci tam
lo tt tpr n fuisse. Si u significare constanter contempnere. qm fo-
cuncta nec exprimere studens. co- rtiter sepe uicerunt. nisi porrecta
pendiosa breuitate succingo. ob- undecuque occasione qua auide
scura facia. et ita plerosque apud desiderauerant. tam libertt hau-
erunt dubia. ut nec dicta credan- sissent. Ostenderunt enim qm
tur. Maxime cu econtrio nos uim egre admisere illa que eatenus
reru n ymagine comendare cu- gesserint. que tam facile indig-
rem. Breuitas atque obscuritas. im- na etia condicione deposuerunt.
mo ut est semp obscura breuitas. Nam quid tam indignum libers
etsi cognoscendi ymagine pfert. et fortibs uiris. qm longe remoti-
aufert tn intelligendi uigore. S; sepe uicti. et adhuc hostis. et dein
ego cu utriuque utandu scia. utinque- minitantis. impio arma depone-
facia. ut qqm alterutru utque temp- paciq: seruire. si n ipso tm annu-
erit. si nec multu pmissa. n mul- ciate pacis sono p corda cunctorum
tu constructa uideant. Explt plog. egra belli tabuisset intentio. et si

Plate 89. BL, MS Royal 6 C.VIII, fol. 26r (*History* of Orosius; from Rievaulx).

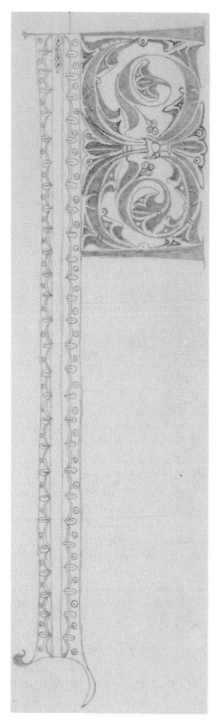

Fig. 38. DCL, MS A.III.4, fol. 4v (19 lines high; from Durham).

Fig. 39. BL, MS Rawlinson C. 329, fol. 193v
(14 lines high; twelfth/thirteenth-century;
from Roche).

'split-petal' initials were taken up by Fountains scribes and used in all their products, not merely copied from exemplars, is however demonstrated by Oxford,
Corpus Christi College, MS D.209, which aside from a *Life* of St Olaf contains
purely Cistercian texts, which cannot have had Durham exemplars.

In the case of Byland, which was founded as a Savigniac house, relations with St
Mary's York, and its growing library, were perhaps more friendly.[46] But here also
intellectual links with Durham, and the copying of Durham exemplars, seem likely.
The strongest evidence is provided by Byland's copies of Palladius's *Opus agriculture*
and the writings of Remigius of Auxerre; these were not common texts, but as both
are in the Durham book-list their exemplars may have come from Durham. The
'split-petal' initials are to be found both in manuscripts which may have been
copied from Durham exemplars and in those which most probably were not,
suggesting that the Byland scriptorium also took up and adapted the motif. In the
first category are BL, MS Royal 5.E.XXII, another copy of the *Sermons* of Gregory
Nazianzenus, and BL, MS Harley 3641, William of Malmesbury's *Gesta Pontificum*. The second group may be represented by BL, MS Additional 35180, a Peter
Cantor manuscript with a beautiful initial.

This adoption of the 'split-petal' motif by the scriptoria of the first Cistercian

---

[46] See above, n. 43.

houses in northern England makes its appearance in books belonging to their daughter-houses hard to interpret. In the absence of more conclusive evidence, it is more likely to be derived from books supplied by the mother-houses than directly from Durham; but the latter cannot be ruled out. Such initials occur in books from Fountains's daughters, Kirkstall and Newminster, and in a group of three books from Newminster's own daughter, Roche (fig. 39). These Roche books are copies of standard patristic works, but two suggest direct influence from Durham because they show the distinctive initial 'I' already discussed which does not appear in surviving books from Rievaulx, Fountains, or Byland. The books in question are Bodl.L, MS Laud misc. 308, volume three of St Augustine's *Commentary on the Psalms* and Bodl.L, MS Laud misc. 145, Lethbertus' *Flores Psalterii*. Evidence from Rievaulx's daughter-houses is much scarcer, but Holm Cultram, founded from Melrose, seems to have adopted the 'split-petal' initials. What is striking is that such initials do not occur in manuscripts from Cistercian houses in southern England. It therefore seems that the northern Cistercians developed their distinctive style of manuscript decoration under strong influence from Durham.

In turning from the Cistercians to Yorkshire houses of other orders, there is a disappointing lack of evidence from the Benedictine abbeys. The late twelfth-century catalogue of Whitby suggests an interest in the classics similar to that at Durham, but all the books have been lost.[47] Similarly, the wealthy Cluniac house of Pontefract may well have had a collection of books, especially after Archbishop Thurstan's retirement there in 1139; but only one twelfth-century book survives. From the Conqueror's foundation at Selby two relevant books have been identified, but neither shows Durham influence.[48] This is disappointing as the presence of a *Life* of St German, Selby's patron saint, in the Durham book-list suggests contact between the two. Nevertheless, Selby seems to have looked to Canterbury for inspiration for its manuscripts, to judge from the initials in its copy of Bede.[49]

Most difficult of all to interpret are the surviving books of St Mary's York, which was also the recipient of royal patronage. Recent work has suggested that St Mary's may well have had a good patristic collection in the twelfth century.[50] Some nine books survive, including copies of Plato's *Timaeus* and Ovid's *Epistolae ex Ponto*, both showing an interest in relatively unusual classical works of which the former at least was available at Durham. This makes it interesting that BL, MS Burney 220, the copy of Ovid, from the mid-twelfth century, has both the 'split-petal' motif (fig. 40), and a rather feeble version of the 'clove-curl'. Late twelfth-century books, copies of recent theological works, have no distinctive motifs and appear to be either the work of itinerant professionals, or gifts. Earlier in the twelfth century, however, St Mary's also seems to have been in touch with Canterbury; BL, MS

---

[47] A late-twelfth-century Whitby library-catalogue is printed in *Cartularium abbathiae de Whitby, ordinis S. Benedicti, fundatae anno MLXXVIII*, ed. J.C. Atkinson (SS 69; 1879), p. 341.
[48] Ker, *Medieval Libraries*, p. 177.
[49] This is Bodl.L., MS Fairfax 12.
[50] Richard Sharpe, pers. comm.

Fig. 40. BL, MS Burney 220, fol. 7 (8 lines high;
mid-twelfth-century; from St Mary's York).

Fig. 41. BL, MS Arundel 218, fol. 1 (5 lines high; late
twelfth-century; from Guisborough).

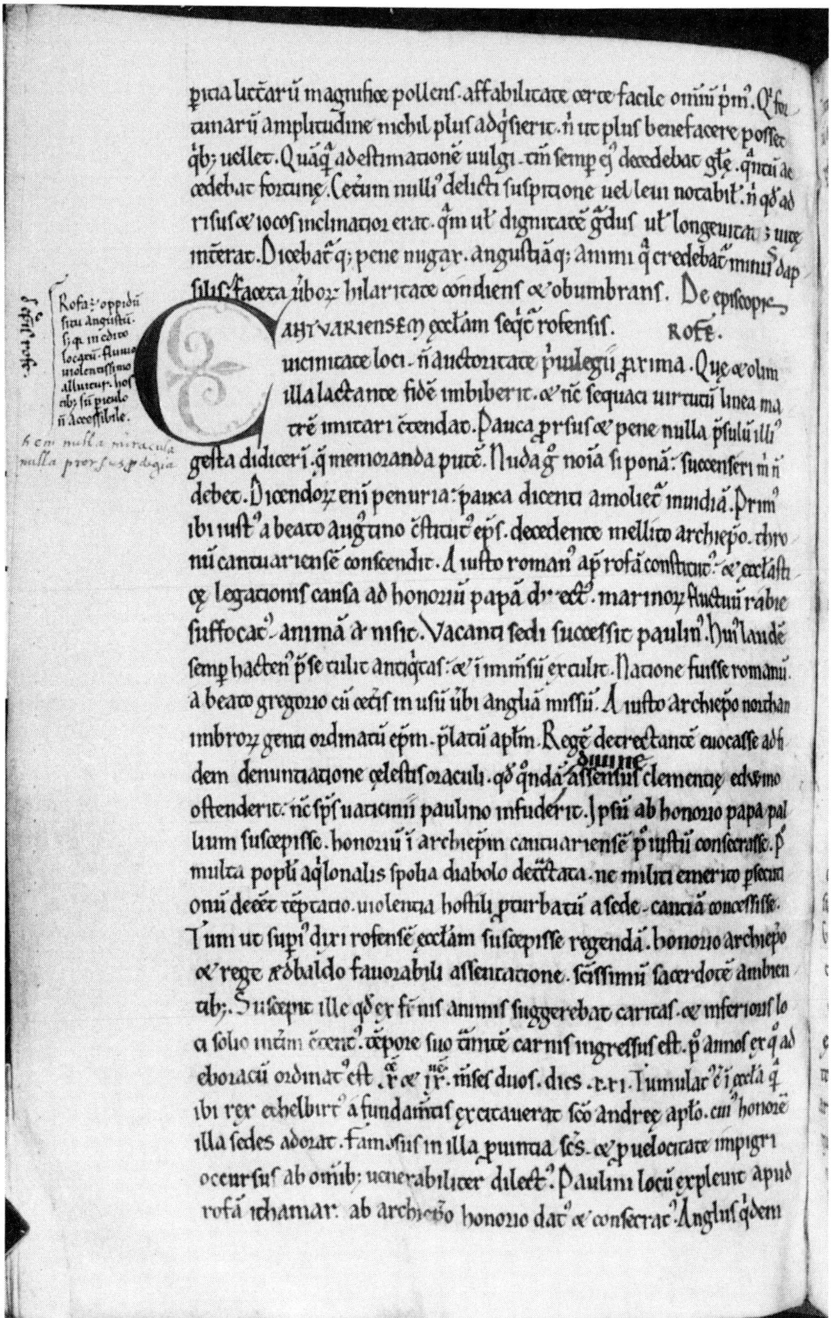

Plate 90.   BL, Cotton MS Claudius A.V, fol. 84v (William of Malmesbury, *Gesta pontificum*; from Bridlington).

Harley 56, the St Mary's copy of Osbern's *Life* of St Dunstan, has a marginal diagram suggesting knowledge of the tombs at Christ Church. This manuscript is complex, since its main initial has a motif very close to the 'split-petal'.[51] This would again suggest some Durham influence at York itself.

The evidence of Durham influence on the Yorkshire Augustinian houses is stronger, although contacts with the Cistercian houses mean that it could have come indirectly. From Kirkham, copies of Bede's *Historia ecclesiastica* and Possidius show both 'split-petals' and 'clove-curls'. They also have more complex initials using dragons and interlace of kinds to be found in rather earlier Durham manuscripts, and absent in Cistercian ones.[52] From Guisborough there is also evidence of interest in the works of Bede, and a manuscript decorated with 'clove-curl' initials of very Durham appearance (fig. 41).[53] From Bridlington there is a copy of William of Malmesbury's *Gesta pontificum*, with 'split-petal' initials (pl. 90). From North Ferriby the evidence is less clear, but its copy of the *Paradisus*, a popular collection of saints' *Lives* which occurs also in the Durham book-list, has 'split-petal' initials. On the other hand Cistercian influence is also clear, perhaps not surprisingly given the influence of Ailred and the move of Waldef, with his friend Everard, from Kirkham to the Cistercian houses of Melrose and Holm Cultram.[54] Interest at Kirkham in Ailred's writings is demonstrated by BL, Cotton MS Vespasian B.XI, a copy of Ailred's *Life* of Edward the Confessor, with very Cistercian initials. Similarly, the Cistercians are known to have encouraged the historian, William of Newburgh; and the initials of the Newburgh copy of William's own work are also very Cistercian in appearance.[55]

From this mass of material it is now possible to suggest answers to the questions posed at the beginning. It does indeed seem that Durham manuscripts exerted considerable artistic influence, and moreover that they did so over a region extending from the Scottish borders down to the Humber, and including Cumbria. However, it is possible to go further, and to suggest two phases of development, in both of which Durham played a crucial role. In the fifty years following the Conquest, Durham appears as only one of the leaders in the movement to reintroduce formal Benedictine monasticism, to build up libraries and to establish scriptoria. During this period the other monasteries, especially those in receipt of royal patronage, looked to Lanfranc's Canterbury at least as much as to Durham. But during the next half-century Durham took a leading role within an evolving network of personal, intellectual, and spiritual contacts with newer houses, especially those of the reforming orders. Through this network, Durham played a central part in the development of a distinctive, northern style of book production and decoration, which lasted into the thirteenth century.

---

[51] Temple, 'Twelfth-Century Psalter', p. 197. For illustration, see Lawrence, 'Cistercian Manuscripts'.
[52] These are, respectively, BL, MS Additional 38817 and BL, MS Arundel 36.
[53] This is BL, MS Arundel 218, containing works by Alcuin.
[54] For the careers of Waldef and Everard, see D. Baker, 'Legend and reality: the Case of Waldef of Melrose', *Studies in Church History* 12 (1975), pp. 59–82.
[55] This is BL, MS Stowe 62.

The Bible of Hugh of le Puiset
(Durham Dean and Chapter Library, MS A.II.1)

DOMINIC MARNER

INTRODUCTION

ONE OF THE MOST richly decorated manuscripts housed in the Dean and Chapter Library at Durham is the late twelfth-century Bible which now has the pressmark A.II.1. The Bible itself was commissioned by one of the great patrons of the arts in Durham: Hugh of le Puiset. Elected Bishop of Durham in 1153, he enjoyed one of the longest episcopacies in the cathedral's history, and is remembered primarily as a prodigious builder.[1] Hugh III, lord of le Puiset, vicomte of Chartres, and count of Corbeil, was his father, while his uncles included King Stephen and Henry of Blois. His wealth and background were reflected in the elaborate stoles, maniples, censers, and candelabras that he gave to the monastery.[2] Furthermore, his generous patronage of the arts must be understood, to some degree, as his desire to emulate his philanthropic uncle Henry at Winchester.

A medieval library list records that he donated over seventy manuscripts to the monastery, which included the classics, theology, ecclesiastical law, service books and a few miscellaneous texts, of which a handful are extant.[3] By its sheer size and expense, the most magnificent of these is a four-volume giant bible, the Puiset Bible, now housed in Durham Dean and Chapter Library. But despite its grandeur, the place of the Puiset Bible in the context of other giant Romanesque Bibles (either in England or France) has not been established. Indeed, the manuscript has received very little attention from medieval historians, particularly when one considers the quantity of material written about other Romanesque Bibles such as the Winchester Bible, the Gifford Bible, or the Lambeth Bible.[4]

---

[1] Puiset rebuilt Durham Castle which had been partly destroyed by fire. He renewed an area of the city walls, and built the Elvet bridge. He also rebuilt some of the episcopal residences and, of course, built the Galilee Chapel.

I would like to thank Sandy Heslop, John Mitchell, and Nalini Persram for their criticisms and comments. I would also like to acknowledge the Royal Historical Society and the Social Science and Humanities Research Council of Canada for their financial support.

[2] *Wills and Inventories illustrative of the History, Manners, Language, etc. of the northern counties of England*, ed. J. Raine (SS 2; 1835), p. 3.

[3] Ibid., p. 4.

[4] W. Oakeshott, *The Two Winchester Bibles* (Oxford, 1981); C. Donovan, *The Winchester*

Questions concerning the production of the manuscript, the number of scribes involved and their specific scribal characteristics, the quire arrangements, the textual peculiarities, and the illuminations are all important and worthy avenues of investigation. However, the present contribution is limited to an analysis of several images which warrant special attention because of their unusual subject matter. This idiosyncracy suggests that, for some reason, the texts which they accompany were of particular interest to those involved in the book's production.

Unfortunately a great many of the illuminations have been excised, which makes it very difficult to grasp the overall pictorial content of the original manuscript, and to discover if there was an underlying theme or pattern of thought for the choice of subjects. In volume I, eleven initials have been cut out: one historiated initial remains, it begins II Samuel (fol. 173), and only one decorated initial to Ruth survives (fol. 150v). Likewise twelve of the initials in volume II are missing, leaving four historiated initials – Epilogue to Lamentations, Ezekiel seated (fol. 61v), Amos seated (fol. 109), and Obadiah kneeling (fol. 112) – and six decorated initials (fols. 101, 103, 112v, 118, 126v, 142v). Although volumes III and IV have not escaped destruction, considerably more historiated and decorated initials remain compared with the first two volumes. Volume III has eight missing initials but retains five historiated – Solomon speaking to his son at the beginning of Proverbs (fol. 4), a king saying *Vanitas* before a shrouded corpse (fol. 16), Ezra seated (fol. 94v), Haman hanging (fol. 109), and the initial which begins I Maccabees (fol. 131v). Volume IV has ten missing initials. However, ten historiated initials survive (fols. 2, 10, 29, 40, 41, 72, 114v, 121v, 128v), as do eight decorated (fols. 28v, 95v, 96, 105, 126v, 133, 137v, 140v) and a set of decorated canon tables under arcades (fols. 4–9v). It is apparent from this summary listing that a total of fifty-one initials have been excised, leaving only fifteen decorated and twenty historiated initials. We must therefore approach any conclusions concerning the overall artistic look of the manuscript with caution.

C.M. Kauffmann described the subjects of the historiated initials in the Puiset Bible as 'the standard ones' which compare closely to those found in the Winchester and Gifford Bibles.[5] Although this is the case with a few initials, for instance the battle scene before I Maccabees, the initial of Solomon teaching before Proverbs, and the three portraits of the prophets, which are all similar to scenes in the Gifford Bible, the similarities end there. This is partly because of the insufficient number of extant initials needed to make a fair assessment of their similarities and differences, and, more importantly, because those initials which do remain have enough variation to suggest a conspicuous lack of 'standard' themes.

Bible (London, 1993); J.M. Sheppard, *The Gifford Bible: Bodleian Library MS Laud misc. 752* (New York, London, 1986); C.M Kauffmann, 'The Bury Bible', *Journal of the Warburg and Courtauld Institutes* 29 (1966), pp. 60–81; C.R. Dodwell, *The Great Lambeth Bible* (London, 1959). For further bibliography see W. Cahn, *Romanesque Bible Illumination* (New York, 1982), pp. 259–63.
[5] C.M. Kauffmann, *Romanesque Manuscripts 1066–1190* (London, 1975), no. 98, pp. 121–2.

The initial which prefaces II Samuel illustrates the point. The Puiset Bible depicts David mourning, with Saul and Jonathan lying before him. The Gifford Bible depicts the Amalekite offering the crown and then his death. The Winchester Bible depicts the Amalekite taking Saul's crown, then David rending clothes, and finally the Amalekite's death. The Lambeth Bible depicts the battle on Mount Gideon and the death of Saul. The Dover Bible (CCCC, MS 3–4) depicts the same scenes as the Winchester Bible, while the somewhat earlier Rochester Bible (BL, MS Royal I.C.VII) simply depicts David as the harpist.[6]

All of these manuscripts have a similar grand scale, but the diversity of their often elaborate illuminations suggests that those responsible for either commissioning or making these Bibles were interested in creating exceptionally luxurious books, each with individual status and without rival.

Although the initials of the Puiset Bible have some common subjects with other giant Bibles, there are some notable oddities, even in the limited extant sample. It is the argument of this essay that through an analysis of these exceptional initials one can gain a glimpse into the creative process of the illuminator, and, in the broader context, begin to appreciate the ambitions of the patron: namely, the desire on the part of Hugh of le Puiset for an elaborate, impressive and unique Bible.

THE CORINTHIAN EPISTLES, Volume IV, fols. 114v and 121v
(pls. 91 and 92)

Two peculiar images begin the two Pauline Epistles to the Corinthians. They are peculiar because within the bowl of the initial 'P' the illuminator has chosen to depict not Paul, as is the custom, but other figures. The initial to I Corinthians contains Sosthenes before the city of Corinth. He holds a scroll in one hand in which he proclaims: *Ego sosthenes frater ecclesiae*, while his other hand indicates the gesture of speech.

Sosthenes is mentioned twice in the New Testament (Acts 18:17 and I Cor. 1:1) but there is some uncertainty as to whether the references are to a single person or to different people. In Acts he is referred to as the 'ruler of the synagogue' in Corinth, while in I Corinthians he is placed next to Paul as a co-author of the Epistle. Although there is no proof, it is quite likely that they refer to the same person. According to Acts Sosthenes was brought before the judgement seat by the Jews because Gallio, the governor, dismissed the charges against Paul (Acts 18:12). Sosthenes was then seized and beaten, possibly by the Jews themselves. If this Sosthenes was the same as the co-author of I Corinthians, he must by then have converted, as St Paul mentions him as a Christian of good standing, whose name is well known in Corinth.

Unlike Sosthenes, the person depicted in the initial to II Corinthians is not identified on the scroll which he holds. However, his dramatic pose, as if he were

---

[6] For further comparisons see the subjects listed in Kauffmann's list of Old Testament iconography in Romanesque Bibles, ibid., pp. 40 ff.

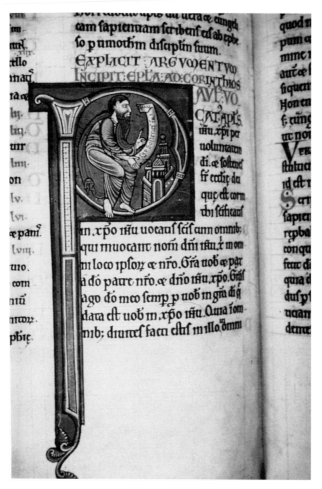

Plate 91.   DCL, MS A.II.1, vol. IV, fol. 114v
(the 'Puiset Bible').

running (or leaping), and his appearance, which is not that of St Paul, suggest that he is the messenger who carried Paul's letter. Paul mentions that he sent Timothy to the Corinthians (I Cor. 4:17) to remind them of his teachings, and in the Marcionite prologue which prefaces I Corinthians, Timothy is mentioned as the epistolary messenger.[7] Finally, he is mentioned in the opening remarks of II Corinthians (1:1). There can be little doubt that this figure represents Timothy.

The depiction of a messenger in twelfth-century Pauline Epistles is extremely rare. In fact, one of the earliest examples of the inclusion of a messenger comes from the first quarter of the thirteenth century in an initial for Galatians (Reims,

[7] '. . . euangelicam sapientiam scribens eis ab epheso per timotheum discipulum suum.'

Plate 92. DCL, MS A.II.1, vol. IV, fol. 121v
(the 'Puiset Bible').

Bibliothèque Municipale, MS 34–36, Vol. III, fol. 138).[8] It has been argued that the introduction of a messenger in this manuscript is the culmination of a genre of images in which the epistolary nature of the text gradually becomes the focus of the initials. Eleen argues that the designers of Pauline initials became increasingly interested in stressing the epistolary aspect of the text rather than Paul's authorship or any of the various themes which might be represented. This concern led artists to examine the opening passages of the texts in order to find 'hints as to the circumstances in which they were written and sent'.

[8]   L. Eleen, *The Illustration of the Pauline Epistles in French and English Bibles of the Twelfth and Thirteenth Centuries* (Oxford, 1982).

The first expressions of this can be found in the scenes where Paul is shown sending a letter and the recipients are shown receiving it.[9] This subject becomes more common in the second half of the twelfth century and reaches its height of popularity in the thirteenth century. According to Eleen, a key manuscript in this development is a commentary on the Epistles by Peter Lombard, made between 1160 and 1170 (Paris, Bibliothèque Ste Geneviève, MS 77), in which several scenes elucidate the idea of authorship and the communication of a message. Indeed, this seems to be the case in the Puiset Bible for I and II Corinthians. Sosthenes as co-author is presented in I Corinthians, and Timothy, the messenger of Paul, in II Corinthians. Both authority and the epistolary form of the text are stressed.

ECCLESIASTES, Vol. III, fol. 16 (pl. 93)

In terms of the decoration of these giant Bibles, I have become particularly interested in the way in which images relate to texts and the way in which the written or spoken word interacts with visual images. I am concerned, for example, with the way in which speech scrolls were introduced into late twelfth-century manuscript images, and gradually became used in interesting and novel ways to explain images, integrate images to the text more fully, or in some fashion to expand or gloss the text.[10] An example of the use of a speech scroll can be found in volume III, on fol. 16, in an historiated initial which prefaces the book of Ecclesiastes.

The image depicts two figures clearly engaged in a discussion. Their dialogue is represented both by their speech gestures and by the introduction of words, which are either written directly on the painted background, as in the figure on the left, or inscribed on a scroll, held in the hand of the figure on the right. In one account it has been incorrectly described as a preacher pointing out to the king a passage from Job (10:19).[11] Unfortunately the accompanying instruction to the artist does not help with regard to the identity of the figures.

Given that from his mouth come the first words of Ecclesiastes, *Vanitas*, one can assume that the crowned king to the left is Solomon in his guise as preacher. Likewise, the figure to the right may be interpreted as Job (even though he is not

---

[9] Paris, Assemblée Nationale, MS 2, fol. 281. Eleen, op. cit., fig. 62.

[10] D. Marner, 'Written Scrolls, Blank Scrolls, Literacy and Inspiration', unpublished paper presented at *Subversions Objects*, Association of Art Historians Annual Conference, Leeds, 1992.

[11] 'Engl. Bibel, Durham Cath. Libr. A.II.1 Vol. III fol. 16, um 1150, der Prediger weist den Kg auf die im Totenamt zit. Stelle Jo 9,19 (sic)' [English bible, Durham Cathedral Library A.II.1, Vol. III, fol. 16, about 1150, the Preacher points out to the king from Job 9.19 a passage from the burial mass]: J. Paul and W. Busch, 'Prediger', *Lexikon der christlichen Iconographie* (Rome, Freiburg, Basle, Vienna, 1971), III, cols. 456–57. A significant clue to the identities of the figures may be found in the marginal instruction to the artist which reads *Rex (?)...*, but the identity of the second figure remains obscured by the missing letters.

Plate 93. DCL, MS A.II.1, vol. III, fol. 16r (the 'Puiset Bible').

depicted in the traditional emaciated manner), as he holds the words which were spoken by him: *de utero translatus ad tumulum*, or 'from the womb to the tomb'.

This phrase refers to Job's desire to have been born dead, and therefore to be taken directly from the womb to the tomb. In the first two chapters of Job Satan tests him by inflicting Job with many nasty ailments. Finally, at the end of chapter 2 we learn of three of Job's friends: Eliphaz of Teman, Bildad of Shuah and Zophar of Naamath, who went to see Job whom they hardly recognize. They sit with him for seven days and nights without speaking a word. Chapter 3 begins with Job breaking the silence and launching into the first of a series of speeches: cursing the day of his birth. The significant and related themes of this first speech revolve around the concept of *de utero translatus ad tumulum*. First Job laments:

> Why did I not die new-born, not perish as I left the womb? Why were there two knees to receive me, two breasts for me to suck? Had there not been, I should now be lying in peace, wrapped in restful slumber, with the kings and high viziers of earth who build themselves vast vaults, or with princes who have gold and to spare and houses crammed with silver, or put away like a still-born child that never came to be, like unborn babes that never see the light . . . (3:11–16).

Then in 10: 18–22: 'Why did you bring me out of the womb? I should have perished then, unseen by any eye, a being that had never been, to be carried from womb to tomb.'

Although the phrase written on the scroll has no direct link to Ecclesiastes, by way of a commentary it does seem to fit the 'gloom and doom' scenario presented in Ecclesiastes, and mirrors some statements in the text such as 'Naked he came, when he left his mother's womb, and naked still death finds him; nothing to show for all his long endeavour' (5:14), and perhaps, 'I say it were better for him never to have come to the birth.' (6:5). However, the closest textual link must be with 4:2: 'So rather than the living who still have lives to live, I salute the dead who have already met death; happier than both of these is he who is yet unborn and has not seen the evil things that are done under the sun.'

The annoyingly vague marginal instructions to the artist would have left him with a considerable degree of artistic licence, and this freedom of choice is reflected in the unprecedented, yet appropriate, introduction of Job's words. This explanation would account for the shrouded corpse which lies directly below Job and which seems to be connected to him in terms of its placement and its coloration.

Placing Solomon and Job, who are historically unrelated, together as participants in a discussion or dispute is also unprecedented in the repertoire of medieval Biblical illumination. A parallel may be the placement of prophets in roundels from the Tree of Jesse iconography, but even there the prophets are not actually discussing anything, they are simply proclaiming the coming of Christ.

A more convincing parallel may be the iconography of the 'Disputing Prophets', examples of which may be found on the Romanesque door jambs of the Abbey Church of St Madeleine at Vézelay (1120–32), or the carved prophets on the early Gothic choir screen at Bamberg Cathedral (1220–30), both of which ultimately derive from early Christian sources. In these examples the prophets turn in pairs towards each other and, with animated gestures, engage in a discussion.

The introduction of the shrouded corpse into the scene is also unusual. This is an attempt by the artist to find a visual equivalent to what one of the protagonists is saying, or thinking, or desiring, and, as such, he is trying to communicate in visual terms Job's sense of anxiety and despair.

LAMENTATIONS, Vol. II, fol. 61v (pl. 94)

A fascinating initial begins an Epilogue to Lamentations. R.A.B. Mynors describes it as follows: 'Epilogue to Lamentations. Bust of naked man in centre, four half-figures of men around him'.[12] Mynors presents no interpretation or explanation of the image or of the text it prefaces. In C.M. Kauffmann's catalogue of English Romanesque manuscripts this particular image is conspicuous by its absence from his list of initials in the Puiset Bible, as is any mention of the accompanying text. Since the image is on a comparable scale to those which begin the major books of the Bible, and thus has similar visual 'weight', and since, furthermore, there is virtually no mention of it in the published sources, nor is there a marginal instruction to the artist,[13] an interpretation may be appropriate.

[12] *DCM*, p. 84, pl. 49.
[13] A variety of marginal instructions faintly remain in Volumes II and III. For a list of these see *DCM*.

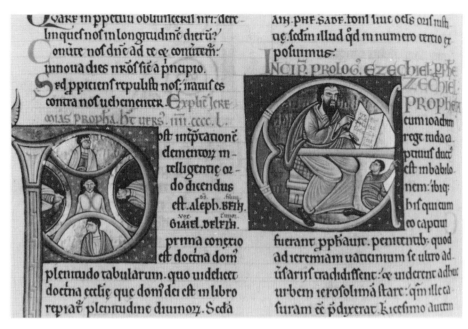

Plate 94. DCL, MS A.II.1, vol. II, fol. 61v (the 'Puiset Bible').

The book which immediately precedes this image is Lamentations, a text which was thought to have been written by Jeremiah and which acts in a way as an appendage to the book of Jeremiah. It is because the Lamentations mourn the Babylonian conquest of Jerusalem and the destruction of the Temple in 587 BC that medieval commentators viewed them as poems expounding the notion of purification through suffering, in a similar vein to the story of Job.[14]

Furthermore, in the original Hebrew the first four of the five books of Lamentations has an acrostic form: a consecutive letter of the Hebrew alphabet begins each verse of the first four books, while the last book, although not acrostic in form, has precisely twenty-two verses, matching the number of letters in the Hebrew alphabet. The reader is reminded of this acrostic structure by the placement of the letters of the Hebrew alphabet in red after each verse.

The epilogue text is part of St Jerome's commentary on the Book of Lamentations in which he discusses the meaning of the Hebrew letters of the alphabet.[15] There is a rather large section of material which both precedes and succeeds this text in the entire commentary. The commentary is written out in its entirety in the prefatory material to the Psalms later in the manuscript, although textual variations may suggest a different model for the two texts.

What is distinctive about the epilogue text is that it does not incorporate all

[14] E.A. Matter, 'The Lamentations Commentaries of Hrabanus Maurus and Paschasius Radbertus', *Traditio* 38 (1982), at pp. 137–8.
[15] *Epistula XXX ad Paulum*, CSEL 54 (1910).

twenty-two letters of the alphabet, but stops after *Sade*, the eighteenth letter. A further superscripted meaning of the individual letters is introduced.[16] If the model for this text was the correct version used for the commentary prefacing the Psalms, the scribe would not have made such a mistake.

Remarkably, an almost exact duplicate of this text occurs in the Lambeth Bible, complete with the superscripted elements. Both texts begin and end at precisely the same place. The only variations are in spelling: *conexio/connexio* and *reperiator/repperiator*. The textual similarities point to a common model.[17]

The question which arises from this examination involves that of the relationship between text and image. A simple connection one may make between the image and the text it precedes is that the four figures refer to the *elementa*, or letters of the alphabet, possibly the four first letters – *Aleph, Beth, Gimel, Deleth* – which are seen next to it. However, the problem with this association is that it does not account for the central naked figure, nor does it account for the more complicated sets of relationships between the figures represented.

Assuming that images were created with a conscious intention and within a particular context, they must have some kind of meaning. It is therefore important to articulate accurately the visual conventions being employed in this image. In the first place, the semi-circular bands used to separate the marginal figures from the central figure were a common medieval convention for distinguishing between the heavenly realm and the earthly realm. This convention can be found in a variety of media throughout the Middle Ages; it signifies a major separation of one mode of being from another. (The figure in the centre therefore differs ontologically from the others.) This difference is accentuated by the depiction of the figure as an archetype – naked and frontal – and thus cosmic. The central figure is also frontal while the marginal figures are in profile. In the twelfth century the juxtaposition of frontal and profile figures often signifies the general theme of beauty versus ugliness; in this case, the thematic variation is heavenly perfection versus worldly imperfection. By their difference the marginal figures occupy a terrestrial realm and not the cosmic space of the central figure. The relationship between the backgrounds to these terrestrial figures forms a vertical and horizontal axis, the vertical axis being defined by the gold background, and the horizontal axis by the dark blue background and white dots.

A common theme of both the text of Lamentations and Jerome's commentary is that of the Hebrew alphabet and the acrostic structure. The image in question,

[16] The origin of the superscripted elements remains obscure. They occur in table form prefacing the Psalms in the Puiset Bible and also in a Bible from St Albans (CCCC, MS 48, fol. 121).

[17] Because of the textual differences between the two commentaries within the Puiset Bible, and because of the textual similarities with the Lambeth Bible, it is possible that the Bible itself was not copied from a single exemplar, but put together from separate texts. The large amount of prefatory material to the Psalms, the inclusion of this Epilogue to Lamentations, and the 'placing' of the preface to I Maccabees after the text of Maccabees, suggests that on the one hand there was more than one 'exemplar', and on the other that the production of the manuscript was somewhat hurried.

which is divided into five parts (four of which are visually equal and subordinate to the fifth), can be correlated to the structure of Lamentations: the first four books have an acrostic structure while the fifth, although not an acrostic, has twenty-two verses, matching the number of letters in the Hebrew alphabet.

Is it possible that the image functions as a diagrammatic representation of the acrostic structure of Lamentations? If so, how would the parts of the image match the structure of Lamentations? In order to match image with text one would have to establish an order of correspondence. As such, the central naked figure would correspond to the fifth book of Lamentations, as the common element of the figure and the book is the unusual status each is accorded. The figure, by being depicted naked and frontal, significantly differs from the clothed and profile figures, while the fifth book is the culminating text, the so-called prayer of Jeremiah, which has no acrostic structure unlike the first four books.

As to the central figure's identity, the last two verses of the fifth book may provide a clue: 'Restore us to thyself, Lord, that we may be restored! Renew our days as from the beginning' (5:21);[18] 'Or have you utterly rejected us? Are you very angry with us?' (5:22).[19] In verse 21 there is a lament for the time of the beginning, a renewal of the days *sicut a principio*, that is, of the time of innocence, prior to the Fall, the time of the Innocent Adam. The significance of this verse will be discussed later. In verse 22 the author asks God if He has rejected humanity, or if He is angry with humanity, a phrase which must have brought to mind Christ's final cry on the cross: 'My God, my God, why hast thou forsaken me?' (Matthew 27:46).[20]

It would seem that the central figure is that of Christ. This is for three reasons. First, the figure is located at the juncture of the vertical and horizontal axis, in other words at the implied centre of the arms of a cross. Second, the last verse of Lamentations is an allusion to Christ's final cry on the cross, and third the figure has a 'cosmic' status. This suggestion is strengthened further when one considers the chiastic structure of the image. It is placed within the bowl of the letter 'P' and is formed in such a way as to imply not only the form of a cross, but that of an 'X' as well, the 'X' and the 'P' being the familiar Chi-Rho symbol of Christ.

What remains to be discovered is an account of the different backgrounds of the vertical and horizontal arms of the cross, and for the introduction of figures into these spaces. What is the significance of having two different backgrounds? In twelfth-century illuminations, and indeed elsewhere in the Puiset Bible, similar gold and coloured backgrounds can be found with no obvious symbolic meaning. An author portrait, like the image which prefaces the prologue to Ezekiel next to this image, might have a gold, or possibly dark blue, or even red background. However, these backgrounds tend to be uniform, that is, of gold or blue in entirety. In the image concerned here, it seems the illuminator has deliberately chosen to make the vertical arms with a gold background and the horizontal with a dark blue

---

[18] 'Converte nos, Domine, ad te et convertemur; innova dies nostros, sicut a principio.'
[19] 'Sed proiiciens repulisti nos, iratus es contra nos vehementer.'
[20] 'Deus meus, Deus meus, ut quid dereliquisti me?'

background. For this reason these backgrounds can be considered significant to an understanding of the image as a whole.[21]

In the Middle Ages, it was quite common to consider gold as the symbol of light; if this was the intention of the illuminator one can interpret this vertical arm as one of light, and the horizontal arm as one of darkness. This visual metaphor can be expanded to accommodate the notion of day and night along vertical and horizontal axes respectively (the cluster of dots on a dark ground thus representing the stars). If the gold background alludes to light and day, appropriately one may speculate that the uppermost and lowermost sections signify the east and the west, or the rising and the setting of the sun, and therefore the temporal parameters of the day. Following this logic the dark backgrounds with 'stars' might signify the north and the south, or the temporal parameters of the night. Considering the orientation of medieval maps where the east was placed at the top, the west at the bottom, the north to the left and the south to the right, this would seem a plausible explanation of the differing backgrounds.

There are several implications in considering the terrestrial figures of this image as personifications of the regions of the world. It was St Augustine who first observed that the regions of the world, when translated into Greek, form an acrostic of the word ADAM (*Anatole*, east; *Dysis*, west; *Arktos*, north; *Mesembria*, south).[22] This is why, in contemporary microcosm/macrocosm schematic diagrams, the letters A,D,A,M are often written much larger at the points corresponding to the east, west, north and south respectively, and why often a nude male figure is placed at the centre of the cosmos.[23] Augustine's observation that the regions of the world named in Greek are an acrostic of the word ADAM was developed in the early twelfth century by Honorius Augustodunensis (1075 or 1080 to *c.*1156).[24] He believed that the reason the four regions of the world were so represented was because the world came from Adam. That is, from Adam's feet came the earth, from his bones the stones, from his nails the trees, from his hair the grass, and so on. Thus the fragmented Adam was strewn over the whole world. And hence the reason why, in the Greek language, the four regions are an acrostic of his name.

Given Augustine's discovery, it is possible to suggest that the central figure in this image may be Adam. Yet this does not contradict nor undermine the earlier suggestion of the presence of Christ in the image, for the identification between Christ and Adam is evident in St Paul's characterization of Adam as Adam *Vetus*

[21] The notion that the background can contribute to the meaning of an image is discussed by Sixten Ringbom, 'Some Pictorial Conventions for the Recounting of Thoughts and Experiences in Late Medieval Art', in *Medieval Iconography and Narrative. A Symposium* (Odense, 1980), pp. 38–69, especially 47 ff.
[22] Augustine commentary on Psalm 95: *PL* 37, col. 1236.
[23] M.-T. d'Alverny, 'Le cosmos symbolique du XIIe siècle', *Archives d'histoire doctrinale et littéraire du moyen âge* 28 (1953), pp. 31–81. Also cf. Oxford, St John's College, MS 17, fol. 7v.
[24] E.M. Sanford, 'Honorius, Presbyter and Scholasticus', *Speculum* 23 (1948); 'Honorius Augustodunensis, *De neocosmo*', ed. R.D. Crouse (unpublished Ph.D. thesis, Harvard University, 1970); see also A. Esmeijer, *Divina Quaternitas. A Preliminary Study in the Method and Application of Visual Exegesis* (Amsterdam, 1978).

and the crucified Christ as the new Adam, the Adam *Novus* (1 Cor. 15:45). In this image the visual reference is Christ's placement at the centre between the implied vertical and horizontal arms of the cross.[25]

The central figure's dual identity is apparent from the adjoining text of Lamentations, and involves the link between text and image, cross and map. This ambivalence is the crux of the matter. The figure is both Adam and Christ. The textual allusion to Adam occurs in verse 21, where there is a lament for the time of the beginning, a renewal of the days *sicut a principio*, that is, of the time of innocence, prior to the Fall, the time of the Innocent Adam. The final verse gives the allusion to Christ. The image, therefore, is a response to the final question of Lamentations, a question which is central to Christianity. It visually answers the question with a diagrammatic representation of the microcosm-macrocosm relationship, the conventions concerning which would have been familiar to the reader. The image, therefore, reassures the reader that God has not abandoned the world and reminds the reader that Christ through his death on the cross redeemed the world and in so doing saved humanity and re-created, as it were, a time of innocence, *a principio*. Given the importance of Lamentations in the commemoration of the suffering and death of Jesus as re-enacted in the Holy Week Liturgy, this image seems to make a great deal of sense.

The implication of this account is that the problem of how to determine which of the terrestrial figures might correspond to each of the first four books of Lamentations is greatly reduced. The order would simply follow the letters of Adam's name. In other words east would correspond to the first book of Lamentations, west to the second, north to the third and south to the fourth.

A factor which reinforces this particular correlation is the number of verses in the books of Lamentations. Although the books are identical in their acrostic structure, book three has three times as many verses as the other books. It has sixty-six verses, not twenty-two. The change in the number of verses has been visually noted by the illuminator. Three of the four figures are conveyed as young men signified by their clean shaven faces, and are placed in the positions of the first, second and fourth books of Lamentations, each having twenty-two verses, while the one personifying the north, that of the third book (sixty-six verses), is represented as an old man, denoted by possessing a beard.

---

[25] This quadrapartite cosmic scheme can also relate to the Holy Scriptures. The relation between Creation and Scriptures has been frequently noted by exegetes, and must have been familiar to the reader. The harmony of the Creation was disturbed by the Fall, and this necessitated a second Creation by means of a second revelation of the Word, the Scriptures. This concept of God's two-fold revelation was extremely widespread. Scriptures and Creation, *scriptura/creatura* and *lux/mundus* are like two books. Honorius Augustonensis even relates the cardinal points to the Evangelists: north – Matthew, west – Luke, south – John, and east – Mark. See *PL* 172, cols. 833–4.

CONCLUSION

Like many medieval manuscripts the Puiset Bible has suffered the loss of some of its finest illumination. As a result the historian can never hope to reconstruct the original manuscript or to discover the possible themes or patterns of thought involved in determining the choice of subjects depicted. Indeed a great many of the initials which preface the books of the Bible in the late twelfth century tend to be decorative and those which are historiated tend to be rather straightforward. Therefore, the role of the patron in choosing specific subject matter to be illustrated is problematic. An equally difficult task is to determine the role of the illuminator's creative impulse.

Out of the remaining thirty-five illuminations in the Puiset Bible I have chosen to discuss four. These four are exceptional in that each image is unprecedented in the repertoire of biblical illumination and each points to a considerable degree of sophistication on the part of the makers of this manuscript. Whether this complexity was the result of Hugh of le Puiset's role as patron, or the result of the illuminator's inventive mind, cannot be determined. However, it is clear that the grand scale, numerous illuminations and iconographic novelty of this manuscript must have satisfied Puiset's desire for an elaborate, impressive and visually provocative Bible.

The Shape and Meaning of the Old English Poem 'Durham'

D. R. HOWLETT

T HE LAST extant Old English poem composed in the traditional metre, entitled 'Durham' by modern editors, was written sometime before Symeon of
Durham had completed *De exordio et procursu Dunelmensis ecclesiae*, not later than
1109.[1] Margaret Schlauch has classified the poem as an *encomium urbis*, a genre
transmitted from the Greeks by Romans to medieval rhetoricians. She has mentioned the 'curiously rigid tenacity of form in this as in many other school-boy
exercises' and described the poem as 'little more than a class-room assignment'.[2] It
is nonetheless a well wrought exercise, which exhibits structural features derived
from the text of the Hebrew Old Testament and the Greek New Testament through
the Latin Bible, recurrent in all the finest Old English poetry composed between
the seventh century and the twelfth.[3]

These features include, first, parallelism, statement of ideas followed by restatement of ideas in the same order, as Isaiah 1:10:

  e   d   c   b   a

שִׁמְעוּ דְבַר־יְהוָה קְצִינֵי סְדֹם

  e'   d'   c'   b'   a'

הַאֲזִינוּ תּוֹרַת אֱלֹהֵינוּ עַם עֲמֹרָה׃

a   b   c   d   e

ακουσατε λογον Κυριου αρχοντες Σοδομων.

a'   b'   c'   d'   e'

προσεχετε νομον Θεου λαος Γομορρας.

a   b   c   d   e

audite uerbum Domini principes Sodomorum

---

[1] *Sym. Op.* I, 221–2. 'Durham', ed. E.V.K. Dobbie in *The Anglo-Saxon Minor Poems*, The
Anglo-Saxon Poetic Records: A Collective Edition (New York, 1942), VI, pp. xliii–xlv (intro-
duction), 27 (text), 151–3 (notes). H.S. Offler, 'The Date of Durham (*Carmen de Situ
Dunelmi)*', *Journal of English and Germanic Philology* 61 (1962), pp. 591–4.

[2] M. Schlauch, 'An Old English *Encomium Urbis*', *Journal of English and Germanic Philology*
40 (1941), p. 14.

[3] See my *British Books in Biblical Style* (forthcoming).

       a'   b' c'   d'   e'
percipite auribus legem Dei nostri populus Gomorrae.

     a   b   c   d   e
Hear the word of the Lord, you rulers of Sodom.

     a'   b'   c'   d'   e'
Give ear to the teaching of our God, you people of Gomorrah.

An example in English nursery rhyme is

> To market, to market, to buy a fat pig,
>   home again, home again, jiggety jig.
> To market, to market, to buy a fat hog,
>   home again, home again, jiggety jog.

The features include, secondly, chiasmus, statement of ideas followed by restatement of ideas in reverse order, as Lamentations 1:1:

        aii   ai   ai   aii
הָיְתָה כְּאַלְמָנָה   εγενηθη ως χηρα

        bii   bi   bi   bii
רַבָּתִי בַגּוֹיִם   πεπληθυμμενη εν εθνεσιν

        b'ii   b'i   b'i   b'ii
שָׂרָתִי בַּמְּדִינוֹת   αρχουσα εν χωραις

        a'ii   a'i   a'i   a'ii
הָיְתָה לָמַס׃   εγενηθη εις φορον.

       a i   a ii
facta est quasi uidua   a   How like a widow she has become
       b i   b ii
domina gentium   b   she that was great among the nations;
       b'i   b'ii
princeps prouinciarum   b'   she that was a princess among the cities
       a'i   a'ii
facta est sub tributo.   a'   has become a vassal.

An example in English nursery rhyme is

> As I was going to Saint Ives
>   I met a man with seven wives;
>   each wife had seven sacks;
>   each sack had seven cats;
>   each cat had seven kits.
>   Kits,
>   cats,
>   sacks,
> and wives,
> how many were going to Saint Ives?

John Henry Newman's hymn is in the same form:

> Praise to the Holiest
>   in the height
>   and in the depth
> be praise,
>   in all His words
>   most wonderful,
>   most sure
>   in all His ways.

Here is an example from the New Testament, the Prologue to Saint John's Gospel:

A1	In the beginning	Εν αρχηι
2	was	ην
3	the Word,	ο λογος
4	and the Word	και ο λογος
5	was	ην
6	with God	προς τον θεον
7	and	και
6'	God	θεος
5'	was	ην
4'	the Word;	ο λογος
3'	He	ουτος
2'	was	ην
1'	in the beginning with God.	εν αρχηι προς τον θεον.
B1	All things	παντα
2	through Him were made	δια αυτου εγενετο
3	and	και
2'	without Him was made	χωρις αυτου εγενετο
1'	not one thing.	ουδε εν.
C1	What was made in Him	ο γεγονεν εν αυτωι
2	life was	ζωη ην
3	and	και
2'	the life was	η ζωη ην
1'	the light of men.	το φως των ανθρωπων.
D1	And the light in the darkness shines	και το φως εν τηι σκοτιαι φαινει
1'	and the darkness has not overcome it.	και η σκοτια αυτο ου κατελαβεν.

A1	In principio
2	erat
3	Verbum
4	et Verbum
5	erat
6	apud Deum
7	et
6'	Deus
5'	erat
4'	Verbum;

```
3'      Hoc
2    erat
1'  in principio apud Deum.
B1   Omnia
2      per ipsum facta sunt
3        et
2'      sine ipso factum est
1'    nihil.
C1   Quod factum est in ipso
2      uita erat
3        et
2'      uita erat
1'    lux hominum.
D1   Et lux in tenebris lucet
1'   et tenebrae eam non comprehenderunt.
```

The features include also composition in mathematical ratios by which ancient and medieval men believed God to have created the universe: symmetry, 1:1; duple ratio, 2:1; extreme and mean ratio, 0.61803 and 0.38197; sesquialter ratio, 3:2; sesquitertian ratio, 4:3; and sesquioctave ratio, 9:8. These are discussed in Plato's *Timaeus* §§ 31–2, in Euclid's *Elements* II 11 and VI 30, in Boethius *De Institutione Arithmetica* II 52 and *De Institutione Musica* I 10, all texts known in the Latin West during the early Middle Ages.

One reason for association of topography, architecture, history, arithmetic, music, geometry, and astronomy in poetry is that all these subjects are found together in the cosmogony of Job 38:4–7:

Where were you when I laid the foundation of the earth?	ubi eras quando ponebam fundamenta terrae?
Tell me, if you have understanding.	indica mihi si habes intellegentiam
Who	quis
determined	posuit
its measurements;	mensuras eius,
surely you know!	si nosti,
Or who	uel quis
stretched	tetendit
the line upon it?	super eam lineam
On what were its bases	super quo bases illius
sunk,	solidatae sunt
or who	aut quis
laid	dimisit
its cornerstone,	lapidem angularem eius
when the morning stars sang together	cum me laudarent simul astra matutina
and all the sons of God shouted for joy?	et iubilarent omnes filii Dei.

Here is the text of 'Durham' transcribed from Cambridge, University Library, MS Ff.1.27, p. 202 column b and arranged in lines of verse.

De situ Dunelmi et de sanctorum reliquiis quae ibidem
continentur carmen compositum

Is ðeos burch . breome   geond Breotenrice
steppa gestaðolad   stanas ymbutan
wundrum . gewæxen .   Weor . ymbeornad .
ea yðum . stronge .   7 ðer inne wunað
feola fisca . kyn .   on floda gemonge .   5
7 ðær gewexen is   wudafæstern micel .
wuniad in ðem wycum   wilda deor monige
in deope dalum   deora ungerim .

Is in ðere byri eac   bearnum gecyðed .
ðe arfesta   eadig Cudberch .   10
and ðes clene   cyniuges heafud
Osuualdes Engle leo .   7 Aidan biscop .
Eadberch . 7 Eadfrið .   æðele geferes .
Is ðer inne midd heom .   7 ðelwold . biscop .
7 breoma bocera . Beda .   7 Boisil abbot .   15
ðe clene Cudberte   on gecheðe
lerde . lustum .   7 he wis lara wel genom .
Eardiæð . æt ðem eadige   inin ðem minstre
unarimeda .   reliquia .
ðe monia wundrum ge.wurðað.   ðes ðe writ . seggeð .
Midd ðene Drihnes . wer   domes bideð .   21

3 *ymbeornad* with *d* altered from *n*. 5 *fcola* with *c* added above the line.
15 *beda* corrected from *beba* by dotting the second *b* and adding *d* above
the line.

The first part begins with a capital letter in *Is* and ends with a punctuation mark
after line 8. The second part has capital letters in its first, sixth, tenth, and
thirteenth lines, and it ends with a punctuation point. The punctuation, which
may at first sight appear erratic, is sensible. Of the forty-two half-lines in the poem
twenty-five end with punctuation marks: 3a–b, 4a, 5a–b, 6b, 8b, 9b, 10b, 12a–b,
13a–b, 14a–b, 15a–b, 17a–b, 19a–b, 20a–b, 21a–b. In more than half the lines the
scribe has further marked the metrical structure by placing a point before the last
word in a half-line at 1a, 3a–b, 4a, 5a, 14b, 15a, 17a, 20a–b, 21a–b. Note the
points also in 13a and 18a.

The poem survives also in a transcript of British Library, Cotton MS Vitellius
D.XX made before the library fire by the Reverend G. Nicolson, archdeacon of
Carlisle, published by George Hickes, arranged in half lines.[4]

2 *Steopa*. 3 *ymb eornað*. 4 *Ean. strong*. 5 *Fisca feola kinn. gemong*.
6 *ðere. no is*. 6 *Wuda festern mycel*. 7 *Wuniað in þem wicum*. 8
deopa. 9 *im. gecyðed*. 10 *Cuðbercht*. 11 *clæne cyninges heofud*. 12
Osualdes Engla. bisceop. 13 *Ædbercht 7 + Ædfrid*. 14 *mid. Æðelwold*

4 G. Hickes, *Linguarum Vett. Septentrionalium Thesaurus Grammatico-Criticus et Archaeo-
logicus* (Oxford, 1705), Pars I, pp. 178–9.

bisceop. abbet. 16 *clæne Cuðberchte + On gicheðe.* 17 *his.* 18 *Eardiað.*
mynstre. 20 *ðær monige.* no *ðes. writa.* 21 *mid. drihtnes.*

Each half line is introduced with a capital letter, and each is concluded with a
punctuation point.

Recently another transcript by Francis Junius from an unknown and apparently
lost manuscript has been printed from Stanford University Libraries, MS Misc.
010.[5]

Page 1a:

Is ðeos burh + byrig	Est haec urbs
breome + breme.	inclyta, celebris
geond {beat?} breoton-	per Britannici
rice stowa gesta-	regni loca sta-
þolad.	tuta, fundata.
stanas ymbutan.	lapides circumcirca
wundrum gewæxen.	miri creverunt.
weor + deor, hic videtur	
antiquū fluvii nomen sub-	
stituendū quod proxima[6]	
ad hosce literarū ductus	
accedit.	
weor ymbeornað	Weor circumfluit
{amnicis fluctibus praeceps}	amnicis fluctibus
ea yðum stronge.	praeceps.
& ðær inne wunað	& in eo habitant
feala fisca cynn	multa pisciū genera
on floda gemonge.	inter fluenta.

Page 1b:

& ðær gewæxen is	ibi quoque succrevit
wuda fæstern +	sylvarum munimentum
western micel.	+ desertum ingens.
wunað in ðæm wycum	morantur in istis refugiis
wylda deor monige.	ferae multae.
in deoredalum	in variis ferarum parti-
	tionibus (in the severall
	walkes of the forrest)
+ in deorewealdum	in ferarum nemoribus
deora ungerim.	fera innumera.
is in ðære byri eac	est in eâ urbe etiam
bearnum gecyðed	pueris memoratus
se arfæsta eadig	pius beatus
cuðberht, & ðes	Cuthbertus. &

[5] D.K. Fry, 'A Newly Discovered Version of the Old English Poem "Durham"', in *Old English and New, Studies in Language and Linguistics in Honor of Frederic G. Cassidy,* ed. J.H. Hall *et al.* (New York and London, 1992), pp. 83–96.
[6] ? *lege proxime.*

clǽne cyninges hea-
fud oswaldes.
engle leo.
nisi forte malis
engle leof.

casti regis ca-
put Oswaldi,
Anglici leonis,

Anglis cari.

Page 1c:

& aidan biscop.
Eadberht, & Ead-
frið. {& ðǽre}
& ðelegeferes. forte
& ðere geferas.
is ðere nine mid heom.
   ex historiâ istius saeculi petendū quis sit
   iste Nine & quomomodo[7] paullo post re-
   pisuenda[8] sint quaedam nomina propria
   ab imperitis librariis mutilata.
& þelwold f. æðelwold
biscop. & breoma
bocera Beda.
& Bosil abbod.
ðe clǽne Cuþberht
on gechete lǽrde
   ex historiâ forte, poterit erui num istud
   gechete intelligendū sit de loco insti-
   tutionis, {and} vel de facultate aliquâ.
lustum forte ponitur pro lustlice. Alacriter,
   cum quadā animi voluptate.quam
   expositionē vidētur possotare[9] {antithesis}
   quae sequuntur, & Cuthberti docilitatem
   testantur.
& he wislara wel genom.

& Aidanus episcopus.
Eadbertus & Ead-
fridus.

& eorum socii.
Est ibi Nine cum iis.

& Æthelwoldus
episcopus, & celebris
scriptor Beda.
& Bosil abbas.
qui purum Cuthbertum
in   docuit.

& ille sapientiae do-
ctrinam bene imbibit.

Page 1d:

Eardreð & ðem eadige
imuðem. forte ymb þem
mynstre unarimeda
reliquia ðe monia
wundra gewyrcað.
ðes ðe writ secgeð.
mid ðene drihtnes
andweardnes bydeð.

is in ðǽre byri eac be ear-
nungum gecyged se arfǽsta

. . . . .
      circa mo-
nasterium innumerabiles
reliquiae, quae multa
miracula operantur,
prout scripta testantur,
in iis qui Domini
praesentiam expectant
   vel implorant.

---

7 ? *lege quomodo vel quoquomodo.*
8 ? *lege restituenda.*
9 ? *lege pessumdare.*

eadig cuþberht.
{Est} In isthac urbe ob merita quoque
invocantur pius beatus Cuthbertus.

From these three copies we may attempt to restore the original form of the verses, assuming only that they were grammatically, syntactically, and orthographically internally consistent. To the right of the text the first column states the number of lines, the second the number of words, the third the number of syllables, and the fourth the number of letters.

De situ Dunelmi et de sanctorum reliquiis quae ibidem continentur carmen compositum

Is ðeos burch . breoma . geond Breotenrice .		6	10	33
steopa . gestaðolad . stanas . ymbutan .		4	11	29
wundrum . geweaxen . Weor . ymbeorneð .		4	9	28
ea yðum . strong . and ðer inne . wuniað .		7	10	28
feola fisca . kyn . on floda . gemong .	5	6	10	26
and ðer . geweaxen is . wudufæstenn . micel .		6	12	32
wuniað in ðæm . wicum . wilda deor . monige .		7	12	31
in deopum . dalum . deora . ungerim .		5	10	25
		45	84	260
Is in ðære byri . eac . bearnum . geciged .		7	12	29
ðe arfæsta . eadig . Cuðbercht .	10	4	8	23
and ðæs clænan . cyninges . heafud .		5	9	26
Oswaldes Engla hleo . and Aidan bisceop .		6	11	32
Eadbercht . and Eadfrið . æðele . geferes .		5	11	31
Is ðer inne . midd heom . Æðelwald . bisceop .		7	11	32
and breoma bocera . Beda . and Boisil . abbud .	15	7	13	33
ðe clænan . Cuðberchte . on . gecigde .		5	10	27
lerde . lustum . and he wis lara wel . genom .		8	12	31
Eardiað . æt ðæm eadige . inin . ðæm minstre .		7	12	32
unarimeda . reliquia .		2	9	17
ðær monige wundrum . gewurðað . ðæs ðe writ . seggeð .		8	14	39
Midd ðone Drihtnes . wer . domes . bidað .	21	6	10	29
		77	142	360

Both the heading and a notice by Symeon of Durham[10] refer to the division of the poem into two parts, a description of Durham and an account of its relics:

illud Anglico sermone compositum carmen, ubi cum de statu hujus loci, et de sanctorum reliquiis quae in eo continentur agitur, etiam reliquiarum Bedae una cum caeteris ibidem mentio habetur.

Lines 1–8 form the first part of the poem, *de situ Dunelmi*, a verse paragraph within which is a parallelism.

---

10 *LDE*, bk. 3, ch. 7, *Sym. Op.* I, 89.

a	wundrum geweaxen	a'	and ðer geweaxen is
b	Weor ymbeorneð ea yðum strong	b'	wudufæstenn micel
c	and ðer inne wuniað	c'	wuniað in ðæm wicum
d	feola fisca kyn	d'	wilda deor monige
e	on floda gemong	e'	in deopum dalum

Lines 9–21 form the second part of the poem, *de sanctorum reliquiis*, a verse paragraph within which is a chiasmus.

a	in ðære byri
bi	geciged
ii	eadig
c	Cuðbercht
d	ðæs clænan
e	heafud
fi	Aidan bisceop
ii	Eadbercht and Eadfrið
g	Is ðer inne midd heom
f'i	Æðelwald bisceop
ii	Beda and Boisil
e'	abbud
d'	ðe clænan
c'	Cuðberchte
b'i	on gecigde
ii	ðæm eadige
a'	inin ðæm minstre

The first part of the poem is linked to the second part by parallelism.

1	Is ðeos burch breoma geond Breotenrice	1'	Is in ðære byri eac bearnum geciged
2	and ðer inne wuniað	2'	Is ðer inne midd heom
3	wuniað in ðæm wicum	3'	Eardiað æt ðæm eadige
4	in deopum dalum	4'	inin ðæm minstre
5	deora ungerim.	5'	unarimeda reliquia

Besides these parallels in the same order, other diction of the second part further echoes that of the first. Compare *breoma* 1 with *breoma* 15, *wundrum* 3 with *wundrum* 20, *wudufæstenn* 6 with *arfæsta* 10, and *monige* 7 with *monige* 20.

In the first part of the poem the first line alliterates on *b*, the fourth on vowels, the penultimate on *w*, and the last on *d*. In the second part the first line alliterates on *b*, the fourth on vowels, the penultimate on *w*, and the last on *d*.

There are further connections in the first part between *gestaðolad* 2a and *geweaxen* 3a, *ymbutan* 2b and *ymbeorneð* 3b, *ymbeorneð* 3b and *wuniað* 4b, *strong* 4a and *gemong* 5b, *wicum* 7a, *dalum* 8a, and *ungerim* 8b; and in the second part between *geciged* 9b and *gecigde* 16b, *Cuðbercht* 10b and *Cuðberchte* 16a, *heafud* 11b and *abbud* 15b, *bisceop* 12b and *bisceop* 14b, *Cuðberchte* 16a and *gecigde* 16b, *lustum* 17a and *genom* 17b, *eadige* 18a and *minstre* 18b, *unarimeda* 19a and *reliquia* 19b, *gewurðað* 20a, *seggeð* 20b, and *bidað* 21b.

The entire poem occupies twenty-one lines, which divide by extreme and mean ratio and by sesquialter ratio at 13 and 8. The first part, *de situ Dunelmi*, contains eight lines and forty-five words. The number 8 divides by extreme and mean ratio and by sesquialter ratio at 5 and 3; the number 45 divides by sesquialter ratio at 27 and 18. The verses divide at the parallelism. The first five lines describe Durham and the Wear, two and one half lines each. The last three lines describe the surrounding wood. The first five lines contain twenty-seven words. The last three lines contain eighteen words.

The second part, *de sanctorum reliquiis*, contains thirteen lines, seventy-seven words, and 143 syllables. The number 13 divides by extreme and mean ratio and by sesquialter ratio at 8 and 5; the number 77 divides by extreme and mean ratio at 48 and 29, the number 143 at 88 and 55. The verses divide at the crux of the chiasmus. The first five lines 9–13 name five saints, and the last eight lines name four saints in the four lines 14–17 and refer to countless relics in the four lines 18–21. The twenty-ninth word from the beginning and the forty-eighth word from the end are *ðer inne* at the crux of the chiasmus. The fifty-fifth syllable from the beginning is the last of *ðer inne*.

The recurrence of words and ideas in the poem illustrates well known ratios of musical theory. The principal idea of the poem is the site of Durham. The twenty-one lines of the poem divide by sesquialter ratio at 13 and 8; the 122 words of the poem divide by sesquialter ratio at 73 and 49. The eighth line from the end begins *Is ðer inne* 14, of which the first word is the seventy-third of the poem. From *Is ðeos burch* 1 to *Is in ðære byri* 9 inclusive there are forty-nine words. Those forty-nine words divide by sesquialter ratio at 29 and 20. From *Is ðeos burch* 1 to *ðer inne* 4 inclusive there are twenty words. From *Is ðeos burch* 1 to *ðer* 6 inclusive there are twenty-nine words. After *ðer* 6 the last of *Is in ðære byri* 9 is the twentieth word. After *ðer inne* 4 the last of *Is in ðære byri* 9 is the twenty-ninth word. The fifty-fourth word of the poem is *arfæsta* 10. Fifty-four words divide by sesquialter ratio at 32 and 22. The thirty-second word of the poem is *wudufæstenn* 6.

From *eadig* 10 to *eadige* 18 inclusive there are forty-nine words, which divide by duple ratio at 33 and 16. From *eadig* to *Eadfrið* inclusive there are sixteen words, and thereafter to *eadige* inclusive there are thirty-three words. From *Cuðbercht* to *Cuðberchte* inclusive there are thirty-four words, which divide by extreme and mean ratio at 21 and 13. From *Cuðbercht* to *Eadbercht* inclusive there are thirteen words, and thereafter to *Cuðberchte* there are twenty-one words.

The 122 words of the poem divide by sesquitertian ratio at 70 and 52. After *monige* 7 *monige* 20 is the seventieth word.

The twenty-one lines of the poem divide by symmetry at 11; the 122 words of the poem divide by symmetry at 61 and 61. In the eleventh line after *ungerim* 8 *unarimeda* 19 occurs. Between them are sixty-one words, half the words of the poem.

The 122 words of the poem divide by extreme and mean ratio at 75 and 47. Between *breoma* 1 and *and breoma* 15 there are seventy-five words. From the beginning to *breoma* 1 and from *and breoma* 15 to the end there are forty-seven words.

The eleventh word of the poem is *wundrum* 3. The 111th word is *wundrum* 20, after which there are eleven words to the end of the poem.

There are no indications here that the poet thought 'Durham' was a last feeble gasp of an expiring tradition of verse composition. Nor is it. The work is more competent and craftsmanly than any modern critic has yet supposed.

Index

The locations of places in Great Britain are given with reference to pre-1974 county boundaries. References to manuscripts have been grouped under the heading 'manuscripts'.

CORRIGENDA

The Durham Mint before Boldon Book

p. 382, line 3. *For* pp. 382–91 *read* pp. 388–91.

p. 384, lines 12–13. *For* the four pennies of the *Paxs* type (BMC William I type VIII) found *read* pennies of the *Paxs* type (BMC William I type VIII), four of which were found.

p. 385, line 13. *For* (first documented, in 1195/6) *read* (first documented in 1195/6).

p. 388, line 36 (penultimate line of text). *For* approximate *read* approximately.

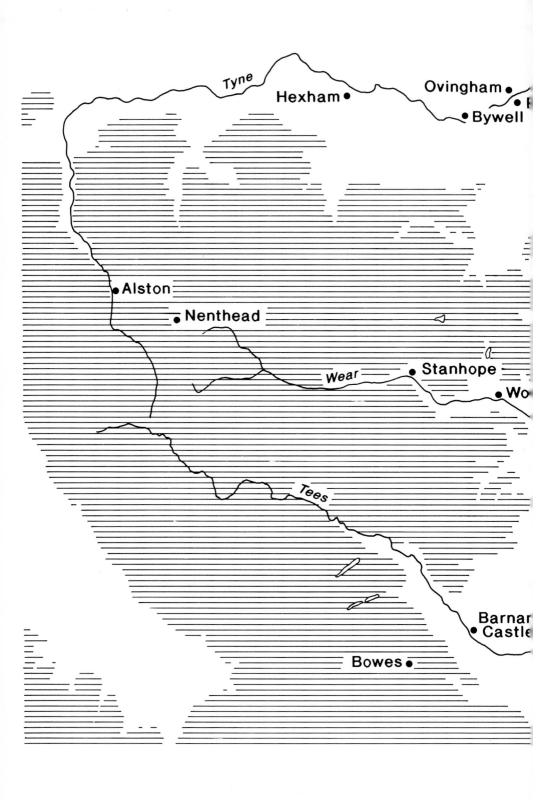

BETWEEN TYNE
AND TEES

Tynemouth •

Newcastle •
Jarrow •
Gateshead

Monkwearmouth •

er-le-Street •

Finchale Abbey •

Easington
Haswell • Durham • •

Brancepeth •

Hart •

Bishop Auckland •

Billingham •
Bishopton • Norton •
drop

Gainford •
Sadberge •
• Darlington

10 km

≡ Land over 244m